DATE DUE

SE 25 '0			

DEMCO 38-296

Smith, Currie & Hancock's
COMMON SENSE
CONSTRUCTION LAW

Smith, Currie & Hancock's
COMMON SENSE
CONSTRUCTION LAW

EDITORS
Neal J. Sweeney
Thomas J. Kelleher, Jr.
Philip E. Beck
Randall F. Hafer

JOHN WILEY & SONS, INC.

New York / Chichester / Brisbane / Toronto / Singapore / Weinheim

Library of Congress Cataloging in Publication Data

Smith, Currie & Hancock
    Smith, Currie & Hancock's common sense construction law / Smith,
Currie & Hancock.
      p. cm.
    Includes index.
    ISBN 0-471-01031-6 (cloth : alk. paper)
    1. Construction contracts–United States. 2. Construction
industry–Law and legislation–United States.
KF902.S919 1997
343.73'078624–dc20
[347.30378624]   96-27813

Printed in the United States of America

10 9 8 7 6 5 4 3

To Overton A. Currie and Luther P. House, Jr.—our partners, our teachers, and our friends

CONTENTS

13 Proving Costs and Damages 269

14 Resolution of Construction Disputes 293

PREFACE

The attorneys of Smith, Currie & Hancock have practiced construction law and government contracts over the course of four decades. During that time, we have conducted hundreds of construction and government contract law seminars for clients, trade associations, colleges and universities, and professional groups. Our consistent goal throughout those efforts has been to provide a practical, common sense perspective to the legal issues affecting the construction industry. This book is in many respects a culmination and refinement of those educational efforts and the common sense approach they entail.

Construction law is an accessory to the construction industry—theories, principles and some strict rules that contribute to the smooth running of the construction process. When that process falters and disputes arise, construction law provides a variety of procedures with varying degrees of formality for the resolution of those disputes. Construction law is not just for lawyers. Individuals in responsible positions in the industry must be cognizant of what the law requires of them and what they can expect and require from others. Nor can lawyers focus on legal rules and procedures to the exclusion of the *business* of construction and expect to effectively represent and assist their clients. Construction law and the business of construction are inextricably intertwined. We hope this book reflects this interrelationship in the topics it tackles and the various perspectives and approaches it employs.

Claims and disputes are addressed, as they must be in any complete and competent analysis of the competitive construction environment. But this book is not only about resolving disputes once they arise. It is intended to provide the kind of insight and understanding needed to *avoid* claims and disputes. Reasonable recognition of the contractual allocation of rights, risks and responsibilities, coupled with a spirit of communication and teamwork in the execution of the work, is far more likely to culminate in a successful project than an atmosphere rife with confrontation and dispute. Of course, the possibility of claims and disputes cannot be ignored. Careful attention and planning is required to avoid disputes and to deal effectively with them when they become inevitable.

Common Sense Construction Law is a general teaching tool and is not a substitute for the advice of your attorney. Specific concerns and problems require the timely attention of legal counsel familiar with construction law.

However, this book will help to expand your knowledge and awareness of construction law issues that exist everyday in construction. It may not provide all the answers, but you will be better equipped to ask the right questions. To make these materials more useful to you, we have included checklists, sample forms, and summary "Points to Remember" for each chapter.

We thank our clients, who have shared their insights and concerns and provided the opportunities for experience and learning that are shared in this book. We also owe much gratitude to the construction industry as a whole for allowing us as construction attorneys to participate in the challenges of the industry to avoid and resolve problems. We hope this work will contribute to the worthy goals of the industry. We also hope that this book helps the reader pursue their interests in and commitments to construction from concept to completion.

SMITH, CURRIE & HANCOCK

Atlanta, Georgia
January 1997

SMITH, CURRIE & HANCOCK'S CONSTRUCTION LAW AND GOVERNMENT CONTRACTS DEPARTMENT

This book represents the joint efforts of many individuals over many years. The law firm of Smith, Currie & Hancock is a nationally recognized leader in the field of construction law and the resolution of the varied legal problems facing the industry. For more than 30 years, Smith, Currie & Hancock has represented clients in construction and government contract matters throughout all 50 states and around the world. With 40 attorneys, Smith, Currie & Hancock's Construction Law and Government Contracts Department is believed to be the largest group of attorneys practicing exclusively in the area of construction. As a group, they represent hundreds of lawyer years of experience in construction.

Many of the firm's construction attorneys have engineering degrees in addition to their legal education, and some worked in the construction industry prior to pursuing their law degrees. Others joined Smith, Currie & Hancock after serving in the Army, the Navy and the Air Force as government contracts and procurement lawyers or have extensive specialized training in public procurement.

Smith, Currie & Hancock has represented clients from the entire spectrum of the construction industry: contractors, subcontractors, construction managers, owners (public and private), architects, engineers, sureties, insurance companies, suppliers, lenders, real estate developers and others. They include multinational and *Fortune* 500 companies and trade associations representing billion-dollar industries, as well as local and regional clients doing business on a much smaller scale.

In addition to serving clients nationwide, Smith, Currie & Hancock attorneys have published numerous articles in trade magazines and other periodicals and have authored or co-authored dozens of books on construction and public contract law. In addition, its construction lawyers maintain a heavy schedule of lectures and seminars sponsored by various trade associations, colleges and universities, including the U.S. Army Corps of Engineers, Georgia Institute of Technology, Auburn University, the American Bar Association, the Practicing Law Institute and the Associated General Contractors.

OVERTON A. CURRIE: Born in Hattiesburg, Mississippi, on November 28, 1926. BBA, University of Mississippi, 1948 (Valedictorian); LL.B., University of Mississippi, 1949 (Valedictorian); B.D., Emory University, 1958; LL.M., Yale University, 1958 (Class Marshall, Valedictorian). Associate Editor *Mississippi Law Journal,* 1948–1949. County Prosecuting Attorney, 1952–1955. Member: Board of Directors and Approved Arbitrator for Government and Construction Contract Disputes, American Arbitration Association; American Bar Association, Public Contract Law Section, National Chairman, 1971–1972; Construction Cases Litigation, Litigation Section, National Chairman, 1978–1979; State Bar of Georgia; Mississippi State Bar; Lawyers Club of Atlanta; The Association of Trial Lawyers of America; Atlanta Bar Association.

LUTHER P. HOUSE, JR.: Born in Bethpage, Tennessee, on December 18, 1933. Managing Partner of Smith, Currie & Hancock. Phi Beta Kappa graduate of the University of Kentucky, 1955, and its College of Law. Assistant Editor of the *Kentucky Law Journal,* 1957. Recipient of a Master of Laws degree from Yale Law School. Author and lecturer on all phases of construction contracting. Chair of Forum Committee of the Construction Industry of the ABA, 1991–1992. Former Air Force legal officer engaged in trial work (for which he received two commendations) and government contracts. Member: American Bar Association and other professional societies.

GLOWER W. JONES: Born in Atlanta, Georgia, on May 4, 1936. A.B., Dartmouth College, 1958; LL.B., Emory University, 1963 (with distinction); Bryan Honor Society. Editor-in-Chief of Emory Section of the *Georgia Bar Journal,* 1962–1963. Atlanta Bar Association Engineer-Lawyer Relations Committee Chairman, 1984–1985; Editorial Board of Georgia Bar Journal, 1975–1979. International Construction Procurement Committee Chairman, 1990–1992, Public Contract Law Section, American Bar Association; International Bar Association International Sales and Related Commercial Transactions Committee Chairman, 1992–1996; International Bar Association UNCITRAL Legal Guide for International Industrial Works Projects Committee Chairman, 1990–1992; Articles: "Win Punitive Damages in Arbitration," ABA *Journal of the American Bar Association,* May 1987. "Warranties: U.N. Convention on Contracts for the International Sale of Goods Compared to U.S. Uniform Commercial Code on Sales," *International Business Lawyer,* December 1989 [17 I.B.L. 497]; *Alternative Clauses to Standard Construction Contracts,* James E. Stephenson, Editor, Chapter author, John Wiley & Sons, New York, 1990; "The U.S. Perspective on Procedures for Subsurface Ground Conditions Claims," *The International Construction*

Law Review, April 1990 [1990 I.C.L.R. 155] Lloyd's of London Press, Ltd.; *Construction Subcontracting: A Legal Guide for Industry Professionals,* Chapter author, John Wiley & Sons, 1991; "Negotiating the Architectural Design Contract for the Owner," [1991 I.C.L.R. 451]; "Construction Contractors: The Right To Stop Work," [1992 I.C.L.R. 310]; "Impact of the Vienna Convention in Drafting International Sales Contracts," [20 I.B.L. 421] 1992; *Remedies for International Sellers of Goods,* United States Chapter, Sweet & Maxwell, London, 1993; *Legal Aspects of Doing Business in North America,* Georgia Chapter, Kluwer Law and Taxation Publishers, Deventer, Netherlands, 1991; "Construction and Project Management—The Structure and Its Impact on Project Participants/USA—The Experience and Trends," 10 ICLR 425 (1993); "Performance Guarantees of Construction Contracts: Surety Bonds Compared to Letters of Credit As Vehicles to Guarantee Performance," 11 ICLR 3 (1994). Member: American Bar Association; International Bar Association and other professional societies.

ROBERT B. ANSLEY, JR.: Born in Atlanta, Georgia, on March 6, 1939. B.A., Vanderbilt University, 1962; J.D., Emory University, 1965; Bryan Honor Society. Co-Editor-in-Chief, *Journal of Public Law* and Emory Section, State Bar Journal of Georgia, 1965. Co-author: "Differing Site (Changed) Conditions," *Briefing Papers* No. 71-5, Federal Publications. Admitted: U.S. Supreme Court; Supreme Court of Georgia; Court of Appeals of Georgia; U.S. Court of Appeals for the Federal Circuit; U.S. Court of Federal Claims; U.S. District Court (N.D. of Georgia); U.S. District Court (M.D. of Georgia). Member: State Bar of Georgia; American Bar Association, Public Contract Law Section and Tort and Insurance Practice Section; Atlanta Bar Association; Lawyers Club of Atlanta.

BERT R. OASTLER: Born in Atlanta, Georgia, on October 19, 1933. B.S., Civil Engineering, Duke University, 1956; J.D., Emory University, 1966; Bryan Honor Society. Associate Editor, *Journal of Public Law.* Practiced structural steel design at Newport News Shipbuilding & Drydock Company, was assigned to construction design and building in the United States Air Force. Engaged in the building construction business in Atlanta, Georgia, as estimator and project manager for five years. Lectured on construction litigation, arbitration and government contracts procurement law for Federal Publications, Inc., Associated General Contractors, Emory University and Georgia Institute of Technology, Atlanta, Georgia. Member: American Bar Association; American Trial Lawyers Association; Georgia Trial Lawyers Association.

AUBREY L. COLEMAN, JR.: Born in Little Rock, Arkansas, on December 11, 1942. B.A., Tulane University, 1964 (*cum laude*); LL.B., Vanderbilt University, 1967; Order of the Coif; Managing Editor, *Vanderbilt Law Review,* 1966–1967; Phi Beta Kappa. Co-author: Georgia Construction Law, Professional Education Systems, 1986. Author and lecturer on various aspects of construction law and construction claims preparation, presentation, and defense, including participation in programs presented by Georgia State University, University of Kentucky Law School, Professional Education Systems, Inc., and Federal Publications, Inc.

THOMAS E. ABERNATHY, IV: Born in Chattanooga, Tennessee, on February 18, 1941. B.A., Vanderbilt University, 1963; J.D., Vanderbilt University, 1967; Phi Alpha Delta; Omicron Delta Kappa. Co-author: "Differing Site (Changed) Conditions," *Briefing Papers* No. 71-5, Federal Publications, Inc., October, 1971; "Inspection under Fixed-Price Construction Contracts," *Briefing Papers* No. 76-6, Federal Publications, Inc., December, 1976. Author: "EPA Construction Grants: Rights and Remedies for the Disappointed Bidder," 11 *Pub Contr. Newsletter* 4, 1976; "Changed Conditions," *Construction Briefings,* No. 84-12 Federal Publications, Inc., December, 1984; *Construction Business Handbook* (Second Edition), McGraw-Hill, Inc., 1984; "Developments in Federal Construction Contracts," *Wiley Construction Law Update,* John Wiley & Sons, Inc., 1992–1995; "Resolving Government Construction Claims without Litigation," 93-10 *Briefing Papers,* Federal Publications, September 1993. Lecturer on construction and government contract matters to various professional groups. Member: Atlanta, Tennessee and Federal Bar Associations; American Bar Association, Public Contract Law Section, National Chairman, 1983-1984; Fellow, American College of Construction Lawyers; State Bar of Georgia; Lawyers Club of Atlanta.

PHILIP L. FORTUNE: Born in High Point, North Carolina, on November 11, 1945. B.A., University of North Carolina at Chapel Hill, 1967, Gamma Beta Phi; J.D., University of Toledo, 1970 (Valedictorian). Comments Editor, *University of Toledo Law Review;* Instructor of Federal Procurement Law, Emory Law School, 1972. Author and lecturer on construction law, bonds, liens and preparation of claims, including participation in programs presented by Georgia Tech, Five County Builders & Contractors Association, Inc., Ft. Myers, Florida, and various professional groups. Lecturer on various aspects of the hazardous waste and environmental protection laws and regulations including Superfund. Member: Atlanta, Georgia and American Bar Associations; American Trial Lawyers Association.

THOMAS J. KELLEHER, JR.: Born in Malden, Massachusetts, on August 22, 1943. A.B., Harvard University, 1965 (*cum laude*); J.D., University of Virginia, 1968; Co-Author: *Construction Litigation: Practice Guide with Forms,* John Wiley & Sons, 1984; "Inspection under Fixed Price Construction Contracts," *Briefing Papers,* No. 76-6, Federal Publications, Inc., December 1976; "Preparing and Settling Construction Claims," *Construction Briefings,* No. 83-12, Federal Publications, Inc., December 1983. Writer and lecturer on construction law and federal government contract law for Federal Publications, Inc. Instructor, Assistant Chief, Procurement Law Division, The Judge Advocate General's School, U.S.

Army, 1970–1973. Member: State Bar of Georgia; Virginia State Bar; American Bar Association, Public Contract Law Section.

FRANK E. RIGGS, JR.: Born in Hattiesburg, Mississippi, on August 9, 1948. B.A., University of Southern Mississippi, 1971 (with honors); J.D., University of Virginia, 1974; Omicron Delta Kappa; Phi Delta Phi. Lecturer on various aspects of construction law including construction claims preparation, presentation and defense. Member: Atlanta and American Bar Associations, Public Contract Law Section and Litigation Section; Forum Committee on the Construction Industry; State Bar of Georgia; Lawyers Club of Atlanta; The Association of Trial Lawyers of America; Georgia Trial Lawyers Association.

RONALD G. ROBEY: Born in Savannah, Georgia, on August 12, 1952. B.A., Centre College and University of Kentucky, 1974 (with distinction); J.D., University of Kentucky, 1977; Order of the Coif. Lead Articles Editor, *Kentucky Law Journal*, 1976–1977. Author: "Construction Management—Avoid Being a Fiduciary," *Contractor Profit News*, October 1986; "A Telephone Sub-Bid Is Enforceable," *Contractor Profit News*, June 1985. Co-Author: *Winning Strategies in Construction Negotiations, Arbitration and Litigation*, Construction Contracts, Practicing Law Institute, 1986.

WILLIAM E. DORRIS: Born in Dublin, Georgia, on April 10, 1955. B.A., University of Kentucky, 1976 (with distinction); Phi Beta Kappa; J.D., University of Kentucky, 1979 (with distinction); *Kentucky Law Journal*, 1977–1979; Order of the Coif. Co-author: *Construction Litigation: Practice Guide with Forms*, John Wiley & Sons, 1984; "Understanding Construction Contracts: A Myriad of Special Clauses," *Arbitration Journal*, Volume 41, 1–14, March 1986; "Construction Acceleration Clauses," *Construction Briefings*, No. 87-8, Federal Publications. Member: State Bar of Georgia; State Bar of Kentucky.

BRIAN G. CORGAN: Born in Oakland, California, on August 31, 1954. B.A., Tulane University, 1976; J.D., Tulane University, 1979 (*summa cum laude*); Order of the Coif. Notes Editor, *Tulane Law Review*, 1977–1979. Co-author: *Construction Litigation: Practice Guide with Forms*, John Wiley & Sons, 1984; "Building Construction," *Deposition Strategy, Law and Forms*, Matthew Bender, 1985.

CHARLES W. SURASKY: Born in Columbia, South Carolina, on May 15, 1951. B.A., University of South Carolina, 1973 (*cum laude*); J.D., George Washington University, 1978 (with honors). *George Washington Law Review*, 1976–1978. Admitted to practice in Georgia, Florida, South Carolina and the District of Columbia.

JOHN T. FLYNN: Born in Orange, New Jersey, on December 18, 1946. B.A., Texas Tech University, 1968; J.D., University of Texas, 1970; LL.M., George Washington University, 1977; Phi Delta Phi. Author: "Patent Infringements: The Composition of Reasonable and Entire

Compensation Under 28 U.S.C. 1498," *The Air Force Law Review,* Volume 20, Number 2, 1978; "The Rule Contra Proferentum in the Government Contract Interpretation Process," *Public Contract Law Journal,* Volume II, Number 2, 1980. Member: Florida State Bar; State Bar of Texas; State Bar of Georgia; U.S. Court of Military Appeals; U.S. Claims Court; American Bar Association, Public Contract Law Section.

JAMES F. BUTLER, III: Born in Buffalo, New York, on July 25, 1951. A.B., Duke University, 1977; J.D., University of Kentucky, 1981. Member: State Bar of Florida, State Bar of Georgia, Kentucky Bar Association, and State Bar of Texas; American Bar Associations, Litigation Section and International Law Section; Forum Committee on the Construction Industry; The Association of Trial Lawyers. Co-author: *Alternative Clauses to Standard Construction Contracts,* John Wiley & Sons, 1990; *Design-Build Contracting Handbook,* John Wiley & Sons, 1992; *The AGC Environmental Risk Management Procedure Manual.*

JOSEPH C. STAAK: Born in Philadelphia, Pennsylvania, on June 16, 1952. B.S., Civil Engineering, Georgia Institute of Technology, 1974; J.D., University of Georgia, 1981 (*cum laude*); *Georgia Law Review,* 1979–1981; Design and Construction Engineer, U.S. Air Force, 1974–1978.

HUBERT J. BELL, JR.: Born in Elberton, Georgia, on September 24, 1942. B.A., Davidson College, 1966; M.A., Pacific Lutheran University, 1974; J.D., University of Georgia, 1981 (*cum laude*); Order of the Coif. Author: "Inadvertent Disclosure of Privileged Material," *Georgia State Bar Journal,* Volume 18, Number 4, May 1982; Co-author: "The Economic Loss Rule: A Fair Balancing of Interests," *The Construction Lawyer,* Volume 11, Number 2, April 1991; "Current Status of Economic Loss Rule," *Wiley Construction Law Update,* John Wiley & Sons, 1992. Lieutenant Colonel, U.S. Army 1966–1978, U.S. Army Reserve 1978–1987, Federal Procurement Officer, Department of Defense Contracts Auditor, Department of the Army General Staff (Aviation Systems Procurement Officer). Member: American Bar Association, Public Contract Law Section, Chairman, Construction Division, 1995–Present, Litigation Section; Forum Committee on the Construction Industry; National Contract Management Association, Director 1984–1985.

PHILIP E. BECK: Born in Salisbury, North Carolina, on November 8, 1956. B.S., University of Tennessee, 1978 (high honors), M.B.A., University of Tennessee, 1981; J.D., University of Tennessee, 1981; Order of the Coif; Moot Court Board; Omicron Delta Kappa; Beta Gamma Sigma; Phi Kappa Phi. Law Clerk to the Honorable Houston Goddard, Tennessee Court of Appeals, 1980–1981. Co-author: "The Owner Contemplating Litigation and Its Alternatives," *Construction Litigation: Representing the Owner,* John Wiley & Sons, 1984, and Second Edition, 1990; "The Contractor Contemplating Litigation and Its Alternatives," *Construction*

Litigation: Representing the Contractor, John Wiley & Sons, 1986, and Second Edition, 1992; *Wiley Construction Law Update,* John Wiley & Sons, 1992–1997. Author of numerous trade publication articles and frequent guest speaker for various trade associations.

NEAL J. SWEENEY: Born in Paterson, New Jersey, on November 1, 1957. B.A., Rutgers University, 1979 (with high honors); J.D., George Washington University, 1982 (with honors). Notes Editor, *George Washington Journal of International Law & Economics.* Editor: *Wiley Construction Law Update,* John Wiley & Sons, 1992–1997; *Construction Subcontracting: A Legal Guide for Industry Professionals,* John Wiley & Sons, 1991. Co-author: "Holding Subcontractors to Their Bids," *Construction Briefings,* No. 86-3, Federal Publications; "Avoiding and Dealing with Subcontractor Default," *Construction Briefings* No. 87; "Winning Strategies for Proving & Pricing Claims," *Proving & Pricing Construction Claims,* Second Edition, John Wiley & Sons, 1996, and numerous trade publication articles. Lecturer for Associated General Contractors, Federal Publications, and Risk and Insurance Management Society.

JAMES K. BIDGOOD, JR.: Born in Dublin, Georgia, on December 31, 1951. B.S., Civil Engineering, Georgia Institute of Technology, 1974; M.B.A., Phillips University, 1980; J.D., Emory University, 1983 (with distinction); *Emory Law Journal;* Order of the Coif; U.S. Air Force, 1974–1980.

RANDALL F. HAFER: Born in Camden, New Jersey, on March 15, 1950. B.S., Georgia State University, 1975 (*cum laude*); J.D., University of Tennessee, 1983 (with high honors); Student Materials Editor, *Tennessee Law Review,* 1982–1983; Order of the Coif; Phi Kappa Phi. Co-author: Chapter 5, "Performance of Construction and Design Contracts," *Construction Law,* Matthew-Bender, 1986; Chapter 2, "Construction Contracts," in *Negotiating Real Estate Transactions,* Wiley, 1988; Chapter 16 in *Alternate Clauses to Standard Construction Contracts,* Wiley, 1990; and Chapter 11, "Selecting a Third-Party Neutral" in *Alternative Dispute Resolution in the Construction Industry,* Wiley, 1991. Co-editor: *Construction Subcontracting: A Legal Guide for Industry Professionals,* Wiley, 1991.

S. GREGORY JOY: Born in Richmond, Virginia, on March 15, 1959. B.A., University of Virginia, 1981 (with high distinction); Phi Beta Kappa; Raven Honor Society; J.D., University of Virginia, 1984; Moot Court Board.

ROBERT C. CHAMBERS: Born in Cornelia, Georgia, on February 12, 1958. B.S.C.E., Georgia Institute of Technology, 1979 (high honors); M.S.C.E., 1980 (Study Emphasis: Geotechnical Engineering); J.D., University of Georgia, 1985 (*magna cum laude*); Order of the Coif. Co-author: "Changed Conditions," *Construction Briefings,* No. 84-12, Federal Publications.

KARL DIX, JR.: Born in Iron Mountain, Michigan, on November 3, 1957. B.S., Economics, The Wharton School of Finance and Commerce at the University of Pennsylvania, 1980 (*magna cum laude*); J.D., Cornell Law School, 1983 (*cum laude*). Captain, U.S. Army Corps of Engineers, Contract and Procurement and Office of the Chief Trial Attorney, 1983–1987; Army Meritorious Service Medals for Contract Appeals work. Member: New York State and Georgia State Bar.

WILLIAM ROBERT POPLIN, JR.: Born in Greenville, South Carolina, on January 24, 1961. B.A., Political Science and Business, University of South Carolina, 1983 (*magna cum laude*); J.D., University of South Carolina, 1986. Co-author: "Building Construction," *Deposition Strategy, Law and Forms,* Matthew Bender, 1986; "General Contractors Agreements," *Engineering News-Record* 1987. Member: State Bar of Georgia; State Bar of Texas; State Bar of Alabama; State Bar of South Carolina.

JOSEPH PAUL HENNER: Born in Bristol, Virginia, on November 20, 1963. B.A., History and Government, University of Virginia, 1985; J.D., University of Tennessee, 1988. Member: State Bar of Georgia Bar; Atlanta Bar Association. Co-author: *1994 Supplement to Alternative Clauses to Standard Construction Contracts,* John Wiley & Sons.

JOHN E. MENECHINO, JR.: Born in Islip, New York, on March 6, 1964. B.A., University of South Carolina, 1986 (*magna cum laude*); J.D., University of South Carolina, 1989; Phi Beta Kappa. Co-author: *Alternative Clauses to Standard Construction Contracts,* John Wiley & Sons, 1990; "Federal Government Subcontracting," *Construction Subcontracting: A Legal Guide for Industry Professionals,* John Wiley & Sons, 1991. Member: American Bar Association; State Bar of Georgia; Atlanta Bar Association.

GEORGE PAPAIOANOU: Born in Drexel Hill, Pennsylvania, on April 8, 1960. B.S., United States Naval Academy; M.S., Civil Engineering, Georgia Institute of Technology; J.D., Temple University. Lieutenant, U.S. Navy Civil Engineer Corps, served as Assistant Resident Officer in Charge of Construction and Contracting Officer, 1982–1991. Licensed Professional Engineer. Member: National Society of Professional Engineers; American Bar Association; State Bar of Georgia.

R. RANDY EDWARDS: Born in Atlanta, Georgia, on March 9, 1961. B.S., University of Alabama, 1984; M.A., University of Alabama, 1992; J.D., University of Alabama, 1992. Senior Editor, *Alabama Law Review.* Admitted: Georgia Court of Appeals; United States District Courts Northern District Georgia, Northern District Alabama, Middle District Alabama; Alabama Supreme Court; Contract Adviser, National Football League Players Association, 1992. Member: State Bar of Georgia; American Bar Association.

WILLIAM L. BAGGETT, JR.: Born in Birmingham, Alabama on May 3, 1962. A.B., Dartmouth College, 1984 (*magna cum laude*); Phi Beta

Kappa; J.D., Vanderbilt University, 1987. Articles Editor, *Vanderbilt Law Review,* 1986–1987. Law Clerk to the Honorable Albert J. Henderson, Senior Circuit Judge, United States Court of Appeals for the Eleventh Circuit, 1987–1988. Admitted: United States Court of Appeals for the Eleventh Circuit; United States Court of Appeals for the Sixth Circuit; United States District Court for the Middle District of Tennessee; United States District Court for the Northern District of Georgia; Supreme Court of Tennessee; Supreme Court of Georgia; Court of Appeals of Tennessee and all Tennessee state trial courts. Member: American Bar Association; Tennessee Bar Association; State Bar of Tennessee; State Bar of Georgia.

R. LEE MANN, III: Born in Fitzgerald, Georgia, on April 17, 1963. B.S., Industrial Engineering, Georgia Institute of Technology, 1985 (with highest honors); Industrial Engineer, McDonnell Douglas Missile Systems Company, 1985–1992; J.D., University of Georgia, 1995 (*magna cum laude*); Order of the Coif; Woodruff Scholar. Managing Editor, *Georgia Law Review.* Member: American Bar Association; State Bar of Georgia; State Bar of Florida.

PETER C. BROWN: Born in Dallas, Texas, on October 28, 1967. B.A., University of Dayton, 1989 (*cum laude*); J.D., University of Kentucky, 1996. Associate Editor, *Kentucky Law Review;* President, Moot Court Board. Admitted: Supreme Court of Georgia; United States District Court for the Northern District of Georgia. Member: State Bar of Georgia; Atlanta Bar Association.

REMER CRAIG DANIEL: Born in Macon, Georgia, on August 1, 1968. B.S., Building Construction, Georgia Institute of Technology, 1993 (with highest honors); Real Estate Title Abstractor, Martin, Snow, Grant and Napier, 1993; J.D., Walter F. George School of Law, Mercer University, 1996. Member: State Bar of Georgia.

GENE J. HEADY: Born in Poughkeepsie, New York, on January 25, 1958; B.S., Engineering (major: Electrical Contracting), University of Hartford, 1981; Kappa Mu Honorary Engineering Society; J.D., Texas Tech University School of Law, 1996 (*cum laude*); Phi Delta Phi. Editor-in-Chief, *Texas Tech Law Review,* 1995–1996; Editor, *Texas Tech Legal Research Board,* 1995–1996; Author: "Stuck Inside These Four Walls: Recognition of Sick Building Syndrome Has Laid the Foundation to Raise Toxic Tort Litigation to New Heights," 26 *Tex. Tech. L. Rev.* 1041 (1995) (republished in *Legal Handbook for Architects, Engineers and Contractors,* Clark Boardman Callaghan, 1996). Co-author: 1996 Georgia Supplement to *Fifty State Construction Lien and Bond Law,* John Wiley & Sons, 1992. Student Editor: *Texas County Court Bench Manual,* Texas Association of Counties, 1996; *Bench Book for The Texas Judiciary,* Texas Center For The Judiciary, 1996. Member: American Bar Association Forum on the Construction Industry; State Bar of Texas.

MARK V. HANRAHAN: Born in Jackson Heights, New York, on May 7, 1957. B.S., Building Construction, Auburn University, 1979; J.D., Georgia State University College of Law, 1996 (*cum laude*); Phi Delta Phi. Associate Lead Articles Editor, *Georgia State University Law Review*. Member: State Bar of Georgia.

RICARDO A. PRICE: Born in Cleveland, Ohio, on November 19, 1963. B.S., Aerospace Engineering, United States Naval Academy, 1985 (Honorary National Merit Scholar); M.S., Aerospace Engineering, University of Maryland, 1986; J.D., Vanderbilt University School of Law, 1996 (Elliot E. Cheatham Scholar). Fighter Pilot, U.S. Navy, 1986–1991, Desert Shield veteran. Registered Professional Engineer.

1

BIDDING ON
THE CONTRACT

1.1 INTRODUCTION

The bidding process is often the general contractor's first exposure to the particular project and the owner of that project. Bidding procedures vary widely, depending on whether the owner is public or private. The vast majority of federal, state and municipal contracts are awarded pursuant to public bidding. Competitive bidding, although less prevalent in the private sector, is used by many private owners as a means of obtaining an advantageous price while still maintaining some degree of control over the quality of the successful awardee. While private owners are rarely, if ever, "required" to use competitive bidding procedures, for those private owners who do choose to solicit competitive bids for a project, both the owner and potential bidders should pay close attention to general principles of public bidding, because most of the same considerations are present whether the project is public or private.

1.2 GENERAL CONSIDERATIONS IN BIDDING ON PUBLIC CONTRACTS

The essential characteristics of public contracts at all levels are similar. Public contracts generally are awarded to the contractor presenting the "lowest responsible and responsive" offer or the "lowest and best offer." In other words, a successful bid will usually be the bid that represents the lowest price from a responsible bidder and that meets the specifications provided by the owner or contracting agency. The following materials discuss in greater detail the elements of the typical successful bid.

1.3   AWARD TO THE "LOW BIDDER"

Some who engage in competitive bidding assume that an owner has the legal obligation to award the construction contract to the lowest bidder. This belief, however, is only partially accurate in public contracting, and generally not true in private contracting. A contractor's bid, in a legal sense, is simply an offer to perform work; until that offer is accepted by the owner, no enforceable obligation arises.[1] Highlighting this idea that the bid itself is only an *offer* to perform, the owner's Invitation for Bids (IFB) will usually contain a provision to the effect that "the owner reserves the right to reject any or all bids." This provision is designed to put contractors on notice in the bidding documents that the owner may choose not to "accept" any of the bid "offers."[2]

While the federal government must take into account factors other than price in the evaluation process, the relative pricing of bids is of great importance in federal procurement, because federal agencies are obligated to accept the bid that is the most financially advantageous to the federal government (so long as that bid is responsive to the terms of the solicitation and the bidder is a responsible contractor). According to 10 U.S.C. § 2305(b)(3), agency heads are to award contracts "to the responsible bidder whose bid conforms to the solicitation and is most advantageous to the United States, *considering only price and the other price-related factors included in the solicitation.*" (emphasis added)

The federal concern for securing the most financially advantageous bid is well-illustrated by the evaluation of bids responding to solicitations with multiple items. Bids presented on this type of solicitation generally must be evaluated based both on the *unit* price offered by a bidder and on the *total* price. In *S. J. Groves & Sons Co.*,[3] the Comptroller General stated that "where awards [sic] on a combination of schedules is contemplated the award made must result in the lowest cost to the Government to carry out the mandate of 10 U.S.C. § 2305(c). . . ."[4] As a result, a federal agency may actually be required to make *multiple* awards if different bidders offer the lowest unit price on different specific items or if the prices of individual items is lower than the total price offered by another bidder.

---

[1] As was pointed out in 1 Williston on contracts (4th ed. Lord 1990), at § 4:10:

> Often tenders or bids are advertised for by public corporations, municipalities, counties or states or private corporations. The rules governing such bidding are analogous to the rules governing auction sales. Thus, an ordinary advertisement for bids or tenders is not itself an offer, but the bid or tender is an offer which creates no right until accepted.

[2] However, some courts have found that a "reservation of right to reject all bids" clause will not permit an arbitrary rejection of bids, particularly when the bids meet the terms of the solicitation and the rejection is intended primarily to avoid a bid protest. *See Pataula Elec. Membership Corp. v. Whitworth*, 951 F.2d 1238, 1243–44 (11th Cir.), *cert denied sub nom. Georgia Power Co. v. Pataula Elec. Membership Corp.*, 506 U.S. 907, 113 S. Ct. 302, 121 L. Ed. 2d 225 (1992), *decision overruled sub nom., Flint Electrical Membership Corp. v. Whitworth*, 68 F.3d 1309 (11th Cir. 1995) *decision modified at* 77 F.3d 1321 (11th Cir. 1996); *Cianbro Corp. v. Jacksonville Transp. Auth.* 473 So.2d 209 (Fla. 1st DCA 1985).

[3] Comp. Gen. Dec. B-184260, 76-1 CPD ¶ 205.

[4] *Id.* at 23.

Even though the relative prices offered by bidders are of great importance to federal procurement officials, a contractor submitting the low bid generally has no vested interest in the award of that contract.[5] Nevertheless, such a contractor cannot be denied the contract unless the denial would be in the best interest of the public. A further qualification to the importance of price is that even if the bidder on a federal contract does not present the lowest bid, the bid is entitled to fair consideration.[6] Where a federal agency fails to consider adequately a bidder's proposal, the bidder may be entitled to recover bid preparation costs.[7]

Most state and local governments are also bound to award their contracts to the lowest and best bidder. Most states and many localities have enacted statutes or ordinances mandating award to the lowest bidder whose bid meets the technical requirements of the solicitation.[8] Some courts addressing state and local public competitive bidding statutes, regulations, ordinances and guidelines have held that such provisions can create a protected property interest in favor of the lowest responsible, responsive bidder in the expectation of award if the solicitation is subject to competitive bidding requirements protected by federal and/or state law.[9] Other courts interpreting state and/or local competitive bidding requirements have found that the lowest responsible, responsive bidder does not have a protected property interest in the award of the contract.[10] The determination of whether a protected property interest exists turns on the nature of the state or local law, regulation or ordinance.[11]

If a protest is contemplated, the contractor should first determine whether the state's or locality's procurement is governed by a competitive bidding statute or regulation, and, if so, what the regulation permits or requires.

1.4 THE "RESPONSIBLE" BIDDER

The terms "lowest responsive and responsible" or "lowest and best" bidder, as used in statutes, are not confined to the lowest dollar bid. Indeed, the words "responsible" or "best" are as important as the word "lowest."

---

[5] However, courts in some jurisdictions have found that the contractor submitting the lowest responsible, responsive bid does have a protected property interest under state or local law in contract award. *See Pataula Elec.* fn. 2, *supra.*

[6] *Keco Indus., Inc. v. United States,* 192 Ct. Cl. 773, 428 F.2d 1233 (1970); *Heyer Products Co. v. United States,* 135 Ct. Cl. 63, 140 F. Supp. 409 (1956).

[7] *Continental Business Enter., Inc. v. United States,* 196 Ct. Cl. 627, 452 F.2d 1016 (1971).

[8] *See, e.g.,* Florida Statutes § 337.11 and Florida Statutes Chapter 287; Official Code of Georgia Annotated § 36-10-2.

[9] *See, e.g., Pataula Elec.,* fn. 2, *supra; L & H Sanitation, Inc. v. Lake City Sanitation, Inc.,* 585 F. Supp. 120 (E.D. Ark. 1984), *aff'd on other grounds,* 769 F.2d 517 (8th Cir. 1985); *Teleprompter of Erie, Inc. v. City of Erie,* 537 F. Supp. 6 (W.D. Pa. 1981); *Three Rivers Cablevision, Inc. v. City of Pittsburgh,* 502 F. Supp. 1118 (W.D. Pa. 1980).

[10] *See, e.g., Key West Harbor Dev. Corp. v. City of Key West,* 987 F.2d 723 (11th Cir. 1993); *Corner Constr.Corp. v. Rapid City School Dist. No. 51-4,* 845 F. Supp. 1354 (D. S.D. 1994).

[11] *See, e.g., Pataula Elec.,* fn. 2, *supra.*

Responsibility determinations focus on whether the contractor has the necessary technical, managerial, and financial capability and integrity to perform the work. A "responsible" bidder is a contractor who is capable of undertaking and completing the work in a satisfactory fashion. Public contracting authorities will consider a number of factors in determining whether a contractor is responsible. These factors, falling into two general categories, are also relevant to a private owner's evaluation of prospective contractors.

First, a contractor must have the ability to perform the work required by the solicitation. In determining the ability of a contractor to perform, public contracting authorities will take into account the contractor's financial resources, facilities and equipment, experience and licenses and permits. The second general category of responsibility standards addresses the contractor's desire and reliability to perform the contract. In this category, procurement officials will consider the ethical integrity of the contractor and the contractor's ability to perform and complete previous projects.

In federal procurement, Federal Acquisition Regulation (FAR) §9.104-1 specifies that a contractor must demonstrate the following qualifications in order to be considered responsible:

(1) Have adequate financial resources to perform the contract, or the ability to obtain them;

(2) Be able to comply with the required or proposed delivery or performance schedule, taking into account all existing commercial and governmental business commitments;

(3) Have a satisfactory performance record;

(4) Have a satisfactory record of integrity and business ethics;

(5) Have the necessary organization, experience, accounting and operational controls and technical skills, or the ability to obtain them;

(6) Have the necessary production, construction and technical equipment and facilities, or be able to obtain them; and

(7) Be otherwise qualified and eligible for award under applicable laws and regulations.

The determination of responsibility is based on the contractor's ability to perform the specified work as of the time work is to commence, not at the time of bidding. Therefore, a bidder does not have to demonstrate the ability to perform at the time the bid is submitted. Rather, a bidder will be deemed responsible if the bidder has or can obtain the apparent ability to perform the work as of the date work is to begin.[12]

A contractor's "ability to obtain" certain elements listed in the FAR can be particularly important for small contractors. The General Services Board of Contract Appeals, deciding a protest involving automated data processing

---

[12] Comp. Gen. Dec. B-176227, 52 Comp. Gen. 240, 1972 CPD ¶ 97.

engineering services, held that the Federal Aviation Administration (FAA) had improperly determined that an offeror was not responsible.[13] The FAA cited the small business offeror's lack of in-house general and administrative (G&A) service personnel. According to the Board, the FAA was required to consider whether the services could be obtained through alternative means as permitted by FAR §9.104-1. In this case, the offeror demonstrated its ability to provide G&A services through a subcontract arrangement.[14]

All available facts, whether or not submitted with the bid, should be submitted by the contractor and considered by the government to resolve responsibility questions. Since a public official is making a quasi-judicial decision when determining whether a bidder is "responsible" within the meaning of the governing statute, the bidder is entitled to the prerequisites of due process. Therefore, a finding by a public body that a bidder is not responsible should be supported by a record establishing (1) the facts upon which the decision was based, (2) details of the investigation that disclosed these facts, and (3) the opportunity that was offered to the bidder to present its qualifications.

Generally, the contractor will be entitled to an informal hearing on the matter, although a formal hearing may be prescribed by statute. The contractor is normally entitled to present evidence in its own behalf. Once a decision is made, however, the courts generally will not reverse the agency's decision and require award of the contract, except where there has been a clear violation of the law. In *Ward La France Truck Corp. v. City of New York,*[15] for example, the court found that requirements of a fair hearing had not been observed. The court, however, did not order award of the contract to the affected bidder; instead, it returned the matter to the public body for reconsideration.

In the federal procurement setting, the Comptroller General has in recent years refused to entertain challenges to responsibility determinations absent an allegation of fraud on the procuring agency's part. The result has been the tacit acceptance of agency determinations in the vast majority of cases.[16] However, where an agency determination of nonresponsibility is so unreasonable as to be arbitrary and capricious, the affected bidder will be permitted to recover its bid preparation costs.[17]

1.5 THE "RESPONSIVE" BIDDER

Public contract bids usually will not be successful unless the bids comply with all material requirements of the solicitation. Responsiveness differs from responsibility because responsiveness focuses on whether the bid, as submitted, is an offer to perform the exact tasks spelled out in the bid invitation and

[13] *Universal Automation Leasing Corp.,* GSBCA 11268-P, 91-3 BCA ¶ 24,255.
[14] *Id.* at 121,271.
[15] 7 Misc. 2d 739, 160 N.Y.S.2d 679 (Sup. Ct. 1957).
[16] 54 Comp. Gen. 66 (1974).
[17] *L. A. Anderson Constr. Co.,* GSBCA 6235, 82-1 BCA ¶ 15,507.

whether acceptance will bind the contractor to perform in strict conformance with the invitation.[18]

Failure of a contractor carefully to comply with all the requirements for competitive bidding may result in the bid being declared "nonresponsive," or if an award has been made, may render the contract voidable or prevent the contractor from recovering full compensation for work performed. In determining the responsiveness of bids, the bidder's intent must be clearly ascertainable from the face of the bid.[19] However, in order to rise to the level of nonresponsiveness the deviation must be considered *material.*

A deviation is considered to be material if it gives one bidder a substantial competitive advantage that prevents other bidders from competing equally. A contractor bidding on public work must generally take the contract as presented. Any qualification of a bid that limits or changes one or more of the terms of the proposed contract subjects the contractor to the risk of being held nonresponsive. For example, in *Lift Power, Inc.,*[20] a contractor was found to be nonresponsive where it reserved the right in the bid to change the price if costs should increase.[21] Obviously, such a qualification, if accepted by the owner, could have given the contractor an unfair price advantage over other bidders.

The majority of rules concerning bid responsiveness are aimed at preventing a contractor from having "two bites at the apple." In other words, the concept of "bid responsiveness" is used to guard against a low bidder having the opportunity, after bids are opened and all prices are revealed, to accept or reject award based on some contingency that the bidder created itself, and which only applied to, and works to the advantage of, that bidder.

The prohibition against a bidder having "two bites at the apple" applies most often where a defect in the bid or an ambiguity in a solicitation subjects the intended bid to differing interpretations. For example, in *Caprock Vermeer Equip., Inc.,*[22] a bidder for an equipment supply contract included in its bid descriptive literature upon which was written the word "optional." The Comptroller General found that there were two interpretations of the bid, at least one of which rendered the bid nonresponsive. The Comptroller General, therefore, upheld the government's rejection of the bid.

A bid will also be considered nonresponsive if the bidder attempts to make the bid contingent upon some act or event. In *Hewlett Packard,*[23] the General Accounting Office (GAO) found a bid to be nonresponsive where the bidder sent a transmittal letter stating that the bid was contingent upon the removal of a contract clause. The Comptroller General found that the contingency

---

[18] *Prestex, Inc. v. United States,* 162 Ct. Cl. 620, 320 F.2d 367 (1963); *East Side Constr. Co. v. Town of Adams,* 329 Mass. 347, 108 N.E.2d 659 (1952).

[19] *Jarke Corp.,* Comp. Gen. Dec. B-231858, 88-2 CPD ¶ 82.

[20] Comp. Gen. Dec. B-182604, 75-1 CPD ¶ 13.

[21] *See also, Kipp Constr. Co.,* Comp. Gen. Dec. B-181588, 75-1 CPD ¶ 20.

[22] Comp. Gen. Dec. B-217088, 85-2 CPD ¶ 259.

[23] Comp. Gen. Dec. B-216530 (Feb. 13, 1985).

rendered the bid nonresponsive because the bidder sought to change the terms of the contract to the bidder's sole advantage.

A bid will also be considered nonresponsive where the bidder deviates from the bidding requirements by failing to acknowledge addenda, particularly where the addenda contain a statutorily required provision.[24] Also, an oral rather than written acknowledgment of an amendment is unacceptable.[25]

According to the Comptroller General, nonresponsive bids also include bids that fail to acknowledge an amendment that would impose a new legal obligation (even if it would have no effect on price),[26] and which fail to certify that a small business product will be provided.[27]

A determination that a bid was nonresponsive because it was materially unbalanced was upheld by the Comptroller General even though the bidder contended the "unbalancing" resulted from allocating technical evaluation and preproduction costs to first articles.[28] The Comptroller General said that, where costs necessary to produce the first articles also are a necessary investment in the production quantity, the costs should be amortized over the total contract rather than allocated solely to the first articles. The reason for rejecting "front-loaded" bids is that the greatly enhanced first article prices will provide funds to the firm in the early period of contract performance, and will be, in essence, an interest-free loan to which the contractor is not entitled.[29]

Rejection of a bid for nonresponsiveness may also be proper when the principal on the bid bond submitted by the bidder is not the same legal entity as the offeror on the bid form. Generally, a surety can only be obligated on a bid bond if the principal named in the bond fails to execute the contract. The refusal of another entity to contract with the awarding authority does not result in a forfeiture of the bid bond. Defective bid bonds constitute a substantial deviation ordinarily requiring rejection of the bid as nonresponsive because such bonds do not protect the public body but enable bidders to get out of contracts with impunity.[30]

While many deviations such as those noted above may be considered "material," minor irregularities may be waived by the awarding authority.[31] This long established policy permitting waiver of minor irregularities or informalities preserves the focus of competitive bidding on lowest price by discouraging questions over matters not affecting the substance of the bid.[32]

The basic rule observed in connection with minor irregularities is that the defect or variation in the bid must have trivial or negligible significance when

---

[24] See Grade-Way Constr. Co. v. United States, 3 F.P.D. ¶ 95 (Ct. Cl. 1985).

[25] Alcon, Inc., Comp. Gen. Dec. B-228409, 88-2 CPD ¶ 114.

[26] American Sein-Pro, Comp. Gen. Dec. B-231823, 88-2 CPD ¶ 209.

[27] Delta Concepts, Inc., Comp. Gen. Dec. B-230632, 88-2 CPD ¶ 43.

[28] M. C. General, Inc., Comp. Gen. Dec. B-228334, 87-2 CPD ¶ 572.

[29] Fidelity Technologies Corp., Comp. Gen. Dec. B-232340, 88-2 CPD ¶ 511.

[30] See Yank Waste Co., Comp. Gen. Dec. B-180418, 74-1 CPD ¶ 190; but see Comp. Gen. Dec. B-178824 (Aug. 16, 1973).

[31] 51 Comp. Gen. 62 (1971).

[32] 41 Comp. Gen. 721 (1962); Faist v. City of Hoboken, 72 N.J.L. 361, 43 Vroom 361, 60 A. 1120 (N.J. Sup. 1905).

contrasted with the total cost or scope of the invitation for bids. Deviations affecting price, quantity, quality, or delivery/completion are generally material and merit especially stringent standards to protect against any bidder obtaining a competitive advantage.[33] For an irregularity in a bid to be waived, it must be so inconsequential or immaterial that the bidder does not gain a competitive advantage after all bids have been exposed. Thus a minor irregularity may be found where the bidder fails to initial a price change in its bid before bid opening,[34] fails to mark its bid envelope with the solicitation number, date and time of bid opening,[35] or fails to provide incidental information requested by the invitation.[36]

The determination of what constitutes a minor informality generally is left to the discretion of the contracting officer,[37] and courts often give contracting officers broad discretion as to what constitutes a minor irregularity. For example, one court in Maryland held that a bidder's failure to furnish a bid bond was not a material irregularity necessitating bid rejection.[38] In that case, the court characterized the governing considerations as follows:

> Of course, bidders should make every effort to comply as strictly as possible with specifications. On the other hand, *it is the duty of an administrative agency to secure the most advantageous contracts possible for the accomplishment of its work.* A bidder's variation from specifications will not exclude him from consideration for the award of the contract unless it is so substantial as to give him a special advantage over the other bidders. In judging whether or not the omission or irregularity in a bid is so substantial as to invalidate it, the court must be careful not to thwart the purpose of competitive bidding by declaring the lowest bid invalid on account of variations that are not material.[39] (Emphasis added.)

(As noted above, the court's conclusion that a bid without a required bid bond did not constitute a "special advantage over the other bidders" is inconsistent with the great majority of such decisions.[40])

Another far-reaching example of a procuring agency's exercise of discretion to award to the low bidder despite a potential bid irregularity arose in *Pullman Inc. v. Volpe.*[41] There, the court upheld "clarifications" made by the low bidder after bid opening on the ground that the clarifications demonstrated that the bid conformed to and did not alter the specifications.

[33] *See Prestex, Inc.* fn. 18, *supra;* 40 Comp. Gen. 321 (1960); FAR § 14.405.
[34] Comp. Gen. Dec. B-211870, 31 CCF ¶ 71,615 (Aug. 23, 1983).
[35] Comp. Gen. Dec. B-210251, 30 CCF ¶ 70,804 (Jan. 24, 1983).
[36] Comp. Gen. Dec. B-215162, 64 Comp. Gen. 8 (1984).
[37] *Excavation Constr., Inc. v. United States,* 204 Ct. Cl. 299, 494 F.2d 1289 (Ct. Cl. 1974).
[38] *Board of Educ. of Carroll County v. Allender,* 206 Md. 466, 112 A.2d 455 (Md. Ct. App. 1955).
[39] *Id.* at 460, citing *George A. Fuller Co. v. Elderkin,* 160 Md. 660, 665, 154 A. 548 (1931).
[40] *George Harms Constr. Co. v. Ocean County Sewerage Auth.,* 163 N.J. Super. 107, 394 A.2d 360 (N.J. Super. 1978); *Thorp's Mowing,* Comp. Gen. Dec. B-181154, 74-2 CPD ¶ 37.
[41] 337 F. Supp. 432 (E.D. Pa. 1971).

In contrast to the two cases just cited, a number of Comptroller General decisions have helped define what are more typically considered to be minor informalities:

(1) The omission of unit prices under circumstances where they could be calculated by dividing total prices by estimated quantities;[42]

(2) The insertion of the wrong solicitation number on a bid bond;[43]

(3) The omission of a principal's signature on a bid bond when the bond is submitted with a signed bid;[44]

(4) An ambiguous bid price if the bid is low under all reasonable interpretations;[45]

(5) A failure to include required information on affiliates;[46]

(6) A failure to acknowledge an amendment to the solicitation that would not have a material impact on price,[47] or only a trivial impact on price;[48]

(7) A failure to acknowledge an amendment reducing the quantity of items to be ordered where the amendment imposed no obligations not already in the original invitation and had no impact on the bid price;[49] and

(8) A failure to provide equipment description information where the solicitation did not make it clear a failure would result in bid rejection.[50]

Finally, the General Services Board of Contract Appeals (GSBCA) classified as minor informalities a bidder's failure to include with the bid evidence of an agent's authority and the failure to set out the corporate name on each page on which an entry had been made.[51]

1.6 GENERAL CONSIDERATIONS IN BIDDING ON PRIVATE CONTRACTS

Few rules exist in private contract bidding that obligate the owner to award to a particular contractor. While a private owner is not bound by statute to operate under the "lowest responsible, responsive" bidder approach, the owner is likely to consider many of the same factors when reviewing the bids. The private owner may select a contractor based on any criteria it deems

---

[42] *GEM Eng'g. Co.,* Comp. Gen. Dec. B-231605.2, 88-2 CPD ¶ 252.

[43] *Kirila Contractors, Inc.,* Comp. Gen. Dec. B-230731, 88-1 CPD ¶ 554, G. C. ¶ 239.

[44] *P-B Eng'g Co.,* Comp. Gen. Dec. B-229739, 88-1 CPD ¶ 71.

[45] *NJS Dev. Corp.,* Comp. Gen. Dec. B-230871, 88-2 CPD ¶ 62.

[46] *A & C Bldg. & Indus. Maintenance Corp.,* Comp. Gen. Dec. B-229931, 88-1 CPD ¶ 309.

[47] *Adak Communications Sys., Inc.,* Comp. Gen. Dec. B-228341, 88-1 CPD ¶ 74.

[48] *Star Brite Constr. Co.,* Comp. Gen Dec. B-228522, 88-1 CPD ¶ 17 ($2,000 out of a $118,000 difference between low and second low bid).

[49] *Automated Datatron, Inc.,* Comp. Gen. Dec. B-231411, 88-2 CPD ¶ 137.

[50] *Houston Helicopters, Inc.,* Comp. Gen. Dec. B-231122, 88-2 CPD ¶ 149.

[51] *Federal Sys Group, Inc.,* GSBCA 9548-P, 88-3 BCA ¶ 21,021.

appropriate. The private owner is generally under no obligation to make award to the lowest bidder, and might attempt to negotiate an even lower price once the low bid has been determined. Moreover, private owners are generally under no duty to disclose the bases for their decisions. Private owners may open bids outside the presence of all bidders. The private owner may require the bidders to provide a wide variety of information concerning the contractor's ability to perform the project. In addition, the private owner may or may not require the contractor to provide a bid bond or payment and performance bonds to guarantee performance.

As with public bidding, the contractor will want to present itself as a responsible business that is responsive to the owner's needs and that will perform at a reasonable price. The contractor should also be careful to determine whether the owner will be able to meet payment obligations and to provide promised logistical support. The private owner presents a much greater financial risk than a public body with its tax base. Additionally, the contractor should carefully review all specifications and plans presented by the owner, because the private owner may not have the resources to provide the review necessary to find and eliminate potential, and costly, design problems.

1.7   PRIME CONTRACTOR BID MISTAKES

Bid mistakes are a fairly common occurrence in the rush of competitive bidding situations. Contractors do not work under ideal conditions in the hurry to meet the deadline for submitting bids. Most courts recognize that honest, sincere people, even in the exercise of ordinary care, can make mistakes of such a fundamental character that holding the contractor to the bid would be fundamentally unfair.[52]

The rationale behind allowing a contractor to withdraw an erroneous bid lies in the principle that, in most cases where performance has not yet commenced, the owner can be returned to the status quo, and will suffer no injury if withdrawal of the bid is permitted. The mere fact that the owner will have to accept a bid at a higher price generally is not viewed as the type of "injury" that would justify holding the contractor to his mistaken bid. If the contractor is low due only to a mistake, the owner would get an unearned windfall if it could force the contractor to perform at the mistakenly low price.[53]

1.8   ELEMENTS FOR RELIEF FROM A BID MISTAKE

Despite the general availability of equitable relief, not every bid mistake will entitle a contractor to retract its bid. To justify the court's intervention, a contractor generally must satisfy the following criteria:

---

[52] *Kenneth E. Curran, Inc. v. State,* 106 N.H. 558, 215 A.2d 702 (1965).
[53] *M. F. Kemper Constr. Co. v. City of Los Angeles,* 37 Cal.2d 696, 235 P.2d 7 (1951).

(1) The mistake is of such consequence that enforcement would be unconscionable;

(2) The mistake must relate to the substance of the consideration, that is, a "material" feature;

(3) The mistake must have occurred regardless of the exercise of ordinary care; and

(4) It must be possible to place the other party in status quo.[54]

This test has been adopted in a number of cases.[55] For example, the Arizona Court of Appeals held, in *Marana Unified School Dist. No. 6 v. Aetna Casualty & Sur. Co.*,[56] that a contractor would be allowed to withdraw its bid containing a bid mistake in excess of $300,000 without forfeiting its bid bond because the mistake: (1) was large; (2) related to a material matter; (3) resulted from an honest mathematical error; and (4) did not seriously prejudice the owner.

Other cases suggest a fifth requirement—timely notice. When there has been a unilateral mistake, prompt notification to the other party concerning the error may be crucial in determining whether the contractor will be allowed to withdraw its bid.[57] Relief from a bid mistake is most easily obtained where notification of the mistake is given before the bid has been accepted.[58]

Even if award has already been made, relief may be available if the contractor acts promptly. In *School Dist. of Scottsbluff v. Olson Constr. Co.*,[59] a public owner sued a contractor and its bonding company because the contractor refused to enter into a school facilities contract. The contractor had submitted a bid of $177,000, and its bid had been accepted and award made. The only other bid was $203,700. When the contractor's vice-president learned of the discrepancy in the two bids he immediately suspected an error. He examined the estimate sheets and found that a clerk, though experienced in preparing bids, had inadvertently entered an amount of "$2,628," instead of "$26,289," for the structural steel, resulting in an error of approximately $23,000. The owner was notified at once of the error, but insisted on compliance with the bid. Only four days had elapsed between the bid opening and notification of the mistake.

The court held that the contractor was entitled to retract the bid. Although the contractor's bid had been accepted and the contract awarded to it, the contract had not been signed and performance had not started.

[54] *Kenneth E. Curran*, fn. 52, *supra.*
[55] *Dick Corp. v. Associated Elec. Co-op., Inc.*, 475 F. Supp. 15 (W.D. Mo. 1979), *Clinton County Dep't. of Public Works v. American Bank & Trust Co.*, 83 Mich. 259, 268 N.W.2d 367 (Ct. App. 1978), *rev'd on other grounds*, 406 Mich. 85, 276 N.W.2d 7 (Mich. 1979); *Puget Sound Painters, Inc. v. State*, 278 P.2d 302 (Wash. 1954).
[56] 144 Ariz. 159, 696 P.2d 711 (Ariz. Ct. App. 1984).
[57] *M. F. Kemper Constr. Co.*, fn. 53, *supra.*
[58] *Clinton County Dep't. of Public Works*, fn. 55, *supra.*
[59] 153 Neb. 451, 45 N.W.2d 164 (Neb. 1950).

If a contractor waits too long to request relief, courts may be reluctant to allow the mistake to be corrected. For example, a contractor who made a $317,000 arithmetical error in its 15.8 million dollar Florida state highway bid was not entitled to an increase in its contract price, despite the Florida Department of Transportation's knowledge of a possible error. The contractor did not sue for correction of the mistake until twenty-one months after bid opening, with the project three-quarters complete.[60]

Courts regularly emphasize the requirement that the bid mistake must not have resulted from any culpable negligence on the part of the contractor.[61] The burden is placed on the contractor to establish the absence of such negligence in bid preparation.[62] In addition, courts often make a distinction between (1) errors of a mathematical, typographical or clerical nature (e.g., incorrect transposition of figures to the bid sheet); and (2) errors in judgment (e.g., incorrectly estimating the amount of steel required for the project). Generally, relief will be available in the courts for clerical errors, but not for errors in judgment.[63]

An example of the application of this concept is found in a recent Comptroller General decision, *Matter of Continental Heller Corp.*[64] Continental Heller submitted the apparent low bid on a contract for construction of a Navy training building. Prior to contract award, Continental Heller notified the Navy that it had made a mistake in its bid by including only $50,000 for profit rather than the intended $500,000. In support of its claim, Continental Heller submitted, among other things, its bid preparation work sheets showing the $500,000. The Comptroller General sustained Continental Heller's bid protest because its bid preparation documents provided clear and convincing evidence of a clerical error and the specific amount of the intended bid. Continental Heller was thus allowed to receive the contract at the corrected price.

A contractor who realizes prior to award that the bid contains a material error should take certain steps to safeguard its chances of obtaining relief. First, the contractor should immediately notify the owner or public contracting official awarding the contract of the error, preferably in writing, but if time will not permit, then orally, followed promptly by a written request for modification or withdrawal with documentation supporting the assertion of a mistake.[65]

---

[60] *Dep't of Transp. v. Ronlee, Inc.*, 518 So.2d 1326 (Fla. 3d DCA). *See also, Chris Berg, Inc. v. United States*, 192 Ct. Cl. 176, 426 F.2d 314 (1970); *Dick Corp.*, fn. 55, *supra; C.N. Monroe Mfg. Co. v. United States*, 143 F. Supp. 449 (E.D. Mich. 1956).

[61] *See Kenneth E. Curran*, fn. 52, *supra; Liebherr Crane Corp. v. United States*, 810 F.2d 1153 (Fed. Cir. 1987).

[62] *See, e.g., State Bd. of Control v. Clutter Constr. Corp.*, 139 So.2d 153 (Fla. 1st DCA 1962), and *Ex parte Perusini Constr. Co.*, 242 Ala. 632, 7 So.2d 576 (1942).

[63] *Balaban–Gordon Co., Inc. v. Brighton Sewer Dist., No. 2*, 41 A.D.2d 246, 342 N.Y.S.2d 435 (App. Div. 4 Dept. 1973).

[64] Comp. Gen. Dec. B-230559 (June 14, 1988).

[65] 38 Comp. Gen. 218 (1958); Comp. Gen. Dec. B-167649 (Oct. 3, 1969).

Once the owner has been notified, an informal conference should be requested to discuss the bid mistake, at which time the contractor needs to present evidence supporting its request for modification and withdrawal. This evidence should include statements (preferably affidavits) explaining the mistake, copies of the bid, original worksheets, subcontractor quotations, published price lists and any other data used in preparing the bid that establishes (1) the existence of the error, (2) the manner in which it occurred, and (3) the intended bid. The contractor should gather this information as quickly as possible and secure it until the presentation to the owner.[66]

If the error is detected after award, the contractor faces greater difficulty in modifying or withdrawing its bid. An error discovered after award should be brought to the owner's attention immediately in the same manner as if discovered prior to award. However, the likelihood of successfully reforming the bid is much more remote.[67]

In private contracting, a contractor has no vested right to withdraw an erroneous bid. However, a contractor's right to retract its bid, when equitable criteria are met, is not affected by a statutory prohibition or restriction against withdrawal of public bids. Similarly, when equitable conditions are satisfied, a bidder may be entitled to recover its bid deposit.[68]

1.9   OWNER'S DUTY IF BID MISTAKE IS SUSPECTED

The owner may also have a duty to notify the contractor that there may be an error in the bid if the circumstances are sufficient to place the owner on notice of a possible error. For example, in *Hudson Structural Steel Co. v. Smith & Rumery Co.,*[69] a contractor's bid for steel roof framing was so much less than the actual cost of furnishing framing for two buildings that the owner, who was also an experienced contractor, knew immediately that the bidder had interpreted the specifications as covering only one building. The *Hudson* court found the facts sufficient to have put the owner on notice, and to impose upon him the additional duty to inform the contractor of his suspicions. As a general rule, the existence of a wide range between the low bid price and the other bid prices is generally sufficient to put the recipient of the bid on notice of a possible error. Similarly, a substantial variation in the bid from the owner's estimate of the approximate cost can also put the owner on notice of a possible error.[70]

---

[66] *Continental Heller Corp.*, fn. 64, *supra.*
[67] *Edgemont Constr. Co.*, ASBCA 23794, 80-2 BCA ¶ 14,468.
[68] *See Rushlight Automatic Sprinkler Co. v. City of Portland*, 189 Or. 194, 219 P.2d 732 (1950).
[69] 110 Me. 123, 85 A. 384 (1912).
[70] *See, e.g.*, Comp. Gen. Dec. B-170190 (July 21, 1970); *Moffett, Hodgkins & Clark Co. v. City of Rochester*, 178 U.S. 373 (1900).

1.10 WITHDRAWAL VERSUS REFORMATION OF MISTAKE IN BID

While the right to withdraw a mistaken bid is recognized under most states' laws, the right to correct is often not available. The courts of some states have recognized that an erroneous bid should be reformed where the bid was the lowest bid before and after reformation.[71] Other courts have held that a bid is properly rescinded where the bidder makes a unilateral mistake.[72]

The right to withdraw and the opportunity to correct a mistaken bid are more well established under federal law. FAR § 14.406 describes in detail the procedures for dealing with bid mistakes and the circumstances in which a bid may be withdrawn or corrected. To guard against mistakes, the contracting officer must review all bids and must notify a bidder if an apparent mistake is found or if there is a reason to believe there is a mistake.[73]

Even if the bidder verifies the accuracy of its bid, relief for mistake may still be allowed where the government's request for verification does not alert the bidder to the basis for the government's belief that the bid is erroneous.[74] If a contractor's mistake is known or should have been known by the contracting officer, then award of a contact is tantamount to bad faith and constitutes overreaching. Under such circumstances, relief may be appropriate if the contracting officer does not properly verify the contractor's price.[75]

In federal procurement, bidders are permitted to alter their bids to correct mistakes so the government can enjoy the cost benefits of a downward correction.[76] If a downward correction would displace the low bid, the bidder must present clear and convincing evidence, ascertainable substantially from the invitation and the bid itself,[77] which establishes both the existence of the mistake and the dollar amount of the bid actually intended by the contractor.

Where the low bidder seeks to increase its bid and still remain low, it must also present clear and convincing evidence of the mistake and its actual intended bid. However, the evidence it can present is not limited to the solicitation and the bid itself, and can include statements, a file copy of the bid, original worksheets, subcontractor quotations and published price lists.[78] However, even if there is evidence to support such a correction, the correction may be disallowed if it brings the low bidder too close to the second low bidder.

Finally, federal statutes and regulation expressly provide for relief from mistakes after award. The Contract Disputes Act of 1978 authorizes contracting officers and the boards of contract appeals to grant relief to contractors who allege a mistake in bid after award. The contractor's claim for relief is

---

[71] *Chris Berg, Inc.*, fn. 60, *supra. Dick Corp.*, fn. 55, *supra; C.N. Monroe Mfg. Co.*, fn. 60, *supra.*

[72] *See Clinton County Dep't of Public Works*, fn. 55, *supra; Wil-Fred's, Inc. v. Metropolitan Sanitary Dist. of Greater Chicago*, 372 N.E.2d 946 (Ill. App. 1978); *Baltimore County v. John K. Ruff, Inc.*, 281 Md. 62, 375 A.2d 237 (1977).

[73] FAR § 14.406-2; *BCM Corp. v. United States*, 2 Cl. Ct. 602 (1983).

[74] *P.T. Serv. Co.*, GSBCA 7589, 85-3 BCA ¶ 18,430.

[75] *Chemtronics, Inc.*, ASBCA 30883, 88-2 BCA ¶ 20,534.

[76] *P K Contractors, Inc.*, B-205482, 82-1 CPD ¶ 368.

[77] FAR § 14.406-3(a).

[78] FAR ¶ 14.406-3(g)(2); *Coleman Indus. Constr. Co.*, Comp. Gen. Dec. B-207682, 82-2 CPD ¶ 213.

handled by the contracting officer as any other claim.[79] Under the regulations, the contracting officer has the authority to rescind a contract or to modify the contract by deleting the item involved in the mistake or by increasing the price.

1.11 BID PROTESTS

The federal government, as well as virtually all other governmental entities, primarily uses formal advertising and competitive bidding in the award of public construction contracts. The historical preference for the competitive bid system was rooted in the reasoning that sealed bids, independently submitted, result in the lowest cost to the owner and best protect the public interest. The issue of bid protests arises almost exclusively in connection with competitively bid contracts—predominantly at the federal level, but to an increasing degree at the state and local government levels. In bidding on projects for public owners, contractors must rely not only upon their own evaluation of the invitation for bids, but also on a proper application of competitive bidding procedures by the owner. Increased competition for contracts, combined with economic cycles that reduce the total volume of contracts available for bidding, have forced both contractors and their attorneys to become knowledgeable about the rules governing competitive bidding, the enforcement of competitive bidding rules, and related bid protest rules and regulations.

The nature and degree of formality of competitive bidding procedures varies greatly among states and localities and with the type of owner involved. However, some general guidelines, primarily developed from federal competitive bidding procedures, are applicable to many situations. Increased use of competitive bidding at state and local levels has resulted in the development of the American Bar Association (ABA) "Model Procurement Code" for state and local government. This proposed Code attempts to further standardize competitive bid procedures for public construction contract awards.

The guiding principle in bid protests is quick action, since most regulations specify that such action must be taken within a few days. In addition, under some circumstances, the contracting authority may award the contract while the protest is still pending. Once the award is made, the reviewing body can be expected to be reluctant to reverse the decision of the awarding authority. Thus obtaining a favorable ruling on the merits of a bid protest may prove to be an empty victory if the contract itself has already been awarded to another bidder.

1.12 FILING THE PROTEST ON A FEDERAL PROJECT

When a contractor who has submitted a bid on a public contract believes that the bidding rules and regulations applicable to the particular procurement

---

[79] *See* FAR § 14.406-4.

have not been followed, it may want to protest award of the contract. The protesting contractor generally will base the protest on the successful bidder's failure to meet one or more of the bidding requirements previously discussed: lowest bid, responsibility and responsiveness to the solicitation.

In the federal contract arena, a protestor has many options for filing a bid protest. A bid protest may be filed with:

(1) The Comptroller General of the General Accounting Office (GAO)
(2) The General Services Board of Contract Appeals (GSBCA) for automated data processing contracts
(3) The agency involved
(4) The United States Court of Federal Claims (preaward)
(5) The United States District Courts (postaward)

1.13 PROTESTS TO THE GAO (COMPTROLLER GENERAL)

The following is a summary of the important initial time constraints and factors to consider in filing a protest with the GAO. *Keep in mind that these regulations are subject to change (including the initial deadline for filing a protest) and that the current bid protest regulations as published in the Federal Register and the Code of Federal Regulations must be followed to assure a valid protest.*[80]

Any "interested party" may file a protest with the GAO alleging an irregularity in the solicitation or award of a federal government contract to which a federal agency is a party. An "interested party" is an actual or prospective bidder or offeror whose direct economic interest would be affected by the award of a contract or by the failure to award a contract.[81] In several cases, protestors who did not even submit offers were, nevertheless, held to be interested parties. For example, protestors precluded from submitting a proposal because of short response time and restrictive specifications,[82] or otherwise denied the opportunity to compete,[83] have been allowed standing to protest.

Protests based upon alleged improprieties in a solicitation that are apparent prior to bid opening must be filed prior to bid opening.[84] As a result, the Comptroller General has held that protests regarding improprieties apparent prior to bid opening are untimely even if submitted with a bid,[85] or proposal.[86] In procurements where proposals are requested, alleged improprieties that

---

[80] *See* 4 C.F.R. § 21.0, *et seq.*
[81] 4 C.F.R. § 21.0(a).
[82] *Vicksburg Fed. Bldg. Ltd. Partnership,* Comp. Gen. Dec. B-230660, 88-1 CPD § 515.
[83] *Afftrex, Ltd.,* Comp. Gen. Dec. B-231033, 88-2 CPD ¶ 143; *REL,* Comp. Gen. Dec. B-228155, 88-1 CPD ¶ 125.
[84] 4 C.F.R. § 21.2 (a)(1).
[85] *Fredrico Enter., Inc.,* Comp. Gen. Dec. B-230724.2, 88-1 CPD ¶ 450.
[86] *Darome Connection,* Comp. Gen. Dec. B-230629, 88-1 CPD ¶ 461, 30 G.C. ¶ 234.

do not exist in the initial solicitation but are subsequently incorporated into the solicitation must be protested not later than the next closing time for receipt of proposals after the incorporation.[87]

Generally, other protests must be filed not later than fourteen calendar days after the basis of the protest is known or should have been known, whichever is earlier.[88] This means that most protests, the bases of which become apparent at bid opening, must be filed within fourteeen days after bid opening.

Under 4 C.F.R. § 21.1(b), a protest must be in writing and addressed to General Counsel, General Accounting Office, 441 G Street, NW, Washington, D.C. 20548, Attention: Procurement Law Control Group. The protest must include the name, address, telephone number and facsimile number of the protestor, be signed by the protestor or its representative, identify the contracting agency and the solicitation and/or contract number, include a detailed statement of the legal and factual grounds of the protest, including copies of all relevant documents, set out all information establishing that the protester is an interested party, set out all information establishing the timeliness of the protest, and specifically request a ruling by the Comptroller General and state the form of relief requested.[89]

A protest shall not be deemed filed unless it is actually received by the GAO within the time for filing and is accompanied by a certificate that a copy of the protest, together with relevant documents not issued by the contracting agency, was concurrently served upon the contracting agency and the contracting activity (a contracting activity is the subelement of the contracting agency that actually issued the solicitation and/or contract).[90] No formal briefs or other technical forms of pleadings are required.[91]

The Comptroller General has held that a protest received in the GAO's *Office of Congressional Relations* within the time required by the GAO rules was timely filed even though the protest was not routed to the GAO Procurement Law Control Group until after the protest period had expired.[92] The Comptroller General said the protest was timely since it was actually received by the GAO in accordance with 4 C.F.R. § 21.2. However, it is highly advisable to make sure your protest is timely delivered to the Procurement Law Control Group.

The GAO has permitted consideration of untimely protests raising significant issues. For example, the Comptroller General invoked his discretion to consider an untimely protests under the "significant issue" exception in *Reliable Trash Serv. Co.*,[93] since the record clearly indicated that bids could not have been evaluated on a common basis. In *Associated Professional Enter.*,

---

[87] 4 C.F.R. § 21.2(a)(1).
[88] 4 C.F.R. §§ 21.0(e) and 21.2(a)(2).
[89] 4 C.F.R. § 21.1(c).
[90] 4 C.F.R. §§ 21.0(g) and 21.1(e).
[91] 4 C.F.R. § 21.1(f).
[92] *McLaughlin Enter., Inc.*, Comp. Gen. Dec. B-229521, 88-1 CPD ¶ 232.
[93] Comp. Gen. Dec. B-234367, 89-1 CPD ¶ 535.

Inc.,[94] however, the Comptroller General held that the "good cause" exception to the timeliness rule will be limited in future cases to circumstances in which a compelling reason beyond the protestor's control prevents timely filing.

The GAO must notify the contracting agency of the protest within one working day after receipt of a protest.[95] Under most circumstances, when the contracting agency receives notice of a protest from the GAO prior to award, it will not award a contract while the protest is pending.[96]

The head of the contracting activity who is responsible for award of a contract may authorize the award notwithstanding the protest: (1) upon a written finding that urgent and compelling circumstances that significantly affect the interest of the United States will not permit waiting for the protest decision; (2) after the Comptroller General is advised of the finding; and (3) award of the contract is otherwise likely to occur within thirty days after the making of the finding.[97]

A contractor who is awarded a federal agency contract may begin performance of the contract and engage in any related activities that result in obligations being incurred by the government under the contract unless the contracting officer responsible for award of the contract withholds authorization to proceed with performance of the contract.[98] A contracting officer may withhold an authorization ot proceed with performance of the contract if the contracting officer determines in writing that (1) a protest is likely to be filed and (2) the immediate performance of the contract is not in the best interest of the United States.[99]

If the federal agency awarding the contract receives notice of a protest in accordance with the bid protest requirements within ten days after the date of the contract award or within five days after the debriefing date offered to an unsuccessful offeror for any debriefing that is requested and required, the contracting officer may not authorize performance of the contract to begin while the protest is pending, or if authorization for contract performance to proceed was not withheld pending award, then the contracting officer shall immediately direct the contractor to cease performance under the contract and to suspend any related activities that may result in additional obligations being incurred by the government.[100] Contract performance that has been suspended by reason of a protest generally may not be resumed while the protest is pending.[101] However, the head of the procuring activity may authorize performance of the contract after notice of the protest where the head of the procuring activity (1) makes a written finding that performance of the

---

[94] Comp. Gen. Dec. B-235066.2, 89-1 CPD ¶ 480.
[95] 31 U.S.C. § 3553(b)(1); 4 C.F.R. § 21.3(a).
[96] 31 U.S.C. § 3553(c) and (d); 4 C.F.R. § 21.6; 48 C.F.R. part 33.
[97] 31 U.S.C. § 3553(c)(2) and (3).
[98] 31 U.S.C. § 3553(d)(1).
[99] 31 U.S.C. § 3553(d)(2).
[100] 31 U.S.C. § 3553(d)(3)(A) and (d)(4).
[101] 31 U.S.C. § 3553(d)(3)(B).

contract is in the best interest of the United States or urgent and compelling circumstances that significantly affect interests of the United States will not permit waiting for the protest decision and (2) after the Comptroller General's office is notified of that finding.[102]

The protest may initially be filed with the contracting agency and a subsequent protest to the GAO may be filed within fourteen days of formal notification or actual or constructive knowledge of initial adverse agency action (unless the contracting agency imposes a more stringent time for filing).[103]

In most cases, the protested agency is to issue an agency report regarding the bases for the protest within thirty-five days of notice of the protest to the agency.[104] The protester may submit comments to the GAO on the agency report within fourteen days of receipt of the report.[105]

The GAO is required to render a decision within 125 days after the protest is filed.[106] The remedies available to the GAO include recommendations to the contracting agency with any of the following remedies:

(1) refrain from exercising options under the contract;
(2) terminate the contract;
(3) recompete the contract;
(4) issue a new solicitation;
(5) award a contract consistent with statutes and regulations; or
(6) such other recommendations as the GAO determines necessary to promote compliance.[107]

If the GAO determines that applicable statutes or regulations have not been followed, it may find the protestor entitled to bid preparation costs, protest costs and reasonable attorneys' fees.[108] However, the Comptroller General, in *Princeton Gamma-Tech, Inc.*,[109] has held that costs incurred in connection with the agency level protest cannot be reimbursed under the GAO's rule permitting reimbursement of costs for a prevailing protester.

1.14 PROTESTS TO THE GSBCA

The GSBCA hears and decides bid protests involving procurements conducted under the Brooks Act (40 U.S.C. § 759) for automated data processing equip-

[102] 31 U.S.C. § 3553(d)(3)(C).
[103] 4 C.F.R. § 21.2(a)(3).
[104] 4 C.F.R. § 21.3(c).
[105] 4 C.F.R. § 21.3(h).
[106] 4 C.F.R. § 21.9.
[107] 4 C.F.R. § 21.8(a).
[108] 4 C.F.R. § 21.8(d).
[109] Comp. Gen. Dec. B-228052.5, 89-1 CPD ¶ 401.

ment (ADPE) software, maintenance services and supplies.[110] The jurisdiction of the GSBCA is concurrent with that of the GAO for these protests.[111] The GSBCA has no jurisdiction to hear protests involving procurements under the Warner Amendment exceptions to the Brooks Act by which the Department of Defense and other agencies purchase certain intelligence-related and command and control ADPE.[112]

The GSBCA decided to combine its ADPE protest rules with its existing procedures governing contract disputes, although some GSBCA rules apply only to protests while others apply only to appeals.[113] As a result, the GSBCA protest procedures are considerably more formal and structured than the GAO procedures.

A protest may be filed by any interested party (same definition as with the GAO)[114], but the GSBCA provides for intervention in a protest by other interested parties and intervening agencies.[115]   It also has created a new category of "permissive intervenor."[116] An intervenor of right may intervene within four days of receipt of the protest, while a permissive intervenor may do so at any time.[117]

A "ground of protest" based on improprieties in the solicitation that are apparent before bid opening or the closing time for receipt of bids or proposals must be filed before bid opening or the receipt of proposals deadline.[118] Alleged improprieties that are subsequently incorporated into the solicitation must be protested no later than the next closing time for receipt of proposals.[119] Otherwise, a ground of protest must be filed with the Board within ten *working* days after the basis for the protest is known or should have been known.[120] Filing occurs upon receipt by the office of the Clerk of the Board during the Board's working hours.[121]

The ground of protest must contain grounds for the protest supported by specific allegations, documents or affidavits, a statement of the basis of the Board's jurisdiction, and whether the protestor specifically requests a suspension hearing and a hearing on the merits.[122] If requested by an interested party, including the protestor, a suspension hearing will be held to determine whether the Board should suspend the GSA Administrator's procurement

---

[110] 40 U.S.C. 759(f)(1); *Government Contracts Reporter* ¶ 23,465 (Commerce Clearing House, Inc., 1994).
[111] 40 U.S.C § 759; 4 C.F.R. § 21.5(d); 48 C.F.R Subpart 33.1 and § 6101, et seq.
[112] 10 U.S.C. § 2315.
[113] 48 C.F.R. § 6101.1, *et seq.*
[114] 40 U.S.C. § 759(f)(9)(B); 48 C.F.R. § 6101.1(b)(6).
[115] 40 U.S.C. § 759(f)(6)(A).
[116] 48 C.F.R. §§ 6101.1(b)(7) and (9) and 6101.5.
[117] *Id.*
[118] 48 C.F.R. § 6101.5(b)(3).
[119] *Id.*
[120] 48 C.F.R. § 6101.5(b)(3).
[121] 48 C.F.R. § 6101.1(b)(5).
[122] 48 C.F.R. § 6101.7.

authority or his delegation of procurement authority for the protested procurement until the Board can decide the protest on the merits.[123] A suspension hearing will be held within tend days of the filing of the protest if the protest is filed before contract award and the hearing is requested by an interested party.[124] If requested by an interested party, a suspension hearing will be held within five working days of the date the protest is filed for protests filed within ten calendar days of the date of contract award or within five calendar days after debriefing of the unsuccessful offeror.[125]

The GSBCA rules require that the Board issue a decision within sixty-five working days unless its chairman determines that a longer period would be required.[126] The decision of the Board, unlike a decision by the GAO, may be appealed to the Court of Federal Claims under the procedures set out in the Contract Disputes Act of 1978.[127] (Direct judicial review of a GAO protest decision is not available.)

An additional factor should be considered in deciding whether to file a protest related to an ADPE procurement with the GAO or the GSBCA. The protestor may not be aware that a Department of Defense procurement is made under the authority of the Warner Amendment exception to the Brooks Act, in which case the GSBCA has no authority to hear the protest. Therefore, the protest may be timely filed with the GSBCA (within ten calendar days) but, by the time it is determined that the GSBCA lacks authority to decide the protest, the ten working days during which the protest may be filed with the GAO may have expired, leaving the protestor without an effective administrative remedy. Under these circumstances the contractor is left to an action for injunctive relief in the United States District Court under the doctrine of *Scanwell Laboratories, Inc. v. Shaffer,*[128] if award has not been made, or to a suit in the United States Court of Federal Claims in a postaward situation.

1.15 PROTESTS TO THE CONTRACTING AGENCY

A disappointed bidder may initially submit a bid protest to the agency that is involved in the procurement. Federal regulations do not discuss in detail the procedures for agency protests, but some general guidelines are discussed at FAR Subpart 33.1.

Agency protests may be filed before or after contract award by a bidder or a prospective bidder if its direct economic interest is affected by the award.[129]

---

[123] 40 U.S.C. § 759(f)(2)(A); 48 C.F.R. § 6101.19.
[124] 40 U.S.C. P 759(f)(2)(A).
[125] 48 C.F.R. § 6101.19(a)(2).
[126] 48 C.F.R. § 6101.29.
[127] 40 U.S.C. § 759(f)(6)(A).
[128] 424 F.2d 859 (D.C. Cir. 1970).
[129] FAR § 33.101, *et seq.*

The protestor must submit the protest in writing.[130] The agency receiving the protest must respond in writing.[131]

It is probably advisable to submit a protest at a level within the contracting agency or contracting activity higher than the contracting officer because decisions of the contracting officer may be the very decisions in question. Therefore, it may be advisable to protest to the head of the agency or the head of the procuring activity with a copy being sent to the contracting officer.

If a protest is submitted prior to contract award, the award will be withheld while the protest is pending unless there is a determination: (1) that the need for the services or supplies is urgent; (2) that the failure to make an award quickly will delay delivery or performance unduly; or (3) that a prompt award will otherwise be in the best interest of the government.[132] Bidders are to be notified of a protest when the award is withheld and asked to extend the effective period of their bids, if necessary.[133]

If an award has been made before the protest is received by the contracting agency, there is no need for the contracting officer to suspend performance or terminate the award.[134] The contracting officer should attempt to obtain an agreement from the contractor to suspend performance without cost to the government pending the protest if it is likely that the award will be invalidated and delay will not adversely affect the government's interest.

If the protest involves the interpretation of a particular provision of the solicitation and bids have not been received before the protest is resolved, then the contracting officer may amend the solicitation and provide additional time for the submission of bids if bids have not yet been received. An agency that sustains a protest prior to award but after receiving bids may award the contract to the successful protestor or reject all bids and resolicit.

If the protest is received after award of the contract, the contracting officer has the authority to terminate the award or permit the award to stand if that is in the best interest of the government.

Bidders are often reluctant to protest to the contracting agency because the agency is being asked to judge the actions of its own employees. Protests to the GAO or in federal court provide more of an opportunity for a "neutral, third party review" of the agency's actions and positions. Furthermore, agency protests are likely to be less successful than protests to the GAO or the GSBCA if the basis for the protest involves an unusual issue or one that is not a clear violation of applicable laws or regulations. The contracting agency is likely to ratify the actions of its employees if there is any basis for such actions.

However, there are circumstances where an agency protest may be advantageous to a bidder. An agency protest may be less costly and time consuming if the protest is unquestionably valid because the agency may act quickly to

---

[130] FAR § 33.101.
[131] FAR § 33.102 and 33.103(b)(5).
[132] FAR § 33.103(a).
[133] FAR § 33.103(a)(3).
[134] FAR § 33.103(a)(4).

correct any deficiency so as not to delay the commencement of work on the particular project. Additionally, an agency protest may be used when the time has expired to submit a protest to the GAO or the GSBCA. Generally, there are no time limits for submitting a protest to the contracting agency, unlike the GAO and GSBCA, which have short limitation periods for the submission of protests. (Again, the protestor should submit a protest as soon as it becomes aware of the basis for the protest because the likelihood of success declines significantly once the award has been made.)

Additionally, agency protests may be useful where the protest is filed well before bids are to be received. In such a situation, the protestor may have the opportunity to attempt to obtain a quick decision from the contracting agency, and if that decision is adverse to the protestor's position, the protestor may then seek relief in another forum such as the GAO or GSBCA. However, the filing of an agency protest will not toll the time periods for filing protests with the GAO or GSBCA, so the protestor must be prepared to file a timely appeal to the GAO or GSBCA (as appropriate) if it does not receive a quick response to its agency protest.

1.16 BID PROTESTS IN COURT

As noted, one of the most important aspects of bid protests is quick action. From the standpoint of the protestor, it is imperative to prevent the award or performance of the disputed contract from going any further than it has at the time the decision to pursue a protest is made. The further along the award and/or performance on the contract, the less likely that a court will be willing to grant injunctive relief to suspend any further performance.

Often, a contractor will want to obtain a temporary restraining order and injunction to prevent the award and/or commencement of the contract to another bidder. (This is particularly true on state and local projects where award is not automatically stayed and in federal contracts where the agency has indicated it intends to award despite the automatic stay regulation[135] or because the agency claims award and performance is in the agency's best interests and urgent and compelling reasons exist to start performance.)

An injunction suspends any further activity on the contact, whether award or performance, while the court or appropriate agency has the opportunity to decide the merits of the protest. Although the automatic stay provisions of the Competition in Contracting Act diminish the need for injunctive relief in federal government procurements, there will still be situations in which such relief is required. In addition, although federal courts give substantial deference to GAO decisions,[136] a protestor may want the court involved to review the administrative decision rendered by the GAO. Most importantly,

---

[135] 4 C.F.R. § 21.6; 31 U.S.C. §§ 3553(c)(2) and (d)(3)(c).
[136] *Honeywell, Inc. v. United States,* 8 FPD ¶ 46 (Fed. Cir. 1989), 31 GC ¶ 135; *Shoals Am. Indus., Inc. v. United States,* 877 F.2d 883 (11th Cir. 1989).

court action may provide the only vehicle to pursue a protest beyond "agency level" in state and local procurements.

The U.S. Court of Federal Claims is the appropriate court for the protesting bidder seeking injunctive relief against a federal agency or activity. The Federal Court Improvement Act of 1982 (FCIA), P.L. No. 97-164, 96 Stat. 25, created the U.S. Claims Court (now the Court of Federal Claims) and Court of Appeals for the Federal Circuit to replace the U.S. Court of Claims. In addition, the FCIA granted the U.S. Claims Court (Court of Federal Claims) "exclusive jurisdiction" to decide preaward federal contract disputes.[137] Previously, only federal district courts had jurisdiction over bid protests. The district courts' jurisdiction was based upon the *Scanwell* doctrine, named for the first case in which the federal courts took jurisdiction over a federal bid protest.[138]

Because of the FCIA, the courts have held that only the U.S. Court of Federal Claims, and not the federal district courts, has jurisdiction over bid protests that arise *prior* to award.[139] The federal district courts still possess jurisdiction over *postaward* disputes under the *Scanwell* doctrine.[140] A complaint that involves a contract for which no award has been made but that is improperly filed in a federal district court may be transferred to the Court of Federal Claims.[141]

1.17 BID PROTESTS TO STATE AND LOCAL AGENCIES

For state or local projects, absent specific procedures, a bid protest similar to that described above should be delivered to the awarding authority and other involved parties. For example, in connection with federally funded projects at the local level (such as Environmental Protection Agency (EPA) sewage treatment projects), notice of the protest should be sent to the grantor as well as the grantee, usually the local awarding authority. Also, the protestant should consult any pertinent federal statutes or regulations governing protests of federally funded state or local contracts (such as the EPA Construction Grant Regulations for EPA treatment projects).

Thereafter, it is essential to prepare, as quickly as possible, a comprehensive statement with supporting documentation stating the detailed basis for the protest. This presentation should be submitted to all concerned parties.

A protestor should determine whether the state or local agency has a protest procedure. If so, that procedure should be followed carefully if an administrative protest is desired or required. However, in a situation where

---

[137] 28 U.S.C. § 149(a)(3).
[138] *Scanwell Laboratories, Inc.*, fn. 122, *supra.*
[139] *United States v. John C. Grimberg Co., Inc.*, 702 F.2d 1362 (Fed. Cir. 1983).
[140] *Id.; see also, American Dist. Telegraph v. Department of Energy*, 555 F. Supp. 1244 (D.C.D.C. 1983).
[141] *See, e.g., F. Alderete General Contractors, Inc. v. United States*, 2 Cl. Ct. 184, *rev'd on other grounds*, 715 F.2d 1476 (Fed. Cir. 1983).

a contract may be awarded or work may proceed before the protest is resolved, the protestor may have to seek a temporary restraining order or other injunctive relief in court to prevent award or to prevent the public body from proceeding with work.

1.18 BID BONDS

In connection with public contracts in particular, it is frequently required that each bidder provide security with the bid that will guarantee execution of the contract in the event that the bidder is awarded the contract.[142] In some instances a cash deposit is required. More commonly, the security called for is in the form of a "bid bond."[143] These bonds commonly provide that if the contractor does not execute the contract, the surety will be liable to the owner only to the extent of the difference between the contractor's bid and the lowest amount for which the owner may be able, in good faith, to award the contract within a reasonable time. A further limit generally is the penal sum of the bond.[144]

Federal contracts usually require that a bid bond (also known as a "bid deposit") be provided to guarantee contractor performance. As the Court of Claims noted in *Anthony P. Miller, Inc. v. United States:*[145]

> It is well established that in the event of a default by a bidder the United States may retain the bid deposit as liquidated damages unless the amount is so large or disproportionate as to constitute a penalty.

States may require bid bonds on their construction contracts as a matter of law or public policy. While not all states have statutory provisions requiring bid bonds, the power of public agencies to require such bonds is not generally dependent upon statute. Thus it is generally conceded that a municipal corporation or other public agency or body that has been empowered to let a contract, as well as the state itself, may require the contractor to furnish a surety bond, although express statutory authority for such a requirement is lacking.[146]

A summary of the major provisions of all state laws concerning public bonds may be found in the *Credit Manual of Commercial Laws,* published

---

[142] *See Diamond Int'l Corp.,* Comp. Gen. Dec. B-180426, 74-2 CPD ¶ 139 (1974).

[143] *See, e.g., Bolivar Reorganized School Dist. No. 1, Polk County v. American Sur. Co. of N.Y.,* 307 S.W.2d 405 (Mo. 1957).

[144] *See Brown v. United States,* 152 F. 964 (2nd Cir. 1907) and *Bd. of Educ. of Union Free School Dist. No. 3 v. Maryland Casualty Co.,* 277 A. D. 936, 98 N.Y.S.2d 865 (App. Div. 4 Dept. 1950) (in the context of the difference in cost exceeding the penal sum of the bond).

[145] 161 Ct. Cl. 455, 468 (1963).

[146] *Union Indem. Co. v. State,* 217 Ala. 35, 114 So. 415 (1927); *Southwestern Portland Cement Co. v. Williams,* 32 N.M. 68, 251 P. 380 (1926); *Foster v. Kerr & Houston,* 133 Mass. 389, 179 A. 297 (1907).

by the National Association of Credit Management and updated annually. Although the practice is perhaps more common in connection with public contracts, bids on private contracts are also occasionally required to be accompanied by bid bonds.

The surety's liability on a bid bond stems from the failure of the contractor to enter into a contract with the owner (whether private or public) upon the basis of his bid as submitted. The contractor's liability to the surety in turn rests upon express indemnity provisions included in such bonds, pursuant to which the contractor agrees to reimburse the surety for any amounts the surety is held liable for under the bond or, in the rarer case, upon common law principles of indemnity.

The extent of liability under a bid bond is usually a fixed sum specified in the bond or the difference between the bid submitted by the defaulting contractor and the next lowest bidder or the price at which the owner is forced to contract.[147] For example, in *Board of Educ. of Community United School Dist. No. 303 v. George S. Walker Plumbing & Heating, Inc.*,[148] summary judgment was awarded the owner for the difference between the lowest bidder's bid and the second bidder's contract price because the lowest bidder, whose bid was accepted, refused to enter into a contract. With respect to the contractor's risks, it should be noted that the surety also received summary judgment against the contractor for indemnification at the same time. Indemnification between the contractor and surety usually arises out of the express obligations in the bond itself.

Courts have given various treatment to the limit of the surety's liability to the owner pursuant to the bond. In *A. J. Colella, Inc. v. Allegheny County*,[149] the amount of recovery was limited to the penal sum of the bid bond although the difference between the amount of the bid and the amount at which the county ultimately let a contract greatly exceeded the penalty of the bond.

Other cases have held that the penal amount of the bid bond is in effect a liquidated damages provision. Thus, upon failure of the low bidder to enter into a contract, the owner was entitled to recover the penal sum of the bond, even though the difference between the defaulting contractor's bid and the eventual contract price was less.[150]

Several defenses have been argued by a defaulting contractor and its bid bond surety when the contractor has refused to enter into a contract and there has been a call on the bond. Under appropriate facts, the contractor may successfully argue that there has been a material change in the contract upon which the bid was submitted. Such was the case in *Northeastern Constr. Co. v. City of Winston-Salem*,[151] where after bid opening the municipal authority

---

[147] *Brown*, fn. 144, *supra.*
[148] 5 Ill. App. 3d 418, 282 N.E.2d 268 (1972).
[149] 391 Pa. 103, 137 A.2d 265 (Pa. 1958).
[150] *See Bellefonte Borough Auth. v. Gateway Equip. & Supply Co.*, 442 Pa. 492, 277 A.2d 347 (1971) and *City of Lake Geneva v. States Improvement Co.*, 45 Wis. 2d 50, 172 N.W.2d 176 (1969).
[151] 83 F.2d 57 (4th Cir. 1936).

eliminated approximately 15 percent of the work. Furthermore, the contractor and its surety may also be released where the contractor made a material mistake in its bid as well as where bid conditions are not met.[152] *See also Hennepin Pub. Water Dist. v. Petersen Constr. Co.,*[153] where the contract was not awarded within the prescribed statutory period.

In some circumstances, contractors may have claims against their sureties if, after execution of the bid bond and before award, the surety refuses to execute the necessary payment and performance bonds for the contractor who is the low bidder. While the giving of the bid bond ordinarily does not obligate the surety to furnish additional bonds, some contractors have claimed against their bid bond surety for the surety's refusal to issue the other bonds necessary for the contractor to accept award.

In attempting to assert such a claim against the surety, the contractor might use an estoppel argument if sufficient facts can be presented to indicate that words or conduct on the part of the surety were relied upon by the contractor to the contractor's detriment.[154] In addition, even though the surety company, where a standard form of application is used, is not obligated to furnish payment and performance bonds upon the furnishing of the bid bond, the contractor might be able to introduce evidence tending to show that the writing of payment and performance bonds is customary after the writing of the bid bond.[155]

1.19 "BID SHOPPING"—DOES THE PRIME CONTRACTOR HAVE AN OBLIGATION TO THE SUBCONTRACTOR WITH THE LOWEST PRICE?

One of the most emotional issues connected with the prime contractor/subcontractor relationship involves "bid shopping" by the prime contractor. "Bid shopping" refers to actions taken by the prime contractor after award of the prime contract to reduce subcontractor prices by "shopping" the lowest bid in a particular craft from subcontractor to subcontractor. One court has referred to such postaward conduct as "bid chiseling" and defined "bid shopping" or "bid peddling" as those actions occurring before award of the prime contract.[156]

Although "bid shopping" has been described as "the purest form of competition," virtually all subcontractors and suppliers categorically reject the possibility of *any* virtue in the practice. See Orrick, "Trade Associations Are

---

[152] *See* 52 A.L.R.2d 792.
[153] 54 Ill. 2d 327, 297 N.E.2d 131 (Ill. 1973).
[154] *See generally Reynolds v. Gorton,* 30 Misc.2d 216, 213 N.Y.S.2d 561 (Sup. Ct. 1960).
[155] *Commercial Ins. Co. v. Hartwell Excavating Co.,* 89 Idaho 531, 407 P.2d 312 (1965).
[156] *People v. Inland Bid Depository,* 233 Cal. App. 2d 851, 44 Cal. Rptr. 206 (Cal. App. 5th Dist. 1965).

Boycott Prone—Bid Depositories as a Case Study."[157] Indeed, bid shopping has been condemned by The Code of Ethical Conduct of The Associated General Contractors of America (Pub. 1947, reprinted 1970). However, it remains present in the industry, and the difficult position of the subcontractor is magnified by the lack of available legal theories to bind the prime.

As a result of the various criticisms that have been leveled at bid shopping, several measures have been taken to eliminate, or at least, minimize, the practice. The first of these measures has been the establishment of local bid depositories for subcontractor bids. However, a number of depository by-law provisions necessary for the effective operation of bid depositories have been held to violate state and federal antitrust laws because of their restrictive effect on competition among both subcontractors and general contractors. In *Mechanical Contractors Bid Depository v. Christiansen,*[158] treble damages were awarded the plaintiff for antitrust violations by use of a bid depository.[159]

A second measure to combat bid shopping (which addresses any post-award bid shopping) has been the statutory or contractual requirement that the prime contractor list in its bid the subcontractors whom it intends to use.[160] Where listing is required, there may be a statutory duty not to substitute.[161] Only when a subcontractor is unable or unwilling to perform will substitution be permitted, and the prime contractor must seek consent to substitute from the awarding authority.[162] The requirement of subcontractor listing has in some instances resulted in actions by subcontractors against prime contractors.[163]

Federal regulations requiring subcontractor listing have been abandoned. The General Services Administration employed a subcontractor listing requirement for several years but eliminated the requirement in 1984.

In the absence of organized measures like bid depositories or subcontractor listing requirements, what measures are available to subcontractors to counteract the effects of bid shopping? Subcontractors bringing suits against "shopping" prime contractors generally base their actions on two theories of recovery:

(1) That the prime contractor through its acts (principally by using the subcontractor's bid in its own bid to the owner) has "accepted" the bid of the subcontractor, and has thereby entered into a subcontract; and/or

---

[157] 19 Hastings L. J. 505 (1968).

[158] 352 F.2d 817 (10th Cir. 1965), *cert. denied,* 384 U.S. 918 (1966).

[159] *Id., but see Cullum Elec. & Mechanical, Inc. v. Mechanical Contractors Ass'n of South Carolina,* 436 F. Supp. 418 (D.S.C. 1976), *aff'd,* 569 F.2d 821 (4th Cir.), *cert. denied,* 439 U.S. 910 (1978) (four-hour bid plan approved).

[160] *See, e.g.,* California Subletting and Subcontracting Fair Practices Act, Annotated California Codes, Public Contract Code, § 4100, *et seq.*

[161] *Id.* at § 4107.

[162] *See Southern California Acoustics Co. v. C. V. Holder, Inc.,* 71 Cal. 2d 719, 456 P.2d 975, 79 Cal. Rptr. 319 (1969).

[163] *Id.*

(2) That the conversations and negotiations between the subcontractor and the general contractor have created an oral agreement for performance of the subcontracted work.

Such subcontractor actions have generally not met with great success. The first theory of recovery set out above was rejected in *Williams v. Favret*[164] and in *Merritt-Chapman & Scott Corp. v. Gunderson Bros. Eng'g Corp.*,[165] where the court found, despite the fact that the subcontractor's bid had been listed as a part of the bid on the prime contract, that there had never been the requisite "meeting of minds" in negotiations between the prime and subcontractor, and thus no contract had resulted. The naming of Gunderson, the subcontractor, in the prime contractor's bid was found to make no difference in the result. Correspondingly, the argument for an oral contract is generally defeated by the Statute of Frauds, which requires that certain types of contracts be in writing.

The general lack of success of subcontractors in proving that a contract exists with the prime contractor prior to execution of a formal written subcontract or purchase order should not, however, leave the impression that there is no possibility of a prime contractor's being found contractually obligated to a subcontractor under appropriate circumstances. One of the common problems in proving a contract is to establish that there is a sufficiently specific agreement between the parties.

A reasonably specific agreement is necessary for enforcement. However, detailed items such as the precise scope of the work to be performed, the period of performance, and so on, are subjects that may not be discussed in preliminary negotiations. Nonetheless, many such details can be supplied from various sources. For example, certain items will be contained in the general and special conditions of the prime contract, the specifications, and in the drawings as set out in the bid documents. These details may be adopted by reference. Contract terms can also be proved by reference to custom and usage. Terms defining exactly what work is included in the contract and establishing a price for that work may be confirmed in writing without an elaborate document. A one-page letter or memorandum may succinctly encompass the few remaining details sufficient for a contract, and, if signed by the general contractor, can very well serve as an enforceable contract.

1.20 HOLDING SUBCONTRACTORS TO THEIR BIDS TO PRIME CONTRACTORS

Prime contractors can be faced with the unfortunate situation of having relied on a low subcontractor bid only to discover after award of the prime contract

---

[164] 161 F.2d 822 (5th Cir. 1947). A subcontractor was successful, when compelling facts were present, in *Electrical Constr. & Maintenance Co. v. Maeda Pacific Corp.*, 764 F.2d 619 (9th Cir. 1985).
[165] 305 F.2d 659 (9th Cir.), *cert. denied,* 371 U.S. 935 (1962).

that the subcontractor is unwilling to perform at the price originally bid. Although the prime contractor's formal, written bid has been accepted and the prime contractor is bound to the owner, the prime contractor has no contract with the subcontractor and is faced with making up the shortfall himself. Under the doctrine of promissory estoppel, however, the subcontractor may be bound to the prime contractor as if a subcontract had actually been executed.[166]

1.21 Doctrine of Promissory Estoppel

The doctrine of promissory estoppel is set forth in the Restatement (Second) of Contracts 2d (1981) as follows:

> A promise which the promisor should reasonably expect to induce action or forbearance on the part of the promisee (or a third person) and which does induce such action or forbearance is binding if injustice can be avoided only by the enforcement of the promise. The remedy granted for breach may be limited as justice requires.

The leading case regarding the application of the doctrine of promissory estoppel to subcontractors' bids is *Drennan v. Star Paving Co.*[167] Drennan, a general contractor, was preparing to bid on a school project in California. Star Paving Company submitted to Drennan a bid on the paving portion of the school job. Star's bid was submitted by telephone on the day that Drennan had to submit its bid to the school district. Because Star's bid was the lowest received on the paving work, Drennan included Star's price in its computation of the overall costs of the project, and submitted the total as its bid to the school district. Drennan was awarded the contract, as it had submitted the lowest general bid.

The next day Drennan visited the offices of Star and before he had the opportunity to do more than introduce himself, an officer of Star informed Drennan that Star was revoking its bid. Drennan indicated that he had used the bid in computing his own overall bid, and that he expected Star to carry out the work in accordance with the terms of Star's bid. Upon Star's refusal to do so, Drennan was forced to obtain a contract for the paving work from a different company at an increase in the price. Drennan sued Star for the amount of the price increase. The court applied the doctrine of promissory estoppel to rule that Star had become bound to the terms of its offer as a result of Drennan's detrimental reliance on the promises contained in the offer.

Indeed, subcontractors may be bound not only by the price given in their quote but also to subcontract terms deemed to be standard in the industry.

---

[166] *See* O. Currie and N. Sweeney, "Holding Subcontractors to Their Bids," *Construction Briefings*, No. 86-3, February 1986, Federal Publications, Inc.
[167] 51 Cal.2d 409, 333 P.2d 757 (1958).

For example, in *Crook v. Mortenson-Neal*,[168] a subcontractor whose bid was accepted balked at the scheduling and bonding requirements in the subcontract prepared by the general contractor. The court stated that:

> At the time [the subcontractor] bid on its subcontract, it should have expected to be bound by reasonable additional terms governing standard conditions implicit in the relationship between subcontractor and general contractor. Both industry custom, as expressed in standard form subcontracts, and the circumstances surrounding the particular project, dictate the kinds of provisions [the subcontractor] should reasonably have expected in its final subcontract.

The majority of courts now hold that a contractor may enforce a subcontractor's bid under a promissory estoppel theory.[169] (However, other courts have rejected the *Drennan* reasoning. For example, in *Home Elec. Co. of Lenoir v. Underdown Heating and Air Conditioning Co.*,[170] the court ruled as a matter of law that a subcontractor was not bound to its bid. The court was disturbed by the one-sided arrangement caused by promissory estoppel; the prime is allowed to enforce the subcontractor's price, while the subcontractor has no recourse if it is not awarded the subcontract. The court reasoned that prime contractors can avoid the problem by securing a contract with a subcontractor at the outset, conditioned on a successful bid to the owner.[171])

1.22   *Elements of the Doctrine of Promissory Estoppel* In order to hold a subcontractor to its bid under the doctrine of promissory estoppel, the contractor must show:

(1) A clear and definite offer by the subcontractor to perform the work at a certain price;

(2) A reasonable expectation by the subcontractor that the prime contractor will rely on the subcontractor's price in preparing the prime contractor's bid;

(3) Actual reliance by the prime contractor on the subcontractor's bid; and

(4) Detriment to the general contractor as a result of reliance on the subcontractor's bid and the subcontractor's subsequent refusal to perform.[172]

---

[168] 727 P.2d 297 (Alaska 1986).

[169] *See Allen M. Campbell Co., Gen. Contractors, Inc. v. Virginia Metal Indus., Inc.*, 708 F.2d 930 (4th Cir. 1983); *Hoel-Steffen Constr. Co. v. United States*, 231 Ct. Cl. 128, 684 F.2d 843 (1982); *James King & Son, Inc. v. De Santis Constr. No. 2 Corp.*, 97 Misc. 2d 1063, 413 N.Y.S.2d 78 (Sup. Ct. 1977); *Jenkins & Boller Co. v. Schmidt Iron Works, Inc.*, 36 Ill. App. 3d 1044, 344 N.E.2d 275 (Ill. App. 2d Dist. 1976); *E. A. Coronis Assocs. v. M. Gordon Constr. Co.*, 216 A.2d 246 (N.J. 1966).

[170] 86 N.C. App. 540, 358 S.E.2d 539 (N.C. App. 1987), *aff'd*, 322 N.C. 107, 366 S.E.2d 441 (N.C. 1988).

[171] *See also Anderson Constr. Co. v. Lyon Metal Products, Inc.*, 370 So.2d 935 (Miss. 1979).

[172] *Preload Technology, Inc. v. A. B. & J. Constr. Co.*, 696 F.2d 1080 (5th Cir. 1983); *E. A. Coronis Assocs.*, fn. 165, *supra*.

1.23 Clear and Definite Offer   Generally, a subcontractor submits its price to the general contractor as an offer to do the work at a specific price. However, the requirement that there be a clear and definite offer to perform a certain part of the work for a particular price prevents the application of the doctrine of promissory estoppel where a subcontractor or supplier offers only an estimate of the cost of the work to the prime contractor, without intending to make a definite offer to perform the work at that price.[173]   Likewise, where the bid is made expressly revocable or subject to revision, there is no clear and definite order.[174]

1.24 Subcontractor Expects Reliance   In order for the doctrine of promissory estoppel to apply to a subcontractor's bid, it must be reasonable for the subcontractor to have expected the general contractor to rely on the subcontractor's bid in the preparation of the prime contractor's overall bid. In order to prove that this was the expectation of the subcontractor, or else that it reasonably should have been his expectation, the courts have, in cases like *Constructors Supply Co. v. Bostrom Sheetmetal Works, Inc.,*[175] allowed the prime contractor to introduce testimony as to the ordinary customs and practices of the construction industry in this regard. Of course, evidence may also be presented to demonstrate a subcontractor's actual knowledge that a prime would use its quotation in submitting a bid for the overall project.[176]

1.25 General Contractor's Reliance Is Reasonable   Another fundamental requirement for the application of promissory estoppel is that the prime contractor's reliance on the subcontractor's bid must have been *reasonable.* Again, ordinary customs and practices of the construction industry can be relied on to establish the reasonableness of such reliance. Where the allegedly mistaken bid does not differ substantially from the other bids received and there is no obvious mathematical error in the bid, then the general contractor's reliance will normally be considered reasonable.

However, if the subcontractor's bid is much lower than other subcontract bids received on the same work, the prime contractor's reliance upon that bid may be unreasonable.[177] Furthermore, reasonable reliance will not be found where the general contractor misleads an inexperienced subcontractor into believing that the subcontract work can be performed at a price suggested by the general contractor, but, in fact, that price underestimates the true cost of performance.[178]

---

[173] *See N. Litterio & Co. v. Glassman Constr. Co.,* 319 F.2d 736 (D.C. Cir. 1963).

[174] *Preload Technology, Inc.,* fn. 168, *supra.*

[175] 291 Minn. 113, 190 N.W.2d 71 (1971).

[176] *Debron Corp. v. Nat'l Homes Constr. Corp.,* 493 F.2d 352 (8th Cir. 1974).

[177] *Edward Joy Co. v. Noise Control Prod., Inc.,* 111 Misc.2d 64, 443 N.Y.S.2d 361 (Sup. Ct. 1981); *Anderson Constr. Co.,* fn. 167, *supra.*

[178] *Architects & Contractors Estimating Serv., Inc. v. Smith,* 164 Cal. App. 3d 1001, 211 Cal. Rptr. 45 (Cal. App. 4th Dist. 1985).

However, if a prime contractor is confronted with an unusually low bid which it has not suggested, and verifies the bid, the prime contractor's reliance may be shown to be reasonable.[179]

Even if it can be established that the subcontractor's bid was mistaken, the subcontractor may be bound. In *Constructors Supply Co. v. Bostrum Sheetmetal Works, Inc.*,[180] the court found that a bid that was ten to eleven percent lower than the other subcontract bids was not self-evidently mistaken, and the general contractor was reasonable in relying upon it.[181]

1.26 Problems with the Statute of Frauds

It is common in the construction industry for a general contractor to receive subcontract bids on the date that the general contract bid is required to be submitted. Often these subcontract bids will be given over the telephone at the last minute, because the subcontractors wish to prevent general contractors from engaging in preaward "bid shopping." As a result, the general contractor is often in a position where it must rely upon these oral bids, with the possibility of substantial financial exposure should the subcontractors refuse to perform. The question therefore arises whether a general contractor, who is invoking the doctrine of promissory estoppel to enforce a subcontractor's bid, is barred by the Statute of Frauds if the subcontractor's bid is oral.

The Statute of Frauds is the designation for an English statute (29 Car. II, c. 3) passed in 1677 that has been adopted in one version or another in nearly every state. Its primary characteristic is that no legal action can be maintained on certain contracts in excess of a minimum dollar amount (often $500.00) or where the contract performance period is beyond a minimum period of time (often one year) unless the contract is in writing or evidenced by a writing signed by the party against whom the contract claim is asserted.[182]

The courts have split as to whether the Statute of Frauds defense is overcome by the promissory estoppel argument. In numerous cases, the Statute of Frauds has been held not to apply to subcontractor bids enforced under the doctrine of promissory estoppel.[183] However, in *Anderson Constr. Co. v. Lyon Metal Products, Inc.*,[184] the court ruled that a prime contractor was barred by the Statute of Frauds from recovering damages for a subcontractor's failure to honor its oral bid.

---

[179] *H. W. Stanfield Constr. Corp. v. Robert McMullan & Son, Inc.* (Cal. App. 4th Dist. 1971), 92 Cal. Rptr. 669; *Preload Technology*, fn. 168, *supra*.

[180] *Constructors Supply Co.*, fn. 171, *supra*.

[181] *See also, Saliba-Kringlen Corp. v. Allen Eng'g Co.*, 15 Cal. App. 3d 95, 92 Cal. Rptr. 799 (Cal. App. 2d Dist. 1971).

[182] *Black's Law Dictionary*, Fifth Edition, page 595 (West Publishing 1979).

[183] *See, e.g., Allen M. Campbell Co.*, fn. 165, *supra*; *Ralston Purina Co. v. McCollum*, 271 Ark. 840, 611 S.W.2d 201 (Ark. App. 1981).

[184] 370 So.2d 935 (Miss. 1979).

1.27 Damages

Assuming that the general contractor has established all the elements of an action based upon promissory estoppel, what is the measure of damages that it may receive from the subcontractor? In most cases, the measure has been the difference between the price at which the original subcontractor bid the work and the price that the general contractor has had to pay to obtain a replacement subcontractor.[185]

A somewhat different formulation of damages was used in *Constructors Supply Co. v. Bostrum Sheetmetal Works, Inc.*[186] In that case, the court found that the general contractor had not attempted to bid shop the defendant subcontractor. As a result, the general contractor was held entitled to recover its damages from the subcontractor. However, the court found that the general contractor had engaged in bid shopping on other subcontracts for the same project, and as a result, had saved a certain amount of money. The damages awarded to the general contractor for the difference in cost between the defendant subcontractor's bid and the cost of obtaining a replacement subcontractor were reduced by the amount that the general contractor had saved by bid shopping on other subcontractors. This case illustrates the extent to which some courts dislike the practice of bid shopping, and the danger that bid shopping poses to a general contractor who may want to use promissory estoppel to obtain damages from a subcontractor who has withdrawn its bid and refused to perform.

POINTS TO REMEMBER

Award of Competitively Bid Public Contracts

· Such contracts are generally awarded to the low bidder as long as:
  · The low bidder is financially, technically and historically responsible to perform the work; and
  · Its bid is responsive to the solicitation.
· Minor irregularities in the bid can be waived.
· Material irregularities may not be waived.

Bidding on Private Contracts

· Owner generally has broad discretion in selecting contractor.

Elements of a Mistaken Bid

· The error must be large in comparison to overall bid price.
· The mistake must relate to an important or "material" aspect of the work.

---

[185] *See, e.g, C & K Eng'g Contractors v. Amber Steel Co.,* 23 Cal.3d 1, 587 P.2d 1136, 151 Cal. Rptr. 323 (1978); *James King & Son, Inc.,* fn. 165, *supra.*
[186] *See* fn. 171, *supra.*

· The mistake cannot be the product of the bidder's own negligence:
  · Relief is more likely for mathematical error.
  · Relief is less likely for subjective estimating error.
· The owner must be capable of being returned to the status quo.
· Timely notice of the mistake must be given.

Potential Relief from Bid Mistakes (Maximizing the Mistaken Bidder's Potential for Success)

· Notify the owner or public contracting official *immediately* upon discovery of the mistake.
· Request modification or withdrawal of bid *in writing*.
· Request immediate *conference* with owner or public contracting official to discuss the mistake.
· Put together *evidence* of the mistake to present to owner or public contracting official including:
  · Affidavits of those individuals involved in bid preparation explaining the mistake
  · Copies of the bid
  · Original worksheets
  · Subcontractor quotes
  · Published price lists or trade cataloges
  · Any other data used to prepare the bid
· Gear presentation to *prove:*
  · The existence of the mistake
  · How the mistake happened
  · The bid that was intended

Efforts to Relieve Bid Shopping

· Bid depositories
  · Not very successful
· Subcontractor listing requirements
  · Not frequently used

Holding the Subcontractor to its Bid—Promissory Estoppel

· Promissory estoppel requires a clear and definite offer from subcontractor.
· Subcontractor must expect general contractor to rely on subcontractor's bid.

- General contractor must actually rely on subcontractor's bid.
  - General contractor's reliance on subcontractor's bid needs to be reasonable:
  - General contractor may not rely on obviously mistaken bid.
  - General contractor may not mislead subcontractor into unfairly low price.
- Damages, if subcontractor refuses to perform in accordance with bid, include difference between the bid and ultimate subcontractor price.

2

INTERPRETING
THE CONTRACT

2.1 THE IMPORTANCE OF CONTRACT INTERPRETATION

The "contract" is the foundation of virtually every relationship in the construction industry. Contract interpretation is the process of determining what the parties agreed to in their contract. It involves deciding the meaning of words, filling in gaps, and resolving conflicts. The more familiar you are with the basic rules of contract interpretation, the better your chances are of avoiding the numerous problems that frequently arise during the negotiation and performance of construction contracts.

2.2 WHAT IS A "CONTRACT"?

A "contract" may be succinctly defined as a set of promises. If a contract is enforceable, the law requires the performance of these promises and provides a remedy if they are not performed. Every contract must satisfy the following conditions to be enforceable:

(1) There must be a real agreement between the parties, that is, a true "meeting of the minds" on the subject matter of the contract;
(2) The subject matter must be lawful;
(3) There must be sufficient consideration;
(4) The parties must have the legal capacity to contract; and
(5) There must be compliance with legal requirements regarding the form of the contract; for example, some contracts must be made in writing.

The law will refuse to enforce a contract that fails to meet any of these requirements. Practical considerations, however, require recognition. For example, even if an oral contract is enforceable, the complexities of the construction business make reliance on an oral agreement a risky proposition.

The promises that constitute a contract may do more than just impose duties on the promisor and grant rights to the promisee. They may also operate to allocate certain risks that would ultimately make performance by one party more difficult or expensive. Thus a court, when interpreting a contract, may speak not only in terms of contractual duties and rights, but also in terms of which party assumed the risk of certain contingencies.

2.3 THE GOAL OF CONTRACT INTERPRETATION

The goal of contract interpretation is to ascertain and enforce the intent of the parties at the time of contracting. It is rarely possible to determine what was in the minds of the parties at the time of contracting. Therefore, courts rely upon the objective manifestations of the parties.

A primary contract interpretation rule, which has several facets, is that the *reasonable, logical meaning* of the contract language will be presumed to be the meaning intended by the parties. This reasonable and logical meaning rule overrides all other rules of contract interpretation.[1]

According to this rule, contract language is interpreted as it would be understood by a reasonably intelligent and logical person familiar with the facts and circumstances surrounding the contract. Courts use two sources of information in determining this objective intent: (1) the language used by the parties in the contract; and (2) the facts and circumstances surrounding contract formation.

2.4 DEFINING CONTRACT TERMS

Contract interpretation starts by defining the contract's terms. These definitions come from three sources. First, the parties may have defined the terms within the contract. Second, technical terms are given their meaning within various industries and trades. Third, general terms are given their widely accepted meanings. Each of these sources of definitions are discussed below.

2.5 Terms Defined by the Parties

It is common practice for parties to define the terms they use in a contract. These agreed-upon definitions are the clearest manifestations of the parties' intent. Therefore, courts will generally abide by the parties' definitions.[2]

---

[1] *Alvin Ltd. v. United States Postal Serv.,* 816 F.2d 1562 (Fed. Cir. 1987); *Norcoast Constructors, Inc. v. United States,* 448 F.2d 1400 (Ct. Cl. 1971).
[2] *See, e.g., Guy F. Atkinson Co.,* ENGBCA 4891, 86-1 BCA ¶ 18,555.

2.6 Technical Terms

Terms may acquire nonstandard or technical meanings in certain industries or trades. These meanings may differ substantially from the meanings generally associated with those terms. Technical meanings will override generally accepted meanings when circumstances indicate that the parties intended to use the technical meaning of the term.[3]

2.7 Generally Accepted Definitions

Terms will be given the meanings generally ascribed to them, that is, unless the parties have defined a term otherwise or intended for a term to have a technical meaning.[4]

2.8 INTERPRETING THE LANGUAGE OF THE CONTRACT

The following sections examine the legal rules generally applicable to interpreting the language of a contract once its individual terms have been defined in accordance with the principles discussed in the prior section.

2.9 The Contract Must Be Considered as a Whole

A fundamental principle of contract interpretation is that a contract must be considered as a whole, giving effect to all of its parts.[5] Each part of the agreement should be examined with reference to all other parts, because one clause may modify, limit, or illuminate another.[6] Similarly, where several documents form an integral part of one transaction, a court may read these together with reference to one another even where the documents involved do not specifically refer to one another. A similar rule applies to documents annexed to the contract or incorporated in it by reference. Therefore, interpretation that leaves portions of the contract meaningless will generally be rejected. Likewise, if a contract is to be read as a whole, its provisions should, if possible, be harmonized.

2.10 Order of Precedence

It may be impossible to interpret a contract without avoiding a conflict. Construction contracts are complex, containing many provisions that are often drafted by different people. When two or more provisions conflict, however,

---

[3] *See, e.g., P. J. Dick Contracting, Inc.,* PSBCA 1097, 84-1 BCA ¶ 17,149.
[4] *See, e.g., Sauter Constr. Co.,* ASBCA 22338, 78-1 BCA ¶ 13,092.
[5] *Julius Goldman's Egg City v. United States,* 697 F.2d 1051 (Fed. Cir. 1983); *McDevitt Mechanical Contractors, Inc. v. United States,* 21 Cl. Ct. 616 (1990).
[6] *Plaza Dev. Serv. v. Joe Harden Builders, Inc.,* 365 S.E.2d 231 (S.C. Ct. App. 1988); *Yates v. Brown,* 170 S.E.2d 477 (N.C. 1969).

contract interpretation rules establishing an order of precedence may resolve the conflict.

The general conditions of most contracts include an "order of precedence" clause expressly stating which provisions take precedence over others in case of conflict.[7] For example, the order of precedence clause may state that the specifications generally take precedence over the drawings, special conditions take precedence over general conditions, and so on. However, in federal government contracts, provisions required by law generally cannot be altered by such a clause.

In the absence of an order of precedence clause, general common law rules of precedence will apply. For example, it is a basic rule of contract interpretation that general terms and provisions in a contract yield to specific ones.[8] It is also a uniform rule of contract interpretation that when specific requirements of contractual performance or specific recitals of contractual definitions are itemized and spelled out, that which is not expressly included is thereby excluded.[9] Additionally, handwritten terms take precedence over typewritten terms, which in turn take precedence over printed terms.[10]

2.11 THE FACTS AND CIRCUMSTANCES SURROUNDING CONTRACT FORMATION

Courts frequently interpret a contract based upon the facts and circumstances surrounding the contract's formation. This evidence comes in three forms: (1) evidence of discussions and conduct; (2) evidence of the parties' prior dealings; and (3) evidence of custom and usage in the industry.

2.12 Discussions and Conduct

The parties' discussions and conduct can be persuasive when interpreting a contract. For example, a contractor may become aware of a possible ambiguity at a prebid conference and request a clarification. Such a clarification may serve as proof that the parties agreed upon the resolution of a possible ambiguity and upon a common interpretation of the contract.

Similarly, one of the parties may make its interpretation of the contract known to the other party. This can be done expressly through discussions or impliedly by its actions. If the other party, knowing this interpretation, remains silent or does not object, then this interpretation will be binding.

---

[7] *See, e.g., Hensel Phelps Constr., Co. v. United States,* 886 F.2d 1296 (Fed. Cir. 1989).

[8] This rule is generally known as *ejusdem generis.* For application of the rule, *see Corso v. Creighton Univ.,* 731 F.2d 529 (8th Cir. 1984).

[9] This rule of contract law is generally known as *expressio unius. See* 17A *Corpus Juris Secundum* Contracts, § 312.

[10] *See, e.g., Wood River Pipeline Co. v. Willbros Energy Servs. Co.,* 738 P.2d 866 (Kan. 1987).

Evidence of the parties' discussions and conduct before, and at the time, a written contract is signed ("parol evidence") may not, however, be admissible. Reducing a contract to writing has legal consequences. Traditionally, the law has imposed certain rules that govern the use of evidence external to the terms of the contract to interpret or vary it. This is often termed the "parol evidence rule."[11]

The first question that must be answered to determine the admissibility of parol evidence is whether the contract is a final and complete expression of the parties' agreement. Parol evidence may be used to make this determination. If the contract is final and complete, normally parol evidence cannot be introduced into evidence to vary or contradict its unambiguous terms.[12] For example, in one case, a contractor was not allowed to rely upon an alleged prebid oral extension of time to establish an acceleration claim when such evidence would contradict the express provisions of the parties' written contract.[13] However, if a term is ambiguous, courts may hear extrinsic evidence concerning the parties' negotiations to ascertain the intention of the parties at the time of contracting.[14]

2.13 The Parties' Prior Dealings

If parties have dealt with each other previously, a court will look at prior behavior and practices to help interpret their current contract. Although evidence of an established pattern of prior dealings can be introduced to aid a court, it cannot be used to vary or modify the clear, express terms of a written contract. The "parol evidence rule" prevents such a use of extrinsic evidence.

The admission of prior dealings serves the purpose of showing what the parties intended by the language in the contract. For example, in a recent case, a Pennsylvania court interpreted an ambiguity in a contract as to the meaning of the term "positive shielding" in favor of the contractor based on the "conduct of the parties" throughout a prior project. The court allowed extrinsic evidence as to the parties' conduct to determine the parties' intent in using the term.[15]

As previously stated, extrinsic evidence is not generally admissible to show that one party intended something entirely different from what was clearly stated in the contract. A prior course of dealing may, however, show that the contract is not the final and complete agreement of the parties.[16]

---

[11] *See Lower Kuskokwim School Dist. v. Alaska Diversified Contractors, Inc.*, 734 P.2d 62 (Alaska 1987).

[12] *Rothlein v. Armour and Co.*, 377 F. Supp. 506, 510 (W.D. Pa. 1974). *See also Fuller Co. v. Brown Minneapolis Tank & Fabricating Co.*, 678 F. Supp. 506 (E.D. Pa. 1987).

[13] *Lower Kuskokwim School Dist.*, fn. 11, *supra.*

[14] *Taylor Freezer Sales Co., Inc. v. Hydrick*, 227 S.E.2d 494 (Ga. Ct. App. 1976); *Federal Realty Inv. Trust v. Belk-Tyler of Elizabeth City, Inc.*, 289 S.E.2d 145 (N.C. Ct. App. 1982).

[15] *Department of Transp. v. IA Constr. Corp.*, 588 A.2d 1327 (Pa. Commw. Ct. 1991).

[16] *Restatement of Contracts, 2d* §§ 209–210.

Prior conduct may also amount to waiver or estoppel. A party may be prevented from enforcing an explicit contract requirement if in prior dealings it did not require compliance with the requirement.[17]

2.14 Custom and Usages in the Industry

Customs of a particular industry may be introduced to show that the parties intended for an ordinary word to take on a specialized meaning.[18] Such evidence is admissible even though the term, on its face, is unambiguous.[19]

A party seeking to assert a trade custom practice must present substantial evidence that the custom is well established.[20] One method of establishing trade custom is to introduce the interpretations of other bidders on the contract.[21]

Similarly, a technical word will be given its ordinary meaning in the industry unless it is shown that the parties intended to use it in a different sense. The appropriate meaning of ambiguous technical terms may also be clarified by the introduction of extrinsic evidence. For example, in a classic case, a Texas Appellate Court allowed the introduction of evidence of custom to establish the intended meaning of the contract term "working days," as it related to the owner's right to assess liquidated damages for delay in completion.[22] More recently, the United States Court of Appeals for the Federal Circuit relied on trade practice to interpret patently ambiguous rebar requirements in a federal government construction contract.[23]

2.15 RESOLVING AMBIGUITIES

The rules of contract interpretation discussed above may not resolve every ambiguity in a contract. If an ambiguity remains, courts will apply one of the following two risk allocation principles to resolve the conflict: (1) the ambiguity should be construed against its drafter; and (2) the ambiguity should be construed against the party who failed to request a clarification of the ambiguity. These principles are discussed below.

2.16 Construction against the Drafter

The risk of ambiguous contract language is generally allocated to the party responsible for drafting the ambiguity unless the nondrafting party knew of

---

[17] *L. W. Foster Sportswear Co. v. United States*, 405 F.2d 1285 (Ct. Cl. 1969).

[18] *See, e.g., Rosenberg v. Turner*, 98 S.E. 763 (Va. 1919).

[19] *Gholson, Byars & Holmes Constr. Co. v. United States*, 351 F.2d 987 (Ct. Cl. 1965); *Haehn Management Co. v. United States*, 15 Cl. Ct. 50 (1988), *aff'd*, 878 F.2d 1445 (Fed. Cir. 1989).

[20] *W. G. Cornell Co. of Washington D.C., Inc. v. United States*, 376 F.2d 299 (Ct. Cl. 1967).

[21] *See Eagle Paving*, AGBCA 75-156, 78-1 BCA ¶ 13,107.

[22] *Lewis v. Jones*, 251 S.W.2d 942 (Tex. Ct. App. 1952).

[23] *Fortec Constructors v. United States*, 760 F.2d 1288 (Fed. Cir. 1985).

or should have known of, the ambiguity.[24] Several requirements must be met for this principle to apply.

First, there must truly be an ambiguity; that is, the contract must be susceptible to two reasonable interpretations. Thus a nondrafting party's interpretation need not be the only reasonable interpretation for this principle to apply.[25] Second, one of the two parties must have chosen the ambiguous contract language. Third, the nondrafting party must demonstrate that it relied on its own interpretation.[26]

2.17 Duty to Request Clarification

An ambiguous contract provision will not be construed against its drafter, however, if the nondrafting party fails to clarify a patent ambiguity prior to bidding. Ambiguities are either *patent* or *latent.* A patent ambiguity is one that is readily apparent from the wording of the contract.[27] In contrast, language containing a latent ambiguity initially appears to be clear and unambiguous, but actually contains an inherent ambiguity that becomes apparent after a close examination or presentation of extrinsic facts.[28]

A bidder generally has an obligation to seek a clarification of patent (obvious) ambiguities or inconsistencies that appear in the bid documents. For example, in one case, bid documents contained a clause requiring prospective bidders to inform the contracting officer of discrepancies in the plans and specifications. The United States Court of Claims held against a contractor who failed to comply with that requirement and later sought to rely on an ambiguity in its claim.[29] The court held that the bidder had an affirmative obligation to call to the government's attention an "obvious omission, inconsistency or discrepancy of significance" in a specification if the bidder intended to take advantage of it. In that case, the bidder did not alert the contracting officer to a patent and glaring discrepancy and the court barred the contractor from recovering any damages caused by the discrepancy in the specification.[30]

The difficulty here is determining whether an ambiguity was patent *prior to bidding.* One factor used to make this determination is whether other bidders requested a clarification.[31]

---

[24] The technical name for this interpretive rule is *contra proferentem.* For a thorough discussion of this principle in the context of government contracts, *see* John T. Flynn, "The Rule of Contra Proferentem in the Government Contract Interpretation Process," 11 Pub. Cont. L.J. 379 (1980). *See also United States v. Turner Constr. Co.,* 819 F.2d 283 (Fed. Cir. 1987).

[25] *Bennett v. United States,* 371 F.2d 859 (Ct. Cl. 1967); *Gall Landau Young Constr. Co.,* ASBCA 25801, 83-1 BCA ¶ 16,359; *Malone,* ASBCA 30384 & 30385, 87-2 BCA ¶ 19,758.

[26] *Fruin-Colnon Corp. v. United States,* 912 F.2d 1426 (Fed. Cir. 1990).

[27] *See Big Chief Drilling Co. v. United States,* 15 Cl. Ct. 295 (1988).

[28] *See AWC, Inc.,* PSBCA 1747, 88-2 BCA ¶ 20,637.

[29] *Beacon Constr. Co. of Mass. v. United States,* 314 F.2d 501 (Ct. Cl. 1963).

[30] 314 F.2d at 504. *See also, Big Chief Drilling Co.,* fn. 27, *supra.*

[31] *See W. M. Schlosser Co., Inc.,* VABCA 1802, 83-2 BCA ¶ 16,630.

2.18   IMPLIED CONTRACT OBLIGATIONS

Every contract contains implied obligations in addition to obligations expressly set forth in the contract. These implied obligations allocate particular risks between the parties in the absence of contract clauses addressing those risks. Two of the most significant of these implied obligations are discussed below.

2.19   Duty to Cooperate

From the contractor's standpoint, perhaps the most important implied contract obligation is an owner's implied duty of cooperation. In an old but often cited case, the United States Court of Claims, in awarding a contractor damages for owner-caused delays, thoroughly reviewed the generally accepted authorities supporting the duty to cooperate in the context of a construction contract and stated:

> [I]t is, however, an implied provision of every contract, whether it be one between individuals or between an individual and the Government, that neither party to the contract will do anything to prevent performance thereof by the other party or that will hinder or delay him in its performance.[32]

There are numerous factual situations illustrating this implied duty to cooperate.[33]

This duty also encompasses the obligation to coordinate the activities of other parties with whom the owner has contracted but who lack a direct contractual link with the contractor. For example, the owner has an implied *duty to coordinate* the work of parallel prime contractors.[34]

In a school project in New York, separate contracts were let for the general construction, heating, electrical and plumbing portions of the work. Numerous times during the progress of the work, the plumbing contractor notified the State of New York that it was being delayed by the general contractor's lack of progress. In awarding the plumbing contractor damages, the New York Court of Claims made the following observations:

---

[32] *George A. Fuller Co. v. United States,* 69 F. Supp. 409 (Ct. Cl. 1947). *See also Coatesville Contractors & Engineers, Inc. v. Borough of Ridley Park,* 506 A.2d 862 (Pa. 1986).

[33] *See Lewis-Nicholson, Inc. v. United States,* 550 F.2d 26 (Ct. Cl. 1977) (U.S. Government breached implied obligation not to unreasonably delay road construction contractor when it failed to properly stake work site); *Gulf, Mobile and Ohio R.R. Co. v. Illinois Central R.R. Co.,* 128 F. Supp. 311, *aff'd,* 225 F.2d 816 (5th Cir. 1955) (railroad that asked Interstate Commerce Commission to order the abandonment of a certain route may not later plead that such an order relieves it of the duty to cooperate in the performance of a contract); *Griffin Mfg. Co. v. Boom Boiler & Welding Co.,* 90 F.2d 209 (6th Cir.), *cert. denied,* 302 U.S. 741 (1937) (owner and operator of plant had a duty not to delay or obstruct the installation of equipment by seller of equipment); *Great Lakes Constr. Co. v. United States,* 96 Ct. Cl. 378 (1942) (contractor may recover for unwarranted delays in construction of federal building caused by government).

[34] *See, e.g., Baldwin-Lima-Hamilton Corp. v. United States,* 434 F.2d 1371 (Ct. Cl. 1970).

But to avoid liability, the State must at least show some effort to carry out its obligation to see that the work progresses properly and is properly coordinated within the purview of the contract. Here the State failed in this obligation and unreasonably failed to supervise, coordinate and see to the progress of the work.[35]

Thus, when an owner fails to provide necessary coordination, it must generally respond by paying delay or disruption damages.[36] This principle also applies to general contractors in their coordination of subcontractors.

Naturally this implied duty is a fertile source of controversy among owners, general contractors and subcontractors. In an effort to avoid this potential liability for damages, many owners and general contractors have inserted a no-damages-for-delay provision in their contracts, attempting to protect themselves from delay damages attributable to certain specified causes. Such clauses typically provide that in the event of delay, the contractor or subcontractor will be entitled to a time extension only.

However, a court may limit the operation of such a no-damages-for-delay clause upon the showing of a party's fraud, concealment or active interference with performance of a contract.[37] Similarly, a court may not enforce such a clause if it concludes that the cause of the delay is not one of those enumerated in or contemplated by the parties in the contract.

2.20 Warranty of Plans and Specifications

Another very important implied obligation is that the party (usually the owner) furnishing the plans and specifications impliedly warrants their adequacy and sufficiency.[38] This doctrine, now recognized in virtually every state, was first propounded by the United States Supreme Court in *United States v. Spearin,* where the Court stated:

> [I]f the contractor is bound to build according to plans and specifications prepared by the owner, the contractor will not be responsible for the consequences of defects in the plans and specifications.[39]

In the typical situation of owner furnished plans and specifications, the Spearin Doctrine means that the contractor will not be liable for an unsatisfactory final result if the contract documents are followed. This implied warranty

---

[35] *Snyder Plumbing & Heating Corp. v. State,* 198 N.Y.S.2d 600, 604 (Ct. Cl. 1960).

[36] *See Gasparini Excavating Co. v. Pennsylvania Turnpike Comm'n,* 187 A.2d 157 (Pa. 1963); *L. L. Hall Constr. Co. v. United States,* 379 F.2d 559 (Ct. Cl. 1966); *Freeman Contractors, Inc. v. Central Sur. & Ins. Corp.,* 205 F.2d 607 (8th Cir. 1953).

[37] *See Newberry Square Dev. Corp. v. Southern Landmark, Inc.,* 578 So.2d 750 (Fla. 1st DCA 1991); *DAL Constr. Corp. v. City of N.Y.,* 485 N.Y.S.2d 774 (App. Div. 1985); *Corinno Civetta Constr. Corp. v. New York,* 502 N.Y.S.2d 681 (1986).

[38] *See, e.g., Ordnance Research, Inc. v. United States,* 609 F.2d 462 (Ct. Cl. 1979); *State Highway Dep't v. Hewitt Contracting Co.,* 146 S.E.2d 632 (Ga. 1966).

[39] 248 U.S. 132, 136 (1918).

applies to owner-furnished plans and specifications even though the owner's architect or engineer actually prepared the plans and specifications.[40]

In a recent Indiana case, a federal court of appeals enforced the Spearin Doctrine, holding that an owner impliedly warranted the suitability of specified exterior face bricks.[41] The court refused to accept the owner's argument that its implied warranty of design was "trumped" by the contractor's express warranty against defective materials.

The Spearin Doctrine can be used, not only defensively, protecting a contractor encountering problems, but also offensively. A contractor or subcontractor may recover for delays, extra work, disruption and constructive changes when there are errors in the plans and specifications.[42] In one case, a Louisiana court held that this warranty allowed a subcontractor to recover from the general contractor for defects in the specifications that necessitated repairing breaks in a sewer line. The court further held that the general contractor was entitled to indemnity from the owner for any amounts paid to the subcontractor.[43] Generally, in federal government contracts all delays due to defective plans are considered to be compensable.[44]

The implied warranty applies with the most force to design specifications, but it also applies to performance specifications with a lesser impact. An owner is not responsible for a contractor's difficulty in achieving a performance specification unless the specification's requirements are either impossible or commercially impracticable to achieve.[45]

The Spearin Doctrine also applies in design-build projects. However, since the contractor controls the design, the contractor, not the owner, impliedly warrants the adequacy and sufficiency of the design. In one case involving a design-build or "turn-key" construction contract, a court held that where the contractor assumed responsibility for the employment of the architect and the preparation of plans and specifications at its own expense, the contractor was responsible for the design of the project and assumed the risks of any defects or deficiencies in the design.[46]

An implied warranty of plans and specifications claim will only be successful if the claimant can prove that the defective plans or specifications caused the requested damages.[47] The claimant must also prove that it reasonably relied upon the plans and specifications. For example, a claimant who knew or should have known of the defect prior to bidding cannot successfully pursue an implied warranty claim.[48]

[40] *Greenhut Constr. Co., Inc.*, ASBCA 15192, 71-1 BCA ¶8845.

[41] *Trustees of Indiana Univ. v. Aetna Casualty & Sur. Co.*, 920 F.2d 429 (7th Cir. 1990).

[42] *See USA Petroleum Corp. v. United States*, 821 F.2d 622 (Fed. Cir. 1987); *R. M. Hollingshead Corp. v. United States*, 111 F. Supp. 285 (Ct. Cl. 1953).

[43] *Keller Constr. Corp. v. George W. McCoy & Co.*, 119 So.2d 450 (La. 1960). *See also W. F. Magann Corp. v. Diamond Mfg. Co., Inc.*, 775 F.2d 1202 (4th Cir. 1985).

[44] *See Chaney and James Constr Co. v. United States*, 421 F.2d 728 (Ct. Cl. 1970).

[45] *Intercontinental Mfg. Co. Inc. v. United States*, 4 Cl. Ct. 591 (1984).

[46] *Mobile Hous. Env't v. Barton and Barton*, 432 F. Supp. 1343 (D. Colo. 1977).

[47] *See Felton Constr. Co.*, AGBCA 406-9, 81-1 BCA ¶ 14,932.

[48] *See Johnson Controls, Inc. v. United States*, 671 F.2d 1312 (Ct. Cl. 1982); *Allied Contractors, Inc. v. United States*, 381 F.2d 995 (Ct. Cl. 1967).

POINTS TO REMEMBER

- A contract should be entered into and performed with an awareness and understanding of the principles of contract interpretation.
- Contracts should be written.
- Contracts should fully:
  (1) Allocate risks between the parties.
  (2) Embody the parties' entire agreement.
- Important contract terms should be defined.
- A contract should contain an order of precedence clause.
- Reliance upon prior or contemporaneous discussions and conduct, prior dealings and industry usages is risky. The terms of the contract itself should address these issues explicitly.
- The drafter of the contract must be aware that when both parties to a construction contract submit a reasonable interpretation of an ambiguous provision, in most cases, the contract language will be construed against the drafter.
- Contractors have an obligation to inform owners of patent ambiguities or inconsistencies in bid documents.
- Every contract contains implied obligations in addition to those obligations expressly stated in the contract.
- Two of the most important implied obligations are the duty to cooperate and the duty to furnish accurate and adequate plans and specifications.

3

THE UNIFORM COMMERCIAL CODE AND THE CONSTRUCTION INDUSTRY

3.1 THE UNIFORM COMMERCIAL CODE

The Uniform Commercial Code (UCC or Code) is a system of rules governing a wide variety of business transactions and commercial instruments. These include, among others, the sale of goods, negotiable instruments, bulk transfers, letters of credit, and certain credit transactions involving security interests. In the construction context, the Code primarily affects transactions involving the sale of materials or equipment.

The UCC was developed by a group of legal scholars and practitioners in an effort to lend uniformity to the state laws governing such transactions, which often involve parties in two or more states. The UCC has been adopted by forty-nine states, the District of Columbia, and the Virgin Islands. The lone holdout, Louisiana, has adopted all but Article 2 (sale of goods) and Article 9 (secured credit transactions). The UCC has been adopted in substantially the same form from state to state, resulting in considerable uniformity of law in the affected kinds of business transactions. Almost all states, however, have modified the UCC to some extent. In addition, although the UCC has not been enacted as federal statutory law, some federal courts have considered the UCC as representative of federal law applicable to federal government supply contracts.[1]

3.2 APPLICABILITY OF THE UCC TO CONSTRUCTION

The UCC article most frequently encountered in the construction industry is, by far, Article 2, which deals with the sale of "goods." In fact, Article 2 will be involved to some extent in virtually every construction project.

[1] *See Padbloc Co. v. United States,* 161 Ct. Cl. 369 (1963).

Article 2 of the Code governs transactions involving the sale of "goods," which the Code defines as "all things (including specially manufactured goods) which are movable at the time of identification to the contract for sale."[2] Given this broad definition of "goods," it would seem that the UCC should apply to any contract involving the sale of materials, equipment, tools, and so on, in connection with a construction project.

Many construction-related contracts involving the sale of "goods" also involve the furnishing of labor or other services. Contracts for services generally are governed by a separate body of contract law, which in all states except Louisiana is based on the common law. Since the UCC does not apply to contracts for the sale of services, it is not always easy to determine whether the UCC is applicable. Where the contract calls exclusively for the furnishing of materials, equipment, or other "goods," the UCC clearly applies. Where the contract calls exclusively for the furnishing of labor or other services, the UCC clearly does not apply.

Many contracts, however, are "hybrid" in nature, that is, they call for the furnishing of *both* goods and services. The courts have employed several methods to determine whether the UCC applies to a "hybrid" construction contract. *Most courts* have adopted an approach that evaluates whether the *predominant nature* of the contract is a sale of goods with labor incidentally involved or a contract for services with the furnishing of goods incidentally involved. If the main purpose of the contract is the sale of goods, the UCC is applicable, even though labor or other services are required in connection with the sale.[3] A few courts have applied the UCC to just the portion of a "hybrid" contract pertaining to goods, even if the contract was predominantly a labor contract.[4] This approach is applied especially where the goods are supplied separately and could have been purchased off-the-shelf by the buyer.[5]

---

[2] § 2-105.

[3] *See, e.g., United States v. City of Twin Falls, Idaho*, 806 F.2d 862 (9th Cir. 1986), *cert. denied sub nom., City of Twin Falls, Idaho v. Envirotech Corp.*, 482 U.S. 914 (1987) (contract to furnish and install sludge control equipment governed by Article 2); *Pittsburgh–Des Moines Steel Co. v. Brookhaven Manor Water Co.*, 532 F.2d 572 (7th Cir. 1976) (sale and installation of million-gallon water tank governed by Article 2); *Bonebrake v. Cox*, 499 F.2d 951 (8th Cir. 1974) (sale and installation of bowling alley equipment governed by Article 2); *Standard Structural Steel Co. v. Debron Corp.*, 515 F. Supp. 803 (D. Conn. 1980), *aff'd*, 657 F.2d 265 (2d. Cir. 1981) (sub-subcontract to design and fabricate steel was contract for sale of goods with services incidentally involved); *Meyers v. Henderson Constr. Co.*, 370 A.2d 547 (N.J. 1977) (contract to supply and install overhead doors governed by Article 2); *Mennonite Deaconess Home & Hospital, Inc. v. Gates Engineering Co.*, 219 Neb. 303, 363 N.W.2d 155 (1985) (installation of one-ply roof membrane governed by Article 2); *Port City Constr. Co. v. Henderson*, 266 So.2d 896 (Ala. App. 1972) (contract for sale of concrete and "all labor to pour and finish" held to be a sale of goods); *Gulf Coast Fabricators, Inc. v. Mosley*, 439 So.2d 36 (Ala. 1983) (sale and erection of prefabricated metal building governed by Article 2); *Colorado Carpet Installation, Inc. v. Palermo*, 668 P.2d 1384 (Colo. 1983) (installation of carpet a sale of goods); *Town of Hooksett School Dist. v. W. R. Grace & Co.*, 617 F. Supp. 126 (D.N.H. 1984) (Code applied without discussion to sale and installation of asbestos insulation).

[4] *See, e.g., Foster v. Colorado Radio Corp.*, 381 F.2d 222 (10th Cir. 1967).

[5] *Anthony Pools v. Sheehan*, 455 A.2d 434 (Md. 1983) (supply of diving board governed by UCC even though construction of swimming pool was not).

There is no hard and fast rule to determine whether the UCC applies to a hybrid construction contract. Generally speaking, the UCC is more likely to be applied to a hybrid construction contract that does not require the performance of labor or other services *at the job site*. The UCC also is more likely to be applied where the hybrid contract is entered into by way of a purchase order rather than a subcontract. The UCC is less likely to apply to a prime contract with an owner, which is usually deemed to be a contract primarily for services. These general rules of thumb are subject to exceptions, however, and should not be relied upon to predict with certainty whether the UCC will apply to any particular transaction.

3.3 MODIFYING UCC OBLIGATIONS

Even when the UCC applies, the buyer and seller may, by agreement, alter nearly all the terms of the UCC. Section 1-102(3) of the UCC expressly provides that the effect of provisions and obligations of the Code may, except where specifically limited, be varied by agreement of the parties. In addition, some Code sections specify that parties may "contract out" of that particular section of the UCC. Certain obligations cannot be limited or disclaimed by agreement of the parties. These are the obligations to act in good faith, with diligence, with due care, and in a reasonable manner. These obligations are implied in all transactions covered by the UCC. Section 102(3) does provide, however, that the parties may determine by agreement the standards by which performance of these obligations is to be measured.

3.4 CONTRACT FORMATION UNDER THE UCC

The traditional common law rules of contract formation provide that a contract is formed by an offer and an acceptance of that offer. Under the common law, an offer is rejected unless the acceptance is, in effect, its "mirror image." For example, under the common law, if the "acceptance" contains terms in addition to or differing from those contained in the offer, it is treated as a rejection of the offer and as a counteroffer. If the parties then perform, the terms of the counteroffer constitute the agreement. Article 2 governing the sale of goods changes this result and attempts to bring the process of contract formation into line with the realities of business practices relating to the sale of goods.

3.5 Total Agreement on All Terms and Conditions Is Not Required

Departing from the formal offer-acceptance structure of the common law, Article 2 focuses upon the practical conduct of the parties. Under the UCC, a contract for the sale of goods may be formed in any manner sufficient to show agreement, including conduct by the parties that establishes the existence of a contract.[6]

Under § 2-207, an acceptance no longer is required to be a "mirror image" of the offer. Instead, even though it may contain different or additional terms, a definite expression of acceptance or a written confirmation sent within a reasonable time will operate as an acceptance *unless* the acceptance is expressly made conditional upon the offeror's acceptance of the additional terms. Additional terms are treated as proposals for additions to the contract. These will become part of the contract unless the offer limits acceptance to its terms or the offeror timely objects to the additional terms. Finally, as mentioned above, the parties' conduct may be sufficient to establish a contract despite major unresolved conflicts in the written offer and acceptance. Total agreement between the parties on all terms is not required. In such a case the contract consists of the terms upon which the parties agree, along with the implied terms (price, time, etc.) provided elsewhere in Article 2 and discussed in the next section.

3.6 The Requirement for a Written Contract

Section 2-201 provides that contracts for the sale of goods valued in excess of $500 are not enforceable unless there exists some writing "sufficient to indicate that a contract for sale has been made between the parties and signed by the party against whom enforcement is sought." This rule has several exceptions and can be satisfied in several ways. For example, the requirement of a writing is also satisfied where one party, within a reasonable time, sends a written confirmation of the contract to the other party and the receiving party has reason to know of the contents of the confirmation and fails to give written notice of objection to its contents within ten days after receipt.[7] The writing requirement does not apply when:

(1) The goods are specially manufactured for the buyer and the seller has started manufacturing or procuring the goods;

(2) The opposing party admits in court papers the existence of the contract; or

(3) The goods have been received and accepted, or payment has been made and accepted.

Of course, the best way to ensure compliance with the requirement for a written contract is to formalize the contract into a document signed by both parties. This often is impractical or not customary practice, such as ordering

---

[6] *See* § 2-207(3).

[7] *See Atlas R. Constr. Co. v. Commercial Stone Co.,* 33 D&C 3d 477 (Pa. Ct. Comm. Pl. 1984) (contractor's lawyer's demand letter sent to stone supplier three and one-half months after breach of oral contract held timely written confirmation of oral contract).

supplies or materials by telephone. In such cases, either party may be able to back out if none of the above exceptions apply.

3.7 Withdrawal of an Offer

The Code, unlike the common law applicable to a contract for services, allows a buyer or seller to hold an offer open even if the other party does not pay to keep it open. Section 2-205 provides that a written offer to buy or sell goods that gives assurances that the offer will be held open is irrevocable for the stated period or for a reasonable period not exceeding three months.

3.8 Filling Gaps in Essential Contract Terms

Ideally, parties to a contract for the sale of goods will agree, in writing, on all essential contract terms. This agreement may come after extensive negotiations during which the terms are openly presented and discussed. The UCC recognizes, however, that a contract may be formed without extensive negotiations. To alleviate possible problems arising from "gaps" in the contract, Section 2-204(3) provides that a contract will not fail for indefiniteness merely because the parties have left one or more terms open. However, the parties must intend to make a contract, and a reasonably certain basis must exist for formulating a remedy in the event of a breach.

Under the UCC, the quantity of goods bought and sold usually is the only essential contract term. The courts will even imply a reasonable price[8] and enforce the contract if the parties have agreed on other essential terms. Except in the case of a "requirements" or "output" contract, the courts will not fill in the "gap" by implying a "reasonable" quantity of goods.[9] The courts will enforce a contract with "gaps" such as no delivery date by implying a reasonable date based on the circumstances.

[8] *D. R. Curtis Co. v. Mathews,* 653 P.2d 1188 (Idaho App. 1982); *Irby Constr. Co. v. Shipco, Inc.,* 548 F. Supp. 1023 (D. La. 1982) (place of delivery); *Beiriger & Sons Irrigation, Inc. v. Southwest Land Co., Inc.,* 705 P.2d 532 (Colo. App. 1985) (time of delivery).

[9] A "requirements" contract is one in which the buyer expressly or implicitly agrees to obtain all of the requirements for a certain kind of goods from the seller. In certain circumstances a "requirements" contract may be useful to a contractor purchasing construction materials. Where it would be difficult to estimate accurately the quantity of material required, the supplier may simply agree to meet the contractor's requirements; that is, to supply all the material the contractor needs to perform the contract. Should the quantity exceed that which was reasonably contemplated, the courts limit the quantity, at the contract unit price, to a reasonable amount. If the buyer does not in fact require any of the goods, there is no obligation under a requirements contract to take or pay for any quantity. An "output" contract calls for the buyer to purchase all of the seller's output of a certain kind of goods. In the construction setting, the "output" contract is rarely encountered. *Brem-Rock, Inc. v. A. C. Warmack,* 28 Wash. App. 483, 624 P.2d 220 (1981) (sand and gravel requirements contract upheld despite being "harsh bargain"); *R. A. Weaver & Assoc., Inc. v. Asphalt Constr., Inc.,* 587 F.2d 1315 (D.C. Cir. 1978) (subcontract to supply and install crushed limestone).

In addition to implied terms, a court may also take notice of customary practices in the industry. Section 2-208 provides that express terms of the contract may be interpreted in light of the parties' conduct, course of dealing, trade usage, or course of performance. This Code section recognizes that the parties themselves know best what they meant by their agreement and that their actions under the agreement are the best indication of what was meant.

3.9 Warranties under the UCC

The Code provides for three kinds of warranties for the protection of buyers of goods:

(1) *Express Warranty:* This is a written explanation of what the goods can and cannot do.[10]

(2) *Implied Warranty of Merchantability:* This provides that the goods will be fit for ordinary use; it is considered a part of all contracts regardless of whether it is written in the contract.[11]

(3) *Implied Warranty of Fitness for the Intended Purpose:* When the seller has or should have knowledge of the buyer's out-of-the-ordinary needs and sells goods to specifically satisfy those needs, this implied warranty arises regardless of whether it is written in the contract.[12]

3.10 Warranty Disclaimers

The Code sets forth specific rules governing attempts by the seller to disclaim warranty coverage.[13] Generally, the language of the disclaimer clause must conform to the suggested wording provided by the Code. The case law dealing with this subject has developed to the point where sellers have little trouble including an enforceable disclaimer provision in their form contracts. While language stating that "there is no implied warranty of merchantability or any other implied warranty that extends beyond the express warranty included in this contract" is more common, it is sufficient for a seller to state as a disclaimer of all warranties that the goods are "as is" or "with all faults."

Often more important than warranty disclaimers are limitations on damages when warranties are breached.[14] Sellers typically seek to limit recoverable damages by substituting an alternative measure of damages such as limiting the buyer's remedy to a return of the goods and repayment of the price or repair and replacement of the defective goods.[15] To provide an effective bar

---

[10] § 2-313.

[11] § 2-314.

[12] § 2-315.

[13] § 2-316.

[14] §§ 2-718, 2-719.

[15] *Salt River Project Agricultural Improvement and Power Dist. v. Westinghouse Elec. Corp.*, 143 Ariz. 368, 694 P.2d 198 (1984) (disclaimer of UCC contract remedies and limitation on damages upheld where $4.5 million turbine failed).

to the recovery of consequential damages, that is, business losses other than those incurred to obtain conforming goods, the seller must provide that the alternative remedy is exclusive of all other remedies. If the alternative remedy is not expressly exclusive, then the stated remedy is considered merely to be one of many forms of relief. A UCC disclaimer, however, is not necessarily effective to eliminate tort liability, that is, for negligence or strict liability in tort, although such liability can be *waived* in a properly drafted contract term.[16]

Finally, Code § 2-719(2) gives the buyer recourse to all other remedies provided by the Code when the exclusive or limited remedy fails of its essential purpose. In other words, the buyer is not bound by a limited remedy that fails to work. The most common limited remedy is repair or replacement of defective goods. If the defect cannot be repaired or replaced within a reasonable time, the buyer can sue for damages.[17]

3.11   Statute of Limitations and Commencement of the Warranty Period

Generally, a warranty period begins when tender of delivery is made. Tender of delivery is "an offer of goods under a contract as if in fulfillment of its conditions even though there is a defect when measured against the contract obligation."[18] Similarly, a cause of action for breach arises when the breach occurs and, in the case of the delivery of defective goods, a breach occurs upon tender of delivery. The statute of limitations begins to run when the cause of action arises, which generally occurs upon tender of delivery.[19]   Typically, the Code statute of limitations is four years.[20]

There are, however, several important instances in which the general principles discussed above do not apply. First, as discussed earlier, the timing of both the commencement of the warranty period and the running of the statute of limitations can be altered by agreement. For example, both events may be made contingent upon acceptance of the goods by the buyer after a reasonable period for inspection.

A second instance arises when the seller makes repair attempts that ultimately prove unsuccessful. Sometimes such repair efforts are considered to

---

[16] *Id.*

[17] *Chatlos Sys., Inc. v. NCR Corp.,* 635 F.2d 1081 (3d Cir. 1980) (ineffective repair of computer system over one and one-half year period was failure of repair remedy); *Garden State Food Distrib., Inc. v. Sperry Rand Corp.,* 512 F. Supp. 975 (D.N.J. 1981); *but see Kaplan v. RCA Corp.,* 783 F.2d 463 (4th Cir. 1986) (repair remedy did not fail where seller replaced defective antenna immediately); *Flow Indus., Inc. v. Fields Constr. Co.,* 683 F. Supp. 527 (D. Md. 1988) (late delivery of pump not necessarily a failure of essential remedy). Even if the limited remedy fails and the buyer is entitled to sue for damages, a contract clause excluding consequential damages may still be effective. *Id.*

[18] *Standard Alliance Indus., Inc. v. Black Clawson Co.,* 587 F.2d 813 (6th Cir. 1978), *cert. denied,* 441 U.S. 923 (1979).

[19] *South Burlington School Dist. v. Calcagni-Frazier-Zajchowski Architects, Inc.,* 410 A.2d 1359 (Vt. 1980) (breach of contract to supply roof materials occurred on delivery).

[20] § 2-275.

"toll," or suspend, the running of the statute of limitations. The effect of repair attempts varies greatly from state to state. Some states hold that repair efforts do not suspend the running of the limitation period.[21] Other states hold that the limitation period does not run during the seller's repair efforts.[22] The key factor in determining whether a seller's repair efforts toll the running of the statute is whether the seller made promises or assurances to the buyer that the defects could be repaired. Such assurances will be examined by the court to see if they caused the buyer to forebear from filing suit.[23]

The party seeking to avoid the running of the limitations period may argue that because the defect could not be discovered until some point after tender of delivery, there was a warranty of future performance. The courts generally have rejected this argument, however, unless the warranty required more in the way of future performance than merely meeting the contract specifications.[24] One example of a construction project warranty that extends to future performance is the typical ten- or twenty-year roof warranty. Express language such as "bonded for up to twenty years" may provide a warranty of future performance.[25] The failure of concrete forms to withstand specified loads was not a breach of a warranty of future performance.[26]

A special problem exists with regard to the statute of limitations where the purchase agreement provides that the seller will indemnify and hold the buyer harmless from claims and losses arising from the sale of, or the buyer's use of, the goods. The statute of limitations generally does not begin to run on a breach of an indemnification agreement until the seller refuses to honor it, even though delivery of the goods was made much earlier in time.[27]

3.12 DEALING WITH THE OTHER PARTY'S INSOLVENCY

Under the UCC, a party is insolvent if it has ceased to pay its debts in the ordinary course of business, cannot pay its debts as they become due, or is deemed insolvent under federal bankruptcy law.

---

[21] *E.g., K/F Dev. & Inv. Corp. v. Williamson Crane & Dozer Corp.,* 367 So.2d 1078 (Fla. 3rd DCA), *cert. denied,* 378 So.2d 350 (Fla. 1979).

[22] *E.g., Ontario Hydro v. Zallea Sys., Inc.,* 569 F. Supp. 1261 (D. Del. 1983).

[23] *See Weeks v. Slavick Builders, Inc.,* 180 N.W.2d 503 (Mich. App. 1970), *aff'd,* 181 N.W.2d 271 (1970).

[24] *See Safeway Stores, Inc. v. Certainteed Corp.,* 710 S.W.2d 544 (Tex. 1986) (containing an extensive listing of cases supporting the "universal rule in other jurisdictions [that] an implied warranty does not fall under the exception in the Code because, by its nature, it cannot explicitly extend to future performance").

[25] *Little Rock School Dist. of Pulaski County v. Celotext Corp.,* 264 Ark. 757, 574 S.W.2d 669 (1978). *See Mittasch v. Seal Lock Burial Vault, Inc.,* 344 N.Y.S.2d 101 (N.Y. 1973) (warranty that a burial vault would provide "satisfactory service at all times" was a warranty of future performance).

[26] *Raymond-Dravo-Langenfelder v. Microdot, Inc.,* 425 F. Supp. 614 (D. Del. 1976).

[27] *See, e.g., Tolar Constr. Co. v. GAF Corp.,* 267 S.E.2d 635 (Ga. App. 1980), *rev'd on other grounds,* 271 S.E.2d 811 (Ga. 1980).

Upon discovering the buyer's insolvency, the seller may:

(1) Stop delivery if the goods are still in transit;
(2) Refuse delivery unless the buyer pays cash for the delivered goods and all prior deliveries; or
(3) Reclaim the goods:
    (a) within ten days, if the buyer received the goods on credit while insolvent; or
    (b) anytime, if the buyer misrepresented its solvency in writing to the seller within three months prior to delivery.

The right to reclaim the goods is an important right under the Code. There are, however, limitations on this right to reclaim.

The first restriction operates in all circumstances. If the buyer has resold the goods to a good-faith purchaser, the original seller's right to reclaim is foreclosed. Thus, in the construction context, if an insolvent subcontractor accepts delivery of materials, equipment, or other goods that will not be incorporated into the project (within ten days or a longer period in some instances), the contractor or owner can protect its interest in the goods by promptly paying the subcontractor for the goods.

There are, however, potential drawbacks to this course of action. First, payment to an insolvent subcontractor is generally not a wise course of action unless the subcontractor has already performed the work (as opposed to merely purchasing supplies that will later be incorporated into the project) for which it is entitled to be paid. Second, it is not permissible to take action to cut off the seller's right to reclaim the goods when the subcontractor's insolvency is obvious. Thus, unless the subcontract requires such prompt payment and the contractor has in fact made prior payments for materials in such prompt fashion, a sudden hasty payment to a subcontractor could be viewed as evidence that the contractor knew of the subcontractor's insolvency and was attempting in bad faith to impair the seller's ability to reclaim. The better course of action considering the mentioned drawbacks would be to work directly with the seller to obtain possession and title to the goods.

The converse situation occurs when a buyer is faced with an insolvent seller. Under § 2-502, a buyer may take possession of specially manufactured goods, or goods specifically identified as intended for the buyer, subject to one very important condition: the buyer must have made at least partial payment for the goods and the seller must have become insolvent within ten days after the first payment. This condition is extremely restrictive. The buyer may, however, acquire a security interest by complying with Article 9 of the Code and thereby obtain rights to the goods when the seller's insolvency occurs later than ten days after the first payment.

3.13 RISK OF LOSS

The Code provides a comprehensive scheme for allocating risk of loss by agreement of the parties. Once it is determined which party bears the risk of loss, then insurance for the goods in transit and in storage can be arranged accordingly.

Section 2-509(1) covers risk of loss where neither party is in breach of contract as follows:

(1) Where shipment is by a carrier, risk of loss passes to the buyer on delivery to the carrier unless the contract requires delivery at a particular destination, in which case the risk of loss passes to the buyer when the carrier tenders delivery at that destination.

(2) Where the goods are held by a third party in a bailment, the risk of loss passes on tender of documents of title or when the bailee acknowledges the buyer's right to possession. Thus it is possible, for example, for the risk of loss to pass to the buyer for construction materials that are stored off-site in a warehouse over which the buyer has no control.

(3) In all cases not covered by (1) and (2), the risk of loss passes to the buyer on receipt of the goods if the seller is a merchant, or on tender of delivery if the seller is not a merchant. Thus, for example, where a supplier ships in its own trucks, the risk of loss passes upon the buyer's receipt of the goods.

The Code allows any of these provisions to be changed by agreement of the parties.[28] A contract that specifies "F.O.B. (free on board) place of shipment," also known as a "shipment" contract, places the risk of loss on the buyer as soon as the goods are placed in the possession of a common carrier.[29] Conversely, a contract that specifies "F.O.B. place of destination," also known as a "destination" contract, leaves the risk of loss on the seller until the delivery of the goods is tendered at the named destination.[30]

3.14 INSPECTION OF THE GOODS

The Code provides that if the seller is required or authorized to send the goods to the buyer, the buyer has the right before acceptance to inspect the goods at any reasonable time and place and in any reasonable manner.[31] The

---

[28] In a typical purchase order or sales order form, the risk of loss is covered by delivery terms, such as "F.O.B."
[29] § 2-319(1)(a).
[30] § 2-319(1)(b).
[31] § 2-513(1).

parties may agree to modify the time, place, or even the right of inspection by inserting appropriate terms in the contract.[32]

Inspection and payment are linked together by the Code, though the parties may agree otherwise by contract. Where the buyer is to pay on or after delivery of the goods, the buyer has the right to inspect before payment. Absent an opportunity to inspect, there is no obligation to pay. The buyer, however, may lose the right of inspection by agreement or by conduct showing waiver.

The buyer may contract away its right to inspection by agreeing to cash on delivery (C.O.D.) payment terms or other similar terms. C.O.D. requires payment before delivery, which effectively precludes inspection.[33] Where payment before inspection is required by the contract, payment does not necessarily constitute acceptance or defeat the right to a later inspection and assertion of the buyer's rights and remedies.[34] Denial of the right of inspection is a breach of contract. Thus, if the contract does not allow the seller to ship C.O.D., the seller is in breach if it ships C.O.D. because this denies the right of inspection.[35]

The buyer may waive the right to inspect by an unreasonable delay in the inspection.[36] Whether a delay in inspection is reasonable or is so unreasonable as to amount to a waiver depends on the facts and circumstances of the transaction. In addition to the need to inspect within a reasonable time, the buyer must also give notice of any defect within a reasonable time or be barred from any remedy.[37]

The right of inspection includes the right to make tests of the goods, including testing requiring the destruction of a small amount of the goods. Use of the goods for either destructive and nondestructive testing is not considered to be acceptance of the goods so long as the testing is necessary and reasonable.

The buyer must bear the expenses of inspection and testing but may recover those expenses from the seller if the goods fail the inspection and are rejected.[38]

3.15 REJECTION OF GOODS

If the goods or the seller's tender of delivery fail in any respect to meet contract requirements, the buyer may accept or reject the goods or any part of them.[39] If the buyer rejects some or all of the goods, the buyer must do so within a reasonable time and give notice to the seller.[40] If the buyer fails to

---

[32] *Id.*

[33] § 2-513(3).

[34] § 2-512.

[35] 4 Anderson, UCC § 2-513:13 (1983).

[36] *Michael M. Berlin & Co. v. T. Whiting Mfg., Inc.,* 5 UCC Rep. Serv. 357 (N.Y. Sup. Ct. 1968).

[37] § 2-607. *See* Section 3.16 below.

[38] § 2-513(2).

[39] § 2-601.

[40] § 2-602(1).

state a particular reason for rejection, the buyer cannot rely on the reason to justify rejection if the seller could have cured the defect with notice.[41]

3.16 ACCEPTANCE AND NOTICE OF BREACH

One of the most important Code sections for construction projects is § 2-607, which governs the buyer's conduct upon acceptance of goods. § 2-607(a) provides that the buyer must pay for any accepted goods. This may seem to be an obvious requirement. It is true that where there are no problems with quantity, quality, or timeliness, the buyer usually pays in the ordinary course of business. The impact of § 2-607(a) is felt when there are problems, but the buyer has failed to protect its interests. In that case, the buyer must pay for accepted goods.[42] The significance of § 2-607(a) is highlighted by the meaning of "accepted" goods and the notice requirement for preserving remedies.

"Acceptance" of goods is defined in § 2-606. A buyer "accepts" goods by knowingly taking nonconforming goods or by doing any act inconsistent with the seller's ownership.[43] For example, using construction materials in performing the work ordinarily would constitute acceptance.

The other aspect of § 2-607 that warrants attention is the notice requirement. Section 2-607(3) requires the buyer to give notice of any breach within a reasonable time or be *barred from any remedy*. In other words, the buyer cannot sit idly by while defective goods are used in the work. The buyer must give notice within a reasonable time to preserve its remedies under the Code.[44] Failure to give notice bars any remedy.[45] To be "reasonable," the notice must be given within sufficient time to give the seller a chance to remedy the breach and minimize damages.[46]

3.17 ANTICIPATORY REPUDIATION/ADEQUATE ASSURANCE OF PERFORMANCE

When one party has reasonable grounds for feeling insecure about the other party's ability or desire to fully perform a contract calling for future perfor-

---

[41] § 2-605(1).

[42] *Economy Forms Corp. v. Kandy, Inc.*, 391 F. Supp. 944 (N.D. Ga. 1974), *aff'd*, 511 F.2d 1400 (5th Cir. 1975) (general contractor was obligated to pay for concrete forms despite any alleged defects).

[43] *See Meland v. Intermountain Sys., Inc.*, 712 P.2d 1295 (Mont. 1985) (buyer accepted goods by erecting entire building after discovering incorrect lengths in parts of prefabricated metal building).

[44] *Smith-Wolf Constr., Inc. v. Hood*, 756 P.2d 1027 (Colo. App. 1988) (subcontractor gave reasonable notice of breach of warranty of methods and rates of application of waterproofing product).

[45] *Town of Hooksett School Dist.*, fn. 3, *supra*. (school failed to give notice of breach of implied warranty after learning about problems associated with asbestos installed 25 years earlier).

[46] *Metro Inv. Corp. v. Portland Road Lumber Yard, Inc.*, 501 P.2d 312 (Or. 1972) (notice of siding defects not untimely although given two years after the defect was discovered).

mance, that party has a right to require adequate assurance of full perfor-mance.[47] The adequacy of any assurance is determined according to commer-cial standards. The term "commercial standards," as well as the notion of insecurity, may be defined by agreement of the parties to avoid many of the problems of interpretation inherent in this section.

The party seeking adequate assurance may make a demand on the other party, who then has the duty to provide adequate assurance of performance within a reasonable time (but no longer than thirty days). A failure to provide adequate assurances within a reasonable time is a repudiation of the contract. The party seeking assurances (the aggrieved party) is entitled to take action to mitigate its damages pursuant to § 2-610. The aggrieved party may: (1) await, for a commercially reasonable time, performance by the repudiating party; (2) resort to any remedy for breach even though the aggrieved party has stated it will await performance; or (3) simply suspend its own performance. In practice, the aggrieved party cannot demand more than "adequate" assur-ances of performance. Otherwise, if the other party refuses to meet those demands, a court may find the demanding (aggrieved) party to be in breach.

The demanding party may ask for additional security, but not so much as to modify the essential terms of the contract. For instance, the seller cannot demand payment in advance when the contract expressly or impliedly provides for a thirty- to sixty-day billing cycle and other security is offered. On the other hand, verbal assurances by a buyer that payment *eventually* will be made is not adequate when the seller is demanding that payment be made on time. As an example of adequate assurances, a buyer may present assurances from its banker, a letter of credit, establish an escrow account for future payments, or even offer a mortgage on other property.

3.18 EXCUSE OF SELLER'S PERFORMANCE BY FAILURE OF PRESUPPOSED CONDITIONS

Purchase order and sale agreement forms usually contain a *force majeure* clause. A typical *force majeure* clause excuses nonperformance by either the buyer or the seller caused by an act of God, war, strike by common carrier, and other causes beyond the control of the parties. A *force majeure* clause is lawful and enforceable.

Where there is no *force majeure* clause, the Code provides that a late delivery or nondelivery will be excused if the seller's performance has been made impracticable by the occurrence of a contingency, the nonoccurrence of which was a basic assumption of the contract, or by good faith compliance with a domestic or foreign governmental regulation.[48] Where the seller's total capacity to perform is not affected, the seller must allocate production and

---

[47] § 2-609.
[48] § 2-615(a).

deliveries among its customers.[49] In addition, the seller must notify the buyer of delay or nondelivery and the amount of any allocation of available deliveries.[50] If the impracticability affects the agreed manner of delivery and a reasonable substitute is available, the buyer must accept the reasonable substitute.[51]

"Impracticability" under this Code section means "commercial impracticability," which is a broader ground for excusing performance than is available under the common law applicable to a construction contract.

As noted previously, § 2-615 does not apply to the typical construction contract.[52] Thus, the contractor or subcontractor should be wary of contracting for performance that is excused only in case of a *force majeure* event, such as a flood, while the seller of key material or equipment may be excused by mere commercial impracticability. The Code allows the parties to impose greater obligations on the seller by contract.[53] From the general contractor's or subcontractor's point of view, it would be important to impose performance obligations on the seller at least as great as those imposed on the contractor or subcontractor.

Increased costs do not constitute commercial impracticability unless they are due to an unforeseen contingency. Mere unexpected difficulties and expenses do not excuse performance unless they are so extreme that they would be outside the contemplation of the parties.[54] A severe shortfall of raw materials or supplies due to war embargo, or unforeseen shutdown of a major source of supply, which either causes a large increase in cost or prevents the seller from procuring basic supplies, however, may constitute commercial impracticability.[55]

3.19 BUYER'S REMEDIES

If the seller fails to deliver, or delivers nonconforming goods, the buyer may either purchase replacement goods ("cover") or seek specific performance (to force delivery of the goods by the seller).

The measure of damages in the event of cover is the difference between the contract price and the amount actually paid for the substitute goods. An alternate measure of damages is the difference between the contract price and the market price. This measure can be used to establish that a cover price was unreasonably high or low. However, where the two measures of damages differ only marginally, the party seeking damages may recover the more favorable amount.

[49] § 2-615(b).
[50] § 2-615(c).
[51] § 2-614(a).
[52] *Helms Constr. & Dev. Co. v. State,* 97 Nev. 500, 634 P.2d 1224 (1981).
[53] § 2-615.
[54] *Sachs v. Precision Prods. Co.,* 257 Or. 273, 476 P.2d 199 (1970).
[55] *Swift Textiles, Inc. v. Lawson,* 135 Ga. App. 799, 219 S.E.2d 167 (1975).

Specific performance is a buyer's remedy where the goods are otherwise unavailable or the price of replacement goods has increased so dramatically that it obviously would be a poor business practice to cover. Further, specific performance is an extraordinary remedy that may be available from a court in an expedited time frame.

The buyer must provide the seller with prompt notice of rejection or revocation of acceptance. Failure to provide prompt notice will almost always constitute wrongful rejection/revocation by the buyer.[56] Prompt notice is important because the seller has the right to cure the defects and tender the repaired goods as conforming to the contract as long as the time for performance has not expired.[57] Although the seller's right to cure does not extend to major repairs, the definition of "major" in the commercial construction context will vary, depending upon the cost and nature of the goods.

3.20   SELLER'S REMEDIES

Where the buyer wrongfully rejects or revokes acceptance of goods, or fails to make payment, or repudiates the contract, the seller may stop delivery, resell the goods, and sue for losses from the resale, recover damages, or cancel the contract.[58] A seller's damages may also include incidental costs incurred in transportation, care, and custody of the goods involved in stopping delivery and any resale.[59]

POINTS TO REMEMBER

The following key points should be noted:

- *Article 2 of the Uniform Commercial Code (UCC)* applies to virtually every construction project to some extent.
- Although Article 2 of the UCC does not apply to contracts for the sale of construction services, it does govern *transactions involving the sale of "goods,"* which are defined as "all things . . . which are movable at the time of identification to the contract for sale."
- Where a contract involves the sale of both goods and services, most courts will look to the *predominant nature* of the contract to determine whether the UCC applies.
- Most of the terms imposed by the UCC *may be modified* by mutual agreement of the parties.

[56] §§ 2-601, 2-714(1).
[57] § 2-508.
[58] § 2-703.
[59] § 2-710.

- Some of the traditional common law rules governing contract formation do not apply under the UCC, making it *easier to establish the existence of a binding contract.*
- The UCC provides for three kinds of warranties for the protection of buyers of goods: *express warranties;* the *implied warranty of merchantability;* and the *implied warranty of fitness for the intended purpose.*
- *Disclaimers of warranties* are possible, but there are *limitations* on what warranties can be disclaimed, and *special language* may be required.
- The UCC grants certain rights in the event the buyer is *insolvent.*
- The UCC also contains a comprehensive scheme for allocating the *risk of loss* between the contracting parties.
- Other specific issues expressly addressed by the UCC include the buyer's right to *inspect* the goods; the circumstances under which a buyer may *reject* the goods; the buyer's obligations and rights upon *acceptance* of the goods; the requirements governing *notice of a breach;* and a party's rights upon learning that the other party is not likely to perform ("*anticipatory repudiation*").
- Most purchase orders and sales agreements contain a "*force majeure*" clause; in the absence of such a clause, the UCC provides that late delivery or nondelivery will be excused if the seller's performance has been made impracticable by the occurrence of a contingency, the nonoccurrence of which was a basic assumption of the contract, or by good faith compliance with a governmental regulation.
- And, finally, the UCC sets forth the *remedies* that are available to a buyer or seller should the other party breach the agreement.

4

THE AUTHORITY AND RESPONSIBILITY OF THE PROJECT ARCHITECT/ENGINEER

Design is an integral part of the construction process, and many construction disputes have their genesis in real or perceived design problems. In addition, the project design professional, whether an architect or engineer, also plays a pivotal role in the administration of the project and the contractor's contract with the owner, with responsibilities in contract interpretation, approval of payment, and inspection and acceptance of the work. For these reasons, recognition of the relative rights and responsibilities of the project design professional is essential to an understanding of the legal relations that govern a project.

The services performed by architects and engineers in connection with construction projects overlap to such an extent that in many cases it is difficult to draw a distinction between them.[1] Federal government agencies use the term "Architect-Engineer" to refer to both types of services, and their contracts are generally similar in form and content. There is also a definite trend among the larger professional design firms to provide both architectural and engineering services within the same organization. Otherwise, an individual architect or engineer will be primarily responsible for a project while subcontracting various portions of the design and/or construction supervision to other consultant firms.

For the purposes of this chapter, the two professions will be considered interchangeable, as the principles discussed are in most cases applicable to both.[2] The term "design professional" will be used throughout this chapter to refer to the project architect and/or engineer.

---

[1] *Georgia Assoc. of the AIA v. Gwinnett County,* 233 S.E.2d 142 (Ga. 1977).
[2] *See generally* Abbett, *Engineering Contracts and Specifications* (Wiley, 4th ed. 1963).

4.1 STANDARD OF RESPONSIBILITY OF THE DESIGN PROFESSIONAL

The specific scope of the design professional's authority and responsibility on a particular project is defined by its contract with the owner. The design professional and the owner have a direct contract—contractual privity—which is typically lacking in the relationship between the contractor and the design professional. Contractual privity allows the owner to sue the design professional directly for damages attributable to a breach of contract. No breach of contract action is available to contractors against the design professional. Contractors may only sue the owner for breaches of contract. When seeking remedies directly against the design professional, contractors must resort instead to actions based on legal theories such as negligence, third-party beneficiary, and breach of implied warranty. The pros and cons of employing these theories are discussed later in this chapter.

Design professionals, like other professions, are not expected to be perfect. Regardless of whether a claim is asserted by the project owner, the contractor or some third party, the liability of a design professional is gauged by a professional negligence or malpractice standard. One court explained: "Architects, doctors, engineers, attorneys, and others deal in somewhat inexact sciences and are continually called upon to exercise their skill and judgment in order to anticipate and provide for random factors which are incapable of precise measurement. The indeterminate nature of these factors makes it impossible for professional service people to gauge them with complete accuracy in every instance." Thus, "doctors cannot promise that every operation will be successful; . . . and an architect cannot be certain that a structural design will interact with natural forces as anticipated." Instead, "the law has traditionally required, not perfect results, but rather the exercise of that skill and judgment which can be reasonably expected from similarly situated professionals . . . ."[3] The design professional is not liable for mere errors in judgment; in order for liability to be established, the offense must rise to the level of a failure to exercise reasonable care and professional skill. If the design professional represents a specialization and experience in a particular area, the design professional will likely be held to a higher standard. In addition, the description of the design professional's efforts may be so specific as to the final performance of the completed project that those representations can amount to an express warranty of the design with the resulting contractual liability in lieu of a professional negligence standard.

4.2 THE AUTHORITY OF THE DESIGN PROFESSIONAL

During design development, the design professional generally acts as an independent contractor to the owner. Thus the design professional typically is not

[3] *City of Moundsview v. Walijarvi*, 263 N.W.2d 420 (Minn. 1978).

considered an agent of the owner and cannot bind the owner with regard to third parties. However, when the design professional assumes inspection and supervisory responsibilities during project construction, the design professional often becomes the owner's agent and can act on its behalf, unless the contract between the parties clearly provides that the design professional's status shall be only that of an independent contractor.[4] According to the law of agency, the supervisory authority of the design professional at the job site can be actual, implied, and/or apparent.

4.3 Actual Authority

"Actual authority" refers to that authority which the owner expressly confers upon the agent or allows the agent to believe it possesses. A design professional's actual authority is usually outlined in its contract with the owner and limited to specific functions. For example, on a typical construction project, the design professional does not, by virtue of its position, have any authority to make or modify contracts on the owner's behalf, or to materially change the work.[5] The owner can, however, grant the design professional actual authority to take these actions by so providing in its contract.

It is common for the contract between the owner and the contractor to specify the extent of the design professional's authority to act as agent for the owner. Unfortunately, most contracts do not isolate this information in any single area of the contract. Language pertaining to a design professional's authority can often be found in different sections of the general conditions, in the specifications and even on the plans. It is important for a design professional to know when he or she is empowered to act on behalf of the owner and when only the owner has authority to act. Many disputes arise because either the design professional, the contractor or the owner failed to understand the limits of the design professional's duties. All three construction parties should be familiar with the design professional's actual authority as expressed in its contract with the owner and/or the plans and specifications.

4.4 Implied Authority

Closely related to the concept of actual authority is that of "implied authority." Implied authority gives the design professional the authority to perform acts that are incidental to its exercise of actual authority. In other words, implied authority allows the design professional to do those things that are considered reasonable and necessary for the exercise of its actual authority. The design professional may bind the owner with these acts even though they are not expressly set forth in the contract.

[4] J. Acret, *Architects and Engineers: Their Professional Responsibilities* § 8.1 (McGraw-Hill 1977).
[5] *Crown Constr. Co. v. Opelika Mfg. Corp.*, 480 F.2d 149 (5th Cir. 1973).

For example, if a contract gives the design professional the responsibility to "review and approve" pay requests, the design professional also possesses the implied authority to reject pay requests. As this example illustrates, determination of those acts that are reasonable and necessary, and therefore implied, is often a matter of common sense. This is not always the case, however. Assume that the design professional has the actual authority to decide whether to require the *contractor* to post payment and performance bonds. Does the design professional also have the implied authority to represent to a *potential subcontractor* that a payment bond will be required? At least one court considering this question has held an owner responsible for such a representation by the design professional because the circumstances implied that the design professional had the authority to do so.[6]

4.5 Apparent Authority

"Apparent authority" is a concept distinct from that of actual and implied authority through which parties can unwittingly expand the scope of the design professional's authority. Apparent authority arises when an owner acts in a way that leads a contractor (or other third parties) to reasonably believe that the design professional has authority beyond that which it actually possesses. If, based on the owner's actions, a reasonably prudent third person would assume that the design professional has the authority that the owner holds it out as having, the owner will be bound by the design professional's acts, just as the owner is bound by the acts of the design professional exercising its actual authority.

For example, suppose a design professional is expressly authorized to issue written change orders with the owner's signature. If a design professional issues written change orders without the owner's signature but with the owner's knowledge and consent, the owner will be bound by these change orders, as the design professional had the apparent authority to issue them. However, a contractor must be particularly careful when relying upon the apparent authority of a design professional to approve changes or additional work without the owner's consent. It is always best to obtain the owner's signature on change orders and "extras."

The dilemma of apparent authority with respect to a design professional's issuance of change orders has been addressed by the American Institute of Architects (AIA) through evolution of AIA Document 201. Prior to 1976, AIA Document A201, "General Conditions of the Contract for Construction," provided that the design professional had the authority to issue a written change order without the owner's signature if the design professional had written authority that could be furnished to the contractor upon request. The 1976 version of A201, however, altered this provision to require that change orders be signed jointly by the owner and the architect. The 1987 edition of A201 goes one step further by requiring that change orders be prepared by the architect and signed by the owner, architect and contractor. A change order signed by only the archi-

---

[6] *Bethlehem Fabricators, Inc. v. British Overseas Airways Corp.,* 434 F.2d 840 (2d Cir. 1970).

tect and owner is now referred to as a "Construction Change Directive."[7] In any event, the AIA General Conditions do not give the design professional authority to issue changes without the owner's signature.

Unless the contract provides otherwise, it has generally been held that the design professional does not have authority to alter the plans and/or specifications without the owner's consent. For instance, in a 1915 case,[8] an architect directed a contractor to dispense with wainscoting in the corridors of a building. Upon the building's completion, the owner had another contractor put in wainscoting and deducted this cost from the amount due the original contractor. In a suit by the original contractor against the owner, the court found in favor of the owner, holding that the contractor's reliance upon the architect's directive was not reasonable. This principle still applies today, unless the contractor can establish apparent authority of the design professional to alter the plans and/or specifications through the actions of the owner.

Similar disputes frequently arise in connection with a design professional's verbal orders for extra work or changes when the contract requires a written change order. Generally, the owner is not bound by such oral authorizations unless the owner waives the written change order requirement.[9] For example, where a design professional had orally instructed the contractor to use a more expensive type of material, the contractor was not entitled to recover any additional cost because the design professional did not have the authority to direct the change.[10] In that case, the contract provided that no changes resulting in added cost could be authorized by the architect, and that any such changes could be made only by a written order of the owner signed by the architect.

A design professional who issues orders that are beyond its authority subjects itself to a risk that it may ultimately be held responsible, and thus liable, for the consequences. Modern courts have demonstrated an increasing willingness to hold design professionals responsible for their actions and not let them hide behind concepts of agency, especially when a contractor has acted reasonably in relying on the design professional.

Owners are also exposed to liability when their design professionals issue orders beyond the scope of their authority. While the contract gives owners some protection, such protection does not extend to any acquiescence, waiver or conduct by the owner that gives the design professional apparent authority to act.

4.6 COMMON SUPERVISORY AND ADMINISTRATIVE FUNCTIONS OF THE DESIGN PROFESSIONAL

The design professional's contract with the owner often requires the design professional to perform supervisory and administrative functions during construction. Sometimes, particularly when the federal government is involved,

---

[7] *See* AIA Document A201, § 7.3. (1987 ed.).
[8] *Smith v. Board of Educ.*, 85 S.E. 513 (W. Va. 1915).
[9] *See* Chapter 6.
[10] *Iowa Elec. Light & Power Co. v. Hopp*, 266 N.W. 512 (Iowa 1936).

responsibility for the supervision and/or administration of construction is placed with the owner or an independent construction manager, instead of the design professional.

The following section will focus on the five common aspects of the design professional's supervisory and administrative roles during construction:

(1) Interpretation of the plans and specifications;

(2) Review and approval of shop drawings and submittals;

(3) Inspection and testing;

(4) Issuance of certificates of progress or completion in connection with the contractor's right to payment; and

(5) Resolution of disputes between the owner and the contractor.

4.7 Interpretation of the Plans and Specifications

The plans and specifications commonly generate many questions on construction projects. Minor issues often arise because there is no detail or specification that covers a specific element of work. It is rare for every detail of the work to be expressly set forth in the plans and/or specifications. Thus parties are forced to interpret the contract requirements based on the original intent of the parties, industry practice, code requirements and course of dealing. However, at some point issues of simple contract interpretation can cross the line and become issues of defective specifications, ambiguities and oral changes. Even experienced construction professionals can run into circumstances where it is difficult to differentiate between interpretation of the specifications and modification of the specifications. However, reasonable judgment and open communication can generally resolve most interpretation issues, thus leaving only the true defective specification problems to be resolved.

The supervising design professional normally has the authority to interpret the plans and specifications. This authority theoretically gives the design professional some degree of control over the work as it progresses, and assures flexibility in order to solve problems and maintain consistency throughout the project. But responsibility and potential liability accompany this authority. An architect can be held liable to an owner for negligent interpretation of the plans and specifications. This is true even where an owner uses the unique design of a separate design consultant. For instance, in one case, an architect was found liable for a faulty design that had been recommended to the owner by an expert engineer. The court viewed the architect's act of affixing his stamp of approval on the plans as acknowledgement of an affirmative duty to review the plans to ensure that they were architecturally sound. The court reasoned that if the architect did not have the expertise to review the engineer's plans, he should have abstained from doing so.[11]

The design professional's authority to interpret the contract requirements does not include the authority to place additional burdens or liabilities upon

---

[11] *South Dakota Bldg. Auth. v. Geiger-Berger Assoc.*, 414 N.W.2d 15 (S.D. 1987).

the owner or the contractor by modifying contract terms. For example, on one job, a dispute arose over a design professional's interpretation of the contractor's obligation to provide additional fill. Although the plans and specifications contained no reference to such additional fill, the architect determined that the contractor was required to provide it without additional compensation. The court deciding the dispute held that the architect did not have the power, express or implied, to add to or take away from the contractual rights or liabilities of either party under the contract.[12]

In addition to the literal wording of the contract documents, the design professional's discretion in interpreting the plans and specifications is limited by general practice and trade custom in the construction industry. For example, a subcontractor was entitled to additional compensation for performing certain painting work beyond normal custom, despite a contrary interpretation of the subcontract by the architect. The court stated that, although the architect had been given authority to make final decisions regarding the meaning of plans and specifications, the architect could not render a decision that is not in accordance with industry custom or trade usage.[13]

This same principle applies in the federal arena. A contractor on a government project is entitled to rely on industry custom and practice in the absence of any contractual provision to the contrary. In one case, the United States Court of Claims awarded damages to a contractor for costs incurred in meeting higher standards than required under a reasonable interpretation of the contract specifications. The contractor was directed to construct wooden concrete forms within tolerances that were not set forth in the specifications and that were more restrictive than necessary to meet the specified tolerances for the finished concrete. The contract only specified that the "forms shall be true to line and grade." The court relied upon common trade practices to support the contractor's award. The court reasoned that the federal government must state in clear and unambiguous language any intention to alter industry custom or trade usage with respect to required tolerances.[14]

The design professional's power to interpret contract requirements also carries with it the duty to render such interpretative decisions honestly and in good faith. Practically speaking, the design professional is working for the owner. Thus it may be difficult at times for the design professional to exercise independent judgment. Furthermore, the design professional is often placed in the awkward position of having to judge the adequacy of its own work product—the plans and specifications. A sense of professional pride combined with a reluctance to go to the owner for extra money to correct an omission or mistake in the design can sometimes affect a design professional's decision in the field. Courts understand this inherent problem and consequently recognize circumstances under which the failure of a design professional to perform its administrative duties honestly and in good faith diminishes or nullifies its authority to interpret contract requirements or arbitrate contract disputes.

---

[12] *Tomlinson v. Ashland County*, 173 N.W. 300 (Wis. 1919).
[13] *John W. Johnson, Inc. v. J. A. Jones Constr. Co.*, 369 F. Supp. 484 (E.D. Va. 1973).
[14] *Kenneth Reed Constr. Corp. v. United States*, 475 F.2d 583 (Ct. Cl. 1973).

4.8 Review and Approval of Shop Drawings and Submittals

The design professional generally reviews data submitted by the contractor, such as samples, shop drawings, production data and schedules. These submittals form the "bridge" between the contract documents and the constructed project.[15] Such documentation also keeps the design professional, as well as the owner, aware of the processes and methods to be used by the contractor and the contractor's understanding of the contract's requirements.

As with the other duties of the design professional, the design professional's review of submittals has legal consequences. To the extent that they are not specified in the contract documents, the selection of processes and methods of performance are generally the contractor's responsibility. One question that arises frequently is whether the design professional's approval of these processes and methods relieves the contractor of its responsibility to comply with the specifications. Generally, it does not.[16] The design professional does not have the authority to change the specifications by approving shop drawings submitted by the contractor, and the owner is not bound by any such approval.[17]

In one case, for example, a contractor with a design-build contract hired a design professional to do the design work and review shop drawings.[18] The contractor later awarded work to a subcontractor, who was required to submit shop drawings to the contractor for review and approval. The contractor then gave the drawings to the design professional, who erroneously approved them. After the work had been performed in accordance with the shop drawings, problems were discovered and the subcontractor had to perform remedial work. The subcontractor subsequently sued the design professional for its negligence. The court held in favor of the design professional, stating that the design professional owed no duty to the subcontractor, who was responsible for meeting all of the requirements of its subcontract. The subcontractor had no right to rely on the design professional's approval of its shop drawings, because the design professional was hired to provide services only to the contractor, not to subcontractors.

The AIA General Conditions of AIA Document A201 (1987 ed.) are specific as to the design professional's liability for approving contractor submittals that change the specifications. The General Conditions relieve the contractor of responsibility for *deviations* from the contract documents contained in submittals, if and only if:

> [T]he Contractor has specifically informed the Architect in writing of such deviation at the time of submittal and the Architect has given written approval to the specific deviation.

[15] See Sweet, *Legal Aspects of Architecture, Engineering and the Construction Process* 104 (West 1977).

[16] *Community Science Technology Corp.,* ASBCA No. 20244, 77-1 BCA ¶ 12,352.

[17] *Fauss Constr., Inc. v. City of Hooper,* 249 N.W.2d 478 (Neb. 1977).

[18] *Lutz Eng'g Co. v. Industrial Louvers, Inc.,* 585 A.2d 631 (R.I. 1991).

Occasionally, courts do impose liability on a design professional for approving shop drawings that deviate from the contract documents. For example, in one case, the contract documents called for ten (10) gauge steel to be used for stair pans. The contractor submitted shop drawings showing fourteen (14) gauge steel, which the design professional approved. Workmen later walked onto the pans and were injured when the landing pan collapsed through the framework. The court held in favor of the workmen and against the design professional, finding that the contract did not relieve the design professional of liability for its negligence in failing to detect the error.[19]

The design professional also has an obligation to review and act upon a shop drawing or submittal within a reasonable time. To the extent the contractor is delayed or hindered by the design professional's failure to approve or reject a submittal, the owner, and perhaps even the design professional, may be liable to the contractor.[20]

4.9 Inspection and Testing

Frequently the design professional is given the authority to inspect work for conformity to contract requirements. In performing its inspection duties, the design professional acts as agent for the owner. As a part of this responsibility, the design professional has the implied authority to reject work. Disputes typically arise when the design professional rejects work that the contractor believes complies with the contract. Factual disputes in this area cover every aspect of construction and generally turn on issues of contract interpretation, workmanship and sufficiency of materials.

Improper rejection of work generally will not expose the design professional to liability to the contractor, because the design professional is usually acting on behalf of the owner. However, incorrect or negligent inspections that result in improper rejection of the work, and thus liability of the owner to the contractor, may generate an action by the owner against the design professional.

Other issues arise when the design professional fails to inspect work or fails to timely detect nonconforming work as the work proceeds. Often contractors, believing their work to be satisfactory, will build on top of or add on to nonconforming work, making corrections and/or remedial work much more difficult. Who should be responsible when corrections to nonconforming work are more expensive because the problem is discovered so late—the contractor who improperly constructed the work or the design professional who failed to timely catch the error?

The AIA General Conditions, AIA Document A201 (1987 ed.), and most other construction contract forms, limit the scope of the owner's and design professional's duty to inspect the work. The primary responsibility for contract

---

[19] *Jaeger v. Henningson, Durham & Richardson,* 714 F.2d 773 (8th Cir. 1983).
[20] *See, e.g., E. C. Ernst, Inc. v. Manhattan Constr. Co. of Texas,* 551 F.2d 1026 (5th Cir. 1977), *cert. denied,* 434 U.S. 1067 (1978); *Prichard Bros., Inc. v. Grady Co.,* 436 N.W.2d 460 (Minn. Ct. App. 1989).

compliance and for control of construction means, methods and techniques remains with the contractor. This obligation is contained in the AIA Document's means and methods clause. An engineer generally does not have to supervise or inspect construction when not required to do so by the contract.[21]

For example, in a Texas case, a supervising engineering firm was found not liable for a contractor's failure to use adequate supports when pouring a concrete slab, a failure that resulted in the death of a construction worker when the slab collapsed.[22] The court relied on the engineer's contract, which specified that the firm was not responsible for the contractor's construction methods or for safety at the job site.[23]

The means and methods clause, however, does not always absolve the design professional of all liability. In another Texas case, the court held the architect liable for failing to adequately inspect a project despite exculpatory contract language stating that the architect would "not be responsible for the Contractor's failure to carry out the work in accordance with the contract documents." The court reasoned that an architect who was paid to protect the owner from construction defects should be held responsible for failing to detect defective work.[24]

The scope of a design professional's potential liability for job site accidents caused by unsafe working conditions continues to trouble many courts. Generally the design professional's obligation to monitor the quality of the work is weighed against the contractor's responsibility to control the means and methods of its performance. The courts usually resolve this issue by closely examining the language of both the design professional's contract and the construction contract.[25]

In an illustrative case, a court considered whether a design professional could be held liable for a fire caused by the contractor's deficient performance.[26] The design professional had entered into a standard AIA design contract that provided the following:

> The Architect shall visit the site at intervals appropriate to the stage of construction . . . to become generally familiar with the progress and quality of the Work and to determine in general if the Work is proceeding in accordance with the Contract Documents. However, the Architect shall not be required to make exhaustive or continuous on-site inspections to check the quality or quantity of the Work. On the basis of such on-site observations as an architect, the Architect shall keep the Owner informed of the progress and quality of the Work, and

[21] *Goette v. Press Bar & Cafe, Inc.*, 413 N.W.2d 854 (Minn. Ct. App. 1987).

[22] *Rodriquez v. Universal Fastenings Corp.*, 777 S.W.2d 513 (Tex. App.—Corpus Christi 1989, no writ).

[23] *See also Davis v. Lenox School*, 541 N.Y.S.2d 814 (N.Y. App. Div. 1989).

[24] *Hunt v. Ellisor & Tanner, Inc.*, 739 S.W.2d 933 (Tex. App.—Dallas 1987, writ denied).

[25] *Shepherd Components, Inc. v. Brice Petrides-Donohue & Assoc.*, 473 N.W.2d 612 (Iowa 1991); *Moore v. PRC Eng'g, Inc.*, 565 So.2d 817 (Fla. Dist. Ct. App. 1990); *Marshall v. Port Auth. of Allegheny County*, 568 A.2d 931 (Pa. 1990).

[26] *Diocese of Rochester v. R-Monde Contractors, Inc.*, 562 N.Y.S.2d 593 (N.Y. Sup. Ct. 1989).

shall endeavor to guard the Owner against defects and deficiencies in the Work of the Contractor.

The fire was caused by the contractor's improper placement of insulation around light fixtures, which the design professional had not detected. The court rejected the argument that the design professional was not obligated to catch the defect in the work. Despite the general disclaimers in the AIA standard contract, the court found that the design professional had a duty to be generally knowledgeable of the quality and quantity of work in order to evaluate payment applications. The design professional was not relieved from liability simply because the contractor had failed to perform its work correctly. While the design professional was not a guarantor of the contractor's performance, it still had the responsibility to keep abreast of the quality of work.

The design professional is obligated to take action when it discovers or should have discovered the contractor's defective workmanship. The design professional can be held liable to the owner for inspection and approval of a contractor's faulty and/or nonconforming work. For instance, an architect was held liable to a building owner for the cost of repairing interior wall coverings damaged as a result of inadequate waterproofing that was observed and approved by the architect.[27]

In another case, a homeowner sued the architect for habitually neglecting its duties to inspect and approve the contractor's work.[28] The architect argued that, while contractually obligated to perform "general supervision of the construction work," its fee did not include "the cost of superintendence by a full-time inspector or Clerk of the Works." The court held for the homeowner, noting that:

> The term "general supervision," as used in the instant agreement, must mean something other than mere superficial supervision. Obviously, there can be no real value in supervision unless the same be directed toward securing a workmanlike adherence to specifications and adequate performance on the part of the contractor.[29]

Similarly, in *Central School Dist. No. 2 v. Flintkote Co.,*[30] the court required a trial on the issue of whether the design professional properly inspected a roof. The owner had employed a "Clerk of the Works" to make inspections, and the design professional contended that this eliminated any duty on his behalf to inspect the work. The court rejected this argument, holding that if the architect could rely solely on the Clerk in this regard, then:

> [T]he owner would be deprived of the professional judgment which he had the right to expect. The owner's retainer of a "Clerk of the Works" for full-time,

---

[27] *Dan Cowling & Assoc., Inc. v. Board of Educ.*, 618 S.W.2d 158 (Ark. 1981).
[28] *Pancoast v. Russell*, 307 P.2d 719 (Cal. Ct. App. 1957).
[29] *Id.* at 722.
[30] 391 N.Y.S.2d 887 (N.Y. App. Div. 1977).

on-site services, constituted a protection that is an addition to and not a substitute for the contractual and professional obligations of the architect.

From the standpoint of the contractor, a design professional's periodic inspection of construction work and failure to object to nonconforming materials and workmanship may, under the right circumstances, establish a constructive acceptance of the work and preclude an owner from refusing to pay the contractor.[31] Although no hard and fast rule applies in these situations, the contractor is more likely to prevail if it can show either a reasonable reliance on the design professional to detect nonconforming work or fault on the part of the design professional or owner.

For example, an architect failed to inspect a subcontractor's repairs to work that the architect had originally found inadequate. The court held that the architect's failure to inspect the remedial work and specify any additional corrections constituted a waiver of the contractual requirement that work be performed to the satisfaction of the architect. The court would not allow the owner-contractor to raise this contract provision as a defense in a suit brought by the subcontractor for breach of contract.[32]

4.10 Issuance of Certificates of Progress or Certificates of Completion

Another duty commonly required in a design professional's contract is the issuance of certificates of progress or completion, which generally are connected to the owner's duty to make payments to the contractor. This type of contract requirement is valid, despite the fact that the design professional acts as the agent of the owner.[33]

Common issues that arise from this duty involve the acceptance of the work by the design professional's approval of pay requests and the liability of the design professional for the improper failure to approve progress payments. As with the issues relating to inspection of the work, the analysis of these payment issues is dependent upon the particular contract language and the specific facts.

Contract language typically places full responsibility of meeting the requirements of the contract on the contractor. Thus contracts usually state that payment to the contractor does not constitute acceptance of the work and does not waive the owner's right to demand full contract compliance from the contractor. AIA Document A201, for instance, attempts to avoid the implication that the contractor has performed in accordance with the contract documents due to approval of payment applications in the following provision:

> The issuance of a Certificate for Payment will constitute a representation by the Architect to the Owner, based on his [the Architect's] observations . . . and

[31] *Milaeger Well Drilling Co. v. Muskego Rendering Co.,* 85 N.W.2d 331 (Wis. 1957).

[32] *Hartford Elec. Applicators of Thermalux, Inc. v. Alden,* 363 A.2d 135 (Conn. 1975).

[33] *Friberg v. Elrod,* 296 P. 1061 (Or. 1931).

the data comprising the Application for Payment, that the Work has progressed to the point indicated; that, to the best of his knowledge, information and belief, the quality of the Work is in accordance with the Contract Documents . . . and that the Contractor is entitled to payment in the amount certified.

Despite the careful wording of such clauses, the design professional's certificate of progress or completion may still benefit the contractor. *Fuchs v. Parsons Constr. Co.*[34] was a breach of contract action brought by the owner against the contractor for failure to comply with the plans and specifications. The court held that the design professional's certificate of completion was an effective defense to the owner's claim of noncompliance unless there was proof of fraud, gross negligence or bad faith on the part of the design professional in issuing the certificate.

The requirement that the design professional issue a certificate prior to contractor payment may be excused or waived by the parties under certain circumstances. In one case, the court found that neither the owner nor the contractor had relied on a design professional's certificate as a basis for making or receiving progress payments for completed excavation work. Consequently, the provision in the contract requiring a certificate prior to final payment was deemed waived, and neither party could insist on strict compliance with the contract requirement.[35]

An architect cannot delegate the responsibility of certifying progress payments to another architect and escape liability for a defective building. In *Sheetz, Aiken & Aiken, Inc. v. Spann, Hall, Ritchie, Inc.,*[36] the Alabama Supreme Court held that the project architect's duty, as inspecting architect, was to verify that the contractor performed the work in accordance with the plans and specifications, whereas the duty of the architect hired to certify progress was merely to determine the amount owed to the contractor for direct construction costs, not to insure a defect-free building.

A number of cases confirm the design professional's duty to use the care of one skilled in his profession when issuing payment certificates, and the design professional can be held liable for damages resulting from a failure to act accordingly. For example, in a California case, the owner asserted that the architect was negligent in issuing certificates of payment without first ascertaining whether the contractor had fully paid its subcontractors and materialmen. The court held that the architect, under its contract, should have protected the owner by making certain that all bills were paid or by insisting on lien waivers from suppliers.[37]

The design professional's negligence in approving pay requests and issuing progress certificates may also expose it to liability to third parties who have a financial interest in the project. These parties are typically lending banks

---

[34] 111 N.W.2d 727 (Neb. 1961).
[35] *Palmer v. Watson Constr. Co.,* 121 N.W.2d 62 (Minn. 1963).
[36] 512 So.2d 99 (Ala. 1987).
[37] *Palmer v. Brown,* 273 P.2d 306 (Cal. Ct. App. 1954).

and sureties. For example, an architect was found liable in one case to the contractor's surety for its negligence in issuing a substantial completion certificate. Under the contract, the architect could require the contractor to present evidence that payroll and material bills had been paid before releasing retained funds. The architect, however, failed to enforce this requirement. Consequently, the contractor collected its retainage and then defaulted, leaving the burden of completing the work and satisfying claims on the surety.[38]

The court rejected the argument that the architect could not be held liable because there was no privity of contract between the architect and the surety. The court relied on a negligence theory and ruled that the design professional owed a duty to ascertain whether the contractor had paid the bills to both the owner and the surety, for whose mutual benefit and protection contractor funds were retained. The surety's failure to take steps to ascertain whether outstanding bills were being paid by the contractor did not constitute contributory negligence, because the surety had a right to assume that the retainage would not be released until the contract was fully performed.

Furthermore, in *Peerless Ins. Co. v. Cerny & Assoc., Inc.,*[39] the court determined that a surety was subrogated to any claim that the owner would have against the architect for negligent certification of progress payments. Similarly, in *Westerhold v. Carroll,*[40] the Missouri Supreme Court confirmed that an architect can be held liable to the indemnitor of a contractor's surety for certifying payments in excess of the value of work performed.

The design professional's certification of progress payments has also been used by subcontractors as support for claims against the general contractor. In one case, the prime terminated a subcontractor for deficient performance.[41] The subcontractor, however, noted that the prime contractor had sought and obtained progress payments for the subcontractor's work. The subcontractor argued that the design professional's certification of the subcontractor's work was strong evidence that the work was satisfactory. The prime was placed in the difficult position of arguing either that the payment applications were not representations that the work was acceptable, or that the design professional's approval of the payments did not constitute a binding acceptance of the work. The court found the applications to be evidence of the subcontractor's satisfactory performance and held for the subcontractor.[42]

4.11 Arbitration of Disputes

Another major function that may be performed by the design professional pursuant to a contract provision is the arbitration of disputes between the

---

[38] *National Sur. Corp. v. Malvaney,* 72 So.2d 424 (Miss. 1954).

[39] 199 F. Supp. 951 (D. Minn. 1961).

[40] 419 S.W.2d 73 (Mo. 1967).

[41] *Sweeney Co. of Maryland v. Engineers-Contractors, Inc.,* 823 F.2d 805 (4th Cir. 1987), *in dictum.*

[42] *See also Magnolia Constr. Co. v. Mississippi Gulf South Eng's, Inc.,* 518 So.2d 1194 (Miss. 1988) (entitling third parties to rely on an architect's certification of progress).

owner and contractor. For instance, the design professional is at the center of the dispute resolution process under the AIA Document A201 General Conditions (1987 ed.), which requires that all claims be initially submitted to the design professional in writing.[43] The submission of claims is considered a "condition precedent to arbitration or litigation of a Claim between the Contractor and Owner as to all such matters arising prior to the date the final payment is due."

In contracts that contain provisions requiring disputes to be referred to the design professional for decision, questions arise as to whether the design professional's decision is binding, and if not, at what point a party can initiate arbitration or litigation. Generally, courts are reluctant to give the design professional the final and binding power to resolve disputes unless the contract is clear and unambiguous in giving the design professional such power. Courts recognize that design professionals may be partial to the owner and are therefore hesitant in enforcing what would amount to a waiver of a party's right to its day in court (or arbitration).

More difficult issues tend to arise with contracts that require claims to be submitted to the design professional for decision prior to a party's initiating litigation. How long must a contractor wait for a decision from the design professional before litigation may be commenced? What if the design professional repeatedly asks for additional documentation to support the claim, thus delaying a decision? Courts typically will not consider initial referral of a claim to the design professional a condition precedent to litigation unless the contract clearly states otherwise.[44] Furthermore, if the contract requires the design professional to render its decision within a certain period of time, the commencement of litigation would be appropriate after the time for a decision has elapsed. If no time is specified, a reasonable time is often assumed. Some courts have held that the design professional's role as arbitrator of disputes between owner and contractor ends once the work is completed.[45]

When the design professional assumes the impartial role of an arbitrator, the design professional is well protected against actions brought by owners and contractors as a result of its decisions.[46] The design professional is afforded this immunity because of its performance of a quasi-judicial function.[47] However, this immunity is limited to those acts of the design professional done while in a judicial capacity. Thus the crucial question is whether the particular challenged act was within the scope of the design professional's duties as an arbitrator. For example, at least one court has ruled that an architect cannot be held liable for failure to exercise care in the issuance of a final certificate when such an act is inside the scope of the architect's authority as arbitrator.[48]

---

[43] AIA Document A201 § 4.3.2 (1987 ed.).

[44] *Shook of W. Va., Inc. v. York City Sewer Auth.,* 756 F. Supp. 848 (M.D. Pa. 1991).

[45] *Id.; Tsombikos v. Brager,* 559 N.Y.S.2d 460 (N.Y. Sup. Ct. 1990).

[46] *Lane v. Geiger-Berger Assoc.,* 608 F.2d 1148 (8th Cir. 1979).

[47] *Lundgren v. Freeman,* 307 F.2d 104 (9th Cir. 1962).

[48] *Blecick v. School Dist. No. 18,* 406 P.2d 750 (Ariz. Ct. App. 1965).

In *Blecick,* the court found that the architect's refusal to issue a final certificate referred to an act done in their capacity as arbitrators.[49]

In another case, a contractor alleged that when he pointed out defects in the plans and specifications, the design professional who had prepared the documents became enraged. The design professional intentionally and maliciously undertook to bankrupt the contractor and to interfere with contractual relations between the contractor and the owner. The contractor claimed that the design professional issued contradictory instructions, changed plans and specifications without regard to added cost or delay, interfered with the contractor's coordination of its subcontractors and withheld progress payments. The contractor sought $200,000 actual damages and $250,000 in punitive damages against the design professional. The design professional's claim of immunity based on its status as an arbitrator was not an adequate defense, because the challenged acts were clearly outside the scope of the arbitrator's function.[50]

Distinguishing between protected arbitrator functions and the other functions of the design professional is a difficult task. The deliberate or negligent misuse of the design professional's powers as arbitrator may allow a party to ignore the design professional's decision. In *Brezina Constr. Co. v. South Dakota Dep't of Transp.,*[51] a state engineer's unreasonable behavior caused the court to negate his authority to classify and quantify a contractor's excavation work. The contractor agreed to construct a bridge and reconstruct a section of state highway. All "unclassified excavation" was to be performed at a unit price of $3.50 per cubic yard. Rock excavation was to be performed at five times that price. When the contractor unexpectedly struck rock and notified the State in accordance with the contract requirements, the Department's engineer (who was designated as the final arbiter of contract disputes) was uncommunicative and delayed visiting the job site to measure the extent of the rock encountered.

The court agreed that the engineer had authority under the contract to determine the quantity of rock, but found that the parties were not bound by an engineer's decision that is "manifestly arbitrary or rendered in bad faith." On the basis of the engineer's intentional failure to conduct a timely inspection, the court awarded the contractor damages for the uncompensated rock excavation. The engineer's failure to exercise its powers as arbitrator in good faith rendered the engineer's decision meaningless.

4.12 OTHER DESIGN PROFESSIONAL DUTIES

The administrative duties of the design professional previously discussed are found in many private construction contracts and illustrate the design professional's basic responsibilities and obligations on a project. However, these

---

[49] *Id.*
[50] *Craviolini v. Scholer & Fuller Associated Architects,* 357 P.2d 611 (Ariz. 1960).
[51] 297 N.W.2d 168 (S.D. 1980).

general duties of the design professional may be supplemented by the inclusion of specific provisions in the specifications, such as the following:

(1) If soil conditions are such that, *in the opinion of the Architect,* yard hydrants cannot be secured, use bridles.

(2) Defects in the extension of existing gas lines must be repaired *to the satisfaction of the Architect.*

(3) The entire jacking and shoring *procedure is subject to review by the Architect.*

(4) Set manhole castings in fresh bed of mortar and carefully adjust elevation *or as directed by the Architect.*

(5) Concrete surfaces shall be finished to a true and even plane well within limits of best trade practice and to the satisfaction of the Engineer.

4.13   THE DESIGN PROFESSIONAL'S LIABILITY TO THE CONTRACTOR

Under certain circumstances, the failure of the design professional to properly perform its supervisory or administrative responsibilities may result in liability for resulting damages to the owner. These same acts or omissions by the design professional may also form the basis for an action by the contractor against the owner and/or the design professional.

With increasing frequency, design professionals are being held directly liable to contractors under various legal theories. The most prevalent of these theories involves the design professional's negligent breach of a duty owed to the owner and/or the contractor.

4.14   Negligence and the "Economic Loss Rule"

The negligent breach of a duty by one person often injures another person. Such harm may include an injury to the person, an injury to property, or an injury to a business interest of some type, often referred to as "economic loss." It has long been established that a person may sue in negligence for personal injuries and property damage even where the person has no privity or contractual relationship with the defendant.[52] However, courts have been more reluctant to allow parties to recover in negligence for *economic loss* where there is no privity between the parties to the lawsuit. This limitation on negligence actions is called the "Economic Loss Rule."

Some jurisdictions have rejected the Economic Loss Rule outright, reasoning that a person should not have to suffer personal injury or property damage in order to recover for damage caused by another's wrongful acts. Other courts have based rejection of the Economic Loss Rule on the theory that a

---

[52] *MacPherson v. Buick Motor Co.,* 111 N.E. 1050 (N.Y. 1916).

person has a duty to avoid creating a foreseeable risk of harm—regardless of whether such harm is to property, person or business interest.

Although the Economic Loss Rule is still recognized in more than twenty jurisdictions in the United States and was unanimously upheld by the United States Supreme Court in 1986,[53] the Rule is losing strength in the courts and is undergoing continuous modification in order to allow parties, such as contractors, to recover for economic harms caused by another's negligence.

Some courts have recognized that when the contractor, or another person not a party to the design professional contract, relies on the guidance or expertise of the design professional to carry out particular construction responsibilities, the design professional has a duty to render this guidance in a professional manner. The design professional's negligent breach of this duty gives the contractor or other third party the right to sue the design professional directly. Third parties have been allowed to recover damages for the design professional's: (1) negligent preparation of a soils report,[54] (2) negligent failure to prepare an environmental impact statement,[55] (3) preparation of defective plans and specifications,[56] and (4) negligent performance of a water percolation test.[57]

Some courts place a duty on the design professional toward the contractor based on the design professional's inherent power over the contractor. For example, in *United States ex rel. Los Angeles Testing Laboratory v. Rogers & Rogers,*[58] a contractor was delayed in completing the work because the architect negligently interpreted certain concrete tests. Stating that "[t]he power of the architect to stop the work alone is tantamount to a power of economic life or death over the contractor," the court allowed the contractor to recover damages for delay directly from the architect.

The key factors for some courts that permit negligence actions against the design professional for solely economic losses are the *foreseeability* of harm and the *special relationship* between the design professional and the contractor. Many of these courts recognize a cause of action against the design professional in favor of the contractor while adhering to the Economic Loss Rule with respect to other third-party plaintiffs.[59]

If the design professional has agreed to perform supervisory tasks on a construction project, the contractor has a right to rely on that supervision.[60] In one case, the contractor claimed that the architect inspected and approved certain roof trusses that were improperly designed and caused the roof to collapse. The court found that when it is foreseeable that a contractor may

[53] *East River S.S. Corp. v. Transamerica Delaval, Inc.,* 476 U.S. 858 (1986).
[54] *Davidson & Jones, Inc. v. New Hanover County,* 255 S.E.2d 580 (N.C. Ct. App. 1979).
[55] *COAC, Inc. v. Kennedy Eng'rs,* 136 Cal. Rptr. 890 (Cal. Dist. Ct. App. 1977).
[56] *Donnelly Constr. Co. v. Oberg/Hunt/Gilleland,* 677 P.2d 1292 (Ariz. 1984).
[57] *Southeast Consultants, Inc. v. O'Pry,* 404 S.E.2d 299 (Ga. Ct. App. 1991).
[58] 161 F. Supp. 132 (S.D. Cal. 1958).
[59] *McClain v. Harveston,* 263 S.E.2d 228 (Ga. Ct. App. 1979).
[60] *See Day v. National U.S. Radiator Corp.,* 128 So.2d 660 (La. 1961).

sustain economic loss as a result of the design professional's negligent performance of its contractual duties to others, the contractor may sue the design professional directly for such negligence. The court recognized that each participant in a construction project must rely on the performance of others, and thus each is obligated to perform its duties with due care. The contractor was entitled to recover from the project architect any costs caused by the architect's negligence.[61]

It appears that courts allowing recovery for economic losses under a negligence theory will not distinguish between cases where a design professional's duties are deemed "supervisory" and those where the design professional's duties are "administrative." For instance, in *Dickerson Constr. Co. v. Process Eng'g Co.,*[62] the project architect's duties were defined by the contract as administrative. The court concluded that neither "supervision" nor "administration" connoted a higher or lower standard of duty than "inspection." The court further held that the basic question was whether the design professional had exercised reasonable care in making whatever observations and inspections it had actually made on the project. In another case, the architect himself testified that "supervision" and "administration" at the job site constitute the same set of obligations.[63]

Even in the jurisdictions rejecting the Economic Loss Rule, the design professional may successfully defend against the claim alleging contributory negligence on the contractor's part. Also, the third party asserting the negligence claim against the design professional must be able to prove that the design professional's negligence *proximately caused* the injury or damage. For instance, a Florida appellate court held that an architect was not liable to a subcontractor for negligently advising the owner to reject the subcontractor's request for a substitution. According to the court, because the owner made the final decision on the subcontractor's request, the architect was not the "proximate cause" of the subcontractor's damages.[64]

In some cases, courts may be unwilling to allow a contractor to sue the design professional if the contractor could not sue the owner for the same claim. For example, in one case, the contractor sued the architect for delay damages caused by the architect's negligent failure to provide construction power for more than a year during performance. The contractor could not sue the owner because a no damages for delay clause in the construction contract precluded recovery against the owner. The court held that the contractor could not circumvent the restrictions of this clause by suing the design professional for negligence, reasoning that the no damages for delay clause was broad enough to include claims against the design professional.[65]

---

[61] *Shoffner Indus., Inc. v. W. B. Lloyd Constr. Co.,* 257 S.E.2d 50 (N.C. Ct. App. 1979).

[62] 341 So.2d 646 (Miss. 1977).

[63] *Kleb v. Wendling,* 385 N.E.2d 346 (Ill. App. Ct. 1978).

[64] *McElvy, Jennewein, Stefany, Howard, Inc. v. Arlington Elec., Inc.,* 582 So.2d 47 (Fla. Dist. Ct. App. 1991). *See generally* Bell & House, *Current Status of Economic Loss Rule, in* 1992 Wiley Construction Law Update 239 (Currie & Sweeney eds., 1992).

[65] *Bates & Rogers Constr. Co. v. Greeley & Hansen,* 486 N.E.2d 902 (Ill. 1985).

Assuming the project is in a jurisdiction that recognizes the contractor's right to sue the design professional in negligence for economic loss, the contractor still faces a tough battle to recovery. In general, it is much easier to establish owner liability for defective design under contract and warranty theories than it is to prove professional negligence on the part of the design professional.

Negligence is determined by evaluating the acts and/or omissions of the alleged wrongdoer according to a specific standard of care. Design professionals are required to exercise the skill, judgment, and reasonable care possessed and practiced by those in the same profession.[66] This standard varies according to local practice.[67] A design professional's deviation from established standards of care as announced in trade journals and manuals published by professional organizations such as the AIA, the National Society of Professional Engineers (NSPE) and the American Consulting Engineers Council (ACEC) is often considered evidence of negligence. Such evidence is not conclusive, however, and proof of professional malpractice usually requires expert testimony by someone in the same field. Some jurisdictions have even passed statutes that require parties suing a professional for negligence to attach to their complaints an affidavit from a professional in the same field substantiating the malpractice claim.

Usually, design professionals have "shallow pockets" as compared to owners. Consequently, contractors and third parties whose claims are fairly large probably have a better chance of recovering their damages by suing the owner, if such action is possible. "Errors and omissions" liability insurance, however, which is available to architects and engineers, increases a party's opportunities with respect to recovery against a design professional, and at the same time protects design professionals from large judgments in negligence actions.

The questions that often arise in relation to a design professional's malpractice insurance can affect both the professional and the parties trying to reach the proceeds of the policy. The majority of these problems involve interpretation of the scope of coverage to determine whether the design professional is protected from the particular claims alleged. Errors and omissions insurance policies are very specific as to the negligent acts that are covered. For instance, if an architect or engineer performs services on a project that deviate from "basic" architectural or engineering services (i.e., construction management), it is unlikely that negligence claims associated with those services would be covered under the typical malpractice liability policy. Also, design professional policies expressly exclude from coverage certain acts that are not considered "insurable risks" because they involve conscious and deliberate conduct on the part of the professional. Such exclusions include the design professional's failure to complete drawings or specifications on time and the professional's commission of intentional torts. Because professional liability insurance cover-

---

[66] *Overland Constructors, Inc. v. Millard School Dist.*, 369 N.W.2d 69 (Neb. 1985).
[67] *Collins Co. v. City of Decatur*, 533 So.2d 1127 (Ala. 1988).

age is so limited, an insurance company will not entertain claims of a design professional's general negligence in the performance of its duties.

4.15   Intentional Torts

Although undoubtedly less common than actions for negligence, lawsuits for intentional torts can also present problems for design professionals. Such suits are generally based on the intentional interference with the contractual relationship between owner and contractor. Because negligence theories are now more widely recognized as tools for recovery of economic loss, the intentional tort theory is used much less frequently.

In one case, a court held that an architect's totally unjustified and therefore arbitrary refusal to issue a certificate of performance subjected it to intentional tort liability.[68] In another case, a court found that the architect willfully and wrongfully interfered with a school construction contract by inducing the school district to default the contractor.[69] The court further held that if the plaintiff contractor could demonstrate malicious intent on the part of the architect, it could recover punitive as well as compensatory damages.[70]

An architect will not always be held liable for tortious interference with contractual relations merely because the design professional recommends that the contractor replace a subcontractor. But where the evidence shows that a design professional's actions were arbitrary and specifically undertaken for the purpose of interfering with the contractor's business, the contractor will have a valid cause of action.[71]

4.16   Third-party Beneficiary

Another theory that may be available to the contractor is the argument that the contractor is a "third-party beneficiary" of the contract between the owner and the design professional. This theory, for the most part, has been unsuccessful in the courts.

A "third-party beneficiary" is a party who is not one of the original contracting parties but who may bring an action to enforce the provisions of the contract. To do so, however, the third party must have been an "intended beneficiary" of the contract. In other words, the contract must have been entered into with an *intent* to confer a *direct* or *immediate benefit* on the *third party who claims to be a beneficiary.* Such an intent is difficult to prove, as there is a strong presumption that people customarily contract for their own benefit.[72] When third parties are benefited by an agreement, but their benefit

---

[68] *Unity Sheet Metal Works, Inc. v. Farrell Lines, Inc.,* 101 N.Y. S.2d 1000 (N.Y. Sup. Ct. 1950).

[69] *Lundgren,* fn. 47, *supra.*

[70] *See also Craviolini,* fn. 50, *supra.*

[71] *John W. Johnson, Inc. v. Basic Constr. Co.,* 292 F. Supp. 300 (D.D.C. 1968), *aff'd,* 429 F.2d 764 (D.C. Cir. 1970).

[72] *Peter Kiewit Sons' Co. v. Iowa S. Util. Co.,* 355 F. Supp. 376 (S.D. Iowa 1973).

is not the specific purpose of contractual performance, they are referred to as "incidental beneficiaries." Despite their benefited status, incidental beneficiaries do not have a legal right to bring an action to enforce the provisions of the contract.[73]

As a practical matter, a contractor is more likely to succeed in an action in tort than in a contract action as a third-party beneficiary to the contract between the owner and the design professional. For example, in a Florida case,[74] a contractor claimed to be a third-party beneficiary to the design professional–owner contract. The court held that, in most cases, provisions in the contract between owner and architect that call for supervision or administration by the architect are intended for the benefit of the owner, and the general contractor is only an incidental beneficiary. However, the court did recognize that the design professional could be liable to the contractor for negligence.

Likewise, in a Louisiana case,[75] the contractor's claims against the project architect were predicated upon both tort and third-party beneficiary grounds. The contractor alleged unreasonable delays occasioned by improperly prepared plans, late delivery of plans and working drawings, untimely change orders and improperly issued correction data by the design professional. The court, while finding the tort claims supportable, dismissed the contractor's third-party beneficiary claims.

In those situations where the design professional has undertaken to perform a duty owed by the owner to the contractor, the contractor may assert a third-party beneficiary claim to enforce performance of the architect-owner contract.[76] The court determines whether a contractor is a third-party beneficiary by examining the apparent intent of the contracting parties.[77]

Also, there may be circumstances in which the design professional assumes *extra* responsibilities to the contractor by its conduct. An example is where the architect has no contractual duty to the owner to make extensive and thorough on-site inspections but nevertheless does make such inspections.[78] Proper performance of assumed duties may still be enforced through third-party beneficiary actions.

By carefully drafting the contract, a design professional can avoid third-party beneficiary claims. For example, AIA Document A201 (1987 ed.), Article 1, ¶ 1.1.2 provides:

---

[73] *Engle Acoustic & Tile, Inc. v. Grenfell,* 223 So.2d 613 (Miss. 1969); *Valley Landscape Co. v. Rolland,* 237 S.E.2d 120 (Va. 1977).

[74] *A. R. Moyer, Inc. v. Graham,* 285 So.2d 397 (Fla. 1973).

[75] *C. H. Leavell & Co. v. Glantz Contracting Corp. of La.,* 322 F. Supp. 779 (E.D. La. 1971).

[76] *See, e.g., Owen v. Dodd,* 431 F. Supp. 1239 (N.D. Miss. 1977).

[77] *See* 17 Am. Jur. 2d, Contracts §§ 302, *et seq.; see also Malta Constr. Co. v. Henningson, Durham & Richardson, Inc.,* 694 F. Supp. 902 (N.D. Ga. 1988) (upholding third-party beneficiary theory by a general contractor against supplier of shop drawings under contract with a subcontractor).

[78] *Krieger v. J. E. Greiner Co.,* 382 A.2d 1069 (Md. 1978).

> The Contract Documents shall not be construed to create a contractual relationship of any kind (1) between the Architect and the Contractor, (2) between the Owner and a Subcontractor, or Sub-subcontractor, or (3) between any persons or entities other than the Owner and Contractor.

Such clauses are usually judicially enforced.[79]

A court might be persuaded by a third-party beneficiary argument where it is needed to salvage a cause of action. In most cases, however, the same act that would constitute the basis for a third-party beneficiary action would also constitute a negligence action, and a more likely basis for relief.[80]

4.17 Statutes of Repose

With the increase in scope of liability for design professionals and the prospect of perpetual liability, courts and legislatures have limited the length of time during which a claim for damages may be brought against design professionals. Generally, certain claims may be brought only within specific time frames. These time frames are typically set forth in statutes of limitations and are typically triggered by the discovery of the act or omission giving rise to the claim. Conversely, statutes of *repose* are intended to establish an outer time limit beyond which the design professional cannot be held liable for design and construction defects. Thus a party who discovers its claim after the expiration of the statute of repose period is barred from asserting that claim despite the existence of an otherwise applicable statute of limitation.

Often, injury and resulting liability relating to construction projects do not surface until many years after the work has been completed and accepted. Most states have enacted special statutes of repose that deal with claims associated with the design and construction of a project. Although the language of statutes of repose varies from state to state, design professionals such as architects and engineers fall within the purview of these statutes. Usually, the statutes are phrased generally, so as to bar claims against "any party who designs or furnishes an improvement to real property" that are brought after the specified time.[81] Therefore, a contractor suing a design professional for damages sustained in connection with the project must institute an action that complies with the applicable statute of repose.

All of the statutes of repose apply to tort claims, such as those brought under negligence or intentional tort theories. Many of the statutes also time-bar contract claims. Thus a party suing a design professional on a third-party beneficiary theory must also pay close attention to any applicable statute of repose.

Statutes of repose for design and construction claims usually take one of two forms. The majority of the statutes set a maximum time after completion

---

[79] *See, e.g., Michigan Abrasive Co., Inc. v. Poole,* 805 F.2d 1001 (11th Cir. 1986); *Sheetz, Aiken & Aiken,* fn. 36, *supra; Federal Mogul Corp. v. Universal Constr. Co.,* 376 So.2d 716 (Ala. Civ. App. 1979).
[80] *See, e.g., Engle Acoustic & Tile,* fn. 73, *supra.*
[81] *See* Ark. Stat. Ann. § 37-2-37 (Supp. 1985).

of the construction beyond which no claims may be brought that relate to the design and/or construction of the project.[82] The second type of statute also sets a maximum time after project completion for bringing a claim; however, these statutes also specify a shorter period of time after the cause of action accrues within which such action must be brought.[83]

Some statutes of repose specifically define when the statute begins to run. Others are left for judicial interpretation. The statute may begin to run, depending on the jurisdiction, upon completion of the project, substantial completion of the project, termination of the design of the improvement, or termination of the construction services.[84] Furthermore, a few statutes can be triggered by other events such as the date of actual possession by the owner of the improvement, the date of the issuance of a certificate of occupancy, or the date of completion or termination of the contract between the design professional or the contractor and the owner.[85]

4.18 ASSUMPTION OF DESIGN LIABILITY BY THE CONTRACTOR

Traditionally, the design professional is responsible for defects and other problems associated with the design of a project and may be held liable therefor. There are several ways, however, that a contractor may assume design liability. When this happens, a contractor may be required to bear not only its own costs incurred by a defect, but also those extra costs incurred by the owner or other parties related to the defect.

The most common situation where a contractor assumes the risks of design defects is on "design/build" projects.[86] A "design/build" contractor performs the tasks ordinarily assigned to the design professional, in addition to its construction duties. Design/build contracts are attractive to owners because they create a single source for design liability. These contracts also relieve the owner from being caught between the design professional and a contractor with respect to design disputes. In addition to assuming the risks of defects and design, a design/build contractor also assumes the risk that construction of the project will cost more than originally anticipated at the time of contracting with the owner. As long as the performance criteria provided by the owner are not impracticable, a design/build contractor will be held liable for excessive costs incurred by the owner on account of extended construction time.[87]

An owner does not receive complete immunity from design liability by entering into a design/build contract with a contractor. An owner may be

---

[82] *See* Mo. Ann. Stat. § 516.097 (Vernon Supp. 1986).

[83] *See* Mass. Gen. Laws Ann. Ch. 260 § 2B (West Supp. 1986).

[84] *See, e.g.,* Fla. Stat. § 95.11(3)(c) (1982); Ga. Code § 9-3-51 (1981); Mo. Ann. Stat. § 516.097 (Vernon Supp. 1986); Mont. Code Ann. § 27-2-208 (1985); N.J. Stat. Ann. § 2A: 14-1.1 (West Supp. 1985).

[85] *See, e.g.,* Colo. Rev. Stat. § 13-80-127 (Supp. 1985); Ill. Ann. Stat. Ch. 110 § 13-2-14 (Smith Hurd Supp. 1986).

[86] *Mobile Hous. Env'ts v. Barton & Barton,* 432 F. Supp. 1343 (D. Colo. 1977).

[87] *Ruscon Constr. Co.,* ASBCA No. 39586, 90-2 BCA ¶ 22,768.

subject to liability for design defects depending on the level of the owner's technical expertise, the owner's active participation in the design process, and the information provided by the owner at the outset of the project. Because the design/build scenario represents such a deviation from the traditional allocation of design risks, both owner and contractor should pay special attention to the language and terms of the contract.

Contractors performing in the traditional setting of design/bid/build may still assume design liability. One way in which this happens is by the contractor's compliance with performance specifications or criteria provided by the owner. While performance specifications dictate the result to be achieved by the contractor, they do not tell the contractor how to accomplish the desired result. Consequently, the contractor is responsible for the costs associated with achieving the end result specified by the performance criteria.

It is not uncommon for the design and performance specifications to be in conflict with one another. If a contractor recognizes such a conflict or has sufficient knowledge to recognize it, at a minimum, the contractor must notify the owner and/or the design professional in order to excuse itself from design liability resulting from the conflict. For example, in *Regan Constr. Co. & Nager Elec. Co.,*[88] the performance criteria provided by the owner for air handling units could only be met by one particular unit on the market, which the contractor incorporated into the construction. The unit, however, did not fit into the space allotted by the overall design. As a result, the contractor incurred extra costs associated with accommodating the unit. In an action against the owner, the Board of Contract Appeals held the contractor liable for the extra costs, reasoning that the contractor should have discovered the conflict between the design and performance specifications earlier.

Another specification issue that may give rise to contractor liability for design involves the use of a "brand name or equal" specification by the owner. Use of the brand name product by a contractor will not automatically relieve the contractor of liability for noncompliance. In other words, a defect in design that results from a contractor's use of a brand name as specified in a "brand name or equal" specification is not included in the owner's implied warranty of the adequacy of the specifications. As long as the contractor has a choice of products, the contractor must bear the burden of meeting compliance requirements.[89]

As discussed earlier in this chapter, the shop drawings form a bridge between the contract documents and the complete project. The shop drawings contain the details necessary to fabricate material and install work in the field and are the responsibility of the contractor. In preparing the shop drawings, there is always a risk that the contractor will alter the original design in translating the design as represented by the plans and specifications to the shop drawings. When such a modification or alteration to the design occurs, the contractor may be subject to liability for any resulting damages.

[88] PSBCA No. 633, 80-2 BCA ¶ 14,802.
[89] *Florida Bd. of Regents v. Mycon Corp.,* 651 So.2d 149 (Fla. Dist. Ct. App. 1995).

One of the common duties of a design professional on a project is to review and approve contractor submittals, including shop drawings. However, if shop drawings prepared by the contractor change the original design and are later approved by the design professional, the contractor may still be held responsible for impacts to the overall construction caused by the change.[90] It is possible for the contractor to shift this type of design liability back to the owner by immediately bringing any changes or modifications to the design by shop drawings to the attention of both the owner and the design professional.

Finally, contractors should be wary of standard contract clauses that expose the contractor to potential liability for design defects. For instance, many contracts contain a catchall interpretations clause, which requires the contractor to supply any and all necessary labor and materials that may be reasonably inferred from the plans and specifications to achieve a complete project. If the contractor fails to provide such labor or materials and a defect results, the contractor may be held liable.

Contractors are often assigned the responsibility of reviewing the design and notifying either the owner or the design professional of errors and omissions. Many courts have found contractors liable for failure to disclose patent defects—that is, obvious defects of which the contractors knew or should have known. As is the case with other issues concerning patent defects, what a court may consider "patent" depends on the circumstances surrounding the particular project and the expertise of the contractor on the job.

POINTS TO REMEMBER

- Parties can avoid many construction contract disputes by understanding the authority, responsibility and duties of the design professional on the project.
- In any given case, a design professional may have authority to do certain things on the job site because:
  (1) It is expressly stated in the contract documents (actual authority);
  (2) It is incidental or necessary to the exercise of the design professional's actual authority (implied authority); or
  (3) The acts of the owner would lead a reasonable person to believe the design professional had such authority (apparent authority).
- During construction, the project design professional is generally responsible for:
  (1) The initial interpretation of the plans and specifications;
  (2) Reviewing and approving shop drawings and other submittals;

---

[90] *Fauss Constr., Inc. v. City of Hooper,* 249 N.W.2d 478 (Neb. 1977).

(3) Inspection and testing;

(4) Reviewing the contractor's pay requests and certifying progress and completion; and

(5) Arbitrating certain disputes between the owner and the contractor.

· On most jobs, the design professional does *not* have authority

(1) To make changes to the work;

(2) To direct the operations of the contractor; or

(3) To deviate from the requirements of the contract.

· Remember that some contracts, such as the AIA contract documents, may emphasize the design professional's role as "administrative" and otherwise seek to insulate the design professional from potential liability to the contractor or the owner for interpreting, reviewing, inspecting, approving and performing other functions set out in the contract documents.

· The design professional may be liable in some states to the contractor for economic losses suffered due to negligent performance of the design professional's duties and responsibilities even though there is no contract between the design professional and the contractor. The applicable law on this issue must be reviewed in each case to determine if a cause of action is available and, if so, what damages are recoverable.

· The contractor may assume design liability in certain situations. To avoid such liability, the contractor should always notify the owner and the design professional about inconsistencies between the design and the performance specifications, as well as any changes to the design resulting from the shop drawings.

5

SUBCONTRACT ADMINISTRATION AND DISPUTE AVOIDANCE

The prime contractor is responsible for the satisfactory and timely completion of the work. Yet much of the work will be done by subcontractors and suppliers. Successful project performance depends as much on the legal and business relationship between the general contractor and the subcontractors and suppliers as on anything.

Unsatisfactory performance by a subcontractor often generates disputes among the general contractor, that subcontractor and the owner, and possibly other subcontractors. Disputes also arise between the general contractor and the subcontractor from problems for which the *owner* may be responsible. Similarly, a failure to perform by the prime contractor affects everyone involved with the project.

These disputes are the things of which lawsuits are made. Unfortunately, litigation is costly and time consuming, and it rarely produces a decision at the time the problem arises.

Contract administration between the general contractor and subcontractors and suppliers and dispute avoidance are the subjects of this chapter. In an effort to help you identify and prevent problems from the outset, this chapter focuses on areas where general contractor and subcontractor problems often originate.

5.1 DISPUTE AVOIDANCE BEGINS AT THE BIDDING STAGE

5.2 The Importance of the Low Price

Price is an important consideration in selecting a subcontractor, but it is not the only one. The lowest cost subcontract may turn out to be the most expensive one if the subcontractor is unwilling or unable to do the work.

A prospective subcontractor should also consider the general contractor's overall pricing strategy. Unfortunately, you will never be sure how the prime is pricing the project before the bid but history may give a workable indication whether the general can be expected to underprice the contract with the expectation of negotiating even lower subcontract prices after award or of making up deficiencies on extras.

5.3 Know with Whom You Are Dealing

Dealing with irresponsible or unscrupulous contractors very likely will result in disputes. Avoidance of such problems begins at the bidding stage, when both general contractors and subcontractors identify potential contractors with whom they will bid and are willing to enter into contracts for the work.

All contractors should consider the following factors.

5.4 Reputation   A contractor can avoid numerous headaches and possible losses simply by investigating the past performance record of a potential prime contractor or subcontractor. Unreliable contractors can be avoided at the outset by dealing with reputable individuals with a proven ability to perform, by running credit checks, and by inquiring about the experiences of other owners and contractors.

Even a cursory investigation may yield clues to potential problems. For example, engaging a subcontractor with a reputation for shoddy or defective work may force the prime to remedy an unsatisfactory work-product at its own expense. A subcontractor may find that a prime has a history of slow performance so that its subs are forced into extended schedules or so that payment delays are frequently encountered. A particularly litigious contractor may refuse to negotiate a settlement in the event of a disagreement, disrupting the project schedule by refusing to work, and possibly forcing you to incur the expense of arbitration or a court battle.

5.5 Financial Resources   A contractor that lacks adequate working capital brings a myriad of problems to the project, even without a default. For example, suppliers concerned about the contractor's ability to pay may hold deliveries until they receive payment. Laborers may refuse to work because they are not timely paid. These problems can have an impact on other work.

The ultimate concern is the financial resources of the prime contractor, who may be called upon to finance part of the performance. For instance, the contractor may be forced to finance corrective work for defects by other subcontractors, or to continue to perform in the face of differing site conditions or changes in the work while negotiations or litigation resolve ultimate entitlement to payment. If the prime contractor does not have sufficient financial resources to continue performance and pay its subcontractors and suppliers in the face of delayed payments from the owner, there is the potential of a prime contractor failure, which will affect everyone involved with the project.

That prospect warrants considerable attention by subcontractors and suppliers to the reputation and resources of the contractors with whom they do business.

A subcontractor with insufficient working capital may be encouraged to front-end load pay requests so that payment may be made for work not yet performed or for more than the work actually performed is worth. If an overpaid subcontractor defaults, the cost to complete, combined with the sum already paid the defaulting subcontractor, may be substantially greater than the amount originally allocated by the prime for the work. The difference, of course, may come out of the prime's pocket.

5.6 *Experience and Qualifications*   State and local laws require licensing of general contractors and certain subcontractor trades. The licensing requirements provide minimal assurance of the contractor's competence, but the investigation should not stop there.

You should inquire about the contractor's experience on projects of similar type and size to the one being bid. The best residential electrical subcontractor in the county is not necessarily the best subcontractor for a high-rise hotel project. That subcontractor's reputation may be built on his *personal* integrity and quality of his work, which are laudable achievements. But they do not necessarily assure that subcontractor has the experience to manage the work of fifteen other electricians and coordinate with other trades, which a high-rise hotel project will require.

The subcontractor may find by inquiring of other subcontractors and suppliers that a general contractor has considerable experience in one type of project, but that the experience is different from the requirements of the prospective project. Or the subcontractor may learn that the prime contractor is already overcommitted on existing contracts, which may affect its performance on a new project.

The general contractor must also explore the subcontractor's experience in light of special performance requirements for the particular project. For example, if the specifications only give performance criteria, the subcontractor must be able to produce engineering and design details to meet the criteria, in a timely manner. If a subcontractor proposes to sub-subcontract out the engineering or design work, it is appropriate to investigate the credentials and experience of the proposed designer or engineer.

Some building product and component suppliers condition the warranty of their products upon installation or application by an approved (certified) subcontractor. In some cases such requirements are not necessary and intended only to inflate the cost of the work. But the applicable warranty law must be reviewed before dismissing the supplier's or manufacturer's requirements because the limitations may be valid. The general contractor could find that his subcontractor is insolvent and the supplier has no warranty obligation for the failure of a roof or wall system because its product was installed by an unauthorized subcontractor. By contrast, if the work is performed by an approved installer, the general contractor may be protected both by the supplier's periodic inspections and by warranties of both the product and the installation.

5.7   Union versus Nonunion Status   A general contractor's choice of a union or nonunion subcontractor generally depends on his own union status. If a union subcontractor and a nonunion general contractor contract for a project, the subcontract should contain provisions dealing with labor relations on the work site and give the general contractor the right to terminate the subcontractor if labor problems delay or impede the progress of the work.

A subcontractor should carefully consider its contract right to time extensions in the event the general contractor or another subcontractor has labor problems that affect its work.

One option available to contractors, which has become more feasible in recent years due to favorable National Labor Relations Board (NLRB) decisions, is to operate "double-breasted."[1] In general, a double-breasted contractor is a union contractor who forms a second, separate company that operates "open-shop." In essence, there are two employers—one union, one nonunion. This form gives the contractor the advantage of being able to operate without a union where this is feasible, while at the same time, continuing operation of the union company where the use of union labor sources is required. Double-breasted operation does not, of course, guarantee freedom from labor problems, and the cost of maintaining two separate companies may be prohibitive for some organizations. The use of a double-breasted operation also requires careful adherence to technical labor law requirements. Nonetheless, double-breasted operations can be an effective alternative for a contractor who wants to compete with open-shop contractors in some areas, while maintaining good relations with the union where union labor predominates.

5.8   Problem Areas in Subcontract Bidding

When is there an enforceable agreement between a prime contractor and subcontractor? The simple answer is only when both parties have signed the subcontract agreement. This simple answer may also be wrong.

For example, a prime contractor who has relied on a subcontractor's telephone bid may be entitled to enforce that bid even though the parties have not *signed* an agreement. A letter of intent, or a telephone conversation, may give rise to binding obligations, and refusal to execute a subcontract agreement following a letter of intent or a telephone bid may be a breach itself.

Oral agreements can be binding, although they may be unenforceable in certain transactions. When a transaction involves primarily the sale of goods, a binding contract may arise under the Uniform Commercial Code (UCC) when the parties have agreed to the material terms, even though disagreement exists with respect to other important terms of the "contract."[2]

[1] *Gerace Constr., Inc.*, 193 NLRB 645 (1971).
[2] *See* Chapter 3 regarding the UCC.

5.9 *Enforcement of Subcontractor Bids* Practically every prime contractor and subcontractor has had a subcontractor or supplier revoke its bid or proposal after the prime or sub has relied on it in committing to a contract of its own. This problem has generated as much litigation between prime contractors and subcontractors as almost any other problem facing the construction industry.

Many early cases held that the subcontractor was not bound to the prime contractor, or similarly, the supplier was not bound to the subcontractor, unless the parties had actually signed a contract document.[3] Therefore, bids and proposals could be withdrawn up until the parties were actually bound by formal documents.

In recent years, many courts have held a subcontractor bound to the prime who notifies the subcontractor within a reasonable time after award that its bid was relied on in obtaining the prime contract award and the prime intends to use the subcontractor for the project.[4] What constitutes a reasonable time for acceptance of an offer depends on the circumstances.[5]

The trend toward binding subcontractors to the prime contractor based upon the bidder's proposal, even without a contract document, is a response to the hardship to the contractor if it is awarded a contract based on the sub's proposal, but the sub is not obligated to proceed with performance. Many contractors seek to avoid this problem by requiring that companies who submit prices also agree that their proposal will not be revoked for the same period of time allowed for award of the prime contract in the owner's bid documents.

5.10 *Subcontractor Rights against the Prime Contractor* Although subcontractors may be responsible to general contractors who rely on their bid, general contractors are less frequently bound to enter into subcontracts with subcontractors whose prices they used.[6]

The fact that the prime contractor used the sub's proposal in its bid to the owner does not, under the usual circumstances, give rights to the subcontractor like those which the prime contractor may have to bind the sub to a contract. However, each set of circumstances must be judged on its own merits. An

---

[3] *See, e.g., Anderson Constr. Co. v. Lyon Metal Prods.,* 370 So.2d 935 (Miss. 1979).

[4] *See, e.g., Allen M. Campbell v. Virginia Metal Indus., Inc.,* 708 F.2d 930 (4th Cir. 1983); *Allied Grape Growers v. Bronco Wine Co.,* 203 Cal. App. 3d 432, 249 Cal. Rptr. 872 (5th Dist. 1988); *Arango Constr. Co. v. Success Roofing, Inc.,* 730 P.2d 720 (Wash. App. 1st Div. 1986)(refusing to follow the *Anderson* case); *Drennan v. Star Paving Co.,* 333 P.2d 757 (Cal. 1958); *Home Elec. Co. v. Hall & Underdown Heating and Air Conditioning Co.,* 366 S.E.2d 441 (N.C. 1988) (the North Carolina Supreme Court refused to follow the *Campbell* case).

[5] *See Piland Corp. v. REA Constr. Co.,* 672 F. Supp. 244 (E.D. Va. 1987) (subcontractor not bound by telephone bid where general contractor failed to notify it of acceptance within industry's customary thirty-day period).

[6] *See Williams v. Favret,* 161 F.2d 822 (5th Cir. 1947). *But see Electrical Constr. v. Maeda Pac. Corp.,* 764 F.2d 619 (9th Cir. 1985) (court reversed trial court's holding that general contractor not bound to accept subcontractor's low bid). *See generally, Steeltech Bldg. Prod., Inc. v. Edward Sutt Assoc., Inc.,* 559 A.2d 228 (Conn. App. 1989) (court upheld trial court's determination that oral agreement was enforceable by contractor against owner).

argument has successfully been made that if the prime contractor sends the sub a letter of intent or other clear statement that it intends at that point to have the subcontractor perform the proposed work for a mutually acceptable price, and the subcontractor actually begins performance at the prime's request, then there is the basis to find that the parties have entered into a contract, even though it is not completely reduced to writing. Under these circumstances, a subcontractor may be entitled to recover damages for breach of contract if the prime contractor later withdraws its commitment.

5.11 PREPARATION OF THE SUBCONTRACT AGREEMENT

The subcontract, for purposes of this discussion, refers to the contract document between parties at any level below the prime contract where the owner is usually a party. The subcontract includes the contract between the prime contractor and a subcontractor and also the contracts between a subcontractor and sub-subcontractor, at all levels. Contracts with vendors who only supply materials and do little or no work on the project site are often subject to the principles of law in the UCC, which are discussed in Chapter 3.

At the outset, you should decide whether to use a standard subcontract form or, instead, to draft your own subcontract form.

Form subcontracts, developed by the American Institute of Architects (AIA) and the Associated General Contractors of America, Inc. (AGC), are widely utilized in the industry. Form subcontracts have the advantage of being relatively inexpensive and fairly widely accepted. Their primary disadvantage is that they may not address specific items of concern to the contracting parties. For that reason, contractors may choose to develop their own forms.

An adequate subcontract form should, at a minimum, accomplish the following:

(1) Define the exact undertakings of the subcontractor so that there can be no dispute about the work the subcontractor is to perform, including standard of quality and performance time.

(2) Detail the terms and conditions of payment, including the method of computing progress payments, terms of payment for stored material, due dates for pay requests, handling of interim retainage, and the final payment.

(3) Anticipate the areas of trouble or dispute, and define the consequences if work is not performed properly and on time.

(4) Specify the relief that the innocent party is entitled to receive.

(5) Avoid favoring one party to such an extent that the other party will decline to sign the proffered form or refuse to perform under its terms.

A subcontract should be tailored to fit the needs of a particular project. But a collection of uncoordinated provisions from various unrelated form contracts can result in a "monster," which may create substantial unanticipated problems for both parties.

Such monsters are typically created in one of two ways. The first is a "cut-and-paste" operation by which various provisions are borrowed from different subcontracts and brought together in one document without being reconciled or analyzed for consistency. The second is an "inclusion" operation, by which the contractor includes (either expressly or by reference) in its subcontract the conditions of the prime contract, the general conditions it has prepared specially, and perhaps some standard form conditions, such as the AIA A201 General Conditions. The theory is that "more is better." The result often is quite different—a hodgepodge of documents that are not consistent or coordinated.

A subcontract form should be prepared by someone competent for the task and should be tailor-made for the conditions of each project. Also, it should be periodically reviewed in light of lessons learned through experience and changes in the law.

Unlike terms of many public contracts, which are set by law or regulation, there are no "standard" subcontract terms. The following points should be considered in drafting the terms of a subcontract.

5.12 "Flow-Down" Obligations

A flow-down clause, which contractually ties, for instance, the subcontractor to the prime as the prime is bound to the owner, is imperative.[7] Since subcontractors at every level are bound together on the project by a series of contracts, the contracts should all contain flow-down clauses. The absence of a flow-down clause can leave the contractor exposed to liability, but unable to demand of the subcontractor the performance that it is required to undertake.

In return for this protection, the prime contractor is generally willing to give the subcontractor the same rights with regard to making claims, protest and notice that the prime has against the owner up the contract ladder. In other words, the rights and duties flow both ways—upward to the prime contractor, as well as downward to the subcontractors at each level. This tends to keep the parties on an even basis, even though there is no privity of contract between the owner and the subcontractors.

5.13 Scope of the Work

Every subcontract must set out as clearly and definitively as possible the work to be performed by the subcontractor. Realistically, it is very difficult to define all of the subcontractor's work so the subcontract form should also refer to all contract documents between the owner and prime contractor.[8]

---

[7] *See generally,* Construction Briefing No. 85-5 (Hoe, Oliver and Abbott, "Flow-Down Clauses in Subcontracts").

[8] Construction Briefing No. 85-7 (Braude and Patin, "Subcontract Incorporation by Reference Clauses").

The general contract bid items are often too general to incorporate by reference into the subcontract as the definition of the scope of work. This practice should be avoided. The work description must explicitly define responsibilities for the scope of work and must also define the responsibilities each contractor assumes for its own activities.

Scope of Work Checklist

Keep in mind that the scope of work is not simply the items of performance activities for the project that are subcontracted out, but includes the responsibilities for the facilities, and for contract administration. Therefore, the detailed description of the actual project work to be performed by the subcontractor, supplemented by an incorporation of the owner's description of the work from the general contract, must be supplemented with revisions that address other contingencies such as the following:

(1) An explanation of items listed in the subcontract scope of work, which may differ from the plans or technical specifications; for example:

(a) Items of work that appear in the specifications may be excluded by the subcontractor in its bid;

(b) Items of work may be specifically listed to clarify a possible ambiguity as to which trade is responsible for performance; and

(c) Items that may not be listed in the plans or technical specifications but that are necessary for a complete job and are included in the scope to be performed by the subcontractor.

(2) A clause that clarifies that the subcontractor agrees to furnish, without extra charge, all work, labor, materials, and equipment not mentioned or shown in the contract documents that are nonetheless generally included under a particular class of subcontract or fairly implied by the subcontract as necessary for the satisfactory completion of the project (including work necessary to conform to all laws, ordinances, orders, rules, regulations, and requirements).

(3) A section that provides a method of interpretation of the subcontract document. This may include an agreement to allow the architect to resolve any conflicts between various subcontract provisions, plans, and specifications. The form of the contract may require the architect to resolve differences of interpretation under that contract so a drafter may chose to carry that responsibility through into the subcontract.

If a general contractor elects to divide a certain item of work between subcontractors, two additional considerations arise. First, extreme care must be used in defining each subcontractor's scope of work to assure that no aspect of the work is omitted. Second, the contractor must realize that responsibility for coordinating the efforts of these subcontractors will fall on the contractor who has divided the work. Efforts to avoid this responsibility by subcontract disclaimers generally are ineffective and cause problems because authority is not delegated to make the assignment of responsibility effective.

5.14 Payment Obligations

The prime contractor's obligation to make progress payments or pay retainage to the subcontractor before the prime receives the corresponding payment from the owner is almost inevitably an area for disputes.

5.15 *The Case against the Paid when Paid Clause* The AIA Standard Subcontract Form of Agreement (AIA Document A401, 1987 ed.) provides in Article 11.3 that if the contractor does not receive payment from the owner for any reason that is not the fault of the subcontractor, the contractor shall pay the subcontractor the amount computed for the progress payment according to the contract, *on demand.* This widely used standard form of agreement adopts the rationale of many courts that have limited the application of paid when paid clauses.

One example of a paid when paid clause is: "The total price to be paid to subcontractor shall be . . . no part of which shall be due until five (5) days after owner shall have paid contractor therefore . . . ."[9] The variations are almost unlimited. The prime contractor in this example was not released from its payment obligation even though the owner filed bankruptcy before final payment. There are a number of reasons why the clause should not be applied to excuse payment under all circumstances.

First, the intent of the parties must be examined. In most cases, the subcontractor has no privity of contract with the owner, and usually has no opportunity to deal with the owner in bidding or at any time during performance. The subcontractor looks to the prime for coordination with other trades and for use of site facilities, for scheduling, for interpretation of the plans and specifications, and for payment for the work. If it is the intention of the parties that the sub will look only to the owner for payment, that intention must be clearly expressed.

Second, the payment clause in the contract must be examined. Look for specific circumstances mentioned in the contract such as the delay of progress payments because of default of the subcontractor in the AIA A401 contract, or a reference to the owner's insolvency as a condition excusing nonpayment. If the payment clause deals with the amount, timing, method of payment and other essential provisions, without reference to specific conditions excusing payment, then it is likely that the court will decide the payment to the subcontractor is not conditioned on payment from the owner under all circumstances.

Finally, many courts have simply held that an interpretation of the contract terms that would require the subcontractor to wait for an indefinite period of time until the prime contractor has been paid by the owner, an event that

---

[9] *Thomas J. Dyer Co. v. Bishop Int'l Eng'g. Co.,* 303 F.2d 655 (6th Cir. 1962).

may never occur, is simply an *unreasonable construction*. The subcontractor may be forced to wait some reasonable period of time, but to require it to wait indefinitely or to forego payment under circumstances that the sub cannot control, has led many courts to refuse to enforce paid when paid provisions.[10]

5.16   The Case for the Paid when Paid Clause   Other states have taken a stance more favorable to the prime contractor and upheld the subcontract payment provision making the owner's payment to the prime contractor a condition precedent to the prime's obligation to pay the subcontractor for work performed.[11]

As an example, a prime contractor was excused from the obligation to pay until it had received payment when the subcontract provided: ". . . payments will be made [to the subcontractor] from money received from the owner only and divided pro rata [among] all approved accounts of subcontractors, labor and materials."[12] This payment clause set up a fund consisting of money received from the owner, out of which subcontractors were to be paid, and made the fund the *only source* from which subs were to be paid. This provision was enforced as a paid when paid clause, relieving the prime contractor of the obligation to advance monies for progress payments to the subcontractor, because it showed the intent of the parties that the subcontractors' payments were *only* to come from the fund created by payments from the owner. The subcontractors were not relying upon the prime contractor's credit for payment.[13]

In an effort to avoid being required to make payments to subcontractors even though payment has not been received from the owner, many prime contractors now include a provision in their subcontracts making payment by the owner a "condition precedent" to the prime's obligation to pay its subcontractors.[14] The contract provision must clearly show that the express condition is the mutual intent of the parties and demonstrate that the parties have in mind that payment might not be received from the owner so that the subcontractor assumes that risk as a part of its negotiated contract terms.

The following should be kept in mind in drafting or reviewing contract language on the terms of payment:

Payment Clause Checklist

(1) *Conditions for Payment:* What conditions precedent must be met before the subcontractor is entitled to payment? For instance, the prime contract may require that all work meet the approval of the architect and the owner before payment is considered.

---

[10] *See also Southern States Masonry, Inc. v. J. A. Jones Constr. Co.,* 507 So.2d 198 (La. 1987); *Kawall Corp. v. Capolino Design and Renovation,* 54 A.D.2d 941, 388 N.Y.S.2d 346 (2d Dept. 1976).
[11] *See A. A. Conte, Inc. v. Campbell-Lowrie-Lautermilch Corp.,* 477 N.E.2d 30 (Ill. App. 1985); *Sasser & Co. v. Griffin,* 133 Ga. App. 83, 210 S.E.2d 34 (Ga. App. 1974).
[12] *Sasser,* fn. 11, *supra.*
[13] *Pace Constr. Corp. v. OBS Co.,* 531 So.2d 737 (Fla. App. 1988); *Wilson v. Post-Tensioned Structures, Inc.,* 522 So.2d 79 (Fla. App. 1988).
[14] *St. Paul Fire & Marine Ins. Co. v. Georgia Interstate Elec. Corp.,* 370 S.E.2d 829 (Ga. App. 1988).

(2) *Computing the Amount:* The method of determining the amount of progress payments should be clearly described. The contract terms should describe how to determine the basis of payment, such as a percentage of the total estimated value of labor, materials, and equipment incorporated into the work, and a percentage of the value of materials suitably stored, less the aggregate of previous payments.

(3) *Paid When Paid:* Is payment to the subcontractor conditioned upon payment by the owner for the same work? If this is the parties' agreement, state that the owner's payment is a "condition precedent"; that the subcontractor expressly accepts the risk that the owner may not pay the contractor; that the subcontractor relies for payment on the credit and ability of the owner to pay; and that the prime contractor's payment bond surety will be obligated only to the same extent as the prime contractor.

(4) *Final Payment Terms:* After the subcontract is fully completed, when will the subcontractor receive its final payment, and what are the conditions to be met before final payment will occur? These conditions may include:

(a) The owner and architect accept the work in writing;

(b) The contractor is fully paid by the owner; and

(c) A release is executed by the subcontractor for the contractor.

5.17 Changes to the Payment Terms Must Also Account for the Surety
After the contract is signed, the potential for problems is not over for the parties in the administration of their agreement. The most obvious problems are caused by delay in payment or a dispute over the amounts earned for progress payments or for extra work. Careful draftsmanship and thoughtful consideration in advance will provide the parties contract terms to measure and guide their performance. However, the sub and prime may find that unexpected circumstances during performance may require a change in their expected payment procedures. If their actions to accommodate the new circumstances are not carefully considered, unexpected results may follow.

For example, the prepayment of a subcontractor may discharge the subcontractor's performance bond surety from liability. If a subcontractor falls behind schedule and is financially unable to increase its work force to regain the lost time, the prime may consider prepaying the subcontractor to finance the additional crews needed to regain the schedule, while expecting to deduct the amounts advanced from later progress payments.

In one case, a prime contractor agreed to this arrangement but failed to obtain the approval of the sub's payment and performance bond surety.[15] When it sued the surety for the amounts prepaid to the subcontractor, the surety defended on the basis that the prepayments materially altered the subcontract and operated to discharge the surety from its obligations.[16]

[15] *Southwood Builders, Inc. v. Peerless Ins. Co.,* 366 S.E.2d 104 (Va. 1988).
[16] *See also Brunswick Nursing & Convalescent Center, Inc. v. Great Am. Ins. Co.,* 308 F. Supp. 297 (S.D. Ga. 1970).

The prime contractor's payment bond surety may take the same position if the prime contractor is in default of its payment obligations after agreeing to alter the payment terms of its contract without gaining the prior consent of the surety.

The point for all parties is that the payment terms must carefully be considered when initially entering into the contract, and any change must be reviewed for its impact on the present obligations between the parties and the rights and obligations of sureties and other payment guarantors who may be affected.

5.18 Subcontractor Default Clause

5.19 *The Right to Terminate*

5.20 The AIA Documents Virtually all construction contracts expressly recognize the right to terminate the contract for the default of the other party in certain specific circumstances. These provisions also recognize the right of the innocent party to recover damages flowing from the default and resulting termination. Section 7.2.1 of AIA Document A401 (1987 ed.) specifically provides that the contractor may terminate the subcontractor upon seven days notice if the subcontractor "persistently or repeatedly fails or neglects to carry out the work in accordance with the Subcontract Documents or otherwise to perform in accordance with this Agreement." The AIA Subcontract Form A401 also gives the subcontractor the right to terminate for the same reasons the contractor can terminate its contract with the owner or for nonpayment for sixty days or more.

5.21 Implied Termination Rights Even in the absence of an express termination provision, there generally exists an implied right to terminate a contract and sue for damages if the other party has materially breached the contract. It is nonetheless important that the prime contractor have the right to terminate a subcontract (and that a subcontractor be able to terminate a subsubcontractor's right to proceed) under certain circumstances, and this right must be spelled out in detail, with notice requirements and cure rights specifically delineated. Although the discussion below focuses on the prime contractor/subcontractor relationship, the principles stated are equally applicable to a subcontractor/sub-subcontractor agreement.

5.22 Alternatives to Termination The subcontract termination clause should provide flexibility to the prime contractor, so that the extreme act of termination is not the contractor's only option in dealing with a subcontractor's default. The subcontract must expressly reserve the prime's right to pursue alternatives in lieu of termination, such as paying the subcontractor's suppliers and subcontractors, or supplementing the subcontractor's work force. A termination for default is the construction industry equivalent of capital punishment. It is an option not to be invoked lightly, and only after careful consideration of other options. Some of the options for termination are discussed in the Default Clause Checklist, which follows.

5.23   Termination for Convenience

5.24   Consequences of Improper Termination   Whether the subcontractor was actually in default at the time of termination is usually a fact question. The facts will determine whether the termination was proper or improper. If proper, then the prime contractor will be entitled to damages, including cost of completion; if improper, then the subcontractor may recover as damages the profit it would have made if allowed to complete, or if there would be no profit, it may recover damages on a *quantum meruit* basis. If the subcontract contains only a "termination for default" option, the prime contractor may be exposed to significant subcontractor claims if the termination is later deemed improper, even if the prime contractor acted with a good faith belief that the termination was justified.

5.25   Termination for Convenience Clauses   To protect the prime contractor in such circumstances, the inclusion of a provision for the "termination for convenience" of the sub is recommended. This provision allows the prime to terminate the sub *with or without cause*. If one party terminates another for convenience, the terminated party has the right to an equitable adjustment that will return that party to its precontract condition.

5.26   Limits to Termination for Convenience Rights   While a typical termination for convenience clause appears to give one party the absolute right to terminate another for whatever reason, there is a conflict as to whether the termination must be made "in good faith." At least one court has held that there are circumstances in which a termination, even under a seemingly unrestricted termination clause, may not be allowed where done in bad faith.[17] Other courts have been hesitant to hold that there is a good faith requirement for the exercise of a termination for convenience right.[18] The question of whether there is a good faith requirement for termination without cause remains to be resolved in many jurisdictions.[19] It is therefore a point that may be argued by any contractor who may have been terminated "in bad faith." In federal contracting, it is clear that the government's right to terminate a contract for its convenience is limited to situations in which "bad faith" or "abuse of discretion" cannot be demonstrated.[20]

5.27   Considerations in Drafting Subcontract Default Clause   Some of the considerations that should be addressed when drafting or reviewing a

[17] *Randolph v. New England Mut. Life Ins. Co.*, 526 F.2d 1383 (6th Cir. 1975).
[18] *Niagara Mohawk Power Corp. v. Graver Tank & Mfg. Co.*, 470 F. Supp. 1308 (N.D.N.Y. 1979).
[19] *Id.*
[20] *C.F.S. Air Cargo, Inc.*, ASBCA 36113, 91-1 BCA ¶ 23,583, *aff'd*, 944 F.2d 913 (1991).

subcontract default clause are set out below. Use this checklist to determine if and how your subcontract addresses major issues in a default situation.

Default Clause Checklist

(1) *Obligation to Proceed:* In the event of a dispute, can the subcontractor be required to carry out its work under the direction of the contractor? Even so, if the subcontractor's refusal to proceed under protest is "reasonable" (e.g., where paving in cold weather might subject the subcontractor to later liability on its express warranty), it is possible that the subcontractor may successfully argue that the resulting default termination was improper.[21]

(2) *Notice:* Does the subcontract specifically outline requirements for notice to the subcontractor if the subcontractor fails to comply with the contractor's instructions or the terms of the subcontract? In the absence of an express notice provision, some courts may find an implied duty to notify the subcontractor prior to termination and to give the subcontractor an opportunity to cure the default.[22]

(3) *Cure Right:* The length of time within which the subcontractor will be given the chance to cure a default should be specified. Some definition of an effective cure (e.g., a complete correction of the default, or an approved, written program for curing the default and reasonable progress in implementing such a program) is also helpful. Subcontractors should review the clause to verify that the contract does expressly provide a right to cure a default.

(4) *Contractor Options:* A well-drafted default clause will give a contractor several different options in dealing with a potential subcontractor default. If there is no cure within the specified time period, these options might include:

(a) Supplementing the subcontractor's workforce;

(b) Having a second subcontractor take over a portion of the subcontractor's work;

(c) Making direct payments to subcontractor suppliers, sub-subcontractors, and laborers;

(d) Accelerating the work; or

(e) Subcontract termination (i.e., taking possession of the subcontractor's materials, tools, etc., and completing the subcontractor's work with another subcontractor).

The subcontract should clarify that the decision to first pursue one or more of these options does not prejudice the prime's right to later terminate or to claim damages against the subcontractor or its surety.

(5) *Payment Rights:* What effect will a default have on payment to the subcontractor? This clause might include provisions giving the contractor the right to deduct all monies expended and costs incurred, direct and indirect

---

[21] *Wilson v. Kapetan, Inc.,* 595 A.2d 369 (Conn. App. 1991).
[22] *McClain v. Kimbrough Constr. Co.,* 806 S.W.2d 194 (Tenn. App. 1990).

(including attorneys' fees), as a result of the subcontractor's default, from all amounts otherwise owed to the subcontractor. Also, if the amounts owed to the subcontractor are not enough to cover such expenses, the termination clause would obligate the subcontractor to promptly pay upon demand the full amount of the difference.

(6) *Good-Faith Defense:* If the prime contractor is mistaken about the subcontractor's default or failure to cure such default, but acts on a good faith belief, will the contractor be liable for additional subcontractor damages (e.g., anticipated profits)? To minimize this risk, the termination clause might convert the termination to a "termination for convenience" and limit the contractor's exposure to the value or cost of the work in place, plus a reasonable profit and overhead markup on that work. The clause could expressly exclude the subcontractor's right to unearned profit, unexpended overhead and other damages.

(7) *Proof of Termination Costs:* What information from the contractor will be sufficient to demonstrate the amount of money owed the contractor as a result of the default?

(8) *Default Triggering Events:* How does the subcontract define those subcontractor acts and omissions that will justify prime contractor action under the Termination Clause? Careful drafting is required to anticipate the potential problems that might give rise to a contractor's need to invoke the termination clause. In the absence of an express provision justifying a subcontract termination, a contractor must prove that the subcontractor "materially breached" the subcontract.

(9) *Faulty Workmanship Proof:* The current version of the AIA subcontract requires that, when faulty workmanship, materials, or equipment is asserted as the basis for a subcontractor default, the project architect must first determine that the subcontractor's work is not in accordance with the prime contract requirements. From the contractor's perspective, this requirement is unduly restrictive. For the subcontractor's viewpoint, this provision offers a layer of protection against an improper termination.

(10) *Use of Subcontractor Resources:* Does the termination clause effectively preserve the contractor's right to take over the subcontractor's materials, tools and equipment in order to complete the subcontract work? Does the clause preserve the contractor's right of access to subcontractor information (e.g., as-built information) and the option to accept an assignment of subcontractor contracts with suppliers, equipment dealers and sub-subcontractors?

(11) *Flow-Down Limitations:* Does the subcontract anticipate that the termination of the subcontract may result from a termination of the prime contract by the owner? In a properly drafted flow-down clause, a prime contractor may attempt to limit its exposure to termination damages and expenses to whatever damages or costs the contractor is able to collect on the subcontractor's behalf from the owner.

5.28   No Damages for Delay, Except as Paid by the Owner

A contractor may be able to limit delay claim exposure to its subcontractors in proportion to the owner's liability to the prime. In *Dyser Plumbing Co. v. Ross Plumbing & Heating, Inc.,*[23] a Florida appellate court upheld a contract clause that limited a subcontractor's delay damages to a percentage of an amount paid by the owner. The court ruled that the subcontract's terms clearly and unambiguously established the extent of any recovery by the subcontractor for delay damages.

If a general contractor hopes to limit a subcontractor's claim for delays to those that are paid by the owner, the subcontract should expressly set out this limitation. The considerations outlined earlier in this chapter at Section 5.14 are equally applicable to the determination of the payment rights of the subcontractor confronted with such a subcontract provision.

Obviously, these same considerations apply when a subcontractor is drafting its sub-subcontracts and purchase orders.

5.29   Changes

One of the areas of frequent disputes in construction is the contract's changes clause. For the owner and contractor, it is important that the subcontract specify a procedure for allowing changes to the contract. The subcontractor's primary concern is that it be guaranteed the right to be paid for work that it views as "extra." In addition, the subcontractor is frequently concerned that it not be required to finance, for an extended period of time, a significant amount of "extra" work while waiting for (1) a determination of whether the work is "extra" and, if so, (2) a determination of the work's reasonable value. The parties' competing interests lead to frequent disputes.

In judging the completeness and fairness of the subcontract changes clause, contractors and subcontractors should look for the following:

Subcontract Changes Clause Checklist

(1) *The Right to Order Changes:* The contractor should verify that the subcontract clearly states the contractor's right at any time, on written order, without notice to the surety and without invalidating the subcontract, to make changes in the work contracted for and the subcontractor's duty to proceed with the work as directed by the contractor's written order. There is no implied right to order contract changes.

(2) *Notice Requirements:* In the event the subcontractor is faced with an "informal" direction to perform additional work, the subcontract should set out express notice requirements and stated consequences for the failure to observe those notice requirements.

---

[23] 515 So.2d 250 (Fla. App. 1987).

(3) *Specific Timetable for Change Order Resolution:* The contractor and subcontractor both should be concerned that the subcontract specify a timetable and specific steps for the resolution of the adjustment of the subcontract price and schedule. The contractor does not want to surprise the owner with subcontractor claims that remain unknown or unquantified until the end of the job. The subcontractor does not want to finance extra work for a prolonged period. The duties and rights of the parties in the event the work is performed prior to an agreement on price must be detailed.

(4) *Pricing Limitations:* The parties should be aware of any limitations on the allowable adjustment to the subcontract price, for example: the amount allowed by the owner; the amount of the subcontractor's initial estimate; the amount determined by the project architect or some other "final decision maker;" overhead and profit limitation clauses; or other conditions precedent to a price adjustment.

(5) *Pricing Proof:* The subcontract should identify the subcontractor's duty to provide cost data, certifications, and any other information necessary to support its proposal. Section 5.3 of A401 (1987 ed.) requires the subcontractor to submit claims for additional costs in a manner and time sufficient to allow the general contractor to submit this information, if need be, to the owner under the terms of the prime contract.

(6) *Binding Effect of the Change Order:* Frequently, the subcontract will grant audit rights to either the owner or the general contractor, so as to hold open the possibility of reopening a change order in the event of defective or inadequate pricing by the subcontractor.

(7) *Emergency Changes:* The subcontract should provide alternate change order procedures, rights, and duties in the event of the need to implement a change during an emergency that endangers life or property.

(8) *Oral Change Orders:* What is the effect of oral orders or directives that are believed to be changes, and what are the parties' duties and obligations under such circumstances? Does the subcontract require that the subcontractor obtain a written work order prior to performing extra work? Such requirements are common and can be enforceable.

(9) *Working under Protest:* From the contractor's perspective, it is important that the subcontractor be obligated to proceed with the directed work, even if the subcontractor disputes the value of the work or if the contractor denies that the work is "extra." Such a subcontract clause can be enforceable. For example, in *Keyway Contractors, Inc. v. Leek Corp.,*[24] a Georgia court enforced a contract provision requiring that the work continue despite pending disputes. Following a dispute over payment, the subcontractor abandoned the work site. The court found that the subcontractor's action constituted a material contract breach. The subcontractor confronted with such a clause must look for some express or implied limit to the obligation

---

[24] 189 Ga. App. 467, 376 S.E.2d 212 (1988).

to perform work for which it may not be paid. In addition, the subcontractor must be certain that it has the right to proceed "under protest," and that it understands the procedural requirements for preserving that right.

(10) *Change Order Authority:* Does the subcontract contain limitations on the authority of contractor representatives to direct changes? Limitations as to who has the authority to direct changes, and limits on the amount of change order authority entrusted to a contractor representative are common.

(11) *Alternative Methods for Fixing Change Order Amounts:* Does the subcontract provide unit prices for change order work, or pricing limitations in connection with "force account" work? Since it is likely that many change order amounts will not be agreed upon in advance, the subcontract should provide alternate routes to fixing the change order amount.

(12) *Time Extensions:* The changes clause should require that the subcontractor quantify the time impact, as well as the cost impact, of changes to the work. Subcontractors must make themselves aware of subcontract clauses that would deprive them of time extensions made necessary by changes unless the time extension request is presented in a specified format, with specified support, or in a certain timeframe.

5.30   Subcontractor's Indemnification of the Contractor

Traditionally, subcontracts have imposed very broad hold-harmless obligations on subcontractors. Courts in recent times have been reluctant to enforce overly broad indemnification clauses as a matter of public policy. Some state legislatures have also taken steps to limit the effects of indemnity agreements.[25] For example, § 13-8-2 of the Official Code of Georgia (1981) invalidates any attempt to require a contacting party to hold another party harmless from liability arising solely from the latter's own acts. Accordingly, while a broad, general indemnification clause is important, it should be drafted after consideration of the applicable state laws and decisions. Similarly, a clause that is enforceable in one state may be void in a neighboring state. Therefore, prime contractors should be cautious when doing work outside of their home state. Subcontractors should look for provisions that provide that the contract is to be governed by the laws of a particular state.

Subcontract indemnity clauses come in many shapes and sizes. The clauses are typically long and cumbersome to read and understand. Consider the following potential problem areas in drafting or reviewing a subcontract:

Subcontract Indemnity Clause Checklist

(1) *Scope of Indemnity:* What types of claims and damages are covered? Is the indemnity clause limited to damages arising out of any injury to any person, or any death at any time resulting from such injury, or any damage

---

[25] *See, e.g.,* Florida Stat. ¶ 725.06.

to any property, which may arise (or which may be alleged to have arisen) out of or in connection with the work covered by the subcontract? Do the damages covered go beyond those connected with property damage or personal injury? Do the damages covered include attorneys' fees and consequential damages? Care in defining the scope of the damages covered is critical for the contractor and subcontractor alike.

(2) *Persons Protected:* Is the indemnity obligation owed only to the contractor, or does it include other named parties or groups? How broad is the definition of the protected class?

(3) *Conduct Creating the Indemnity Obligation:* Is the indemnity obligation limited to damages that flow solely from the conduct of the subcontractor? Does the indemnity obligation arise if the subcontractor is only partially responsible for the damage? Does the subcontract attempt to place the indemnity obligation on the subcontractor even if the damages do not result in any part from the subcontractor's negligence?

(4) *Insurance Availability:* Some types of risks that are assigned to subcontractors through indemnity clauses may be transferred to insurance policies. However, contractors and subcontractors frequently fail to assess and compare the risks presented by indemnity clauses with their insurance coverage.

(5) *Public Policy Limits:* As previously mentioned, several states have taken the position that broad form indemnity agreements (i.e., those obligating one party to indemnify another for all loss, even if caused solely by the indemnitee's own negligence) are void as against public policy. Illinois, Georgia, New York, Minnesota, California and Michigan have such "anti-indemnity" statutes. Depending upon the jurisdiction involved, these anti-indemnity statutes may not preclude the contractor's requiring that the subcontractor obtain insurance to cover the negligent acts of the contractor.[26] Check to see that the protection you hope to gain by your subcontract indemnity clause is not taken away by applicable laws.

(6) *Clarity of the Parties' Intent:* Since indemnity provisions tend to reverse the generally preferred rule that wrongdoers should pay for their own mistakes, courts often construe strictly the indemnity language. Loose language used in defining the indemnity obligation may result in a restrictive reading of the scope of the parties' indemnity agreement. Understand the scope of the risk that is intended to be the subject of the indemnity clause and define it clearly.

(7) *Collection Rights:* Typically, the subcontract may give the contractor the right to withhold from any payment otherwise due the subcontractor such amounts as may be "reasonably necessary" to protect it against damages covered by the indemnity clause. From the subcontractor's perspective, it is desirable to place some safeguards on the process and timetable for determining indemnity losses and some limits (e.g., indemnity payments will be limited

---

[26] *See Jokich v. Union Oil Co. of Cal.,* 574 N.E.2d 214 (Ill. App. 1 Dist. 1991); *Holmes v. Watson-Forsberg Co.,* 471 N.W.2d 109 (Minn. App. 1991).

to the amount of available insurance) on the exposure assumed under the subcontract.

5.31 Labor Affiliation

It is important that the prime contractor have the right to determine whether a project will be open shop or union and to require, insofar as permitted by applicable law, its subcontractors to abide by this policy. The prime should retain the right to require a subcontractor to perform, or be terminated, even if the subcontractor's workers refuse to work as a result of a dispute that involves the general contractor and its employees (not the subcontractor's). The following should be addressed in any subcontract:

(1) *Advice Regarding Labor Practices:* The subcontractor's obligation to keep itself and the prime contractor fully advised of all pertinent local and regional labor agreements and practices, including any local labor union contract negotiations occurring during the term of the subcontract.

(2) *Collective Bargaining Agreements:* In the event the subcontractor has a collective bargaining agreement either locally or nationally with a labor union engaged in local negotiations or if the subcontractor will be affected, either directly or indirectly, by the outcome of local negotiations, is the subcontractor obligated to join such negotiations, if legally permissible, and participate or associate itself with the local contractor or contractors involved in the negotiations in an endeavor to resolve the labor dispute?

(3) *Labor Harmony:* The obligation that all labor used throughout the work shall be acceptable to the owner and the contractor and of a standing or affiliation that will permit the work to be carried on harmoniously and without delay to the project, and that will in no case or under any circumstances cause any disturbance, interference or delay to the progress of the building, structures or facilities, or to any other work being carried on by the owner or the contractor in any other town or city in the United States.

(4) *Labor Agreements:* The subcontractor's obligation to recognize and comply with all agreements of the contractor with local building trade councils and/or separate unions concerning labor and working conditions and otherwise applicable to the work, insofar as these agreements do not conflict with or violate any local, state, or federal laws or properly constituted orders or regulations.

(5) *Termination Rights:* The contractor's right to terminate the subcontract and proceed in accordance with the provisions of the subcontract if the subcontractor's work or the contractor's work is stopped or delayed or interfered with by strikes, slowdowns, or work interruptions resulting from the acts of or failure to act by the employees of the subcontractor, or if the subcontractor breaches other applicable labor provisions in the subcontract.

(6) *Work Stoppages:* The contractor's remedies when the subcontractor's employees engage in a work stoppage solely as a result of a labor dispute

involving the contractor or others and not in any manner involving the subcontractor.

5.32 Disputes Procedures

5.33 Arbitration Considerations   The determination to accept or include an arbitration provision in a contract or subcontract involves both practical and legal considerations. This decision must be made before the subcontract is executed. If the subcontract does not contain an arbitration provision, disputes arising thereafter will be arbitrated only if both parties so agree. Such an agreement may not be easy to obtain after the dispute has arisen.

On the other hand, if an arbitration agreement is contained in the subcontract, it will probably be enforceable under federal and, perhaps, state laws. The contractor cannot avoid arbitration at that point over the subcontractor's objection.

Some contracts contain provisions requiring arbitration at the sole election of the contractor. Such unilateral provisions have been enforced by some courts and rejected by others.

It is generally desirable that the prime contractor tie the subcontractor to the same remedies and disputes process as binds the prime contractor to the owner. Whether in court, arbitration, an administrative disputes process (board hearing), or an alternative disputes resolution procedure (e.g., mediation), the subcontractor should be required to pursue diligently and exhaust those remedies and to be bound by the determination of its claims or rights under the specified disputes procedure.

Disputes Clause Considerations

In drafting or reviewing subcontract provisions governing the resolution of disputes, the following matters should be addressed:

(1) *Flow-Down Effect of Dispute Resolution:* To what extent is the determination of any issue under the terms of the contract between the owner and the contractor binding on the rights of the subcontractor? From the contractor's perspective, the ability to "flow-down" the impact of a binding decision under the Owner/Contractor Agreement is critical.

(2) *Subcontractor Participation in Owner/Contractor Disputes Procedures:* Is the subcontractor obligated to assist the contractor in the prosecution or defense of a proceeding under the terms of the general contract? Is the subcontractor obligated to reimburse the prime contractor for any portion of the costs and legal fees incurred? Even if the subcontractor is not a named party to the dispute proceedings, if the subcontractor's rights will be effected by the outcome, it will want the right to participate in the proceedings.

(3) *Decision Making Authority:* Does the subcontractor have any control, under the terms of the general contract over the prosecution and defense of

any proceeding that involves or relates to the subcontract? Does the subcontractor have any protection against an unreasonable compromise of its dispute position?

(4) *Obligation to Continue Working:* Is the subcontractor obligated to proceed with the work as directed by the contractor pending resolution of any dispute under the terms of the general contract or any dispute between the contractor and its subcontractor?

(5) *Disputes Not Involving the Owner:* Does the subcontract contain provisions, such as an arbitration clause, that control the resolution of disputes between the contractor and the subcontractor and that are not related to the owner or controlled by the terms of the general contract?

(6) *Third-Party Claims:* Does the subcontract contain provisions addressing the subcontractor's right or duty to proceed against third parties to recover claims for damages? Such clauses are increasingly popular, not only in subcontracts, but in owner/contractor agreements as well.

(7) *Mandatory Pursuit of Administrative Remedies:* Does the subcontract contain provisions requiring the subcontractor to exhaust any contractual disputes process prior to instituting or prosecuting any statutory remedy or action against the contractor or the contractor's surety?

(8) *Mandatory Alternative Dispute Resolution (ADR) Procedures:* In recognition of the high cost and uncertainty of litigation and other "formal" disputes procedures, many in the construction industry are searching for less costly, less divisive and quicker means for resolving disputes. Any ADR procedure should be detailed in the subcontract.

(9) *The Appointment of Final Decision Makers:* Contracts and subcontracts often attempt to designate some individual as having the authority to make "final and binding" decisions with respect to certain types of disputes. Identify such attempts prior to contracting and be wary of their impact.

5.34 Federal Government Projects

If the prime contract is with the federal government, or one of its agencies, certain provisions in the contract become more important, and there are other provisions—perhaps unnecessary in private work—that need to be included in the subcontract form. The same may be true with respect to state governments and their agencies. Any contractor who works with a particular governmental agency or agencies would be well advised to consult an attorney concerning what, if any, additional provisions should be included in its standard subcontract form due to the particular way in which that agency conducts its construction contracting business.

The following examples of contract provisions may be useful additions to subcontracts on federal government projects:

(1) *Termination for Convenience:* The government's exercise of its rights under this clause has a significant substantive and procedural effect on the

contractor's rights and remedies, including express directions to the contractor concerning its subcontractors and suppliers. The federal government's duty to reimburse the contractor for certain subcontractor/supplier claims may depend on the negotiations between the contractor and subcontractor/supplier concerning the effect of a termination for convenience.

(2) *Cost and Pricing Data:* The subcontract/purchase order should address the subcontractor's/supplier's obligation to provide "Cost or Pricing" data or other cost and claim certifications required by or necessary under the terms of the general contract. To the extent that the contractor relies upon and/or is liable to the federal government due to data, information, or certificates provided by the subcontractor or supplier, the subcontract or purchase order should address the issues of indemnity, costs of defense, and so on, related to any government claim. In addition, the clause should address the extent and duration of audit rights by any party and any needed flow-down requirement.

(3) *Flow-Down Consistency:* Particular care must be given to flow-down clauses needed to promote the consistency of the prime contract and the subcontracts for proper administration of a subcontract or purchase order under a government contract. In addition, numerous social and economic clauses must be incorporated into specific subcontracts and purchase orders and further flowed down to lower tiers. Satisfaction of these requirements dictates the careful drafting of an appropriate flow-down provisions and a review of the terms of the government contract.

5.35 SHOULD SUBCONTRACTORS BE BONDED?

A performance bond is a guaranty (based on the terms of the bond) that the subcontractor will perform the contract. It is usually intended to mean that if the subcontractor defaults or fails to complete the project, the surety will complete performance or pay damages up to the limit of the penal sum of the bond. (For a more complete discussion of performance and payment bonds, see Chapter 11.)

A *labor and material* payment bond helps assure that labor and materials used in the course of the subcontractor's work will be paid for by the surety if not by the subcontractor. A payment bond creates alternatives to the filing of liens on the project property and helps protect the prime contractor from liability to the various tiers of sub-subcontractors and suppliers.

In the past, it was not unusual for prime contractors to require bonds of subcontractors, and for subcontractors to require bonds of sub-subcontractors. However, in recent years, these bonds have become more expensive, and sometimes more difficult to obtain.

As a result, the question of whether subcontractors should provide bonds has become somewhat more complicated. The general contractor may decide at the outset that the subcontracted work will be bonded, no matter which subcontractor is chosen to do the work. But bonds are expensive, and the project budget may not be able to justify this across-the-board decision to require bonds of every subcontractor. If cost is a factor, it may be appropriate to assess on a case-by-case basis whether subcontract bonds will be required.

Other alternatives may provide some assurance of the subcontractor's performance without involving the expense of a bond. For example, the subcontractor may be willing to post a letter of credit in lieu of a bond; another entity, perhaps a parent company, may be willing to provide a guaranty of performance; or the subcontractor may allow the prime to hold an increased level of retainage.

The prime contractor who decides to have its subcontractors bonded must be aware of the exact language of the bonds. No statutory requirements exist for subcontractors' bonds. They are considered to be common law bonds, and their wording controls the obligations of the surety.

Subcontractor performance bonds can be worded so that they protect or benefit only the prime contractor, and do not provide a direct right of action by third-party subcontractors and suppliers. Alternatively, the bond may expressly state that subcontractors and suppliers can maintain a direct action against the surety. Otherwise, a court may well find that the bond does not create such a right of action in third parties.

If bonds are to be provided, separate payment and performance bonds should be required. The contractor obtains greater protection by requiring two separate bonds. If the bonds are not separate, the penal sum provides the maximum liability of the surety for *both* the payment and performance bonds. For example, if a payment and performance bond is in the total penal amount of $1,000,000, the surety is generally liable for no more than $1,000,000 even though the cost to complete the subcontractor's performance together with the claims of materialmen and suppliers totals more than $1,000,000. However, if a performance bond is obtained in the amount of $1,000,000 and a payment bond is obtained in the same amount, the general contractor obtains potential protection of $2,000,000, with $1,000,000 for performance and $1,000,000 for payment.

It is essential that the surety providing the bonds be financially viable and responsible, since bonds from a deficient surety offer little or no protection. Consequently, the subcontract form should contain the limitation that the bonds will be provided by an "acceptable surety."

5.36 DISPUTE AVOIDANCE BY DILIGENT PROJECT ADMINISTRATION

Disputes often can be avoided or minimized by effective project management, by both the prime contractor and the subcontractors. An understanding of some important obligations and rights is critical to dispute avoidance or resolution.

5.37   General Contractor's Duty to Coordinate the Work

Subcontractors are normally engaged by the general contractor to perform various "trade" portions of the work. For the project to proceed smoothly and without unreasonable interference, the activities of the general and of each subcontractor must be sequenced and coordinated so that all can perform their portion in a prompt and an efficient manner.

The general contractor usually assumes this responsibility for coordination, which is similar to the responsibility of the owner in the coordination of parallel prime contractors. Since the general contractor is customarily the only party in direct privity with all of the subcontractors, that contractor generally has the duty to coordinate.

5.38   Implied Duty to Cooperate

The duty to cooperate with subcontractors and coordinate their work is implied, even though the subcontract may not expressly provide that the prime or general contractor must respond in damages for any delay or extra cost incurred by a subcontractor as a result of a breach of this duty. Subcontract provisions such as a "no damages" clause may, however, modify, limit or shift this implied responsibility or the damages for breach of this duty.[27]

The implied duties to cooperate and coordinate require the general contractor to take reasonable measures to protect a subcontractor from delays or interference by the general contractor or other subcontractors. For example, in *Johnson v. Fenestra, Inc.*,[28] a subcontractor contracted to install panels on the exterior of a building under construction and the prime agreed to furnish these panels. However, the prime contractor delivered defective panels. Several months elapsed before the correct panels were provided, and the delay prevented the subcontractor from completing work before winter weather set in. The court held that the subcontractor was entitled to damages for being forced into winter work, and that the subcontract necessarily implied that the prime would supply panels in time and in quantities that were consistent with the parties' understanding that there would be a "prompt beginning and an early completion" of the job.

The obligation to reimburse for delay and extra cost may arise from provisions that require the prime to perform some act preparatory to the subcontractor's work. In *Manhattan Fireproofing Co. v. John Thatcher & Son,*[29] the prime agreed that the building under construction would be made available to the concrete subcontractor so that the concrete work could be done "in one operation" and completed by a stated date. However, because the prime delayed the job and was late in turning over the building, the subcontractor was required to divide its work into several phases. The court, in awarding

---

[27] See *Crawford Painting & Drywall Co. v. J. W. Bateson Co.*, 857 F.2d 981 (5th Cir. 1988).
[28] 305 F.2d 179 (3rd Cir. 1962).
[29] 38 F. Supp. 749 (W.D.N.Y. 1941).

the subcontractor delay damages, held that the provision that the work could be "done in one operation" required the prime contractor to protect the subcontractor from the type of disruption delay experienced on the job.

5.39 Implied Duty to Coordinate

It is not enough for the general contractor to insure that its own forces do not interfere with the subcontractors. The duty to coordinate includes an additional requirement that the general contractor take reasonable steps to avoid interference *between subcontractors*. This requires the contractor to (1) schedule the work of all subcontractors so that the work of different trades can be sequenced as contemplated at the time of bidding and (2) take reasonable steps during performance to maintain the schedule.

A general contractor's responsibility for coordination of all subcontractors is illustrated in *J. J. Brown Co. v. J. L. Simmons Co.*[30] There, the plastering subcontractor claimed damages for the prime's failure to provide heat in buildings where the plastering work was to be performed. The prime contended that other subcontractors were responsible for the failure to provide heat. The court held that the prime had a duty "to keep the work in such state of forwardness as to enable the subcontractor to perform within a limited time" and that the delays of other subcontractors were the prime's responsibility and would serve as no defense to the plastering subcontractor's suit.

5.40 Limitation of Liability

A prime contractor may be able to limit liability by disclaiming the responsibility of coordination to subcontractors, as illustrated by *Crawford Painting & Drywall Co. v. J. W. Bateson Co.*[31] Bateson was the prime contractor on a hospital building project for the Army Corps of Engineers. Bateson's subcontract with Crawford included a clause in which Bateson disclaimed liability for any delay or disruption to Crawford's work.

After excessive change orders were issued, work was significantly delayed. Crawford sued Bateson, and at trial introduced evidence that Bateson withheld from its subcontractors the actual project schedule and extensions to that schedule which Bateson had negotiated with the Corps. Crawford alleged that Bateson took advantage of the subcontractors in administering the project and in negotiating claim settlements. The jury awarded Crawford $7 million, but the United States Court of Appeals reversed the jury award and dismissed the lawsuit. The court held that Bateson's actions amounted to nothing more than a failure to coordinate the subcontractors, and Bateson had disclaimed this responsibility in its subcontract. Crawford could not recover.

---

[30] 2 Ill. App. 2d 132, 118 N.E.2d 781 (1954).
[31] Fn. 27, *supra*.

Although the general contractor can be held answerable for its interference with or failure to coordinate subcontractors, the general may not be liable for delays or interference over which it has no control and that were unforeseeable at the time of contracting. In *Southern Fireproofing Co. v. R. F. Ball Constr. Co., Inc.,*[32] the court held that a contractor was not liable for damages caused to a subcontractor by delays attributable to subsurface conditions that were unknown to the parties at the time of subcontracting. A similar result was reached when a prime contractor was held not liable for damages caused by delays that were due to inclement weather.[33]

Success in coordination depends largely on open and accurate communication between the general contractor and all subcontractors. The general must establish some method to both discover what is going on at the job site (e.g., what problems the subcontractors are having and the problems they anticipate), and to relay suggestions, recommendations and requirements to the subcontractors to avoid or solve the problems. Efforts to develop these communications must begin at the preconstruction conference and continue throughout the contract period.

5.41 Pay Applications and Partial Lien Waivers

When a general contractor receives a pay application from a subcontractor, it should generally require a partial waiver of liens covering work for which payment is requested. At the end of a project, total lien waivers should be required. Subcontractors should obtain similar partial and total lien waivers from their lower tier subcontractors and suppliers. Lien laws vary greatly from state to state, so advice of counsel who is familiar with the applicable lien law should always be obtained. Generally, waivers of lien are strictly construed, must be in writing, and must clearly express the potential lien claimant's unambiguous intent to waive lien rights.

Contractors must not confuse a lien waiver with a release of claims. A lien waiver, unlike a release, generally benefits only the property owner by protecting it from the claim of lien. It does not absolve the contractor from its obligations to the lien claimant.[34] The general contractor should consider using a form that both waives lien rights *and* releases the contractor from subcontractor's claims at least to the extent of payment actually received.

5.42 Prime Contractor Financing of Subcontractors

The question of whether a prime should provide financial aid to an ailing subcontractor, and, if so, to what extent, usually arises when an unbonded subcontractor is on the verge of default.

---

[32] 334 F.2d 122 (8th Cir. 1964).
[33] *Ben Agree Co. v. Sorensen–Gross Constr. Co.,* 365 Mich. 185, 111 N.W.2d 878 (1961).
[34] *See, e.g., David Shapiro & Co., Inc. v. Timber Specialties, Inc.,* 233 S.E.2d 439 (Ga. App. 1977).

A prime contractor has several obvious reasons for wanting to help a faltering subcontractor. First, the prime is obligated to complete the project by a specified time. A work slowdown prior to default and delay while obtaining a completion subcontractor may extend the project beyond the completion date. Second, the prime has the obligation to keep the work in a state of readiness so that other subcontractors can proceed efficiently. A failure to coordinate the work may subject the general to delay damage claims by these subcontractors. Third, the defaulting subcontractor may be unable to answer in damages to the prime for the effect of its default.

Other advantages may be gained by working out some form of financial assistance for a troubled subcontractor. The value of maintaining continuity on the job may justify the cost of financial assistance. The subcontractor's personnel have a basic familiarity with the project, and work experience would eliminate the need for another learning curve for replacement workers. The defaulting subcontractor may have executed fixed price purchase orders that could be lost if the sub is terminated, causing the completing subcontractor's cost (and correspondingly the cost to the general contractor) to increase. Also, there may be a shortage of available subcontractors in particular trades and geographic areas at any given time, making it difficult or even impossible for the prime to find a suitable replacement subcontractor.

All these considerations suggest that it may be prudent for a prime contractor to consider providing financial assistance to an unbonded subcontractor faltering on the verge of default. This assistance may come in the form of advanced payments, reduced retainage, guarantees of payment to sub-subcontractors or suppliers, and the like. While these techniques may help the subcontractor complete the job, they also create potential risks by reducing the contractor's financial security in the subcontractor's performance or creating an obligation for the prime contractor that is larger than anticipated.

Different considerations are involved when the faltering subcontractor is bonded, and these problems are reviewed elsewhere. As a general matter, any payments the surety makes to a distressed subcontractor do not result in a credit to the surety against the penal sum of the performance bond.[35] But the prime contractor who lends financial assistance runs a risk of having the surety later claim to be discharged by reason of a material increase in the bonded risk.

5.43 Remedies for Defective Performance

Contract law generally provides that where the performance of a builder is defective, the agreed contract price is subject to a deduction for the costs to remedy the defects. The same rule applies between prime contractors and subcontractors.[36]

---

[35]*See Caron v. Andrew,* 133 Cal. App. 2d 402, 284 P.2d 544 (1955).

[36] "The builder . . . may be entitled to a deduction or setoff against such compensation [as is owed the subcontractor] for expenses incurred or damages sustained by reason of the subcontractor's failure to comply with his contract." 17A C.J.S., Contracts, § 368 at p. 390.

If a subcontractor fails to perform its work, the prime contractor may perform the work, backcharge the subcontractor, and deduct the backcharge from the subcontractor's progress payments.

The measure of the prime contractor's damages generally is the reasonable cost of remedying the defects, that is, the cost of making the subcontractor's work conform to the contract.[37] Where the prime contractor retains a portion of the subcontract price, the measure of damages is the reasonable cost of completing the contract and repairing the subcontractor's defective performance less the part of the contract price still unpaid.[38]

A prime contractor's decision to perform the subcontractor's work assumes that the subcontractor is in default. That assumption carries with it some risk. The contractor runs the risk of guessing wrong as to whether or not the subcontractor has substantially performed in the first instance and whether the backcharge is valid in the second. In making such an error, the contractor may, itself, be committing a material breach of the subcontract.[39]

5.44   Remedies for Delayed Performance

When a subcontractor fails to complete the work covered by its subcontract within the time specified, and the delay in completion is not excusable, the prime contractor is entitled to recover any resulting, foreseeable damages. A delay is excusable if it results from an event or omission for which the subcontractor is not responsible. Under certain circumstances, the subcontractor's unexcused delay may warrant termination of the subcontract.

Termination of a sub for late performance is only proper if the delay is not excusable. When a subcontractor is delayed because of the prime contractor's failure to schedule or coordinate other trades on the project, the delay is excusable and does not warrant a default termination.

In *Tribble & Stephens Co. v. Consolidated Serv., Inc.,*[40] the court held that a subcontractor was wrongfully terminated since the delay in prosecuting its work was excusable. In *Tribble,* the court relied upon evidence showing that the contractor had ordered the subcontractor to relocate electrical junction boxes as a result of another subcontractor's work. In addition, a delay in completing the soffits, which was not in the subcontractor's scope of work, prevented the subcontractor from installing the light fixtures. Finally, certain owner-furnished material arrived late and impeded the subcontractor's wiring in certain areas of the project.

Typically, the liquidated damages assessed by the owner against the prime contractor constitute the owner's measure of damages for delays, although the owner may be able to recover actual damages. A prime contractor may be able to protect itself from liquidated damages when the delay is caused by a subcontractor and the subcontract contains an appropriately worded

---

[37] *Sorensen v. Robert N. Ewing,* 8 Ariz. App. 540, 448 P.2d 110 (1968).
[38] 448 P.2d at 114.
[39] *Howard S. Lease Constr. Co. v. Holly,* 725 P.2d 712 (Alaska 1986).
[40] 744 S.W.2d 945 (Tex. App. 1987).

subcontract provision. For example, in *Taos Constr. Co., Inc. v. Penzel Constr. Co.,*[41] the court ruled that a subcontract's "pass on" of liquidated damages from the prime to its subcontractor was valid.

Krauss v. Greenbarg[42] also illustrates the prime contractor's rights to recover damages caused by a subcontractor's delay. Krauss, the subcontractor, sued Greenberg for the value of material furnished in connection with work under a government contract that contained a liquidated damages clause. The prime contractor had been charged by the owner for liquidated damages for delays that were attributable to the subcontractor. Therefore, the prime counterclaimed against the subcontractor, raising the question of whether consequential damages could be recovered for breach of a subcontract.

The damages were allowed because the court found that assessment of liquidated damages by the owner in the event of late completion was within the contemplation of the subcontracting parties. However, unless the subcontract language controlling the subcontractor's liability for delay damages is carefully written, a prime contractor's recovery for delays caused by the subcontractor may be limited to the liquidated damages paid to the owner.[43]

5.45 Relationship between Subcontractor and the Owner—May the Prime Contractor Assert the Subcontractor's Rights against the Owner?

There is normally no "privity of contract" between the owner and any subcontractor. As a result, the owner and subcontractor generally cannot sue each other for breach of contract. In addition, the owner's only payment obligation is to the prime contractor under the terms of their contract. The prime contractor in turn, however, has a corresponding contractual obligation to make payment to its subcontractors.[44]

In connection with federal government contracts, it is permissible for a prime contractor to bring an action against the government on behalf of a subcontractor who has been injured by government action or inaction. This "sponsorship" rule applies to appeals before the various agency boards of contract appeals as well as before the Court of Federal Claims. This right was confirmed in *United States v. Blair,*[45] where the United States Supreme Court stated that "Respondent [the prime contractor] was the only person legally bound to perform his contract with the Government and he had the undoubted right to recover from the Government the contract price for the tile, terrazzo,

---

[41] 750 S.W.2d 522 (Mo. App. 1988).
[42] 137 F.2d 569 (3rd Cir. 1943).
[43] *Industrial Indem. Co. v. Wick Constr. Co.,* 680 P.2d 1100 (Alaska 1984).
[44] *Utschig v. McClone,* 16 Wis.2d 506, 114 N.W.2d 854 (1962); *Marion Mach. Foundry & Supply Co. v. Colcord,* 174 Ark. 90, 294 S.W. 361 (1927).
[45] 321 U.S. 730 (1944).

marble and soapstone work whether that work was performed personally or through another."

This same theory may also be available as a basis for an action by a prime contractor on behalf of its subcontractor against a nonfederal government owner, where the prime, in effect, acts as a conduit for the cause of action.[46]

The subcontractor may be entitled to recover from both the prime and the owner when both are found to be responsible for damages. In *Rome Hous. Auth. v. Allied Bldg. Materials, Inc.,*[47] the court held that the trial court was correct in awarding delay damages to a subcontractor apportioned equally between the contractor and the owner as a result of their failure to resolve disputes in a timely manner. In *Mobil Chem. Co. v. Blount Bros. Corp.,*[48] a general contractor, acting as construction manager, and an owner were found equally liable for damages to subcontractors resulting from their joint decision to accelerate. The court admonished the general contractor because its "first construction schedule was prepared by an employee innocent of the ability to prepare such a schedule for a complex project."[49] The message is clear: The prime contractor's right to insist that subcontractors perform in accordance with the project schedule carries with it a corresponding obligation to ensure that the schedule is accurate, realistic and consistent with the parties' agreement.

In *Wexler Constr. Co. v. Housing Auth. of Norwich,*[50] the general contractor was not allowed to sue on behalf of a subcontractor. In that case the court implied, however, that the Blair doctrine was inapplicable only because there existed an implied contract between the subcontractor and the owner, and thus there was no reason why the subcontractor could not bring the action directly.

5.46   The Prime Must Be Liable to the Subcontractor for the Pass Through Claim—The Severin Rule

Many courts have held that a prime contractor can maintain a suit on behalf of one of its subcontractors only if it has reimbursed its subcontractor for the latter's damages or remains liable for such reimbursement in the future.[51]

Exceptions to this rule have been made since the decision was first rendered. In 1965, the Court of Claims held that the rule does not apply when subcontrac-

---

[46] *See Robert E. McKee, Inc. v. City of Atlanta,* 414 F. Supp. 957 (N.D. Ga., 1976); *St. Paul Dredging Co. v. State,* 259 Minn. 398, 107 N.W.2d 717 (1961).

[47] 355 S.E.2d 747 (Ga. App. 1987).

[48] 809 F.2d 1175 (5th Cir. 1987).

[49] *Id.* at 1177.

[50] 149 Conn. 602, 183 A.2d 262 (1962).

[51] *See J. L. Simmons Co. v. United States,* 304 F.2d 886 (Ct. Cl. 1962); *Severin v. United States,* 99 Ct. Cl. 435 (1943), *cert. denied,* 322 U.S. 733 (1944).

tors' claims are asserted as an equitable adjustment under the provisions of a prime contract with the federal government.[52]

5.47 States Have Adopted the Severin Rule

Some state courts have adopted the Severin rule as their own. For instance, the Georgia Supreme Court held that a general contractor may not recover on behalf of its subcontractors absent proof of liability to those subcontractors.[53] Thus, if a subcontract absolves a general contractor of liability to its subcontractor for delay damages, the general contractor is precluded from bringing an action to recover for delays on behalf of the subcontractor.

The North Carolina Court of Appeals has created an absolute bar to subcontractor claims against the North Carolina Department of Transportation (DOT) even if the claim is brought by the general contractor and regardless of whether the general contractor is or will ultimately be liable to the subcontractor for the damages in question.[54] In reaching this decision, the court specifically disregarded considerations of the Severin rule. Rather, the court based its decision upon the language contained in § 108-6 of the *Standard Specifications for Roads and Structures* issued by the North Carolina DOT, providing that a subcontractor will not have any claim against the DOT by reason of the approval of the subcontract by the DOT, interpreting this section to preclude even claims by general contractors on behalf of a subcontractor.

5.48 CONCLUSION

Avoidance of subcontract disputes demands diligent subcontract administration and constant vigilance on the part of the prime contractor.

Dispute avoidance begins at the bidding or negotiation stage of the project. Prime contractors should investigate their potential subcontractors in light of the subcontractor's ability to contribute to the overall success of the project. Subcontractors should be equally diligent in checking out the prime.

The subcontract document should accurately express the parties' agreement. Whether a form subcontract or a specially drafted document is used, the subcontract should be consistent with the requirements of the general

---

[52] *Blount Bros. Constr. Co. v. United States*, 348 F.2d 471 (Ct. Cl. 1965).

[53] *See also Kinsington Corp. v. State*, 253 N.W.2d 781 (Mich. App. 1977); *Buckley & Co. v. State*, 356 A.2d 56 (N.J. Super. 1975); *Univ. of Alaska v. Modern Constr., Inc.*, 522 P.2d 1132 (Alaska 1974); *Tully & DiNapoli, Inc. v. State*, 272 N.Y.S. 2d 667 (N.Y. Ct. Cl. 1966); *D. A. Parrish & Sons v. County Sanitation Dist. No. 4*, 344 P.2d 883 (Cal. App. 1959); *Department of Transp. v. Claussen Paving, Co.* 273 S.E.2d 161 (Ga. 1980).

[54] *Warren Bros. Co. v. North Carolina Dep't of Transp.*, 307 S.E.2d 836 (N.C. App. 1983).

contract and address problems that may affect the progress and performance of the work.

Finally, diligent project administration should achieve early detection of problems, which will help avoid disputes or, at least, minimize their consequences.

POINTS TO REMEMBER

Subcontract Default Clause

- Prior to contracting, utilize a Default Clause Checklist to identify the terms and verify the adequacy of a subcontract termination for default clause.
- Notice of default and the right to cure may be implied by some courts, even in the absence of express language in the default clause.
- The right to terminate a subcontract for the contractor's convenience may be restricted in some courts by a "good faith" requirement in the exercise of the termination right.

No Damages for Delay, Except as Paid by the Owner

- A properly drafted subcontract flow-down provision may limit a subcontractor's right to recover delay damages.
- Subcontractors should carefully review the owner/general contractor contract documents to determine, prior to contracting, the risk assumed by the subcontractor through broad-form subcontract flow-down clauses.

Changes

- Prior to contracting, utilize a Changes Clause Checklist to verify the adequacy and fairness of a subcontract changes clause.
- Clauses that attempt to limit the type and amount of additional costs (e.g., overhead, profit, indirect losses) recoverable as a result of contract changes are increasingly popular and potentially dangerous.
- Take the sample checklists outlined in this chapter, expand and tailor them to suit your particular practices and industry needs, and require their use in prescreening each potential contract.
- At the beginning of each job, outline for your project management the contract procedures (e.g., notice requirements, time limits, cost support requirements, etc.) that will govern and limit your change order rights.

Subcontract Indemnification

- In some states, clauses requiring one party to hold another party harmless from liability arising solely from the latter party's own acts are void, as against public policy.

· Use a Subcontract Indemnity Clause Checklist to determine, in advance of contracting, the exact scope of any indemnity obligation created in the subcontract.

Labor Affiliation

· Insuring labor harmony on the project should be one of the goals of a properly drafted subcontract.
· Use the Labor Affiliation Checklist in this chapter to help identify the manner in which labor issues are treated in your subcontract.

Subcontract Disputes Procedures

· The contractor should be careful that its subcontract disputes procedure is consistent with any disputes procedure required in the owner/contractor agreement.
· If the subcontractor is to be bound by determinations made as a result of owner/contract disputes, the subcontract should spell out the subcontractor's rights or duties of participation in that disputes procedure.
· Less traditional disputes resolution procedures can be less expensive and less time consuming; consider such alternative disputes procedures prior to contracting.

Federal Government Projects

· Standard subcontract forms utilized in private work are often inadequate for problems inherent to public contracting.
· Before doing public contract work, have your subcontract reviewed for any necessary inclusion of contract clauses (e.g., cost and pricing requirements) peculiar to government contracting.

6

CONTRACT CHANGES

6.1   WHAT IS A CHANGES CLAUSE?

Construction projects are rarely built exactly as they were originally designed. The "changes" clause in a construction contract allows an owner to make alterations in the work while the project is underway. A changes clause encompasses not only changes specifically designated as such, but may also come into play when questions arise concerning inspection, acceptance and warranties, as well as defective specifications, differing site conditions, impossibility of performance, and acceleration. In short, a changes clause is often an umbrella provision, involving numerous aspects of performance under the contract. No other clause more clearly illustrates the uniqueness and complexity of a construction contract.

A changes clause would appear to depart from established contract law principles involving contract modifications. The common rule is that a contract cannot be modified unless all parties to the contract agree to the modification. One party cannot unilaterally modify the agreement.

However, a changes clause does not violate principles of contract law because it is an agreement between both parties that one of the parties has the right to make changes. This agreement is recognized by the courts because it universally provides that compensation will be adjusted if the changes require extra work.

A typical changes clause provides that an owner may order extra work or make changes to the existing work, by altering, adding to or deducting from the work, with commensurate adjustments in the contract price and performance time. Subcontract forms usually contain a similar provision allowing for the adjustment of contract obligations at the subcontract level.

A "change order" provision, as the changes clause is sometimes called, gives the owner the flexibility that is necessary to adapt actual conditions to the end product sought—for example, to correct errors in the plans and specifications or to take advantage of newly developed construction techniques and materials. On the other hand, the changes provision does not, in general, work to the contractor's detriment. Instead, a contractor can generally use the changes clause to obtain adequate additional compensation, both in terms of additional money and performance time when a change increases the contractor's cost or performance time.

Changes clauses often specify the method for determining the amount of additional compensation for changed or extra work. Payment for changed work is often on a lump sum, unit price, or time-and-materials (cost-plus) basis.

Although owners often want to negotiate the total amount of extra compensation the contractor is to receive before the work is done, owners nevertheless typically provide in their changes clauses that the contractor can be required to proceed with the work without an agreement in advance as to the compensation. This protects the owner against possible work stoppages or delays that might result while negotiations are underway. For example, the General Conditions in The American Institute of Architects (AIA) document A201 (1987 ed.) provides for the "construction change directive," which is signed by the owner and the architect and requires the contractor to proceed with changed work.[1] Once the construction change directive is signed by the contractor, it becomes a "change order."

This type of provision can be just as important for the general contractor to assure that subcontractors do not stop work during a changes dispute with the general contractor. Thus a provision requiring subcontractors to continue work during change order negotiations should be included in all subcontracts.

In the event of a change for which the price is to be negotiated at a later date, the contractor can protect itself by keeping complete documentation, including records of all expenditures associated with the changed or extra work. These costs should be documented using separate cost codes for the changed work when possible. The ultimate cost may be certified by the project architect or engineer and generally includes a reasonable allowance for the contractor's overhead and profit.

The contractor also is entitled usually to an appropriate extension of the contract time whenever the contract sets out a specific completion date and the changed work delays completion of the work. Whether or not the contract contains a liquidated damages provision, an appropriate adjustment in the time of performance may be set out in the written change order. It is also critical for the contractor to document the extension of performance time required by the change if no agreement can be reached.

6.2 RECOVERY UNDER THE CHANGES CLAUSE

There are four primary factors to consider in attempting to assess the ability of a contractor to recover under the changes clause:

[1] A201, § 7.3 (1987 ed.).

(1) Is there changed or extra work?

(2) Who is authorized to order changes?

(3) When are written change orders required?

(4) When is written notice of a claim for additional compensation resulting from extra work required?

Each factor is discussed in detail below.

6.3 Is There Changed or Extra Work?

In many cases the parties to a contract will not be able to agree whether certain orders from the owner constitute "changes" under the changes clause. Determining the answer to this question usually depends upon the unique plans, specifications and contract provisions for each job. As a general rule, a contractor is required only to perform in accordance with its original agreement; and, if the owner orders work that is beyond what was required in the original agreement, the changes clause will entitle the contractor to additional compensation.[2]

It is important to remember that the changes clause also applies to changes that *decrease* the cost of or time required for performance. For example, if the owner decreases the contractor's scope of work, the changes clause may entitle the owner to a decrease in the contract price or time.[3]

The basic rules of contract interpretation discussed in Chapter 2 often play an important role in a court's resolution of a dispute as to whether certain work ordered by the owner constitutes changed or extra work. One of the most important rules of contract interpretation with regard to this matter is that a written contract is construed most strongly against the person who prepared it.[4]

In other words, when a contract is subject to two or more reasonable interpretations (i.e., when the contract is ambiguous), it will be construed against the author. Typically, the construction contract is drafted by the owner or its agent (such as the project architect). Thus, in order for a contractor to recover for extra work, it is not generally necessary that its interpretation of the contract be the only reasonable interpretation, or even the most reasonable interpretation. Rather, if the contractor's interpretation is reasonable, and the ambiguity was not "patent" (i.e., obvious), then the contractor's interpretation should generally prevail over an equally reasonable interpretation advanced by the drafter of the ambiguous contract documents.[5]

---

[2] *See, e.g., E. C. Ernst, Inc. v. Koppers Co., Inc.,* 476 F. Supp. 729 (W.D. Pa. 1979), *modified,* 626 F.2d 324 (3rd Cir. 1980); *W. R. Ferguson, Inc. v. William A. Berbusse, Inc.,* 216 A.2d 876 (Del. 1966); *Jones v. Pollock,* 208 P.2d 1031 (Cal. App. 1949).

[3] *See, Ragnar Benson, Inc. v. Bechtel Power Corp.,* 651 F. Supp. 962 (M.D. Pa. 1986) (subcontractor required to credit contractor for savings realized by the use of a more economical cleaning method).

[4] *Lytle v. Freedom Int'l Carrier, S.A.,* 519 F.2d 129, 134 (6th Cir. 1975); *Cincinnati Bengals, Inc. v. Bergey,* 453 F. Supp. 129, 149 (S.D. Ohio 1974).

[5] *See Bennett v. United States,* 371 F.2d 859 (Ct. Cl. 1967).

6.4 Who Is Authorized to Order Changes?

The changes clause in most construction contracts identifies who can order changes to the work. Typically, the owner reserves to itself the right to order changes to the work. Many contracts, however, allow the architect/engineer to order minor changes that do not affect the contract price but require the owner's approval for changes affecting the price. In federal government contracts, the contracting officer or an authorized representative is the only person authorized to order changes on behalf of the government.

Ideally, the individuals having authority to order changes would be specified in the contract. However, contract documents do not always clearly establish who can order changes. This can be a significant problem if it is not feasible for a contractor to wait for a final change order to be processed through the owner before beginning additional work. As a result, the contractor must rely on assurances by the design professional or other owner representatives that additional costs will be paid. The problem is that these persons may not have the legal authority to alter significantly the plans and specifications or to impose additional obligations on the owner without the owner's prior consent.[6]

If the contract is not clear on this point, an understanding should be reached at the preconstruction conference as to the individuals authorized to order changes and the extent of their authority.

A lack of clear direction in the contract as to who is authorized to direct compensable changes can cause harsh results if the person directing the change is found to lack the necessary authority. For example, in *Nether Providence Township School Auth. v. Thomas M. Durkin & Sons, Inc.,*[7] the construction contract required that changes be approved in writing by the School Board. During performance, a disagreement arose as to whether certain work was required under the contract. Two members of the School Board signed a letter to the contractor ordering the contractor to proceed with the disputed work and stating that the disagreement would be resolved at a later time. The court ruled that the letter was neither valid authorization under the terms of the contract nor a waiver of those terms. The court concluded that the contractor was not entitled to additional compensation because it had never been given instructions by the School Board, the party with such authority under the contract.

The *Nether Providence* decision is an unfortunate example of what can happen when a contractor does not follow the requirements of the changes clause. That case involved a public body spending tax dollars, and the court felt compelled to strictly follow the contract requirements. Although there are several ways (discussed below) the contractor in *Nether Providence* might have been allowed to recover, the case confirms that a contractor accepts

---

[6] *See, e.g., Smith v. Board of Educ.,* 85 S.E. 513 (W. Va. 1915) (where the contractor was subsequently held responsible for the installation of an item that was specified in the contract and that had been omitted pursuant to the instructions of the architect).

[7] 476 A.2d 904 (Pa. 1984).

substantial risk when it departs from strict compliance with requirements of the changes clause.

The contractor who performs extra work at the direction of someone other than the person designated in the contract has two primary legal theories for obtaining recovery under the changes clause. The lack of actual express authority may be overcome by: (1) the implied or apparent authority of the architect/engineer (or other representative of the owner), or (2) ratification of the architect/engineer's acts by the owner. These theories are discussed below.

6.5 Implied Authority In preparing plans and specifications, the achitect/engineer's role is generally that of an independent contractor. However, in providing supervisory functions on a project, including processing change orders for extra work, the architect/engineer may function as the owner's agent. (See Chapter 4 for a general discussion of the architect/engineer's authority). In an extra work situation, the question often becomes whether the architect/engineer has the "implied" authority to order extra work on the owner's behalf, even though the contract does not give the architect/engineer "express" authority.

The term "implied authority" relates to an agent's authority to do whatever acts are incidental to, or necessary, usual or proper for, the exercise of the express authority delegated to him by the principal. For example, does an engineer who has the express authority to direct a change in the grade of a railroad also have the *implied* authority to enter into a supplemental contract to accomplish the work? In *Lafayette Ry. Co. v. Tucker,*[8] it was held that the engineer did have such implied authority.[9] In federal government contracts, a contractor may not rely upon implied or apparent authority; the person ordering the changed work must have *actual* authority to do so.

6.6 Apparent Authority In contrast to implied authority, the term "apparent authority" refers to the situation where the architect/engineer (or other owner representative) acts in such a manner as to lead the contractor to reasonably believe that he has authority beyond that that he actually possesses. If a reasonably prudent contractor would believe that the architect, for example, has the authority that the owner holds the architect out as having, then the owner may be bound by the architect's acts. For a more complete discussion of these agency principles, see Chapter 4 and *Wells Fargo Business Credit v. Kozloff*[10] and *AAA Tire & Export, Inc. v. Big Chief Truck Lines, Inc.*[11]

It is often difficult for a court to determine the scope of an agent's authority. Nonetheless, an error in this determination can prove disastrous. Such was

---

[8] 27 So.447 (Ala. 1900).
[9] *But see Albert Steinfield & Co. v. Broxholme,* 211 P.473 (Cal. App. 1922) (a different result was reached on similar facts).
[10] 695 F.2d 940 (5th Cir. 1983).
[11] 385 So.2d 426 (La. App. 1980).

the case in *Missouri Portland Cement Co. v. J. A. Jones Constr. Co.,*[12] which involved a contract to erect three steel cement storage silos. The plans and specifications contained notations that each of three silos was to be welded to six supporting columns by a continuous field weld at all points of contact. The connecting points were secured temporarily by high-tensile steel bolts. The owner's representative on the site was not a registered professional engineer, and his main function was to act as liaison between the owner and the contractor. When work had progressed to the point of welding the connections between the silos and columns, the general contractor's superintendent asked the owner's job site representative whether the connections should be welded or caulked to keep water out and prevent rust. The representative instructed the contractor to caulk the connections; as a result, the weld was never made. Subsequently, at the time of initial loading, one silo collapsed, causing extensive damage to the other two silos.

The general contractor was held liable for breach of contract because the court determined that the owner's representative was not authorized to exercise control over the structural requirements of the job, and had no actual, implied or apparent authority to interpret the plans or to authorize any deviation from the requirements of the plans. The general contractor was, however, entitled to indemnification by the steel erection subcontractor who was the party actually responsible for the failure to comply with the plans.

6.7 Ratification by the Owner Although the architect/engineer (or other owner representative) may not originally have had the authority to order particular items of extra work, it may be possible to establish that the agent's actions were "ratified" or approved by the owner subsequently. As emphasized in the case of *Kirk Reid Co. v. Fine,*[13] however, for the theory of ratification to apply it is critical that the owner have actual knowledge of the change he is claimed to have ratified.[14]

6.8 Summary The best and safest course of action for the contractor is to perform no extra or changed work without a valid (and written) order from a person authorized in the contract to order such work under the changes clause. Failure to comply with the contract changes clause in obtaining proper authorization can jeopardize the contractor's claim for extra compensation under the changes clause.

6.9 When Are Written Change Orders Required for Extra Work?

Questions often arise regarding oral orders for extra work where the contract specifically requires authorization to be by written change order only. Most construction contracts today provide that the contractor shall not proceed

---

[12] 323 F. Supp. 242 (M.D. Tenn. 1970), *aff'd,* 438 F.2d 3 (6th Cir. 1971).
[13] 139 S.E.2d 829 (Va. 1965).
[14] *Id.* at 834–835.

with any extra or changed work until a written change order has been signed by both parties. Such provisions can be valid and binding on the parties, and, if not satisfied, may prevent the contractor from recovering compensation for changed or extra work.[15] For this reason, the contractor should demand a written change order, or at least a written work directive, before performing changed or extra work.

An instructive example is found in *Environmental Util. Corp. v. Lancaster Area Sewer Auth.*[16] In that case, a contractor was not allowed to recover for extra work performed because it did not have written orders for the work. In *Southern Roadbuilders, Inc. v. Lee County,*[17] one Florida court denied recovery for changed work without a written change order, even though the contractor had been given oral directives by the county-owner to perform such work. The court based its decision on sovereign immunity, stating that the public treasury cannot be used to pay for claims that do not arise out of a statutorily authorized written agreement. Another Florida court, however, rejected the *Southern Roadbuilders* decision.[18]

While obtaining a written change order before executing any changed work is desirable, since it protects both owner and contractor, it is frequently ignored in practice. The contractor often cannot stop work, sometimes for weeks, while a formal change order is processed. Realities make it necessary for the contractor to rely on the assurances of the owner's representative or the architect/engineer that a change order will be forthcoming. Perhaps in recognition of this reality, the 1987 edition of the A201 General Conditions provide that the contractor is to proceed with changes directed by the owner and architect in a construction change directive before there is an agreement on pricing for the change.[19]

Even without such language, a contractor may obtain relief in certain situations. A court will sometimes look for a means of avoiding enforcement of the written work order requirement when it leads to a particularly inequitable result for a contractor who has performed work without a written change order. Various methods and theories have been used for this purpose.

Some courts have recognized a distinction between an "extra," which is work not required at all under the contract, and "additional work," which itself is not precisely required by the contract, but is a necessary extension of other work that is specified. Where the contractual written change order requirement covers only "extra" work, a court might characterize the work

[15] *See, e.g., Plumley v. United States,* 226 U.S. 545 (1913); *see generally,* 13 Am. Jur. 2d, Building and Construction Contracts, § 22 (1964).

[16] 453 F. Supp. 1260 (E.D. Penn. 1978).

[17] 495 So.2d 189 (Fla. 2d DCA 1986).

[18] *See Champagne-Webber, Inc. v. City of Ft. Lauderdale,* 519 So.2d 696 (4th DCA Fla. 1988). *See also City of Mound Bayou v. Roy Collins Constr. Co., Inc.,* 499 So.2d 1354 (Miss. 1986) (city waived right to have change orders in writing because of prior payments for verbally directed changes and the engineer's bad faith); *Huang Int'l, Inc. v. Foose Constr. Co.,* 734 P.2d 975 (Wyo. 1987).

[19] A201, §7.3 (1987 ed.).

as "additional" work for which the contractor could recover despite not having a written order.[20]

A contractor can also sometimes avoid the harsh results of the written change order requirement if the owner waives, modifies, or abandons the written change order requirement. Courts (focusing on the ultimate question of recovery) have used the theories interchangeably. The decisions are not altogether consistent as to what particular acts or conduct are sufficient to waive or modify, the requirement for a written change order.

The general principle is that the written change order requirement can be waived or modified not only by express words, but also by acts or conduct of the parties which by implication waive or otherwise derogate the writing requirement.[21] A waiver or modification of the written order requirement is most easily established where the owner has made progress payments for some of the extra work without insisting on a written order.[22]

Similarly, repeated verbal orders for changes from the owner can create a modification or waiver of the written change order requirement. For example, in *Consolidated Fed. Corp. v. Cain,*[23] the court concluded that an owner who verbally ordered several changes could not contend that the contractor breached the contract by requesting additional compensation for those changes. The court recognized that the contract required written change orders but concluded that the owner waived that requirement by repeatedly ordering changes verbally.[24]

A waiver or modification has been found based solely on the owner's oral promise to pay for extra work and the contractor's performance based on that promise.[25] In *Udevco, Inc. v. Wagner,*[26] a contractor was allowed to recover when the court found that the owner made an express oral waiver of the writing requirement and the contractor relied on the statement in doing the work. Yet, in a Texas case, a subcontractor lost a claim against its prime contractor because of the absence of a written change order, even though the prime's representative promised that "they would take care of it down the line."[27]

Knowledge of the extra work on the part of the owner, who does not object to it, has been held to permit payment to the contractor for extra work even

---

[20] *See Roff v. Southern Constr. Corp.,* 163 So.2d 112 (La. App. 1964); *DeMartini v. Elade Realty Corp.,* 52 N.Y.S.2d 487 (1943).

[21] *See* Annotation, "Effect of Stipulation in Private Building or Construction Contract, That Alterations or Extras Must Be Ordered in Writing," 2 *A.L.R.*3d 620, (19658 supp. 1995).

[22] *See Union Bldg. Corp. v. J & J Bldg. Maintenance,* 578 S.W.2d 519 (Tex. Ct. App. 1979). *See also Custom Builders, Inc. v. Clemons,* 367 N.E.2d 537 (1977) (where the owner only refused to pay for some selected extras without a written order); *Safer v. Perper,* 569 F.2d 87 (D.C. Cir. 1977); *W. E. Garrison Grading Co. v. Piracci Constr. Co.,* 221 S.E.2d 512 (N.C. App. 1975).

[23] 394 S.E.2d 605 (Ga. App. 1990).

[24] *See also Allen & O'Hara, Inc. v. Barrett Wrecking, Inc.,* 898 F.2d 512 (7th Cir. 1990); *Eastline Corp. v. Marion Apartments, Ltd.,* 524 So.2d 582 (Miss. 1988).

[25] *Udevco, Inc. v. Rocky Wagner,* 678 P.2d 679 (Nev. 1984); *Meadows v. Kinser,* 603 S.W.2d 624 (Mo. App. 1980); *Carolina Mechanical Contractors, Inc. v. Yeargin Constr. Co.,* 198 S.E.2d 224 (1978).

[26] 678 P.2d 679 (Nev. 1984).

[27] *Austin Elcon Corp. v. Avco Corp.,* 590 F. Supp. 507 (W.D. Tex. 1984).

though the contract provided that extras were required to be performed upon written order only.[28] However, mere knowledge on the part of the owner often will not be enough to convince a court that the writing requirement has been waived.

Generally, a modification may be compensable without a written change order where:

(1) The work was orally ordered or authorized by the owner (rather than by the design professional), or

(2) The owner has orally agreed or promised to pay additional compensation for the work in question, or

(3) The owner has accepted the work in question upon its completion, or

(4) The parties to the contract, throughout its performance, have entirely or repeatedly disregarded the writing requirement.

While the legal theories of waiver, modification, and estoppel may, in many instances, provide relief where the contractor has not obtained a contractually required written change order, these theories present significant proof problems. The safer course is for the contractor to insist on written authorization (if not a formal change order) before proceeding with the work, rather than relying on the oral assurances of the architect/engineer or the owner that the contractor will be compensated for his effort. A contractor can get some protection by confirming, in writing to the owner, that the work being performed is in addition to that required under the contract and that the contractor anticipates additional compensation in money and time for the extra work.

6.10 When Is Written Notice of a Claim for Additional Compensation Resulting from Extra Work Required?

Owners typically include provisions in construction contracts requiring that they be notified in writing within a certain period of time if the contractor intends to file a claim for performing work that the contractor considers to be beyond the contract requirements. For example, AIA Document A201 (1976 ed.) requires written notice to the architect within twenty days after the occurrence of the event giving rise to the claim and before commencing the work (except in emergency situations).[29]

---

[28] *Annot.,* 2 A.L.R.3d at 658.

[29] A201, § 12.3.1 (1976 ed.) states: If the Contractor wishes to make a claim for an increase in the Contract Sum, *he shall give the Architect written notice thereof within twenty days after the occurrence of the event giving rise to such claim.* This notice shall be given by the Contractor before proceeding to execute the Work, except in an emergency endangering life or property in which case the contractor shall proceed in accordance with Paragraph 10.3. No such claim shall be valid unless so made. If the Owner and the Contractor cannot agree on the amount of the adjustment in the contract sum, it shall be determined by the Architect. Any change in the contract sum resulting from such claim shall be authorized by change order. (Emphasis added.) This time limitation is twenty-one days in ¶ 4.3.3 of A201 (1987 ed.).

Provisions requiring written notice of claims serve to protect the owner by allowing the owner an opportunity to evaluate the situation before the work is performed and the costs are incurred. Such provisions in subcontracts provide similar protection to the general contractor.

The contractor's failure to give the required notice of a claim for additional compensation may bar recovery of such additional compensation.[30] However, provisions in construction contracts relieving the owner of liability unless notification is given within a specified time may be waived or modified in much the same fashion as the written change order requirement. For example, in *Transpower Constructors v. Grand River Dam Authority*,[31] the contractor on a transmission line project submitted a claim for additional compensation for changes made in the work. The owner denied the claim on the grounds that the contractor had failed to comply with contractual provisions regarding notice and documentation of claims. The court found that, in every other instance where the contractor had requested additional compensation, the owner and its engineer had approved payment notwithstanding that those claims had not been presented in compliance with the provisions relied upon by the owner in this case. Accordingly, the court held that the owner had waived the provisions regarding notice and documentation, and upheld the contractor's claim.

In *Macri v. United States*,[32] a general contractor was to provide the foundation upon which a subcontractor was to erect certain tanks. The subcontractor complained of defects in the foundation that would delay the subcontractor's performance and increase costs. After unsuccessfully attempting to repair the foundation, the general contractor ordered the subcontractor to proceed. The court allowed the subcontractor to assert a claim for extras, since the general contractor had knowledge of the subcontractor's claim and could not claim surprise or prejudice due to the subcontractor's failure to comply with the written notice provision.[33]

In summary, a failure to give prompt written notice may prevent a contractor from recovering compensation to which he otherwise would be entitled. Later disputes can be minimized by prompt written notice to the owner, or the architect/engineer, of any action (or inaction) on the part of the owner (or his representatives) that increases cost or time.

6.11   "CONSTRUCTIVE CHANGES"

One author has described the constructive change concept as "[owner] conduct which is not a formal change order, but which has the effect of requiring the

---

[30] *See, e.g., Linneman Constr. Co. v. Montana-Dakota Utils. Co., Inc.*, 504 F.2d 1365 (8th Cir. 1974).
[31] 905 F.2d 1413 (10th Cir. 1990).
[32] 353 F.2d 804 (9th Cir. 1965).
[33] *See also General Specialties Co. v. Nello L. Teer Co.*, 254 S.E.2d 658 (N.C. App. 1979) (court characterized the owner's oral agreement to an extra as a waiver of the formal notice requirement); *Nat Harrison Assoc., Inc. v. Gulf States Utils. Co.*, 491 F.2d 578, *reh'g denied*, 493 F.2d 1405 (5th Cir. 1974) (party to whom written notice was to be given waived the written notice requirement because it had knowledge of the extra work and did not object to it).

contractor to perform work different from that prescribed by the original contract, but in theory, which could have been ordered under the changes clause."[34]

Although the term "constructive change" first arose in government contracts and is used less frequently in connection with private construction contracts, the general concept is well known. Courts simply use different terminology and legal theories to achieve the same result. Three such legal theories are typically employed in the private owner context:

(1) Directed work (which is most analogous to pure "constructive change" analysis)
(2) Breach of contract
(3) Implied contract[35]

The underlying concept is essentially the same whether the owner is a public or private entity, and similar rules apply in both spheres.

"Constructive changes" typically fall into one of three general categories:

(1) The drawings or specifications are defective and, as a result, the contractor is required to perform extra work;
(2) The owner or its representative misinterprets the contract, for example, where work that actually satisfies contract requirements is erroneously rejected or where an unreasonably high standard of performance is required; or
(3) The owner denies the contractor a justified time extension, requiring compliance with the original completion schedule, and thereby forces the contractor to accelerate performance.[36]

Each of these three categories is discussed below.

6.12 Defective Plans and Specifications

A "constructive change" arising in connection with defective plans and specifications has its basis in what is referred to in Chapter 2 as the Spearin Doctrine. This doctrine provides that, when an owner supplies the plans and

---

[34] C. Gusman, " 'Constructive Change'—A Theory Labeled Wrongly," 6 Pub. Cont. L. J., 229 (January 1974). As Gusman explains:

The "constructive change" doctrine . . . is a recognition that an informal requirement for performance of additional work is substantially equivalent to a formal requirement and must, therefore, be governed by similar principles.

[35] For cases illustrating these theories, respectively, see *Udevco*, fn. 25, *supra*; *Denton Constr. Co. v. Missouri State Highway Comm.*, 454 S.W.2d 44 (Mo. 1970); and *V. L. Nicholson Co. v. Transcon Inv.& Fin. Ltd.*, 595 S.W.2d 474 (Tenn. 1980).
[36] Gusman, fn. 34, *supra*, at 232.

specifications for a construction project, the contractor cannot be held liable for an unsatisfactory final result attributable solely to defects or insufficiencies in those plans and specifications. This doctrine assumes the absence of any negligence on the contractor's part and that the contractor made no express warranty with regard to the suitability of the plans and specifications. Under this principle, an implied warranty exists for owner-furnished plans and specifications that if the contractor complies with them, a satisfactory product will result.[37] The delivery of defective plans and specifications is therefore a breach of the implied warranty, absolving the contractor from liability for unsatisfactory results or delays in completion.

The second aspect of the Spearin Doctrine, the right of a contractor to recover its additional costs when defective plans and specifications necessitate extra or remedial work, has found similar acceptance. The general principle has been stated as follows:

Where defects in the plans and specifications, the sufficiency of which is not warranted by the contractor, necessitate extra work or materials to complete the contract, the contractor may recover therefor from the owner. (Emphasis added.)[38]

For example, in *Fairbanks North Star Borough v. Kandick Constr., Inc.,*[39] the plans and specifications on a roadway project understated the amount of excavation of material to be removed and disposed of away from the project site. The court found that the owner had breached its implied warranty of the adequacy of the plans and specifications, and allowed the contractor to recover its extra costs since the contractor had reasonably relied upon the defective plans and specifications. In *Keller Constr. Corp. v. George W. McCoy & Co.,*[40] the court held that the owner warranted the sufficiency of the plans and specifications to the general contractor, and this warranty carried over to a subcontractor, entitling the subcontractor to recover from the general contractor for defects in specifications that required repairing breaks in a sewer line. The court further held that the owner had to indemnify the general contractor for any amounts so paid to the subcontractor. *See also Adams v. Tri-City Amusement Co.,*[41] where the walls of a building collapsed because the plans and specifications did not make allowances for wet soil conditions. The court held that the contractor was entitled to recover the reasonable value of the work to reconstruct the wall.

6.13   Misinterpretation of Plans and Specifications by the Owner

The second category under the "constructive change" concept relates to misinterpretation of the plans and specifications by the owner or its representatives.

---

[37] *R. M. Hollingshead Corp. v. United States,* 111 F. Supp. 285 (Ct. Cl. 1953).
[38] 13 Am. Jur. 2d, Building and Construction Contracts, § 19 (1964).
[39] 795 P.2d 793 (Alaska 1990).
[40] 119 So.2d 450 (La. 1960).
[41] 98 S.E. 647 (Va. 1919).

This type of constructive change arises from the owner's implied duty not to hinder or delay the contractor in the performance of his work, which is an implied obligation contained in every contract.[42]

This type of "constructive change" arises where, for example, the contract clearly specifies a particular method of performance or allows the contractor to select the method, but the architect or engineer requires a different, more expensive method than that contemplated by the contractor at the time he prepared his bid. For example, in *H. I. Homa Co.*,[43] a constructive change was found to result where the contracting officer rejected a bar-type progress chart that satisfied the contract's Progress of Work Clause, and instead required the contractor to provide a CPM Schedule.

In *Charles Meads & Co. v. City of New York*,[44] a contract to build a public library gave the contractor the option of performing the work in a certain manner. When the architect required the contractor to use a more complicated and expensive method to attain the same result, the court held that the city was liable for the contractor's extra costs. A similar principle was applied in *S. Hanson Lumber Co. v. Moss*,[45] where the contractor was entitled to additional compensation when the owner wrongfully refused to allow the use of the material specified in the contract, and instead required a more expensive type of material.

This type of constructive change can also arise from the owner's interpretation of a contract ambiguity in his favor. For example, in *American Asphalt, Inc.*,[46] a contractor was found to be entitled to additional costs of removing excavated soil where the government-prepared plans were ambiguous as to whether the excavated materials were to remain on site. The government's plans appeared to indicate the material would remain on site as fill material, but the government intended to show finish grade of paving, not the level for additional fill. The contractor had made no allowance in the bid for the removal of this soil.

6.14   Acceleration

The third category of "constructive change" involves the situation where the owner refuses to give the contractor a time extension to which the contractor is contractually entitled, thereby forcing the contractor to "accelerate" its work efforts in an attempt to maintain the original work schedule (possibly to avoid liquidated damages).[47]

---

[42] *See George A. Fuller Co. v. United States,* 69 F. Supp. 409 (Ct. Cl. 1947).
[43] ENG BCA Nos. PCC-41, PCC-42, 82-1 BCA ¶ 15,651.
[44] 181 N.Y.S. 704 (1920).
[45] 111 N.W.2d 681 (Iowa 1961).
[46] ASBCA No. 37349, 91-2 BCA ¶ 23,722.
[47] *See Howard J. White, Inc. v. Varian Assoc.,* 2 Cal. Rptr. 871 (Cal. App. 1960), *Siefford v. Housing Auth. of City of Humboldt,* 223 N.W.2d 816 (Neb. 1974).

In *Norair Eng'g Corp. v. United States*,[48] the United States Claims Court succinctly recognized three elements that must be proved to recover for the increased costs of acceleration under a changes clause:

(1) That any delays giving rise to the order were excusable (thus entitling the contractor to a time extension);
(2) That the contractor was ordered to accelerate; and
(3) That the contractor in fact accelerated performance and incurred extra costs.

The *Norair* court held that the contractor could recover its acceleration costs even though the project was over 500 days "late" because the contractor was entitled to approximately 700 days of time extension and had to accelerate to finish "only" 500 days behind schedule.[49]

This type of constructive change can also arise when an owner's incorrect interpretation of the contract requires the contractor to accelerate. For example, in *Rogers Excavating*,[50] an earthwork contract required the contractor to start work within four days after receipt of the Notice to Proceed and finish all work in ninety days. The contractor submitted a proposed schedule showing mobilization to start within four days but actual excavation not starting until forty days after Notice to Proceed. The owner refused to accept this schedule and required the contractor to start excavation work within the four-day period. The court found this to be an acceleration justifying additional compensation because mobilization was found to be "work" as it was defined in the contract. (However, the contractor ultimately lost the case because it had failed to give the required notice that it considered the owner's action to create a claim situation.)

The term "acceleration" is best known in federal government contracts.[51] However, the same result is achieved, usually under a breach of contract theory, where the private owner fails to grant an extension of time promptly or properly. As the court stated in *Wallace Process Piping Co. v. Martin-Marietta Corp.*:[51A]

> The order to complete additional work without an extension of time, which made necessary a work week in excess of 50 hours, was a change within the meaning of Paragraph 4, the Changes Clause of the contract. The refusal of Martin upon demand timely made by Wallace for an equitable adjustment constituted a breach of contract.

---

[48] 666 F.2d 546 (Ct. Cl. 1981).
[49] *See also Continental Heller Corp.*, GSBCA No. 7140, 84-2 BCA ¶ 17,275.
[50] AGBCA No. 79-180, 83-2 BCA ¶ 16,701.
[51] *See, e.g., Ensign-Bickford Co.*, ASBCA No. 6214, 60-2 BCA ¶ 2817.
[51A] 251 F. Supp. 411, 418 & 19 (ED. Va. 1965).

6.15 "CARDINAL CHANGES"

The changes clause of a construction contract does not give the owner an unrestricted right to order extra work. Changed work or extra work must be within the general scope of the original contract.

As a simple example, an owner who contracts for the construction of a house cannot require the contractor, by change order, to build a second house. Such extra work is totally beyond the scope of the original agreement. This would be an example of a "cardinal change." However, a change order requiring the addition of a room or the finishing of the basement probably would be valid under the changes clause. The difficult questions, of course, involve those cases that fall somewhere between the two extremes.

The term "cardinal change" refers to a change or changes ordered by the owner that are beyond the scope of the contract, and therefore constitute a material breach of contract.[52] If a change is a cardinal change, the owner is in breach of its contract and the contractor can either refuse to perform or can perform and be paid the reasonable value for the work. However, if a contractor refuses to perform a proper change, incorrectly thinking it to be a cardinal change, it will be in breach for refusing to perform.

If the contractor is confronted with an undertaking *substantially different* from that originally contemplated due to the extensive changes ordered by the owner or dictated by the owner's actions, then a cardinal change may exist. The contractor has the right to disregard the contract agreement in a cardinal change situation and seek compensation for the reasonable value of all his services.

In *County of Cook v. Harms,*[53] the court discussed the concept of cardinal change in great detail:

> Obviously, under a contract to construct a framed building at stipulated prices, a party could not be required to construct a stone or brick building, at prices to be fixed by the architect of the other party, by the use of these words in the contract. Nor could a party, by virtue thereof, contracting to build a small and inferior brick or stone building, be required to construct a large and superior stone or brick building. The mere combination of proportions and quantities, even of materials of the same class or grade, may be so different in different buildings of the same dimensions, that a party would not make the same bid, or be able, without financial loss, to construct them all for the same price.
>
> The terms stated in the writing were, we think, the controlling inducement to the contract, and the "changes, additions and alterations" therein provided for must have been contemplated and intended to be but such as were incidental to the complete execution of the work as described in the plans and specifications, and therefore of only minor and trifling importance, for otherwise some definite

[52] *Keco Indus., Inc. v. United States,* 364 F.2d 838 (Ct. Cl. 1966).
[53] 108 Ill. 151 (1883).

mode of determining what prices should be paid for them would also have been prescribed by the writing. We think any material departure from the plans and specifications with reference to which the contract was made, which resulted in a new and substantially different undertaking, cannot be regarded as within the meaning of this language. . . .

We cannot admit that a party entering into a contract to do a given work at stipulated prices, can, by the use of these words in the written contract, be made to do a different and more expensive work at prices to be named altogether, or in large part, by the architect of the other party.[54]

In *C. Norman Peterson Co. v. Container Corp. of Am.,*[55] a contractor brought an action for breach of contract and for the reasonable value of the labor and materials used after experiencing cost overruns at a paper mill modernization project. The court found that the owner, by imposing hundreds of changes upon the contractor, so altered the scope of the work under the original contract that the owner had abandoned the contract. Accordingly, the guaranteed maximum cost provision of the contract was inapplicable and the contractor was entitled to recover the reasonable cost of its work. The court justified basing the contractor's damages on the total cost method because the owner was to blame for preventing the contractor from making a detailed showing as to how the damages claimed were caused by the breach.

A cardinal change may also result from physical conditions encountered by the contractor that were not expected and that fundamentally change the scope of the work. For example, in *Universal Contracting & Brick Painting Co. v. United States,*[56] a contractor entered into an agreement with the federal government calling for paint removal. After contract award, the contractor discovered that the paint contained asbestos. The contractor claimed that this constituted a "cardinal change" entitling the contractor to damages for breach of contract. (This would also constitute a differing site condition entitling the contractor to additional compensation, but the notice provision is more strictly construed than under a changes clause.) The government moved for summary judgment, contending that the presence of asbestos in the paint was not a substantial enough circumstance to constitute a "cardinal change." The court denied the government's motion, ruling that the contractor's claim presented a legitimate claim of "cardinal change" that could be decided only by a trial.

The question of whether a particular change (or group of changes) is sufficient to constitute a cardinal change is a matter of degree—and often is very subjective. The basic tests for a cardinal change are:

(1) Whether the type of work was within the contemplation of the parties when they entered into the contract, and

(2) Whether the job as modified is still the same basic job.

---

[54] *Id.* at 159–60.
[55] 218 Cal. Rptr. 592 (Cal. App. 1985).
[56] 19 Cl. Ct. 785 (1990).

6.16 IMPACT COSTS FOR NUMEROUS CHANGES MADE DURING THE PROJECT

Contractors occasionally will encounter a project where the owner makes many changes on the job, no one of which, alone, could be considered a cardinal change, and then discover, only after agreeing to many of these changes, that the agreed prices for the changes are not adequate to compensate the contractor for the disruption and inefficiency created by the large volume of changes. This situation can occur when the contractor prices a change based on the direct costs to perform the work and does not account for the adverse impact of the change on performing unchanged work.

Generally, a contractor is bound by the terms of signed change orders. Thus, if the change orders state that they reflect all the compensation the contractor is entitled to receive for the changed work—for both its direct and indirect costs—the contractor may have little legal recourse. For example, in *Vanlar Constr., Inc. v. County of Los Angeles,*[57] a contractor brought an action against the county to recover impact costs arising out of the cumulative effect of numerous change orders. The court held that Vanlar was not entitled to impact costs, emphasizing that all of the change orders and supplemental agreements entered into between the contractor and the owner included direct and indirect costs. The court further pointed out that if Vanlar contemplated a future claim for impact costs, it was legally obligated to request that a reservation clause be inserted in each change order and supplemental agreement.

A contractor who is concerned about the possible impact costs of numerous changes on the job should consider adding a clause to proposed change orders stating that the change order covers only the direct costs of the changed work and that the contractor reserves the right to claim impact costs later.

6.17 IMPOSSIBILITY/IMPRACTICABILITY

The legal theory of "impossibility" provides relief in appropriate situations from the usual common law principle that a party must either perform the contract or respond in damages, even though performance proved to be more onerous or expensive than anticipated. The impossibility doctrine permits a contractor to walk away from a contract without penalty if performance is impossible or so impracticable as to be virtually impossible. The rationale frequently used for excusing a contracting party on the basis of impossibility is that the contract contains an implied condition that performance as contemplated by the parties will in fact be possible at the time performance is due.[58]

---

[57] 217 Cal. Rptr. 53 (Cal. App. 1985).
[58] *Faught v. Platte Valley Pub. Power & Irrigation Dist.,* 51 N.W.2d 253 (Neb. 1952).

The theory of commercial impracticability is related to the doctrine of impossibility. In the leading case of *Mineral Park Land Co. v. Howard,*[59] the court described the concept as follows:

> *A thing is impossible in legal contemplation when it is not practicable; and a thing is impracticable when it can only be done at an excessive and unreasonable cost.* . . . We do not mean to intimate that the defendants could excuse themselves by showing the existence of conditions which would make the performance of their obligations more expensive than they had anticipated, or which would entail a loss by them. But where the difference in cost is so great as here, and has the effect, as found, of making performance impracticable, the situation is not different from that of a total absence of earth and gravel. (Emphasis added.)

In *Mineral Park Land,* the contractor was excused from performing under a gravel excavation contract when the cost of performance proved to be twelve times that originally anticipated.

It is generally stated that the doctrine of impracticability requires *objective* impracticability. Subjective impracticability is not sufficient.[60] Thus a contractor must show that performance would be impractical for other reasonable contractors rather than merely impractical for it because of its particular abilities or circumstances.[61] For example, in *Piasecki Aircraft Corp. v. United States,*[62] the court refused to apply the doctrine, cautioning that the doctrine of impracticable performance may be invoked "only when the [contractor] has exhausted all its alternatives" and when all methods of performance are "commercially senseless."

While the concept of impossibility generally serves as a defense to excuse a contractor's performance under a contract, it may also be applicable under the changes clause. For example, when the plans and specifications require the use of certain materials that subsequently prove impossible or impracticable to obtain, the contractor is necessarily forced to find a substitute. This substitution is a compensable change to the extent it increases the contractor's cost of performance. In *McIntyre v. United States,*[63] the contract required approved Colorado marble, but marble satisfying the specifications was unavailable in Colorado. The court held that the contractor was entitled to the extra costs incurred in obtaining marble from Tennessee, even though government permission to obtain it from the alternate source was subject to the condition that there would be no additional cost chargeable to the government.

A similar rule seems to apply with regard to methods of performance.[64] However, the government contract appeals boards and the United States Court of Claims have held that a method of performance dictated by the

---

[59] 156 P. 458 (Cal. 1916).
[60] *See, e.g., Pauley Petroleum, Inc. v. United States,* 591 F.2d 1308 (Ct. Cl. 1979).
[61] *Koppers Co. v. United States,* 405 F.2d 554 (Ct. Cl. 1968).
[62] 667 F.2d 50 (Ct. Cl. 1981), *cert. denied,* 444 U.S. 898 (1981).
[63] 52 Ct. Cl. 503 (1917).
[64] *See Hol-Gar Mfg. Corp. v. United States,* 360 F.2d 634 (Ct. Cl. 1966).

contract must be followed, even though performance may be more difficult (though short of impossible) or less efficient than anticipated. For example, *Natus Corp. v. United States*[65] involved an $8.5 million contract to produce a portable steel airplane landing mat. The contractor argued that production in accordance with government specifications was commercially "impracticable" and that, as a result, it was entitled to an equitable adjustment. Despite the problems that the plaintiff encountered in developing a suitable production process, the court found that an alternative process, though less economical, appeared to be workable. In the words of the court:

> *The law excuses performance (or, in the case of Government contracts, grants relief through a change order) where the attendant costs of performance bespeak commercial senselessness; it does not grant relief merely because performance cannot be achieved under the most economical means.* (Emphasis added.)[66]

POINTS TO REMEMBER

The following key points should be noted:

- *Change order disputes* arise when the contracting parties disagree about:
  - The original scope of the work, or
  - Compliance with notice requirements, or
  - Who has authority to order changes.
- *Authority* issues arise when a person who has no actual express authority orders a change for which the owner must pay because:
  - The person had implied authority, or
  - The person had apparent authority, or
  - The owner ratifies the change order.
- *The lack of the written notice/written change order* often required by a contract does not necessarily defeat a claim for extra compensation if the requirement for a writing has been waived by agreement or conduct of the parties.
- Owners must pay the cost of *constructive changes* that occur when the owner, without issuing a written order, directs the contractor to perform additional work to complete or remedy defective plans and specifications, to meet a higher standard of performance, or to change or accelerate its schedule, or to alter the sequence of work from that which the contractor had otherwise planned.
- *Cardinal changes* are those changes or accumulations of changes that so greatly exceed the scope of the contract as to create a material breach of contract.

[65] 371 F.2d 450 (Ct. Cl. 1967).
[66] *Id.* at 457.

· *Impact costs* refer to the cumulative or "ripple" cost effect of numerous changes, and can be recovered in addition to the cost of the underlying changes if the contractor has appropriately reserved its right, in each signed change order, to recover later-incurred impact costs.

· *Impossible or commercially impracticable* conditions can excuse a contractor from performance; contractors generally must show that performance was impracticable for a reasonable contractor in order to prove that it was impossible or commercially impracticable to perform.

7

DIFFERING SITE
CONDITIONS

A common source of disputes between owners and contractors is the cost of remedying site conditions that are materially different from those contemplated at the time the contract was bid. Not only do unanticipated site conditions often generate extra costs, they can also substantially delay and disrupt the project. Unfortunately, such delays usually occur at the front end of a job where the overall impact is often the worst.

7.1 DIFFERING SITE CONDITION DEFINED

A *differing site*—or *changed condition* as they are sometimes called—is a physical condition encountered in performing the work that was not visible and not known to exist at the time of bidding and that is materially different from the condition believed to exist at the time of bidding. Often, this condition could not have been discovered by a reasonable site investigation. Examples of "changed condition" or "differing site condition" problems include soil with inadequate bearing capacity to support the building being constructed; soil that cannot be reused as structural fill; unanticipated groundwater (static or percolating); quicksand; muck; rock formations (or excessive or insufficient quantities of rock); and artificial (man-made) subsurface obstructions.

7.2 RESPONSIBILITY FOR DIFFERING SITE CONDITIONS

Under a traditional contract risk allocation analysis, a prudent contractor would be expected to protect itself against unforeseen conditions by including a contingency factor in its bid. The basic flaw in this approach is that a contractor cannot accurately value a true unknown. Even if included, the bid contingency may end up being totally inadequate, or, alternatively, grossly conservative. The one constant is that including any contingency increases bid prices and thus works to the detriment of the owner if adverse conditions are not encountered. In other situations, the contingency may prove wholly inadequate to cover the contractor's actual increased costs.

To alleviate some of the problems associated with unexpected subsurface conditions, "differing site condition" clauses have become a common feature in many construction contracts. The underlying reason for the presence of this widely used provision has been explained by many courts including the United States Court of Claims (now the U.S. Claims Court) in *Foster Constr. C.A. & Williams Bros. Co. v. United States:*[1]

> The purpose of the changed conditions clause is thus to take at least some of the gamble on subsurface conditions out of bidding.
>
> Bidders need not weigh the cost and ease of making their own borings against the risk of encountering an adverse subsurface condition, and they need not consider how large a contingency should be added to the bid to cover the risk. *There will be no windfalls and no disasters.* The Government benefits from more accurate bidding, without inflation for risks which may not eventuate. It pays for difficult subsurface work only when it is encountered and was not indicated in the logs. (Emphasis added.)

Despite this logic, both private and public owners often choose not to include a changed condition clause in their contracts. Some owners, in fact, go the opposite direction, by including clauses that purport to place all possible risks of a "bad" site on the contractor. These "exculpatory" clauses or disclaimers would seem to invite bidders to include contingencies in their bids.

The absence of a changed conditions provision in the contract, however, does not necessarily mean that a contractor will be denied relief if adverse site problems arise. Several theories of recovery have been advanced in such cases. The most prominent of these theories are: (1) breach of warranty, (2) breach of a duty to disclose available information, (3) mutual mistake, (4) innocent misrepresentation, and (5) fraud. These theories are discussed briefly below following a more detailed review of the principles involved in changed condition problems.

7.3 STANDARD DIFFERING SITE CONDITIONS CLAUSES

Virtually all of the "standard" form contracts between owners and contractors contain some type of differing site conditions clause. The first such standard clause appeared in 1927 in the federal government's standard fixed-price

[1] 435 F.2d 873, 887 (Ct. Cl. 1970).

construction contract. Its purpose was, and is today, to place the risk of reasonably unexpected site conditions on the federal government—granting a price increase and time extension to contractors required to deal with such conditions.[2]

7.4 Federal Government

The text of the differing site conditions clause used in federal government contracts [Federal Acquisition Regulation (FAR) § 52.236-2] provides:

Differing Site Conditions
(Apr 1984)

(a) The Contractor shall promptly, and before the conditions are disturbed, give a written notice to the Contracting Officer of (1) subsurface or latent physical conditions at the site which differ materially from those indicated in this contract, or (2) unknown physical conditions at the site, of an unusual nature, which differ materially from those ordinarily encountered and generally recognized as inhering in work of the character provided for in the contract.

(b) The Contracting Officer shall investigate the site conditions promptly after receiving the notice. If the conditions do materially so differ and cause an increase or decrease in the Contractor's cost of, or the time required for, performing any part of the work under this contract, whether or not changed as a result of the conditions, an equitable adjustment shall be made under this clause and the contract modified in writing accordingly.

(c) No request by the Contractor for an equitable adjustment to the contract under this clause shall be allowed, unless the Contractor has given the written notice required; *provided,* that the time prescribed in (a) above for giving written notice may be extended by the Contracting Officer.

(d) No request by the Contractor for an equitable adjustment to the contract for differing site conditions shall be allowed if made after final payment under this contract.

7.5 Other Standard Forms

The American Institute of Architects (AIA) and the Engineer's Joint Contract Documents Committee (EJCDC), [consisting of: the American Consulting Engineers Council (ACEC); the American Society of Civil Engineers (ASCE); the Construction Standards Institute (CSI); and the National Society of Professional Engineers (NSPE)] standard contract forms also contain differing site condition provisions:

---

[2] *See generally* Currie, Ansley, Smith and Abernathy, *Differing Site [Changed] Conditions,* Briefing Papers No. 71, October 1971, Federal Publications, Inc.; Currie, Abernathy and Chambers, *Changed Conditions,* Construction Briefings No. 84-12, Federal Publications, Inc.

The AIA A201 (1987 ed.) Contract Clause

4.3.6 *Claims for concealed or unknown conditions.* If conditions are encountered at the site which are (1) subsurface or otherwise concealed physical conditions which differ materially from those indicated in the Contract Documents or (2) unknown physical conditions of an unusual nature, which differ materially from those ordinarily found to exist and generally recognized as inherent in construction activities of the character provided for in the Contract Documents, then notice by the observing party shall be given to the other party promptly before conditions are disturbed and in no event later than twenty-one (21) days after first observance of the conditions. The Architect will promptly investigate such conditions and, if they differ materially and cause an increase or decrease in the Contractor's cost of, or time required for, performance of any part of the Work, will recommend an equitable adjustment in the Contract Sum or Contract Time, or both. If the Architect determines that the conditions at the site are not materially different from those indicated in the Contract Documents and that no change in the terms of the Contract is justified, the Architect shall so notify the Owner and the Contractor in writing, stating the reasons. Claims by either party in opposition to such determination must be made within twenty-one (21) days after the Architect has given notice of the decision. If the Owner and the Contractor cannot agree on an adjustment in the Contract Sum or the Contract Time, the adjustment shall be referred to the Architect for initial determination, subject to further proceedings pursuant to Paragraph 4.4.

The EJCDC Contract Clause (EJCDC Document 1910-8, 1983 ed.): Physical Conditions:

4.2.1 *Explorations and Reports:* Reference is made to the Supplementary Conditions for identification of those reports of explorations and tests of subsurface conditions at the site that have been utilized by ENGINEER in preparation of the Contract Documents. CONTRACTOR may rely upon the accuracy of the technical data contained in such reports, but not upon nontechnical data, interpretations or opinions contained therein or for the completeness thereof for CONTRACTOR's purposes. Except as indicated in the immediately preceding sentence and in paragraph 4.2.6, CONTRACTOR shall have full responsibility with respect to subsurface conditions at the site.

4.2.2 *Existing Structures:* Reference is made to the Supplementary Conditions for identification of those drawings of physical conditions in or relating to existing surface and subsurface structures (except Underground Facilities referred to in paragraph 4.3) which are at or contiguous to the site that have been utilized by ENGINEER in preparation of the Contract Documents. CONTRACTOR may rely upon the accuracy of the technical data contained in such drawings, but not for the completeness thereof for CONTRACTOR's purposes. Except as indicated in the immediately preceding sentence and in paragraph 4.2.6, CONTRACTOR shall have full responsibility with respect to physical conditions in or relating to such structures.

4.2.3 *Report of Differing Conditions:* If CONTRACTOR believes that:

4.2.3.1. any technical data on which CONTRACTOR is entitled to rely as provided in paragraphs 4.2.1 and 4.2.2 is inaccurate, or

4.2.3.2. any physical condition uncovered or revealed at the site differs materially from that indicated, reflected or referred to in the Contract Documents,

CONTRACTOR shall, promptly after becoming aware thereof and before performing any Work in connection therewith (except in an emergency as permitted by paragraph 6.22), notify OWNER and ENGINEER in writing about the inaccuracy or difference.

4.2.4 *ENGINEER's Review:* ENGINEER will promptly review the pertinent conditions, determine the necessity of obtaining additional explorations or tests with respect thereto and advise OWNER in writing (with a copy to CONTRACTOR) of ENGINEER's findings and conclusions.

4.2.5 *Possible Document Change:* If ENGINEER concludes that there is a material error in the Contract Documents or that because of newly discovered conditions a change in the Contract Documents is required, a Work Directive Change or a Change Order will be issued as provided in Article 10 to reflect and document the consequences of the inaccuracy or difference.

4.2.6 *Possible Price and Time Adjustments:* In each such case, an increase or decrease in the Contract Price or an extension or shortening of the Contract Time, or any combination thereof, will be allowable to the extent that they are attributable to any such inaccuracy or difference.

If OWNER and CONTRACTOR are unable to agree as to the amount or length thereof, a claim may be made therefor as provided in Articles 11 and 12.

An examination of these three clauses (the federal government's, the AIA's and the EJCDC's) reveals a basic similarity with minor but important differences.

7.6 Types of Conditions Covered

While the FAR and EJCDC clauses define differing site conditions as "subsurface" or "subsurface or latent physical conditions," the AIA clause uses the phrase "concealed conditions . . . below the surface of the ground or . . . concealed or unknown conditions in an existing structure."

Generally these clauses cover the same types of situations, although it is possible to imagine a few conditions where the wording would make a difference. A review of some of these situations stresses the importance of *reviewing the exact language* of the differing site condition clause to determine what situations are covered. For example, where actual grade elevations turn out to be lower than those shown on the contract drawings (requiring additional fill to meet the grade requirements), a contractor should be able to recover under the FAR clause's "latent physical conditions" language.[3] But recovery under the AIA clause's "concealed conditions . . . below the surface of the ground or . . . in an existing structure" language might be more difficult.

---

[3] *See Anthony P. Miller, Inc. v. United States,* 422 F.2d 1344 (Ct. Cl. 1970).

7.7 Type I and Type II Changed Conditions

Both the AIA and the FAR provisions identify two distinct types of unantici-pated conditions that are compensable. These are usually designated as Type I and Type II changed conditions.

A Type I changed condition is, in the language of AIA Document A201, a condition that is at "variance with the conditions *indicated* in the contract documents. . . ." The FAR speaks of such conditions as "differing materially from those indicated in the contract."

The FAR clause describes a Type II changed condition as "unknown physi-cal conditions at the site, of an *unusual* nature, which differ materially from those ordinarily encountered and generally recognized as inhering in work of the character provided for in the contract . . ." The language in AIA Docu-ment A201 is quite similar.

The EJCDC clause addresses only the "Type I" changed condition situa-tion—in other words, a condition that is different than *indicated* in the contract documents. As a result, the contractor performing under an EJCDC contract arguably assumes more risk with regard to possible differing site conditions than it would under a contract containing either the FAR or AIA clauses. However, the "newly discovered conditions" language found at provision 4.2.5. of the EJCDC may still make it possible to claim for "unusual" or Type II changed conditions, even if the contract was silent as to the particular condition encountered.

7.8 Notice Requirements

Differences also exist among these standard clauses with respect to notice requirements. The FAR requires that the contractor stop work and give notice upon hitting an unexpected condition, and *before* disturbing it, so that the government's representative will have an opportunity to inspect and evaluate the condition. The EJCDC clause, with its "promptly notify" language, ap-pears to be closer in intent to the FAR than it is to AIA Document A201, which only requires that notice of a claim for equitable adjustment be given to the owner within twenty-one days *after* "first observation of the condition." Regardless of the exact language, it is almost always preferable that the owner (or its agent, such as the project architect or engineer) be notified immediately when materially different conditions are encountered. By giving the owner the option of investigating the condition and, if appropriate, determining how best to proceed, the contractor greatly increases the likelihood of resolving any resulting claim in an expedient and mutually acceptable manner.

7.9 OPERATION OF THE DIFFERING SITE CONDITIONS CLAUSE

A differing site conditions clause provides a mechanism for dealing with an adverse, changed condition situation. However, a contract adjustment is not automatic. To obtain an adjustment under such a clause, one must first establish that the situation falls within the coverage of the clause. Before examining what typically must be proven, it is important to remember what one is *not* required to prove.

If you are a contractor, notification of a suspected differing site condition does not mean that you are attempting to prove fault, bad faith or defective design by the owner or its representative. There are simply some situations where differing, unanticipated conditions are encountered. This is especially true when dealing with subsurface work, or with older structures where only sketchy construction history is available.

An example of this situation is found in the terms of many agreements between soils engineers and owners. For example, standard language recommended by the ASFE (formerly known as the Association of Soil and Foundation Engineers) in its suggested form contract between a geotechnical consultant and an owner (CLIENT) reads:

> CLIENT *recognizes that subsurface conditions may vary from those observed at locations where borings, surveys, or explorations are made, and that site conditions may change with time.* Data, interpretations, and recommendations by GEOTECHNICAL ENGINEER will be based solely on information available to GEOTECHNICAL ENGINEER. GEOTECHNICAL ENGINEER is responsible for those data, interpretations, and recommendations, but will not be responsible for other parties' interpretations or use of the information developed. (Emphasis added.)

The presence of a differing site conditions clause allows the contractor to be reimbursed for its reasonable additional costs, regardless of the owner's knowledge or ignorance of actual conditions. By including a differing site conditions provision, the owner has assumed a portion of the risk of such conditions in exchange for the contractor not being forced to include a contingency in its bid.

The converse is also true: The owner is entitled to a cost reduction if conditions prove less onerous than expected. Although such downward adjustments are rare, they do occur. Such credits are consistent with the clauses' central purpose, which is to base the owner's cost and the contractor's compensation on the reasonable value of the work actually performed, thereby eliminating unnecessary risks to each party.

7.10 Recovery for a Type I Changed Condition

In order to recover for a Type I changed condition—one where actual conditions are at variance with the conditions "indicated" by the contract documents—the contractor must show:

(1) That certain conditions are *indicated* by the plans, specifications and other contract documents;

(2) Its *reliance* on the physical conditions *indicated in the contract;*

(3) The nature of the *actual* conditions;

(4) The existence of a *material variation* between the conditions indicated and the conditions actually encountered;

(5) That *notice,* as required by the contract, was given; and

(6) That the change resulted in additional performance costs and/or time, as demonstrated by satisfactory *documentation* or proof.

The initial emphasis in Type I changed condition situations is on what conditions were "indicated" in the contract. Some statement or representation must be contained in the contract as to what conditions could be expected, and the actual conditions must differ from that statement or representation.

What is meant by "indicated in the contract" has been defined by numerous case decisions. It is not required that the indications (upon which the contractor is entitled to reasonably rely) be affirmatively expressed on the plans or in specific contract provisions. Instead, such indications may be a mere inference based upon reading the contract as a whole. Thus the contractor may be able to compare actual conditions, not only with the express representations in the contract documents, but also with all reasonable inferences and implications that can be drawn from those documents. As was pointed out in *Metropolitan Sewerage Comm. v. R. W. Constr., Inc.,*[4] it is not required that the contract indications be "explicit or specific, but only enough to impress or lull a reasonable bidder not to expect the adverse conditions actually encountered."

In certain situations, a contract indication may be found from documents that are not a part of the contract. For example, one Federal Court of Appeals has held that soil borings were a "contract indication" *even though* the borings were not a part of the contract documents. This court held:

> The test boring logs do not have to be strictly considered "a part of the contract documents" (which the Appendix states they are not) to be binding on the [owner] to the extent of their own accuracy. We can accept the [owner's] argument that the Appendix is not an item listed in the Table of Contents (but is in addition to the Table of Contents) and therefore the Appendix is not a part of the contract. However, the differing site conditions clause need not be interpreted to limit reimbursements to situations where the logs themselves are necessarily a part of the contract. The clause entitles the contractor to reimbursement when there are "conditions at the site differing materially from those indicated in this contract." Even though the logs may not be included in the contract, they are "indicated" in the contract . . . .[5]

Examples of situations where *express* representations of conditions in the contract documents were found to have differed materially from the actual conditions encountered include:

---

[4] 241 N.W.2d 371 (Wis. 1976).

[5] *City of Columbia v. Paul N. Howard Co.,* 707 F.2d 338, 340 (8th Cir. 1983).

(1) *Muddy Versus Dry Conditions:* The contract documents stated that when "test holes were drilled in the area, no water was noted in any of the test holes." During construction, the contractor encountered "subsurface mud covered by a cracked and deceptively dry looking surface . . ." The Supreme Court of Idaho found the subsurface mud to be materially different from the dry conditions indicated by the contract documents and affirmed the contractor's recovery for a Type I differing site condition.[6]

(2) *Variance from Anticipated Blow Counts:* Soil conditions with actual blow counts that were one-third to one-half the strengths indicated by the contract borings constituted a changed condition. The contractor that encountered this condition during the construction of two underground garages was entitled to additional compensation.[7]

(3) *Limitations on Access:* A playground construction contract called for the contractor to furnish a certain brand of playground equipment, and included a drawing showing the placement and orientation of the equipment. The contractor, in reliance on the drawing, believed that it would be possible to use a dump truck and backhoe to bring in and spread sand after the equipment was in place. However, this proved impossible, and the sand had to be spread by hand. Since the contractor used the specified brand-name equipment it was justified in relying on the government's drawing, and was entitled to an equitable adjustment for a Type I changed condition.[8]

(4) *Hard Clay Versus Soft Mud:* The contract specifications required the contractor to remove soft mud, silt and sand in a river dredging project. When the contractor encountered hard, undisturbed clay instead of the soft materials specified, the contractor was entitled to an equitable adjustment for a Type I differing site condition.[9]

(5) *Excavated Materials Not Suitable as Fill:* Where the contract specifications required that soil materials located on site be excavated, and reused as fill, but the specified excavation and recompaction was prevented by the physical properties of the soil, which differed materially from the contract indications (which problem was also further impacted by an abnormal amount of rainfall), the contractor was entitled to an equitable adjustment for a Type I changed condition.[10]

Some examples of nonexpress, or *implied,* contract indications are the following:

(1) *Hidden Roof System Not Disclosed:* A roofing contractor who was required to demolish and remove an existing roofing system in addition to

---

[6] *Beco Corp. v. Roberts & Sons Constr. Co.,* 760 P.2d 1120 (Idaho 1988).
[7] *Baltimore Contractors, Inc. v. United States,* 12 Cl. Ct. 328 (April 30, 1987). *See also Granite-Groves v. Washington Metro. Area Transit Auth.,* 845 F.2d 330 (D.C. Cir. 1988).
[8] *Torres Constr. Co.,* ASBCA 25697, 84-2 BCA ¶ 17,397.
[9] *C. J. Langenfelder & Son, Inc.,* Maryland Department of Transportation 1000 (August 15, 1980).
[10] *Southern Paving Corp.,* AGBCA 74-103, 77-2 BCA ¶ 12,813.

the roof indicated in the contract specifications and drawings was determined to have a valid Type I differing site conditions claim. Nothing contained in the contract specifications or drawings indicated the existence of the additional roof system. Further, an inspection of the roof revealed no evidence that any additional roofing work had been performed after the as-built drawings had been prepared.[11]

(2) *Suitable Equipment for Work:* The Armed Services Board of Contract Appeals upheld a differing site conditions claim, holding that the "compaction, and clearing and grubbing" requirements were sufficient contract indications. The Board held that, while the contract documents made no express representation regarding subsurface conditions, the compaction and clearing and grubbing requirements led the contractor to reasonably believe it could utilize heavy equipment to perform its work. The Board stated that "where, as here, design requirements cannot be met and procedures and equipment reasonably anticipated cannot be used, the situation represents a classic example of a Type I differing site condition."[12]

(3) *Unanticipated Sloughing of Soils:* A tunneling contractor who encountered "running" ground conditions that were not disclosed by the contract soils information was granted relief under the differing site conditions clause for encountering a Type I condition. The contractor was required to grout in order to stop the sloughing.[13]

(4) *Dry Conditions Implied by Specified Construction Procedures:* When the construction procedures and design requirements set forth in the contract documents, read as a whole, indicated subsurface conditions permitting excavation "in the dry," but actual conditions made it impossible or impracticable to excavate in this manner, a changed condition was held to have been encountered.[14]

(5) *Implied Thickness of Concrete Floor:* The comparison of a 6-inch drain connection shown on the drawings with a cross section of concrete floors on the same drawings indicated the concrete floors were about 6-inch thick. When 12-inch concrete floors were encountered, a changed condition claim was allowed.[15]

7.11 Recovery for a Type II Changed Condition

Type II changed conditions differ significantly from those discussed above. Under a Type II situation, it is possible to recover even where the contract

---

[11] *Southern California Roofing Co.,* PSBCA 1737 et al., 88-2 BCA ¶ 20,803.

[12] *Kinetic Builders, Inc.,* ASBCA 32627, 88-2 BCA ¶ 20,657.

[13] *Shank-Artukovich v. United States,* 13 Cl. Ct. 346 (September 29, 1987).

[14] See *Foster Constr., C.A. v. United States,* 193 Ct. Cl. 587 (1970). *But see Tricon-Triangle Contractors,* ENG BCA 5113, 88-1 BCA ¶ 20,317 (denying a Type I differing site conditions claim where the presence of groundwater could be implied from the contract provision requiring the contractor to maintain a dewatering system).

[15] *J. E. Robertson Co. v. United States,* 437 F.2d 1260 (Ct. Cl. 1971).

is *silent* about the nature of the condition. To establish a Type II changed condition, one must show that the conditions encountered were *unusual* and differed materially from those reasonably anticipated, given the nature of the work and the locale.

To qualify as sufficiently "unknown and unusual," the condition encountered by the contractor does not have to be in the nature of a geological freak—for example, permafrost in the tropics.[16] Instead, all that is generally required is that the unknown physical condition be one that was reasonably unanticipated, based upon an examination of the contract documents and the site.

The key to recovery for a Type II changed condition is the comparison of actual conditions with what was reasonably expected at the time of bidding. This inquiry into reasonable expectations will raise questions of the contractor's *actual and constructive* knowledge of working conditions in the particular area. For example, awareness of a condition at the site which is common knowledge to other contractors working in the area, and thus reasonably ascertainable by inquiry, may be attributed to the contractor. Moreover, a contractor's failure to visit the work site, particularly when alerted to potential problems by the plans and specifications, and the resulting failure to discover obvious physical conditions, may indicate that the bidder's judgment was simply a "guess . . . premised in error," which forms no basis for recovery as a Type II changed condition.[17]

The following are examples of Type II changed conditions:

(1) *Subsurface Water:* A water table found to be much higher than reasonably could have been anticipated has been held to be a changed condition, where dry and stable subsurface conditions were reasonably anticipated (but not indicated).[18]

(2) *Buried Timber/Rubble:* In leveling land that had been cleared, a contractor was held to have had no notice of buried timbers, although the contract required the disposal of surface stumps, roots and other trash encountered. The buried trees thus constituted a Type II changed condition.[19] Similarly, submerged piling in a dredge-filled land area warranted changed conditions relief.[20] Another case that reached the opposite result held that the presence of buried stumps should have been anticipated because the site was in a fill area that contained some protruding stumps, new sprouts and new branches— indicating growth from buried stumps.[21]

---

[16] *See Ruff v. United States,* 96 Ct. Cl. 148 (1942); *Western Well Drilling Co. v. United States,* 96 F. Supp. 377 (D. Cal. 1951).

[17] *See L. B. Samford, Inc.,* GSBCA 1233, 1964 BCA ¶ 4309.

[18] *Loftis v. United States,* 110 Ct. Cl. 551 (1948).

[19] *Morgan Constr. Co.,* IBCA 299, 1963 BCA ¶ 3855.

[20] *Caribbean Constr. Corp.,* IBCA 90, 57-1 BCA ¶ 1315.

[21] *Gilloz Constr. Co.,* W.D. BCA ¶ 826 (1944).

(3) *Undersized Floor Joists:* A contractor entered into an agreement with the federal government to renovate certain family housing units. Rather than encountering 2 × 8 floor joists, as would normally be encountered, the contractor found that over 80% of the joists were much closer to seven inches in height. This required substantial shimming and other modifications, which resulted in extra costs. The contractor did not have a Type I differing site condition claim, as the contract plans did not give an exact representation as to the size of the floor joists. However, since the actual dimensions of the joists differed significantly from the conditions an experienced contractor would reasonably expect to encounter on a project of this type, the undersized joists did constitute a compensable Type II differing site condition.[22]

(4) *Oversized Walls:* In performing a contract to renovate an existing hospital, the contractor encountered a four-course-thick brick and masonry wall on the interior of the hospital. Such a massive wall was unusual for an interior partition; therefore, the contractor recovered the extra costs associated with the removal of the wall as a Type II differing site condition.[23]

(5) *Utilities:* When a contractor discovered that a third party had performed previous wiring in such a way that the phasing and wiring required by its contract could not be accomplished without extra work, this unknown condition warranted payment.[24] An undisclosed sewage line encountered in attempting to dig a manhole has been judged a changed condition.[25] Similarly, a differing site condition was found to exist when a contractor installing conduit pipe under an airfield perimeter road encountered a sewer line that was not indicated on the contract documents and was not a condition that would generally be expected.[26] However, in a different case where a contractor encountered sewers, gas lines, water lines, and coaxial cables which were not shown on the plans, a changed conditions claim was denied because the site was in a heavily built-up area and manholes were shown on the plans.[27]

(6) *Peculiar Structural Conditions:* A dock painting contractor was entitled to an equitable adjustment for extra work due to unusual conditions that reasonably could not have been anticipated at the time of contracting. The additional work was caused by peculiar structural features of the dock to be painted that, in combination with the air pressure from incoming tides, caused a continuous water seepage or mist over the dock. Neither the contract documents, nor the contractor's prebid site inspection, nor the contractor's experience as a painting contractor was sufficient to provide notice of this unusual condition.[28]

---

[22] *Kos Kam, Inc.*, ASBCA No. 24684, 88-1 BCA ¶ 20,246.
[23] *Hercules Constr. Co.*, VABSCA No. 2508, 88-2 BCA ¶ 20,527.
[24] *Dodson Elec. Co.*, ASBCA 5280, 59-2 BCA ¶ 2342.
[25] *Neale Constr. Co.*, ASBCA 2753, 58-1 BCA ¶ 1710.
[26] *Unitec, Inc.*, ASBCA 22025, 79-2 BCA ¶ 13,923.
[27] *H. Walter Schweigert*, ASBCA 4059, 57-2 BCA ¶ 1433.
[28] *Warren Painting Co.*, ASBCA 18456, 74-2 BCA ¶ 10,834.

(7) *Miscellaneous Items:* Where the contractor encountered beer cans, live ammunition and ladies' underwear in cleaning a duct system in a military barracks, the contractor was granted relief for a Type II changed condition.[29]

A Type II differing site condition may result not only from a variance in the type or quantity of a material encountered, but also from the unusual performance of an expected material. Thus, even though clay was expected to be encountered, when—as a result of percolating water—the clay behaved in an unusual, erratic fashion, with an unexpected tendency to slide, there was a changed condition.[30] In the same vein, the unexpected shrinkage of soil, which materially increased the number of cubic yards of earth in a dam, was an unexpected property of the soil that constituted a changed condition.[31] Similarly, a contractor was allowed to recover for the additional cost of handling a subsurface water condition, although subsurface water was to be expected, when the place where it was encountered and the rate of its flow were unusual and unforeseeable.[32]

7.12 STUMBLING BLOCKS TO RECOVERY

7.13 Site Investigations

Bid invitations commonly require contractors to visit the site prior to submitting their bids. Construction contracts routinely require the contractor to warrant that it has made a site inspection. One example of this type of clause reads as follows:

> The Contractor shall be fully aware of all conditions that might affect successful completion of the work. Before submitting his proposal he shall examine the site and compare the actual conditions on site with those shown or represented by the plans and specifications, and shall determine the existence of all physical features, obstructions above or below the ground, ground elevations, etc., on or adjacent to the site, that might affect the work. No allowance will be made for the Contractor's failure to adequately familiarize himself with all conditions and no claim will be permitted for relief due to unforeseen conditions.

Such a requirement does not automatically nullify the effect of a differing site conditions clause if one is present, and does not necessarily obligate the contractor to discover hidden conditions at its peril.[33] A contractual requirement that the contractor make a site investigation does not obligate bidders to discover hidden subsurface conditions that would not be revealed by a

---

[29] *Community Power Suction Furnace Cleaning Co.,* ASBCA 13803, 69-2 BCA ¶ 7963 (1969).
[30] *Paccon, Inc.,* ASBCA 7643, 1962 BCA ¶ 3546.
[31] *Guy F. Atkinson,* IBCA 385, 65-1 BCA ¶ 4642.
[32] *Norair Eng'g Corp.,* ENG BCA 3568, 77-1 BCA ¶ 12,225.
[33] *Farnsworth & Chambers Co. v. United States,* 171 Cl. Ct. 30 (1965).

reasonable preaward inspection.[34] The adequacy of the site investigation is measured by what a reasonable, intelligent contractor, experienced in the particular field of work involved, could be expected to discover—not what a highly trained expert might have found.[35]

The term "site" investigation is generally interpreted to mean, essentially, "sight" investigation, and to not extend to making independent subsurface investigations.[36] However, this is not always the case. The contractor will be responsible for being aware of all information reasonably made available to it, as well as all information that could be gained by a "reasonable" site inspection under the circumstances. For example, in *Cook v. Oklahoma Bd. of Pub. Affairs*,[37] the Oklahoma Supreme Court overturned a contractor's recovery on a differing site conditions claim where the contractor had neglected to attend *prebid conferences* where site conditions were discussed and only made a cursory drive-through of the site.

Likewise, the Armed Services Board of Contract Appeals held, in *Tri-Ad Constructors*,[38] that a contractor was not entitled to an equitable adjustment for installing more electrical cable than anticipated because the contractor failed to conduct a prebid site inspection as required by the contract. From its reading of an electrical wiring diagram, the contractor believed that seven electrical substations were located immediately above the main bank of underground ducts running between two switching stations. Had the contractor made an inspection of the site, it would have immediately seen that the electrical substations, each the size of an automobile, were offset some three hundred feet from the main line, requiring loops between this duct bank and each substation. The contractor was charged with the knowledge obtainable from a reasonable site inspection, as the ASBCA concluded that even the most cursory inspection would have revealed the need for additional cable between each substation and the main ductline.[39]

In addition to requiring that a contractor conduct a reasonable site investigation, some bid solicitations also require a contractor to review documents concerning the site conditions that are made available for inspection prior to bidding, but that are not provided to the contractor in the bid package. If the contractor fails to review the available documents before submitting its bid, it may later be precluded from recovering for conditions that are different than expected, but that could have been determined from a review of the

[34] *Warren Painting Co., Inc.*, ASBCA 18456, 74-2 BCA ¶ 10,834; *John G. Vann, et al. v. United States*, 190 Ct. Cl. 546, 573 (1970); *Maintenance Eng'rs*, ASBCA 17474, 74-2 BCA ¶ 10,760 (1974).
[35] *Stock & Grove, Inc. v. United States*, 493 F.2d 629 (Ct. Cl. 1974); *Commercial Mechanical Contractors, Inc.*, ASBCA 25695, 83-2 BCA ¶ 16,768.
[36] *See, e.g., Condon-Cunningham, Inc. v. Day*, 258 N.E.2d 264 (Ohio isc. 1969).
[37] 736 P.2d 140 (Okla. 1987).
[38] ASBCA No. 34732, 89-1 BCA ¶ 21,250.
[39] *See also McCormick Constr. Co. v. United States*, 18 Cl. Ct. 259 (1989) (denying a contractor's differing site condition claim because a reasonable site investigation would have revealed the possible subsurface condition).

documents made available.[40] For example, a contractor's differing site conditions claim was denied on the ground that the contractor had failed to review records of previous dredgings that contained information regarding the nature of the materials to be dredged and that were available to the contractor prior to bidding.

7.14 Exculpatory Clauses

Contracts frequently contain broad exculpatory clauses that disclaim any liability for the accuracy of plans, specifications, borings and other subsurface data. One such clause reads as follows:

> Boring logs and results of other subsurface investigations and tests are available for inspection. Such subsurface information, whether included in the plans, specifications, or otherwise made available to the bidder, was obtained and is intended solely for the owner's design and estimating purposes. This information has been made available only for the convenience of all bidders. Each bidder is solely responsible for all assumptions, deductions, or conclusions which he may make from his examination of this information.

Many courts have held that these clauses do not have the sweeping effect the drafter of the clause may have desired. Courts normally will not allow such clauses to eliminate the relief provided to the contractor by the differing site conditions clause.[41] For example, in *Woodcrest Constr. Co. v. United States*,[42] the United States Court of Claims allowed a contractor to recover under the changed conditions clause despite the extremely broad exculpatory provisions in the contract. The court stated:

> The effect of an actual representation is to make the statements of the Government binding upon it, despite exculpatory clauses which do not guarantee the accuracy of a description . . . . Here, although there is no (express) statement which can be made binding upon the Government, there was in effect a description of the site, upon which plaintiff had a right to rely, and by which it was misled. Nor does the exculpatory clause in the instant case absolve the Government, since broad exculpatory clauses . . . cannot be given their full literal reach, and, "do not relieve the defendant of liability for changed conditions as the broad language thereof would seem to indicate."[43] [G]eneral portions of the specifications should not lightly be read to override the Changed Conditions Clause . . .[44]

---

[40] *McCormick Constr. Co. v. United States,* 18 Cl. Ct. 259 (1989); *Stuyvesant Dredging Co. v. United States,* 834 F.2d 1576 (Fed. Cir. 1987).

[41] *See Metropolitan Sewerage Comm. v. R. W. Constr., Inc.,* 241 N.W.2d 371 (Wis. 1976); *Roy Strom Excavating & Grading Co., Inc. v. Miller-Davis Co.,* 501 N.E.2d 717 (Ill. App. 1986); *Contra Cruz Constr. Co. v. Lancaster Area Sewer Auth.,* 439 F. Supp. 1202 (E.D. Pa. 1977).

[42] 408 F.2d 395 (Ct. Cl. 1969).

[43] *Fehlhaber Corp. v. United States,* 151 F. Supp. 817, 825, 138 Ct. Cl. 571, 584 (1957), *cert. denied,* 355 U.S. 877, 78 S. Ct. 141, 2 L. Ed. 2d 108.

[44] *United Contractors et al. v. United States,* 368 F.2d 585, 598, 177 Ct. Cl. 151, 165-166 (1966).

Even where a contract lacks a differing site conditions clause *and* contains extensive exculpatory language, it may still be possible for the contractor to recover *if* it can show, for example, that an independent subsurface investigation was not feasible, and that it was thus forced to rely on information provided by the owner.[45] For example, in *Raymond Int'l, Inc. v. Baltimore County, Md.*,[46] the county solicited bids for repairs to the piers of a bridge. Even though the contract documents required the contractor to verify all dimensions in the contract documents, the court held that to require the contractor to make tests to verify the information supplied by the county placed an undue burden on the contractor. The court allowed the contractor to recover the increased costs incurred due to misrepresented conditions in the contract documents.

However, in some states, courts have taken a more literal approach in upholding such disclaimers. In Virginia, for example, one court held that a disclaimer concerning subsurface conditions was to be strictly enforced.[47]

7.15 Notice Requirements

The purpose of the notice requirement for changed conditions is to alert the owner to the existence of the condition and provide the owner an opportunity to evaluate its potential impact on the project. Such an evaluation may cause the owner to make changes in the design or alter the contractor's method of performance.

While it is always advisable for a contractor to comply fully with the notice provisions of the contract, the lack of strict compliance may be excused by the courts. The underlying purposes of the contract requirements may be satisfied by *substantial compliance* with the terms of the notice requirement, or by *actual knowledge* of the condition by the owner or its agent, or if the owner has suffered *no prejudice* from the contractor's failure to give written notice.

Examples of cases where contractors were allowed to recover for a differing site condition despite the lack of strict compliance with the notice requirements include the following:

(1) In *Brinderson Corp. v. Hampton Rd. Sanitation Dist.*,[48] the contractor encountered extremely wet subsurface conditions that it contended differed from the soil conditions presented in the contract documents. However, the contractor failed to give written notice in accordance with the contract until after the wet soils had been disturbed and at least partially removed. An owner's representative was present on site at the time the unusual conditions were first encountered and inspected the conditions. The court stated that the

---

[45] *See, e.g., Robert E. McKee v. City of Atlanta,* 414 F. Supp. 957 (N.D. Ga. 1976).
[46] 412 A.2d 1296 (Md. Ct. Spec. App. 1980).
[47] *McDevitt & Street Co. v. Marriott Corp.,* 713 F. Supp. 906 (E.D. Va. 1989).
[48] 825 F.2d 41 (4th Cir. 1987).

owner had *actual knowledge* of the conditions and, therefore, the purpose of the notice requirement was satisfied. The court held that the contractor should be allowed to proceed to the merits of its differing site condition claim, despite the lack of timely written notice.

(2) In *Pat Wagner,*[49] the contract called for the installation of water meters and additional service lines to an existing water system. After the contractor began work, it realized that the existing lines were copper rather than galvanized steel as indicated by the contract documents. The contractor was forced to tie into the existing system with more expensive copper pipe. Although Wagner failed to issue written notice, the federal government's inspectors were fully aware of the discovery of copper pipe in the existing system. Therefore, the federal government was *not prejudiced* by lack of written notice and recovery was allowed.

(3) In *Leiden Corp.,*[50] the board allowed recovery under the differing site conditions clause where the contracting officer had constructive notice of the conditions at the site because *actual knowledge* of the changed conditions was imputed to the contracting officer's construction representative on-site and thereby to the contracting officer.

7.16 Recordkeeping Requirements: Proving Damages

Even when a differing site conditions clause is present in the contract, the contractor still must prove how much the unanticipated condition cost in order to be compensated. The importance of good recordkeeping and the level of detail that may be required by a court are illustrated by the decision in *Ray D. Lowder, Inc. v. North Carolina State Highway Comm.*[51]

In *Lowder,* the contractor's first job superintendent had kept daily reports showing the progress of the work, the number of men, and the equipment on the job. The second superintendent did not show this information on his daily reports. When the contractor was preparing a differing site conditions claim, it rehired the first superintendent to go over the daily reports and prepare a cost summary.

The court held that this cost summary was inadmissible, and would not let the contractor use it to prove damages. Further, the court held that the daily reports themselves were incomplete and unreliable because even the ones that the first superintendent had filled out did not show how many hours each machine was in operation, whether any machines were broken down for part of the day or even used that day at all.

The *Lowder* case emphatically demonstrates the need for (1) complete, (2) detailed, and (3) accurate cost records. It is almost certain that, because of the differing site condition it encountered, the contractor in *Lowder* spent

---

[49] IBCA No. 1612-A-82, 85-2 BCA   18,103.
[50] ASBCA No. 26136, 83-2 BCA ¶ 16, 612.
[51] 26 N.C. App. 622 217 S.E.2d 682 (1975).

a great deal more money than it was able to prove with reasonable certainty under the criteria set down by that particular court. A complete and detailed recordkeeping system would have provided the very proof that the court found lacking. Remember that the law does not grant recovery for "possible" losses; it requires "reasonable certainty" as to amount.

7.17   RELIEF IN THE ABSENCE OF A CONTRACT PROVISION

The lack of a differing site conditions clause does not necessarily preclude recovery by the contractor. Instead, a contractor may base a claim on legal theories such as misrepresentation, breach of warranty, or mutual mistake. These theories are sometimes used even when the contract contains a differing site conditions clause. For example, if the clause has been rendered inoperative by the contractor's failure to give notice or to adhere to the clause's express requirements, these legal theories may provide an alternative avenue for recovery.

7.18   Misrepresentation

Misrepresentation or fraud (i.e., intentional misrepresentation) on the part of the owner may afford a contractor a basis for recovering the extra costs incurred due to the fact that actual conditions encountered were not as they were represented. A contractor may also be able to recover, even when the owner has made no affirmative misrepresentation, on the basis that the owner has breached its duty to disclose available information:

(1) If the owner makes an accurate representation but does not disclose facts that materially qualify the facts disclosed;

(2) If the facts are known or accessible only to the owner, and the owner knows they are not known to or reasonably discoverable by the contractor; or

(3) If the owner actively conceals information from the contractor.[52]

Some courts have shown a willingness to allow the standard site investigation and disclaimer clauses to undercut a contractor's action for misrepresentation. Other courts are not nearly as harsh, and allow the contractor to utilize the owner's misrepresentations as a basis of liability in spite of site investigation and disclaimer clauses.[53]

In construction, misrepresentations relating to the amount or character of the work to be performed under the contract, or the cost of its performance,

---

[52] *Warner Constr. Corp. v. City of Los Angeles,* 466 P.2d 996, 1001 (Cal. 1970). *See also, L. I. Waldman & Co. v. State,* 41 N.Y.S.2d 704 (Ct. Cl. 1943); *Davis v. Commissioners of Sewerage,* 13 F. Supp. 672 (W.D. Ky. 1936).

[53] *See, e.g., Fattore Co. v. Metropolitan Sewerage Comm.,* 454 F.2d 537 (7th Cir. 1971); *Metropolitan Sewerage Comm. v. R.W. Constr., Inc.,* 241 N.W.2d 371 (Wis. 1976).

may give the contractor grounds to rescind the contract or to sue for damages under a fraud theory.[54] Usually, however, statements of this nature are ruled to be mere estimates or approximations that would not support a fraud action. Each of these cases is controlled by the specific facts and circumstances.

In *Robert E. McKee Inc. v. City of Atlanta*,[55] the United States District Court for the Northern District of Georgia discussed the application of the theory of misrepresentation to changed conditions situations. The city had supplied the contractor with inaccurate information concerning the quantity of rock excavation required by the project. The court noted that a mere showing by the contractor of subsoil conditions not expected by either party would not automatically release the contractor from its obligations under the contract (and therefore the financial risk of the extra rock excavation). The court also recognized that the contract placed the burden of uncertainty on the contractor. Nevertheless, the court held that the city could be held liable if the contractor could show: (1) that it was not reasonably able to discover the true facts through investigation, and (2) that the misrepresentation was material. Thus the theory of misrepresentation may be available to a contractor even if it has "assumed" the risk of changed conditions in the contract.[56]

7.19 Duty to Disclose

A theory of recovery closely related to the theory of misrepresentation is a theory of recovery based upon the failure of an owner (most often a public owner) to satisfy the duty to disclose all available information. For example, when the public owner had an engineering report in its possession that noted the presence of saturated soil conditions not otherwise known to exist or otherwise represented by the contract, the failure to make this information available to bidders supported recovery against the owner.[57]

In *Pinkerton & Laws Co., Inc. v. Roadway Express, Inc.*,[58] the court recognized the legal validity of a contractor's claim based upon the owner's failure to disclose information concerning soil moisture and compaction criteria which the court found important to a contractor's ability to prepare a responsive bid. Interestingly, the *Pinkerton* case involved a private owner, not a public owner or governmental authority, unlike most cases where an owner has been held liable under a duty to disclose theory.

7.20 Breach of Implied Warranty

A contractor's right to recover for differing site conditions is sometimes premised upon the owner's implied warranty of the adequacy of the plans and

---

[54] *Busch v. Wilcok,* 46 N.W. 940 (Mich. 1890).

[55] Fn. 45, *supra.*

[56] *See also, Raymond Int'l, Inc. v. Baltimore County, Md., et al.,* 412 A.2d 1296 (Md. Ct. Spec. App. 1980).

[57] *P. T. & L. Constr. Co. v. New Jersey Dept. of Transp.,* 531 A.2d 1330 (N.J. 1987).

[58] 650 F. Supp. 1138 (N.D. Ga. 1986).

specifications. This warranty stems directly from the 1918 United States Supreme Court decision in *United States v. Spearin.*[59] In essence, this decision holds that the contractor should be able to construct the project in accordance with the plans and specifications, and if so performed, the project should be acceptable; that is, where the owner furnished the contractor plans and specifications that are inadequate, the owner has breached an implied duty. This principle has become so widely associated with this case that the owner's implied warranty of the adequacy of the plans and specifications is sometimes referred to by courts as the Spearin Doctrine.

7.21   Mutual Mistake

"Mutual mistake" is another legal doctrine under which a contractor may obtain relief from a changed condition. Under the mutual mistake theory, a contractor that can show the existence of a factual condition, of which *both* the contractor and the owner were unaware, and that goes to the "very essence" of the contract, may be successful in having the contract rescinded and in having the actual cost paid on a *quantum meruit* (literally "as much as he deserves"; in practice, the "reasonable value" of the materials and services furnished) basis. In *Long v. Inhabitants of Athol,*[60] the amount of work to be done under a sewer contract was stated "approximately" by the owner and the contractor's bid was based on this "approximation." When it became apparent that the construction of the project would require much greater quantities of work than estimated, the court found that a mutual material mistake existed, warranting a rescission of the contract.

POINTS TO REMEMBER

The following key points should be noted:

- *Differing site conditions* or *changed conditions* are a common source of construction disputes.
- A differing site condition or changed condition may be *defined* as a physical condition encountered in performing the work that was not visible and known to exist at the time of bidding and that is materially different from the conditions believed to exist at the time of bidding.
- Under *traditional contract law,* the contractor *generally* assumes the risk of differing site conditions of which neither party is aware.
- *When the contractor assumes the risk* of differing site conditions, the contractor should, in theory, include *a contingency* in its bid to cover the risk—the inclusion of this contingency means that the contractor will

---

[59] 248 U.S. 132 (1918).
[60] 82 N.E. 665 (Mass. 1970).

receive a *windfall* if no differing site condition is encountered, but could suffer a *disaster* if the contingency is not sufficient to cover the cost of a significant differing site condition which is encountered.

- In recognition of this fact, the federal government and many public and private owners elect to use a *differing site condition clause* in their construction contracts which place the risk of differing site conditions on the owner.

- Some of the *standard differing site condition clauses* encountered in the construction industry are quoted and discussed in Chapter 6—these include the differing site condition clause contained in the standard federal government construction contract, the clause contained in the American Institute of Architects' Standard Form AIA 201 (1987 edition), and the clause contained in the EJCDC Standard Form.

- Many differing site condition clauses recognize two distinct types of differing site conditions: a *Type I changed condition,* which is a condition that is at variance with the conditions indicated in the contract document; and a *Type II changed condition,* which is a condition unusual in nature that differs materially from the conditions ordinarily encountered in performing the type of work called for by the contract in the geographic area where the project is located.

- Most differing site condition clauses contain *notice requirements,* requiring the contractor to stop work and provide the owner prompt notice upon encountering a differing site condition, before disturbing it, so that the owner will have an opportunity to inspect and evaluate the condition. Failure to give the required notice may jeopardize a contractor's ability to receive fair compensation for the additional costs incurred as a result of the differing site condition.

- A contractor who encounters a differing site condition should be careful to *follow the procedures* outlined in the contract's differing site condition clause in order to ensure that proper compensation is received.

- *Good recordkeeping* is critical to a contractor's ability to recover the costs resulting from a differing site condition.

- To *recover for a Type I changed condition,* a contractor must generally show (1) certain conditions are indicated by the contract documents; (2) the contractor relied on the physical conditions indicated in the contract documents; (3) the actual conditions encountered materially vary from those indicated; (4) proper notice was given; and (5) the change in condition resulted in additional performance costs and/or time, as demonstrated by appropriate documentation.

- To *recover for a Type II changed condition,* a contractor must generally show that (1) conditions were encountered which were unusual and differed materially from those reasonably anticipated, given the nature of the work and the locale; (2) proper notice was given; and (3) the change resulted in additional performance costs and/or time, as demonstrated by appropriate documentation.

- *Examples* of some of the kinds of Type I and Type II changed conditions which have been recognized as a basis for additional compensation to a contractor by various courts and administrative boards are provided in this chapter.
- Some construction bid documents contain a *site investigation clause* which requires the contractor to perform a thorough site investigation and examination of existing conditions prior to submitting its bid.
- Where a set of contract and bid documents contains both a site investigation clause and a differing site condition clause, the contractor's ability to recover costs resulting from unanticipated conditions will depend upon whether the condition was one a reasonable, intelligent contractor, experienced in the particular field of work involved, could be expected to discover based upon a *reasonable site investigation.*
- In interpreting site investigation clauses, the term "*site*" is often interpreted to mean, essentially, "*sight*", and to not extend to requiring an independent subsurface investigation; however, this is not always the case.
- While many public and private owners utilize differing site condition clauses to assume the risk of different site conditions, thereby eliminating the need for the contractor to include a contingency in its bid, other owners take the opposite approach by including in their contracts various *exculpatory clauses* which purport to place the risk of differing site conditions squarely on the contractor.
- An *example of an exculpatory clause* is a clause providing that even subsurface information provided by the owner to the contractor may not be relied upon by the contractor and will not provide a basis for a claim for additional compensation should the information prove incorrect.
- *Courts have held* that such explanatory clauses are generally enforceable, but have very narrowly construed them and limited their effect. Some courts have even said that such clauses will not be enforced if it was not feasible for a bidder to perform an independent subsurface investigation.
- Even *in the absence of a differing site condition clause,* a contractor *may* be able to recover additional costs resulting from a differing site condition if the contractor can establish the facts necessary to support the legal theories of misrepresentation, breach of warranty, or mutual mistake; or can establish superior knowledge and a duty to disclose on the part of the owner.
- A contractor should *never assume* that he either will or will not be compensated for differing site condition clauses without a careful review of his contract, the specific conditions involved, and all surrounding circumstances.

8

DELAYS

Disputes involving delayed or accelerated construction progress are widespread in the construction industry. Time means money. Interest rates, inflation and extended field and home office overhead are everyday concerns for owners and contractors. Delays and suspensions, and the acceleration that may be required to overcome them, are primary contributors to the cost overruns that plague many projects. Some delays are the result of occurrences beyond the control of either the contractor or the owner. However, many delays result from one party or the other's failure to fulfill its contractual obligations. It is crucial for owners, contractors, subcontractors and any entity involved in the construction process to be able to recognize and distinguish among the various types of delays and to understand their rights and responsibilities in each type of situation. This chapter will look at the types of delays that may be encountered and the parties' respective rights and obligations.

8.1 THE NATURE OF DELAY CLAIMS

The legal rights and obligations associated with the concept of delay arise from either an express contractual obligation to perform by a given date or within a specified timeframe, or the implied obligation in every contract that one party will not delay, hinder or interfere with the performance of the other party. A party to a contract who hinders or prevents performance by the other party, or renders it impossible, may not benefit from this wrong. This rule of law prevents one party from taking advantage of its own contract breaches. The same rule also provides a basis for the recovery of costs generated by delays that are the fault or responsibility of one of the contracting parties.

Common causes of delays include inclement weather, labor disputes, untimely equipment delivery, defective specifications, changes and differing site conditions. These delays often increase both the time required to perform the contract work and the cost of the work.

8.2 CONTRACT TIME

8.3 Time Is of the Essence

Most contract documents provide that "time is of the essence." This clause ensures that an owner can recover delay damages for missed milestone or completion dates by making time a material requirement of the contractor's obligation. In the absence of such a clause, a court may decide that delay damages are not recoverable.

8.4 Contract Commencement and Completion Date(s)

The first factor to be analyzed in assessing a delay claim is the date on which work was to have been completed. Contracts usually specify the performance period either by setting forth commencement and completion dates or by stating that work should be completed within some number of days after the notice to proceed or commencement of work. Many contracts also include interim milestone dates, which specify the dates on which certain portions of the work are to be completed. An inability to meet interim dates may provide the basis for actual or liquidated delay damages, termination of the contract, or an acceleration directive. All parties should take great care to clearly define these time periods, and the consequences for failure to meet any dates, to avoid misunderstandings and disputes.

Where a contract contains a specific date for the commencement of work, the owner may be deemed to have warranted that the worksite would be in a sufficient state of readiness so the contractor could begin work on that day. If the contractor is not allowed to commence work on that date, the owner may be liable for delay damages. Owners often include a statement in the contract that the specified commencement date is only a projection or estimate in an attempt to avoid liability for any such delay.

8.5 Substantial Completion

Most contract documents define "substantial completion" of the work as "the stage in the progress of the work when the work or a designated portion thereof is sufficiently complete . . . so the owner can occupy or utilize the work for its intended use." Generally, an owner may not assess, and a contractor is not liable for, delay or liquidated damages after substantial completion. Thus even when a contractor has not completed the work called by its contract, or has performed such work in a defective manner, the owner may be estopped from collecting delay or liquidated damages if there has been substantial performance.

8.6 EXCUSABLE DELAYS VERSUS COMPENSABLE DELAYS

Obviously, a construction delay raises the issue of who should bear the responsibility and cost of that delay. In deciding these questions, courts or arbitration panels look both to the causes of the delay and to the express and implied obligations and assumptions of risk in each particular contract.

The legal consequences of a given delay are dependent upon a determination of responsibility for that delay. Construction delays fall into two major categories: excusable and nonexcusable. An "excusable delay" is one that provides a basis under the contract for an extension of the contract performance time. Excusable delays can be either compensable (time and money) or noncompensable (time only).

8.7 Excusable Delays

Generally, the contract dictates whether a delay is excusable—that is, whether a time extension is due. Typical examples are differing site conditions, design problems, changes, unanticipated weather, strikes and acts of God. When unanticipated outside forces delay completion of the work, the delay is "excusable" under the terms of most contracts.

Most contracts enumerate with specificity the types of excusable delays for which a time extension is due. However, the types of excusable delays for which time extensions are due vary from contract to contract. Some contracts are designed to list exhaustively each type of excusable delay, while others conclude the enumeration with such catch-all phrases as "causes beyond the control, and without the fault or negligence, of the contractor." Each party to a construction contract must have a clear understanding of the intended scope and operation of the clause when requesting time extensions or entertaining time extension requests.

8.8 Compensable Delays

Compensable delays are excusable delays for which the innocent party is entitled, not only to a time extension, but also to additional compensation for the resulting costs. For example, where an owner is the cause of a delay, the contractor is entitled to both compensatory damages and a time extension, if the contract documents do not include any provision exonerating the owner from liability for such delays.

Building contracts do not usually require a contractor to utilize all of the allowed time. Recognizing this, courts have held an owner liable for delaying the contractor where, even though the project was finished within the contractually allotted time, the contractor was prevented from achieving an early finish. Thus timely completion does not necessarily preclude the recovery of delay damages, where a reasonable schedule would otherwise have allowed early completion.

8.9 TYPICAL CAUSES OF DELAY

8.10 Compensable Delays

8.11 Defective Drawings or Specifications An owner is generally held to impliedly warrant the plans and specifications he provides to the contractor.[1] If such plans are erroneous or are insufficient to allow the contractor to perform the contract work in accordance therewith, the owner may be liable for time extensions and delay damages.

8.12 Failure to Provide Access The owner is generally required to provide the contractor access to the work site in a timely and properly sequenced fashion. However, in order to limit its exposure, the owner may insert an exculpatory clause into the construction contract or request that the contractor waive its rights or expressly assume the risk of restricted access.[2]

8.13 Improper Site Preparation Closely related to the owner's duty to provide the contractor with access to the work site is the owner's duty to prepare the work site properly.[3] In regard to this duty, an owner may require the contractor to inspect the work site prior to beginning work. Should the contractor fail to discover site preparation problems that a reasonable inspection would have revealed, or should it fail to raise any objections in a timely manner, the contractor may be precluded from recovering delay damages.[4]

8.14 Failure to Supply Materials or Labor Many construction contracts make the owner responsible for supplying materials and equipment to the

[1] *United States v. Spearin,* 248 U.S. 132, 39 S. Ct. 59, 63 L. Ed. 166 (1918); *Gilbert Pacific Corp. v. State By and Through Dep't of Transp., Highway Div.,* 822 P.2d 729 (Ore. App. 1991); *Frontier Found., Inc. v. Layton Constr. Co., Inc.,* 818 P.2d 1040 (Utah App. 1991).

[2] *A. Kaplen & Son, Ltd. v. Housing Auth.,* 42 N.J. Super. 230, 126 A.2d 13 (1956). *See also Burgess Constr. Co. v. M. Morrin & Son,* 526 F.2d 108 (10th Cir. 1975); *Weber Constr. Co. v. State,* 37 A.D.2d 232, 323 N.Y.S.2d 492 (1971), *aff'd,* 30 N.Y.2d 631, 282 N.E.2d 331, 331 N.Y.S.2d 443 (1972); *Broome Constr., Inc. v. United States,* 492 F.2d 829 (Ct. Cl. 1974).

[3] *E. C. Nolan Co. v. State,* 58 Mich. App. 294, 227 N.W.2d 323 (1975); *Jennings v. Reale Constr. Co.,* 175 Conn. 16, 392 A.2d 962 (1978) (suit by subcontractor against contractor); *Columbia Asphalt Corp. v. State,* 70 A.D.2d 133, 420 N.Y.S.2d 36 (1979); *Commonwealth v. General Asphalt Paving Co.,* 46 Pa. Commw. 114, 405 A.2d 1138 (1979); *Fehlhaber Corp. v. State,* 69 A.D.2d 362, 419 N.Y.S.2d 773 (1979).

[4] *See A. E. Ottaviano, Inc. v. State,* 110 N.Y.S.2d 99 (1952); *Public Constrs., Inc. v. State,* 55 A.D.2d 389, 390 N.Y.S.2d 481 (1977). *See Camarco Contractors v. State,* 22 A.D.2d 833, 253 N.Y.S.2d 827 (1964); *Morrison-Knudsen Co. v. United States,* 84 F. Supp. 282 (Ct. Cl. 1949).

contractor. Should the owner breach this duty or fail to provide the materials or equipment in a timely manner, the owner will generally be liable for delay damages. The owner may be able to shift the responsibility for such delays, however, by including an exculpatory clause in the contract specifically addressing this situation.

8.15 Failure to Provide Plans/Approve Shop Drawings The owner (except on a design/build project) is typically responsible for providing plans and specifications to the contractor. Should the owner fail to provide the plans and specifications in a timely manner, or to timely approve a contractor's shop drawings, the owner may be liable for the resulting delay to the project.

8.16 Failure to Coordinate Prime Contractors When an owner elects to contract with multiple prime contractors to construct a project, many jurisdictions recognize a duty on the part of the owner to coordinate the work of the separate prime contractors. Thus the owner may be responsible to one prime contractor for delays caused by another. Even where the owner attempts to shift this duty to one of the prime contractors, the owner still may be liable for delays if that contractor is not also given the power to enforce its responsibilities.[5]

8.17 Failure to Give Timely Orders for Work If the owner fails to issue the notice to proceed within the time frame agreed to in the contract (or within a reasonable time if the contract does not specify a time), the owner will generally be liable for delay. This rule also applies to delays in authorization for extra work, delays in responding to requests for information and any unreasonable failure to approve materials.

8.18 Failure to Make Timely Payments to Contractors Should the owner fail to make timely payment, the contractor may elect to terminate the contract as specified therein, or continue with the contract work and seek damages. The contractor can generally recover interest on the late payments, and in some jurisdictions may also be able to recover its consequential damages suffered due to late payment.

8.19 Failure to Inspect Under the typical contract, an owner may have the right or duty to inspect the contractor's work as it progresses. The owner may be liable to the contractor for inspections that are unreasonably intensive or repetitious, and for a failure to inspect timely and promptly.[6]

---

[5] *Shoffner Indus. v. W. B. Lloyd Constr. Co.*, 42 N.C. App. 259, 257 S.E.2d 50 (1979), *review denied*, 298 N.C. 296, 259 S.E.2d 301 (1979).
[6] Abernathy and Kelleher, "Inspection under Fixed-Price Construction Contracts," Briefing Papers, Federal Publications (Dec. 1976), pp. 6–8.

8.20 Suspensions A suspension is a form of delay resulting from the owner's interruption of the course of the work for a period of time. The term is primarily encountered in federal government contracts, where the standard "suspension of work" clause provides, in part:

(a) The Contracting Officer may order the Contractor in writing, to suspend, delay or interrupt all or any part of the work of this contract for the period of time that the Contracting Officer determines appropriate for the convenience of the Government.[7]

The presence of this type of clause benefits both the contractor and the owner. It provides the owner the right to halt construction temporarily, if, for example, the owner experiences funding or right-of-way problems. In addition it provides that the contractor will be fairly compensated for the resulting additional costs and extended performance time. Recovery is also expressly allowed under federal government contracts in delay situations where no formal affirmative suspension order is issued, but where the effect of the owner's action or inaction is the same.

Contractors performing on federal government contracts have been allowed to recover under either the express or constructive suspension provisions for costs generated by: (1) government delays in making the site available; (2) delays in issuing change orders; and (3) delays caused by defective plans and specifications.

8.21 Excessive Change Orders When the owner orders an excessive or unreasonable amount of changed or extra work, the contractor may be allowed to recover its resulting delay damages. These damages are commonly referred to as "impact costs."

8.22 Failure to Accept Completed Work Should the owner unreasonably refuse to make final acceptance of the contractor's work, the owner may be liable for the contractor's damages.

8.23 Acceleration "Acceleration" is a term describing the situation when an owner requires a contractor to complete by a date earlier than the contract completion date, as that date should be extended for excusable delays. "Directed acceleration" occurs when an owner consciously directs a contractor to complete earlier than the contract completion date. "Constructive acceleration" is the term utilized in the more frequently encountered situation when an owner fails to grant a contractor time extensions to which it is entitled, and the contractor is required to achieve, or strive for, an earlier completion than the properly extended contract completion date. Thus acceleration may

---

[7] United States Government Standard Form 23A, "General Provisions—(Construction Contract)."

be a by-product of delay or other factors that justify a time extension that is not formally granted by the owner.

The essential elements of a claim for constructive acceleration follow:

(1) Excusable delay;

(2) Timely request for a time extension;

(3) Failure or refusal to grant request;

(4) Conduct by owner that is reasonably construed as requiring the contractor to complete on a schedule that has not been properly extended;

(5) Effort by the contractor to accelerate performance; and

(6) Additional costs incurred by the contractor as a result of the acceleration.

If these elements are proven, the contractor is entitled to recover the costs incurred in accelerating its performance.

Acceleration damages usually take the form of premium time pay, the costs of additional tools and equipment required for the added crew, and the costs of labor inefficiency that may occur due to longer hours or increased crew sizes, which complicate work procedures.

8.24 Excusable Delays

8.25 *Weather* Under most contracts, unusually severe adverse weather can give rise to an excusable (but not compensable) delay. Unusually severe adverse weather is adverse weather that is unusual for the time of year and the place it occurred. This may be shown by comparing previous years' weather with the weather experienced by the contractor. The mere fact that the weather is harsh or destructive is not sufficient if the contractor reasonably should have anticipated that type of weather at the time and place it occurred. Some bad weather is always to be expected. If the contract period is 600 days, the contractor obviously does not have a right to expect 600 dry, sunny days with all of his subcontractors working at full force.

8.26 *Acts of God* Under most contracts, delays caused by Acts of God—floods, hurricanes, tornadoes, or earthquakes—fall into the excusable delay category, entitling the contractor to an extension of performance time. Thus usually neither party is obligated to the other for additional costs resulting solely from Acts of God.

8.27 *Labor Problems* Similarly, delays resulting from most, but not all, strikes and labor disturbances generally constitute excusable delays. If the strike is in effect or anticipated at the time of contracting, it may be determined, that because the labor problems were foreseeable, the contractor should have made a provision for them in the contract. Likewise, when a strike is provoked by an unfair labor practice on the part of the contractor, the delay might not be considered to be due to a "cause beyond the contractor's control."

With some exceptions, delays resulting from labor shortages not caused by labor disputes will not be excused. Similarly, a time extension generally will not be granted when its necessity results from subcontractor or supplier delays, because responsibility for their actions is generally assumed by and attributed to the contractor.

8.28 CONCURRENT DELAY

Concurrent delays are delays that occur, at least to some degree, during the same period of time. The term is used in construction as a term of art that refers to the situation when a compensable delay and an unexcusable delay occur at the same time or during overlapping time periods. For example, the term would apply when a contractor cannot commence work on the second phase of a project because the owner has failed to obtain a necessary right-of-way, and, simultaneously the contractor is also prevented from commencing the second phase by its own failure to timely complete precedent work in the first phase.

This phenomenon of "concurrent delay" creates interesting legal issues with regard to assessing responsibility for the overall project delay. This issue may be further complicated if the delay periods are of different lengths, the delay periods are not totally concurrent, or the delays have a different impact in terms of the number and types of work activities they affect and the severity of that impact.

8.29 Early View—No Recovery by Either Party

Until recently, when project performance was concurrently delayed by both a compensable delay and an unexcusable delay, neither party was allowed any affirmative recovery from the other; that is, the owner was not entitled to recover liquidated or actual damages for the period of delay and the contractor was not entitled to recover delay damages. Thus, in *J. A. Jones Constr. Co. v. Greenbriar Shopping Center,*[8] when the prime contractor caused delay through the failure of its subcontractors and materialmen to timely perform, and the owner caused delay by changes to the design and late issuance of drawings, the court held that neither party was entitled to any affirmative recovery. In such a case, the owner and contractor both bore their own costs even though one may have been responsible for more delay than the other.

8.30 Modern Trend—Apportionment of Delay Damages

Due in part to the advent of sophisticated scheduling techniques, such as critical path method (CPM), it is generally easier than it once was to accurately

---

[8] 332 F. Supp. 1336 (N.D. Ga. 1971), *aff'd,* 461 F.2d 1269 (5th Cir. 1972).

segregate the impact of concurrent delays. Logically, if the impact of one delay exceeds that of the other, the party responsible for the lesser impact should be allowed to recover damages for the excess impact. Accordingly, the courts recently have shown a willingness to allocate responsibility for concurrent delay as between owner and contractor. If the effects of concurrent delay cannot be segregated, however, no damages will be awarded.

8.31 THE CLAIMS PROCESS

8.32 Contractual Prerequisites

8.33 *Requirement of Notice* Most construction contracts require that any claim for additional compensation or performance time be preceded by written notice to the owner or architect within a definite period of time after the delay-causing event. A notice requirement is imposed to protect the interest of the owner, who may be unaware of the causes of the particular delay and thereby precluded from taking immediate measures to rectify the situation and mitigate its cost. Failure to give prompt notice may result in a waiver of the contractor's rights, or result in a time-consuming litigation effort that may ultimately prove unsuccessful.

Formal notice may be unnecessary when the owner has actual or constructive knowledge of the problem, or when the lack of notice does not prejudice a legitimate owner interest. However, the contractor should never knowingly forego written notice on the assumption that one of those conditions is present. Some courts view notice as a condition precedent to recovery. The contractor who gives the owner prompt written notice of delays and disruptions that are the owner's responsibility increases its opportunity to recover the costs generated by those problems.

8.34 Rights and Remedies

8.35 *Extra Time* A contractor is generally entitled to extra time for any excusable delay that occurs during the execution of project work. The contractor should beware of clauses that purport to limit its remedy for delay to time extensions, precluding the recovery of monetary delay damages.

8.36 Delay Damages

8.37 No-Damages-for-Delay Clause Despite the widely recognized right of a contractor to recover damages stemming from delayed or out-of-sequence work caused by the owner, the owner (or the general contractor if the claimant is a subcontractor) may succeed in asserting one of several possible defenses to a delay claim. The most notable potential defense is the *no-damages-for-delay* clause.

A no-damages-for-delay clause typically provides that the owner will not be liable for monetary damages resulting from any delays, or resulting from certain specified types of delays. Most clauses of this kind provide that a contractor's only relief for delays covered by the clause is a time extension. As a general rule, no-damages-for-delay clauses are legally valid and enforceable.

Such provisions do not, however, always constitute an absolute bar to recovery. The law of most states in this area was summarized well by the court in *Corinno Civetta Constr. Corp. v. City of New York:*[9]

> A clause which exculpates a contractee from liability to a contractor for damages resulting from delay in the performance in the latter's work is valid and enforceable and is not contrary to public policy if the clause and the contract of which it is a part satisfy the requirements for the validity of contracts generally. The rule is not without its exceptions, however, and even exculpatory language which purports to preclude damages from all delays resulting from any cause whatsoever are not read literally. Generally, even with such a clause, damages may be recovered for: (1) delays caused by the contractee's bad faith or its willful, malicious or grossly negligent conduct, (2) uncontemplated delays, (3) delays so unreasonable that they constitute an intentional abandonment of the contract by the contractee, and (4) delays resulting from the contractee's breach of a fundamental obligation of the contract.

A number of other courts have established that a contractor may recover delay damages despite the presence of such a clause in the contract, provided the delay:

(1) Was of a kind not contemplated by the parties in the contract clause;
(2) Was such as to amount to an abandonment of the contract;
(3) Was the result of fraud, bad faith or arbitrary action;
(4) Was the result of active interference with the contractor's work on the part of the owner (or active interference by the contractor where a subcontractor seeks recovery); or
(5) Was unreasonable.

When applying a no-damages-for-delay clause, most courts have adopted a policy of strict construction in determining whether the particular delay was within the contemplation of the parties. In addition, some state legislatures have passed statutes limiting the enforceability of no-damages-for-delay clauses.

In order to avoid the harsh consequences of a no-damages-for-delay clause, some courts have recognized a distinction between "delays" and "hindrances." In one case, a court held that a no-damages-for-delay clause that did not include the term "hindrance" only barred the contractor from recovering the

[9] 67 N.Y.2d 297, 493 N.E.2d 905, 502 N.Y.S.2d 681 (1986).

cost of an idle (as opposed to inefficient) work force.[10] Therefore, the contractor could recover damages that resulted when the owner "merely" hindered the contractor's work, with *hindering* defined as conduct that impedes, obstructs or slows progress. Thus it can be argued that virtually any act or omission by the owner that impedes, obstructs or slows the work of the contractor is a hindrance and falls outside the operation of a no-damages-for-delay clause.

Some courts have held that a contractor can recover delay damages despite the presence of a no-damages-for-delay clause when the delay is caused by the active interference of the owner, or by the owner's negligent performance of its contractual obligations. These courts have stated that an owner may become liable for delay where it arbitrarily interferes with the progress of the work or unreasonably fails to progress it, takes some action not contemplated by the parties to the contract, or otherwise actively or negligently causes an unreasonable delay, resulting in damage to the contractor.

A distinction should be made between a mere "hindrance" and "active interference." Although a hindrance involves active obstruction by the owner, it is lesser in degree than active interference. In order to constitute active interference there must be reprehensible conduct on the part of the owner in the form of bad faith, evil motive or total disregard for the consequences. A hindrance, on the other hand, only requires some degree of impeding the contractor's work.

8.38 Contractor Damages A contractor's damages for delay may include the following elements:

(1) Liquidated damages

(2) Inefficient or idle labor

(3) Inefficient or idle equipment

(4) Acceleration and overtime

(5) Extended field office overhead

(6) Unabsorbed or underabsorbed home office overhead

(7) Escalated material and labor costs

(8) Legal fees

(9) Interest

(10) Loss of profits

(11) Loss of bonding capacity

8.39 Owner Damages The damages that an owner may recover for delayed completion are often fixed by a liquidated damages clause. Such a provision relieves the contractor of liability for the actual damages flowing from a breach

---

[10] *John E. Green Plumbing & Heating Co. v. Turner Constr. Co.,* 742 F.2d 965 (6th Cir. 1984), *cert. denied,* 471 U.S. 1102.

and replaces this with liability in a fixed amount for each day that project completion is inexcusably delayed. A liquidated damages provision is valid if it appears that, at the time of contracting, the provision was not intended to establish a penalty, but rather to establish a reasonable approximation of the amount of actual damages that would result from a delay but that would otherwise be difficult to ascertain or prove. If a liquidated damages provision does not appear to represent an attempt to reasonably approximate foreseeable actual damages, but appears to be intended as a penalty, the owner will not be able to recover liquidated damages and will have to prove its actual damages resulting from the delayed completion.

A liquidated damages provision may operate to the benefit of the contractor. For example, in the case of *Georgia Ports Auth. v. Norair Eng'g,*[11] the owner, as a result of a contractor-caused delay, incurred actual damages in the amount of approximately $140,000 plus the value of the lost use of the project for the delay period of 177 days. Nevertheless, the court held that the owner could not recover its actual damages, but was limited to recovery under the contract's liquidated damage provision for 177 days at $500 per day, or a total of $88,500.

In *Industrial Indem. Co. v. Wick Constr. Co.,*[12] the Alaska Supreme Court held that a standard pass-through liquidated damages clause in a subcontract agreement limited the prime contractor's recovery for delay damages against the subcontractor to the amount in which the general contractor was liable to the owner for liquidated damages. As a result, the trial court's award of damages to the general contractor was substantially reduced.

Liquidated damages provisions should be considered carefully by all parties to a construction contract. Often the stipulated per diem amount is substantially less than the actual delay damages an owner may sustain. In such cases, the liquidated damages clause may provide a contractor a welcome safety net for late completion due to inexcusable delay.

The types of actual damages that an owner may be able to recover in the absence of a liquidated damages clause include:

(1) Lost revenues due to delayed occupancy
(2) Increased engineering and inspection costs
(3) Increased financing costs and interest
(4) Legal fees

8.40 Delay Claims Analyses A CPM analysis is often used to assess or present a delay claim. Basic project documentation is often critical to establishing the validity of the analysis. The following checklist itemizes many of the sources of information to be evaluated when preparing, or attempting to rebut, a delay claim:

---

[11] 195 S.E.2d 199 (Ga. App. 1973).
[12] 680 P.2d 1100 (Alaska 1984).

(1) Estimate
(2) Original schedules
(3) Schedules used on the project: from two-week look ahead schedules to CPM logic diagrams and tabular printouts
(4) As-built schedules
(5) Daily reports
(6) Diaries
(7) Manpower and manloading reports
(8) Cost accounting records
(9) Scheduling meeting minutes
(10) Material and equipment delivery tickets
(11) Job photographs and videotapes
(12) As-built drawings
(13) Shop drawing logs
(14) Project correspondence
(15) Change orders
(16) Contract documents
(17) Pay applications
(18) Internal memoranda

When evaluating a potential claim for delay, the following checklist is a useful tool for reviewing the pertinent factual information:

(1) *Accuracy:* Are the schedules used for the project accurate? Were they agreed upon and used by the parties, or were they issued for "internal purposes" only? Courts give great weight to schedules to which the parties have agreed previously.

(2) *Abandonment of Schedule:* Was the selected scheduling technique abandoned during performance? If so, why? A contractor who committed by contract to a particular scheduling technique might be precluded from proving its claim with that technique if it did not meet its scheduling commitments.

(3) *Current Schedule:* Was the schedule updated and kept current on a regular basis? Schedules often change dramatically over the course of a project.

(4) *Changes:* Was the schedule revised to reflect the effect of change orders? The schedule should show whether the change impacted work along the critical path or consumed float. A change order impact analysis is a handy tool for negotiating the price of a change.

(5) *Change Order Compensation:* Was additional overhead included in the change order? Even if the changed work only affects float, it may result in less effective resource utilization or involve unforeseen overhead or job staffing.

(6) *Cross-References:* Are the project records tied into the project schedule by work activity code or designation? Doing so provides data for subsequent updates and for the preparation of an accurate as-built analysis.

(7) *Float Ownership:* Does the contract bar the contractor from seeking compensation, time extensions, or both for delays that consume only float time?

(8) *Coordination Responsibility:* Who is the party responsible for coordinating and scheduling?

(9) *Scheduling Experts:* Get expert or in-house scheduling assistance early. This may aid in efficient recordkeeping and assist in minimizing the effect of a delay.

(10) *Choosing an Expert:* An expert should be well versed in:

(a) The theory and output of all scheduling techniques used,

(b) The estimating process used and its relation to the contractor's resources,

(c) The contractual relationships among owner, designers, contractors, subcontractors and suppliers,

(d) Good project recordkeeping and cost accounting, and

(e) The design and construction of the type of work involved.

POINTS TO REMEMBER

The following key points should be noted:

- Most big-dollar construction disputes are based upon changes—either *delay or acceleration*—to the construction schedule.
- Most construction contracts contain an *express obligation* that the contractor will complete the work by a given date or within a specified time frame, which is accompanied by an *implied obligation* that neither party will do anything to delay, hinder, or interfere with the performance of the other.
- *Common causes of delays* include inclement weather, labor disputes, untimely equipment delivery, defective specifications, changes, and differing site conditions. Which party bears *responsibility* for each of these types of delays depends upon the language of the contract and the surrounding circumstances.
- The presence of a *"time is of the essence"* provision in a contract should not be viewed as mere "boiler plate"; it triggers the recovery of delay damages.
- An understanding of several *key terms* is important in discussing who bears responsibility for construction delays:

  An *excusable delay* is a delay that entitles the contractor to a time extension under the terms of the contract;

  A *nonexcusable delay* is a delay that does not entitle the contractor to a time extension;

An excusable delay may be either *compensable* or *noncompensable;*

A *compensable delay* is a delay which is not only excusable (entitling the contractor to a time extension), but also entitles the contractor to additional compensation for the resulting cost;

A *noncompensable,* but *excusable, delay* is one for which the contractor is entitled to a time extension but no additional compensation.

· To *determine* whether a given delay is an excusable and/or a compensable delay, one must carefully study the contract, the nature of the delay, and all surrounding circumstances.

· *Examples* of some of the types of delays which *may* constitute excusable delays are weather, Acts of God, and labor problems.

· Most construction contracts require the contractor to provide the owner *prompt written notice* of any excusable or compensable delay; a contractor's failure to provide such notice may jeopardize the contractor's right to a time extension and/or additional compensation.

· *Examples* of some of the causes of delay which *may* constitute compensable delays include delays due to defective drawings or specifications, the owner's failure to provide access, improper site preparation by the owner or a parallel contractor, the owner's failure to timely supply owner-furnished materials or labor, the owner's failure to timely provide plans and approved shop drawings, the owner's failure to properly coordinate parallel prime contractors, the owner's failure to make timely payments, the owner's failure to perform timely inspections, the owner's suspension of the work, excessive change orders, and the owner's failure to timely accept complete work.

· *Acceleration* is another common source of construction claims and disputes. Acceleration may take two forms:

> *Directed acceleration;* and
> *Constructive acceleration.*

· *Directed acceleration* describes a situation where the owner consciously directs the contractor to complete the work earlier than the contractually required completion date.

· *Constructive acceleration* describes the situation which is more difficult to identify but far more common—the situation where an owner fails to grant a contractor a time extension to which it is entitled, thereby requiring the contractor to complete, or attempt to complete, the work by an earlier date than the contractually required completion date, as properly extended. Thus, constructive acceleration is, in effect, a possible byproduct of an excusable delay.

· The *essential elements of a claim for constructive acceleration* are as follows:

(1) An excusable delay;

(2) A request for a time extension;

(3) The owner's failure or refusal to grant the request;

(4) Conduct by the owner that is reasonably construed as requiring the contractor to complete on a schedule that has not been properly extended;

(5) An effort by the contractor to accelerate performance in order to meet the non-extended schedule; and

(6) Additional costs incurred by the contractor as a result of the acceleration.

- If the contractor can establish each of these six elements of a constructive acceleration claim, the contractor is generally entitled to additional compensation *even though* the contractor may have been *unsuccessful* in his attempt to complete the work by the non-extended completion date.

- *Examples* of acceleration damages include premium time pay, the cost of additional tools and equipment required for added crews, and the cost of the labor inefficiency that may occur due to the longer hours or increased crew sizes or numbers.

- Another important concept is that of *concurrent delay;* this is a term of art that refers to the situation where two different delays occur simultaneously or in overlapping time periods and one of the delays is a compensable delay, while the other is an nonexcusable delay. The phenomenon of concurrent delay creates an interesting legal issue as to which party should bear responsibility for project delays under such circumstances.

- The *early view* stated by the courts and administrative boards regarding concurrent delay was that neither party was allowed any affirmative recovery from the other in the case of concurrent delay.

- The *modern trend* is to apportion responsibility for project delays between the parties whenever it is possible, using modern, sophisticated scheduling techniques such as Critical Path Method (CPM) scheduling, to segregate the impact of the concurrent delays.

- Some construction contracts contain a type of exculpatory clause referred to as a *no-damages-for-delay clause.* A no-damages-for-delay clause typically provides that the owner will not be liable to the contractor for monetary damages resulting from any delays or from certain specified types of delay.

- As a *general rule,* no-damages-for-delay clauses are legally valid and *enforceable;* however, courts often narrowly construe such provisions and create various judicial exceptions to the general rule of enforceability in order to avoid harsh results.

- *Some common exceptions* to the general rule that no-damages-for-delay clauses are enforceable which have been recognized by various courts, provide that no-damages-for-delay clauses will not be enforced to preclude the contractor from recovering delay damages for the following types of delay:

(1) Delays of a kind not contemplated by the parties in the contract provision;

(2) Delays which were of such a type and magnitude as to amount to an abandonment of the contract;

(3) Delays which were the result of fraud, bad faith, arbitrary action on the part of the other party;

(4) Delays which were the result of active interference with the contractor's work on the part of the other party; and

(5) Delays which were unreasonable.

- Some *state legislatures* have also passed statutes limiting the enforceability of no-damages-for-delay clauses.

- The harsh consequences of a no-damages-for-delay clause can also sometimes be averted by drawing a *distinction* between a "delay" and a "hindrance", "disruption", "resequencing", "acceleration", and "contract change".

- Some of the *types of damages* a contractor may be able to recover as delay damages include liquidated damages, inefficient or idle labor costs, idle equipment costs, acceleration and overtime costs, extended field office overhead costs, unabsorbed or underabsorbed home office overhead costs, escalated material and labor costs, legal fees, interest, lost profits, and damages resulting from lost bonding capacity.

- When a contractor fails to complete a project within the contractually specified time, as properly extended for any excusable delays, the *owner may recover delay damages* from the contractor. These damages may take the form of liquidated damages (if the contract contains a valid liquidated damages provision), or, in the absence of a liquidated damages provision, actual damages.

- The *types of actual damages* an owner may be able to recover in the absence of a liquidated damages provision include lost revenues due to delayed occupancy, increased engineering and inpsection costs, increased financing costs and interest, and legal fees.

- A *good scheduling analysis* and *good documentation* are critical to the successful presentation of any delay claim.

9

INSPECTION,
ACCEPTANCE
AND WARRANTIES

This chapter discusses three methods to help insure quality throughout the construction project: (1) inspections, (2) acceptance, and (3) warranties. As demonstrated below, quality inspections performed by experienced personnel can reduce poor quality construction and limit costly corrective procedures. Similarly, acceptance procedures should identify obvious defects and other nonconforming work in a prompt manner to reduce its impact on the project. Finally, the contract and the law usually impose warranties on all members of the industry to allocate responsibility for defective work.

9.1 INSPECTION

9.2 Introduction

The owners of both private and public projects generally employ representatives to inspect the quality of the contractor's work. In private construction, inspections are generally performed by an architect/engineer specially retained by the owner. In public construction, however, inspections are often handled by government-employed inspectors.

Inspection is for the protection of the owner and not the contractor; therefore, the owner has no duty to inspect. Owners often place the burden of inspections and quality control on the contractor by requiring the contractor to submit quality control plans. Failure to inspect effectively, however, may impact the owner's rights under applicable warranties once the project is accepted. Furthermore, the owner cannot, with impunity, perform inspections in such a manner as to delay or disrupt the contractor's work or to alter the requirements of the contract.

9.3 Standard Inspection Clauses

The rights and responsibilities of the owner and contractor in a typical construction project are illustrated by the standard provisions regarding inspections. The standard clause used in federal construction contracting, entitled "inspection of construction," is set forth in Federal Acquisition Regulation (FAR) § 52.246-12. The standard clause used in private construction is contained in AIA Document A201 (1987 ed.) [hereinafter cited as A201], Article 12, "uncovering and correction of work."

The federal clause specifies that the owner has the right to inspect "at all reasonable times before acceptance to ensure strict compliance with the terms of the contract." The clause clearly provides that the inspection is solely for the owner's benefit and does not constitute or imply acceptance of the contractor's work. The contractor, therefore, is not relieved of the responsibility of insuring compliance with contract requirements merely because the government has conducted inspections.

Other standard federal government contract clauses impact the inspection issue. The "material and workmanship" clause provides that materials employed are to be new and "of the most suitable grade" unless the contract provides otherwise; that references to products by trade name are intended to set a standard of quality and not to limit competition; that anything installed without required approval may be rejected; and that work must be performed in a "skillful and workmanlike manner."

The "permits and responsibilities" clause in the standard federal contract, FAR § 52.236-7, requires the contractor to take proper safety and health precautions for the purpose of protecting the work, the workers, and the persons and property of others. The clause also states that the contractor is responsible for damages to persons or property caused by the contractor's fault or negligence, and places responsibility upon the contractor for all materials and work prior to acceptance by the government.[1]

Likewise, Article 10 of AIA Document A201 makes the contractor responsible for initiating, maintaining and supervising all safety precautions and programs in connection with the performance of the contract.[2]

However, the contractor is not an insurer, and therefore it is not always responsible for certain job site injuries. For example, in Georgia, an architect was denied recovery against the contractor when the architect fell off a ladder. The court stated that a contractor must use ordinary care not to cause injuries; the architect, however, has the same duty. The problem with the ladder was obvious and the architect should have known better than to use it. Therefore, the architect recovered nothing.[3]

The standard federal "use and possession prior to completion" clause provides that the owner may take possession of or use a partially or totally

[1] *See* FAR § 36.507.
[2] A201 § 10.1.1.
[3] *Morris v. Barnet,* 381 S.E.2d 597 (Ga. Ct. App. 1989).

completed portion of a project without being deemed to have accepted the work. Prior to such possession or use, the contracting officer must provide the contractor with a list of work remaining to be done on the relevant portion of the project. Even where the owner fails to list a particular defect or item of work, however, the contractor must still comply with the contract terms.[4] The AIA General Conditions also provide for possession prior to completion.[5]

9.4 Costs of Inspection

Although the owner normally bears its own inspection costs, the contractor is required to bear the expense of providing the inspector with those facilities, labor or material reasonably necessary to perform the test or inspection.[6] However, several circumstances exist in which the contractor may be reimbursed for expenses incurred for inspection or testing. For example, if the owner increases the cost of conducting the inspection or test by changing the location or requiring special inspection devices, the contractor may recover additional costs.[7]

As previously stated, the owner may examine completed work and require the contractor to remove or tear out the work. If the work is defective or does not conform to the specifications, the contractor must pay the costs of both the inspection and correction of the work. If, however, the work is satisfactory, the contractor is entitled to a price adjustment for the additional costs and a time extension if completion is delayed.

The cost of reinspection is generally assigned to the party whose action or inaction resulted in the reinspection.[8] If, for example, the contractor's work was not sufficiently complete at the time of the original inspection, the contractor must pay the costs of reinspection. Similarly, if the reinspection is the result of an earlier rejection, the contractor is responsible for the additional costs.[9] Before any reinspection, however, the owner must provide a reasonable notification and amount of time for the contractor to correct or complete the work.

Paragraph 12.2.5 of AIA Document A201 requires the contractor to "bear the cost of correcting destroyed or damaged construction, whether completed or partially completed, of the Owner or separate contractors caused by the Contractor's correction or removal of work which is not in accordance with the requirements of the Contract Documents." Paragraph 12.3.1 authorizes the owner to accept defective work and reduce the contract price to take the defective work into account.

---

[4] *See* FAR § 52.236-11.
[5] *See* A201 § 9.9.
[6] *See Tecon Corp. v. United States,* 411 F.2d 1262 (Ct. Cl. 1969).
[7] *See Gordon H. Ball, Inc.,* ASBCA 8316, 63-1 BCA ¶ 3925; *Corbetta Constr. Co.,* ASBCA 5045, 60-1 BCA ¶ 2613.
[8] *See Okland Constr. Co.,* GSBCA 3557, 72-2 BCA ¶ 9675.
[9] *See Minnesota Mining and Mfg. Co.,* GSBCA 4054, 75-1 BCA ¶ 11,065.

9.5 The Owner's Right to Inspect

9.6 The Right, Not the Duty The contractor's best friend is contemporaneous inspection, which allows the owner or its representative to monitor the work on a daily basis and inspect for deviations from the plans and specifications. If the owner or its representative reasonably objects, performance can be modified to make it acceptable with minimal cost. If the owner fails to object, waiver of the deficiency may be inferred. In the event of an ambiguous requirement, the owner's acquiescence to the work as performed may show that the owner agreed with the contractor's interpretation at the time of performance.[10]

Cognizant of the risks of overlooking defects during inspection, owners have sought to minimize contractors' ability to rely on owners' inspections. Thus, the 1976 edition of AIA Document A201 provided in § 9.4.2, with regard to the effect of issuing a Certificate for Payment:

> . . . [B]y issuing a Certificate for Payment, the Architect shall not thereby be deemed to represent that he has made exhaustive or continuous on-site inspections to check the quality or quantity of the Work. . . .

The 1987 edition of § 9.4.2 has been changed to add that issuance of a Certificate of Payment also will not indicate that the architect has "reviewed copies of requisitions received from Subcontractors and material suppliers and other data requested by the Owner to substantiate the Contractor's right to payment."

The standard federal "inspection and acceptance" clause, cited above, is more specific: "Any such inspection and test is for the sole benefit of the Government and shall not relieve the Contractor of the responsibility of providing quality control measures. . . ." This provision makes clear that no inspection duty is imposed upon the government; rather, the government has the right to inspect should it so desire.

The owner would have an affirmative duty to inspect the work where the contract specifically contemplates or requires the owner to perform certain tests during the work.[11] The failure of the owner to inspect or test in accordance with contract terms may cause it to lose some of its specific rights and remedies, such as the right to reject items or have defects corrected when a reasonable inspection would have uncovered such defects.

9.7 Scope of Inspection The scope of the owner's inspection duties often leads to disputes regarding the interpretation of specifications, quality of workmanship and other "quality" determinations. The scope of an owner's inspection is usually set forth in the contract and, where no specific inspection requirements are set forth, the inspections must be reasonable in scope. In

---

[10] *Milaeger Well Drilling Co. v. Muskego Rendering Co.*, 85 N.W.2d 331 (Wis. 1957).
[11] *See Cone Bros. Contracting Co.*, ASBCA 16078, 72-1 BCA ¶ 9444.

federal government work, the scope of the inspection requirements depends upon the analysis of the type of work to be delivered.

The standard inspection clause generally controls construction contracts. However, the FAR establishes three levels of inspection: (1) only the contractor performs inspections; (2) the "standard" inspection is performed by the government; and (3) "higher-level quality" inspections are performed by the government.[12]

These three levels generally are applied to service and supply contracts. The contractor should discuss the level of such inspection with the Contracting Officer at the preconstruction meeting. In most cases, the government will either perform the standard inspection or the higher level quality inspection. The requirements for the standard inspection are set forth in the inspection clause, which permits: (1) the contractor to establish an inspection system; (2) the government to inspect during performance; and (3) the contractor to maintain inspection records.[13] The higher level quality inspection requirements are generally set forth in special supplementary contract clauses implementing stricter quality control.[14]

Even if the scope of the inspection is set forth in the contract, as a general rule, the federal government contract may impose an unspecified alternative test as a basis for determining contract compliance. The new test must reasonably measure contract compliance. However, if the "specified" test can be viewed as establishing a standard of performance, a different test that increases the level of performance cannot be substituted.[15]

Not only does the government have the right to inspect at all places and times, the government also has the right to reinspect the same performance. Generally, the government may conduct reasonable, continuing inspections at any time prior to acceptance.[16] Exceptions exist with regard to the government's right to reinspect. Multiple inspections cannot be wholly inconsistent. Subjecting the contractor to inconsistent inspections amounts to an unreasonable interference with the contractor's work and entitles the contractor to compensation.[17]

9.8 Rejection and Correction

After inspection, an owner has the right to accept the performance, reject the performance, require correction of nonconforming performance or, in appropriate circumstances, terminate the contract for default. To enforce its rejection/correction remedy, the federal government must provide the contrac-

---

[12] FAR § 46.202.
[13] FAR § 46.2023.
[14] FAR §§ 46.311, 52.246-11.
[15] *Roda Enter., Inc.*, ASBCA 22323, 81-2 BCA ¶ 15,419; *Southwest Welding and Mfg. Co. v. United States*, 413 F.2d 1167 (Ct. Cl. 1969).
[16] *Forsberg & Gregory, Inc.*, ASBCA 17598, 75-1 BCA ¶ 11,176.
[17] *WRB Corp. v. United States*, 183 Ct. Cl. 409 (1968).

tor with notice of the alleged discrepancy within a "reasonable time" after discovery of the defects. The notice must include the reasons for the rejection.[18] When the government fails to provide the reasons for the rejection in the initial notice and the contractor is prejudiced by the failure, the rejection can be overturned as ineffective. Furthermore, a failure to reject the performance in a reasonable time can be interpreted as an implied acceptance of the performance.[19]

If the federal government elects to reject the performance, it must give the contractor an opportunity to correct the defects if they can be cured within the contract schedule.[20] If the Contracting Officer orders correction instead of rejection and replacement, the contractor is entitled to a reasonable time within which to make the correction, without regard to the original schedule.[21]

If the contractor fails to replace or correct rejected work in a timely manner, the government has three remedies. The government can: (1) terminate the contract for default and reprocure the supplies, services or construction; (2) replace or correct the defective supplies, service or construction by contract or using government resources, at the contractor's expense under the inspection clause; or (3) retain the nonconforming supplies, services or construction and reduce the contract price based on the difference in value between the work as delivered and the work contemplated by the contract.[22]

9.9 Limitation on Owner's Inspections

Although the owner has broad rights relating to inspection, a contractor may have various rights and remedies resulting from constructive changes to the contract work, and delays and disruptions caused by the owner's inspections. However, there are particular problems that must be recognized in analyzing inspections related to constructive changes.

9.10 Problems with Authority
Differences in opinion regarding the standards of performance required by the contract or the correct inspection test to be used often cause contractors to claim that they are being required to perform extra work. However, even if the contractor's interpretation was correct and the inspector was wrong, the contractor may be confronted with the argument that the inspector lacked the authority to change the contract and bind the owner.

The issue of the inspector's authority can be complicated. Inspectors seldom have authority to change the contract requirements, but they do have authority to reject work. It is usually held, therefore, that an erroneous rejection is

---

[18] FAR § 46.407(g).
[19] FAR §§ 46.407(g), 52.246-2(f).
[20] FAR § 46.407(b).
[21] *Baifield Indus. Div. A-T-O, Inc.*, ASBCA 14582, 72-2 BCA ¶ 9676.
[22] FAR §§ 52.249-8, 52.249-10, 52.246-2(h), 52.246-4(e), 52.246-12(g), 52.246-2(b), 52.246-4(d), 52.246-12(f).

within their authority and can form the basis of a contract extra. This assumes, of course, proper notice by the contractor and "performance under protest."[23] To avoid disputes over authority, the best procedure to follow is to routinely provide written notice to an authorized owner-representative whenever the actions of an inspector are causing performance and cost beyond those contemplated by the contract.

The federal government frequently argues that its inspectors lack the authority to make a constructive change. In a recent case, the specifications for brick were strict and the contractor's chief mason complied with the requirements by rejecting between 20 and 25 percent of the brick. The manufacturer, the government's on-site representative and the architect agreed that the contractor was being overly critical and told the contractor to stop rejecting brick. Thereafter, the government rejected the brickwork due to an undesirable basketweave appearance and directed the contractor to remove and replace the brick.

The contractor demanded an equitable adjustment for its costs in removing and replacing the brick. The government argued that its on-site representative did not have the authority to direct the contractor to stop rejecting brick. The board of contract appeals held that the inspector's authority depends on the facts and conduct of each case and that the contracting officer can authorize technical personnel (such as inspectors) to give guidance or instruction about specification problems. Therefore, the government was liable for the constructive change that caused the placement of the defective brick.[24]

9.11 Higher Standards of Performance The owner may use any reasonable inspection test. However, it may not adopt a higher standard of performance through the use of inspection procedures or tests that are more stringent than called for by the contract or that are not consistent with industry practice.[25] If higher standards or stricter tests are imposed, the contractor is entitled to additional compensation. Similarly, if the contractor is required by the inspector to use materials or construction methods that are not required by the contract and are more expensive than the contractor's chosen method, a compensable change may result.[26]

Problems may occur in cases where the contract does not clearly define either the standard of workmanship required of the contractor or the standard of inspection to be employed. In such cases, inspectors will often rely upon industry standards and trade customs, or even on subjective standards such as "skillful and workmanlike." Where the use of such criteria actually requires a level of performance in excess of that reasonably contemplated at the time the parties entered into the contract, the contractor may be entitled to extra compensation.

[23] Annot., 2 A.L.R.3d 620, § 22.
[24] *Jordan & Nobles Constr. Co.*, GSBCA 8349, 91-1 BCA § 23,659 (Dec. 31, 1990).
[25] *See Warren Painting Co.*, ASBCA 6511, 61-2 BCA ¶ 3199.
[26] *See, e.g., Jack Graham Corp.*, ASBCA 4585, 58-2 BCA ¶ 1998.

For example, an inspector's use of straightedges and other measuring tools to check stud alignment has been held to amount to a change when no such method was specified in the contract and the normal industry practice was to check alignment by visual inspection.[27]

9.12 Rejecting Acceptable Work An inspector's wrongful rejection of acceptable work involves issues similar to the imposition of increased standards of performance. If work that should have been accepted is "corrected" to a higher standard of quality and additional costs are incurred in the process, a compensable change has occurred.[28]

Where specifications are ambiguous, an inspector's silent acquiescence while the contractor performs in accordance with its own reasonable interpretation of the performance standards may establish that the contractor's approach was reasonable and the work acceptable.[29] Also, if the owner submits to the contractor what purports to be a complete list of defects in the work, the owner may later be prevented from rejecting work that had been corrected pursuant to the list on the ground that its list amounted to a binding interpretation of ambiguous specifications.[30]

Generally, the owner has the right to reject defective work at any time prior to acceptance of the work, and an inspector's observation of nonconforming work does not necessarily preclude later rejection.[31] However, if an owner's delay in rejection of nonconforming work substantially prejudiced the contractor, the owner may be estopped from later rejecting the work.[32] Estoppel will be more likely if the contractor has given clear notice regarding its interpretation of the standards and methods of performance that were used and that later became the subject of the dispute.

9.13 Delay and Disruption In each construction contract there is an implied obligation on the part of the owner not to unduly delay or hinder the work. This duty extends to the owner's exercise of its inspection rights. Thus the standard federal inspection clause states:

> All inspection and tests by the Government shall be performed in such manner as not to unnecessarily delay the work.

This principle is similarly recognized in the AIA Document A201 § 10.1, which requires that the architect "will promptly make such inspection" for final completion. Thus, where unreasonable delay or interference can be dem-

---

[27] *Williams and Dunlap,* ASBCA 6145, 63-1 BCA ¶ 3834.

[28] *See Denton Constr. Co. v. Missouri State Highway Comm'n,* 454 S.W.2d 44 (Mo. 1970); *Byson v. City of Los Angeles,* 308 P.2d 765 (Cal. App. 1957); *Acme Missiles & Constr. Corp.,* ASBCA 13671, 69-1 BCA ¶ 7698.

[29] *See Dondlinger & Sons Constr. Co.,* ASBCA 13651, 70-2 BCA ¶ 8603.

[30] *See Frederick P. Warrick Co.,* ASBCA 9644, 65-2 BCA ¶ 5169.

[31] *Forsberg & Gregory, Inc.,* ASBCA 18457, 75-1 BCA ¶ 11,293.

[32] *See Baltimore Contractors, Inc.,* ASBCA 15852, 73-2 BCA ¶ 10,281.

onstrated on the part of the owner through inspection, a contractor may be entitled to a time extension and recovery of additional costs, or even breach of contract damages.

To determine whether a particular delay was unreasonable, reference must be made to the surrounding facts or circumstances. The basic test is whether the inspector's actions were reasonably necessary to protect the owner's interests, or whether the owner's legitimate objective could have been accomplished by some other, less disruptive, means.[33]

Compensable delays also may be caused by multiple and inconsistent inspections.[34] Likewise, the owner's failure to make a timely inspection after a request by the contractor may result in owner liability.[35]

What may be a timely inspection in one situation will amount to an unreasonable delay in another. For example, in one case, a government inspection three days after the contractor's request was held to be an unreasonable delay, but in another case a ten-day delay was not sufficient to make the inspection untimely.[36]

Unreasonable delays in the review and approval of shop drawings, equipment submittals, material submittals, plans of operations and the government's determinations as to what corrective action is required when defects are discovered have all been held to entitle the contractor to relief. Likewise, when an inspector interferes with a contractor's employees, disrupts the performance sequence or otherwise causes the work to be performed less efficiently, the contractor may be entitled to be reimbursed for the cost of resulting extra work. Such actions may also be construed as a breach of contract.[37]

9.14   Inspection by the Architect/Engineer/Inspector

The party performing the actual inspections has the duty and obligation to perform these inspections adequately and without negligence. Architects, engineers, construction managers, and government inspectors may be liable to the owner, contractor, or other third-parties as a result of failing to fulfill their inspection duties.

Generally, an architect/engineer is required to visit the site at regular intervals, but is not required to perform exhaustive or continuous on-site inspections to check the quality or quantity of the work. The architect/engineer is also generally required to keep the owner informed of the progress of work and to guard the owner against defects and deficiencies in the work.

---

[33] See *S. S. Silberblatt, Inc. v. United States,* 433 F.2d 1314 (Ct. Cl. 1970).
[34] See *WRB Corp. v. United States,* 183 Ct. Cl. 409 (1968); *State Highway Comm'n v. Garton & Garton, Inc.,* 418 P.2d 15 (Wyo. 1966).
[35] See *Larco-Indus. Painting Corp.,* ASBCA 14647, 73-2 BCA ¶ 10,073.
[36] *Compare Kingston Bituminous Prod. Co.,* ASBCA 9964, 67-2 BCA ¶ 6638 with *Fullerton Constr. Co.,* ASBCA 11500, 67-2 BCA ¶ 6394.
[37] See WRB Corp., fn. 34, supra.

In a recent case, an issue existed regarding whether an architect who allegedly failed to make adequate periodic inspections during the work is immune from liability by virtue of a contract provision stating that the architect will not be responsible for the contractor's acts or omissions. The court noted that the architect was required to visit the site periodically in order to be familiar with the progress and quality of the work, to keep the owner informed about the work's progress and quality and to guard the owner against defects in the work. Furthermore, the architect's obligation to issue certificates of payment required him to be familiar with both quantity and quality of work. Therefore, the exculpatory provision excusing the architect from responsibility for construction methods or for the acts or omissions of the contractor did not immunize the architect from liability flowing from a breach of its duty to the owner.[38]

In another case, an architect/engineer firm was held liable to an owner and the contractor's surety for negligently inspecting a roof. Even after repeated warnings by a roofing expert that the roof was not being installed in accordance with the contract specifications, the architect/engineer's resident inspector informed the owner that the roof was fine and that "you don't have to worry about it." In reliance on the inspector's assurances, the owner accepted the building and released all payments to the contractor. A few months later, the roof began to leak and the contractor's attempts to solve the problem were unsuccessful.

The court ruled that the architect/engineer had a duty to inspect the roof construction and to protect the owner against poor work by the contractor. An architect/engineer is required to exercise ordinary professional skills and diligence and this duty is nondelegable. Since the architect/engineer breached its obligation to the owner under the above circumstances, the architect/engineer was liable.[39]

9.15 Inspection by the Contractor

The contractor's inspection duties in the routine performance of a construction contract include not only the inspection of the work in place, but an inspection of job conditions, including job cleanup, potential safety hazards and monitoring the progress of the work and schedule. In addition to its own work, the contractor must inspect performance of its subcontractors and material suppliers. Most large construction contracts impose specific burdens upon the contractor to perform such inspections. However, even if no specific contract burden is applied, prudence dictates that such inspection should be carried out at all levels and in a routine fashion. It should include a regular process

---

[38] *Diocese of Rochester v. R. Monde Contractors, Inc.*, 562 N.Y.S.2d 593 (App. Div. 1989), *aff'd*, 561 N.Y.S.2d 659 (1990).

[39] *URS Co., Inc. v. Gulfport-Biloxi Regional Airport Auth.*, 544 So.2d 824 (Miss. 1989); *but see Watson, Watson, Rutland/Architects, Inc. v. Montgomery County Bd. of Educ.*, 559 So.2d 168 (Ala. 1990).

for reporting and exchanging information in order for the contractor to complete the project promptly, expeditiously and economically.

The contractor may also be required to obtain test results of work in place or materials to be used. Normally these are obtained through designated independent testing laboratories. For example, one usually must make test cylinders of the concrete mix. Sometimes such tests are set forth in the specifications and in other cases they are imposed by industry standards incorporated expressly or impliedly into the contract documents. Such inspections not only satisfy the contractor's obligations to the owner but also help the contractor monitor its own work. They also establish empirical data in the event that disputes later develop or a failure occurs.

In federal government construction, the standard federal inspection clause places primary responsibility for contract compliance on the contractor. In addition, most federal agencies have included provisions in construction contracts that place on the contractor the specific duty to conduct inspections and ensure that the work complies with the plans and specifications. For example, one clause provides:

> The Contractor shall (i) maintain an adequate inspection system and perform such inspections as will ensure that the work performed under the contract conforms to contract requirements, and (ii) maintain and make available to the Government adequate records of such inspections.[40]

Similarly, the contract and applicable regulations may also include various contractor recordkeeping and/or certification requirements.[41] In one case, the board gave a strict interpretation to such a requirement. The contract required the contractor to designate an individual who would be responsible to specifically test each unit before delivery and to issue a certification. Instead, the contractor relied upon the supplier's testing procedure and certification, which did not comply with the contract's requirements. The contracting officer terminated the contractor for default because of failure to provide the required inspection. The default termination was upheld on the ground that the government was entitled to the specific type of inspection set forth in the contract.

9.16   ACCEPTANCE

9.17   General

Acceptance of a project is of great significance. Acceptance generally limits the owner's ability to complain of defects and reject work. Acceptance may also commence the running of warranties. Contractors and owners often dispute when the project is complete, which frequently results in the withholding

---

[40] FAR § 52.246.12(b).
[41] *Acorn Specialty & Supply Co.*, GSBCA 7577, 85-2 BCA ¶ 17,995.

of formal acceptance by the owner. The theory of constructive acceptance, however, has been developed to help contractors avoid the harsh consequences of the unreasonable withholding of formal acceptance. A theory closely related to constructive acceptance is substantial completion. This theory recognizes the point where the owner has basically received the benefit of the bargain, although all technicalities may not have been fulfilled.[42]

It is a well-recognized rule of contract law that a party entitled to performance may waive strict performance.[43] In the context of the construction contract, this means that the owner may acquiesce to the contractor's failure to perform according to the strict terms of the agreement. Such waiver or acquiescence is often established through acceptance. But courts are increasingly reluctant to bar an owner's right to recover for defective construction merely because of "acceptance."[44]

The inspection and acceptance clause in federal government contracts indicates that an acceptance pursuant to the clause becomes final and binding except in the limited situations provided:

. . . Acceptance shall be final and conclusive except for latent defects, fraud, gross mistakes amounting to fraud. . . .[45]

In private construction, if the owner makes final payment, all claims by the owner may be waived except those arising from:

1. liens, claims [made pursuant to the contract's dispute resolution process], security interests or encumbrances arising out of the contract and which are unsettled;

2. failure of the work to comply with the requirements of the contract documents; or

3. the terms of special warranties required by the contract documents.[46]

9.18 Types of Acceptance: Formal versus Constructive

Acceptance has been found to occur under AIA Document A201 when there has been final completion and final payment. In federal contracting, execution of the proper form by an authorized government representative may constitute acceptance. Further, where the owner has taken no positive action to accept or reject, a failure to reject noncomplying work within a reasonable time may constitute a "constructive" acceptance.[47]

---

[42] *J. M. Beeson Co. v. Satori*, 553 So.2d 180 (Fla. Dist. Ct. App. 1989).

[43] *See Trustees of Ind. Univ. v. Aetna Cas. & Sur. Co.*, 920 F.2d 429 (7th Cir. 1990).

[44] *Davidge v. H. H. Constr. Co.*, 432 So.2d 393 (La. Ct. App. 1988).

[45] FAR § 52.246-12(i).

[46] *See* AIA Document A-201 § 4.3.5 (1987 ed.) (similar provision).

[47] *See Havens Steel Co. v. Randolph Eng'g Co.*, 613 F. Supp. 514 (D.C. Mo. 1985), *aff'd*, 813 F.2d 186 (8th Cir. 1987).

In *Tranco Indus., Inc.,*[48] a constructive acceptance was found where the government failed to inspect the painting of fuel tanks for three months. The board ruled that the proper standard for timely acceptance or rejection is "a reasonable time for prompt action under the circumstances." In this case, the board held a three-month delay from paint sample approval to final inspection was unreasonable and that, while a change in contracting officers justified a two-week delay, it did not justify the balance of the government's tardiness.

In contrast, it has long been recognized that mere occupation and use of a structure by the owner does not constitute acceptance or waiver of defects therein.[49] This rule applies as well when the owner has taken possession of the project with the express understanding that defects will be remedied at a later date.[50] The latest edition of AIA Document A201 General Conditions has a new section entitled "Partial Occupancy or Use," which provides that "Unless otherwise agreed upon, partial occupancy or use of a portion or portions of the Work shall not constitute acceptance of Work not complying with the requirements of the Contract Documents."[51]

In federal construction, the concept of constructive acceptance is better developed than in private construction and is recognized in procurement regulations, which define acceptance as:

> . . . [T]he act of an authorized representative of the Government by which the Government, for itself or as agent of another, assumes ownership of existing identified supplies tendered or approves specific services rendered as partial or complete performance of the contract.[52]

Similarly, the "use and possession prior to completion" clause provides that "the Government shall have the right to take possession of or use of any completed or partially completed part of the work . . . ," but that "such possession or use shall not be deemed an acceptance of any work under the contract." However, in certain cases where that clause has not been employed, government use, possession, or control, coupled with a failure to indicate that the work was not complete, amounted to an acceptance.[53] In federal procurement, constructive acceptance (as with formal acceptance) commences the warranty period under the contract.[54]

Moreover, one should also realize that individual contract actions alone may not constitute an acceptance; for example:

· Payment, by itself, does not constitute an implied acceptance;[55]

---

[48] ASBCA 26305, 83-2 BCA ¶ 16,679.
[49] *See Granite Constr. Co.,* ENG BCA 4642, 89-3 BCA ¶ 21,946.
[50] *Brouillette v. Consolidated Constr. Co. of Fl., Inc.,* 422 So.2d 176 (La. Ct. App. 1982).
[51] A201 § 9.9.3.
[52] FAR § 46.101.
[53] *See Bell & Flynn, Inc.,* ASBCA 11038, 66-2 BCA ¶ 5855.
[54] *See Paul Tishman Co.,* GSBCA 1099, 1964 BCA ¶ 4256.
[55] *See Abney Constr. Co.,* ASBCA 26358, 83-1 BCA ¶ 16,246; *G. M. Co. Mfg., Inc.,* ASBCA 5345, 60-2 BCA ¶ 2759.

- Visits by government representatives during fabrication of equipment did not constitute inspection and acceptance;[56]
- The government's failure to inspect is not implied acceptance waiving strict compliance;[57] and
- Mere acceptance of the delivery of the supplies is not an implied acceptance.[58]

The specific facts and circumstances must be viewed in light of the applicable contract language to determine if the owner's actions amount to an acceptance.

9.19 Problem of Authority in Constructive Acceptance

The actual authority of the individual whose action or inaction is being relied upon is a factor that may affect the determination of whether there has been a formal or a constructive acceptance. This is especially true in federal government work since the acceptance will be binding only if made by a person authorized to accept on behalf of the government.[59] In private agency law, an employer may be bound by an employee under the legal theory of apparent authority if the employer has permitted the employee to assume authority or has held the employee out as possessing authority.[60]

Recognizing the importance of effective government control over the conduct of its agents, the boards and courts have generally rejected the apparent authority rule, holding that actual authority is required to bind the government.[61] Even government personnel with official sounding titles such as contract specialists, negotiators, and administrators, personnel who handle the day-to-day contracting activity of the government, generally do not have authority to order additional work or otherwise obligate the government.[62]

9.20 Limitations on the Finality of Acceptance

In order for the owner to waive strict performance or to acquiesce in the deviation from the contract documents through acceptance, the owner or its authorized representative must be aware of the defect or the deviation.[63] However, courts have ruled that an owner waives deviations from the contract where the owner *should have* been aware of the deviations. Whether particular

---

[56] *See J. W. Bateson Co.,* GSBCA 3157, 71-1 BCA ¶ 8820.

[57] *See Waterbury Co.,* ASBCA 6634, 61-2 BCA ¶ 3158.

[58] *See Lox Equip. Co.,* ASBCA 8518, 1964 BCA ¶ 4469.

[59] *See Inter-Tribal Council of Nev., Inc.,* IBCA 1234-12-78, 83-1 BCA ¶ 16,433 (1983).

[60] *See* Restatement (2d) of Agency § 8.

[61] *See Federal Crop Insur. Corp. v. Merrill,* 332 U.S. 380 (1947).

[62] *See, e.g., General Elec. Co.,* ASBCA 11990, 67-1 BCA ¶ 6377, 188 Ct. Cl. 620, 412 F.2d 1215 *mot. for reconsid. denied,* 188 Ct. Cl. 116, 416 F.2d 1320 (1969).

[63] *See Cantrell v. Woodhill Enters., Inc.,* 160 S.E.2d 476 (N.C. 1968). *See also South Carolina Elec. and Gas Co. v. Combustion Eng'g, Inc.,* 322 S.E.2d 453 (S.C. Ct. App. 1984).

acts or conduct amount to an acceptance and thus a waiver of strict performance is a fact question that depends upon the circumstances of each case.

Defects that are not apparent and that cannot be discovered until a later date (i.e., latent defects) are not accepted. This is especially true on federal construction projects.[64] Also, where a contractor knowingly misrepresents the condition or quality of its work with the intent to deceive, the government is considered to have been induced to accept defective work as a result and may recover the costs of repairing such defects from the contractor.[65]

Similarly, where the contractor makes gross mistakes or misrepresents a material fact without the intent to deceive the government, the contractor may be liable for such defects despite government acceptance of the work. One such case involved contractor changes to a drawing that had been previously approved by the government, and the contractor's subsequent failure to alert government officials to the change before the drawing was used in checking the contractor's production run.[66]

Closely related to waiver by acceptance is the issue of whether progress payments constitute a waiver of defects. The jurisdictions appear evenly divided: some state courts rule that partial payments constitute a waiver of defects while other states rule the opposite.[67] The argument for waiver of defects by partial payment is much more persuasive when the defects were known, when the owner or its representative failed to protest and when there was no express agreement to remedy them. Generally, however, the contract will provide that any progress payment will not constitute acceptance of any work not in compliance with the contract documents.[68]

Waiver or acceptance of defective performance by the owner may preclude it from refusing to pay the contractor the reasonable value of the work or its price according to the terms of the contract.[69] Similarly, where the owner accepts the work as being in full compliance with the contract, it is generally not possible to maintain an action later against the contractor to recover for deviations from the contract documents or recoup such damages in an action brought by the contractor for compensation.[70]

9.21 Contract Provisions Related to the Finality of Acceptance

Contracts often include clauses aimed at qualifying the significance of acceptance. For example, to avoid the waiver of contract deviations by completion, final payment and acceptance, AIA Document A201, § 4.3.5.2 (1987 ed.), provides:

[64] *See Kaminer Constr. Corp. v. United States,* 488 F.2d 980 (Ct. Cl. 1973).
[65] *Nasatka & Sons, Inc.,* IBCA 1157-6-77, 79-2 BCA ¶ 14,064.
[66] *See Catalytic Eng'g and Mfg. Corp.,* ASBCA 15257, 72-1 BCA ¶ 9342.
[67] *See* Annotation, 66 *A.L.R.*2d 570 (and authorities cited therein).
[68] *See* A201 § 9.6.6. (1987 ed.).
[69] *See Milaeger Well Drilling Co.,* fn. 10, supra.
[70] *City of Gering v. Patricia G. Smith Co.,* 337 N.W.2d 747 (Neb. 1983); *John Price Assocs., Inc. v. Davis,* 588 P.2d 713 (Utah 1978).

The making of final payment shall constitute a waiver of Claims by the Owner except those arising from:

. . .

2. Failure of the Work to comply with the requirements of the Contract Documents.[71]

In the absence of a nonwaiver contract provision, waiver may still be implied if the owner or its representative had an opportunity during the progress of the work to inspect and reject work or materials that obviously did not comply with the contract requirements but failed to do so.[72] In such a case, failure to object during the progress of the work may amount to a waiver of the defect. However, the mere presence of the owner or the representative at the site does not *necessarily* constitute a waiver, such as when a defect is not readily discoverable.[73]

Similarly, under the standard inspection and acceptance clause in federal contracts, there are several exceptions to the finality of acceptance, such as latent defects, fraud and gross mistakes amounting to fraud. Also, the government has rights under the warranty or guarantee provisions.

9.22 Substantial Completion

Substantial completion has been defined in numerous ways and has been the subject of extensive litigation. Generally, when the owner has the use and benefit of the contractor's work and the project is capable of being used for the intended purpose, substantial completion has occurred.[74]

AIA Document A201, § 9.8, defines substantial completion as follows:

Substantial completion is the stage in the progress of the Work when the Work or a designated portion thereof is sufficiently complete in accordance with the Contract Documents so the Owner can occupy or utilize the Work for its intended use.

The new AIA A201 General Conditions have also made the requirements for substantial completion more akin to those for final completion. The architect is required to inspect the work for any item of work not in accordance with the Contract Documents at the time the contractor considers the work to be substantially complete. The contractor now must correct any item found by the architect to be deficient before a certificate of substantial completion will be issued.[75]

---

[71] *See also* A201 § 9.9.4 (1976 ed.) (same provision).
[72] *See Florida Ice Mach. Corp. v. Branton Insulation, Inc.,* 290 So.2d 415 (La. Ct. App. 1974); *also see Brand S. Roofing,* ASBCA 24688, 82-1 BCA ¶ 15,513.
[73] *See J. W. Bateson Co.,* fn. 56, supra.
[74] *See J. M. Beeson Co.,* fn. 42, supra; *Waynick Constr. Inc. v. York,* 319 S.E.2d 304 (N.C. Ct. App. 1984); *Royal Ornamental Iron, Inc. v. Devon Bank,* 336 N.E.2d 105 (Ill. Ct. App. 1975).
[75] *See* A201 § 9.8.2.

The date of substantial completion is often a crucial date in construction litigation. Basically there are two points connected with substantial completion. First, once substantial completion has been attained, the owner has received essentially what was bargained for and the contractor has substantially performed its obligations; thus, the contractor is usually entitled to the balance of the contract price less the cost of remedying minor defects. Second, liquidated damages may stop after this date.[76]

In many states, substantial completion marks the commencement of a special limitation period, sometimes called a statute of repose, for actions against persons performing or furnishing design, planning, supervision, observation of construction or construction of any improvement to real property. Also, upon substantial completion, the contractor may also recover on the contract and need not rely upon the equitable theory of *quantum meruit* in order to recover for work performed and materials supplied.[77]

9.23   WARRANTIES

It is generally recognized in both commercial law and in government contract law that there are two kinds of warranties applicable to any contractual arrangement. These are: (1) express warranties, which are express promises, either oral or written, and (2) implied warranties, which commercial law implies from the nature of the transaction between the parties unless the contract expressly provides that such warranties are inapplicable.

9.24   Express Warranties

Express warranties relating to construction contract performance can be complex and do not have to be labeled as a warranty or guarantee in order to have the effect of an express warranty. An express warranty has been defined as:

> Any affirmation of fact or any promise by the seller relating to the goods is an express warranty if the natural tendency of such affirmation or promise is to induce the owner to purchase the goods, and if the buyer purchases the goods relying thereon.[78]

In that regard, it is essential that both parties to a construction contract carefully review all the contract plans and documents to determine whether requirements and language that may have the effect of providing an express

---

[76] *See Phillips v. Ben M. Hogan Co.,* 594 S.W.2d 39 (Ark. Ct. App. 1990); *Hungerford Constr. Co. v. Florida Citrus Exposition,* 410 F.2d 1229 (5th Cir.), *cert. denied,* 396 U.S. 928 (1969).

[77] *See Cox v. Fremont County Pub. Bldg. Auth.,* 415 F.2d 882 (10th Cir. 1969); 13 Am. Jur. 2d, Building and Construction Contracts §§ 41, 110.

[78] 8 S. Williston, A Treatise on the Law of Contracts § 970 at 484 (3rd ed. 1964).

warranty are intended and are desirable under all the surrounding facts and circumstances. Without this type of careful review and analysis, the owner may find that it is buying protection that it did not desire. Conversely, the contractor may find that it warranted a certain result or performance and that the risk attending such a warranty was not considered in the preparation of the bid or proposal for the work.

The contractor may "expressly warrant" that the material and workmanship furnished for the project are free from defects for a specified period of time. Liability under these express warranties expands the scope of the contractor's responsibility for defective work beyond the date of final acceptance. Generally, the courts construe these warranties as additions to and *not* substitutions for other responsibilities of the contractor.[79]

AIA Document A201 contains a number of express warranties. The first is a general warranty that guarantees all equipment and materials are new and in conformance with the contract documents and that all work is of good quality. A201 § 3.5.1 (1987 ed.) provides:

> The Contractor warrants to the Owner and Architect that *materials and equipment furnished under the Contract will be of good quality and new unless otherwise required or permitted by the Contract Documents, that the Work will be free from defects not inherent in the quality required or permitted, and that the Work will conform with the requirements of the Contract Documents.* (Emphasis added.)

This express warranty may be limited only by the applicable statute of limitations. Thus the provision could extend the contractor's obligations for a substantial period. Furthermore, this period may be extended even further by the so-called "discovery rule." This rule provides that a cause of action does not accrue, and that the statute of limitations period does not even begin to "tick," until the defect is, or should have been, discovered.[80]

Warranties that expressly state a period of discovery, such as twelve months, generally do not limit other avenues of recovery, and do not work to reduce applicable statutes of limitation.[81]

A warranty is generally not waived by final payment or completion.[82] In addition, A201, § 12.2.2, provides a one-year repair warranty. This one-year warranty is essentially a repair obligation that commences from the date of substantial completion. It does not limit the general warranty of § 3.5.1., nor does it limit the rights under the general warranty of good workmanship.[83]

Additional express warranties may be required in connection with equipment supplied by the contract. Such specific warranties are usually spelled

---

[79] *See Tassan v. United Dev. Co.,* 410 N.E.2d 902 (Ill. App. Ct. 1980).

[80] *See Arst v. Man Barken, Inc.,* 655 S.W.2d 845 (Mo. Ct. App. 1983).

[81] *See Mounts v. Parker,* 727 P.2d 594 (Okla. 1986).

[82] *See A201 § 4.3.5.*

[83] *See Burton-Dixie Corp. v. Timothy McCarthy Constr. Co.,* 436 F.2d 405 (5th Cir. 1971); *Houston Fire and Cas. Insur. Co. v. Riesel Indep. School Dist.,* 375 S.W.2d 323 (Tex. Civ. App. 1964, writ ref'd n.r.e.).

out under the provisions of the specifications to which they apply rather than in the general conditions. They are often in the nature of guarantees of performance and agreement to repair defects for a specified period of time.

The express warranties required by the contract documents generally begin to run from the date of substantial completion.[84] Other special warranties may commence at delivery of the machinery or commencement of operations.

9.25 Implied Warranties

Both commercial and government contracts have been held to contain warranties that are implied by the law for the benefit of one of the parties to the contract. Probably the best known implied warranty in construction is the implied warranty attached to detailed design specifications furnished by one of the parties to the contract.

9.26 *The Owner's Warranty of the Adequacy of the Plans and Specifications* It is a well-settled doctrine of construction that the party who furnishes the plans and specifications impliedly warrants the adequacy and sufficiency of those documents. The United States Supreme Court recognized this doctrine in the case of *United States v. Spearin*.[85] The Court stated in that case that:

> [I]f the contractor is bound to build according to plans and specifications prepared by the owner, the contractor will not be responsible for the consequences of defects in the plans and specifications.[86]

It is important to remember that this so-called Spearin Doctrine can apply to the contractor as well as the owner. For example, in the "design/build" context, the contractor warrants the adequacy of the plans and specifications that it supplies.[87] For a further discussion of the Spearin Doctrine, see other chapters of this manual.

9.27 *Contractor's Implied Warranties* When there are no express warranties made by the contractor, courts will often "imply" a warranty of workmanship. The formulation of the implied warranty differs from jurisdiction to jurisdiction. Courts have stated that contractors warrant that they will perform in a "workmanlike manner and without negligence",[88] or that the work will be done in a "good and workmanlike manner."[89]

---

[84] *See* A201 §§ 9.8.1, 9.8.2.

[85] 248 U.S. 132 (1918).

[86] *Id.* at 136.

[87] *See, e.g., Barraque v. Neff,* 11 So.2d 697 (La. 1942). *See also Segall Co., Inc. v. W. D. Glassell Co., Inc.,* 401 So.2d 483 (La. Ct. App. 1981).

[88] *See Kubby v. Crescent Steel,* 466 P.2d 753 (Ariz. 1970).

[89] *See Moore v. Werner,* 418 S.W.2d 918 (Tex. Civ. App. 1967, no writ); *see also Scott v. Strickland,* 691 P.2d 45 (Kan. Ct. App. 1984); among others.

POINTS TO REMEMBER

The following are practical pointers to remember during the construction of a project. These practical pointers relate to the inspection, acceptance and warranty aspects of a construction project.

Inspection

- Whether you are the owner, architect, contractor or subcontractor, quality assurance is the key to avoiding disputes. The principal obligation for guaranteeing quality is on the contractor. The contractor has the responsibility to comply strictly with the plans and specifications. In government contracts, the contractor has an obligation to establish a system to assure quality performance. However, as the case law demonstrates, the owner and architect can also be liable for costs arising from improper inspections.

- The owner and contractor should consider the cost of inspections at the time of bid. Generally, the owner and contractor are each responsible for their cost of inspection. The contractor has the obligation to assist the owner or the government in inspecting completed work. The owner has the right to conduct reasonable inspections. The owner also has the right to reinspect and reject work that was previously inspected. The owner must remember, however, that it cannot conduct unreasonable or wholly inconsistent inspections.

- The owner's inspection must not unduly delay the contractor's work. The contractor should promptly notify the owner when inspections are required and should also notify the owner or government when the inspections are delaying the contractor's work. As with all construction matters, written documentation regarding delays, hindrances or interferences is a must to protect your rights.

- If a dispute arises regarding whether the work was wrongfully rejected, the contractor should investigate the methods used by the inspector. If work is rejected improperly, a contractor can be entitled to an extension of time and added compensation for the extra work. Again, to protect your interests, whether you are the owner or contractor, written documentation regarding the inspections or written notice of the objection to the type of inspection is crucial.

- A constructive change may occur where an inspector improperly interprets the contract specifications. If an inspector is misinterpreting a contract requirement, the contractor should immediately bring this to the attention of the owner or contracting officer. In federal government contracts, if the contractor gets a ruling from the inspector and not the contracting officer, the contractor might not be entitled to additional costs because the government may argue that the inspector did not have authority to make the constructive change.

Acceptance

- Contractors must differentiate between the authority required in a federal government contract versus a private contract. In a federal government contract, acceptance can only occur when the individual with actual authority accepts the work. Generally, only the contracting officer has actual authority to accept the work. However, in private contracts, most inspectors and other individuals working for the owner can be held to have apparent authority to accept the work.
- Generally, acceptance requires final completion and final payment. However, under certain circumstances "constructive" acceptance can occur where the owner utilizes the area of the project and acts without objections to any of the contractor's performance. Similarly, where a party delays formal acceptance or rejection for an unreasonable time, constructive acceptance can occur.
- Generally, once the work is accepted, a contractor is relieved of responsibility, except where a warranty clause exists. However, a contractor can be liable for latent defects that could not have been discovered at the time of acceptance.
- An owner can be held to have waived a defect when the owner knew or should have known of the defect at the time of acceptance. However, if the contractor makes a knowing misrepresentation with intent to deceive the owner regarding the completion of the work, the contractor may be liable for the results of the defective performance and for fraud.
- An issue related to acceptance is substantial completion. Substantial completion in the construction industry has many legal ramifications. Substantial completion occurs when the owner receives generally what he has bargained for and the contractor is then entitled to recover the contract price minus cost of remedying minor defects. Furthermore, when substantial completion occurs, the owner is generally not entitled to assess additional liquidated damages.

Warranty

- All parties in the construction realm must be very cautious regarding the creation of express warranties. Not only do contracts contain express warranties, but also any affirmation of fact by any member of the construction industry can create an express warranty. Generally, the extent of a party's responsibility under an express warranty is limited only by statutes of limitation. However, in some states, the "discovery rule" can extend the applicable statute of limitation indefinitely.
- The main implied warranty in the construction industry is known as the Spearin Doctrine, which states that the owner warrants the adequacy of the plans and specifications. In the design/build situation, the contractor

can be responsible under the Spearin Doctrine for a subcontractor's and sub-subcontractor's work because the contractor, by entering into a design/build contract, warrants the adequacy of the plans.

· Many other implied warranties can exist in the construction industry. For example, all parties on a construction project have an implied duty to act in good faith to perform the work adequately and in a workmanlike manner.

10

MANAGEMENT AND DOCUMENTATION TECHNIQUES TO AVOID DISPUTES

10.1 THE EVER-PRESENT RISK OF DISPUTES IN CONSTRUCTION

Construction is a dispute-prone industry, and claims are a fact of life. Even successful projects have claims. Claims are a natural outgrowth of a complex and highly competitive process during which the unexpected often happens. Careful organization and coordination of numerous parties is required, and it may then be outside parties who control many of the circumstances and events that generate claims. The potential for claims cannot be ignored. The responsible owner, contractor, subcontractor or designer, as part of doing business, recognizes the need to anticipate claims and to develop effective and affirmative strategies for dealing with them.

The best way to handle claims is to anticipate them and avoid them as much as possible. Despite the uniqueness of each project and its participants, there are certain recurring problems that generate disputes. The past is prologue and some of those recurring problems can be avoided, their impact mitigated, or, at a minimum, some preparation made for the dispute if it should occur. Of course, too much focus on eliminating all risks and anticipating claims and disputes can also create problems and a paralysis that can impair one's ability to do business effectively. A certain element of risk must be recognized and accepted. Risk can only be mitigated, not eliminated.

This chapter focuses on those measures that can be taken at the outset of a project to avoid or effectively prepare for and successfully deal with disputes when they cannot be avoided. Common sense, planning, skill and experience can help identify those strategies for avoiding and effectively dealing with disputes.

10.2 INVOLVING REPUTABLE AND RELIABLE PARTICIPANTS IN THE PROJECT

Construction is a cooperative enterprise involving numerous entities and disciplines, from design professionals, the owner or developer, and lender through the prime contractor, subcontractors and suppliers, each with an integral function. A failure by any participant to perform properly can mean disaster for the entire project and the rest of the participants.

The initial choice of project participants can dictate the destiny of the project and is one of the first steps in avoiding claims. Many headaches and possible losses can be avoided simply by investigating the past performance record of the other parties, rather than looking solely at the lowest price or the opportunity to obtain some work. By dealing with reputable companies and individuals with a proven ability to perform, by running credit checks and by inquiring about the experience of others with that particular company, bad risks and big mistakes can be avoided.

Naturally, the owner is in the best position to control the selection of project participants because under most contracting schemes the owner selects the designer and the contractor. The owner can also have a significant impact on subcontractor selection. The prime contractor, who stands in a similar position to the owner, has the greater control over the selection of subcontractors, as does the architect or lead designer over the selection of its subconsultants. When the choice of a specific party would create a risk of claims or disputes to the extent that any reasonable return is jeopardized, that party should not be used on the project, regardless of price. On the other hand, the prime contractor cannot select the owner or developer of a project. The contractor, however, does decide with whom it wants to do business, as do subcontractors. Sometimes the risks of a project or of doing business with a particular owner are simply too great, and prudence dictates that certain opportunities be foregone. Higher volume and backlog figures are meaningless if they engender unnecessary risks and do not translate to profit. Despite the time crunch and euphoria often associated with the beginning of a project, everyone involved should consider certain key factors when selecting project participants: the financial condition of the parties, their qualification for bonds, evidence of their technical skills and their reputation in the industry. Even a cursory investigation of potential project participants may yield clues to future problems.

Money, if not "the root of all evil," is the source of many disputes and claims that arise on a construction project. The financial resources of the owner are probably of paramount concern. An underfinanced owner virtually dooms any project. Although the possibility of lien rights might provide comfort, if the owner goes under, the likelihood of full and complete payment to the contractor is pretty dim. Considering the preeminent influence of the owner on the success or failure of a project, contractors and architects are wise to subject the owner's background to an informal "prequalification" process, like that used on other project participants, to confirm that the owner has the capacity to meet its commitments. In addition to other independent sources that may be available to obtain information about the owner's finances, subparagraph 2.2.1 of the standard General Conditions published by the American Institute of Architects, AIA Document A201 (1987 ed.), allows the contractor to demand reasonable evidence of the owner's ability to finance the work. Subparagraph 2.1.2 also requires the owner to provide written information regarding title to the property as well as any changes in title, if requested by the contractor.

The financial condition of contractors and subcontractors is also extremely important. A subcontractor who has insufficient working capital may bring a myriad of problems, such as slow deliveries of materials as suppliers grow concerned about the subcontractor's ability to pay. This can have a ripple effect on other work. Similarly, a contractor needing cash flow may front-end load his bid and his pay requests. The early overpayment caused by front-end loading may result in the contractor's default on the latter part of the project as contract funds run out. Unfortunately, there are few, if any, effective remedies against an unbonded, insolvent contractor. The typical action to recover completion costs is often pointless when the default resulted directly from the contractor's financial problems.

An obvious source of financial protection for owners is to require payment and performance bonds. Bonding serves two purposes. First, the contractor's competence and financial well-being are endorsed by the surety's underwriting department, which is also trying to avoid bad risks. If a contractor is incapable of obtaining bonding, it means sureties have a grave concern about its ability to complete a project. That warning is probably best heeded. Second, and more directly, the bonds represent a financial guarantee. A performance bond usually means that if the contractor defaults and fails to complete, the surety will complete performance or pay damages up to the limit of the penal sum of the bond. In contrast, a labor and material payment bond helps assure the owner that labor and materials will be paid for and creates alternatives to the filing of liens on the project.

Even if provided, payment and performance bonds are not a cure-all. It is also necessary to consider carefully the financial stability of the surety itself. Over the years, too many sureties have themselves gone bankrupt. Moreover, even solvent, well-financed sureties are far from an automatic source of relief. Claims under the bond can themselves be the subject of lengthy disputes and litigation.

Of course, there are concerns about technical qualifications that go beyond money. For example, licensing requirements provide some protection from incompetent and inexperienced contractors, particularly in the skilled trades such as electrical and mechanical. Licensing should be deemed a bare minimum requirement, however, and not an endorsement of qualifications for any type of work authorized by a particular license. Inquiries into the contractor's experience on particular types and sizes of projects should also be made.

There is a big difference between installing plumbing in a low-rise apartment building and installing the mechanical systems for a major health care facility. The owner's technical capabilities and qualifications to handle a particular type or size of project are also relevant. However, the owners shortcoming may be offset by the association of capable consultants.

More subjective reports about other parties should also be considered, but perhaps be given lesser weight. For example, engaging a subcontractor with a reputation for shoddy or defective work may result in the prime having to remedy unsatisfactory work at its own expense. A particularly litigious owner may refuse to negotiate a settlement in the event of a dispute in this type of situation, forcing the contractor into more expensive arbitration or court battles.

Even if an owner, designer or contractor appears to have the qualifications and established track record to pass muster as a company, it is important to consider the personnel that will be devoted to the particular project. Companies can be too successful, causing them to be stretched too thin, with all their capable and experienced personnel assigned and consumed by other projects. The company is certainly important, but the individuals representing that company and executing responsibilities and work in the field are no less important.

10.3 DEFINING RIGHTS, RESPONSIBILITIES AND RISKS: THE PARTIES AND THEIR CONTRACTS

A written contract generally provides the foundation for each of the numerous relationships and binds the disparate project participants into a cohesive force to get the job built. Keeping those participants together requires in part anticipating issues and events that might create disputes and detract from the goal of prompt and cost-effective completion. This is done by a combination of allocating risks among the parties, so it is clear who will have to bear the burden if the risk becomes reality, and providing mechanisms for resolving disputes when the risk allocation is not clear or when there is disagreement. A well-drafted contract is another important element in effectively managing a project and avoiding or efficiently dealing with claims.

Clarity, common sense and precision should be employed in the drafting of contract language. Such efforts will hopefully limit later uncertainty and misunderstanding among the parties, and eliminate the need to refer to some third-party decision-maker, in court or arbitration, to determine how the contract will be interpreted. Unreasonable and overly burdensome terms should be avoided as they can unnecessarily drive up the cost of the work through inflated contingencies and may be difficult to enforce. On the other hand, such harsh terms cannot be ignored in an unrealistically optimistic view that they will not be enforced or that circumstances relating to those harsh terms will not arise on the project. The parties must grapple with the tough issues raised by their conflicting interests in the contract preparation stage or face the prospect of much more serious disagreements and disputes during the performance of the contract.

10.4   CONTRACT FRAMEWORK

Establishing the contract framework for the project is a threshold decision that must be made by the owner. The selection depends on a variety of factors, including the owner's needs and its expertise and capabilities. Construction projects have traditionally been designed, bid, built, and paid for within a framework of strictly defined roles, relationships and procedures. This has proven satisfactory for many construction projects, but perceived weaknesses in the traditional method have led to consideration and use of new, alternative methods, such as the various forms of construction management, multi-prime contracting and design/build contracts.[1] The new methods have provided many advantages, but the manner in which they diverge from clearly defined practices and roles requires careful attention in the contract drafting phase to make certain that the advantages in use are not lost through unanticipated problems and disputes.

10.5   STANDARD CONTRACT FORMS AND KEY CONTRACT PROVISIONS

There are a number of available standard contract forms that establish the various relationships on a construction project. The documents published by the American Institute of Architects (AIA) are by far the most widely used and most generally accepted. The Associated General Contractors of America (AGC) and the Engineers Joint Contract Documents Committee (EJCDC) also publish contract documents. The provisions of the AIA documents are generally well understood by developers, architects, contractors, lenders and others involved in the construction process. These common forms permit all parties to focus on critical variables when negotiating construction transactions, and obviate the need to start from scratch with each new construction transaction.

The AIA documents are fairly well integrated, with the terms of the various contracts coordinated with and complementing each other.[2] This consistency enhances the reliability of the AIA documents. The AIA documents have the advantage of familiarity and acceptance in the industry, but do not necessarily meet the needs of each and every project. Some modification may be required

---

[1] *See generally* Bynum, *Construction Management and Design-Build/Fast Tract Construction from the Perspective of a General Contractor,* 46 Law & Contemp. Probs. 25 (1983).

[2] *See generally* J. Sweet, *Sweet on Construction Industry Contracts* (John Wiley & Sons, 3d ed., 1996).

for each specific situation. Moreover, it must be recognized that the AIA documents were drafted by an association that strongly promotes the interests of the architect, often at the expense of the owner and contractor.

Whether reliance is placed on a standard form, a custom-drafted contract, or some combination of the two, certain contract provisions are of critical importance in anticipating, avoiding and resolving claims. They are:

· Payment
· Time for completion and time extensions
· Damages for delay
· Changes in the work
· Termination for default and for convenience
· Changed conditions
· Dispute resolution
· Insurance

Careful attention should also be paid to the use of liquidated damages or no-damage-for-delay clauses, as well as to exculpatory and indemnity provisions, which can weigh heavily in the resolution of claims. It is also worthwhile to consider whether the parties intend for Article 2 of the Uniform Commercial Code (UCC), which governs the sale of goods, to apply to their construction contract.[3] Arbitration as a means of resolving construction claims is discussed separately in Chapter 14.

10.6 AVOIDING AND PREPARING FOR DISPUTES THROUGH PROPER MANAGEMENT AND DOCUMENTATION

The prudent and realistic contractor designs and utilizes systems and procedures to manage, monitor and document the work and progress on the project. These systems serve two important functions. First, they ensure an adequate flow of information to facilitate proper project control and coordination, including adjustments needed to respond to unexpected circumstances. Second, they aid in the compilation of an accurate and complete record of job conditions and problems and their impact on the project. The contractor certainly bears the bulk of responsibility during construction as it installs the work and generally controls the means and methods employed to do so. The architect and owner should not, however, abdicate all responsibility and oversight and totally remove themselves from the construction process in an effort to insulate themselves from liability. They cannot avoid all liability. Moreover, some interaction and monitoring of the construction is always required of the owner and architect and is in their interests. If the owner or the architect becomes

---

[3] See Chapter 3.

too removed from the construction, they can neither anticipate nor promptly address problems requiring their assistance. The level of activity and monitoring will vary, depending on the type and terms of the contract involved, but should not be so active or intrusive as to constitute interference and disruption of the contractor's work. Although it may be somewhat unpleasant to begin a project with an eye to possible future claims, a failure to adopt such prudent management procedures almost ensures that disputes will develop.

10.7   PRUDENT AND RESPONSIBLE ESTIMATING

Efforts to effectively manage work on the project and avoid claims should begin for the contractor before it even mobilizes or reaches the site. Many risks and claims arise not in the field but in the estimating department. Prudent estimating and bidding can avoid a host of performance problems and claims. A project that starts out in the hole because of bad estimating generally cannot climb out. Instead, the hole gets bigger and deeper, expanding the problem and drawing more parties into it.

Failure at any level to accurately perceive and then price the scope of the work or the risks associated with it results in unnecessary losses and difficulties that tend to ripple throughout the project. Estimates and bids should be supported by worksheets and backup documentation of sufficient detail under the circumstances. Such backup and the entire estimating process should be subject to standard forms and procedures and management review to ensure their accuracy.

Overly optimistic estimates based on vague or incomplete designs should be avoided, or at least clearly identified and qualified as such. Performance specifications, which often entail much more responsibility and cost than is initially apparent, are often another soft spot in the estimating effort. The zeal applied to selling the project or submitting an early guaranteed maximum price to satisfy the owner must be balanced with caution against establishing an unrealistic budget or inflated expectations that, regardless of any contractual significance, are bound to cause disappointment, distrust and disagreement when they are not met.

This scrutiny must be applied to bids received from subcontractors as well as those generated in-house. It is not always the case that the contractor may have recourse against the subcontractor. More importantly, the contractor has its own obligations to the owner and other subcontractors and cannot evade that responsibility or liability simply by pointing to the subcontractor who is unable to perform because of an estimating error. Owners should likewise beware of a contractor bid that seems too good to be true—it probably is! Success in initially enforcing a mistaken or reckless bid can reap bitter returns later in the project when the contractor's cash and capital run short.

10.8 ESTABLISHING STANDARD OPERATING PROCEDURES

Construction projects run by the seat of the pants are accidents waiting to happen. Every project should have formalized, standard operating procedures with which all project personnel are familiar. The procedures should identify the specific authority and areas of responsibilities for each project staff position. Ideally, these should be standardized within a company and consistent from project to project. Standard job descriptions can then be used to define the roles of the individuals on a particular project. The standard procedures should cover responsibility for processing change orders and extra work, purchasing and receiving, project documentation, and costs and accounting.

As the project team is being assembled and mobilized and the standard procedures are adjusted, defined and implemented for the particular project, it is a good idea to reexamine the efforts on the project in terms of estimating, scheduling, procurement, cost accounting and the like before construction begins. This reassessment can serve as an additional safeguard for the early identification and correction of problems that might otherwise have a serious impact on the project at some later date if left undetected.

10.9 ESTABLISHING LINES OF COMMUNICATION

The ability of the parties on the project to establish and maintain constructive lines of communications is essential to the success of any project. Prosecution of the work must be recognized as a cooperative effort that demands a team approach rather than adversary conflict. The owner, architect and contractor must establish some method to both discover what is going on at the job site (for example, what problems the subcontractors are having and the problems they anticipate) and relay suggestions, recommendations and requirements as to how these problems can be avoided or solved. Satisfactory communications can be achieved only if the parties have personnel who can develop pleasant and confident working relationships with one another. The subcontractor's workers should have sufficient confidence in the prime contractor's on-site personnel so that they will not hesitate to report difficulties and seek the prime contractor's recommendations as to how those difficulties can be avoided or resolved. Efforts to develop this confidence should begin at the preconstruction conference and should continue throughout the contract period.

An important procedural aid to establishing and maintaining the required lines of communications is regular job meetings. Weekly, bi-weekly, or at least monthly meetings should be scheduled and held. The participants and the frequency of the meetings will depend on their purpose and the status or level of activity on the job. Field coordination meetings should involve the project superintendent, subcontractor superintendents and key foremen. Brief but regular meetings like this can aid the process of coordinating and scheduling the work on a firsthand basis. They can also help identify problem areas and information needed for progress before a situation becomes critical.

Regular meetings between the architect's staff and the contractor are helpful for keeping up on the status of submittals, shop drawings and areas requiring clarifications. Meetings between the contractor, architect and owner should also take place, but probably on a less frequent basis. These meetings can be used to apprise the owner of important developments and to work out contractual issues. Further, the parties can discuss problems that are not being worked out on a more operational level and that require the owner's intervention. The contractor should be wary of allowing the owner to get too far removed from the construction effort.

10.10   PROJECT DOCUMENTATION AND NOTICE REQUIREMENTS

Paperwork on a construction project can be overwhelming, but it is essential. The contractor typically generates and maintains the bulk of the documentation on a construction project, but all participants have an interest in it. Contracts often require that the contractor maintain certain documentation, with copies and/or access available to the owner and others. Project documentation creates an accessible history of the project that serves two roles: (1) planning and managing the project and (2) aiding in resolving claims and disputes.

Related to both these roles of documentation are contractual requirements relating to the timing and content of notice of delays, differing site conditions, defective specifications, and changes. The primary purpose of notice requirements is to allow the parties to assess and manage problems, but failure to comply with such requirements can constitute a legal bar against prosecuting an otherwise legitimate claim.

It is imperative that each contract be scrutinized to determine the applicable notice requirements. Contained in the Appendix to this chapter are *sample* notice checklists for Federal Government construction contracts and the AIA A201 General Conditions (1987 ed.). These are only sample Notice Checklists and should only be used as a starting point for a detailed review of each contract. Regardless of your familiarity with the contract, each contract should be carefully reviewed as special notice requirements are often in "standard" contracts! The checklist should identify the clause, time requirements for notice, the subject of the notice, whether notice must be in writing, and the stated consequences for failing to give notice. The checklist should not be provided to the project staff. Rather, those responsible for giving timely notice should prepare the checklist for every contract. The checklist can be contained on a single sheet of paper, three hole punched, and retained in the project manual.

A sample form for creating a project specific checklist is included in the Appendix. Sample notice letters for certain recurring situations are also included in the Appendix. These are samples only and any actual notice letter must be written in a manner to address the particular facts of the project and the technical requirements of the applicable contract.

Project documentation must be organized and maintained in such a manner that it is a help and not a hindrance to effective project management and prosecution or defense of claims. Routine and uniformity are two essentials to an effective system of project documentation. The procedures should not only be standardized for the project but for the company as a whole. Only with that level of emphasis and indoctrination can all the fruits and benefits of a system be reaped.

The system and procedures must be written down. The length and level of detail of the written description will vary with the size and complexity of the project. Some description may be obviated by the use of computerized tracking systems, such as for cost accounting and tracking submittals. Regardless of how extensive the procedures are, it is imperative that they be clear and specific. If they are vague and general, allowing for personal interpretation and selective application, there will be no system at all. Instead, a hodgepodge of personal recordkeeping and filing systems will result.

Just putting procedures on paper is not enough. The procedures must be reviewed with all levels of personnel who will be responsible for implementation so they are understood, used and enforced. The critical importance of project documentation must be emphasized and that emphasis must be maintained throughout the project and from project to project.

Certain basic information should be maintained and organized in separate files:

- The contract, including all its components, and all change orders or amendments, including a bid or original set of project plans and specifications
- All documents, worksheets and forms associated with the original bid estimate and subsequent revisions
- Subcontractor or vendor files, including bids, subcontracts or purchase orders, together with changes and correspondence
- Project schedules, including the original schedule and all updates
- Insurance requirements and information for all parties

The standard procedures relating to documentation should also address the creation, maintenance and orientation of certain specific types of documentation:

(1) *Correspondence:* Procedures for date-stamping, copying, routing, filing and indexing incoming and outgoing correspondence should be the responsibility of secretarial or clerical support staff, in accordance with standard procedures. A copy of all correspondence should go in a master correspondence file.

The party responsible for responding to or acting on incoming correspondence should be identified. As a matter of routine, the project management should be drilled on the importance of complying with technical notice requirements in the contract. Discussion with other parties should likewise be confirmed in writing to the involved parties with copies to the file. Such confirmation will help immediately resolve any misunderstanding that might exist and also preserve the substance of the discussion if there is a dispute at some later date.

(2) *Meeting Notes:* Regular job coordination meetings between the various parties to the project, on a cumulative basis, probably cover more issues and contribute more to the exchange of information necessary to complete the work than all the correspondence on the project. What occurs at such meetings is therefore of great importance. Someone should be designated to maintain the minutes or notes for each meeting, preferably the same person at each meeting. That person should record the subjects covered, the nature of the discussion, the future actions to be taken and by whom. The name, title and affiliation of each participant should be listed. The notes should be concise but informative. The items discussed should be indexed or designated in a manner so that they can be located for future reference. The notes should then be distributed to all participants and those affected on a regular basis.

A personal computer can be valuable for updating regular meeting notes, as certain items will likely remain open to discussion through several meetings. At the opening of each regular meeting, the notes from the previous meeting can be reviewed to confirm their accuracy and the mutual understanding of the participants. By identifying those items that remain outstanding, the previous week's minutes can also serve as an agenda for the current meeting.

(3) *Job Site Logs or Daily Reports:* Job site logs or daily reports are generally maintained by the project superintendent and can provide the best record of what happens in the field. They help keep management and office personnel informed of progress and problems. In the event of a claim, they are often among the most helpful documents in recreating the progress on the job and as-built schedules.

The daily log or report must be a part of the superintendent's daily routine. If it is too burdensome, it either will be ignored or will detract from the superintendent's primary function of getting the job built. Key information should be elicited briefly and concisely requiring as little narrative as possible. The information covered should include:

- Manpower, preferably broken down by subcontractors
- Equipment used and idle
- Major work activities
- Any delays or problems
- Areas of work not available
- Safety and accidents
- Oral instructions and informal meetings

- A brief weather summary
- Job site visitors

The burden on the superintendent can be eased and the information maintained in a more organized manner by using a standard form. The process can be further expedited by simply allowing the superintendent to dictate entries and having the report typed up by office staff.

All key project personnel, such as foremen, project engineers and project managers, should also be encouraged to maintain personal daily logs and procedures should be established to facilitate this effort. The information they should record should be similar to the job log or daily report but would not be as extensive or detailed.

These types of routine, contemporaneous descriptions of work progress, site conditions, labor and equipment usage and the contractor's ability (or inability) to perform its work can provide valuable information necessary to accurately reconstruct the events of the project in preparation of a claim. In maintaining these reports or logs, project personnel must be consistent in recording the events and activities on the job, particularly those relating to claims or potential claims. Failure to record an event, once the responsibility of a daily report or log is undertaken, carries with it the implication that the event did not occur or was insignificant and also threatens the credibility of the entire log.

(4) *Standard Forms and Status Logs:* There is a constant flow of information between the project participants by means of a variety of media. Drawings are revised, shop drawings are submitted, reviewed and returned, field orders and change orders are issued, questions are asked and clarifications are provided. Cumulatively and individually, these bits and pieces of information are essential for building the job and also for reconstructing the progress of events on paper in the event of a claim. The standard procedures must include the means for providing, eliciting, recording and tracking this mass of data so that it can be used during the course of the job and efficiently retrieved in an after-the-fact claim setting.

Routine transmittal forms should be customized to address specific, routine types of communications in order to expedite the process and ensure required information is provided. For example, separate specialized forms can be prepared for transmittal of shop drawings and submittals, requests for clarifications, drawing revisions and, of course, field orders and change orders. When possible, the forms should provide space for responses, including certain standard responses that simply can be checked off or filled in. At a minimum, the forms should identify the individual sender, the date issued, and specific and self-descriptive references to the affected or enclosed drawings, submittal or specification. If a response is requested by a certain date, that date should be identified on the form.

Ideally, each discrete type of communication or specialized form should be numbered or somehow identified in a chronologically sequential manner, based on the date it is initiated. Shop drawings and submittals, however, are best identified by specification section, with a suffix added to indicate resubmittals. This provides a basis for easy reference and orientation. Copies of the completed forms should be maintained in binders in reverse chronological/ numerical order. Although various project staff members may require working copies, a complete master file should be maintained as a complete reference source and historical document.

In order to maintain the status of and track these numerous and varied communications, which can number many thousands, logs should be maintained. These logs need only address key information such as the number assigned, the date, and a self-descriptive reference. Proposed change orders and change order logs should also identify any increase or decrease in contract amount as well as time extensions. Then logs can be kept on personal computers using inexpensive, commercially available software, or even on a word processor to expedite updating. Logs should be maintained for internal record-keeping and also for distribution to other parties on the project. The logs serve as a reminder of outstanding items and can highlight action required to keep the work progressing.

The contractor should use standard forms and procedures for communications with subcontractors as well as the owner and architect. Ideally, subcontractors should be encouraged to standardize their communications so there will be a more integrated approach for the entire project.

(5) *Photographs and Video Tapes:* Photographs and videotapes are helpful, easy and inexpensive means to monitor, depict and preserve conditions of the work as those conditions change and the work progresses. They are particularly helpful in claims situations. One approach, incorporated in many contracts, is to accumulate a periodic pictorial diary of the job through a series of weekly or monthly photographs and pictures of significant milestones in the construction. This encourages personnel to take photographs of site conditions on a routine basis, perhaps concentrating on problem areas and those areas associated with crucial construction procedures and scheduling. Photographs are also the best evidence of defective work or problem conditions that are cured or covered up and cannot be viewed later.

A professional photographer may be needed at times or required by contract, but generally job site personnel with some instruction are more than capable of handling the photography chores. Cameras capable of producing quality photographs and negatives should be used. However, it is also a good idea to use as a backup a self-developing camera that allows the party responsible for taking pictures to check the content and clarity of the photos while he or she is still at the site and before conditions are altered.

Pictures should always be identified on the back with a notation as to time, date, location, conditions depicted, personnel present and the photographer. This should be done at the time the photograph is taken if a self-developing camera is used. Otherwise, a log should be kept as the photos are taken and the log immediately should be checked when the photos are developed and the appropriate entries made on the back of the prints. Without this information correlated to specific photographs, the utility of the entire effort can be substantially undermined. Negatives should also be retained in an organized, retrievable manner.

Videocassette recorders have become relatively inexpensive and easy to operate. In some situations, videotape can be considerably more informative than a still photograph, such as when attempting to depict an activity or the overall status of the project. Static conditions, however, are best photographed. The availability of a contemporaneous narrative as part of the video can give the after-the-fact viewer a much better idea of what is being depicted and why. A monthly videotape is an excellent way of preserving and presenting evidence. Again, properly trained job site personnel can operate the video recorder and later testify in conjunction with the showing of the tape.

Samples of various types of standard forms to facilitate and monitor project communications and documentation are included in the Appendix to this chapter.

10.11 COST ACCOUNTING RECORDS

The use of effective cost-accounting methods and the maintenance of appropriate cost records can minimize many of the proof problems inherently associated with construction claims. Unfortunately, even though a claimant may be able to prove that an event has occurred entitling it to additional compensation, it will be able to recover only that amount of damages that it can prove with reasonable certainty. Proving the actual dollars lost is crucial to the claim.

Cost-accounting systems utilized by contractors vary drastically in their level of sophistication. More often than not, the accounting function suffers from a lack of priority by senior management until a dispute arises and the claim development process begins. The procedures described earlier to effectively capture and document events or occurrences to prove liability are only half the battle. Without effective accounting systems, the development of a clear, concise and winning claim is haphazard at best. In addition, accounting rules for the construction industry are sometimes subjective and, in many cases, different conclusions can be reached on a single set of circumstances by accounting professionals and business people. With this in mind, it is important that accounting policies and procedures be documented and their application be appropriately monitored for compliance by management. This approach tends to improve the consistency in the manner in which items pertaining to all contracts are accounted for and, therefore, improves the credibility of the way in which matters are treated in developing a claim. Further, and perhaps of primary importance, a good cost-accounting system is invaluable in providing timely information to management for decision-making purposes and for monitoring financial performance.

10.12   MONITORING THE WORK THROUGH SCHEDULING

The prime contractor should continuously monitor the work of all subcontractors to determine that each is meeting its deadlines so that the work of other trades can proceed as originally scheduled. The owner must perform the same task when multiple prime contractors are involved. Even when the contractor has primary scheduling responsibility, which is most often the case, the owner should nonetheless continuously monitor the progress of the work and the scheduling effort. Most prime contracts require the preparation of a bar chart or progress schedule, which provides the easiest means of monitoring the work. The critical path method (CPM) schedule required by the prime contract on many large projects can be even more valuable as a scheduling tool if properly developed, updated and utilized.

The input of subcontractors and all project participants in the development and updating of any project schedule is critical to its usefulness. As a practical matter, a schedule that is developed without the input of the parties actually performing the work may result in an unworkable product, and the schedule as an instrument of coordination will be wasted. By getting the parties to participate in the preparation of the schedule, it becomes a much more meaningful and productive project management device. In addition, through its involvement, each party has in effect admitted what was reasonable and expected of it. If a party later fails to perform or follow the schedule, its ability to dispute the relevance of the project schedule and what was required of that party can be substantially reduced.

A project schedule can be a double-edged sword for the prime contractor, particularly if it is a CPM that shows the interrelationship of all activities and trades. A properly developed schedule can be used to demonstrate how a subcontractor is behind schedule and how its delayed performance is impacting the entire project.[4] Conversely, a subcontractor may also use a project schedule against the prime contractor to show how the subcontractor reasonably expected and planned to proceed with the work and how that plan was disrupted by the prime contractor, another subcontractor or the owner, for which the affected subcontractor is entitled to additional compensation.[5] If the schedule is not properly maintained, updated and enforced so that it bears little relationship to the actual progress of the work or the parties' contractual obligations, it may be dismissed by a court or arbitrators as merely representing "theoretical aspirations rather than practical contract requirements."[6] The heavy use of scheduling information and analysis in resolving claims underscores the importance of preparing, and maintaining through updates, a realistic schedule that secures subcontractor involvement and agreement.

---

[4] *See e.g., Illinois Structural Steel Corp. v. Pathman Constr. Co.,* 23 Ill. App. 3d 1, 318 N.E.2d 232 (1974).
[5] *See United States ex rel. R.W. Vaughn Co. v. F.D. Rich Co.,* 439 F.2d 895 (8th Cir. 1971).
[6] *Id.* at 900.

10.13   CONCLUSION

Effectively dealing with construction disputes begins with a recognition that disputes are best avoided. The identifiable recurring causes of claims permits planning and preparation to try to steer clear of major risks or handle claims responsibly when they cannot be avoided. The same policies and procedures that aid in limiting claims also contribute to comprehensive and effective preparation of claims. The potential for claims cannot be ignored. Skillful and determined management are required both before and during construction to handle the threats and challenges they present.

POINTS TO REMEMBER

- Parties can reduce the risk of construction disputes by dealing with reputable companies that have demonstrated their ability to perform. Careful consideration should be given the prospective project participant's financial strength, bonding capacity, licensing, available project management personnel and experience on similar projects.
- Allocating risks and providing for effective dispute resolution can be accomplished by a well-drafted written contract, particularly when nontraditional construction contract methods are employed.
- Use of generally accepted standard contract forms provide a starting point for parties to negotiate critical variables such as clauses addressing payment terms, time, damages, changes, termination, insurance and dispute resolution.
- Prudent estimating and bidding as well as proper project management and documentation will help reduce the risk that disputes will develop. Moreover, proper project documentation can provide valuable information necessary to accurately reconstruct the events of the project in preparation of a claim. Proper project documentation involves procedures to systematically maintain bidding documents, vendor files, correspondence, meeting notes, job site logs or daily reports, schedules, standard forms and status logs, photographs, and video tapes.
- Company operating procedures should be standardized and consistent from project to project.
- Project participants should establish and maintain open lines of communication by engaging in regular job meetings.
- Because problems of proof are inherently associated with construction claims, maintenance of a good cost-accounting system is crucial.
- A realistic project schedule that secures the involvement and agreement of all project participants should be prepared and routinely updated and maintained.

APPENDIX

1. Sample Notice Checklist–Federal Government Construction Contracts
2. Notice Checklist
3. Sample Notice Letter (all five samples under one document)
4. Request for Information
5. Telephone Conversation Memorandum
6. Daily Report
7. Field Order Status Chart
8. Notice of Backcharge Work to Be Performed
9. Incoming Correspondence Typical Letter Log
10. Outgoing Correspondence Typical Letter Log
11. Request for Information Log
12. Submittal Log

Sample Notice Checklist - Federal Government Construction Contracts

Clause Reference	Subject Matter of Notice	Time Requirements for Notice	Writing Required	Stated Consequences of a Lack of Notice
Changes FAR 52.243-4	Proposal for adjustment.	30 DAYS from receipt of a written change order from the Gov't or written notification of a constructive change by the contractor.	Yes	Claim may not be allowed. Notice requirement may be waived until final payment.
Constructive Changes FAR 52.243-4	Date, circumstances and source of the order & that the contractor regards the Gov't's order as a contract change.	No starting point stated, but notice within 20 DAYS of incurring any additional costs due to the constructive change fully protects the contractor's rights.	Yes	Costs incurred more than 20 DAYS prior to giving notice cannot be recovered, except in the case of defective specifications.
Differing Site Conditions FAR 52.236-2	Existence of unknown or materially different conditions affecting the contractor's cost.	From the time such conditions are identified, notice must be furnished "promptly" and before such conditions are disturbed.	Yes	Claim not allowed. Lack of notice may be waived until final payment.
Suspension of Work FAR 52.242-14	(1) Of "the act or failure to act involved," and (2) Of the amount claimed.	(1) Within 20 DAYS from the act or failure to act by the C.O. (not including a suspension order.) (2) "As soon as practicable" after termination of the suspension, delay or interruption.	(1) Yes (2) Yes	(1) Costs incurred more than 20 DAYS prior to notification cannot be recovered. (2) Claim not allowed, but claim may be considered until final payment.
Termination for Default-Damages for Delay-Time Extensions FAR 52.249-10	Causes of delay beyond contractor's control.	10 DAYS from the beginning of any delay.	Yes	Contractor's right to proceed may be terminated and the Government may sue for damages.
Disputes FAR 52.233-1	Appeal of any final decision by the Contracting Officer (C.O.).	(1) Boards of Contract Appeals - 90 DAYS from receipt of C.O.'s final decision. (2) U.S. Court of Fed. Claims - 1 YEAR from receipt of C.O.'s final decision.	(1) Yes - Notice of Appeal (2) Yes - Filing of Complaint	C.O.'s decision becomes final and conclusive. C.O.'s decision becomes final and conclusive.

Sample Notice - Checklist - AIA A 201 General Conditions (1987)

Time Limits on Claims: Articles 4.3.3, 4.3.7 & 4.3.8.1.	Claims by either party. Contractor claims for time shall include cost estimate; Claims for increase in price due before starting work, except for emergency.	Within 21 DAYS after claimant first recognizes condition giving rise to claim or 21 DAYS after occurrence of event giving rise to claim, whichever is later.	Yes	??????????
Concealed or Unknown Site Conditions: Article 4.3.6	Materially different, subsurface or otherwise concealed physical site conditions.	Promptly, before disturbing the conditions but no later than 21 DAYS after observing such conditions. If the Architect does not agree, a claim must be filed within 21 DAYS.	Yes	??????????
Injury or Damage to Person or Property Article 4.3.9	Claim of injury or damage to property caused by act or omission of other party or agent; claims for added cost or time covered by 4.3.7 & 4.3.8.	Within a reasonable time not exceeding 21 DAYS after first observance. Notice must provide enough detail to permit the other party to investigate the matter.	Yes	??????????
Arbitration Notices and Demands Article 4.5	Demand for Arbitration.	If the Architect's written decision states that it is FINAL but subject to Arbitration, demand for Arbitration of the Claim must be made within 30 DAYS after the date on which the party making the demand received the Architect's written final decision.	Yes. See 4.5.6 regarding need to assert other Claims when filing the Arbitration demand.	Failure to demand Arbitration within the 30 DAY period shall result in the Architect's decision becoming final and binding on the Owner and the Contractor.

General Notes on Preparation of a Checklist

The **Tables** above are sample formats for **Notice Checklists**. Regardless of your familiarity with the contract, each contract should be carefully reviewed as **special notice requirements are often in "***standard***" contracts!** The checklist should identify the clause, time requirements for notice, the subject of the notice, whether notice must be in writing and the stated consequences for failing to give notice. **The checklist should not be provided to the project staff.** Rather, those responsible for giving timely notice should prepare the checklist for every contract. The checklist can be contained on a single sheet of paper, three-hole punched, and retained in the project manual.

NOTICE CHECKLIST - _____ CONTRACT

Clause Reference	Subject Matter of Notice	Time Requirement for Notice	Form of Notice	Consequences of Lack of Notice
Changes Paragraph # _____	Proposal for adjustment	(Sent)(Rec'd) in _____ days Triggering Event: _____ Other Action Required: _____ _____	☐ Written ☐ Certified ☐ Registered Sent to:	
Constructive Changes Paragraph # _____	Date, circumstances and source of the order and that the contractor regards the order as a contract change	(Sent)(Rec'd) in _____ days Triggering Event: _____ Other Action Required: _____ _____	☐ Written ☐ Certified ☐ Registered Sent to:	
Differing Site Conditions Paragraph # _____	Existence of unknown or materially different conditions affecting the contractor's cost	(Sent)(Rec'd) in _____ days Triggering Event: _____ Other Action Required: _____ _____	☐ Written ☐ Certified ☐ Registered Sent to:	
Suspension of Work Paragraph # _____	The act or failure to act involved and the amount claimed	(Sent)(Rec'd) in _____ days Triggering Event: _____ Other Action Required: _____ _____	☐ Written ☐ Certified ☐ Registered Sent to:	
Time Extensions Paragraph # _____	Causes of delay beyond contractor's control	(Sent)(Rec'd) in _____ days Triggering Event: _____ Other Action Required: _____ _____	☐ Written ☐ Certified ☐ Registered Sent to:	
Claims Paragraph # _____	Notice of event or condition giving rise to a claim	(Sent)(Rec'd) in _____ days Triggering Event: _____ Other Action Required: _____ _____	☐ Written ☐ Certified ☐ Registered Sent to:	
Termination for Default Paragraph # _____	Notice of intent to terminate for default	(Sent)(Rec'd) in _____ days Triggering Event: _____ Other Action Required: _____ _____	☐ Written ☐ Certified ☐ Registered Sent to:	
Termination for Convenience Paragraph # _____	Notice of intent to invoke right to terminate for convenience	(Sent)(Rec'd) in _____ days Triggering Event: _____ Other Action Required: _____ _____	☐ Written ☐ Certified ☐ Registered Sent to:	
Injury or Damage to Person or Property Paragraph # _____	Claim of injury or damage to property caused by act or omission of other party or agent	(Sent)(Rec'd) in _____ days Triggering Event: _____ Other Action Required: _____ _____	☐ Written ☐ Certified ☐ Registered Sent to:	
Arbitration Notices and Demands Paragraph # _____	Demand for arbitration	(Sent)(Rec'd) in _____ days Triggering Event: _____ Other Action Required: _____ _____	☐ Written ☐ Certified ☐ Registered Sent to:	
Disputes Paragraph # _____	Appeal of A/E or C.O. Final Decision	(Sent)(Rec'd) in _____ days Triggering Event: _____ Other Action Required: _____ _____	☐ Written ☐ Certified ☐ Registered Sent to:	
Mechanic's Lien Paragraph # _____	Notices to be sent or filed to preserve lien rights	1st Notice Required: _____ Notice Deadline: _____ Other Action Required: _____ Foreclosure Deadline: _____	☐ Written ☐ Certified ☐ Registered Sent to:	

**Sample Notice Letter - Extension of Time For Delays
(and Extra Costs if Appropriate)**

ECC #_____

Addressee:
(To Prime Contractor) or
(Owner and A/E)

Dear:

   We are continuing to pursue the completion of our work as rapidly as is reasonably possible under the current circumstances. We have, however, recently encountered certain *delays* to our performance through no fault of our own and which are beyond our control. We have continued to keep your job representatives informed of these delays and of their affect on overall job completion. You may be assured that we will diligently seek to reasonably minimize the effects of these delays on our work.

   Specifically, we have been delayed in the following particulars:

   Accordingly, we hereby request an extension of [_____ days]* to   our   contract completion to take into consideration the above delays under Clause _____ of the contract provisions.

   **[Such delays have also had a serious effect on costs of performance in that it has created additional time for performance with resultant additional costs for supervision, overhead, rentals, etc., and loss of efficiency for direct labor. Accordingly, this is to place you on notice that we are entitled to additional compensation for all costs flowing from these delays and interference which have been imposed on us through no fault of our own. We will provide you with the specific amount of additional compensation covered by this notice as soon as we research this matter and have computed it.]

Sincerely yours,

Eager Construction Company, Inc.

By _____
   (Title)

*   To be inserted where specific time of delay is known.
**   To be used where extra money is claimed for delay.

Sample Notice Letter - Claim for Extras

ECC #_____

Addressee:
(To Prime Contractor) or
(Owner and A/E)

    Re: (Describe Extra Work)

Dear:

> **Where work is not yet performed**

This is to notify you that (on _____ we will begin) (we are about to begin) this extra work and are expecting to be compensated for it. If you do want us to perform this work as an extra to the contract, please immediately notify us before we incur additional costs in the preparation for performance of this extra work. If we do not hear from you right away, we will proceed on the basis that you agree with our plan to perform this work.

OR

> **Where work already performed**

This work was performed pursuant to your representatives requirement and entitles us to additional compensation. We have proceeded to complete this work so as to minimize the cost of the work and any delay to (our work) (the job). We will be pleased to review this matter with you at your convenience.

We will provide you with a detailed cost breakdown for this added work as soon as we are able to compute it.

        Sincerely yours,

        Eager Construction Company, Inc.

        By _____
                (Title)

Sample Notice Letter - Confirming Change Directive

ECC #_____

DATE

SUBJECT (Contract Name)

Gentlemen:

We were given instructions by (insert name) on (date) (put in time also if pertinent) to (describe work added or changed).

This change order is for work not within the scope of our present contract and we, therefore, request a written modification to cover the added (material, labor, equipment, etc.) required to perform the work as ordered. (Give notice of other factors involved such as delay, acceleration, diversion of men or equipment from contract work, material shortages, etc.)

Our proposal for the added cost resulting from this change order is being prepared and will be submitted for your approval as soon as possible. We cannot determine at this time the effect on contract completion date, or other work under the contract and will advise when a full analysis has been made.

As ordered, we (are proceeding) (have proceeded) at once to (procure materials) (perform the work) in order to complete this change order at the earliest possible time. In the event you do not approve of such action, please advise immediately in order that we may stop this effort and minimize the cost involved.

Your signature at the bottom of this letter will satisfactorily confirm the oral instructions.

Sincerely yours,

Eager Construction Company, Inc.

By _____
(Title)

Confirmation:

The above-stated report of our instruction is confirmed.

Company: _____
By: _____
Title: _____
File No.: _____

Sample Notice Letter - Oral Directions of Extra Work

ECC #_____

DATE

SUBJECT (Contract Name)

Gentlemen:

On the _____ day of _____, 19__, we received certain oral instructions (or orders, approvals, changes, as the case may be) from (insert name). These instructions were confirmed by our _____, 19_ letter and should have been given to us in writing under the terms of our agreement. Your (insert name) has refused to confirm the oral instructions (or orders, approvals, changes, as the case may be) which we have recited in our referenced letter. Accordingly, we must advise that we will not (proceed with) (continue to follow) these verbal instructions unless we receive your immediate written confirmation. In any event, we will expect reimbursement for all costs reasonably incurred in reliance upon your direction.

We understand that it may take time to go through all the steps necessary to bring about a written authorization for extra work, and that sometimes it is more practical to do the work before that written authorization can be obtained. It has been our past practice to try to recognize your need to follow this method of operation. However, in this case, and in order to avoid any misunderstanding, we think it appropriate that you first provide us with a formal written authorization for changed work.

Very truly yours,

Eager Construction Company, Inc.

By _____
            (Title)

NOTE: Where the work already has been performed, it may be important to establish a prior history of reliance by the parties on oral directives. If the work has been fully performed, then the second paragraph should be deleted and the last sentence of the first paragraph replaced with the following:

As you know, we proceeded immediately as directed to perform this additional work. We did so in order to minimize your extra cost, and in the same manner in which we have handled other verbal directives in the past. Consistent with that past practice, we will provide you with our costs as soon as they are fully known and expect your prompt reimbursement.

Sample Notice Letter - Confirming Extra Cost Directive

ECC #_____

DATE

SUBJECT (Contract Name)

Gentlemen:

We were given direction by (name or letter dated _____) on (date) (put in time also if pertinent) to (describe work and specific location). This directive stipulates and orders that we are to complete this work by (date and time).

This directive necessarily (accelerates, delays, diverts men and equipment from contract work, involves inefficiencies, interrupts contract work, involves excessive working hours, shortages, causes manpower shortage for contract work, inefficient working conditions, involves work under hazardous conditions, etc.) and thereby will result in increased cost to _____ on this contract.

Our proposal for the added costs resulting from this directive is being prepared and will be submitted for your approval as soon as possible. We cannot determine at this time the effect on contract completion date and will advise after a full analysis has been made.

Very truly yours,

Eager Construction Company, Inc.

By _____
        (Title)

File No. _____

REQUEST FOR INFORMATION

TO: _____   DATE: _____

_____   PROJECT: _____

_____   _____

ATTENTION: _____

We are this date requesting the following information, clarification or direction:

_____

_____

_____

_____

The above information is needed:

☐   As soon as possible, to avoid disrupting the work

☐   Immediately, to minimize disruption and added costs already being incurred

☐   Not later than _____ or the work may experience disruptions and added costs

Thank you for your prompt attention to this matter.

COMPANY: _____

BY: _____
(Signature and Title)

Response: _____

_____

_____

_____

COMPANY: _____

BY: _____
(Signature and Title)

TELEPHONE CONVERSATION MEMORANDUM

TO: _____   **DATE:** _____

_____   **PROJECT:**_____

_____

I talked to _____

at telephone number _____

regarding _____

_____

_____

_____

To: _____

For your files and use, I am providing you with this confirmation of our telephone conversation described above.

_____
Signature

COPIES TO:

☐ Construction Manager   ☐ Job Superintendent
☐ Project Manager   ☐ Construction Accounting
☐ General Superintendent

A CONFIRMATION LETTER:

☐ Has been sent
☐ Will be sent
☐ Need not be sent

DAILY REPORT

Job or Area: _____ **Date:** _____

Weather Conditions:
_____
_____
_____

Temperature:

High: _____ **Low:** _____

KCC No.	Major Equipment and Use
_____	_____
_____	_____
_____	_____
_____	_____
_____	_____

PERSONNEL	G. Foreman	Foreman	Journeyman	Apprentice	Labor	New Hires	Laid Off
Carpenters							
Laborers							
Operators							
Finishers							
Teamsters							
Pipe Fitters							
Pipe Laborers							

Work Performed Today: _____
_____
_____
_____

Remarks: *(Such as testing, conflicts, verbal instructions, delays, safety problems, visitors)*
_____
_____
_____
_____

Major Equipment and Materials Received:

Item	Carrier	Description

Subcontractors   **Work Performed and Number of People**
_____
_____

Superintendent: _____

FIELD ORDER STATUS CHART

PAGE NO. _____

PROJECT NAME: _____
PROJECT NUMBER: _____
OWNER: _____
CONTRACTOR: _____

STATUS DATE: _____

Job No.	Owner's Field Order #	Authorized By	Date of Order	Description of Work	Work Performed By	Date Work Started	Date Work Completed	Comments on Work	Invoice No.	Date of Bill	Amount of Bill	Amount Paid
									1.			
									2.			
									1.			
									2.			
									1.			
									2.			
									1.			
									2.			
									1.			
									2.			
									1.			
									2.			
									1.			
									2.			
									1.			
									2.			

To:

To keep you aware of the status of added work directed in the field, we will submit updates of this status chart as frequently as is practical. With this form you should be able to track our planned start dates for field work and the status of the work. In the absence of a field order number from you, we will assign our own field order number to each field directive.

NOTICE OF BACKCHARGE WORK TO BE PERFORMED

Location: _____ **Backcharge No.:** _____

Charge To: _____ **Subcontractor No.:** _____

Date: _____ **P.O. Reference:** _____

Description: _____

_____

_____

_____

_____

_____

_____

_____

_____

Notes:

☐ Labor shall be charged at actual costs plus ____% to cover payroll additives.

☐ Material shall be charged at actual delivered cost.

☐ Equipment rental shall be charged at prevailing job site rates of the area.

☐ ____% shall be added to items _____ for indirect costs, overhead, supervision and administration.

APPROVALS

_____ _____ _____
Representative   Date   Supplier/Subcontractor

INCOMING CORRESPONDENCE
TYPICAL LETTER LOG

Maintain Separate Log for General Correspondence on Each Major Subcontractor and Supplier

INCOMING CORRESPONDENCE FROM _____
(Contractor/Supplier)

| | | | | Reply Required | | Reply | |
Ref. No.	Date	Subject	Author	Yes	No	Ref. No.	Date

Page No. _____

OUTGOING CORRESPONDENCE
TYPICAL LETTER LOG

Maintain Separate Log for General Correspondence on Each Major Subcontractor and Supplier

OUTGOING CORRESPONDENCE TO _____
(Contractor/Supplier)

Ref. No.	Date	Subject	Author	Reply Required Yes	No	Reply Ref. No.	Date

Page No. _____

REQUEST FOR INFORMATION LOG

Maintain Log for Each Request for Information

RFI #	Regarding	Subcontractor/ Vendor	Date Submitted	Date Response Required	Actual Response Date	Days Overdue	Notes	

Page No._____

SUBMITTAL LOG

Maintain Log for Each Submittal

Submittal No.	Sub-contactor/ Vendor	Specification Section	Date Submitted	Date Response Needed	Actual Response Date	Status	Resubmittal Date	Response Date	Status	Notes	
										Page No. ___	

11

PAYMENT BOND CLAIMS

11.1 PAYMENT BOND CLAIMS

Payment bonds provide additional payment security to those providing services and materials to a construction project. Through the payment bond, the surety essentially guarantees that payment will be made if the terms of the bond and the contract, which form the basis of the transaction, are fulfilled. The surety's financial obligation to guarantee payment is further limited to the penal sum or amount of the bond.

Payment bonds are typically required by statute on public works projects to replace the protection of lien rights, which generally do not exist on public work projects. Payment bonds may also be required by the owners on private projects to help insulate the owner from lien claims. General contractors may also require subcontractors to provide payment bonds to likewise provide additional security against payment claims from lower tier subcontractors and suppliers.

There is frequently some overlap between the scope and protection of lien rights and the manner in which payment bond statutes and payment bonds are construed under a state's law. Nonetheless, lien rights and the technical requirements associated with liens are so heavily legislated and scrutinized by the courts of the various states that it is dangerous to make any generalizations about lien law across jurisdictions. It is instead imperative to consult and be familiar with the specifics of the lien law in the state where the project is located. Such detailed coverage of state lien law is beyond the scope of this chapter and book. Reference to the specifics of state law is also required in dealing with payment bond issues. However, the federal Miller Act, which governs payment bond requirements on construction contracts with the federal government, provides a basis for discussing the basic concepts of payment bonds.

11.2 When Payment Bonds Are Required by Statute

The most prominent statutory regulation of payment bonds is the Miller Act, 40 U.S.C. §§ 270a–270d. The Miller Act requires the contractor to furnish a payment bond to guarantee payment to parties supplying labor and materials to contractors or subcontractors engaged in the construction, alteration, or repair of any public building or public work of the United States. The Miller Act protects subcontractors and suppliers who would otherwise be without a remedy against an insolvent contractor, due to the lack of lien rights against the federal government.

Many states have followed the policies and procedures of the Miller Act by enacting statutes requiring bonds for construction of public works.[1] Where a state statute is patterned after the Miller Act, state courts will often look to federal case law interpreting the Miller Act as persuasive authority to aid in interpretation of the state statute.[2] Although the Miller Acts cases may be persuasive, they are not controlling and the various state courts can render inconsistent decisions on the same issue. This risk reinforces the need for familiarity with a specific state's law to insure that a claimant loses none of its bond rights.

Payment bonds issued on private projects or by subcontractors on public projects are generally deemed to be private bonds, which are not subject to the rigorous statutory requirements of the Miller Act or "little Miller Acts." Nonetheless, some states do have statutes related to such private payment bonds, and such bonds are frequently construed in light of the state's lien law, so familiarity with both the express terms of the bond and the applicable state law is a must.

Where a state statute requiring the furnishing of a payment bond is ignored and no payment bond is required, a subcontractor or supplier may still obtain some relief. Under Georgia law, for example, the government agency will be deemed liable to the extent of the payment bond, had it been furnished.[3] Even absent such a relatively unique statutory provision, a subcontractor or supplier might be able to recover from the public authority on a theory that the governmental agency was negligent in failing to enforce the statutory requirements, and that this negligence proximately caused the subcontractor's inability to recover from the payment bond surety.[4] Some courts, however, deny recovery in spite of the public body's failure to require the mandated bond.[5]

Even if the payment bond is provided, the claimant may have waived its rights to claim against the bond in its contract. Such express waivers are

---

[1] *See, e.g.,* Ala. Code § 39-1-1; Ga. Code § 36-82-100; Fla. Stat. Ann. § 255.05; Ariz. Rev. Stat. Ann. § 34-222; Cal. Civ. Code §§ 3247, 10221; N.C. Gen. Stat. § 44A-25; S.C. Code Ann. §§ 11-25-3020, 11-35-3030.

[2] *See, e.g., General Fed. Constr., Inc. v. D. R. Thomas, Inc.,* 451 A.2d 1250 (Md. 1982); *Rish v. Theo Bros. Constr. Co.,* 237 S.E.2d 61 (S.C. 1977).

[3] *See* O.C.G.A. § 26-82-102.

[4] *See, e.g., Housing Auth. of Prattville v. Headley,* 360 So.2d 1025 (Ala. Civ. App. 1978).

[5] *See Haskell Lemon Constr. Co. v. Independent School Dist. No. 12,* 589 P.2d 677 (Okla. 1979).

enforceable under the federal Miller Act.[6] Waivers of payment bond rights under little Miller Acts, however, are not always enforceable. In *Coastal Caisson Drill Co., Inc. v. American Casualty Co. of Reading Pa.,*[7] a prime contractor on a state bridge project required its subcontractors to sign a subcontract stating that the subcontractor "waives all rights under any bond . . . executed by contractor and its surety." When the owner failed to pay, the subcontractor sued the prime's surety on the statutory public works bond. The court held that the subcontract agreement provision waiving rights against the surety was void as against public policy. The public works statute, requiring prime contractor bonds on such projects, was found to express a strong public policy. The court found that such waivers would undermine the public policy and make a subcontractor reluctant to bid on public projects.

11.3 Who May Claim under a Payment Bond?

Obviously, many parties contribute to the progress of each project. Which of these parties is entitled to the protection of a payment bond? The answer to this question is often found in the express terms of the bond, the controlling statute, and the decisions of the courts construing the bond and statutory language. The language of the Miller Act—"all persons supplying work and materials in the prosecution of the work"—is extremely broad, suggesting that any party with any remote connection to the project could claim entitlement to recover under a payment bond. However, to consider all of these contributing parties as beneficiaries of a Miller Act bond would be extremely impractical and impossible to monitor. As a result of the Miller Act's broad language, the Supreme Court was faced with the issue of the scope of the statute: Where does the Miller Act's protection stop?

In *Clifford F. MacEvoy Co. v. United States ex rel. Tomkins Co.,*[8] the Court held that only two general classes of claimants were entitled to protection of the Miller Act. The first class is composed of all laborers, materialmen, subcontractors and suppliers who deal directly with the prime contractor—the first tier. The court also ruled that the second class of Miller Act claimants encompassed all materialmen, subcontractors and laborers who have a direct contractual relationship with a first-tier subcontractor—the second tier. The effect of *MacEvoy* is to draw the line of Miller Act protection behind those parties who have direct relationships with the prime or first-tier subcontractor. For example, the suppliers of a second-tier subcontractor are not protected by the Miller Act.[9]

---

[6] *See, e.g., United States ex rel. Trans Coastal Roofing Co. v. David Boland, Inc.,* 922 F. Supp. 597 (S.D. Fla. 1996).

[7] 523 So.2d 791 (Fla. Dist. Ct. App. 1988).

[8] 322 U.S. 102 (1944).

[9] *See J. W. Bateson Co. v. United States ex rel. Board of Trustees,* 434 U.S. 586 (1978). *But see D&L Bldg., Inc. v. State ex rel Maltby Tank & Barge, Inc.,* 747 P.2d 517 (Wyo. 1987).

Although the Supreme Court's decision in *MacEvoy* solved one interpretation issue, it did not precisely define the term "subcontractor" for purposes of Miller Act payment bond coverage. In *F. D. Rich Co. v. United States ex rel. Industrial Lumber Co.*,[10] the Supreme Court reiterated the functional definition of "subcontractor" provided by *MacEvoy,* and emphasized that whether a person is a subcontractor relates to "the substantiality and importance of his relationship with the prime contractor."

Lower courts have given the term "subcontractor" a narrow definition under the Miller Act. This limitation of coverage has generally been applied to payment bonds issued pursuant to little Miller Act statutes as well. However, as a *general* matter, any person having a direct contractual relationship with the prime contractor on a project or with a first-tier subcontractor will fall within the scope of the payment bond.

In determining whether a party is a subcontractor, it is important to focus on the contractual relationship between the party at issue and the prime contractor.[11] A party who merely supplies materials will probably fail to qualify as a "subcontractor." A party who installs materials would be far more likely to meet the test. In the gap, however, is the specialty subcontractor, who supplies "customized materials" that are designed or fabricated specially for the project and that have little or no commercial value except for the particular project. In some cases, the provider of "customized" materials may be a subcontractor for Miller Act purposes.[12] In *Lane Constr.*, the court held that a manufacturer was not a supplier, but instead was a subcontractor. The product the manufacturer supplied was custom-made gates for a dam construction project. The sole purpose and usefulness of the gates would be their functioning as an integral portion of the dam.

The distinction between a supplier and subcontractor at the second tier is critical as it will determine whether a claimant is protected by the Miller Act. The Miller Act protects suppliers to federal contractors and subcontractors, but not suppliers to suppliers. For example in *United States ex rel. Gulf States Enter., Inc. v. R. R. Tway, Inc.*, the provider of a bulldozer and operator to run it on a federal construction project was a *supplier,* not a subcontractor, because the provider was not responsible for doing a definable part of the contract performance.[13] The agreement with the contractor was not to do specific work, but rather to provide a dozer and operator at an agreed upon hourly rate "as needed." Because the provider was a supplier and not a subcontractor, the company that owned the dozer and leased it to the provider could not recover unpaid lease payments from the prime contractor's surety under the Miller Act.

---

[10] 417 U.S. 116 (1974).

[11] *Aetna Casualty & Sur. Co. v. United States ex rel. Gibson Steel Co.*, 382 F.2d 615 (5th Cir. 1967).

[12] *See, e.g., United States ex rel. Parker-Hannifin Corp. v. Lane Constr. Corp.*, 477 F. Supp. 400 (M.D. Pa. 1979); *United States ex rel. Newport News Shipbuilding and Dry Dock Co. v. Blount Bros. Constr. Co.*, 168 F. Supp. 407 (D. Md. 1958).

[13] 938 F.2d 583 (5th. Cir. 1991).

Some other factors considered in determining whether a party is a subcontractor under the Miller Act include whether a payment or performance bond was required; whether the price included sales tax; whether progress payments and retainage were withheld; and whether shop drawings and certified payrolls were submitted.[14]

Also arising under the general issue of "who is a subcontractor" is the issue of "telescoping" contractual relationships. A prime contractor will not be allowed to insert a dummy subcontractor between itself and actual performing subcontractors simply to avoid Miller Act liability when those subcontractors or suppliers go unpaid by the dummy subcontractor.[15] However, unless courts find evidence of bad faith or fraud, they will generally not look beyond formal contractual relationships.

Subcontractors are included within the protection of a little Miller Act payment bond, but the scope of the term "subcontractor" varies, and the local act should be consulted. Where there is no statutory definition provided, courts will often apply the definition of "subcontractor" developed under the Miller Act.[16] Other factors that may be considered include the trade customs, whether the materials are specially fabricated, and the extent to which the claimant has assumed responsibility for the prime contractor's performance.[17]

The payment bond used most frequently on private projects, and on many state and local public works, is the American Institute of Architects' (AIA) Document A312 (1984 ed.), which maintains the limitation of claimants down to the second tier: "An individual or entity having a direct contract with the Contractor or with a subcontractor of the Contractor to furnish labor, materials or equipment for use in the performance of the contract." This language will be construed in light of state statutes and court decisions that, as noted, may not be consistent with the Miller Act coverage.

11.4 What Work Qualifies for Payment Bond Coverage?

After determining who is protected by a payment bond, the next issue is what work by that party qualifies for protection. The Miller Act simply provides payment protection for labor and materials furnished "in the prosecution of the work." Courts have generally interpreted this language liberally, holding that it covers not only work incorporated in the project, but also work done for the benefit of the project.[18]

---

[14] *United States ex rel. Consolidated Pipe & Supply Co. v. Morrison-Knudsen Co.*, 687 F.2d 129 (6th Cir. 1982); *United States v. Ellis Constr. Co.*, 398 F. Supp. 719 (E.D. Tenn. 1975); *United States ex rel. Potomac Rigging Co. v. Wright Contracting Co.*, 194 F. Supp. 444 (D. Md. 1961).

[15] *See Continental Casualty Co. v. United States ex rel. Conroe Creosoting Co.*, 308 F.2d 846 (5th Cir. 1962).

[16] *See, e.g., Lennox Indus., Inc., v. City of Davenport*, 320 N.W.2d 575 (Iowa 1982).

[17] *See Tiffany Constr. Co. v. Hancock & Kelley Constr. Co.*, 539 P.2d 978 (Ariz. Ct. App. 1975).

[18] *See United States ex rel. Westinghouse Elec. Supply Co. v. Endebrock-White Co.*, 275 F.2d 57 (4th Cir. 1960); *United States ex rel. Sunbelt Pipe Corp. v. United States Fidelity and Guar. Co.*, 785 F.2d 468 (4th Cir. 1986).

Thus a claimant obtained relief from a Miller Act surety for material that was damaged in transit and then delivered to the project.[19] Although the material was not incorporated into the project itself, the court held that the material was nevertheless furnished "in the prosecution of the work," because the subcontractor had assumed the risk of loss or damage during shipment.[20] Similarly, a supplier recovered for delivery of equipment to a subcontractor in spite of the subcontractor's subsequent removal of the material from the job site and use on another project.[21] Following this general line of cases, state courts have ruled that a supplier need not show that the materials delivered to the site were actually incorporated into the project.[22]

What about material used in construction but not incorporated into the project, such as concrete form work? As a general rule, the Miller Act applies if the material is substantially consumed or rendered useless in the prosecution of the work.[23] This general rule also applies to capital equipment.[24] In addition, the cost of incidental repairs necessary to maintain equipment during its use on the project may be recoverable under a bond.[25] However, substantial "replacement" repairs may not be recoverable under the bond, on the theory that they add value to the construction equipment by extending its useful life beyond the project in question.

Miller Act payment bonds have been interpreted to cover fair rental value of equipment that is leased for use in the prosecution of the contract work, together with incidental repairs.[26] Guarantee work or repairs that become necessary and are performed after substantial completion of the work may also be the subject of Miller Act recovery. Miller Act payment bonds have also been construed to cover transportation and delivery costs.[27] Food and lodging may also be covered when they are a necessary and integral part of performance.[28]

---

[19] See United States ex rel. National U.S. Radiator Corp. v. D. C. Loveys Co., 174 F. Supp. 44 (D. Mass. 1959).

[20] Id.

[21] See Glassell-Taylor Co. v. Magnolia Petroleum, 153 F.2d 527 (5th Cir. 1946).

[22] See, e.g., Solite Masonry Units Corp. v. Piland Constr. Co., 232 S.E.2d 759 (Va. 1977); see also Mid-Continent Casualty Co. v. P&H Supply, Inc., 490 P.2d 1358 (Okla. 1971) (evidence that materials were delivered to project site creates rebuttable presumption that materials were actually consumed in construction).

[23] See United States ex rel. Tom P. McDermott, Inc. v. Woods Constr. Co., 224 F. Supp. 406 (N.D. Okla. 1963).

[24] See United States ex rel. Chemetron Corp. v. George A. Fuller Co., 250 F. Supp. 649 (D. Mont. 1965); United States ex rel. Sunbelt Pipe Corp., fn. 17, supra.

[25] See Massachusetts Bonding & Ins. Co. v. United States ex rel. Clarksdale Mach. Co., 88 F.2d 388 (5th Cir. 1937); Maryland Casualty Co. v. Ohio River Gravel Co., 20 F.2d 514 (4th Cir. 1927), cert. denied, 275 U.S. 570 (1927).

[26] See Friebel & Hartman, Inc. v. United States ex rel. Codell Constr. Co., 238 F.2d 394 (6th Cir. 1956); United States ex rel. Mississippi Rd. Supply Co. v. H. R. Morgan, Inc., 542 F.2d 262 (5th Cir. 1976), cert. denied, 434 U.S. 828 (1977).

[27] See United States ex rel. Benkart Co. v. John A. Johnson & Sons, Inc., 236 F.2d 864 (3rd Cir. 1956).

[28] Brogan v. National Sur. Co., 246 U.S. 257 (1918).

What is covered under "little Miller Acts" may substantially track the interpretation of the federal Miller Act, but deviations exist and are always a risk. The broad definition of "labor, materials or equipment," provided in AIA Document 312A (1984 ed.) is consistent with fairly broad payment bond coverage, but little Miller Acts can be more restrictive. AIA Document A312, for example, expressly contemplates coverage for leased equipment as do some little Miller Acts.[29] Other Little Miller Acts have been construed to not cover rentals.[30]

11.5 Recovery under Payment Bonds for Extra Work or Delay Costs

Work done by a qualifying claimant under a change order is generally within the payment bond's protection. Indeed, recovery for such extra work under the Miller Act does not depend on the prime contractor's ability to recover its costs from the government.[31] Recovery for extra work incorporated into a project by an otherwise qualified claimant is likewise frequently permitted under little Miller Acts.[32] Compliance with contractual and bond notice provisions should be given extra attention in such situations to enhance the claimant's position.

Delay damages, on the other hand, have traditionally been viewed as outside the scope of Miller Act coverage.[33] This traditional restriction on a claim for delay damages under a payment bond does not affect the claimant's general right to collect delay damages from the contractor or subcontractor causing the damage.

Perhaps the largest area of recurring controversy on payment bond coverage relates to delay damages. The traditional rule under the Miller Act was that breach of contract and delay damages were not covered.[34] The more recent trend is to allow recovery of delay damages. For example, in *United States ex rel. Mandel Bros. Contracting Corp. v. P. J. Carlin Constr. Co.,*[35] a federal district court held that the bond claimant could recover costs of delay on a *quantum meruit* ("value added") theory. In that case, the claimant alleged that the general contractor's failure to provide access to the work and to perform work, which restrained the claimant's performance, was such a substantial interference with the claimant's progress that it amounted to an abandonment of the contract. The defendant sureties relied on the traditional cases

---

[29] *See, e.g.,* Pa. Stat. Ann. Title 8 § 193 (a)(2); R.I. Gen. Laws § 37-12-1.

[30] *See, e.g., Johnson v. Gallegos Constr. Co.,* 785 P.2d 1109 (Utah 1990); *Board of Local Improvements v. St. Paul Fire & Marine Ins.,* 350 N.E. 2d 36 (Ill. App. Ct. 1976).

[31] *See United States ex rel. Warren Painting v. J. C. Boespflug Constr. Co.,* 325 F.2d 54 (9th Cir. 1963); *United States ex rel. Kilsby v. George,* 243 F.2d 83 (5th Cir. 1957).

[32] *See, e.g., Hartford Accident & Indem. Co. v. District of Columbia,* 441 A.2d 969 (D.C. 1982).

[33] *See McDaniel v. Ashton-Mardian Co.,* 357 F.2d 511 (9th Cir. 1966); *United States ex rel. Pittsburgh–Des Moines Steel Co. v. MacDonald Constr. Co.,* 281 F. Supp. 1010 (E.D. Mo. 1968).

[34] *See, e.g. United States ex. rel. Pittsburgh–Des Moines Steel Co. v. MacDonald Constr. Co.,* 281 F. Supp. 1010 (E.D. Mo. 1968).

[35] 254 F. Supp. 637 (E.D.N.Y. 1966).

that breaches of contract predicated on delays were not compensable under the Miller Act. The court rejected that argument, however, on the reasoning that a *quantum meruit* claim is one for labor and materials actually furnished in the prosecution of the work, and therefore within the scope of the payment bond.

Other, more recent cases, discard the *quantum meruit* theory and simply find delay damage to be covered under the Miller Act as part of the value of materials and services contributed to the project. In *United States ex rel. Marianna v. Piracci Constr. Co.,*[36] the court allowed a claimant to recover damages resulting from a delay against a Miller Act payment bond. *Piracci* has been followed by the United States Court of Appeals for the District of Columbia.[37] Similarly, the United States Court of Appeals for the Fifth Circuit held that a subcontractor may recover delay costs if they are out-of-pocket increases, that is escalations, against a payment bond surety. However, no profit was allowed.[38] The Fifth Circuit relied on an earlier case, *United States ex. rel. Petrun Constr. Co. v. Harvester's Group Inc.,*[37] in which the Eleventh Circuit Court of Appeals held that a surety must pay a subcontractor on a Miller Act claim for delay damages caused by the general contractor. The result in *Petrun Constr.* is particularly noteworthy because the subcontract itself appeared to preclude delay damages through a no-damages-for-delay clause. The court construed that clause to only be enforceable if the subcontractor was granted time extensions. Based on the finding that the contractor wrongfully and prematurely terminated the subcontractor's participation on the project, the court held that neither the contractor nor its surety could claim protection under the no damages for delay clause. There are, however, other Federal courts which have continued to refuse recovery of delay damages under the Miller Act.[39]

The ability to recover delay damages against a payment bond under state law depends on the jurisdiction, with some states allowing recovery,[40] and others barring it.[41]

11.6 The Effect of Payment Bonds on Lien Rights

Generally, the existence of a payment bond simply provides the subcontractor (or other qualified claimants) with a further right of recovery, in addition to

---

[36] 405 F. Supp. 904 (D.D.C. 1975).

[37] *See United States ex rel. Heller Elec. Co. v. William F. Klingensmith, Inc.,* 670 F.2d 1227 (D.C. Cir. 1981).

[38] *United States ex rel. T.M.S Mechanical Contractors, Inc. v. Millers Mut. Fire Ins. Co. of Texas,* 942 F.2d 946 (5th Cir. 1991).

[39] *See, e.g., United States ex rel. Mobile Premix Concrete, Inc. v. Santa Fe Engineers, Inc.,* 515 F. Supp. 512 (D. Colo. 1981).

[40] *See, e.g. Hartford Acc. & Indem. Co. v District of Columbia,* 441 A.2d 969 (D.C. 1982).

[41] *See, e.g., Lite-Air Prods., Inc. v. Fidelity & Deposit Co. of Maryland,* 437 F. Supp. 801 (E.D. Pa. 1977).

any lien rights.[42] However, in a few jurisdictions the existence of a right to claim under a payment bond abrogates the claimant's lien rights.[43] Most jurisdictions, however, continue to hold that the existence of the right to claim under a payment bond supplements rather than replaces a subcontractor's lien rights.

11.7 The Surety's Defenses to Payment Bond Liability

In any claim against a payment bond, the surety is entitled to assert any defenses of the principal, including the defense of offset or recoupment. The surety may have additional defenses of its own. Generally, the surety's independent defenses may be found in the applicable statute and/or the terms of the bond itself, and include a claimant's failure to comply with notice requirements and time limitations. Although the surety can assert technical defenses relating to the timing and sufficiency of the required notice, the surety must, however, deal with bond claimants in good faith.[44]

If you believe that you have a valid payment bond claim, it is imperative that you review the terms of the payment bond, as well as any applicable statutes, to determine the exact timing, nature, and recipient of any notice or other requirements necessary to secure rights under the bond. Any failure to comply with such requirements may defeat an otherwise valid claim. If you are responding to a payment bond claim, this careful review is equally important.

11.8 *Time of Notice*   Under the Miller Act and most little Miller Act statutes, notice must be sent within a certain number of days from the date the claimant last performed work or supplied materials for which the claim is made. Under the Miller Act, the notice period is ninety days. This ninety-day period is common for little Miller Act statutes as well.[45] The Miller Act notice requirements, however, do not apply to subcontractors and suppliers in direct privity with the prime contractor.

Notice under the Miller Act needs to be sent to the prime contractor; the surety does not have to receive notice.[46] Although the Miller Act requires notice to be sent by registered mail, this requirement may be waived. However, oral notice will generally be insufficient.[47] Since the notice provisions are intended to protect the contractor who provided the payment bond, the written

---

[42] 57 C.J.S. *Mechanics Liens* § 258.

[43] *See Schleifer v. All-Shores Constr. & Supply Co.*, 260 So.2d 270 (Fla. Dist. Ct. App. 1972); *Globe Indem. Co. v. West Texas Lumber Co.*, 34 S.W.2d 896 (Tex. Civ. App. 1930, no writ).

[44] *See Szarkowski v. Reliance Ins. Co.*, 404 N.W.2d 502 (N.D. 1987) (Supreme Court of North Dakota recognized a cause of action by an unpaid subcontractor against a surety for its alleged bad faith refusal to pay on the bond).

[45] *See, e.g.,* Conn. Gen. Stat. § 49-52.

[46] *See Continental Casualty Co. v. United States ex. rel. Robertson Lumber Co.*, 305 F.2d 794 (8th Cir. 1962), *cert. denied*, 371 U.S. 922 (1962).

[47] *See Fleisher Eng'g & Constr. Co. v. United States*, 311 U.S. 15 (1940).

notice must expressly or impliedly inform the contractor that the claimant is looking to it or the surety for payment.[48]

11.9 Time of Lawsuit   A lawsuit to enforce the provisions of a payment bond by any claimant must generally be brought within one year of "the day on which the last of the labor was performed or material was supplied by [claimant]." Under the Miller Act, this one-year rule is considered by federal courts to be jurisdictional in nature and cannot be waived by the surety.[49]

As a result of these important time limitations, a substantial body of law has developed defining "the day on which the last of the labor was performed or material was supplied by [claimant]." For example, in *General Ins. Co. of Am. v. United States ex rel. Audley Moore & Son,*[50] the court refused to regard "inspecting" as within the scope of the term "labor" as used in the Miller Act. Correction of prior work has been held to constitute "labor" within the meaning of the limitation provisions in some cases, if the government has refused to accept the project until such work has been completed. However, correction of defects or warranty work, after completion of the original subcontract work, may not constitute the furnishing of labor or materials for purposes of the Miller Act's limitation provision.[51]

The distinction that arises out of these cases as they affect repair work for purposes of Miller Act limitations is to distinguish "guarantee work" from "punch list work." In other words, work that the government demands to be finished in accordance with the contract plans and specifications by a punch list or other similar devices is considered to be contract work. Therefore, performance of this work will normally toll the limitation provisions of the Miller Act governing when notice must be given and suit must be filed. On the other hand, a contractor's return to the job site to correct work under a warranty or to repair latent defects is regarded by the courts as being warranty work, and not encompassed by the term "labor" in the Miller Act or little Miller Acts.[52]

Remember, however, that in spite of the profusion of case law fixing the date from which the one-year limitations period runs, the issue is ultimately a question of fact. In *Johnson Serv. Co. v. Transamerica Ins. Co.,*[53] the court observed: "Common to all of these decisions . . . is the notion that each case must be judged on its own facts and that sweeping rules about 'repairs' offer little help in the necessary analysis."

[48] *See Bowden v. United States ex rel. Malloy,* 239 F.2d 572 (9th Cir. 1956), *cert. denied,* 353 U.S. 957 (1957).

[49] *See United States ex rel. Soda v. Montgomery,* 253 F.2d 509 (3rd Cir. 1958).

[50] 406 F.2d 442 (5th Cir. 1969), *cert. denied,* 396 U.S. 902 (1969).

[51] *See United States ex rel. Light & Power Util. Corp. v. Liles Constr. Co.,* 440 F.2d 474 (5th Cir. 1971); *see also Johnson Serv. Co. v. Transamerica Ins. Co.,* 485 F.2d 164 (5th Cir. 1973) (involving a private bond, but using Miller Act decisions as precedent).

[52] *See, e.g., United States ex rel. State Elec. Supply Co. v. Hesselden Constr. Co.,* 404 F.2d 774 (10th Cir. 1968).

[53] 485 F.2d 164, 173 (5th Cir. 1973).

11.10 Misrepresented Status of Payments   A surety often raises defensively a materialman's misrepresentation to the contractor of the status of the subcontractor's account. For example, a subcontractor may attempt to induce the materialman to sign lien waivers in order to receive final payment from the prime contractor. To induce the signing of a lien waiver, the subcontractor promises that the materialman will be paid as soon as the subcontractor receives payment from the prime contractor. If a subcontractor does not make good on this promise, because of the intervention of bankruptcy or judgments, courts have held that the materialman has waived its right to payment. In denying relief to the materialman, courts have estopped the materialman from claiming under the bond, because its acts have been relied upon to the prime contractor's and surety's detriment, thereby discharging the prime contractor and surety from any obligation on the bond.[54]

POINTS TO REMEMBER

- A payment bond provides a financial guarantee of payment from the surety to suppliers and subcontractors.
- Payment bonds are most prevalent on public works projects on which they are required by statute to replace the protection of lien rights, which generally do not exist on public projects.
- A payment bond required by statute will generally be construed according to the terms of the statute. Private payment bonds (those not required by statute) are essentially private contractual undertakings in which the terms of the bond will be determinative. In any event, potential claimants should review and be familiar with the terms of the payment bond relevant to a particular project.
- The federal Miller Act governs payment bond requirements for federal construction projects. Most states have enacted "little Miller Acts," which govern payment bonds on state and local projects, which are modeled after the federal Miller Act. Regardless of similarities, claimants should make themselves aware of the requirements applicable to the jurisdiction which governs the project.
- In most jurisdictions, payment bond coverage does not extend beyond second-tier subcontractors and suppliers—subcontractors to subcontractors and suppliers to subcontractors. Under the federal Miller Act and many little Miller Acts, coverage does not extend to suppliers to suppliers.
- Payment bonds, whether statutory or private, involve various notice and timing requirements relating to claims and litigation. Such requirements must be identified and complied with. Failure to comply may bar otherwise valid claims.

[54] *See United States ex rel. Gulfport Piping Co. v. Monaco and Son, Inc.,* 336 F.2d 636 (4th Cir. 1964); *see also United States ex rel. Westinghouse Elec. v. James Stewart Co.,* 336 F.2d 777 (9th Cir. 1964).

12

PERFORMANCE BONDS AND TERMINATIONS

Furnishing performance bonds is an important and everyday fact of life in the construction industry. Long a statutory requirement in public contracting, a bond requirement in private contracts is now common. Just as the owner insists upon performance bonds, prime contractors often require their subcontractors to provide bonds to acquire greater financial security through a surety's involvement. The existence of performance bonds is often the sole salvation of a project, for all concerned with it.

Although performance bonds are important during a crisis, the requirement to provide bonds significantly impacts a contractor's ability to obtain work, serving as a screening device for contractor selection. A surety should not underwrite bonds for contractors who cannot perform, whether because of lack of expertise or lack of adequate finances. If a contractor cannot obtain the required bond, an owner or prime contractor would be wise to seek a contractor that can.

This chapter analyzes claims made under performance bonds and discusses issues and options presented.[1] The fundamentals of the law of suretyship are described as an introduction to the discussion of cases arising under performance bonds. Following the discussion of performance bonds, issues concerning terminations for default and for convenience are addressed.

12.1 PERFORMANCE BONDS

12.2 Fundamentals of Suretyship

A claim on a performance bond involves a default or alleged default on the part of the contractor. Under such circumstances, an understanding of the legal principles involved is imperative.

[1] Payment bonds are discussed at Chapter 11.

12.3 A Performance Bond Is Not an Insurance Policy

To understand the law of suretyship, one must appreciate the distinction between a surety bond and an insurance policy.

A surety bond is not an insurance policy, although in some respects they are similar.[2] "Insurance has been defined as a contract whereby one undertakes to [indemnify] another against loss, damage or liability arising from an unknown or contingent event; whereas *a contract of suretyship is one to answer for the debt, default or miscarriage of another . . . .*"[3]

Two parties enter into an insurance contract, the insurer and the insured. A performance bond, however, involves three parties: The "principal"—the party whose faithful performance is being bonded; the "obligee"—the party for whose protection the bond is being issued; and the "surety"—who together with the principal jointly binds itself to the obligee for the faithful performance of the principal's obligation.

Under this tripartite arrangement, the *principal*—the contractor—remains *primarily* liable to the owner/obligee. The *surety's* obligation is secondary and arises only upon the failure or default of the principal.[4]

12.4 Indemnification—The Bottom Line

Implied within the contract of suretyship is the principal's obligation to reimburse its surety for damages proximately caused by the principal.[5] A far more common source of the principal's liability, however, is an express indemnification agreement required by the surety to induce it to execute a performance bond for the contractor.

Despite the broad language contained in typical indemnity agreements, an indemnitor of a surety is not without certain defenses. The obligation of the surety only comes into play upon the default of the principal. Thus if the principal is not in default, and has not confessed default to the surety, the surety has no liability to the owner/obligee under the bond. If a surety responds to the demands of the owner to remedy the contractor's alleged default, and the surety does so over the contractor's objections, the contractor may nonetheless discharge any liability under the indemnity agreement with the surety by establishing that the owner's termination of the contractor was improper.[6] On the other hand, where the surety has unreasonably failed to accept a favorable settlement offer that would have reduced the indemnitor's exposure, such unreasonable behavior may discharge the indemnitor to the extent that the actual damages sought exceed the settlement offer.[7]

---

[2] See *Lumbermens Mut. Casualty Co. v. Agency Rent-A-Car, Inc.,* 128 Cal. App. 3d 764, 180 Cal. Rptr. 546 (1982).

[3] *Meyer v. Building & Realty Servs. Co.,* 196 N.E. 250, 253 (Ind. 1935); see *United States v. Frisk,* 675 F.2d 1079, 182 n.6 (9th Cir. 1982); *Madison County Farmers Ass'n v. American Employers Ins. Co.,* 209 F.2d 581, 585 (8th Cir. 1954).

[4] See *Meyer,* fn. 3, *supra* at 253.

[5] See, e.g., *Kimberly-Clark Corp. v. Alpha Bldg. Co.,* 591 F. Supp. 198 (N.D. Miss. 1984).

[6] See *Seaboard Sur. Co. v. Dale Constr. Co.,* 230 F.2d 625 (1st Cir. 1956); *Angle v. Banker's Sur. Co.,* 210 F. 289 (N.D.N.Y. 1913).

[7] See *Briggs v. Travelers Indem. Co.,* 289 So.2d 762 (Fla. Dist. Ct. App. 1974).

12.5 *"Common Law" versus "Statutory" Bonds*   Because legal requirements associated with claims on statutory bonds often differ from requirements for a common law bond, it is critical to ascertain whether the bond is a common law or statutory bond. The primary test depends upon an examination of the bond, concentrating upon the obligations imposed upon the principal and its surety. The test requires a comparison of the minimal requirements enunciated in the statute and the language contained within the bond.[8] When the surety's obligations have not been extended beyond the statutory minimum requirements, the bond is statutory.[9] It is important to note that, even though a bond is furnished incident to a public work project, it is not necessarily construed as a statutory bond.[10] Furthermore, merely because a bond fails to reference a particular statute does not automatically render it a common law bond.[11]

12.6 *The Surety's Obligations*   The nature of the surety's obligation is strictly financial as expressed by the terms of the bond itself. The performance bond surety binds itself *jointly and severally* with its principal to pay to the obligee, the owner of the project, a sum certain or penal sum, generally equal to the contract amount. Any such payment, however, is due only if the principal wrongfully and without justification defaults on the primary obligation (the contract) and only to the extent of any loss to the obligee (the owner). Generally, the surety's liability is strictly limited by both the terms of the bond and by the terms of the underlying contract, which is typically incorporated into and made a part of the bond.

Since the express purpose of the bond is to secure the performance of the underlying contract, the bond and the contract are read together.[12] In this manner, the surety's obligations are found in the contract, the plans and specifications and the bond.[13]

Consequently, the surety possesses all nonpersonal defenses, including offset, that would normally be available to the principal.[14] "Since liability of a surety is commensurate with that of the principal, where the principal is not liable on the obligation, neither is the guarantor."[15]

---

[8] *Florida Keys Community College v. Insurance Co. of N. Am.,* 456 So.2d 1250 (Fla. Dist. Ct. App. 1984). Statutory bonds are those that meet the minimal requirements of the statute; common law bonds are those that provide coverage in excess of the minimum statutory requirements.
[9] *Id.*
[10] *Id.*
[11] *Id.*
[12] *Pacific Employers Ins. Co. v. City of Berkeley,* 158 Cal. App. 3d 145, 204 Cal. Rptr. 387 (1984).
[13] J. Milana, *"The Performance Bond and the Underlying Contract: The Bond Obligations Do Not Include All of the Contract Obligations,"* 12 Forum 187, 188 (1976); *see United States Fidelity & Guar. Co. v. Gulf Fl. Dev. Corp.,* 365 So.2d 748 (Fla. Dist. Ct. App. 1978); *St. Paul Fire & Marine Ins. Co. v. Woolley/Sweeney Hotel,* 545 So.2d 958 (Fla. Dist. Ct. App. 1989) (arbitration agreement in contract bound surety); *American Home Assurance Co. v. Larkin Gen. Hosp. Ltd.,* 593 So.2d 195 (Fla. 1992).
[14] *See State Athletic Comm'n v. Massachusetts Bonding & Ins. Co.,* 46 Cal. App. 2d 839, 117 P.2d 80 (1941).
[15] *U.S. Leasing Corp. v. DuPont,* 70 Cal. Rptr. 393, 403, 444 P.2d 65 (Cal. 1968); *see Riley Constr. Co. v. Schillmoeller & Krofl Co.,* 70 Wisc. 2d 900, 905, 236 N.W.2d 195, 198 (1975).

12.7 Extension of Performance Bond Surety's Liability to Third Parties

Although the owner is the intended beneficiary of a performance bond, sureties increasingly are being held liable to other project participants on a third-party beneficiary theory. In these cases, the claimant asserts that the parties to the performance bond intended to confer rights to the claimant as against the surety. For example, a federal court held that the Miller Act's dual requirement of performance and payment bonds would allow suppliers frustrated by the exhaustion of the penal sum on the payment bond to claim alternatively against the performance bond.[16] In reaching this result, the court reasoned that performance of the construction contract, guaranteed by the performance bond, included payment for the work that was the basis of the unpaid supplier's claims.[17]

In addition, parallel primes on multi-prime projects often assert claims against the performance bond of another parallel prime. The performance bond surety traditionally has attempted to defend claims by other prime contractors on the basis that the performance bond was only for the benefit of the named obligee, the owner, and not third parties. This defense has been successful in some cases.[18]

In other instances, the performance bond surety has been held responsible for a multiple prime contractor under a third-party beneficiary theory. In essence, the surety is deemed to guarantee the performance of the principal's obligation to coordinate and cooperate with other parallel prime contractors and protect additional prime contractors from any damages sustained by the principal's failure.[19]

12.8 Increase of the Surety's Liability under a Performance Bond

In addition to claims from third parties, performance bond sureties must be increasingly concerned with additional claims beyond the express terms of the bond and in excess of the penal sum of the bond.

In *Continental Realty Corp. v. Andrew J. Crevolin Co.*,[20] the court extended a surety's performance bond liability on a novel theory. The court held that the surety's failure (1) to complete the project in a timely manner or (2) to

---

[16] See *United States ex rel. Edward Hines Lumber Co. v. Kalady Constr. Co.*, 227 F. Supp. 1017 (N.D. Ill. 1964); *United States ex rel. Blount Fabricators, Inc. v. Pitt Gen. Contractors, Inc.*, 769 F.Supp. 1016 (E.D. Tenn. 1991).

[17] See *Royal Indem. Co. v. Alexander Indus., Inc.*, 211 A.2d 919 (Del. 1965); *Amelco Window Corp. v. Federal Ins. Co.*, 317 A.2d 398 (N.J. Sup. Ct. App. Div. 1974); *Kalady Constr. Co.*, fn. 16, *supra.*

[18] *M.G.M. Constr. Corp. v. New Jersey Educ. Facilities Auth.*, 220 N.J. Super. 483, 532 A.2d 764 (1987); *J. Louis Crum Corp. v. Alfred Lindgren, Inc.*, 564 S.W.2d 544 (Mo. Ct. App. 1978).

[19] See *M. T. Reed Constr. v. Virginia Metal Prods. Corp.*, 213 F.2d 337 (5th Cir. 1954); *see also Aetna Casualty & Sur. Co. v. Doleac Elec. Co., Inc.*, 471 So.2d 325 (Miss. 1985).

[20] 380 F. Supp. 246 (S.D. W.Va. 1974).

pay the cost of completion constituted a breach of the surety's contractual bond obligation independent of the principal's default. Significantly, the obligee recovered damages equal to the actual damages suffered—that is, damages in excess of the penal sum of the bond.

In essence, the surety in the *Crevolin* case became liable for costs that necessarily could have been avoided had the surety performed timely. For instance, water damage occurred to the building when the contractor abandoned the project prior to completing the roof. Had the surety undertaken to perform its performance bond obligations within the fifteen-day period set forth in the agreement, the moisture damage could have been prevented.

In addition to a waiver of the penal sum, a surety's conduct may be so egregious that punitive damages are awarded. The general rule is that punitive damages cannot be obtained in breach of contract actions except in cases where an independent tort exists.[21] However, insurance regulations applicable to surety companies specifically provide in certain instances that punitive damages and penalties or attorneys' fees, or both, may be recovered against a defaulting surety.[22] Where the statute provides for such a recovery, claimants under performance bonds have been able to recover such punitive damages or penalties covered against a defaulting surety.[23] For example, in *Fisher v. Fidelity & Deposit Company*,[24] a vexatious and unreasonable delay in settling a performance bond claim entitled the owner to attorneys' fees and other costs in addition to compensatory damages resulting from the delay.[25]

Questionable conduct on the part of the surety may also give rise to complaints of bad faith, and, consequently, the assertion of tort claims and punitive damages. The legal basis for a claim that a party has acted in bad faith is found in the universal requirement in all contracts that the parties exercise good faith and engage in fair dealing. The surety, therefore, has a duty to act in good faith. When actual malice, fraud or willful and wanton disregard for the obligee's rights are proven, punitive damages may be recovered against the surety.[26]

12.9   The Surety's Defenses to Performance Bond Liability

As previously stated, a surety's liability is coextensive with that of its principal; the surety's liability for the principal cannot be greater than the principal's

---

[21] *Oliver B. Cannon & Son, Inc. v. Fidelity & Cas. Co.*, 484 F. Supp. 1375 (D.C. Del. 1980).

[22] *See generally* 44 Am. Jur. 2d, Insurance, §§ 1798–1799; 47 A.L.R.3d 314.

[23] *See Ray Ross Constr. Co., Inc. v. Raney*, 587 S.W.2d 46 (Ark. 1979).

[24] 466 N.E.2d 332 (Ill. App. Ct. 1984).

[25] *See also* Fla. Stat. Ann. §§ 627.428, 627.756 (1996) (Florida has enlarged an insurer's liability for attorneys' fees for bad faith failure to settle to cover sureties issuing payment bonds).

[26] *See, e.g., Hoskins, et al. v. Aetna Life Ins. Co.* 6 Ohio St. 3rd 272, 452 N.E.2d 1315 (1983); *Riva Ridge Apartments v. Robert G. Fischer Co., Inc.*, 745 P.2d 1034 (Colo. Ct. App. 1987).

liability.[27] Conversely, a defense normally available to the principal, but which the principal is barred from asserting, is likewise unavailable to the surety.[28]

Additionally, the surety may have independent defenses, arising out of the language of the performance bond itself or the circumstances that give rise to the claim. For example, a surety generally is not liable for the acts of the principal that occurred prior to the posting of the bond.[29]

The obligee also has an obligation to perform faithfully and comply with any conditions precedent in order to recover under the performance bond.[30] A failure to do so can result in the discharge of any liability the surety may otherwise have under the bond. In determining the extent of any waiver, discharge or conditions precedent to liability under the bond, the terms of the bond, as well as the terms of the principal's construction contract, must be reviewed.[31]

"Material alteration" or "increase in risk" provides another example of an independent defense.[32] Where the surety does not consent to a material change to the endeavor that it has financially guaranteed, the surety may be discharged, either in whole or to the extent of injury caused by a material alteration. This discharge is based on the theory that the bond only binds the surety to certain risks, and consent of the surety is necessary in order to expand its liability beyond the terms of the bond.[33] In recognition of this doctrine, most bond forms permit the owner and the principal to alter the terms of the underlying construction contract by change orders and provide that the surety consents to such modifications in advance.[34] A surety normally must show harm caused by the alteration.

The surety may also be released from liability under the performance bond when the owner makes unauthorized or premature payments, or fails

---

[27] See Stearns, *Law of Suretyship* (5th ed.); *Village of Rosemont v. Lentin Lumber Co.*, 494 N.E.2d 592 (Ill. App. Ct. 1986); *State Athletic Comm'n v. Massachusetts Bonding & Ins. Co.*, 117 P.2d 80 (Cal. Ct. App. 1941) ("The liability of the contractor is the measure of the surety's liability.") See *Aetna Cas. & Sur. Co. v. Warren Bros. Co.*, 355 So.2d 785 (Fla. 1978); Cal. Civ. Code § 2807 (1993).

[28] See *Indemnity Ins. Co. v. United States*, 74 F.2d 22 (5th Cir. 1934). See also *Rhode Island Hosp. Trust Nat'l Bank v. Ohio Cas. Ins. Co.*, 789 F.2d 74 (1st Cir. 1986).

[29] *Morton Regent Enterprises, Inc. v. Leadtec California, Inc.*, 74 Cal. App. 3d 842, 845, 141 Cal. Rptr. 706, 708 (1977); 74 Am. Jur. 2d, Suretyship, § 29 (Supp. 1985).

[30] See *Easton v. Boston Inv. Co.*, 51 Cal. App. 246, 196 P. 796 (1921).

[31] *Pacific Employers Ins. Co.*, fn. 12, *supra*, at 387.

[32] See, e.g., *Ramada Dev. Co. v. United States Fidelity and Guar. Co.*, 626 F.2d 517 (6th Cir. 1980); *Continental Bank & Trust Co. v. American Bonding Co.*, 605 F.2d 1049 (8th Cir. 1979), *aff'd in part, rev'd in part on other grounds*, 630 F.2d 606 (8th Cir. 1980).

[33] See *Maryland Cas. Co. v. City of South Norfolk*, 54 F.2d 1032 (4th Cir.), *modified*, 56 F.2d 822, *cert. denied*, 286 U.S. 562 (1932); *United States, ex rel. Army Athletic Ass'n v. Reliance Ins. Co.*, 799 F.2d 1382 (9th Cir. 1986).

[34] See, e.g., *Trinity Universal Ins. Co. v. Gould*, 258 F.2d 883 (10th Cir. 1958); *Massachusetts Bonding & Ins. Co. v. John R. Thompson Co.*, 88 F.2d 825 (8th Cir.), *cert. denied*, 301 U.S. 707 (1937).

to withhold retainage.[35] In *Southwood Builders, Inc. v. Peerless Ins. Co.,*[36] a subcontractor posted payment and performance bonds on a courthouse project. The subcontractor fell behind schedule but refused to add another crew to the project. The prime contractor did not terminate the sub, but agreed to pay for the addition of an extra crew and for all additional materials ordered for the job. Such payments were to be deducted from later subcontractor progress payments. The prime contractor did not notify the subcontractor's surety.[37] When the subcontractor was later unable to continue, the prime contractor completed the subcontractor's work and sued the surety to recover the cost of completing. The court held that the prime contractor's advance payment for the subcontractor's men and materials was a "material variation" in the subcontract terms. This released the surety from its bond obligations.

The rationale for this rule is that the surety has relied upon provisions of the contract in executing the bond. Provisions such as payment according to schedule and a retainage requirement in certain percentages benefit the surety. Overpayment by the owner to the contractor may be a discharge of the surety's obligations because such voluntary action by the owner reduces the contract balance available to the surety for completion of the project after a default. This is clearly true when the architect/owner fraudulently certifies progress payments beyond the defaulting principal's actual progress.

Overpayments made in good faith, however, may not discharge the surety. Moreover, unauthorized prepayments made by an owner may not discharge a compensated surety so long as (1) the funds were used in actual construction of the project and (2) the surety was not prejudiced by the prepayments.[38] When an architect has negligently certified progress payments to a contractor, thereby damaging the surety by reducing the contract balance available to the surety upon completion of the work, the surety may have a cause of action against the architect for the resulting damage.[39]

If the principal engages in fraud to induce the surety to issue a bond, the surety cannot assert that defense to a claim by the obligee.[40] If the obligee has perpetrated a fraud on the surety, however, or even participated in it, the surety will be discharged from any obligation.[41] A problem arises when there

[35] *Fireman's Fund Ins. Co. v. United States,* but see *Fireman's Fund . . . ,* 909 F.2d 495 (Fed Cir. 1990) where the court held that release of retainage prior to sub compliance was not a breach of contract and that surety was not a third party beneficiary of any promise made by the government contained in the contract; *Prairie State Nat'l Bank v. United States,* 164 U.S. 227 (1896).

[36] 366 S.E.2d 104 (Va. 1988).

[37] *See Balboa Ins. Co. v. Fulton County,* 251 S.E.2d 123 (Ga. Ct. App. 1978) (overpayments made in reliance on progress payment requests certified by architect).

[38] *See Firemen's Fund Ins. Co.,* fn. 35, *supra; Basic Asphalt & Constr. Corp. v. Parliament Ins. Co.,* 531 F.2d 702 (5th Cir. 1976).

[39] *See Peerless Ins. Co. v. Cerny & Assocs., Inc.,* 199 F. Supp. 951 (D. Minn. 1961); *Sweeney Co. v. Engineers-Constructors, Inc.,* 823 F.2d 805 (4th Cir. 1987).

[40] *Chrysler Corp. v. Hanover Ins. Co.,* 350 F.2d 652 (7th Cir. 1965), *cert. denied,* 383 U.S. 906 (1966).

[41] *Filippi v. McMartin,* 188 Cal. App. 2d 135, 10 Cal. Rptr. 180 (1961); *see also St. Paul Fire & Marine Ins. Co. v. Commodity Credit Corp.,* 646 F.2d 1064 (5th Cir. 1981).

is not active fraud on the part of the obligee, but there is a question about the extent to which the obligee is affirmatively required to disclose facts that would be relevant to the surety. In *Sumitomo Bank v. Iwasaki*,[42] the court held that the obligee does have such an obligation to disclose under the following circumstances:

· The obligee must have reason to believe that the facts materially increase the risk beyond that which the surety intends to assume;
· The obligee has reason to believe such facts are unknown to the surety; and
· The obligee has a reasonable opportunity to reveal such facts to the surety.[43]

The nature and extent of the dealings between the obligee and surety may also be relevant; for example, if over a course of dealing, the obligee knows that the surety relies upon the obligee for certain information, the obligee may have a higher duty to disclose.

12.10 Surety Entitlement to Contract Funds

Upon the failure of the contractor-principal to perform, the surety becomes entitled to the contract funds due and all remaining funds. These funds are due the surety and must be applied to reduce or satisfy any loss by the surety in the performance of the work.[44]

The surety's right to these funds is strong, and is superior to a claim by a financial institution with a security interest in those funds.[45] The surety even has a superior right to the contract funds over a bankruptcy trustee in the event of the bankruptcy of the contractor-principal, at least to the extent of satisfying any loss incurred by the surety.[46]

In some cases, a performance bond surety has been provided with priority to the contract funds before permitting owner set-offs.[47] Because of the potential set-off by the owner, when called upon to honor a bond claim, the surety will ordinarily require agreement of the owner to pay remaining unpaid contract balances to the surety as completion of the project is achieved.

The surety may be limited to the funds from the specific project on which it completed performance. However, a performance bond surety for a contrac-

---

[42] 70 Cal. 2d 81, 73 Cal. Rptr. 564 (1968).

[43] *See* Restatement of Security § 124.

[44] *Aetna Cas. and Sur. Co. v. United States*, 845 F.2d 971 (Fed. Cir. 1988).

[45] *See Prairie State Nat'l Bank*, fn. 35, *supra; Mid-Continent Cas. Co. v. First Nat'l Bank & Trust Co.*, 531 P.2d 1370 (Okla. 1975); *Kansas City, Mo. v. Tri-City Constr. Co.*, 666 F. Supp. 170 (W.D. Mo. 1987); *Interfirst Bank Dallas, N.A. v. United States Fidelity and Guar. Co.*, 774 S.W.2d 391 (Tex. App. 1989, writ denied).

[46] *Pearlman v. Reliance Ins. Co.*, 371 U.S. 132 (1962).

[47] *Trinity Universal Ins. Co. v. United States*, 382 F.2d 317 (5th Cir. 1967), *cert. denied*, 390 U.S. 906 (1968); *Covenant Mut. Ins. Co. v. Able Concrete Pump*, 609 F. Supp. 27 (D.C. Cal. 1984).

tor on two federal government contracts, having incurred losses when it took over and completed performance of the second contract, did state a claim to recover, under the doctrine of equitable subrogation, funds payable by the government to the contractor under an equitable adjustment on the first contract.[48]

12.11 The Effect on the Surety of Arbitration of Construction Disputes

Arbitration has become a favored method of dispute resolution in the construction industry, especially in the private sector. Many standard construction contract forms provide that disputes between the owner and contractor will be resolved by arbitration. Generally, no reference is made to the surety in such provisions. Since arbitration is enforceable only when there is an agreement between the parties to arbitrate, unless the surety has agreed to arbitrate disputes, the mere fact that the principal has entered into an arbitration agreement may not be a basis to compel the surety to arbitrate.[49] The obligee may be forced to pursue relief in two separate forums: in court against the surety and in arbitration against the principal. This creates the problems of additional expense and the risk of inconsistent results. However, a trend seems to be emerging in which sureties that issue performance bonds are required to arbitrate claims asserted against those bonds.

For example, in *Cianbro Corp. v. Empresa Nacional de Ingenieria,*[50] a general contractor sought to compel its subcontractor's surety to arbitrate a dispute arising out of the subcontract, which contained an arbitration clause. As is typical, the surety's bond specifically incorporated the subcontract by reference. Although the surety signed the bonds, it did not sign the subcontract. Nonetheless, the court held that the surety was bound to arbitrate under the arbitration agreement that was incorporated by reference into the bond. In further support of its decision, the court relied upon the strong policy favoring arbitration expressed by Congress in the Federal Arbitration Act.

Although the surety may not be compelled to arbitrate with the owner and contractor, the surety's obligations may be affected by the outcome of owner-contractor arbitration. For example, in *Fidelity and Deposit Co. v. Parsons & Whittemore Contractors Corp.,*[51] a bonded subcontractor defaulted, and the contractor sought damages for breach of contract from the subcontractor and its performance bond surety. The bond incorporated the subcontract by reference. The subcontract provided that all disputes would be submitted to arbitration. The contractor demanded arbitration and the surety objected. The court found that the liability of the surety was predicated on the contract

---

[48] *Transamerica Ins. Co. v. United States,* 989 F.2d 1188 (Fed. Cir. 1993).
[49] *Transamerican Ins. Co. v. Yonkers Contracting Co.,* 267 N.Y.S.2d 669 (Sup. Ct. 1966); *Windowmaster Corp. v. B. G. Danis Co.,* 511 F. Supp. 157 (S.D. Ohio 1981).
[50] 697 F. Supp. 15 (D. Me. 1988).
[51] 397 N.E.2d 380 (N.Y. 1979).

obligation to accept binding arbitration as provided in the subcontract documents.[52]

In addition, a surety has been held bound to an arbitration award against the contractor (its principal) when the surety knew of the arbitration and had the opportunity to participate.[53]

Thus the surety may be bound by the arbitration of disputes concerning the liability of the contractor to the owner, although the surety may retain the right to assert any separate defense in a distinct proceeding. Finally, authority exists for the proposition that an arbitration award is admissible as prima facie evidence of the liability of the surety. However, the surety could still plead any defenses available, including the contention that the arbitration included matters outside of the liability of the surety or matters not covered by the performance bond.[54]

12.12 TERMINATIONS

12.13 Overview

The first portion of this chapter discusses claims on performance bonds. Such claims arise only upon the default or alleged default of the contractor. The surety's involvement is generally the result of the owner's termination of the contract due to the contractor's default.

Virtually all construction contracts expressly recognize the right to terminate the contract for the default of the other party in certain specific circumstances. Such provisions also recognize the right of the innocent party to recover damages resulting from the default and resulting termination.

Even in the absence of an express termination provision, an implied right to terminate a contract generally exists if the other party has materially breached the contract.

In addition, many public contracts and an increasing number of private construction contracts contain "termination for convenience" clauses that authorize the owner (or prime contractor) to terminate the prime contractor (or subcontractors) even in the absence of default. Payments are usually limited to actual cost incurred without payment of standard breach of contract damages or lost profit.

12.14 Termination for Default

The right to terminate a construction contract for default generally arises only when a material or substantial provision of the contract has been breached or a party has failed to perform a material obligation. The rights

---

[52] *See also Kearsarge Metallurgical Corp. v. Peerless Ins. Co.,* 418 N.E.2d 580 (Mass. 1981).
[53] *Von Eng'g Co. v. R. W. Roberts Constr. Co. Inc.,* 457 So.2d 1080 (Fla. Dist. Ct. App. 1984).
[54] *P. R. Post Corp. v. Maryland Cas. Co.,* 271 N.W.2d 521 (Mich. 1978).

and liabilities of the parties are controlled by the common law and by the terms of the contract, which anticipate and provide the termination of further performance upon default. At common law, a minor deviation in performance or failure to meet an objective that is not material to the subject of the contract was not grounds to terminate for default. While such a deviation or failure in performance may give the nonbreaching party a corresponding right to damages, it does not rise to the level of significance that would merit a complete termination of the contract. Determination of the materiality of a breach depends upon the importance of the event or act to the purpose of the contract as a whole or to the basis of the agreement between the parties.

By the terms of the contract, the parties can expand, limit or redefine the grounds for termination for default that exist at common law. They can also provide for the payment of damages and other obligations after the contract is terminated for default.

Federal construction procurement contracts provide an example of the allocation of the rights and duties of the parties upon the occurrence of a default. The standard federal government construction contract affords the government several remedies in addition to the relief generally available at common law. If a contractor fails to perform by the date specified, produces defective or nonconforming work, or refuses or fails to prosecute the work in such a way as to ensure its timely completion, the government may pursue its administrative remedy under the default clause. That is, the government may terminate the contract and complete the work at the contractor's expense. The contractor is also liable for any liquidated or actual damages caused by unexcusable delays in the completion of the work.

At the same time, the commonly used default termination clauses give the contractor the right to contest the default termination. However, the most that a wrongfully terminated contractor can expect by way of relief under a contract with the federal government is compensation under the termination for convenience clause of the contract, which provides a more limited recovery than general breach of contract damages.

The default clause used by the federal government in fixed-price construction contracts is set forth in the Federal Acquisition Regulation (FAR) at §52.249-10. The following is a brief analysis of the major provisions of that clause. Paragraph (a) of the clause provides the basic authority for termination by the federal government, that is, where the contractor refuses or fails to prosecute any or all of the contracted work with sufficient diligence to ensure timely completion, or fails to complete the work within the specified time. In such circumstances, the government is given the right to terminate the contract in accordance with the provisions of the clause. The government then may take over the contractor's work and carry it to completion by a variety of means. Paragraph (a) also establishes the government's right to recover breach of contract damages from the contractor and its surety. Paragraph (b) sets forth the criteria for determining "excusable delay," which provides a major exception to the contractor's exposure to default termination and/or damages for delay.

Section 14.2 of AIA Document A201 (1987 ed.) likewise describes the instances in which an owner may terminate a contractor. In addition to circumstances relating to the contractor's financial situation, the clause identifies the following bases for termination:

[I]f the Contractor:

1. persistently or repeatedly refuses or fails to supply enough properly skilled workers or proper materials;

2. fails to make payment to Subcontractors for materials or labor in accordance with the respective agreements between the Contractor and the Subcontractors;

3. persistently disregards laws, ordinances, or rules, regulations or orders of a public authority having jurisdiction; or

4. otherwise is guilty of substantial breach of a provision of the Contract Documents.

The clause also requires that the architect certify that sufficient cause exists for the termination. Section 14.1 of AIA Document A201 (1987 ed.) provides the contractor with the right to terminate the contract upon the occurrence of certain itemized events.

12.15 Grounds for Default Termination For the most part, the federal clause and the AIA clause merely restate generally what would most likely be material breaches of contract at common law. Specific situations under which sufficient grounds for termination of a construction contract exist are discussed below.

12.16 Refusal or Failure to Prosecute the Work "If the contractor refuses or fails to prosecute the work, or a separable part thereof, with such diligence as will ensure its completion within the time specified in [the] contract," the contract may be terminated for default.[55] However, the government has the burden of proof to show not only a significant lag in performance, but also that the contractor, at the time of the termination, could not have completed performance on time.[56]

The mere fact that the contractor makes little or no progress during one stage of the work may not, alone, support termination. For example, a termination for default was overturned as premature because sufficient time remained in the contract schedule for the contractor to complete performance.[57] Although the factual determinations vary from situation to situation, many cases

---

[55] FAR § 52.249-10(a).
[56] *Litcom Div., Litton Sys.,* ASBCA 13413, 78-1 BCA ¶ 13,022.
[57] *Strickland Co.,* ASBCA 9840, 67-1 BCA ¶ 6193.

have interpreted the standard default clause to require a showing that timely completion was clearly in jeopardy.[58]

12.17 Failure to Complete on Time The contract may be properly terminated if the contractor fails to complete performance on time without excusable delay. As a general rule, time is of the essence, or basic to the terms of a contract that contains fixed or specific performance dates. If timely performance does not occur, the government can immediately terminate *without notice* and without an opportunity to cure.[59] However, when time is not of the essence, late performance is only one of a number of factors to be considered in determining the adequacy of performance and the justification for a default termination. For example, a substantial delay in final completion may not justify a default if the work is sufficiently complete that it can be used for its intended purpose.[60]

12.18 Repudiation by Contractor A termination based on a contractor's repudiation or anticipatory breach of the contract is closely related to the contractor's refusal or failure to prosecute the work. However, when a contractor repudiates the existence of the contract, it is subject to default termination regardless of the previous rate of progress in performance.[61]

To terminate a contract on the basis of a repudiation by the contractor, the owner must have a clear indication from the contractor that it cannot or will not perform the contract. The cases speak in terms of a "positive, definite, unconditional and unequivocal manifestation of intent, by words or conduct, on the part of a contractor" not to perform.[62] In any case, it must be apparent that the contractor is unable to or will not perform the contract. A failure to make progress alone does not constitute anticipatory repudiation absent some objective manifestation of intent not to perform.

The contractor may be considered to have repudiated the contract by refusing to perform during a dispute about contract interpretation.[63] Similarly, a contractor is not entitled to stop work while awaiting issuance of contract modifications or resolution of a request for price escalation for inflation.[64]

In certain circumstances, a contractor's refusal to perform will not be regarded as an anticipatory breach or repudiation of the contract. For example, when contract specifications are impossible to perform, the contractor has a right to stop work on the basis that no other practical alternative exists.[65]

---

[58] *Discount Co., Inc. v. United States,* 554 F.2d 435 (Ct. Cl.), *cert. denied,* 434 U.S. 938 (1977).
[59] *National Farm Equipment Co.,* GSBCA 4921, 78-1 BCA ¶ 13,195; *see Dallas–Fort Worth Regional Airport Bd. v. Combustion Equipment Assocs., Inc.,* 623 F.2d 1032 (5th Cir. 1980).
[60] *Franklin E. Penny Co. v. United States,* 524 F.2d 668 (Ct. Cl. 1975).
[61] *See First Nat'l Bank of Aberdeen v. Indian Indus.,* 600 F.2d 702 (8th Cir. 1979).
[62] *Mountain State Constr. Co. Inc.,* ENG BCA 3549, 76-2 BCA ¶ 12,197.
[63] *Tester Corp.,* ASBCA 21312, 78-2 BCA ¶ 13,373.
[64] *Fraenkische Parkettverlegung R.,* ASBCA 18453, 75-2 BCA ¶ 11,388.
[65] *L. J. Casey Co.,* AGBCA 75-148, 76-2 BCA ¶ 12,196; *Chugach Elec. Ass'n v. Northern Corp.,* 562 P.2d 1053 (Alaska 1977).

Furthermore, a contractor should not be terminated for default where it is reasonably awaiting clarification from the government of drawings, specifications or other central requirements. If the contractor is unable to proceed until it obtains guidance from the government, the delay in work is justified.[66]

The standard changes clause includes only changes "within the general scope of the contract." Changes beyond that scope are termed "cardinal changes." A contractor's refusal to perform a contract because of an actual or constructive cardinal change is not a basis for a default termination.[67]

When the owner materially breaches the contract, the contractor's subsequent repudiation is justified and may not be the basis for default termination. For example, when the owner withholds payments that are due on a contract, the contractor may stop performance.[68]

12.19 Failure to Comply with Other Provisions of the Contract

The failure of the contractor to comply with certain terms of the contract will be a material breach entitling the owner to terminate the contract for default. The owner must first prove that the provision of the contract that has not been performed is material to the contract and also that the failure to perform is a material breach of the contract.

In *Antonio Santisteban & Co., Inc.*,[69] a contractor's failure to furnish a performance bond constituted a material breach. Likewise, some boards have held that a contractor's failure to furnish Miller Act bonds pursuant to 40 U.S.C. § 270a *et seq.* justifies default termination.[70]

12.20 Defenses of the Contractor

12.21 Excusable Delay

Virtually all construction contracts contain some provision excusing delayed performance when specified criteria are met. As an example, paragraph (b) of the default clause used by the federal government provides that termination for default is improper in cases where a contractor's work is delayed by "unforeseeable causes beyond the control and without the fault or negligence of the contractor." The provision continues with a description and examples of typical causes of excusable delay.[71]

12.22 Waiver by the Owner

Another defense that may be available to a contractor faced with default termination is a claim that the owner has waived

[66] *Electromagnetic Indus., Inc.*, ASBCA 11485, 67-2 BCA ¶ 6545.

[67] *Saddler v. United States*, 287 F.2d 411 (Ct. Cl. 1961); *Allied Materials & Equipment v. United States*, 569 F.2d 562 (Ct. Cl. 1978); *Cray Research Inc. v. Department of Navy*, 556 F. Supp. 201 (D.D.C. 1982).

[68] *United States ex rel. E. C. Ernst, Inc. v. Curtis T. Bedwell & Sons, Inc.*, 506 F. Supp. 1324 (E.D. Pa. 1981); *Contract Maintenance, Inc.*, ASBCA 19603, 75-1 BCA ¶ 11,097. See AIA Document A201, § 14.1 (1987 ed.).

[69] ASBCA 5586, et al., 60-1 BCA ¶ 2497.

[70] *H.L. & S. Contractors, Inc.*, IBCA 1085-11-75, 76-1 BCA ¶ 11,878.

[71] See *Crawford Painting & Drywall Co. v. J. W. Bateson Co., Inc.*, 857 F.2d 981, *cert. denied*, 488 U.S. 1035 (5th Cir. 1988).

strict compliance with the contract completion date, or other contract performance provisions, and thereby forfeited its right to terminate. Even if the terms of the contract are specific and state they may not be waived, its terms may be waived by the expression of consent to or the disregard of the failure of performance. A waiver can be effective without further consideration or a new contract agreement.[72] There will be no waiver, however, if the owner's forbearance in terminating was based on misrepresentation by the contractor.[73]

While the right to terminate a contract for default may be waived if not exercised in a timely manner, it can also be expressly reserved. In *Indemnity Ins. Co. of N. Am. v. United States,*[74] the government expressly reserved its right to terminate a takeover surety for default by informing the surety that it was continuing to assess liquidated damages and by providing the surety with a cure notice once the completion date had passed. The failure of the government to terminate the contract immediately after expiration of the completion date did not constitute a waiver under those circumstances.

An owner may not be deemed to have waived a valid basis for a termination for default simply because it relied on a different basis at the time of the termination. In *Joseph Morton v. United States,*[75] the government's decision to terminate for default was upheld on the grounds of the contractor's fraud, even though the government was unaware of the fraud at the time of the termination. In *FJW Optical Sys. Inc.,*[76] the board held a termination for default was valid even though initially there had only been a termination for convenience. However, the Unites States Claims Court has held that, even when a contractor was technically in default, a termination for default may be reversed if the contracting officer's decision was motivated by hostility to the contractor and was not in the best interests of the government.[77]

12.23 Remedies of the Owner When a contractor is terminated for default, the owner may (1) complete the contract work itself, (2) let a contract to another contractor to complete the work, or (3) allow the defaulted contractor's surety to complete construction. Usually an owner will only complete the work with its own employees or forces if the project is substantially complete and little work remains. Otherwise, the owner will commonly enter into another contract or will rely on the surety to complete, assuming the project is bonded and the surety agrees.

Where the owner either completes on its own or through a completion contractor, reasonable steps must be taken to minimize additional costs. This duty to mitigate damages limits the recovery a party can obtain on breach of contract by requiring that reasonable efforts be taken to complete the contract

---

[72] *See Olson Plumbing & Heating Co.,* ABSCA 17965, 75-1 BCA ¶ 11,203.

[73] *W. M. Z. Mfg. Co., Inc.,* ASBCA No. 28347, 85-3 BCA ¶ 18,169.

[74] 14 Cl. Ct. 219 (1988).

[75] 757 F.2d 1273 (Fed. Cir. 1985).

[76] ASBCA 29780, 85-2 BCA ¶ 18,049.

[77] *Quality Env't Sys., Inc. v. United States,* 7 Cl. Ct. 428 (1985).

economically and efficiently.[78] The reasonableness of the owner's actions will be determined in light of the facts and circumstances of each case.

Under the standard performance bond, the defaulting contractor's surety is obliged to indemnify the owner up to the amount of the bond. Although the surety is not obligated to complete the contract work, most sureties will cooperate with the owner in arranging for completion of the contract. In most cases, the surety will be allowed to take over the work unless there is reason to believe that the party proposed by the surety to complete the work is incompetent or unqualified so that the interests of the owner would be substantially prejudiced by its efforts.[79]

Where the surety tenders another contractor to complete the work, the bonds of the surety under the original contract are still effective. In addition, the owner has the benefit of any additional surety bonds provided by the completion contractor.

Where a surety elects to have the work completed by another firm, it cannot prosecute a claim against the federal government under the disputes clause in its own name, because it has not become a party to the contract. Under such circumstances, it must assume the name of the defaulted contractor and submit the claim in a representative capacity.[80]

12.24 *Reprocurement Costs* Under the default clause, the federal government is entitled to recover its "increased costs," that is, those additional costs in excess of the original contract price that are necessarily incurred in completion of the work. However, the government cannot recover the administrative costs of reprocurement.[81]

When the scope of the newly procured work exceeds the coverage of the terminated contract, the government may recover from the defaulted contractor only those additional costs that are attributable to the work in the original contract.[82] Also, the contract appeal boards will generally reduce an award of excess reprocurement costs where the government has failed to mitigate damages.[83] Finally, if the reprocurement contract contains significant deviations from the original contract, no excess costs may be assessed against the defaulting contractor.[84]

In the absence of a default clause in the contract, and often as a supplement to the rights granted by such a clause, the common law rights for breach of contract apply. The owner is entitled to the payment of damages that would put it in the same position as if the contract had not been breached.

12.25 *Delay Damages* The federal government default clause provides that regardless of whether the contractor is terminated for default, the contrac-

---

[78] *Marley v. United States*, 423 F.2d 324, 333 (Ct. Cl. 1970).
[79] FAR §49.404(c).
[80] *Sentry Ins.*, ASBCA 21918, 77-2 BCA ¶ 12,721.
[81] *Evans*, ASBCA 10951, 66-1 BCA ¶ 5316.
[82] *M.S.I. Corp.*, VABCA 599, 67-2 BCA ¶ 6643.
[83] *See, e.g., A & W General Cleaning Contractors*, ASBCA 14809, 71-2 BCA ¶ 8994.
[84] *Blake Constr. Co. Inc.*, GSBCA 4013, et al., 75-2 BCA ¶ 11,487.

tor and its sureties will be liable for damages resulting from the contractor's refusal or failure to complete the work within the specified time.

Absent a liquidated damages provision, the government is entitled to actual damages caused by the contractor's delay. Actual damages include, for example, the cost of keeping a government inspector on the job after the specified completion date.[85]

Where the contract contains a liquidated damages provision, the government is entitled to damages based upon the period between the contract completion date and the actual date of completion, whether by the contractor, the surety, or a reprocurement contractor. The default clause provisions attempt to secure for the government a common law measure of recovery, putting it in as good a position as it would have enjoyed had the delay not occurred. Liquidated damages may be recovered in addition to excess costs of reprocurement.

12.26 Termination for Convenience

The parties to a construction contract may wish to include a clause that will allow one party (usually the owner) the right to terminate another party without cause, that is, for convenience. While the federal government's right to terminate a contract for convenience is generally deemed to be implied as a matter of law, in order for one party to a private commercial contract to do so, it must have an express provision in the contract giving it the right. If one party terminates another for convenience, the terminated party has a right to compensation, which may be limited by the contract's terms.

Although a typical termination for convenience clause appears to give one party the absolute right to terminate another for whatever reason, there is a conflict as to whether the termination must be made in good faith.[86] At least one court has held that there are circumstances in which a termination, even under a seemingly unrestricted termination clause, may not be allowed if done in bad faith.[87]

Other courts have hesitated to hold that there is a good faith requirement in terminations for convenience. A district court in New York, construing New York law, found that "on the basis of existing precedents, that such a [good faith] restriction would probably not be imposed."[88] The court did point out, however, that this conclusion was not critical to its holding in the case because it was probable that the terminating party could show that the termination was not in bad faith.

The question of whether there is a good faith requirement for termination without cause is unresolved in many jurisdictions. It is, therefore, a point that

[85] *B & E Constructors, Inc.,* IBCA 526-11-65, 67-1 BCA ¶ 6239.
[86] *Randolph v. New England Mut. Life Ins. Co.,* 526 F.2d 1383 (6th Cir. 1975).
[87] *Id.* at 1386.
[88] *Niagara Mohawk Power Corp. v. Graver Tank & Mfg.,* 470 F. Supp. 1308 (N.D. N.Y. 1979).

may be viably argued by any contractor who may have been terminated in bad faith.

In the federal procurement context, the government's right to terminate for convenience is extremely broad. Termination is permitted "whenever the Contracting Officer shall determine that such termination is in the best interest of the Government."[89] The provision expresses a right that has long been recognized, even in the absence of a termination for convenience clause in the contract.[90]

Nonetheless, the contracting officer's discretion is not absolute and cannot be exercised in bad faith. Thus a terminated contractor who alleges bad faith by the contracting officer in issuing a convenience termination is allowed to present evidence tending to demonstrate bad faith.[91] "The termination of a contract for the convenience of the government is only valid in the absence of bad faith or a clear abuse of discretion."[92]

In *Municipal Leasing Corp. v. United States,*[93] the United States Claims Court ruled that a finding of bad faith was not necessary to invalidate a termination for convenience. The court held that:

> The termination for convenience clause can appropriately be invoked only in the event of some kind of change from the circumstances of the bargain or in the expectations of the parties.

> The termination for convenience clause will not act as a constructive shield to protect defendant from the consequences of its decision to follow an option considered but rejected before contracting with plaintiff.[94]

Thus, while the government may have broad discretion to terminate for convenience, there must be no bad faith and some changed circumstances must exist to warrant the action.

In federal procurement law, the contractor whose contract is wholly or partially terminated for convenience should be made financially whole by compensation for the direct consequences of the government's termination. Negotiated termination settlements are limited only by the requirements of reasonableness of cost and the original contract price. Individual cost items need not be negotiated.

Additionally, the contractor is entitled to a "fair and reasonable" profit on work performed, unless it can be demonstrated that the contractor would have lost money on the contract.[95] *Anticipatory profits* are not allowed. Profit is allowable only on the work performed.

---

[89] FAR §52.249-2(a).

[90] *United States v. Corliss Steam Engine Co.,* 91 U.S. 321 (1875).

[91] *See National Factors, Inc v. United States,* 492 F.2d 1383 (Ct. Cl. 1974).

[92] *Id.* at 1385.

[93] 7 Cl. Ct. 43 (1984).

[94] *Id.* at 47. *See Torncello v. United States,* 681 F.2d 756 (Ct. Cl. 1982).

[95] *C. W. McGrath, Inc.,* GSBCA 4586, 77-1 BCA ¶ 12,379.

The standard termination for convenience clause entitles the contracting officer to terminate all or part of a contract. Where only a portion of the contract is terminated, the contractor's measure of cost recovery is governed by the same principles applicable to the termination of the entire contract. The contractor may recover costs incurred until the date of the termination, including a fair and reasonable profit, and the cost of settlement with subcontractors, suppliers and the government. The partial termination settlement proposal must be submitted within ninety days after the effective date of the partial termination.

In addition, the contractor is entitled to an equitable adjustment in the price of the work that has not been terminated if it can be shown that the elimination of a portion of the work caused an increase in the cost of the remaining work.

POINTS TO REMEMBER

- Performance bonds are not insurance.
- The language of the bond is critical; read it carefully. It may contain certain claim requirements or refer you to a statute that contains such requirements.
- Determine if the bond is a *"statutory"* or *"common law"* bond—this distinction may affect claim requirements.
- The penal sum of the bond may not always be the surety's limit of liability.
- A surety has all of the defenses of its principal *plus* any additional *"technical"* defenses.
- A surety is *generally* bound by arbitration.
- Termination for default is a remedy of *last resort.*
- Any attempt to terminate usually requires an opportunity to *"cure"* any of *the defects.*
- The *primary defenses* to termination are excusable delay and failure to pay.
- Converting a termination for default to a termination for convenience generally allows the contractor to recover the *costs of performance on the work completed,* plus termination costs.

13

PROVING COSTS
AND DAMAGES

The issue in construction disputes that generally receives the most attention and focus is liability. Does a differing site condition exist? Who caused the delay and is it compensable? However, the issue of damages or costs flowing from the events that give rise to liability is no less important. Too often, the issue of calculating costs and proving damages is given a back seat, with little precision or scrutiny applied until the eve of trial. That approach can result in an entirely misguided claim effort, missed opportunities for settlement, and loss at trial or in arbitration. The inability to prove damages with a reasonable degree of certainty may prevent the claimant from recovering the full amount, or even a substantial portion, of the damages to which it may be entitled. An early and realistic analysis of damages can help determine whether a claim really exists and the best means of preparing and positioning the claim for the affirmative recovery sought.

13.1 BASIC DAMAGE PRINCIPLES

13.2 The Compensatory Nature of Damages

Several basic premises underlie the theory of damages. For example, when a claimant seeks to recover additional costs and damages resulting from another party's breach of contract, the court generally will attempt to put the claimant in the same position it would have been in had the contract been performed by all parties according to its terms.[1] This theory of the measure of damages

---

[1] *E. B. Ludwig Steel Corp. v. C. J. Waddell Contractors, Inc.,* 534 So.2d 1364 (La. App. 1988); *United States for the Use of Morgan & Son Earthmoving, Inc. v. Timberland Paving & Constr. Co.,* 745 F.2d 595 (9th Cir. 1984); *Bennett v. Associated Food Stores, Inc.,* 165 S.E.2d 581 (Ga. App. 1968).

applies to all breach of contract actions—not just those arising from construction contracts.[2] The law of contract damages is compensatory in nature and, as such, is designed to reimburse the complaining party for all "losses caused and gains prevented" by the other party's breach.[3]

In contrast, the goal in a tort (noncontractual wrong) case is to put the injured party in the same position it would have been in had the tort not been committed.[4] In the construction area, tort claims are generally asserted for negligence, misrepresentation and, in rare cases, on the basis of strict liability.[5] Computation and proof of tort damages are often complex, requiring an evaluation of the foreseeability of the injury and the possible contributory or comparative negligence of other parties, or assumption of risk. While tort damages may be broader in scope than contract damages, many courts have limited tort damages to cases involving either personal injury or property damage, and deny recovery for purely economic loss.[6] For these reasons and because most construction claims are based primarily on a breach of contract, this section focuses on the computation of contract damages.

13.3 Categories of Damages

Damages resulting from breach of a construction contract are generally of two basic types: direct and consequential. A third category, punitive damages, only rarely comes into play.

13.4 *Direct Damages*

Direct damages, sometimes referred to as general damages, are those that result from the direct, natural, and immediate impact of the breach, and are recoverable in all cases where proven.[7] In a contractor's case these damages may include idle labor and machinery, material and labor escalations, and extended job site and home office overhead. The owner's direct damages are generally those costs incurred in completing or correcting the contractor's work and the cost of delay, which is either its actual costs in terms of lost rent, loss of use, or liquidated damages.

13.5 *Consequential Damages*

The second category of contract damages is consequential damages, sometimes referred to as special damages. Consequential damages do not flow directly from the alleged breach, but are an indirect source of losses. Consequential damages must have been within the

---

[2] *Meares v. Nixon Constr. Co.,* 173 S.E.2d 593 (N.C. App. 1970).

[3] Calamari & Perillo, *The Law of Contracts,* § 327 (West 1970).

[4] Restatement (2d), Torts, § 901.

[5] For a discussion of the application of strict liability principles in construction litigation, see "Strict Liability and the Building Industry," 33 *Emory L.J.* 175 (1984).

[6] *See, e.g., Casa Clara v. Toppino,* 588 So.2d 631 (Fla. 3d DCA 1991); *Florida Power & Light Co. v. Westinghouse Elec. Corp.,* 510 So.2d 899 (Fla. 1987); *AFM Corp. v. Southern Bell Tel. & Tel. Co.,* 515 So.2d 180 (Fla. 1987); *State v. Mitchell Constr. Co.,* 699 P.2d 1349 (Idaho 1984); *Bates & Rogers Constr. Corp. v. North Shore Sanitary Dist.,* 471 N.E.2d 915 (Ill. App. 1984).

[7] *Spang Indus., Inc. v. Aetna Casualty and Sur. Co.,* 512 F.2d 365 (2d Cir. 1975).

contemplation of the parties when they contracted, or flow from special circumstances attending the contract that were known to both parties. These losses, which are only indirectly related to the breach, may include loss of profits or a loss of bonding capacity. These are more difficult to prove because the causal link between such damages and the act constituting the breach is likely to be tenuous and uncertain.

Recovery of consequential damages for breach of contract requires proof: (1) that the consequence was foreseeable in the normal course of events; (2) that the loss in fact would have occurred; and (3) that the amount of loss can be reasonably ascertained.[8] The first element is satisfied by showing that the particular type of injury was reasonably foreseeable to the other party at the time of contracting. The "reasonably foreseeable" test was originally enunciated in the English case of *Hadley v. Baxendale*,[9] and has since been widely adopted by American courts.[10]

The second element the claimant must prove is that the damages flowed "naturally" or "proximately" from the breach. In laymen's terms, this means that the injury must be the result of the breach rather than some other cause.[11]

The third limitation on the recovery of consequential damages is that the damages sought must not be too remote or speculative.[12] This general requirement is frequently codified under state law. Questions and issues of the "remote and speculative" nature of claimed damages frequently arise when a claimant seeks to recover profits that have allegedly been lost as a result of the breach—for example, as a result of tied-up capital or reduced bonding capacity. Although statutes covering consequential damages may require "exact computation," most courts have taken a somewhat less stringent approach. The court in one such case explained:

> The proof of damages because of breach of a contract must be made with a *reasonable degree of certainty*. The damages, to be recoverable in such a case, must not be remote or speculative. There must be sufficient data produced by the claimant to permit a determination with reasonable certainty of the loss occasioned by the breach relied upon. . . . *Damages are recoverable for losses caused or for profits and other gains prevented by the breach only to the extent that the evidence affords a sufficient basis for estimating their amount in money with reasonable certainty.* (Emphasis added.)

In seeking consequential damages, the claimant assumes a much heavier burden of proof as compared to direct damages. Moreover, many contracts,

---

[8] *Town of North Bonneville, Wash. v. United States,* 11 Cl. Ct. 694 (1987).

[9] 156 *Eng. Rep.* 145 (1854).

[10] *See Bumann v. Maurer,* 203 N.W.2d 434 (N.D. 1972); *Tousley v. Atlantic City Ambassador Hotel Corp.,* 50 A.2d 472 (N.J. Sup. 1947).

[11] *Kline Iron & Steel Co. v. Superior Trucking Co., Inc.,* 201 S.E.2d 388 (S.C. 1973).

[12] *Dileo v. Nugent,* 592 A.2d 1126 (Md. App. 1991); *Baker v. Riverside Church of God,* 453 S.W.2d 801 (Tenn. App. 1970).

and particularly public construction contracts, by their terms exclude claims for consequential damages.

13.6 Punitive Damages Punitive damages, sometimes referred to as exemplary damages, are awarded where there is evidence of oppression, malice, fraud or wanton and willful conduct on the part of the defendant, and are above what would ordinarily compensate the complaining party for its losses. These damages are not compensatory in nature, but rather are intended to punish the defendant for its wrongful behavior or to make an example in order to deter others from similar conduct.[13]

Traditionally it has been held that punitive damages are not recoverable in an action for breach of contract, absent proof of fraud or malicious intent.[14] And this is so even if the breach is intentional.[15]

In some states, however, the courts may permit the award of punitive damages where there is sufficient evidence of "malice" or utter disregard for the rights of others so as to constitute a willful and wanton course of action, or other tortious conduct amounting to fraud.[16] In addition, although the expenses of litigation are not generally allowed as damages in an action for breach of contract, such fees may be awarded if the defendant has acted in bad faith or has been stubbornly litigious, or has caused the plaintiff unnecessary trouble and expense.[17] This rule, which changes the common law of many jurisdictions, has been codified in some states.[18]

13.7 Causation

In order to successfully prosecute a claim, a claimant must establish the liability of the other party, the amount of its own damages, *and* prove that the damages were caused by the acts giving rise to liability. It is essential that the claimant demonstrate causation, meaning that the damages presented flow directly or indirectly from the liability issues presented. Without making this link, even the most thoroughly prepared and well-documented construction claim will not be able to withstand competent cross-examination. It is not essential to establish the extent of the damage with absolute certainty if there is no question as to the fact that damage did occur. While speculative damages are not recoverable, the courts generally recognize that there is a difference in the measure of proof needed to show that the claimant sustained damage and the measure of proof needed to fix those damages.

---

[13] *Tibbs v. Nat'l Homes Constr. Corp.*, 369 N.E.2d 1218 (Ohio App. 1978).
[14] *Roger Lee, Inc. v. Trend Mills, Inc.*, 410 F.2d 928 (5th Cir. 1969); *Otto v. Imperial Casualty & Indem. Co.*, 277 F.2d 889 (8th Cir. 1960); *Smith v. Johnston*, 591 P.2d 1260 (Okla. 1979).
[15] *Pogge v. Fullerton Lumber Co.*, 277 N.W.2d 916 (Iowa 1979).
[16] *Walker v. Signal Companies, Inc.*, 149 Cal. Rptr. 119 (Cal. App. 1978).
[17] *A. W. Easter Constr. Co. Inc. v. White*, 224 S.E.2d 112 (Ga. App. 1976).
[18] *See* O.C.G.A. § 13-6-11.

One reliable method of establishing this link between liability and damages is to prepare an analysis showing the differences between the construction costs as bid and the costs actually incurred. The focus of this type of analysis would be a demonstration that the overruns being claimed did in fact occur in the areas of work where the liability exists and that the costs were incurred because of specific acts of the owner.

13.8 Cost Accounting Records

The problem of calculating and proving damages can be substantially reduced by initiating proper cost accounting at the time the claim is identified. Accounting measures can be established to segregate and carefully maintain separate records. If such a procedure is followed, proof of damages can be reduced to little more than the presentation of evidence of separate accounts. Unfortunately, this ideal situation seldom exists; the problem is not recognized in time to set up separate accounting procedures, or the maintenance of separate accounts is simply not possible because of an inability to isolate costs, or no attempt is made to establish the requisite procedures. These circumstances necessitate the development of some formula that is sufficiently reliable to permit the court or arbitrators to allow its use as proof of damage. If settlement is being sought, the claimant must likewise convince the other side of the validity and reliability of its damage calculations.

13.9 Mitigation of Damages

In a breach of contract action, the amount of recovery is generally limited to those losses and damages caused by the breach that are considered unavoidable.[19] The complaining party may not stand idly by and allow the losses to accumulate and increase, when the losses could have been reduced by reasonable effort or cost. This requirement is known as the "duty to mitigate damages." In construction cases it usually arises where, upon a breach by one of the parties, there is a need for protection of partially completed work, timely reprocurement, assignment of equipment or work crews, reshoring, or reduction of delay costs. In particular, it has been held that an owner who makes no effort to obtain a reasonable contract price upon reprocurement on a defaulted project cannot expect to recover the full difference between the original contract and the inflated costs to complete.[20]

The duty to mitigate calls for reasonable diligence and ordinary care. The party's actions need only be reasonable under the circumstances.[21] The law does not require that the defaulted party undertake extraordinary expense or effort to avoid losses flowing from a breached contract.[22]

---

[19] 22 Am. Jur. 2d Damages § 33.
[20] *Metal Building Products Co. v. Fidelity & Deposit Co. of Md.,* 144 So.2d 751 (La. App. 1962).
[21] *Halliburton Oil Well Cementing Co. v. Millican,* 171 F.2d 426 (5th Cir. 1948).
[22] *T.C. Bateson Constr. Co. v. United States,* 319 F.2d 135 (Ct. Cl. 1963).

13.10   Betterment

A related concept holds that a party cannot expect compensation for *more* than the loss arising from a breach of contract. For example, necessary repairs or replacement of a structure may, in fact, provide the owner with a "better" building than that provided for in the plans and specifications.[23] In such instances, where the owner obtains a "betterment" from the efforts of the contractor, any award of damages for breach must be reduced by the value of the betterment that the owner receives.[24]

13.11   METHODS OF PRICING CLAIMS

There are several basic methods for pricing construction claims. The simplest method is the *total cost method.* The oversimplicity of the total cost method causes it to be frowned upon and accepted only in extreme cases. The *modified total cost method* attempts to address those weaknesses. The other, more complicated but more widely accepted method is the discrete or *segregated cost method.* Finally, there is the *quantum meruit* approach to pricing a claim, which ignores costs and focuses instead on the value of the material and services provided.

13.12   The Total Cost Method

A total cost claim is simply what the name implies. It essentially seeks to convert a standard fixed-price construction contract into a cost-reimbursement arrangement. The contractor's total out-of-pocket costs of performance are tallied and marked up for overhead and profit. Payments already made to that contractor are deducted from that amount, and the difference is the contractor's damages. Of course, this approach can be refined or adjusted to meet particular needs and circumstances, but the basic components and approach remain: costs associated with the basis for the claim are not segregated. The total cost method is well suited for impact disruption claims when the segregation of costs is virtually impossible.

The total cost approach, although preferred by claimants because of the ease of computation, is generally discouraged by the courts because it assumes that the contractor was virtually fault-free and is fraught with uncertainties. For these reasons, numerous court decisions have established fairly rigorous requirements for the presentation of total cost claims:

1. Other methods of calculating damages are impossible or impractical.

2. Recorded costs must be reasonable.

[23] *Main St. Corp. v. Eagle Roofing Co.,* 168 A.2d 33 (N.J. 1961).
[24] *Correlli Roofing Co. v. Nat'l Instrument Co.,* 214 A.2d 919 (Md. App. 1965).

3. The contractor's bid or estimate must have been accurate (that is, contained no underbidding).
4. The actions of the plaintiff must not have caused any of the cost overruns.[25]

The second requirement, the reasonableness of recorded costs, is typically not a difficult assumption to prove. The claimant must demonstrate the appropriateness of costs, the reliability of the contractor's accounting methods and systems, and a relationship to industry practices and standards. Ironically, the more detailed and well documented the claimant's costs are, the more vulnerable the claimant is to an argument that it can use another method for calculating damages and therefore fail to meet the first requirement.

The remaining two requirements are the most difficult to meet. Proving that the contractor's bid was strictly accurate can be challenging. That proof might require a comparison of supplier and subcontractor quotes to bid amounts, as well as the comparison of material quantity estimates to contract drawings. Presenting such an analysis is expensive, often difficult to follow, and easily refutable because most bids rely heavily on assumptions. Due to the nature of the bidding process, many of these assumptions are accumulated in the absence of accurate information.

Establishing that the claimant was blameless for any overruns is perhaps the most difficult aspect of a total cost claim and why the method so rarely succeeds. In this way, the claimant essentially attempts to prove causation by showing that the damages were not its own fault and therefore must be due to the acts of the other party. The premise is easily attacked by demonstrating only a single area of potential blame attributable to the contractor, which could erode the credibility of the entire total cost claim. That is why this method has often been defeated in practice and why parties may instead pursue a "modified" total cost method, as discussed in § 13.9.

Owners probably view contractor total cost claims with even greater suspicion and distrust than the courts, so much so that the credibility of the entire claim and the claimant can be undermined. The difficulties of establishing the prerequisites for use of a total cost calculation in court combined with the skepticism it can generate counsel against use of the total cost method whenever possible.

13.13 The Segregated Cost Method

The segregated cost method of pricing claims is more difficult than the total cost method, but it is a far more accurate, reliable, and persuasive way of presenting damages. Under this approach, the additional costs associated with the events or occurrences that gave rise to the claim are segregated from

---

[25] *Chicago College of Osteopathic Medicine v. George A. Fuller Co.*, 719 F.2d 1335 (7th Cir. 1983); *John F. Harkins Co., Inc. v. School Dist. of Phila.*, 460 A.2d 260 (Pa. Super. 1983).

those incurred in the normal course of performance of the contract. For example, on an extra work claim, the pricing would reflect an allocation (actual or estimated) for the additional labor, materials, and equipment used in performing the extra work. If the project was delayed, costs of field overhead and home office overhead would also be calculated.

The use of this cause and effect methodology most often yields an accurate, well-defined, and defensible presentation of damages. It may, however, be extremely difficult to accomplish in the absence of detailed record keeping and sophisticated cost control systems that segregate changed or impacted work. This method tends to have added credibility when the person presenting the damage shows that the sum of all specifically identified damages does not equal the total difference between the bid cost and total cost (that is, the total cost method). The difference remaining represents the costs related to contractor-caused events that have been excluded from the claim.

13.14 The Modified Total Cost Method

Another general approach to calculating and presenting damages borrows from the concepts of both the specific identification and total cost methods. The modified total cost method employs the inherent simplicity of the total cost approach but modifies the calculation to demonstrate a more direct cause-and-effect relationship that exists between the costs and acts giving rise to liability. The success of the approach often depends upon the extent of the modifications that demonstrate the cause-and-effect dynamics.

The initial step in calculating damages using the modified total cost method involves adjusting the contractor's bid for any weaknesses uncovered during job performance, whether they were judgment or simple calculation errors. A reasonable bid (an as-adjusted bid) is thus established. The recorded project costs are similarly then examined for reasonableness and reductions are made for costs which cannot be attributed to the owner, such as unanticipated labor material cost escalations that are not tied to the alleged basis for liability.

The modified total cost calculation can be further refined by focusing on specific areas of work or cost categories related to the claim issues. For example, if the claim relates to a differing site condition that only affected site work and foundations and not the balance of the project, focus only on those areas in the calculation, and eliminate all the extraneous costs and issues that complicate and dilute the credibility of the pricing.

Although the modified total cost approach is often viewed as a method of avoiding the unfavorable scrutiny generally given to a total cost analysis, recent cases imply that courts and boards of contract appeals apply the same standards of admissibility to modified total cost claims as they have in the past to traditional total cost claims.[26] If the claimant has properly modified the cost calculation and not relied on a simplistic approach, the modified total

---

[26] *Servidone Construction Corp. v. U.S.*, 931 F.2d 860 (Fed. Cir. 1991).

cost method is far more likely to withstand scrutiny and offer a credible means of quantifing a claim.

13.15 *Quantum Meruit* Claims

A final type of damage theory involves an analysis of the "reasonable value" of the work performed. For instance, mechanic's liens allow contractors and subcontractors to recover the reasonable value of labor and materials used in improving property. *Quantum meruit* is also often used in damage claims when a subcontractor does not have a direct contractual relationship with an owner, but the owner has been "unjustly enriched" by work performed by the subcontractor.

Quantum meruit may also be available if there has been a material breach of the contract and the contractor opts to rescind the contract and seek the reasonable value of the benefits.[27] In most states, the contractor is not limited to the price specified in the initial agreement. The proper preparation and presentation of such a claim can often render proof of damages much easier, avoid the problems inherent in seeking a "total cost" recovery on a pure contract breach theory, and bring about recovery in excess of actual contract prices.[28]

13.16 THE CONTRACTOR'S DAMAGES

The following sections are not intended to provide an inclusive listing of categories of potential claims or cost elements, because the cost elements will vary depending upon the circumstances of each case. These elements are examples of the more common types of claim items in construction disputes.

13.17 Contract Changes and Extras

In most instances, a contractor presenting an affirmative claim to the owner will be seeking damages arising from changes in the anticipated quality, quantity or method of work. Obviously, quantity and quality changes are relatively easy to discern. One clear, colorful and effective way of describing such changes is to say that "the owner had the contractor build a Cadillac rather than the Ford required by the contract."

The owner who requires a contractor to perform an additional quantity of work is susceptible to a claim if the contractor has kept accurate records of the amount of work performed and can prove the difference between actual performance and what a reasonable interpretation of the contract would re-

---

[27] *Schulman Investment Co. v. Olin Corp.*, 477 F. Supp. 623 (S.D.N.Y. 1979).

[28] *See, e.g., U.S. for use of Susi Contracting Co. v. Zara Contracting Co.*, 146 F.2d 606 (2d Cir. 1944); *Murray v. Marbro Builders, Inc.*, 371 N.E.2d 218 (Ohio 1977).

quire.[29] However, the contractor who seeks to recover additional costs associated with changes in the anticipated method or sequence of construction, a category that includes delay, disruption and acceleration damages, faces potential problems. These damages are more speculative than those mentioned above, and hence more difficult to understand and prove with reasonable certainty. In addition, the contractor's records may furnish little support for the total claimed impact of a change in the anticipated method or sequence of work.

In recognition of the frequency of disagreements over pricing, contracts frequently include terms that provide the methodology for determining the price of extra or changed work. For example, the American Institute of Architects (AIA) standard form general contract provides several methods of determining costs for changes including: (1) mutual acceptance of a substantiated lump sum price, (2) contract or subsequently agreed upon unit prices, (3) cost plus a mutually acceptable percentage or fixed fee, or (4) a method determined by the architect when the contractor fails to respond promptly or disagrees with the chosen method for adjustment in the contract sum. When a method determined by the architect is employed, the contractor must present an itemized accounting with supporting data and is generally limited to recovery of the costs of labor, materials, supplies, equipment, rentals, bond and insurance premiums, permit fees, taxes, direct supervision and other related cost items.

Based either on common sense or a contract clause, the reasonableness of any claimed cost will be a critical factor in any pricing dispute. In Federal government construction contracting, the controlling guidance on what is a reasonable cost is provided by the following Federal Acquisition Regulation:

FAR § 31.201-3 Determining Reasonableness.

(a) A cost is reasonable if, in its nature and amount, it does not exceed that which would be incurred by a prudent person in the conduct of competitive business. Reasonableness of specific costs must be examined with particular care in connection with the firms or their separate divisions that may not be subject to effective competitive restraints. *No presumption of reasonableness shall be attached to the incurrence of costs by a contractor.* If an initial review of the facts results in a challenge of a specific cost by the contracting officer's representative, the burden of proof shall be upon the contractor to establish that such cost is reasonable.

(b) What is reasonable depends upon a variety of considerations and circumstances, including—

(1) Whether it is the type of cost generally recognized as ordinary and necessary for the conduct of the contractor's business or the contract performance;

(2) Generally accepted sound business practices, arm's length bargaining, and Federal and State laws and regulations;

---

[29] *Sornsin Constr. Co. v. State,* 590 P.2d 125 (Mont. 1978).

(3) The contractor's responsibilities to the Government, other customers, the owners of the business, employees, and the public at large; and

(4) Any significant deviations from the contractor's established practices. (Emphasis added.)[30]

The types of direct damages sought by contractors in connection with the quantity, quality, and method variations discussed above include, among others, the extra costs of labor, materials, equipment and extended job site and home office overhead. The most frequently sought types of consequential damages are lost profits (stemming from reduced bonding capacity), interest on tied-up capital, and damage to business reputation. These types of consequential damages are often sought in connection with delay claims.

13.18 Wrongful Termination or Abandonment

A contractor may be damaged before beginning work if there is a breach of contract by the owner that prevents the contractor from performing the contract. In such a situation, the contractor is entitled to be placed in as good a position as it would have been in had the contract been performed. This generally means that the contractor can seek lost profits.[31] This rule also applies to subcontractors who may be prevented from performing, as in the case of wrongful termination of the subcontract by the general contractor.[32] However, many private and public contracts now contain provisions permitting the owner (or government) to terminate a contract for its own convenience. These provisions typically provide that the terminated contractor is not entitled to recover anticipated lost profits.

Once the contractor begins performance, it may find that the owner (or, if it is a subcontractor, the general contractor) has committed a material breach of some obligation, either express or implied. In these circumstances, and if the breach is a major one, the contractor could treat the breach as terminating his contract, and suspend construction activities and seek to recover damages.

If such an election is made, the contractor could pursue a number of means of establishing damages. First, it might seek to recover out-of-pocket expenses, less the value of any materials on hand, plus lost profits.[33] Alternatively, the contractor might seek recovery based upon the total contract price, less the total cost of performing the contract, plus any expenses incurred in performing until the material breach.

In addition, if there is some reasonable basis for pursuing this method, the contractor might seek the contract price of work performed up until the time

---

[30] 52 FR 19804, May 27, 1987.

[31] *Innkeepers Int'l, Inc. v. McCoy Motels, Ltd.*, 324 So.2d 676 (Fla. 4th DCA 1975); *Cetrone v. Paul Livoli, Inc.*, 150 N.E.2d 732 (Mass. 1958).

[32] *See John Solely & Sons v. Jones*, 95 N.E. 94 (Mass. 1911).

[33] 5 *Corbin on Contracts*, § 1094. *See also Autrey v. Williams & Dunlap*, 343 F.2d 730 (5th Cir. 1965).

of material breach, plus a profit on all unperformed work.[34] Obviously the election that will be made by the contractor will depend upon the applicable rule of damages in the particular jurisdiction, the extent of the contractor's records, whether or not the contractor would have made a profit, and provisions of the construction contract, which may limit the remedies available.

More typically, however, the contractor will continue to perform after the "breach" by the owner (or the general contractor) and will seek to recover damages after completion of the contract.[35]

13.19   Owner-Caused Delay and Disruption

In the "typical" delay-damage case, one of the contractor's tasks is to establish and isolate the period of delay attributable to the adverse party. Once this is done, proof of damages involves itemizing those fixed (ongoing) costs that were incurred during that period of delay. If, however, the period of delay itself cannot be isolated in this manner, the ensuing problems can be difficult. For example, generally courts will not make any effort to apportion damages in a situation where both parties are found to have contributed to the delays in completion of the contract.[36] Thus, where each party proximately contributes to the delay, "the law does not provide for the recovery or apportionment of damages occasioned thereby to either party."[37] All courts, however, do not adhere to this general rule.[38]

In addition to costs directly associated with the extended duration of a project, a project of extended duration also generates indirect costs, costs that present difficult proof problems. Among these costs are labor inefficiency that results from demobilization and subsequent remobilization, loss of learning-curve efficiency, and loss of efficiency when workers work overtime during an acceleration period. Although proving labor inefficiency is a difficult task, excellent studies have been undertaken and the results published on many aspects of this problem. These can often be used as support for a contractor's claim.

One of the more obvious indirect costs attributable to a delay is the home office overhead cost incurred by the contractor. A large number of cases have recognized that home office overhead, like job site overhead, is an element of damage that is recoverable by the contractor in a delay situation.[39] The

---

[34] See M & R Contractors & Builders, Inc. v. Michael, 138 A.2d 350 (Md. 1958).

[35] Underground Constr. Co. v. Sanitary Dist. of Chicago, 11 N.E.2d 361 (Ill. 1937).

[36] See United States v. United Eng'g and Constructing Co., 234 U.S. 236 (1914).

[37] J. A. Jones Constr. Co. v. Greenbriar Shopping Center, 332 F. Supp. 1336 (N.D. Ga. 1971), aff'd, 461 F.2d 1269 (5th Cir. 1972); Malta Constr. Co. v. Henningson, Durham & Richardson, 694 F. Supp. 902 (N.D. Ga. 1988).

[38] See U.S. for use and benefit of Heller Elec. Co., Inc. v. William F. Klingensmith, Inc., 670 F.2d 1227 (1982); see also Inversiones Arunsu S.A., ENG PCA PCC-77 (Nov. 15, 1991; appeal of JEM Dev. Corp., VABCA 3272, 91-2 BCA ¶ 24,010; Wilner v. United States, 23 Cl. Ct. 241 (1991).

[39] See A. E. Ottaviano Inc. v. State, 110 N.Y.S.2d 99 (1952); State v. Feigel, 178 N.E. 435 (Ind. 1931). For a discussion of a recent Federal Government contract case that attempts to limit the amount of overhead and profit a contractor can recover, see Reliance Ins. Co. v. U.S., 931 F.2d 863 (Fed. Cir. 1991).

method most frequently employed to prove extended home office overhead was set out in *Eichleay Corp.*[40] The formula is:

(1) $\dfrac{\text{Total contract price}}{\text{Total billings for full contract period}}$ × Total home office overhead = Home office overhead allocable to the contract

(2) $\dfrac{\text{Allocable overhead}}{\text{Total days of performance (including the delay period)}}$ = Daily contract overhead

(3) Daily contract overhead × Number of days of delay = Amount recoverable

Although the use of the *Eichleay* formula is sometimes questioned, recent decisions point to the strong endorsement of this method by courts and boards of contract appeals.

The *Eichleay* formula is used to compensate a contractor when a delay on a project prevents the contractor from obtaining new business during the delay period. This prevents the infusion of new funds that will absorb the fixed time-related home office overhead costs incurred. Therefore, to recover unabsorbed home office overhead, the contractor generally must show that the delay affected its operations so that it was not practical to undertake other work during the delay period and, as a result, home office costs were not absorbed.[41]

Other delay and disruption types of damages include:

1. Increased or protracted equipment rentals;[42]
2. Increased labor costs, including wage or benefit increments; for example, when an owner-caused delay forces contract performance into a new labor contract period;[43]
3. Increased material costs;[44] and
4. The costs of an idle workforce and equipment.[45]

[40] ASBCA 5183, 60-2 BCA ¶ 2688 (and commonly referred to as the "Eichleay Formula"). For more recent cases ratifying the *Eichleay* approach, *see Williams Enterprises, Inc. v. Strait Mfg. & Welding Inc.,* 728 F. Supp. 12 (D.C. Cir. 1990), *aff'd in part,* 938 F.2d 230 (D.C. Cir. 1991); appeal of *Ciesko Constr. Co.,* ASBCA No. 34199, 88-1 BCA ¶ 20,223; *George Hyman Constr. Co. v. Washington Metro Area Transit Auth.,* 816 F.2d 753 (D.C. Cir. 1987).

[41] *See* appeal of *Gregory Constructors, Inc.,* ASBCA No. 35960, 88-3 BCA ¶ 20,934; appeal of *Ricway Inc.,* ASBCA No. 29983, 86-2 BCA ¶ 918,841.

[42] *See Shore Bridge Corp. v. State,* 61 N.Y.S.2d 32 (N.Y. Ct. Cl. 1946).

[43] *See* appeal of *Weaver Constr. Co.,* ASBCA 12577, 69-1 BCA ¶ 7455.

[44] *See* appeal of *Samuel N. Zarpas, Inc.,* ASBCA 4722, 59-1 BCA ¶ 2170.

[45] *See State v. Feigel,* 178 N.E. 435 (Ind. 1931).

In certain circumstances, a contractor may also be able to recover future profits lost as a result of owner-caused delays. A delay on one project can cause the contractor's bonding capacity to be reduced, which in turn prevents the contractor from bidding on new projects that would generate future profits. Courts, however, generally view such damages as too speculative to allow recovery.[46]

13.20 Owner-Caused Acceleration

Acceleration arises from the requirement that the contractor complete performance of the contract, or a portion thereof, on a date earlier than that originally contemplated and specified by the contract or *required by a properly adjusted schedule.* There are two types of acceleration that may entitle the contractor to damages: (1) "directed acceleration" occurs when the owner requires the contractor to complete the contract before the scheduled completion date; and (2) "constructive acceleration" occurs when the owner refuses to grant the contractor a time extension in the event of owner-caused or other excusable delays. When the contractor must accelerate the pace of performance the contractor's increased costs are generally compensable.[47] These costs may include, among other things, overtime and shift premiums, supervision costs, extra equipment costs, loss of efficiency, overhead, and profit.[48] If prolonged overtime is required, the effect may be an overall decrease in worker productivity for both overtime and regular (straight) time activities.[49]

The contractor must be able to demonstrate that it has incurred extra costs due to the accelerated efforts. For example, where the owner clearly ordered the contractor to accelerate its work, but there was no evidence that the contractor did anything different or suffered any damage as a result of the acceleration order, the contractor's claim for acceleration was denied.[50]

13.21 Defective Drawings or Specifications

Where the owner supplies the plans and specifications to be used in construction, it is usually held to impliedly warrant that the plans and specifications will be adequate to achieve the purposes contemplated.[51] If the plans and specifications are defective or contain omissions, the contractor may incur substantially increased costs of performance. These costs, including the costs

[46] *See, e.g., HHO, Inc. v. United States,* 3 FPD ¶ 130 (Cl. Ct. 1985); *Kenford Co., Inc. v. Erie County, Inc.* 489 N.Y.S.2d 939 (App. Div. 1985); *but see Laas v. Montana State Highway Comm'n.,* 483 P.2d 699 (Mont. 1971).
[47] Appeal of *J. W. Bateson Co.,* ASBCA 6069, 1962 BCA ¶ 3529; appeal of *Tyee Constr. Co.,* IBCA 692-1-68, 69-1 BCA ¶ 7748.
[48] *See* Nash, *Government Contract Changes* (Federal Publications, Inc. 1975).
[49] *See* "Scheduled Overtime Effect on Construction Project," published by *The Business Roundtable* (November 1980).
[50] *Utley-James, Inc. v. United States,* 14 Cl. Ct. 804 (1988).
[51] *U.S. v. Spearin,* 248 U.S. 132 (1918).

of identifying and correcting defects in the drawings or specifications, along with any delay costs arising therefrom, may be recovered if the contractor properly relied upon such drawings in attempting to perform his contractual obligations.[52] In addition, where defective specifications create "wasted effort" and hinder the contractor's performance, the resulting delay may be excusable, and usually no damages can be recovered by the owner in the event of delayed completion.[53]

13.22 Inefficiency Claims

The loss of efficiency can be defined as the increased level of effort required to complete an activity above that reasonably estimated and anticipated by the contractor. If an activity that was reasonably estimated to take eight hours requires sixteen hours due to factors beyond the contractor's control, the overrun in labor (eight hours) is viewed as the inefficiency loss. This is often expressed in the form of a percentage, which, in this case, would be a 50 percent productivity loss. Although loss of efficiency claims most frequently involve significant labor overruns, dramatic overruns in equipment usage and costs can arise from inefficient operations.

Construction projects are perceived as having some inherent degree of confusion. An inefficiency claim must therefore demonstrate that the disruption experience went beyond that reasonably anticipated. Recovery of additional compensation for loss of efficiency requires that the claimant establish the other party's liability for the events giving rise to the claim and the amount of damages associated with those events. Some of the factors that may adversely affect contractor's efficiency are:

· Excessive overtime
· Out-of-sequence work
· Restricted access to the working area
· Trade stacking
· Overmanning
· Excess changes that disrupt the planned sequence of the unchanged work
· Differing site conditions
· Adverse weather
· Acceleration.

Studies conducted by the Business Roundtable's Construction Industry Cost Effectiveness Task Force indicate that overtime impairs productivity

---

[52] Appeal of *Celesco Indus., Inc.*, ASBCA 18370, 76-1 BCA ¶ 11,766; *Hol-Gar Mfg. Corp. v. U.S.*, 360 F.2d 634 (Ct. Cl. 1966); *La Crosse Garment Mfg. Co. v. U.S.*, 432 F.2d 1377 (Ct. Cl. 1970).
[53] *Warner Constr. Corp. v. City of Los Angeles*, 466 P.2d 996 (Cal. 1970); *Souza & McCue Constr. Co. v. Superior Court of San Benito County*, 20 Cal. Rptr. 634 (Cal. 1962).

because of physical fatigue, increased absenteeism, increased likelihood of accidents, and overall reduced quality of work installed.[54] As a general rule, courts and boards have accepted the proposition that overtime results in loss of efficiency.[55]

Weather has a significant impact on construction,[56] if the work is exposed to the elements. The types of weather impacting productivity include rain, abnormal humidity, frozen ground, subfreezing temperatures, extreme heat, and excessive wind. Relief for weather is usually limited to an extension of contract time for completion without any monetary compensation.[57] If an earlier compensable delay forces the contractor to perform work during a period of inclement weather, then the contractor may be entitled to additional time for the delay as well as compensation for loss of efficiency suffered by its labor force.[58]

One of the best ways to demonstrate productivity losses is through the use of data specific to the project. However, such records are generally not maintained on the majority of construction projects. There are many ways to collect productivity data for a particular project at the job site. One example is illustrated by the inefficiency claim presentation in *Barrett Co.*[59] In that case, the contractor noted on a daily basis the events that adversely affected efficient performance and the consequences of those events. This contemporaneous record was described by the board as "well described and documented,"[60] and the contractor recovered the amounts claimed.

Another effective way to establish the loss of efficiency is a comparison of actual production before and after the problem was encountered, referred to as a "measured mile" analysis.[61] This technique is especially effective for a contractor that routinely performs a particular division of the work with its own forces and has historical, as well as job-specific, records. The availability of this approach depends upon the nature and validity of the project documentation system.

In a loss of efficiency claim, the cause-and-effect relationship may be less capable of exact scientific measurement. This does not mean that a loss of efficiency claim is fiction. The effect of a disruption upon a construction project can be devastating in terms of labor dollars or equipment hours expended. In addition, due to the intricate and subtle dependencies between the various trades and activities (the ripple effect) there may be a need for an expert to

---

[54] Business Roundtable Constr. Indus. Cost Effectiveness Task Force, *Scheduled Overtime Effect on Construction Projects* (Nov. 1980).

[55] *See Maryland Sanitary Mfg. Corp. v. U.S.,* 119 Ct. Cl. 100 (1951); *Casson Constr. Co.,* GSBCA No. 4884, 83-1 BCA ¶ 16,523; *Metro Eng'g,* AGBCA No. 77-121-4, 83-1 BCA ¶ 16,143.

[56] National Electrical Contractors Ass'n, *The Effect of Temperature on Productivity* (Feb. 1987)

[57] *Turnkey Enter., Inc. v. U.S.,* 597 F.2d 750, 754 (Ct. Cl. 1979).

[58] *See F. H. McGraw & Co. v. U.S.,* 82 F. Supp. 338 (Ct. Cl. 1949); *Abbett Elec. Corp. v. U.S.,* 162 F. Supp. 772 (Ct. Cl. 1958).

[59] ENGBCA No. 3877, 78-1 BCA ¶ 13,075 at 63,853.

[60] *Id.* at 63,854.

[61] *Goodwin Contractors, Inc.,* AGBCA No. 89-148-1, 92-2 BCA ¶ 24,931.

offer an opinion as to the cause of a disruption and its effect on the project. In *Luria Bros. & Co. v. United States*,[62] the court stated: "It is a rare case where loss of productivity can be proven by books and records; almost always it has to be proven by the opinion of expert witnesses." Thus, the opinion of an expert witness may be required to quantify the nature, cause, and the amount of inefficiency experienced on the project.

Good documentation combined with appropriate historical data or measured mile studies provides an objective basis for the opinions of experts. Expert opinions and testimony may be extremely valuable in laying the foundation for an inefficiency claim and proving damages. However, without corroboration, the cases indicate that it is quite possible that the opinion testimony will be discounted if there is no other independent basis to support the opinions.

13.23 THE OWNER'S DAMAGES

Liability and damages can flow both ways in a construction dispute. The owner's costs can be the same type of costs of construction a contractor incurs if the owner is required to complete the project or remedy defective work. The owner's consequential damages, however, can be very different from that of a contractor and potentially of a much larger magnitude.

13.24 Direct Damages

A contractor can breach a construction contract in a variety of ways: it can fail to commence work at all; it can commence work but fail to complete it as required by the contract (i.e., abandon the project, or fail to complete it within the time period specified by the contract); or it can substantially complete the work, but have deviated from the plans in some major or minor respect. In each of these cases the owner may be entitled to recover damages for the contractor's breach.

Where the contractor has breached the contract by its failure to commence work at all, no consistent method of computing damages has been recognized and applied by the courts. However, one approach, utilized in *Ross v. Danter Assoc., Inc.*,[63] is to compute the difference between the price at which the original contractor agreed to do the construction, and the price at which the owner was able to obtain a replacement contractor or the fair market price of erecting the building.[64]

Where a contractor abandons the work prior to completion, the generally recognized measure of direct damages is the amount it costs the owner to complete the structure in accordance with the terms of the original agreement.

---

[62] 369 F.2d 701 (Ct. Cl. 1966).
[63] 242 N.E.2d 330 (Ill. App. 1968).
[64] *See generally* 76 A.L.R. 2d 805, § 8.

In *Schmidt Bros. Constr. Co. v. Raymond Y.M.C.A. of Charles City,*[65] the court set out what appears to be the majority rule in this regard:

> The contract contained no provision respecting the completion of the building in case of the failure of the contractor to complete the same. Under these circumstances, [the owner] had the right to complete the building and charge the reasonable cost and expense thereof to [the contractor] . . . [The contractor] having abandoned the contract, [the owner] was not required to submit the cost of completing the structure to competitive bidders, nor to complete the same at the lowest possible cost, but had the right to expend such sum for labor and material as was fairly and reasonably necessary to complete the structure in accordance with the contract and the plans and specifications of the architect.

When the contractor fails to complete the contract within the time period specified, the owner may be entitled to damages for delayed completion.[66] The amount of such damages may be stipulated in the contract by a liquidated damages provision. However, where there is no liquidated damages clause, the proper measure of damages for completion delay in construction contracts is generally held to be the loss of reasonable rentals from the property for the period of the contractor's unexcused delay.[67]

Where the contractor has substantially completed work under the contract but has deviated to some extent from the plans and specifications, the measure of direct damages to the owner will generally be based on some variation of one of the following two theories: (1) the *"cost" rule* or (2) the *"value" rule.*[50] The cost rule measures either the cost of completing or the cost of repairing the contractor's work. The value rule measures the difference between the actual value of the building as delivered and the value promised.

Under either of these theories of recovery the owner, like the contractor, must fully document and prove its damages. Where the damage or injury is so slight as to be insignificant, no recovery is allowed.[68]

These two methods of computing damages are widely accepted. However, the "cost to complete" measure appears to be the more commonly used, particularly in those cases where the specific defect or omission of which the owner is complaining can be remedied at reasonable cost and without destroying work that has already been done.[69]

When as a practical matter defects and omissions cannot be remedied except at unwarranted expense and with excessive economic waste, the courts usually apply the "value" rule. This "diminution in value" rule measures damages by calculating the difference between the value of the work if it had

---

[65] 163 N.W. 458 (Iowa 1917).
[66] *Potter v. Anderson,* 178 N.W.2d 743 (S.D. 1970).
[67] *Kaltoft v. Nielsen,* 106 N.W.2d 597 (Iowa 1960); *Hemenway Co., Inc. v. Bartex, Inc., of Texas,* 373 So. 2d 1356 (La. App. 1979).
[68] *General Refrigeration Co. of Lake Charles, Inc. v. Style Home Builders, Inc.,* 379 So.2 1211 (La. App. 1980).
[69] *R.I. Turnpike and Bridge Auth. v. Bethlehem Steel Corp.,* 379 A.2d 344 (R.I. 1977).

been performed in accordance with the contract and the value of the work as it was actually done; or alternatively the difference between the value of the defective structure and the structure if properly completed.

It should also be noted that these two methods of calculating damages can, under some circumstances, be used together to arrive at an acceptable, overall damage figure. Some of the items of damage may properly be calculated under the "cost to complete" approach, while others may be more suited to a "diminution in value" calculation.

13.25 Consequential Damages

The previous discussion has focused on direct damages recoverable by an owner. However, owners, like contractors, can recover consequential damages attributable to a breach under certain circumstances, and based upon adequate proof. An excellent example of such a situation arose in *Northern Petrochemical Co. v. Thorsen & Thorshov, Inc.*[70] There the owner brought an action against the general contractor, the architect, and the structural engineer for defective construction and design. The presence of numerous major defects in design and construction required reconstruction of a major portion of the facility, with a resulting eight month delay in its availability for use. In addition to the costs of reconstruction and the overall diminution in value of the building, the owner was also allowed to recover for the eight month loss of use of the facility because the court determined that the loss was a direct and proximate result of the injury and that the parties could have reasonably contemplated such damages when entering into the contract.

The court also permitted the owner to recover the following damages, as explained by the court:

> *Loss of profits* is an appropriate measure of the damages resulting from the loss of use *when the anticipated profits can be proved to a reasonable, although not necessarily absolute certainty.* In the instant case, the evidence on loss of profits was superbly marshalled and, in part because of the industry-wide inability to produce sufficient extruded plastic film to meet the demand, easily met the burden of reasonable certainty required for recovery of lost profits. . . . [W]e have no trouble finding the proof sufficiently certain to affirm the court's award in the instant case. (Emphasis added).

The contractor must therefore recognize that the risk of substantial consequential damages may exist, depending on the specific details and circumstances of the particular project and contract.

13.26 Liquidated Damages

Owners often include in the bid and contract document, a provision that states the contractor will pay the owner a certain stipulated sum of money for each

[70] 211 N.W.2d 159 (Minn. 1973).

day of delay in contract completion. In theory, the owner and the prospective contractor have agreed at the time of contract formation on the method of calculating the owner's damages in the event of the contractor's breach at a future date. In practice, however, very little negotiation or "agreement" among the parties is experienced. The owner, or its representative, will merely pick a dollar figure that appears to be sufficient to cover any anticipated excess costs arising out of delayed completion, and insert that into the documents. If a dispute subsequently arises as to the application of the liquidated damages provision, the courts will try to determine the reasonableness of the figure by examining the condition and positions of the parties at the time of contract execution, rather than at the time of breach.

A liquidated damages provision is not necessarily invalid merely because it is at variance with the usual legal rules for computing damages or because it allows an innocent party to recover, despite the fact that it is unable to prove exactly the amount of its actual damages. The crucial factors to be considered are:

(1) Whether the liquidated damage amount bears some reasonable relationship to actual or anticipated damages contemplated by the parties *when the contract was made* so that it does not constitute a penalty;[71]

(2) Whether actual damages were difficult to compute at the time the contract was signed;[72] and

(3) Whether the breach in question is one covered by the liquidated damage provision.[73]

Many states now presume that liquidated damage clauses are valid and place the burden on the party challenging the provision to prove that the clause amounts to a penalty.[74] The rationale behind upholding a valid liquidated damages provision has been explained as follows:

> The modern trend is to look with candor, if not with favor, upon a contract provision for liquidated damages when entered into deliberately between parties who have equality of opportunity for understanding and insisting upon their rights, since an amicable adjustment in advance of difficult issues saves the time of courts, juries, parties, and witnesses and reduces the delay, uncertainty, and expense of litigation.[75]

[71] *Ray v. Electrical Products Consol.*, 390 P.2d 607 (Wyo. 1964); *Psaty & Fuhrman Inc. v. Housing Auth. of Providence*, 68 A.2d 32 (R.I. 1949); *Mattingly Bridge Co. Inc., v. Holloway & Son Constr.*, 694 S.W.2d 702 (Ky. 1985); *Georgia Income Property Corp. v. Murphy*, 354 S.E.2d 859 (Ga. App. 1987).

[72] *Mosler Safe Co. v. Maiden Lane Safe Deposit Co.*, 93 N.E. 81 (N.Y. 1910); *Osceola County v. Bumble Bee Constr., Inc.*, 479 So. 2d 310 (Fla. 5th DCA 1985).

[73] *Grant Constr. Co. v. Burns*, 443 P.2d 1005 (Idaho 1968).

[74] *Farmers Export Co. v. M/V Georgis Prois, Etc.*, 799 F.2d 159 (5th Cir. 1986); *Hubbard Business Plaza v. Lincoln Liberty Life Ins. Co.*, 649 F. Supp. 1310 (D. Nev. 1986); *Coe v. Thermosal Ltd.*, 614 F. Supp. 316 (D.C.N.C. 1985).

[75] *Gorco Constr. Co. v. Stein*, 99 N.W.2d 69 (Minn. 1959).

The requirement that liquidated damages be reasonably proportionate to actual damages stems from the fact that courts have traditionally refused to enforce what amounts to a penalty for breach of contract.[76] One primary objection to penalties is that, while the law favors reimbursement for loss, it does not approve of granting windfalls or unearned profits even to an innocent party. To allow an injured party to recover an amount in excess of the actual damages it has suffered would, in effect, put that party in a better position than it would have been in had the contract been performed. This result would be inconsistent with the basic theory of contract damages, as discussed above.

For these reasons, if the liquidated damage amount set by the parties is found to be a penalty, the party seeking to enforce the provision will not be allowed to rely on it, but will instead be required to prove actual damages caused by the breach of contract. Whether a stipulated sum should be upheld as allowable liquidated damages or struck down as a penalty is a question of law that the court must decide.[77]

Another condition that most courts impose in connection with liquidated damages is that the actual damages resulting from the breach must be difficult or impossible to prove. Substitution of damages agreed upon in advance would not be justified if actual damages could be readily measured. For this reason, a liquidated damages provision will not generally be upheld where actual damages are readily ascertainable by some adequate and approved legal standard. However, the reasonableness of the liquidated damages must be viewed at the time of contracting, not at the time of the breach.

The rules governing liquidated damages have wide application in construction contracts, particularly in those situations involving late completion of the contract. The typical liquidated damages provision provides that the contractor will be assessed a certain dollar amount for each day the project remains uncompleted beyond the specified completion date. Such a provision avoids the difficulties of calculating lost revenues that the owner would otherwise be receiving. Where a contractor has been granted time extensions for whatever reason, liquidated damages do not begin to accrue until the period of the extensions has passed.

Three specific factors should be noted in connection with the assessment of liquidated damages. First, liquidated damages cannot be imposed where the owner is the sole cause of a delay suffered by the contractor.[78] Second, because of the difficulties inherent in apportioning responsibility for delays caused by the owner and the contractor, many courts will not assess liquidated damages where a concurrent delay has occurred.[79] Numerous cases have recog-

---

[76] *See, e.g., Dahlstrom Corp. v. State Highway Comm'n of State of Miss.,* 590 F.2d 614 (5th Cir. 1979); *Precon, Inc. v. JRS Realty Trust,* 47 B.R. 432 (D.C. Me. 1985); *Unis v. JTS Constructors/ Managers, Inc.,* 541 So. 2d 278 (La. App. 1989).

[77] *Farmers Export Co., fn 74, supra; United States v. Swanson,* 618 F. Supp. 1231 (E.C. Mich. 1985); *Florence Wagon Works v. Salmon,* 68 S.E. 866 (Ga. App. 1910).

[78] *Com. Department of Transp. v. W. P. Dickerson & Son, Inc.,* 400 A.2d 930 (Pa. Cmwlth. 1979).

[79] *Gillioz v. State Highway Comm'n.,* 153 S.W.2d 18 (Mo. 1941).

nized and applied the principle that the owner-caused portion of the delays so confuses the issue of responsibility for time overruns that liquidated damages cannot fairly be assessed against the contractor.

The third rule is that an owner generally has no right to assess liquidated damages for delay after the contractor has achieved substantial completion of the project. The justification for this rule is that the owner has received essentially what was contracted for, and therefore the assessment of liquidated damages would constitute a penalty.[80]

Similarly, final payment from the owner to the contractor may waive the owner's right to later seek payment of liquidated damages for the contractor's late completion. In *Centerre Trust Co. v. Continental Ins. Co.*,[81] the owner was found to have waived its right to liquidated damages by making final payment, rather than retaining funds to offset accruing liquidated damages. The owner would have been within its rights to withhold all remaining contract balances to recover the accruing liquidated damages if it had not made final payment to the contractor.

Additionally, an owner may waive its right to recover liquidated damages from a contractor by failing to place the contractor in default. In *Sun-Cal, Inc. v. United States*,[82] the General Services Administration ("owner") terminated the contractor for default. The contractor disputed the termination, claiming that the default was not authorized because the original contract completion date had been waived and a new completion date had never been established. The contract between the parties contained a liquidated damages clause that assessed $1,000.00 per day damages against the contractor for each calendar day completion was delayed beyond the contract completion date.

Due to owner delay, the parties had agreed to delay the contract completion date for one month. Although the contractor did not complete the construction by the newly established contract completion date, the owner encouraged the contractor to continue with its work on the project. A new and final contract completion date was never established by the owner.

The court in *Sun-Cal* determined that the owner had surrendered its right to terminate the contractor by failing to enforce the newly established contract completion date within a reasonable time period. The court also determined that the parties failed to agree on a new contract completion date. Consequently, since the owner chose not to place the contractor in default when it did not meet the original contract completion date or the newly established contract completion date, and since a new contract completion date was never reached, the owner could not assess liquidated damages against the contractor.

A liquidated damages provision may occasionally operate to the contractor's benefit. If such a provision is held enforceable, the clause cannot be attacked by the owner merely because the fixed amount turns out to be *less*

---

[80] *See Powers Contracting Co.*, ASBCA 1430 (1953); *Continental Ill. Nat'l Bank and Trust Co., v. U.S.*, 101 F. Supp. 755 (Ct. Cl. 1952).
[81] 167 Ill. App. 3d 376, 521 N.E.2d 219 (1988).
[82] 21 Cl. Ct. 31 (1990).

than the owner's actual damages. In *Brower Co. v. Garrison,*[83] a liquidated damages provision fixed damages at $50 per day and was upheld despite the fact that the owner's actual damages were $230 per day. Thus, a liquidated damages provision, if upheld, will preclude the owner's right to bring an action for actual damages in most situations.

Contractors may include liquidated damages in their subcontracts. Depending upon the wording of the subcontract clause, collection by the prime contractor of liquidated damages from a subcontractor may be limited to the amount the prime contractor has paid the owner.[84]

Finally, there is no apparent reason why a liquidated damages provision cannot be inserted in a contract to cover anticipated damages incurred by the contractor, as a result of owner-caused delay, disruption, and so on. Such clauses are being discussed and utilized more frequently, under the proper circumstances.

POINTS TO REMEMBER

- The general nature of damages principles is to compensate the injured party for its losses and not to create a windfall.
- Direct damages are those costs flowing directly from the wrongful acts of the other party, such as increased costs of project completion.
- Consequential damages are the reasonably foreseeable, but indirect, injury incurred from the contract breaches, such as lost profits on other projects due to lost bonding capacity.
- Punitive damages are not compensatory. Their purpose is to punish the wrongdoer. Punitive damages are generally not recoverable in contract actions or construction disputes.
- Liquidated damages are stipulated amounts that the parties agree will be assessed for a failure of performance, typically late completion. Liquidated damages are generally in lieu of and not in addition to actual (direct and consequential) damages.
- In order to recover for a claim, the claimant must establish liability, the amount of the additional costs incurred, and that there is a causal relationship between the facts giving rise to liability and the damages claimed.
- Every party has an affirmative obligation to mitigate or minimize their damages, even if the damages are the result of another's wrongful conduct. A claimant cannot unreasonably run up extra costs.

---

[83] 468 P.2d 469 (Wash. App. 1979).
[84] *See Mattingly Bridge Co. v. Holloway & Son Constr. Co.,* 694 S.W.2d 702 (Ky. 1985); *Industrial Indem. Co. v. Wick Constr. Co.,* 680 P.2d 1100 (Alaska 1984); *see also Hall Constr. Co., Inc. v. Beynon,* 507 So.2d 1225 (Fla. 1st DCA 1987) (holding that where a purchase order to a supplier contained a pass-through of liquidated damages clause, the contractor's recovery of delay damages was limited to that amount).

- Construction claims are ideally priced using the discrete cost method, in which specific costs are tied to specific acts of the other party. When it is not practical to do so, other less desirable methods such as the modified total cost method and total cost method are available.
- The total cost method is frowned upon by the courts and should only be used if absolutely necessary.
- Good cost accounting is necessary to credibly price and pursue a claim.
- Even with good documentation, the assistance of experts is necessary to calculate and prove damages, particularly when the claim is based on inefficiency costs rather than pure extra work or delay.

14

RESOLUTION OF CONSTRUCTION DISPUTES

The potential for disputes exists on every construction project of any complexity. If the dispute cannot be avoided, quick resolution is preferred, but not always possible. The existence of a dispute or claim does not render protracted litigation inevitable, but its possibility cannot be ignored. Fortunately, many of the approaches that provide the best preparation for a protracted dispute are the same methods that promote prompt resolution and settlement. It is always advisable to try to settle construction disputes before resorting to litigation or arbitration. Anyone who has been involved in a typically costly and time-consuming legal battle will affirm the old adage—"A poor settlement beats a good lawsuit."

14.1 EARLY CLAIM RECOGNITION AND PREPARATION

Before there can be any preparation or prosecution of a claim, the claim must be recognized. Early recognition is required to ensure that notice requirements are met and that documentation to support the claim is maintained. Familiarity with the contract requirements is needed to recognize claims and to avoid unknowingly providing or accepting a nonconforming quantity, quality or method of performance. Consequently, all job site personnel should be familiar with the contract terms, including the plans and specifications, the general conditions and any special provisions, so they can evaluate the performance actually demanded as compared to the performance specified in the contract. In-house educational programs to enhance this ability and better equip job personnel to identify and handle possible claim situations should also be considered.

Of course, a claim should not be asserted for every minor incident or disagreement. Conversely, trying too hard to get along and never filing a claim is not good business either. Part of an effective program of identifying claims requires targeting those incidents that are sufficiently meritorious and substantial to justify the cost of preparing and prosecuting them. Filing claims with little merit or significance will merely waste resources and squander credibility.

Once a determination is made that a claim merits prosecution, comprehensive preparation and organization should be promptly undertaken. The facts, evidence, and documents bearing on the claim should be assembled, organized and reviewed when they are fresh and before they are lost or forgotten. This preparation should be undertaken with an eye toward resolving the claim in the formal setting of an arbitration or litigation, while still seeking early resolution through informal and less onerous means. If early resolution is not achieved, complete preparation at an early stage provides important insight for developing a claim strategy and a factual foundation that can be relied upon, while remaining subject to revision, as prosecution of the claim continues.

The first step in claim preparation should be an exhaustive investigation of the claimant's own records and sources of information about the project and the claim. Project records are generally voluminous. Although the review of the records must be sufficient in scope to cover the documents relevant to the claim and anticipated defenses, it must also be sufficiently focused and specific enough to avoid inundating the claim preparation process with unnecessary and irrelevant documents. There are certain categories of documents that almost always merit some consideration, such as the contract and all change orders, pay applications, daily logs or reports, bonds and insurance policies, correspondence files and internal memoranda. Some further organization of the documents may be required beyond that used during construction in order to make individual documents relating to the claim more readily accessible.

Although documentation is certainly critical in any construction claim, it is not everything. At trial, although the documents will be admitted into evidence, the witnesses and their words, perceptions and recollections will gain the most attention. Those individual resources should not be overlooked in the claim preparation process, but they often are. The more remote claim preparation is from the people actively involved in the field, the more likely there will be unpleasant surprises and inconsistencies as the claim is subjected to greater scrutiny in discovery or at trial. Consequently, the field personnel involved should be interviewed to confirm that management's secondhand understanding about the facts and circumstances of the claim is accurate and complete. To the extent possible, project personnel should be utilized to staff and assist in the claim preparation effort. At a minimum, field personnel should be given the opportunity to review the claim at various stages of preparation, and certainly before it is submitted, to confirm they can vouch for its accuracy.

14.2 CONSULTATION WITH ATTORNEYS AND EXPERTS

Construction claims often require the assistance of experts to help solve problems and to assemble and analyze the facts. Part of a program of prompt and cost-effective claim preparation requires considering the involvement of attorneys experienced with construction claims and other technical experts at an early stage. The use of outside assistance will depend on the size and complexity of the claim, but in most claims such early involvement will facilitate prompt resolution or better preparation for trial and will be worth the investment. Scrimping on experienced and qualified legal and technical support for a claim can prove very costly in the long run.

An attorney experienced in construction claims and litigation can be deemed an "expert" whose advice and guidance at the early stages of a claim is often desirable. The construction attorney who would ultimately be charged with presenting the claim to judge, jury or arbitrators should be consulted to ensure that the claim and supporting documentation and evidence is being assembled and preserved in a manner consistent with favorable resolution of the claim in such a formal proceeding. The construction attorney need not take over the claim effort, but should be consulted to ensure that the claim effort will not be wasted, and that nothing involved in the effort will undercut the claimant's position in any proceeding that may ensue.

An experienced construction attorney can also often suggest competent technical consultants in specialized areas such as accounting and scheduling, and thereby help avoid the expense and frustration of relying on an individual who does not have the proper qualifications to testify in the case. Involvement of an attorney does not presuppose resort to litigation or arbitration. On the contrary, it is simply another element of comprehensive preparation, which hopefully contributes to the early resolution of claims. Early involvement of technical and accounting expertise will likewise enhance claim preparation efforts and hopefully the claimant's leverage in negotiation or persuasiveness at trial.

If it is possible to involve an expert during the actual construction phase, when a claim is merely a probability, that option should be considered. At such an early stage, the expert may be able to suggest ways of mitigating damages or reducing the impact of an injurious condition. The expert may also be able to recommend methods of preserving evidence and of creating demonstrative evidence for use during negotiation, arbitration or trial. Further, testimony based on firsthand observation of the construction will generally be more credible and persuasive than testimony based solely on secondhand input. There is the risk, however, that an expert's involvement in the project may rise to such a level that the credibility of any testimony the expert might provide in the future is compromised as the expert goes from neutral observer to active and adversary participant. This risk can only be weighed on a case-by-case basis.

Construction is a complex process, involving a broad spectrum of scientific and technical disciplines. Resolution of construction claims likewise requires a variety of experts to serve as consultants in the claim preparation or to testify as expert witnesses. There is neither the space nor the need to enumerate the various technical specialties or subspecialties that are often called upon in claim situations. It is important, however, to note and recognize such specialization and to ensure that the right expert is consulted for the particular problem at hand. If a claim merits prosecution, it also merits the best and most qualified technical expert in that subject who is reasonably available.

The immediate concern with technical qualifications must be balanced with the need to have a witness who is capable of persuasive testimony in the formal forum selected for resolution of claims. A technical expert respected in his field may be understood by a technically oriented arbitration panel, but be incomprehensible to a lay jury. It is this type of counterbalancing concerns that must be considered and addressed early in the claim preparation process to avoid difficult surprises and dramatic adjustments in the later stages of the claim, immediately before or during trial.

Delay is a frequent subject of construction claims. Hence, scheduling analysis and scheduling experts are often involved in resolution of claims. Beyond their scheduling expertise, scheduling consultants must have a detailed, working knowledge of the construction process so their analysis reflects the practical problems and difficulties experienced on the construction site and not merely a computer-generated abstraction. Likewise, it is essential that the scheduling expert involved in a claim be provided access to contemporaneous project documentation that accurately reflects the manner in which the work proceeded. Costly and complex as-built scheduling analyses presented in support of claims can be severely undermined if the dates used in the analysis conflict with those contained in project documentation, such as daily reports or monthly schedule updates. The scheduling expert's task and effectiveness can be substantially enhanced and such problems avoided through the maintenance of project documentation as earlier described.

Certified public accountants who are familiar with the construction industry and its financial and accounting practices can also contribute significantly to quantifying and proving the financial consequence of the technical problems that generated the claim. Their involvement is discussed separately below.

14.3 THE USE OF DEMONSTRATIVE EVIDENCE

Demonstrative evidence has the special advantage of presenting in pictorial form abstract, complicated and extensive facts. It can clarify or explain oral testimony or documentary narrative in concrete terms. In addition, demonstrative evidence adds interest and avoids the tedium of a relentless one-dimensional recitation of facts. The simplicity and clarity demonstrative evidence can provide is particularly effective in large, highly technical and complex construction claims. However, the utility of demonstrative evidence should not be overlooked in smaller, more straightforward disputes.

Demonstrative evidence can range from photographs and videos to charts summarizing facts or making comparisons, such as a chart comparing as-planned manpower to as-built manpower in order to graphically depict an overrun. Charts and graphs are often used in connection with scheduling presentations, again usually comparing the as-planned schedule to the as-built schedule, with a focus on those areas that created problems or delays. By displaying this information in an attractive visual way and in combination with other written and oral presentations, the claim can be advanced in a more compelling and persuasive manner. The goal of the demonstrative presentation is lost if it is not clear and understandable or if it is not firmly supported by the facts.

Discussions of the importance and usefulness of demonstrative evidence as a means of persuasion generally are found in trial advocacy materials. But there is no need to hold such a powerful and effective tool in reserve until trial. Demonstrative evidence should be developed and used to simplify the claim and persuade the other side as soon as possible.

14.4 THE COMPONENTS OF A WELL-PREPARED CLAIM DOCUMENT

Simplicity is the key to effective claim preparation and presentation: It promotes prompt understanding, makes the claim more interesting and makes it appear to be well supported. One means of simplifying claim presentation is to use a claim document, that is, a written synopsis of the claim that can be presented to the opposition at the early stages of the dispute. Like essentially every other aspect of claim preparation, the claim document serves two alternate purposes. First, its immediate and primary goal is to bring about a prompt and satisfactory resolution of the claim. Failing that, the second purpose of the claim document is to provide a blueprint or plan for further prosecution of the claim.

The claim document provides an opportunity for the claimant to explain its grievance in a complete and comprehensive fashion. The process of preparing the claim document is an important step in developing a claim strategy because it requires the claimant to refine and synthesize the claim from beginning to end. The claim document should be viewed as telling a story. It should have a clear and definite theme that can be readily communicated, understood and remembered. The theme should be the strongest argument supporting the claimant's theory of recovery. There will certainly be a considerable quantity of facts gathered in support of the claim, but trying to present and argue each and every one of these facts will simply overwhelm and confuse the reader, and the claim document as a tool of persuasion will be a failure. When multiple and unrelated claims are presented in one document, the document must be structured to emphasize the strongest claim.

The primary communicative component of the claim document is the factual narrative. Although this narrative will certainly focus on the claimant's point of view, it should not be expressed in overly argumentative or combative terms. Instead, to the extent possible, the facts presented should be permitted to speak for themselves. The writing style should be clear and precise, but should not read like technical specifications. It is, after all, a story and not simply a recital of a string of facts. The narrative should be comprehensive and logically organized, so it can be used as a resource throughout negotiations and further prosecution of the claim. If the complexity of the matter is such that the narrative is exceedingly long, an executive summary should be prepared.

The factual narrative is often followed by a written discussion of the applicable legal principles that support and illustrate the theories on which the claim is based. Assistance from an attorney experienced in construction claims is generally required to fashion the legal arguments and otherwise to ensure that the factual narrative is presented in a manner consistent with the applicable legal principles. The need for or extent of a legal discussion is generally geared to the expertise or experience of the ultimate decision maker for the opposition. For example, in federal construction contracts, certain theories of entitlement are so firmly established and recognized on all levels that no or only a limited legal discussion is required. In other situations, the legal discussion may be a crucial element in causing the other side to recognize its liability and exposure. A one-time owner may have no idea of what a differing site condition is or why the contractor should be paid for it. On the other hand, claims against local governmental entities that contract regularly may be ruled upon by elected officials who also require an education about construction law before they can be expected to recognize the need to settle a claim.

Pricing the claim and supporting such calculations is every bit as important as establishing liability for the claim. The claim document must recognize the importance of damages and include a specific dollar figure and fairly detailed cost analysis and breakdown. Supporting information and sources should be identified and appended if not too voluminous.

Finally, the claim document should be used to showcase and highlight the most persuasive documentary and demonstrative evidence. The most potent documents should be quoted or even reproduced in their entirety in the body of the narrative. Those documents that do not merit incorporation into the text, but which are referenced and support the claim, can be included in an indexed appendix that is cross-referenced with and organized like the factual narrative. In this manner, the narrative can be reviewed without having to sift through every bit of paper, but that backup is readily available should further review be desired.

In addition to documents, charts, graphs, drawings and photographs, other demonstrative and visual evidence should be incorporated into the claim document to the extent practical. Similarly, consideration should be given to including relevant reports by experts as attachments to the claim document as exhibits, with appropriate references to and quotes from the reports in the narrative.

In certain situations, the nature of the claim or the character or capacity of the opposition may counsel against submitting an extensive claim document. The opposition may not have the financial resources or genuine interest in resolving the claim by negotiation, which is a primary goal of the claim document. Instead, the opposition may seek a one-way flow of information, being willing to receive a detailed presentation of the claim, but unwilling to explain or document any response, defense or counterclaim until trial. The claimant must evaluate whether pursuing the "race for disclosure" by providing a claim document will ultimately eliminate the roadblocks to negotiation and settlement, or simply better equip the opposition to defend the claim, without a commensurate benefit to the claimant. Generally, but not always, a sound, well-documented and prepared claim should be able to withstand and be improved through feedback from the opposition's scrutiny. Moreover, even if the judgment is made that an extensive claim document should not be submitted, that conclusion does not necessarily mean that a claim document should not be prepared for internal use to better synthesize the claim and prepare for whatever proceeding may follow. Of course, if formal claim submission is mandated by the contract, such a requirement should be followed, although the extent of the submission may vary.

14.5 IMPORTANCE OF CALCULATING AND PROVING DAMAGES

The issue in construction disputes that generally receives the most attention and focus is liability. Does a differing site condition exist? Who caused the delay and is it compensable? However, the issue of damages or costs flowing from the events that give rise to liability is no less important. Too often, the issue of calculating and proving damages is given a backseat, with little precision or scrutiny applied until the eve of trial. That approach can result in an entirely misguided claim effort, missed opportunities for settlement and loss at trial or in arbitration. An early analysis of damages can help determine whether a claim really exists and the best means of preparing and positioning the claim for the affirmative recovery sought.

The problem of calculating and proving damages can be substantially reduced by initiating proper cost accounting at the time the claim is identified. Accounting measures can be established to segregate and carefully maintain separate records. If such a procedure is followed, proof of damages can be reduced to little more than the presentation of evidence of separate accounts. Unfortunately, this ideal situation seldom exists; either the problem is not recognized in time to set up separate accounting procedures, the maintenance of separate accounts is simply not possible because of an inability to isolate costs, or no attempt is made to establish the requisite procedures. These circumstances necessitate the development of some formula that is sufficiently reliable to permit the court or arbitrators to allow its use as proof of damage.

If settlement is being sought, the claimant must likewise convince the other side of the validity and reliability of its damage calculations.

14.6 PURSUING NEGOTIATION AND SETTLEMENT

Although claims and disputes are a part of the construction process, they need not and should not dominate the process. When claims and disputes cannot be avoided, efforts should be redoubled to resolve them as quickly as possible. The complexity, time and cost of arbitration and litigation naturally favor negotiation and settlement. An approach favoring prompt resolution should be part of a claims policy, and project personnel and management should be indoctrinated and trained along those lines. Although contract provisions regarding notice of claims and other technical requirements should be complied with, other lines of communication on the project should not be overlooked as a means of bringing a claim to quick settlement and avoiding the need to have the disputes process run its full course. It is far easier and less expensive to resolve problems in the field, where they arose, than in the courtroom. Even if early settlement is not achieved, the negotiations force the claimant to seriously examine the merits of its claim and also reveal the strengths and weaknesses of the claim at an early stage.

Comprehensive and careful preparation greatly enhances the likelihood of early resolution and settlement. A party attempting to settle a claim should know its own case intimately and should have anticipated as many of the opposing party's points as possible without the benefit of discovery. Use of a well-prepared claim document, as discussed above, is helpful both as a starting point and as a reference during settlement discussions. People with firsthand, detailed knowledge of the underlying facts are also an essential part of any negotiating effort. There is simply no substitute for the person who lived with the project's problems on a daily basis.

14.7 THE ARBITRATION ALTERNATIVE

The issue of arbitration is generally contemplated at the conclusion of the claims process. Arbitration is sought when the parties are unable to resolve the claim between themselves. The availability of arbitration as a means of resolving construction claims and disputes, however, must be planned and provided for at the outset of the project, in the contract itself. Otherwise, that alternative will not exist and if the parties cannot agree they will have to look to the courts. Generally, no particular form or special words are necessary to establish an agreement to arbitrate a dispute between the parties. However, there must be a clear indication from the contract language that the parties intended the disputed issue to be subject to arbitration.

To avoid any dispute about the scope of the agreement to arbitrate, it is best to expressly state that all disputes arising from the contract will be arbitrated. For example, the most widely used arbitration clause, contained in the American Institute of Architects (AIA) Document A201 (1987 ed.), specifies that "[a]ny controversy or claim arising out of or related to the contract, or the breach thereof, shall be settled by arbitration in accordance with the Construction Industry Arbitration Rules of the American Arbitration Association."

Arbitration is not new to the construction industry. Contract clauses providing for arbitration of disputes have been commonplace in the construction industry for many years. Although arbitration is generally perceived as a way to avoid the delays and problems associated with litigation, time and many tests have demonstrated the drawbacks as well as advantages of relying on arbitration as a means of resolving construction claims.

14.8 TIME AND COSTS OF ARBITRATION

Avoiding delays normally associated with the courts and crowded dockets and trial calendars is one of the most often-cited benefits of arbitration. On balance, and particularly for smaller claims, arbitration does provide a faster resolution. Under certain circumstances, however, arbitration can also be excruciatingly time consuming and expensive. A dispute over the existence, scope or validity of an arbitration clause agreement itself can engender a protracted court proceeding and appeal before there is a determination of whether and to what extent the parties should proceed with arbitration. In addition, arbitration of larger claims involving multiple parties can match the delays and complexity of the most arcane court proceeding.

Although ultimately dependent on the parties involved and the scope and complexity of the issues, the cost of arbitration may be less than that of a comparable court proceeding. Generally, a shortened period for resolution will keep costs down, but there are certain costs that cannot be avoided. These costs include those usually incurred in trial preparation, such as the examination and analysis of documents, legal research, the use of experts and the development of demonstrative evidence.

The costs that can be avoided in arbitration usually involve certain tradeoffs. For example, if it is not provided for by agreement or statute, discovery is often not available in arbitration.[1] The costs of discovery, which can be substantial, can thus be avoided. The lack of discovery, however, means less preparation for and knowledge of the opposition's case. It can also possibly lead to a less focused hearing, which may then require more time and increased costs. In addition, there are costs that are unique to arbitration, such as

[1] See Tupman, *Discovery and Evidence In U.S. Arbitration: The Prevailing Views,* The Arb. J. (Mar. 1989).

arbitrators' fees, which can be substantial, as well as administrative fees and the cost of meeting rooms.

14.9 Selection of Arbitrators

The qualifications and fairness of each arbitrator is essential to the viability of arbitration as a means of resolving disputes. From a partisan vantage point, the selection of arbitrators can be a major factor in the success or failure of a claim. Many factors must be considered in selecting the arbitrator or arbitration panel. Some of the most important considerations must be addressed long before any claim arises or construction begins, in the drafting of the arbitration clause. Some basic but fairly strategic considerations are the number of arbitrators and the manner in which they are selected.

The fact that arbitrators generally have more expertise in the construction industry than a judge or jury is generally cited as one of the major advantages of arbitration. Of course, this may not be an advantage if the arbitrator's experience and background are contrary to the claimant's. An engineer may view all contractor claims with a jaundiced eye, for example. Despite her expertise, that engineer is not desirable to the contractor-claimant. Conversely, a contractor-arbitrator may be reluctant to enforce a hefty liquidated damages provision as part of an owner's claim.

In terms of numbers, the basic choice is between a single arbitrator and a three-member panel. A single arbitrator costs less and will probably simplify scheduling hearings. On the other hand, a three-member panel would probably be more balanced. The three-member panel generally decides by majority vote, that is, two of the three panel members can render a decision over the objection or dissent of the third member.

Parties to an arbitration are free to agree to their own procedures for arbitrator selection. The procedure is often set forth in the arbitration clause of the contract. Provided both sides agree, the procedures can also be established or changed at the time the claim is submitted to arbitration. The method for selecting arbitrators set forth in the American Arbitration Association (AAA) Construction Industry Arbitration Rules is most widely employed. The AAA procedures provide for selection of one or three neutral and unbiased arbitrators either by mutual agreement between the parties or by administrative appointment if no agreement can be reached. An alternative to the AAA procedures that is sometimes used to select a three-member panel allows each party to select an arbitrator sympathetic to their side. The third arbitrator is then appointed by the two partisan arbitrators and is expected to be neutral. As a practical matter, this process makes the neutral arbitrator the "swing vote" that decides the arbitration.

14.10 Informality and Limited Appeals in Arbitration

The emphasis on the technical expertise of arbitrators usually involves a substantial de-emphasis of legal principles, technicalities, and procedures, including the right of appeal. This aspect of arbitration is often cited as a positive, but the contrary can be argued as well.

In arbitration proceedings, strict rules of evidence do not apply and arbitrators are generally liberal in their acceptance of evidence. This permits an easier and faster presentation of records, correspondence, documents, photographs and live testimony. In fact, the AAA rules encourage arbitrators to accept any and all evidence that may shed light on the dispute. In the more relaxed environment of arbitration, substantive defenses, such as statute of limitations, "no-damage-for-delay" clauses and notice requirements, may be given little weight.

In addition to the arbitrators' being granted considerable latitude in their conduct of hearings and rendering of awards, the right of appeal by means of a challenge of an award is extremely limited in scope. This limited scope of judicial review of arbitration awards is yet another trade-off. Although it certainly curtails a party's rights as compared to the scope of an appeal of a jury verdict, the limited scope tends to reduce the number and length of appeals from arbitration awards. This is, of course, in contrast to the court system with its lengthy and expensive appellate procedures.

14.11 Enforceability of Agreements to Arbitrate

In addition to the arbitration clause in the contract, a party's right to arbitration depends upon its ability to go to court and enforce the agreement to arbitrate. At common law, the courts were jealous of their jurisdiction and protective of a person's right of access to the courts. Today, however, the overburdened court system has made alternative methods of dispute resolution a necessity, and most states have attempted to broaden the right to arbitration either by statute or by court decision.

In addition to state laws, construction arbitration agreements are often enforceable under the Federal Arbitration Act,[2] which is the expression of a strong federal policy favoring arbitration.[3] The Federal Arbitration Act only applies if the arbitration clause is in a contract "evidencing a transaction involving commerce," meaning interstate commerce. Transactions of the type generally involved in a large construction project often satisfy this interstate commerce requirement and come within the scope of the Federal Arbitration Act.[4] If the interstate commerce requirement is met, the Federal Arbitration Act must be enforced, even in state court, and it preempts and supersedes all contrary and inconsistent state law.[5] However, state law incorporated into

---

[2] 9 U.S.C. §§ 1-15 (1970 & Supp. 1989).

[3] *J.S. & H. Constr. Co. v. Richmond County Hosp. Auth.,* 473 F.2d 212 (4th Cir. 1973).

[4] *See, e.g., Pennsylvania Eng'g Corp. v. Islip Resource Recovery Agency,* 710 F. Supp. 456 (E.D.N.Y. 1986); *Electronic & Missile Facilities, Inc. v. United States,* 306 F.2d 554 (5th Cir. 1962), *rev'd on other grounds,* 374 U.S. 167 (1963); *Metro Indus. Painting Corp. v. Terminal Constr. Co.,* 287 F.2d 382 (2d Cir. 1961).

[5] *Perry v. Thomas,* 482 U.S. 483 (1987); *Southland Corp. v. Keating,* 465 U.S. 1 (1981); *Moses H. Cone Memorial Hosp. v. Mercury Const. Corp.,* 460 U.S. 1 (1983).

the contract by a choice of law provision may still affect the manner in which the arbitration proceeds, even if the Federal Arbitration Act is otherwise applicable.[6]

14.12 Special Problems Involving Multiple Parties

A recurring issue in the administration of construction arbitrations is the consolidation of a number of separate arbitrations and multiple parties on the same project into one proceeding. The potential for problems and the desirability of consolidation need to be considered at the time the arbitration clause is being drafted and the contract signed, long before any claim develops. Although the consolidation of court proceedings involving numerous parties is common, few construction contracts presently provide for such consolidated proceedings in arbitration. Even without contractual authorization, however, some courts have required consolidation as an expeditious means to resolve construction disputes.[7] However, the traditional and majority rule appears to be that, without express contractual consent to multiparty arbitrations, courts will not require consolidation.[8] In *Stop and Shop Co. v. Gilbane Bldg. Co.,*[9] the court insisted that, "[I]f multi-party arbitration is to become a standard procedure, arbitration clauses and the rules and procedures of the AAA and other concerned organizations should be redrawn to provide for it."

The arbitration clause contained in AIA Document A201, Article 4.5.5 (1987 ed.), imposes strict limits on consolidation and prohibits consolidation of the owner's claim against the architect in any arbitration between the owner and the contractor. The AIA arbitration clause does, however, allow for a consolidated proceedings involving parallel contractors. The prohibition against joining the architect can put the owner in the unenviable position of having to defend in arbitration the contractor's claim for the architect's defective design, without being able to compel the architect to join the same arbitration as a party. This places the burden of defending the architect's design or conduct on the owner. The prohibition against consolidation also causes the owner to run the risk of inconsistent results as well as extra expenses from duplicative arbitration proceedings. For example, an owner could lose to a contractor's claim of defective design in one arbitration, only to fail to convince a separate arbitration panel that the design was defective and that the architect should therefore reimburse the owner for its loss to the contractor. If the

[6] *Volt. Info. Sciences v. Stanford Univ.,* 109 S. Ct. 1248 (1989).
[7] *See Episcopal Hous. Corp. v. Federal Ins. Co.,* 273 S.C. 181, 255 S.E.2d 451 (1979); *Exber, Inc. v. Sletten Constr. Co.,* 92 Nev. 721, 558 P.2d 517 (1976); *James Stuart Polshek & Assoc. v. Bergen County Iron Works,* 142 N.J. Super. 516, 362 A.2d 63 (1976); *Grover-Diamond Assoc. v. American Arbitration Ass'n,* 297 Minn. 324, 211 N.W. 2d 787 (1973).
[8] *Consolidated Pac. Eng'g v. Greater Anchorage Area Borough,* 563 P.2d 251 (Alaska 1979); *Cumberland Perry Vocational Technical Sch. Auth. v. Boyor & Bink,* 261 Pa. Super. 350, 396 A.2d 433 (1978).
[9] 364 Mass. 325, 304 N.E.2d 429, 432 (1973).

owner wants to avoid this situation, it must be addressed in advance in the arbitration clauses of its contracts with the contractor and the architect.

14.13 LITIGATION

When there is no arbitration provision, the traditional avenue for obtaining relief is litigation. The rules governing court proceedings are quite complex and vary among federal, state, and local courts from jurisdiction to jurisdiction. For this reason, the following discussion presents only a thumbnail sketch of what is involved in "going to court."

14.14 Profile of the Construction Trial

The trial of a construction contract dispute offers a unique challenge to both sides of the case. Complex antitrust cases are perhaps the closest parallel, since both involve numerous parties and virtual mountains of documentation. However, certain problems are unique to construction controversies.

In contrast to the typical civil dispute or crime where the wrong occurred at a single point in time, construction claims generally grow out of an accumulation of events developing over many months or years. To further complicate matters, a single activity constituting a breach of contract may have a "ripple" effect on the remainder of the project, expanding the effect of the breach and entitling the injured party to recover "impact" costs as an additional element of damages. The category of impact damages includes the cost of inefficiency and lost productivity resulting from out-of-sequence or accelerated work. Although at times difficult to prove, such damages can often be substantial.

An added difficulty in a construction case is the large cast of characters, which can include one or more prime contractors, subcontractors, suppliers, the owner, one or more sureties, design professionals, construction managers, lenders and others. As soon as litigation becomes inevitable, the contractor and its counsel must carefully analyze the list of possible parties from the standpoint of liability, financial responsibility, jurisdiction, venue, access to facts and the other factual and legal viewpoints.

In a contract action, the most obvious parties are those who have direct contract relations or "privity" with one another—owner and prime contractor, or prime contractor and subcontractor. However, other parties may become involved. For example, assume that an owner-plaintiff sues a bonded prime contractor for defective work. The owner would also likely join the contractor's surety as a defendant. Assume that the prime contractor believes the defects are not its fault, but the responsibility of one of its subcontractors. Since there was no "privity of contract" between the owner and the subcontractor, the owner could not sue the subcontractor directly. The prime contractor, by virtue of the subcontract, has a direct contractual relationship with the subcontractor and therefore may "join" the subcontractor as a "third-party defendant." This mechanism is referred to as "third-party practice."

This scenario often results in counterclaims by the prime contractor against the owner for delays, defective plans or the like. Every party considering whether to file suit should take into account the defendant's likely counterclaim, which may make it impossible to withdraw from litigation once suit has been filed.

The subcontractor may repeat the process. It may believe one of its subcontractors or suppliers is actually responsible for the defect and may, in turn, join that party as a "fourth-party defendant." What was once a simple, two-party lawsuit can quickly mushroom into one involving numerous parties and their counsel with the attendant increase in complexity, delay and expense.

14.15 The Court System A decision that must be made concurrently with the selection of parties is the choice of the most desirable court or, in legal terminology, the "forum."

From the standpoint of strategy and convenience, it is generally a distinct advantage to be the plaintiff and to select the forum. The plaintiff tells its story first to the judge or jury. The plaintiff also has some latitude in determining where to initiate the lawsuit. Frequently, this allows a convenient or "hometown" location to be selected.

In order to evaluate the factors that bear on the selection of a particular court, it is helpful to have a basic understanding of the various court systems. Essentially, there are two court systems within the United States—one federal and a variety of state court systems. The federal judicial system is comprised of the United States District Courts (approximately 90 in number), the United States Courts of Appeals (12 in number) and the United States Supreme Court.

The federal courts are courts of "limited jurisdiction." In contrast, state courts are courts of "general jurisdiction." The term "limited jurisdiction" refers to the fact that some specific statutory basis must be established before a party can have its case heard in federal court. In other words, jurisdiction is "limited" to those special instances prescribed by law. In contrast, a presumption exists that a state court has jurisdiction over a particular controversy, unless a showing is made to the contrary.

"Subject matter" jurisdiction refers to the power of a court to hear a particular type of case. The subject matter jurisdiction of the federal courts in construction cases typically has a "federal question" or "diversity of citizenship" basis. "Federal question" jurisdiction encompasses disputes arising "under the Constitution, laws or treaties of the United States." The second basis for subject matter jurisdiction in the federal courts—and by far the more common in construction disputes—is the "diversity of citizenship" basis.[10] Diversity in this sense refers to controversies between citizens of different states or between citizens of a state and an alien. To satisfy the jurisdictional

---

[10] *See* 28 U.S.C § 1332(a).

requirement, diversity of citizenship must be complete—that is, all defendants must be from states different from all plaintiffs.[11]

"Diversity" cases are also subject to a $50,000.00 threshold limit on the amount in controversy, exclusive of interest and costs. This means that suits where the realistic recovery is $50,000.00 or less are barred from federal courts even if they are between citizens of different states.

The second facet of jurisdiction—"personal" jurisdiction—focuses on whether the defendant has sufficient contact with the forum state to give the court the right to resolve the dispute. The most common bases for personal jurisdiction include the defendant's physical presence within the jurisdiction, or, in the case of a corporation, the transaction of business within the area of the court's control.

Venue also presents a preliminary problem in any lawsuit. The term "venue" refers to the proper geographic location for bringing suit, rather than which court system has appropriate jurisdiction to hear and decide the case. Venue considerations apply in both federal and state courts, although they tend to be more complex under state law due to the characteristic focus of state statutes on the county of residence of the defendant.

14.16 The Federal Rules of Civil Procedure The Federal Rules of Civil Procedure, which govern all procedural aspects of federal trials from initial pleadings to judgment, are the product of years of study, analysis and recommendations by attorneys and scholars. They represent an effort to provide a workable procedural system. Many states have adopted the Federal Rules in whole or in part for use in their own court systems, or have developed minor variations. Substantial variations in the rules of civil procedure do exist from state to state. This is in contrast to the standardization of the Federal Rules of Civil Procedure for all federal courts across the country. Although local federal district court rules may vary in some particulars, the attorney familiar with the Federal Rules of Civil Procedure will ordinarily not feel handicapped in a district court outside of that attorney's usual geographic area of practice.

14.17 Discovery Discovery under the Federal Rules of Civil Procedure and its counterparts at the state level is designed to eliminate courtroom surprise and foster settlement. Discovery is particularly important in construction litigation because most complicated cases are predicated on vast amounts of files, plans, specifications, engineering data and other volumes of paper. "Discovery" is the statutory means by which a party is able to elicit facts from the opposing party, and thereby narrow issues, pin down the opposition's contentions and generally prepare for trial. The most important discovery devices for construction cases are described below:

(1) *Interrogatories (Fed. R. Civ. R. 33(a)):* Interrogatories are written questions prepared by one party to the lawsuit and directed to another party.

---

[11] *Strawbridge v. Curtiss,* 2 L. Ed. 435 (1806).

Answers are generally prepared with the assistance of the party's counsel. This involvement of counsel in the preparation of written answers often restricts the information provided in response to the interrogatories. Nonetheless, interrogatories are a useful tool for initially obtaining information upon which subsequent discovery can be based.

(2) *Depositions (Fed. R. Civ. R. 30, 31 and 32):* A deposition is the oral examination of any person, whether or not a party to the action, whose knowledge and perspective are important to the case. The deposition allows the questioner a more effective method of obtaining information since questions can be tailored to prior responses of the deponent and the questioner has an opportunity to follow up spontaneously on new avenues of inquiry. Depositions play a crucial part in the development of trial strategy because the testimony is taken under oath and recorded by a stenographer. Since there is an opportunity for cross-examination during the course of a deposition, a deposition transcript may be used at trial when a witness has died in the interim or is otherwise unavailable. The deposition may also be used for the purpose of contradicting or "impeaching" the courtroom testimony of the witness whose testimony contradicts prior deposition statements.

(3) *Requests for Admission (Fed. R. Civ. R. 36):* One party can require another party to the lawsuit to admit, in writing, the truth of certain facts, by means of a formal request for admission. This saves both time and money, and allows the parties to direct their energies toward those issues that are truly disputed.

(4) *Motion for Entry upon Land (Fed. R. Civ. R. 34(a)):* This rule provides a means for one party to request permission to enter a premises for the purpose of inspecting, surveying, photographing, testing or sampling the property or any designated object or operation. The value of this procedure is readily apparent if the contractor has relinquished control over the site, and subsequently needs to photograph site conditions or sample the soil in connection with a differing site condition claim.

(5) *Production of Documents and Things (Fed. R. Civ. R. 34 (a)):* This rule allows a party to compel another party to furnish designated documents (including writings, drawings, graphs, charts, photographs and other data compilations) or tangible objects that have a bearing on the case and that are in the possession of the other party. A request for production under this rule frequently accompanies a set of interrogatories, with the requested documents or objects to be produced or made available for inspection, copying, testing or sampling at the same time that the answers are filed. Production of documents and objects at a deposition can also be required by means of a *subpoena duces tecum.*

14.18 Judge or Jury?   An important decision associated with a trial is the choice between presenting the case to a judge or a jury. This choice lies with the parties. Generally, any party may file a written demand for a trial by jury.[12]

---

[12] *See* Fed. R. Civ. P. 38, 28 U.S.C.

A number of factors enter into the decision. For example, a judge sitting alone may be more likely to admit disputed evidence, which would normally be excluded from consideration by a jury, on the rationale that it is better to let in doubtful evidence than to face reversal on appeal because relevant evidence was not admitted. In such a case, the judge is relying on experience and training to give the evidence only the weight it deserves. On the other hand, a judge is less likely to be swayed by sympathy factors and equities that frequently work in a party's favor before a jury.

The type of construction project may also have a bearing on this decision. A local jury may prove disastrous if the case involves construction of a public facility such as a school or hospital—particularly one funded by local property taxes or levies, or one that is highly controversial. A similar result may occur if the party being sued is a local business concern, for example a subcontractor or supplier, and the plaintiff is an outsider.

Ultimately, the determining factor may be that many construction cases are simply too complex for the average jury—although some trial attorneys will argue that most judges are likewise not familiar, through experience or background, with construction principles. In any event, the complexity of the matter and the relative advantage that may be gained by simplification (or on the other hand, by confusion) are factors to be weighed in deciding whether to proceed before a judge or jury.

14.19   The Trial   The final focal point of the litigation process is the presentation of evidence calculated to persuade the trier of fact of entitlement to relief. Evidence is presented through: (1) live testimony or by deposition if a witness is not available at the time of trial; (2) documentary evidence; and (3) demonstrative evidence. The trial attorney weaves the case by combining the facts with legal theories supporting the client's entitlement.

14.20   Live Testimony   Live testimony is, in most instances, the most persuasive type of proof. It is crucial, however, that witnesses be prepared well in advance of trial to ensure their knowledge of important facts as well as to bolster confidence.

The client must assist counsel in selecting the most effective witnesses. In most cases, effectiveness can be equated with personal knowledge of the facts. Often it is not the president of the company who has this firsthand knowledge, but superintendents or inspectors, who are "in the trenches" on a daily basis, fighting the battle which ultimately winds up in the courtroom. Another important point to consider is that these individuals—who use the unique language of the construction industry in expressing themselves—frequently make excellent witnesses. They have the capacity to translate complicated construction problems into simple, everyday language that is frequently both colorful and persuasive.

Members of management are usually most effective in establishing broad overview points, such as assumptions about labor productivity that ultimately were translated into the bid and how those assumptions and expectations were frustrated.

In addition to field and office personnel, "expert" witnesses are often used. The use of experts is commonplace in construction litigation, especially in the ever-increasing number of complex "delay damages–interference–impact" cases. It is common practice in such cases for an expert to be used to analyze the validity of the critical path method (CPM) or similar schedule originally relied upon by the contractor in submitting his bid, as well as in the preparation of an as-built schedule depicting where and how the job went wrong. Testimony from such an expert is important to quantify the impact of breaches and delays and the assessment of damages.

One pitfall of using expert witnesses in construction cases is the failure to provide the expert with reliable source material, of the kind usually relied upon, to use in forming opinions and conclusions. It is appropriate for the opposing party to inquire into the foundation, facts and data upon which an expert's opinion is based. If it is found that the facts and data are untrustworthy or not of the type an expert would normally rely upon, then the testimony of the expert witness is subject to attack. As a part of its ruling on the admissibility of expert opinion testimony, the trial court will review the reasonableness of the witness' reliance on facts or data, to determine if the expert has deviated from the recognized area of expertise by basing an opinion on untrustworthy material. It is then the responsibility of the court to rule whether the testimony can be received or should be excluded.[13]

Live witnesses—lay and expert alike—are subject to "direct" examination by counsel representing their side of the dispute, and "cross-examination" by opposing counsel. The primary function of direct examination is to place all pertinent facts into evidence for consideration by the trier of fact. To assure that this is properly done, counsel will generally discuss with the witness the types of questions that will be asked, although the answers should be those of the witness.

On cross-examination, opposing counsel has a different goal and will take a different approach in an effort to discredit the witness or the testimony by, for example, pointing out inconsistencies in the testimony or showing bias. A cardinal rule generally followed by attorneys during cross-examination is "never ask a question you don't know the answer to." Given this, it is frequently possible for the construction attorney and the client to anticipate and prepare for most of the questions that will come up during cross-examination.

POINTS TO REMEMBER

· Early claim recognition and preparation with the assistance of "experts" is important to ensure that the claim and supporting documentation and

[13] *Zenith Radio Corp. v. Matsushita Elec. Indus. Co.*, 505 F. Supp. 1313 (E.D. Pa. 1980), *Shatkin v. McDonnell Douglas Corp.*, 565 F. Supp. 9 (S.D.N.Y. 1983).

evidence is assembled and prepared in a manner likely to result in a favorable resolution.

· Preparation and use of demonstrative evidence can be an effective tool in simplifying and advancing a claim in a persuasive manner.

· A well-drafted claim should be an exercise in storytelling that will educate, inform, and hopefully persuade its reader.

· Early analysis of actual damages is essential in determining if a claim really exists and the best means for either advancing the claim or encouraging an early resolution and settlement.

· The advantages as well as the drawbacks of arbitration as a method of dispute resolution should be considered at the time of contracting. If arbitration is desired, it should be provided for in advance.

· Procedures for selecting arbitrators as well as the consolidation of multiple parties should be considered when drafting the construction contract's arbitration clause. Generally, arbitrators are granted considerable latitude in conducting hearings and rendering awards and the right of appeal is extremely limited.

· Enforceability of agreements to arbitrate may be governed by both state and federal laws.

· In the absence of an arbitration provision, the traditional avenue for obtaining relief is litigation. Construction claims are inherently complex. They often involve multiple parties and the governing laws vary widely among federal, state and local jurisdictions.

· Selection of the court that will hear the claim depends on several factors, including the total dollar amount in controversy and the state citizenship of all of the parties.

· The Federal Rules of Civil Procedure provide numerous important discovery devices that are designed to elicit facts and narrow the issues in preparation for trial.

· Parties to a complex construction claim must carefully consider whether to present evidence of the claim to a judge or to demand a jury trial.

· Whether witnesses were actual participants in the project giving rise to a claim or are hired "experts," it is crucial that all witnesses be prepared well in advance of trial to ensure their effectiveness.

15

CONSTRUCTION
INSURANCE

15.1 THE IMPORTANCE OF INSURANCE PLANNING

Insurance is often neglected in construction. Such neglect is a mistake few can afford. Insurance is a crucial consideration in project planning and also as a means of covering losses and minimizing disputes among the parties on the project.

Construction insurance is a highly specialized and complex field—confusing and mysterious to the uninitiated. There is no all encompassing policy or coverage for any project or party to the project. Instead, a web of policies, coverages, exclusions, deductibles, policy limits, and excess and umbrella coverages are stitched together among the parties to cover those relatively limited number of risks that are insurable on the project.

Insurance planning for construction projects is too complex and specialized to be left to the inexperienced lay person. Even those companies that are able to employ full-time insurance specialists or risk managers must rely on professional insurance brokers to assist in the procurement of the proper coverage at a competitive price. Specialized expertise in construction insurance is also required.

This chapter presents an overview of the types of insurance that are available and frequently at issue on construction projects, and the basic scope and framework of the coverages. Practical considerations in responding to potential insurance claims are addressed. Finally, some recurring coverage issues are discussed.

The unique terms of individual policies and the peculiarities of individual state laws limit the generalization that can be made about insurance issues. The broad principles described in this chapter cannot substitute for specific reference to the contracts and the insurance policies actually at issue and the applicable state law.

15.2 TYPES OF INSURANCE

The types of insurance policies that are typically purchased for construction projects and that are discussed in this chapter are commercial general liability, builders risk, and errors and omissions. There are many other forms of insurance that may also come into play on a construction project. These can range from everyday reliance on worker's compensation insurance to a more unusual claim against a corporate officers and directors' liability policy. Although some of the general principles described may apply to those other forms of insurance, this chapter focuses on the three most common forms of insurance relied upon in resolving construction claims.

15.3 Commercial General Liability

Commercial general liability (CGL) protects the policyholder and other named insureds from injuries they cause to others. A CGL policy is "third-party insurance" in that it protects the insured from claims of loss by third parties against the insured and does not protect the insured from losses it directly incurs.

Contractors and subcontractors' CGL policies or other policies usually will address liability for personal injury. Liability for property damage to the project or the work is a far different matter. CGL coverage is far more narrow than the professional liability or the errors and omissions coverage the design professional secures. A CGL policy is "not intended to indemnify the contractor . . . for direct damages resulting because the contractor furnished defective material and workmanship."[1] The insurance industry's rationale for this limited coverage is that business risks that are in the control of the contractor and for which the contractor seeks a profit should not be the subject of insurance. These limitations of coverage are discussed in greater detail below.

15.4 *"Occurrence" versus "Claims-Made" Policies* A CGL policy can be either an "occurrence policy" or a "claims-made policy"; the difference between the two relates to the timing of coverage. Both forms of coverage are acknowledged in ¶ 11.1.2 of the American Institute of Architect's (AIA) General Conditions for Owner-Contractor Agreement, AIA Document A201 (1987 ed.).

An occurrence policy provides coverage regardless of when the claim is actually made provided the insured occurrence took place during the policy period. A claims-made policy is basically the opposite. Its coverage extends to claims made during the policy period, regardless of when the insured risk occurred.

---

[1] *Rafeiro v. American Employers' Ins. Co.*, 5 Cal. App. 3d 799, 808, 85 Cal. Rptr. 701 (1970); *see generally* Bunshoft & Seabolt, "The Contractor's Insurance Coverage Under Its Liability and Builder's Risk Policies," *Construction Litigation; Representing the Contractor* (Wiley 1986).

When changing policies, it is important to avoid any gaps in coverage, particularly if changing from one form of coverage to the other. The risk of gaps in coverage through such a change can be addressed by purchasing an extended reporting period as part of a claims-made policy. However, the insured should make a practice of immediately reporting any potential claims to ensure coverage under an existing claims-made policy.

15.5 Costs of Defense and Deductibles An important distinction between types of CGL policies is whether the cost of defense is excluded from the policy coverage limits. If the cost of defense is excluded or is in addition to the policy limits, the cost the insurance company incurs in defending a claim does not reduce the value of the coverage. For example, if there is a $100,000 claim on which the insurance company expends $25,000 to defend, your coverage is still the full $100,000 policy limit. If the cost of defense is included in the policy limits, the protection afforded is considerably reduced—the risk of costs of litigation fall on you and not the insurance company. In the same example, the $25,000 in defense costs would reduce your liability coverage to $75,000.

Considering the high cost of complex and protracted construction litigation, this cost of defense can easily approach and possibly exceed the actual liability coverage. The extent to which costs of defense can effectively erode insurance protection have caused some states to prohibit or heavily regulate such coverage.

Policy limits define the ceiling of financial protection afforded by insurance, but there is also a floor to that protection—the deductible, which is the loss or expense the insured must absorb before the insurance company has any obligation to pay. The combined effects of a high deductible and policy limits that include the costs of defense can dramatically limit the real financial protection afforded by a CGL policy on many claims.

It is important to remember that although the need to incur the deductible may postpone any direct involvement or payment by the insurance company, the deductible does not postpone the need to provide the insurance company prompt notice of a potentially covered event or claim. Failure to provide the required notice can result in loss of coverage.

15.6 Layers of Insurance CGL coverage is often purchased in multiple layers. The basic coverage is the "primary" policy, with the additional increments of coverage being "excess" or "umbrella" policies. For example, the policy limit on a primary CGL policy may be $1,000,000, another "layer" may provide coverage in the $1,000,000 to $5,000,000 range, and so on. In addition to providing an additional layer of protection in terms of policy limits, an "umbrella" policy may also provide coverage for some additional risks not covered by the primary policy.

The excess carrier typically will have no duty to defend until the primary or other lower coverage is exhausted, similar to the deductible requirement.

However, prompt notice is required to all carriers regardless of when the excess coverage kicks in.

15.7 *Additional Named Insured* The overall impact of CGL coverage on a construction project can be substantially expanded by the inclusion on the policy of other parties as "additional named insureds," who then also enjoy coverage. It is common for owners to require the general contractor and subcontractors to include the owner as an additional named insured on their CGL policies. General contractors likewise typically require subcontractors to name the general contractor. Inclusion as an additional named insured not only provides protection to the named party against claims by third parties, it also protects the additional named insured from subrogation claims by the insurance carrier. Subrogation is the theory by which the insurance company after paying on a covered claim can pursue the rights of the covered party against the party responsible for the damages.

15.8 *Environmental Liability* The potentially far-reaching liability for environmental hazards is an ever-increasing concern in construction. Unfortunately, the protection afforded under a typical CGL policy is significantly limited when compared to the risk. Most CGL policies exclude coverage for all pollution damages except for that which is "sudden and accidental." Policies are available to separately address broader environmental risks, and the products available continue to increase as the insurance industry comes to grips with how to deal with such liability.

15.9 Builder's Risk Insurance

Builder's risk insurance provides coverage for damages to the project during construction. It protects against the insured's loss, as distinguished from compensating the losses of others as with a CGL policy. Builder's risk is typically purchased by the owner, but with coverage extending to the general contractor and subcontractors. See, for example, AIA Document A201, ¶ 11.3.1. The general contractor and subcontractors also have an insurable interest and can procure coverage on their own.

Builder's risk coverage comes in two similar, but different types of policies. You can procure "all risk insurance," which covers everything except that which is identified in the exclusions—and those exclusions can be fairly broad. Or you can procure specified coverage. Although they approach coverage from two extremes, the scope of coverage actually afforded typically is not that different. AIA Document A201 requires the owner to procure "all risk" coverage.

Even though the owner must procure the insurance, under AIA Document A201, the general contractor and subcontractors must bear the cost of minimum deductibles.

15.10 Errors and Omissions Insurance

Errors and omissions (E&O) insurance is professional liability or malpractice insurance, which covers the professional negligence of design professionals. Although the existence of such coverage is often assumed, it is far from a sure thing. The cost of such coverage is substantial, and, like most insurance, ever-increasing. In addition, many design professionals believe that investing in E&O coverage encourages claims rather than protects against them. This perception is perhaps reflected in the standard AIA contract between the owner and architect, which does not even require that the architect procure such coverage.[2]

Owners are increasingly requiring construction managers to carry professional liability coverage similar to that maintained by design professionals. Similarly, design/build contracts often require contractors to obtain the coverage of an E&O policy or require the design member of the team to carry such insurance.

15.11 CONTRACT REQUIREMENTS FOR INSURANCE

Insurance must be planned for each individual project. Although there are certain industry standards regarding which party provides what kind of coverage, insurance is too important and too specialized to assume anything. It is essential that you consult the individual contracts on each project to confirm how insurance requirements are addressed. This review is necessary to confirm that you are complying with the contract and also to verify that others are providing you with the protection you need. It also is important to confirm that those contractually defined requirements are satisfied by all involved. Unexpected gaps in coverage are unpleasant surprises.

15.12 Standard Contract Clause

The typical insurance arrangement is reflected in the AIA General Conditions for Construction, Document A201 (1987 ed.). The contractor procures CGL coverage.[3] The owner will almost always require that it be listed as an additional insured on that policy. The owner can also obtain liability coverage, but is not required to do so.[4] The owner is, however, required to obtain all risk builder's insurance.[5] This builder's risk protection extends to subcontractors on the project.

AIA's Standard Form of Agreement Between Contractor and Subcontractor, AIA Document A401 (1987 ed.) simply leaves a blank for the types of

---

[2] Standard Form Agreement Between Owner and Architect, AIA Document B141 (1987 ed.).
[3] *Id.* ¶ 11.1.1.
[4] *Id.* ¶ 11.2.1.
[5] *Id.* ¶ 11.3.1.

coverage and policy limits required. Ideally, the general contractor would like the subcontractor's insurance to mirror what the general contractor is required to procure. Such broad coverage for subcontractors is often not practical, necessary or cost effective. After certain minimums are applied, the specific nature and scope of a subcontractor's work should bear upon the extent of the coverage required. If particularly hazardous work is required, even greater levels of insurance may be required.

15.13 Waiver of Subrogation

As noted earlier, waiver of subrogation rights is an important component in planning insurance coverage on a project. Subrogation is the theory by which after paying on a claim, the insurance company can pursue the rights of the insured against the party responsible for the damages. By including a waiver of subrogation clause in a contract, the parties can insulate themselves from such subrogation claims, and have any potential claims primarily resolved through insurance. Because the waiver of subrogation can substantially affect the insurance company's risk by cutting off its potential rights to recoup losses on claims, the insurance company should be notified of the inclusion of such waiver in a contract to avoid jeopardizing coverage.[6]

The AIA Document A201 requires the owner and contractor to waive their subrogation rights and additionally requires them to obtain similar waivers with other contracts, hopefully protecting all from subrogation claims.[7] The waiver of subrogation is also incorporated in the AIA's standard subcontract form, AIA Document A401 (1987 ed.).[8]

15.14 Proof of Insurance

It is not sufficient to merely identify what each party is required to do with respect to insurance. The greatest insurance planning is wasted if there is no execution and follow-through in accordance with the plan and contract requirements. Compliance with insurance requirements should be confirmed by certificates of insurances describing the coverage and identifying the insurance company. Proof of insurance by all parties should be a contract requirement.[9]

Proof of insurance should be confirmed as soon as possible, certainly prior to starting work. If a loss occurs prior to procuring the insurance, the ability to get coverage for that event is extremely limited. If a contractor or subcontractor cannot confirm its insurability and procurement of insurance when it

---

[6] *Liberty Mut. Ins. Co. v. Altfillisch Constr. Co.*, 70 Cal. App. 3d 789, 139 Cal. Rptr. 91 (1977).
[7] AIA Document A201, ¶ 11.3.7.
[8] AIA Document A401 ¶ 13.5.
[9] *See, e.g.,* AIA Document A201, ¶ 11.1.3 and AIA's standard subcontract, AIA Document A401, ¶¶ 13.3 and 13.4.

is required to do so at the beginning of the project, the likelihood that it will ever be able to procure the required coverage is substantially reduced.

Failing to promptly require proof of insurance may not only leave gaps in coverage. It also raises the question of whether you should or can terminate a contractor or subcontractor who cannot obtain insurance if you have permitted them to proceed without insurance. In addition to the practical risks and difficulties associated with terminating a contractor or subcontractor, you may be confronted with the argument that failure to procure insurance is not a material breach justifying termination for default or that the insurance requirement was waived by allowing work to proceed without insurance.

15.15 PROMPT ACTION TO PROTECT POTENTIAL COVERAGE

15.16 Sensitivity to Insurance Issues

Effective insurance planning does not only involve the acquisition of coverage. It must also involve sensitizing project personnel to the potential for coverage of losses and claims, and the need to react and preserve such potential relief. Project management personnel should be sufficiently trained and experienced to affirmatively deal with insurance notice requirements. At a minimum, project management personnel must know when to alert others or upper management with expertise or responsibility for insurance matters when potential coverage issues arise on the project. Ideally, there should be at least one resource person in your organization who, through special training and experience, can deal with specific situations and coverage questions beyond the broad concepts introduced in this chapter.

A starting point for effectively dealing with potential coverage issues is obtaining familiarity with all the insurance policies that may apply to your organization as well as the specific project. Reading the policies is essential, but, unfortunately, not necessarily enough. Without some background in insurance, much of the policy language affirmatively describing coverage and the litany of exclusions may not make any sense.

15.17 Immediate Notice

When confronted with a potential loss or claim, the possibility of insurance coverage must be considered first—not last, and only after all other possible avenues of relief or defense have been exhausted.

Prompt notice to the insurance company of a potential claim is of critical importance to satisfy policy requirements and protect coverage. Early consideration of coverage in dealing with claims or losses is also important in developing the documentation or posture that will enhance an argument in favor of coverage on those claims in which coverage may be disputed.

Where there is merely a possibility of coverage, it is nonetheless prudent to put the insurance company on notice as soon as possible. The notice can be conditioned or qualified as the circumstances require. If there ultimately is no coverage or no loss or claim, the notice provided is of no harm. On the other hand, if you fail to provide prompt notice any chance of coverage may be lost due to your delay.

If a claim is asserted against you, you should affirmatively tender the defense of the claim to the insurer. This tender of defense, however, should not preclude you from taking any immediate action necessary to preserve any defense or rights you or the insurer may have.

Lack of timely notice to the insurer can be the basis for loss of coverage in some states, even if the insurer experienced no actual prejudice as a result of the timing of the notice.[10] In most states, however, late tender of the defense will bar recovery of attorneys' fees and cost of defense incurred prior to the tender.

The tender should be as complete and as informative as possible. You should provide copies of demand letters or pleadings and other documents that describe the nature and circumstances of the claim. If the basis for coverage is not entirely clear, it is also a good idea to provide documents or an explanation that highlights or depicts the circumstances that may establish coverage. For example, in tendering a claim under a CGL policy, the property damage or bodily injury of the claimant should be pointed out if it is not obvious.

In preparing any explanation or description that you provide to the insurer, you should bear in mind that the coverage may be disputed or that communication may be subject to discovery in subsequent litigation with the claimant. This concern should not preclude you from taking appropriate action or keeping the insurer informed, but it should be a consideration.

15.18　THE INSURANCE COMPANY'S RESPONSE TO CLAIMS

An insurance company has three basic choices in responding to the tender of the defense of a claim: (1) the tender can be accepted without reservation; (2) the tender can be accepted with a reservation of rights disputing coverage; or (3) the tender of defense can be flatly refused.

Acceptance of the defense without reservation by the insurer is obviously the best result. With the exception of deductibles and policy limits, the claim becomes the financial responsibility of the insurance company. However, you will have to cooperate with the insurer in the defense of the claim and this can have its own financial and administrative burdens in protracted litigation.

15.19　The Insurance Company's Reservation of Rights

If coverage of a claim is subject to some dispute, the insurance company will frequently err in favor of caution by accepting the defense with a "reservation

---

[10] *See* Windt, *Insurance Claims and Disputes: Representation of Insurance Companies and Insureds* 1–23 (Shepards-McGraw 1982).

of rights." In making this reservation of rights, the insurer describes why the claim may not be covered and confirms its right to subsequently refuse coverage if the facts demonstrate no coverage or the insurer's interpretation of the policy prevails in litigation between the insurance company and the insured. In the meantime, the insurer provides the defense. If the insurance company accepts the tender of defense without a reservation of rights, the insurance company will generally be barred from later denying coverage or asserting a reservation of rights.[11]

Unfortunately, the insurer's reservation of rights can create a conflict of interest. In defending the claim under a reservation of rights, the insurance company can protect its interest by defeating or settling the claim on the merits or it can try to push the claim or pursue the defense so that the outcome supports the insurance company's position that there is no coverage. You, as the insured, can end up with liability, but without coverage. The insurance company can thus protect its interests at the expense of its insured's interests. To address the dilemma, many states require that an insurance company defending a claim under a reservation of rights must pay for an independent attorney chosen by the insured to protect the insured's interest in the manner in which the claim is defended.[12]

15.20 Litigation with the Insurance Company

Disputes over coverage can themselves be the subject of separate litigation while the underlying claim is also in dispute. Either you, as the insured, or the insurance company may initiate an action for declaratory relief against the other to resolve the issue of whether or not the underlying claim is covered under the policy. The lawsuit asks the court to declare the rights of the insurer and the insured parties under the policy, so they then know how to deal with the defense of the underlying claim.

The declaratory relief action may be brought while the insurance company is defending the claim under a reservation of rights. If so, the insurance company may seek to stay any litigation of the underlying claim until the declaratory relief action is concluded and the coverage issue is resolved. You, as the insured, will typically want the litigation of the underlying claim to proceed first. As a practical matter, the further the insurance company gets into the defense, the harder it is for it to get out or the more likely the insurance company will participate in some settlement of the underlying claim, which will also invariably include a settlement of the coverage dispute.

Usually, however, it is the insured that has the upper hand on the question of which litigation should go first. In construction cases, there typically are similar or identical factual issues in the declaratory relief action and the litigation of the underlying claim. As the resolution of the underlying claim

---

[11] *Campbell Piping Contractors, Inc. v. Hess Pipeline Co.*, 342 So.2d. 766 (Ala. 1977).
[12] *See, e.g., San Diego Navy Fed. Credit Union v. Cumis Ins. Soc'y, Inc.*, 162 Cal. App. 3d 358, 208 Cal. Rptr. 494 (1984); *see generally* Windt, fn. 10, *supra*, 421–23.

will be more likely to resolve those issues, the insured is in a better position to succeed in getting the declaratory relief action stayed. Of course, if the insurance company has not accepted the defense and the insured faces substantial costs of defending the underlying claim, the insured may want the litigation of the underlying claim stayed while coverage is resolved.

15.21 ROUTINE COVERAGE ISSUES

The language of specific policies, changes to the standard policy language over time, and the divergent views of courts around the country make it difficult and dangerous to presume anything regarding coverage. The application of general principles to specific situations is risky. There are, however, a number of issues that routinely arise, the results of which can be somewhat predicted. These routine issues generally involve the type of occurrences and damages that do not enjoy coverage.

Construction defects generally are not covered under either CGL or Builder's Risk policies. In addition to the specific exclusions that operate to bar coverage for construction defects, there is a public policy in favor of barring protection for one's own defective work. The contractor is provided the incentive to exercise care in performing its work and limiting coverage in this manner keeps the costs of insurance down.[13]

15.22 CGL Coverage Issues

15.23 Continuing Damages Construction related claims often involve a continuing problem, rather than one catastrophic instant, such as a leak or other defect that becomes worse or creates more damage over time. Because several policies may have been in effect over the extended duration of the problem and the resulting damages, the question arises of which or how many policies may afford coverage. On claims-made policies, the coverage will be limited to the policy in effect when the first claim was made against the insured, regardless of whether the damages incurred continue to increase after that policy's period.

If occurrence policies are involved, the coverage is less clear. There are several competing theories that limit coverage to only one of a series of occurrence policies in effect during the continuing damages. One theory provides for "stacking" or multiple coverage by all policies in effect from the time the injury began until it was discovered. Stacking provides the insured the protection of multiple policy limits. This is an area of frequent dispute and can only be addressed by reference to the policies and court decisions that control your dispute.[14]

---

[13] *See Western Employers Ins. Co. v. Arciero & Sons, Inc.,* 146 Cal. App. 3d 1027, 1031–32, 194 Cal. Rptr. 688, 690 (1983).

[14] *See generally,* Bunshoft & Seabolt, fn. 1, *supra,* 196–97.

15.24 *Diminution in Value* Under most CGL policies, physical damage or destruction of tangible property is required for coverage. A recurring issue in construction disputes is whether installation of defective or substandard work or materials constitutes physical damage or destruction or merely diminution in value, which is not covered. This is an issue on which apparently very similar facts have resulted in divergent treatment by the courts in different jurisdictions, even when the operative policy language appears to be identical.

In one case, coverage was found for the diminished value of a building due to defective plaster with the policy requiring "injury to or destruction of property."[15] But in another case, in which the policy required "physical injury to or destruction of tangible property," there was no coverage for the costs of replacing defective studs.[16]

15.25 *Completed Operations* "Completed operations" are typically defined as liability arising for damage or injury incurred after the contractor has completed or abandoned its work. This coverage is acquired by most contractors and subcontractors. Although coverage for completed operations are included in some policy forms, that is not always the case. Failing to obtain or confirm this coverage can end up being expensive.[17]

15.26 *"Care, Custody and Control" Exclusion* Most CGL policies exclude coverage for damages to the property in the "care, custody and control" of the insured.[18] Policies vary on whether this exclusion applies to real and personal property or simply personal property. Regardless of the precise scope of the exclusion, its purpose is to coordinate coverage between CGL coverage, which addresses liability to third parties, and builder's risk coverage, which addresses the insured's own loss.[19]

Because the general contractor will generally be deemed to maintain "care, custody and control" of the entire project, this exclusion is usually effective against general contractors. Subcontractors, on the other hand, are typically performing a discrete scope of work, rather than the entire project, so this exclusion may not always apply to subcontractors.

15.27 *The "Work Product" Exclusion* Most CGL policies also include what are referred to as "work product" exclusions. These exclusions bar coverage for property damage to or arising from the insured's products or its work. These exclusions generally preclude coverage for a contractor's or a subcontractor's cost to repair or replace its own defective work. These exclu-

---

[15] *Havenstein v. Saint Paul-Mercury Idem. Co.*, 242 Minn. 354, 65 N.W.2d 122 (1954).

[16] *Wyoming Sawmills, Inc. v. Transportation Ins. Co.*, 282 Or. 401, 578 P.2d 1253 (1978).

[17] *See, e.g., Casey v. Employers Nat'l Ins. Co.*, 538 S.W.2d 181 (Tex. Ct. App. 1976) (damages caused by waterpipe broken after the subcontractor completed its work not covered).

[18] *See generally* Annotation, "Scope of Clause Excluding from Contractor's or Similar Liability Policy Damage to Property and Care, Custody, or Control of the Insured," 8 *ALR* 4th 563 (1979).

[19] *See Estrin Constr. Co., Inc. v. Aetna Cas. and Sur. Co.*, 612 S.W.2d 413 (Mo. App. 1981).

sions are described as "the heart and soul" of the insurance industry's efforts to avoid assuming the contractor's business risk through the CGL policy.[20]

As with the "care, custody and control" exclusion, the work product exclusion is generally an effective bar to claims by the general contractor as the entire project will typically be the general contractor's "work product." However, if the defective work of Subcontractor A damages the work of Subcontractor B, Subcontractor A may enjoy coverage for Subcontractor B's claim because it does not involve Subcontractor A's work product.[21] Again, the way the contractor addresses this lack of coverage under the CGL policy is through property or builder's risk insurance.

15.28 Contractual Liability Exclusion Virtually all CGL policies contain an exclusion against contractually assumed liability. This inclusion is intended to avoid coverage for contractual obligations, and thereby limit coverage to the insured's own tort liability. The clearest example of contractually assumed liability subject to the exclusion is a claim based on a broad indemnity clause that requires the contractor to indemnify the owner without regard to whether the contractor's negligence caused the loss.

15.29 Builder's Risk Coverage Issues

15.30 Policy Periods Builder's risk coverage generally covers the project during construction. The precise time period of coverage is often the subject of dispute.

Some builder's risk policies describe the policy period in terms of fixed calendar dates. This level of precision can create problems due to the uncertainties of the construction process and the possibility of delays. For example, if the policy expires on a certain date geared to the original contract completion date, delays to the project can result in lack of coverage. This problem can be avoided by extending the policy period before it runs out.

Many builder's risk policies simply describe the policy period as "during construction." In that case, it is well settled that for coverage to commence, some actual physical construction must have started. Defining completion of construction is frequently a more difficult task if it has not been defined in the policy or the construction contract. Completion will frequently be found if the project is sufficiently complete to permit the owner to utilize the structure for its intended purpose. Many policies expressly provide for termination of coverage when the building becomes occupied.

AIA Document A201 (1987 ed.) addresses the potential impact of owner occupancy on coverage by precluding the owner's use of the structure without advising and obtaining the consent of the builder's risk insurer.[22]

---

[20] Bunshoft & Seabolt, fn. 1, *supra,* 210.
[21] *See, e.g., Todd Shipyards Corp. v. Turbine Scrv., Inc.,* 674 F.2d 401, 5th Cir., *cert. denied,* 459 U.S. 1036 (1982).
[22] AIA Document A201 ¶ 11.3.11.

15.31 Fostuitous Loss A fundamental aspect of builder's risk coverage is that it protects only against "fortuitous" losses. This means the loss must be a matter of chance and not something that is certain to occur, such as depreciation or ordinary wear and tear. The losses arising from the insured's deliberate conduct is likewise excluded.[23] However, losses from the negligence of the insured or its employees or subcontractors is considered fortuitous as it is not intended.[24]

15.32 External Cause Some builder's risk policies require that the loss result from an external cause in order to establish coverage. This requirement may also be implied by courts. In general, the external cause requirement excludes damages arising from an inherent defect in the property. This limitation can be viewed as another version of the requirement for a fortuitous loss.[25]

15.33 Exclusions In addition to the coverage issues addressed, many builder's risk policies also contain express exclusions that bar claims for defective design, faulty workmanship and material, latent or inherent defects, equipment breakdown, earth movement and subsidence.

15.34 Concurrent Causes Losses on construction projects often arise from a combination of forces. Some policies specifically exclude coverage in cases of multiple causations.[26] If the issue of multiple causes is not addressed in the policies, the courts are divided on how to resolve the question of coverage. Some courts have held that if at least one cause is not excluded, coverage exists.[27] In other cases, however, courts have gone through the intricate process of identifying the cause that set the other causes in motion and then evaluating the coverage issue from the standpoint of whether or not that "efficient proximate cause" is subject to an exclusion.[28]

POINTS TO REMEMBER

Insurance Planning

- Planning is crucial for avoiding loss and limiting disputes.
- It requires special training and experience.
- The assistance of an insurance professional who is familiar with construction is necessary.

[23] *See Davis v. Hartford Fire Ins. Co.,* 283 N.C. 142, 195 S.E.2d 545 (1973).
[24] *See C. H. Leavell & Co. v. Fireman's Fund Ins. Co.,* 372 F.2d 784 (9th Cir. 1967).
[25] *See Standard Structural Steel v. Bethlehem Steel Corp.,* 597 F. Supp. 164, 191–92 (D. Conn. 1984).
[26] *See* Withers, "Proximate Cause and Multiple Causation in First-Party Insurance Cases," 20 *Forum* 256 (1985).
[27] *See, e.g., Texas E. Transmission v. Marine Office–Appelton & Cox,* 579 F.2d 561, 565 (10th Cir. 1978).
[28] *See Garvy v. State Farm Fire & Casualty Co.,* 48 Cal. 3d 395, 402, 252 Cal. Rptr. 292, 295, 77 P.2d 704, 707 (1989).

Types of Insurance

- Commercial general liability (CGL) insurance:
  - CGL provides protection against claims by third parties and not the insured's own losses.
  - A CGL policy can be a "claims-made" or "occurrence" policy; which type it is determines the timing of coverage.
  - If costs of defense are not excluded from the policy limit, the financial protection afforded can be greatly reduced.
  - Liability insurance can be purchased in multiple layers. Prompt notice is required to all layers.
  - Inclusion of others on CGL policy as additional named insured extends protection and eliminates subrogation claims.
  - CGL coverage affords extremely limited protection against environmental liability.
- Builder's risk insurance:
  - Builder's risk coverage is first-party insurance; it protects against the insured's loss rather than against the claim of third parties.
  - Builder's risk coverage is typically procured by the owner, with protection extended to the contractor and subcontractors.
- Errors and omissions (E&O) insurance:
  - E&O insurance is professional liability insurance for design professionals.
  - Similar insurance is increasingly required for professional construction managers.
  - E&O coverage by the design professional is not always a contract requirement.

Contract Requirements for Insurance

- Never assume insurance coverage; always consult the contracts on the project to confirm how it is set up.
- Typically, the contractor procures CGL coverage with the owner as an additional named insured; the owner procures builder's risk insurance.
- Most construction contracts include "waiver of subrogation" clauses that preclude the insurance company from trying to recoup its losses from others on the project.
- It is imperative to require proof of insurance and to confirm the parties have complied with the contract requirements before they start work.

Prompt Action to Protect Potential Coverage

- Project management personnel should be educated to deal with potential insurance issues and refer them to an appropriate individual with special training in insurance.

- Prompt notice of potential claims should be made to the insurance company to avoid risk of losing coverage.
- The notice or tender of defense should be as complete and informative as possible.

The Insurance Company's Response to Claims

- The insurance company will often accept defense of a claim with a reservation of rights to later deny coverage.
- In that situation, a potential conflict of interest may exist, which requires the insured to retain independent counsel, hopefully at the insurance company's expense.
- Disputes over coverage may have to be resolved through separate litigation, a declaratory judgment action, between the insured and the insurance company.

Routine Coverage Issues

- Construction defects are generally not covered by CGL or builder's risk insurance.
- CGL coverage issues:
  - A claim resulting in continuing damages can raise the question of which of several policies apply.
  - CGL policies generally require physical damage or destruction for coverage so that diminished value is not covered; however, the cases conflict on what constitutes diminished value.
  - Completed operations covers liability for claims arising after the contractor completes its work; it is often, but not always, part of a CGL policy.
  - The exclusion for property under the "care, custody and control" of the insured in effect extends to the entire project for the general contractor, but may be more limited for subcontractors.
  - The "work product" exclusion precludes coverage for the costs of repairing or replacing one's own defective work and its scope is similar to the "care, custody and control" exclusion.
  - CGL policies exclude contractually assumed liability that does not involve the insured's negligence.
- Builder's Risk Coverage Issues:
  - The policy period extends to a specific date or to when the project is completed, which is often the subject of dispute.
  - Builder's risk coverage extends only to "fortuitous" losses and not that which can be expected, such as ordinary wear and tear.
  - The loss must also be the result of some external cause and not an inherent defect in the property.
  - The existence of concurrent causes contributing to a loss may impact coverage.

16

CONSTRUCTION INDUSTRY ENVIRONMENTAL CONCERNS

Contractors who pursue opportunities in the burgeoning environmental clean-up market recognize the risks associated with that work. Unfortunately, the risk of encountering hazardous wastes exists on virtually every construction project. With that risk comes the potential for limitless liability. Preparing and planning for hazardous wastes is therefore an imperative for every construction project.

The scope of the risks of legal liability under a web of federal and state statutes, common law and the associated regulatory burdens must be appreciated and at least generally understood. Contingency plans and management policies must be in place and ready for execution. Contract terms and insurance coverage must be scrutinized in light of the possibility, regardless of how remote, that hazardous wastes could be encountered. The purpose of this chapter is to further sensitize, educate, and alert the reader to the urgent need to be prepared and to expect the unexpected when it comes to hazardous wastes and environmental liability.

16.1 SOURCES OF REGULATION AND LIABILITY

The federal government's regulation and imposition of liability for hazardous wastes is far-reaching and grabs the most media attention. The Comprehensive Environmental Response, Compensation and Liability Act of 1980,[1] commonly known as CERCLA or "Superfund," is the flagship of environmental liability laws, but is far from the only statute that may apply to the construction contractor. In addition to federal law, most states have enacted their own

[1] 42 U.S.C. §§ 9601–9657 (1994).

statutory schemes to regulate and assess liability for hazardous waste problems. Regardless of the existence of any specific statutes, liability may also be imposed under traditional common law theories of tort, nuisance, and trespass. The consequence of running afoul of this web of liability is not limited to civil liability payable by a company, but can involve fines and criminal penalties assessed against individuals. This chapter focuses on the civil liability aspects of CERCLA and other key federal statutes, which, despite their importance, are by no means the only legal requirements that may apply to a situation.

16.2   CERCLA Liability

CERCLA is generally aimed at addressing liability for clean-up costs for past contamination of sites by hazardous wastes. Other federal statutes, such as the Resource Conservation and Recovery Act of 1976 (RCRA),[2] deal with the generation, handling, storage, treatment, and disposal of hazardous wastes from ongoing operations. Because contamination may occur in the process of handling, storing, treating, or disposing hazardous wastes, there can be some considerable overlap between CERCLA and RCRA.

CERCLA is intended to impose liability for clean-up costs on those parties who are responsible for the contamination. Indeed, the parties on whom CERCLA may impose liability are referred to as "potentially responsible parties" or "PRPs." The manner in which "responsible party" under CERCLA has been interpreted by the courts is far broader than the conventional understanding of that term. The breadth of CERCLA liability and the extraordinarily low level at which it is triggered makes it a major threat to any construction contractor. In addition, CERCLA enforcement is not left to the government alone. Private individuals who are forced to incur clean-up costs are authorized to pursue responsible parties to recover those costs.

16.3   *Strict Liability*   Under CERCLA, if you fall within the statutory definition of "responsible party" you are liable. Even if you took all reasonable precautions and operated in a legally and generally acceptable manner, liability attaches. CERCLA imposes "strict liability," which means liability without regard to fault or negligence. Only a few and very limited defenses are allowed under CERCLA. This was no accident; CERCLA was specifically created to deal with the serious need to address environmental damage from hazardous wastes. The tough measures were deemed necessary to fulfill the statute's important remedial purpose.

There is an exception to strict liability under CERCLA for the contractor specifically engaged to clean-up hazardous wastes, called a "response action contractor" or "RAC" that enjoys a limited privilege of immunity from strict liability. This somewhat anomalous response is due to the recognition that

---

[2] 42 U.S.C. §§ 6901–6992 K (1994), as amended.

without some insulation from strict liability, it would be impossible to get any responsible contractor to perform clean-up work. The RAC is not totally relieved from liability under CERCLA; it remains liable under CERCLA for negligence, gross negligence, and intentional wrongdoing in connection with the clean-up. The CERCLA exception to strict liability for RACs only applies to federal statutes and does not in anyway limit the RAC's potential liability, including strict liability, which may be imposed under state law.

16.4 Responsible Parties CERCLA lists four categories of responsible parties. If you fall into one of the categories, you are liable:

(1) the current owner or operator of the facility;

(2) the owner or operator of the facility at the time the hazardous substance was released;

(3) any person who, by contract or otherwise, arranged for the disposal of hazardous substances owned by them or by another party; and

(4) any person who accepted any hazardous substance for transport or disposal that results in a release of hazardous substances.

On their face, the categories are broad. They have been interpreted even more broadly by the courts. These categories do not appear applicable in the context of the contractor who encounters an *unexpected* hazardous waste, as the hazardous waste is not something for which the contractor assumed responsibility, but that is how the strict liability is applied: liability is imposed without regard to fault or negligence. In theory, that means that the contractor who unwittingly stumbles upon and innocently transports hazardous wastes that result in contamination of a site is just as liable for clean-up costs under CERCLA as a contractor who knowingly handles and purposely disposes of hazardous wastes in an illegal fashion. That may sound like a theoretical worst-case scenario that has no relevance in the real world, but it is not. Consider the contractor's treatment in *Kaiser Aluminum & Chemical Corp. v. Catellus Development Corp.*[3]

In the *Kaiser* case, the court held that a site-work contractor could be liable under CERCLA simply by cutting and filling soil on a site that, unbeknownst to the contractor, turned out to have been contaminated by hazardous waste decades earlier. Once the contamination was discovered, the owner sued the developer who had sold the site under CERCLA to recover the costs of the clean up and restoration of the site. The developer responded by also suing the contractor under CERCLA. In its claim, the developer claimed that the contractor had made the situation worse by excavating contaminated soil and then spreading it on uncontaminated areas at the site. The claim against the contractor was initially dismissed, but that decision was reversed on appeal. The court of appeals found that, under the facts alleged, the contractor could

---

[3] 976 F.2d 1338 (9th Cir. 1992).

be an "operator" of the property and also a "transporter" of hazardous substances and therefore liable under CERCLA.

The contractor was hired by the property owner of the site to grade and prepare the site for a housing development. This required certain "excavation" and "dispersal" of some of the material on-site. No material was removed from the site and no material was imported to the site. After the contractor's work was underway, it was discovered that the site and some of the material handled by the contractor was contaminated by hazardous chemicals decades earlier, back in the 1940s.

Liability as an Operator: The court of appeals ruled that the "yardstick" for determining whether a party was an "operator" of a facility was the degree of control the party is able to exert over the activity causing the contamination at the time the contamination occurs. In *Kaiser,* the court found that the activity which produced the contamination was the excavation and grading of the site, which occurred during construction and while the site was under the contractor's control. Therefore, the contractor had sufficient control over this phase of the development to be an "operator" under CERCLA.

The fact that the original contamination of the site took place in the 1940s, decades before the contractor ever moved so much as a shovel of dirt, made no difference to the court. Simply *moving around* contaminated soils to uncontaminated areas of the same site was sufficient to constitute disposal under CERCLA. In reaching this conclusion, the court relied on the broad definition of "disposal" under CERCLA, which includes "the discharge, deposit, injection, dumping, spilling, or placing of any . . . hazardous waste into or on the land . . . ." The court further reasoned that the term "disposal" should not be limited solely to the initial contamination of the site. Instead, consistent with *the remedial purpose* of CERCLA, the term "disposal" should be read broadly to include *subsequent* movement, dispersal or release of hazardous substances during grading, excavations and fill placement. In the court's view, to limit liability for "disposal" to the initial contamination would result in "a crabbed interpretation [which] would subvert Congress' goal that parties who are responsible for contaminating property be held accountable for the costs of cleaning it up."

Liability as a Transporter: The court went on to find the contractor potentially liable as a "transporter" of hazardous substances as well. CERCLA defines "transportation" simply as "the movement of a hazardous substance by any mode." In the court's view, the contractor's movement of contaminated soil in the excavation and grading was well within the definition. The court did note the reference in the statute of transportation "to . . . sites selected by" the contractor, but ruled that transporting hazardous substances to an uncontaminated area of the same site was no different than transporting them to another site.

16.5 *Joint and Several Liability* In addition to strict liability, CERCLA imposes joint and several liability. It is a relatively simple concept with a very significant impact. Joint and several liability means that if you are liable for any part of the damages—in this case clean-up costs—you are liable for all the damages. Thus the party seeking to recoup the costs of clean-up, whether the federal government or a private party, can pursue any responsible party for the entire cost, regardless of the relative contributions of the various responsible parties to the contamination. Not surprisingly, this joint and several liability provision makes deep pockets even bigger targets for prosecution by the government and private litigants.

16.6 *Contribution* The impact of joint and several liability on a responsible party can be diluted by the ability of one responsible party to seek contribution from other responsible parties for the clean-up costs. The contribution provision was added to CERCLA by the Superfund Amendments and Reauthorization Act of 1986 known as SARA.

Contribution means that if just one responsible party is sued, it can bring a separate action against another responsible party that it contends is partially or completely responsible for clean-up costs actually assessed. Frequently, the claimant will itself claim against a number of potentially responsible parties, and those responsible parties are then able to directly assert contribution claims against each other in the same lawsuit. If the claimant has not named all the responsible parties, the responsible party named may be able to bring additional responsible parties into the original lawsuit. Otherwise, a separate contribution action may be initiated by one responsible party against another. If a responsible party has previously resolved its liability for clean-up costs with the federal or state government, it is protected from contribution claims by other responsible parties.

The costs and burdens of CERCLA litigation are so great that they provide considerable financial incentives to a named responsible party to contribute to a settlement, regardless of the strength of its defense. Consequently, once a CERCLA action is initiated, it is generally in the interest of the claimant and each individual potentially responsible party to have as many responsible parties involved in the litigation as soon as possible. In addition, even if a right of contribution from other responsible parties exists, it does not diminish the underlying liability to the party prosecuting the underlying claim for clean-up costs. Consequently, if the other responsible parties are no longer around or lack the financial resources to meaningfully contribute to a settlement or judgment, the deep pocket responsible party can be left to pay the complete tab, regardless of its relative fault.

These are some of the dynamics which have caused many to call for the revamping of CERCLA so that there is less focus on protracted litigation and attorney fees and more dollars actually expended on the clean-up of hazardous wastes.

16.7 Storm Water Runoff

The Clean Water Act[4] makes it unlawful for any *person* to *discharge* any *pollutant* unless a permit for such a discharge is issued under the Clean Water Act. Under its enforcement authority, EPA has interpreted the Act to include the discharge of storm water from construction sites involving more than five acres.[5] The permitting process is expedited by EPA's adoption of a general permit for storm water discharges from construction sites. EPA's general permit does not apply in states that have opted to administer the permit process on their own, but the federal requirements constitute the minimum requirements of such state-administered programs. Contractors must consult with local state agencies and EPA offices to confirm the applicable standards and permitting procedures.

In order to come under EPA's general construction permit, the "operator" of the site must establish a site-specific storm water pollution control plan and then file a "Notice of Intent" with EPA. In most cases, the general contractor will be the operator, along with the owner and developer. The control plan must meet requirements established by EPA or the state, and include storm water control measures, inspection and maintenance of those control measures, and the identity of the contractors or subcontractors who will implement the plan.[6]

When storm water discharges associated with construction are eliminated, the operator may file a "Notice of Termination" of the permit. With the notice, the operator must execute a certificate stating that storm water discharges have ended or that they are no longer the operator of the site. Violators of the Clean Water Act are subject to civil penalties of up to $25,000 per day and criminal penalties of up to $25,000 per day and prison of up to one year.

16.8 Air Quality, Asbestos and Lead

The Clean Air Act[7] requires the EPA to establish outdoor air quality standards. The EPA has set standards for the concentrations of a number of air pollutants, including sulfur oxides, hydrocarbons, carbon monoxide, nitrogen oxides, lead, ozone, and total suspended particulate matter.

Although many construction projects generate relatively few air pollution concerns, certain types of projects, such as renovation and demolition, present grave risks of exposure to airborne asbestos and lead and special risks to workers. These risks are so common and serious that the Occupational Safety and Health Administration (OSHA) has promulgated regulations specifically outlining the safety and health measures to be followed on construction projects involving these substances.[8] The majority of the procedures and require-

---

[4] 33 U.S.C.A. §§ 1251–1376 (1994), as amended.

[5] 40 C.F.R. pts. 122, 123, 124 (1995).

[6] *See EPA's Storm Water Management for Construction Activities-Developing Pollution Prevention Plans and Best Management Practices* (1992).

[7] 42 U.S.C.A. §§ 7401–7642 (1994), as amended.

[8] *See* 29 C.F.R. § 1926.58 (1995) (asbestos); *id.* § 1926.62 (1995) (lead).

ments are similar for both these substances, but there are important differences that cannot be overlooked. There may also be state and local regulations in some cases.

The regulations covering asbestos and lead apply to all construction work involving demolition, renovation, remodeling, repair, or installation of facilities containing these materials, as well as transportation, disposal, and emergency cleanup situations. Each regulation contains an allowable action level, which represents the maximum concentration or quanity of the substance allowable before the contractor must comply with most aspects of the regulation, and a permissible exposure level (PEL), which is the maximum level of exposure to the substance that the contractor's employees can endure without the use of respirators and other protective measures.

Each contractor must initially determine if any employee may be exposed to one of the substances at or above the action level on the job site. This initial determination can be waived, however, when the contractor is able to provide through objective data that its employees cannot be exposed to concentrations of the substance above the action level even in worst-case scenarios, such as by a prework survey demonstrating no actionable level of the contaminate or with lead when the contractor has previously monitored for substance exposures within the last twelve months during work operations conducted under workplace conditions closely resembling the current operation.

When the initial determination shows the possibility of substance exposure at or above the action level, the contractor must conduct health monitoring that is representative of the exposure for each employee in the workplace who is exposed to the substance must notify affected employees of the monitoring results. The contractor must repeat the initial monitoring process whenever there has been a change in process, control equipment, personnel, or work practices that may result in new or additional exposures above the action level limit.

The contractor must employ engineering controls and work practices to reduce and maintain employee exposure to the substances below the PEL to the extent such controls are feasible. Wherever the feasible engineering controls and work practices are not sufficient to reduce the substance concentration below the PEL, the contractor must supplement the controls with respiratory protective devices, protective clothing, changing and shower facilities, special signage and training programs among other measures. The contractor is also required to institute a rigorous medical surveillance program of exposed employees, including blood tests and examinations.

16.9 MINIMIZING ENVIRONMENTAL RISKS

Once the scope of the risk of unanticipated hazardous waste is appreciated, measures to mitigate or protect against that liability must be considered.

Although the risk cannot be totally eliminated, it can be minimized and allocated through proper contract clauses, including indemnity agreements, and proper insurance planning.

16.10 Contract Provisions and Indemnification

The risks associated with unanticipated hazardous wastes on a construction project are so great that they should be the subject of specific contract terms and conditions which allocate the risks among the parties in an appropriate and equitable manner. The need for specific contract clauses is underscored by the extent to which routine contract clauses that sometime impose considerable risks on the contractor for the unknown can be applied to unanticipated hazardous wastes. Consider a site investigation clause that requires the contractor to examine the site and attempts to shift responsibility for concealed or unexpected conditions. What if the unexpected condition is a concealed hazardous waste contamination rather than some additional removal? Likewise, broad indemnity clauses that benefit the owner are generally considered burdensome under routine circumstances. If applied to hazardous wastes situation, they can be devastating. On the other hand, a standard differing site conditions clause may afford the contractor some protection from the costs associated with unanticipated hazardous wastes, but far greater specificity is preferred to ensure protection.

The need for specific contract provisions to address the unfortunate possibility of contamination by hazardous waste has been recognized, but is by no means fully addressed. The American Institute of Architects' Document A201, The General Conditions of The Contract For Construction (1987 ed.), includes provisions which address the discovery of some specific unanticipated hazardous substances and provides indemnity for the contractor for liability arising from work within a contaminated area. Unfortunately, the AIA document's coverage is limited to unexpected asbestos or PCBs, and not the broad range of hazardous waste and potential liability they entail.

The 1990 Standard General Conditions of The Construction Contract published by The Engineers Joint Contract Documents Committee (EJCDC) affords far greater protection by expressly placing the responsibility for virtually all unanticipated hazardous wastes, and not just asbestos and PCBs, on the owner. The EJCDC General Conditions set forth specific procedures for notice by the contractor to the owner about the contamination encountered and the required response by the owner that must be implemented before the contractor can be directed or required to resume the work in the affected area.

Regardless of whether a standard contract form, modified form or custom drafted contract is utilized, it is imperative that the risk of unexpected hazardous waste be specifically allocated and that definitive procedures be set forth so that the parties know precisely how they are to respond and react to the situation if encountered.

Obtaining indemnification for the consequences of hazardous wastes is of critical importance, but is by no means foolproof. Many states have statutes or decisions that limit the scope of enforceability of indemnity clauses. These laws and cases reflect a public policy against allowing anyone to obtain indemnification for their own negligent acts. As liability under CERCLA is strict and without regard to negligence, this limitation may not be applicable in many situations. Nonetheless, it is prudent for the contractor to consider the law applicable to its contract and the extent of the enforceability and any indemnity associated with hazardous wastes.

16.11 Insurance

Once the size of the threat of environmental liability was recognized, insurance coverage rapidly receded. Now, new forms of coverage are becoming available as the insurance market readjusts. Still, coverage is far from complete and often comes at substantial costs. As a general matter, however, standard forms of insurance, such as commercial general liability insurance, will not afford protection for liability associated with hazardous waste. Therefore, specific pollution coverage must be procured.

Complete insurance protection for unanticipated hazardous waste is typically financially impractical to obtain. Evaluating some specific environmental coverage is nonetheless an appropriate step. Insurance planning for construction projects, particularly as it relates to insuring environmental risks, is too complex and specialized to be left to the inexperienced layperson. Even those contractors that are able to employ full-time insurance specialists or risk managers must rely on professional insurance brokers to assist in the procurement of proper coverage at a competitive price. This is particularly true in the environmental insurance market, which continues to experience rapid change and evolution.

16.12 PROPER MANAGEMENT TECHNIQUES

The increasing use and thoroughness of environmental site assessment by owners and lenders will hopefully reduce the likelihood of encountering unexpected contamination, but the risk will always exist. Constant recognition and review of the risk must be maintained on the management level and vigilance and preparedness enforced on the job site in order to guard against the risks of unanticipated hazardous wastes.

16.13 Management Review of Environmental Risks

It is in the interest of each contractor to designate a senior company officer as having overall responsibility for environmental matters. That individual can serve as a resource to the entire company to aid in the evaluation of and protection against unanticipated hazardous wastes on all projects. In order to serve effectively in this capacity, the individual must become thoroughly familiar with the federal and state laws and regulations affecting their company's work. This manager must be able to evaluate the environmental risks not only in light of the existing laws, but also in the specific context of the applicable contract provisions on a particular project, the nature of the construction, the peculiarities of the site and the ability to procure insurance. The official responsible for environmental matters must also have the authority to respond to unacceptable environmental risks directly or through direct reporting to other company officials. Environmental risk management is far too important to the future of every company to delegate it to an individual who lacks the authority to enforce it. The company should also have a specific and mandatory written procedure to be implemented immediately upon encountering unexpected hazardous wastes. The contents of the procedure and the nature of the response are discussed in greater detail below.

One individual cannot possibly stay on top of all risks of unanticipated wastes a contractor may encounter in its on-going operations. All project management personnel, and to a lesser extent all personnel, must be educated and sensitized to the risks. If they do not know how to respond immediately to a situation involving hazardous waste, they must at least appreciate the severity of the situation and recognize the need to seek advice and direction from someone who does know how to respond.

All the planning, evaluation, and efforts to deal with environmental risks on a management level will be wasted if the planning and ability to execute the plan does not extend to each job site and the individuals actually performing work in the field.

16.14   Have a Response Plan

The response of project personnel should not be left to chance. The appropriate response should be set forth in a written mandatory procedure which has been the subject of in-house training and indoctrination. At the outset of each project and before construction starts, the standard procedure should be reviewed and supplemented as neccessary as to the areas of responsibility for specific individuals. The names and telephone numbers should be listed for any federal, state, or local agencies requiring notification or from whom an emergency response may be required. The procedure should also be coordinated with representatives of the owner, design professional and construction manager as well as subcontractors. Although the response will be the primary responsibility of project management personnel, the response cannot be triggered or properly implemented without the aid of all project personnel, including subcontractors and their employees. Once the response plan is developed, it should be reviewed in project meetings, subcontractor coordination meetings, and toolbox safety meetings in the level of detail appropriate for the gathering to ensure that it has been reviewed and understood.

16.15   Immediately Stop Work in the Affected Area

In very broad terms, unanticipated hazardous wastes are typically not the contractor's responsibility. If they are exposed or discovered but not disturbed or released, the hazardous wastes certainly present a problem but, from the contractor's perspective, a problem of limited scope. If, however, the contractor goes beyond merely exposing the hazardous wastes and disturbs them in any manner, the contractor may well have unwillingly thrown itself into one or more of the categories of "potentially responsible parties" under CERCLA, as the contractor did in the *Kaiser* case discussed earlier. That is why the first response to encountering hazardous waste or any unknown substance or material that might be a hazardous waste is to *STOP!* Do no further work in the affected area or any other areas where the same condition might exist. It should be a reflexive response to encountering anything suspicious, whether it is an unusual color in the soil, a faint but unfamiliar odor, or anything out of the ordinary.

16.16   Provide Immediate Notice

The contractor should provide immediate notice to the owner, the design professional and construction manager that a suspected hazardous waste has been uncovered, even if the contractor cannot identify the substance. The initial notice should be verbal, with written confirmation provided as soon as practical thereafter. The notice should make it clear that the unanticipated hazardous wastes are the responsibility of the owner and that the contractor is awaiting direction from the owner as to how to proceed. The contractor should also consider expressly reserving its rights to seek indemnity for any claims arising from the hazardous wastes as well as adjustments in contract time and price based on the work stoppage and any additional response required to deal with the situation.

The owner or its agents should be responsible for reporting the release or spill of a hazardous waste to the appropriate government officials. The contractor, however, may also be deemed a "person in charge" of the site and therefore required to make a prompt report. It is best for the contractor to err in favor of caution and also make a report if there is any uncertainty as to who is required to do so or whether the owner will make the report.

16.17   Do Not Resume Work without Proper Authorization

The contractor should not resume work in the affected areas without written authorization from the owner or design professional *and* the government agency with authority over the situation. Such authorization should be explicit and in writing.

If the owner's response is to direct the contractor to clean-up the hazardous waste, the contractor should insist on specific written instructions on how to accomplish the clean-up and confirmation that the response has been approved by the responsible government agency. The contractor should also require that the owner specifically indemnify the contractor for undertaking the clean-up. Even if the owner obliges on these points, the contractor should consider whether it wants to undertake the additional risks of clean-up work. Remember, the owner's indemnification is only as good as its ability to pay and does not insulate the contractor from claims by third parties. Undertaking the clean-up of hazardous wastes may also cause some problems with the contractor's insurance carrier and surety, even when a specialty clean-up subcontractor is brought in, if clean-up work is not within the contractor's typical line of work on which its insurance and bonding was based.

16.18 CONCLUSION

The risk of incurring liability under CERCLA and other statutes and theories is now a fact of life in the construction industry. It cannot be avoided. All you can do is recognize the risk, and be vigilant and prepared for those situations in which the risk manifests itself.

POINTS TO REMEMBER

- Many overlapping federal and state laws create a complex web of rules relating to hazardous wastes and environmental issues that affect construction. These laws impose legal liability as well as regulatory and reporting requirements.
- Appoint a senior manager or environmental team to become thoroughly familiar with federal, state, and local environmental statutes and regulations and to oversee compliance with these statutes and regulations.
- Educate your workforce regarding these statutes and regulations and what must be done to comply with them.
- Know how far your insurance coverage goes regarding environmental risks and liabilities.
- Assess potential environmental risks for each particular project prior to entering into a contract.
- During contract negotiations, be wary of standardized contract clauses that may impose responsibility and liability for environmental risks upon you. Make sure that the risk of encountering unexpected hazardous substances is allocated within the contract through specifically drafted clauses.

17

BANKRUPTCY IN THE CONSTRUCTION SETTING

17.1 INTRODUCTION

Bankruptcy may strike an owner, a contractor, a subcontractor or a supplier at any time during a construction project. The party filing for bankruptcy (the "debtor") will be processed through the bankruptcy system to a liquidation or reorganization and discharge of debts. In the interim, the bankruptcy may cause a major adverse impact to other parties on the project.

This chapter examines the impact of bankruptcy on three key areas of a construction project: (1) the status of contracts with the debtor, (2) the status of materials in the debtor's possession at the time of bankruptcy, and (3) the status of contract funds and alternate sources of funds. This chapter also suggests approaches to minimize the impact of a bankruptcy on a construction project.

17.2 The Bankruptcy Code

Bankruptcy laws are contained in the United States Bankruptcy Code (the Code), which is codified in Title 11 of the United States Code. The Code provides for two types of bankruptcy, both of which may be encountered on a construction project: A debtor may file under Chapter 11 to "reorganize" or under Chapter 7 to "liquidate."

Under Chapter 11, the debtor remains in control of its business and property as a "debtor in possession" unless there is a good reason for a trustee to be appointed by the court to control the debtor's property. A debtor in possession has considerable discretion and authority to continue operating its business. The debtor must develop and obtain court approval of a plan of reorganization.

Once the plan is approved, the debtor emerges from bankruptcy with a fresh start.

The other form of bankruptcy often encountered on a construction project is a Chapter 7 liquidation. Under Chapter 7, the debtor seeks to liquidate all of its assets, pay a pro rata share of the proceeds of the liquidation to creditors, and then cease to operate. In a Chapter 7 liquidation, the bankruptcy court appoints a trustee to handle the liquidation and winding up of the business.

Under either a Chapter 11 reorganization or a Chapter 7 liquidation, the basic goal is to give the debtor relief from debts that can no longer be paid in the ordinary course of business. Under Chapter 11, the debtor is discharged from (does not have to pay) otherwise lawful debts. Under Chapter 7, the debtor is not discharged but is left with no assets for creditors to pursue.

Another basic goal of bankruptcy law is to give equal treatment to creditors within the same class. There usually are several different classes of creditors, including secured creditors, who have a security interest in property of the debtor, and general unsecured creditors, who have no security interest in property. Within each class, creditors should receive equal treatment so that no one creditor receives more than its fair share of money or other assets from the debtor. Assets of the debtor are protected to facilitate an orderly gathering and distribution of funds to all creditors.

17.3   The Automatic Stay

A fundamental element of the bankruptcy system is the automatic stay, which is a rigidly enforced prohibition against taking any steps that are hostile to the debtor or that affect the debtor's property. The stay allows the debtor in possession or trustee the necessary breathing space to determine what steps to take in the reorganization or liquidation. The automatic stay also prevents any one creditor from obtaining more money or property than other creditors.[1]

The automatic stay prohibits a wide variety of actions to collect debts or property from the debtor. The stay prohibits such actions as: (1) filing a lawsuit or demanding arbitration against the debtor; (2) continuing a lawsuit or arbitration against the debtor; (3) terminating a contract with the debtor due to its insolvency; (4) seizing the debtor's materials, tools, equipment or supplies; (5) filing or foreclosing a lien against the debtor (in some states); and (6) collecting a judgment against the debtor.

The stay is "automatic" because no court order is necessary to implement the stay. The stay is legally in effect from the moment the bankruptcy petition is filed.

17.4   Sanctions for Violation

The Code allows the bankruptcy court to impose sanctions against a creditor for violation of the automatic stay. Such sanctions may include imposition of

[1] 11 U.S.C. § 362.

administrative penalties and attorneys' fees. Violation of the stay in connection with a contract, such as terminating the contract for default, may be treated as a breach of contract. Because the consequences of violating the automatic stay can be severe, a creditor must determine at the outset whether any action it plans to take regarding a bankrupt debtor is a violation of the stay.

17.5 Relief from the Automatic Stay

A creditor is not, however, without avenues for relief from the impact of the automatic stay, particularly with regard to ongoing business or efforts to collect money owed. The Code provides that a creditor may petition the bankruptcy court for relief from the automatic stay to allow the creditor to proceed against the debtor or the debtor's property.[2] For example, a court may grant relief from the automatic stay when the property against which the creditor seeks to take action is of no value to the estate because the debtor has no equity in it. Relief from the stay may also be obtained "for cause."[3]

A debtor lacks equity in the property in question where the value of the property is less than the security interest in the property. An example is when a debtor-subcontractor's earthmoving equipment is pledged as security for a bank loan and the amount of the bank's security interest exceeds the value of the equipment. Under these circumstances, the bank could move for relief from the automatic stay on the ground that the debtor-subcontractor has no equity in the property and, therefore, the property has no value to the estate or to creditors of the estate.

A wide variety of circumstances justify relief from the automatic stay "for cause." For example, a common problem in a construction setting is a failure of the debtor to maintain insurance on equipment. A creditor with a security interest in the equipment could move for relief from the automatic stay to allow foreclosure on the ground that the debtor is not adequately protecting the security interest by maintaining insurance. Another common occurrence justifying relief from the stay concerns a failure to maintain or secure materials or equipment.

Relief from the automatic stay also may be sought to allow arbitration or litigation to proceed in order to determine the amount of a debt owed by the debtor. If relief from the stay is granted, the creditor would not be allowed to proceed to judgment and collection; relief would be granted only to permit the alternate forum (which presumably would be more familiar with construction cases) to determine the amount of the debt. The creditor's pro rata share of the proceeds of the bankruptcy liquidation or reorganization then would be calculated according to the amount of the debt established by the arbitration or litigation proceeding.

In order to obtain relief from the automatic stay, a creditor must file a motion with the bankruptcy court having jurisdiction over the debtor's case.

---

[2] 11 U.S.C. § 362(d).
[3] 11 U.S.C. § 362(d)(1).

The court must take action within thirty days after the motion is filed or the stay is automatically terminated as to the moving party.[4] The thirty-day time limit allows a creditor to shorten what could otherwise be a lengthy process.

17.6 Preferential Transfers

The Code contains several provisions that allow a trustee, and in some cases a debtor in possession, to void a prebankruptcy transfer of property or money from the debtor to a creditor. If a transfer is voided, the creditor is required to pay the money or property back to the debtor's estate. The transfer is voidable if it is a transfer of an interest in the debtor's property:

(1) To or for the benefit of a creditor;

(2) For an antecedent debt of the debtor;

(3) Made while the debtor was insolvent;

(4) Made within ninety days before the date of bankruptcy or one year before the date of bankruptcy if the creditor was an "insider"; and

(5) The transfer allows a creditor to receive more than the creditor would receive under a Chapter 7 liquidation.[5]

The preferential transfer is voidable even if the payment to the creditor was lawfully made to pay a legal preexisting debt. No intent to defraud other creditors is necessary to void a transfer of funds as preferential. Simply stated, a preferential transfer is voidable to prevent one creditor from receiving more than its fair share of property from the debtor.

Preferences include voluntary payments by the debtor,[6] involuntary collections by creditors,[7] signing of a release of claims by the debtor,[8] and garnishments of contract funds owed to the debtor.[9] Filing a mechanics' lien is not a preference because the Code expressly excludes statutory liens from voidability as a preference.[10]

---

[4] 11 U.S.C. § 362(e).

[5] 11 U.S.C. § 547(b).

[6] *Johns v. United Bank & Trust Co. of California*, 15 F.2d 300 (9th Cir. 1926), *cert. denied*, 273 U.S. 753, 47 S. Ct. 457, 71 L. Ed. 874 (1927).

[7] *Wheeler v. Johnson*, 26 F.2d 455 (8th Cir. 1928).

[8] *In re Energy Co-Op, Inc.*, 832 F.2d 997 (7th Cir. 1987) (release of contractual obligations is not considered new value).

[9] *See In re Riddervold*, 647 F.2d 342 (2nd Cir. 1981) (payments made within ninety days prior to filing bankruptcy pursuant to a garnishment writ executed prior to the ninety-day preference period did not constitute a "transfer of property to the debtor" and was not a voidable preference). *See also In re Conner*, 733 F.2d 1560 (11th Cir. 1984) ("transfer" that could be voided occurred when employer was served with summons of garnishment rather than when payments were made).

[10] 11 U.S.C. § 547(c)(6).

17.7 Exceptions to the Voidable Preference Rule

The Code provides for exceptions to the voidable preference rule.[11] Exceptions include: (1) transfers made for new value given to the debtor contemporaneously; (2) payments made in the ordinary course of business; (3) loans made to the debtor to purchase certain property, for example, purchase money security interests; (4) valid statutory liens; (5) consumer type debt payments; (6) payments made on a running or open account in the regular course of business within ninety days prior to filing bankruptcy; and (7) claims of a perfected security interest holder in inventory or receivables.

Perhaps the most important exception is that a contemporaneous exchange of property for new value is not a voidable preference.[12] For example, a release of lien or bond rights in exchange for a payment of past due amounts can be treated as being given for new value so that the payment is not a voidable preference.[13]

Although a waiver and release of lien or bond rights is not universally held to be an exchange for new value,[14] a contractor or supplier receiving a payment from an owner or another contractor in shaky financial condition can improve its chances of keeping the payment even if the payor files for bankruptcy within ninety days of the payment. For example, the contractor or supplier receiving the payment should document that any lien or bond rights that are waived or released as a result of the payment are being given up expressly in exchange for receipt of the funds. The waiver or release language should be worded carefully to state that the waiver or release is contingent upon actual receipt of the funds.

In jurisdictions where a waiver and release are not treated as new value, the contractor or supplier may be able to preserve lien or bond rights by entering into an agreement with the debtor that the waiver and release are contingent upon the paying party not filing for bankruptcy within ninety days after the payment is made. Although the payment still would be treated as a voidable preference, the contractor or supplier at least would retain lien or bond rights. Depending upon the notice and filing requirements in the jurisdiction, it may be necessary to proceed with perfecting lien or bond rights during the ninety day preference period to avoid losing such rights for failure to comply with applicable time limits.

---

[11] 11 U.S.C. § 547(c).

[12] 11 U.S.C. § 547(c)(1).

[13] *Matter of Advanced Contractors,* 44 B.R. 239 (Bankr. M.D. Fla. 1984) (release of lien rights was new value); *In re E. R. Fegert, Inc.,* 88 B.R. 258 (Bankr. 9th Cir. 1988) (release of payment bond right was new value); *see Matter of Fuel Oil Supply Terminaling, Inc.,* 837 F.2d 224, 228 (5th Cir. 1988) (release of letter of credit and collateral was new value).

[14] *In re Hatfield Elec., Co.,* 91 B.R. 782 (Bankr. N.D. Ohio 1988) (subcontractor's waiver of lien rights as to owner's land was not "new value" given in exchange for payment from debtor-contractor); *In re Nucorp Energy, Inc.,* 80 B.R. 517 (Bankr. S.D. Cal. 1987) (forbearance to file lien not "new value").

A second exception to the voidable preference rule relevant to the construction industry concerns payments made in the ordinary course of business.[15] The rationale for this exception is that payments in the ordinary course of business neither drain funds from the debtor's estate nor treat other creditors unfairly because the debtor has received something of value in the form of credit over the short term.

Courts will look to the parties' past dealings to determine whether the payment at issue is consistent with those past dealings.[16] The ordinary course of business exception should apply to a progress payment made to a contractor or subcontractor within the contract payment terms or other terms established between the parties. Where a contractor has made irregular payments to a subcontractor or supplier over the course of the contract at issue or over the course of other contracts between the same parties, those irregular payments may constitute the "ordinary" course of business between the parties and therefore be within the exception to the voidable preference rule.[17] Courts will consider such payments on a case-by-case basis. The closer that a payment is to the ordinary business dealings between the parties, the more likely it is that the court will treat it as an exception to the voidable preference rule.

17.8 Discharge

At the conclusion of a bankruptcy case, the debtor is discharged. The discharge is accomplished by an order that bars the debtor's liability on most claims.[18] Upon discharge, the automatic stay is replaced by a permanent injunction against all judicial proceedings and nonjudicial collection efforts against the discharged debtor. In a Chapter 7 liquidation, an individual is discharged from liability for prepetition debts. Corporations cease to exist under a Chapter 7 liquidation rather than being discharged. Pursuant to Chapter 11, a corporation is discharged by the order confirming a plan of reorganization.[19]

17.9 Nondischargeable Debts

Certain debts of an individual are not dischargeable. Such nondischargeable debts include debts for money, property or services obtained through false statements or fraud, debts obtained through false financial statements upon which the creditor relied and which the debtor provided with the intent to deceive, and debts arising from fraud while the debtor was acting in a fiduciary capacity.[20]

---

[15] 11 U.S.C. § 547(c)(2).

[16] *In re Ewald Bros.,* 45 B.R. 52, 57 (Bankr. D. Minn. 1984) (late payments were not in ordinary course of business because payments never had been made late before).

[17] *See In re White,* 58 B.R. 266 (Bankr. E.D. Tenn. 1986) (mechanical contractor's irregular payments to a supplier were its ordinary course of business).

[18] 11 U.S.C. § 524(a).

[19] 11 U.S.C. § 1141(d)(1)(A).

[20] 11 U.S.C. § 523.

In the construction setting, a construction trust fund statute usually treats all parties having possession of the funds as "trustees." Courts have reached conflicting results when deciding whether a construction trust fund statute creates a fiduciary duty within the meaning of the Code and whether the breach of the fiduciary duty renders a debt nondischargeable.[21] Whether a debtor's violation of a construction trust fund statute results in a nondischargeable debt depends upon the state statute in question and the bankruptcy court's treatment of the statute.

A finding that a debt is nondischargeable leaves the debtor exposed to liability for suit and collection. Any debt owed by a debtor on a construction project should be investigated carefully to determine whether there is a basis for claiming fraud or a breach of a fiduciary duty. Whether a transaction will fall within the nondischargeable debt exception depends upon the facts of the case and applicable state law.

17.10 STATUS OF THE DEBTOR'S CONTRACTS

17.11 Executory Contracts

When a party files for bankruptcy, all "executory" contracts remain in full force and effect. Under the Code, an executory contract is one that involves substantial performance remaining on both sides.[22] To the extent that a failure to complete performance by either party would constitute a material breach of contract, the contract is executory.[23] Generally, a construction contract is considered executory prior to substantial completion. Punchlist work remaining after substantial completion, however, also constitutes a substantial obligation on the part of the contractor. Likewise, payment of retainage is a substantial obligation. Therefore, it is likely that a construction contract after substantial completion but before final completion would be treated as executory.

17.12 Affirmance or Rejection

The Code provides a number of protections for the debtor in possession or trustee to allow an orderly process for dealing with executory contracts. For example, the Code prohibits termination of a contract solely because of insolvency or bankruptcy. A contract clause that gives the right of termination for insolvency or bankruptcy is void and unenforceable.[24] The Code also allows

---

[21] *Matter of Angelle*, 610 F.2d 1335 (5th Cir. 1980) (Louisiana statute making it a crime to misappropriate construction funds did not make debtor-contractor a fiduciary); *In re Johnson*, 691 F.2d 249 (6th Cir. 1982) (Michigan Building Contract Fund Act created trust fiduciary obligation).

[22] 11 U.S.C. § 365.

[23] *In re Alexander*, 670 F.2d 885 (9th Cir. 1982); *In re Ridgewood Sacramento, Inc.*, 20 B.R. 443 (Bankr. E.D. Cal. 1982).

[24] 11 U.S.C. § 365(e); *In re Computer Communications, Inc.*, 824 F.2d 725 (9th Cir. 1987).

a debtor in possession or trustee to affirm or reject an executory contract.[25] Under Chapter 7, the trustee has sixty days to affirm or reject a contract.[26] Under Chapter 11, the debtor in possession can affirm or reject a contract at any time up until the plan of reorganization is approved by the court.

If the debtor in possession or trustee decides to affirm a contract that is in default, any default must first be cured and the other party must be given adequate compensation for damages incurred as a result of the default. In addition, adequate assurance of future performance must be given.[27] As a practical matter, curing existing defaults and giving adequate assurance of performance can be insurmountable obstacles if the debtor's estate is in a condition sufficient to warrant filing for bankruptcy.

The debtor in possession or trustee may affirm or reject an executory contract only in accordance with relevant bankruptcy procedures, which entail petitioning the court for permission to act.[28] If the debtor in possession or trustee fails to obtain court approval for rejection, the contract continues in effect automatically.[29] In the case of a trustee under Chapter 7, the contract continues in effect only until the expiration of the sixty-day period for the trustee to affirm or reject.

If an executory contract is affirmed, performance of contract obligations by both parties can continue in the normal course of business. An affirmed contract creates additional obligations on the part of the debtor in possession or trustee and gives substantial rights to the other party to the contract. All debts and expenses incurred by the debtor's estate for an assumed contract are treated as "administrative expenses" of the estate. Administrative expense is a term of art applied to expenses and debts incurred by the debtor during administration of the bankruptcy estate. An expense or debt must be shown to benefit the debtor's estate in order to be treated as an administrative expense. Ordinary expenses and debts incurred in the course of operating the debtor's business or liquidating the estate will be treated as administrative expenses.[30] These expenses are entitled to high priority in the distribution of funds from the estate.

If, on the other hand, an executory contract is rejected rather than affirmed, the rejection constitutes a breach of contract.[31] This breach of contract is treated as having occurred prior to the filing of the petition in bankruptcy.[32] Thus damages for breach of contract by virtue of the rejection are treated as general unsecured debts entitled to no special treatment or priority.

---

[25] 11 U.S.C. § 365(d)(2).
[26] 11 U.S.C. § 365(d)(1).
[27] 11 U.S.C. § 365(b).
[28] *In re W. T. Grant Co.*, 474 F. Supp. 788, 793 (S.D.N.Y. 1979).
[29] *Id.* at 793.
[30] 11 U.S.C. § 503(b); *In re Ridgewood Sacramento, Inc.*, 20 B.R. 443 (Bankr. E.D. Cal. 1982).
[31] 11 U.S.C. § 365(g).
[32] 11 U.S.C. § 365(g).

17.13 Assignment

Although the debtor in possession or trustee may assign an executory contract,[33] adequate assurance of performance by the assignee must be given.[34] An executory contract may be affirmed and then assigned even if the contract contains a nonassignment clause.[35] However, if applicable state law or non-bankruptcy federal law provides that the other party would have to consent to an assignment of the contract, an executory contract cannot be assigned without consent.[36]

17.14 Minimizing the Impact on Executory Contracts

Between the automatic stay prohibiting termination of a contract in default and the debtor in possession's or trustee's right to affirm or reject a contract, the other party to a contract with a debtor is effectively denied the freedom to take immediate action regarding the contract. Most construction projects require quick decisions and aggressive actions to continue the progress on the work. If a party in bankruptcy continues to perform without difficulty, the bankruptcy may not have any impact. However, if the debtor in possession or trustee ceases performance but takes no action to reject the contract, the impact on the progress of construction can be immediate and severe. Fortunately, certain measures, discussed below, can be taken to minimize the impact of an executory contract on a construction project.

17.15 Terminate before Bankruptcy

In many cases, some advance indication exists that a party on a construction project is about to file for bankruptcy. The problems inherent in having an executory contract can be avoided by terminating the contract before the bankruptcy filing. Of course, the contract must be in default for some reason other than insolvency or impending bankruptcy or the contract must contain a termination for convenience clause. In addition, applicable contract termination procedures must be followed. Any required notice and cure period must run in full before the bankruptcy filing; otherwise, the termination cannot be made final because of the automatic stay.

The right to affirm or reject a contract does not apply if the contract has been breached or terminated before the bankruptcy petition is filed. After

---

[33] 11 U.S.C. § 365(f).
[34] 11 U.S.C. § 365(f)(2)(B).
[35] 11 U.S.C. § 365(f)(1).
[36] 11 U.S.C. § 365(c)(1); *See Matter of West Electronics, Inc.*, 852 F.2d 79 (3rd Cir. 1988) (Government contract is not assignable unless the government consents (41 U.S.C. § 15)); *In re Pioneer Ford Sales, Inc.*, 729 F.2d 27 (1st Cir. 1984) (franchise agreement not assignable under state law without consent); *In re Braniff Airways, Inc.*, 700 F.2d 935 (5th Cir. 1983) (airport landing slots not assignable under local law).

breach or termination, there is no legally existing contract to be affirmed or rejected.

17.16 Exercise Contract Rights

A typical construction contract includes a clause allowing an owner or general contractor (or a subcontractor in the case of a sub-subcontractor in bankruptcy) to supply the necessary labor, materials and equipment to complete the other party's work in the event of a failure of performance. If a contractor or subcontractor petitions for bankruptcy and ceases performing, the other party to the contract can use such a clause to supplement the debtor's forces without violating the automatic stay and without violating the debtor in possession's or trustee's right to affirm or reject the contract. The costs incurred in doing so can be backcharged to the debtor in possession or trustee. If the contract is rejected, costs not recovered as a backcharge become general, unsecured claims against the estate. If the contract is affirmed, costs not recovered as backcharges would be administrative expenses of the estate.

17.17 Seek Relief from the Automatic Stay

If the contract is in default, the other party may petition for relief from the automatic stay to allow termination. The request will force the debtor in possession or trustee to take a position on the contract. A showing that the contract is seriously in default with no hope of cure should establish good cause for lifting the stay. The rule that the stay is lifted automatically if the bankruptcy judge has not ruled within thirty days on a motion to lift the stay puts a time limit on the period of uncertainty surrounding the contract. If, in the meantime, the nonbankrupt party supplements the debtor's forces, the impact of the default on the project can be minimized. As a practical matter, if the debtor's situation is hopeless, the debtor in possession or trustee may not oppose lifting the stay to allow termination.

17.18 Seek a Time Limit on Affirming or Rejecting the Contract

If the debtor continues performing the work and is not in default, no grounds exist for terminating the contract. As previously discussed, merely being insolvent or in bankruptcy is not a ground for termination. However, even if a contract is not in default, the Code allows the nonbankrupt party to petition the bankruptcy court to set a "reasonable" limit on the debtor in possession's or trustee's time to affirm or reject the contract. What is "reasonable" depends on the circumstances of each case. Where the contract is not in default, a request for a time limit to affirm or reject the contract is the only way to shorten the process.

17.19 STATUS OF MATERIAL AND EQUIPMENT

On a construction project, materials and equipment incorporated into the work can easily amount to half the value of the project. At any given moment during construction, materials and equipment needed for the project will be in the possession of suppliers, subcontractors, the contractor or the owner. In addition, materials and equipment may or may not be paid for, depending upon whether the materials are installed, stored, stored at site, in transit, or still in the possession of a supplier.

17.20 Property of the Debtor's Estate

In the event of a bankruptcy, unless the debtor in possession or trustee continues performance, construction materials and equipment intended for the project may be seized by the debtor in possession or trustee and used for reorganization of the estate in the case of a Chapter 11 or in a liquidation of assets in a Chapter 7. Problems with materials and equipment arise primarily where they are sought to be made a part of the debtor's estate rather than allowed to be installed in the project.

The debtor's estate consists of all legal and equitable interest of the debtor in property as of the filing of the bankruptcy petition.[37] The extent and validity of the debtor's interest in property, however, is a question of state law rather than bankruptcy law.[38]

The ultimate use of materials and equipment intended for incorporation into the project depends upon who has possession of materials, whether the materials are paid for, the terms and conditions of the contract and the debtor in possession's or trustee's intentions regarding affirming or rejecting the contract. The debtor's materials for which the debtor has not yet been paid in a progress payment as of the bankruptcy filing will be property of the debtor's estate. If the debtor rejects the construction contract, the materials may be used for a Chapter 11 reorganization or in a Chapter 7 liquidation. If the debtor in possession or trustee affirms the contract, the materials and equipment can be installed and paid for in a progress payment in the ordinary course of business.

17.21 Supplier's Right to Recover Goods

Caution must be exercised in obtaining materials from a debtor in possession or trustee. If the debtor has not paid for the materials or equipment, the supplier of the materials or equipment can repossess them. Under the Code, a supplier of goods can regain possession of materials delivered to an insolvent debtor if the supplier demands their return within ten days after the debtor's

---

[37] 11 U.S.C. § 541(a)(1).
[38] *In re Livingston,* 804 F.2d 1219 (11th Cir. 1986).

receipt of the goods.[39] Although the automatic stay does not apply to the supplier's reclaiming of the goods, suppliers must be extremely diligent in exercising the right to recover goods. The ten-day demand period is obviously very short, and the right to recover goods cannot be exercised if the debtor was solvent at the time of delivery.

An owner, contractor, or subcontractor must be alert to the possibility that stored materials or equipment for which payment has been made may be seized by the supplier for nonpayment. The safe course is to make sure that the goods were delivered more than ten days prior to payment. After the ten-day grace period has run, the automatic stay prohibits seizure (with certain narrow exceptions). Even if the materials or equipment are covered by a security agreement giving the supplier a security interest in the goods, the supplier cannot repossess them without obtaining relief from the automatic stay.[40]

The supplier can recover materials and equipment only where the goods are still in the debtor's possession.[41] Materials and equipment that have been incorporated into the work are not subject to seizure. Stored materials and materials stored at the site would be at risk, depending on the contract terms governing possession, risk of loss and title to the goods.

17.22   Stored Materials

Special problems arise where materials have been paid for but have not been permanently incorporated into the work. The debtor in possession or trustee can claim that stored materials are property of the estate because the debtor has some legal or equitable interest in them even if they have already been paid for in a progress payment.[42] The contrary argument is that the debtor's estate no longer has any legal or equitable interest in the materials or equipment because the debtor received full value upon payment.

The owner, contractor, or subcontractor can protect itself to a certain extent against claims to stored materials by inserting appropriate clauses in the contract. One alternative is to insert a clause in the contract that treats stored materials as a bailment arrangement. As a "bailee," the debtor would not have any property interest in the materials or equipment. Lacking a property interest, the debtor in possession or trustee would have no right to hold the property.[43] Another alternative is inclusion of a clause that provides that title to stored materials passes to the owner or general contractor upon payment. Under such a clause, the debtor in possession or trustee would be unlikely to prevail in claiming that the debtor's estate has a property interest in the

---

[39] 11 U.S.C. § 546(c).

[40] 11 U.S.C. § 362(d).

[41] *In re Rawson Food Service, Inc.*, 846 F.2d 1343 (11th Cir. 1988).

[42] *See In re A-1 Hydro Mechanics Corp.*, 92 B.R. 451, 457 (Bankr. D. Haw. 1988).

[43] *Matter of Ray Slattery, Inc.*, 54 B.R. 642 (Bankr. D. N.J. 1985).

goods.[44] Clauses affecting title and possession of materials and equipment must be coordinated carefully with clauses on insurance and risk of loss.

17.23 Voiding Unperfected Security Interests

The Code gives a debtor in possession or trustee authority to void unperfected security interests in property.[45] Under the Code, a debtor in possession or trustee obtains a secured interest in property in which the debtor has any interest other than naked possession. If the debtor in possession or trustee voids an unperfected security interest in property, the Code-provided security interest takes priority and allows seizure of the goods. This provision of the Code is known as the "strong-arm" provision.

The strong-arm provision has been applied to construction materials to allow a trustee to seize materials provided by a general contractor for a debtor-subcontractor to install on the project. Even though title to the materials remained in the general contractor, the general contractor's interest was treated as a mere security interest, which the trustee was allowed to void because a Uniform Commercial Code (UCC) financing statement had not been filed as to the general contractor's security interest. Thus, the trustee was entitled to possession of the materials.[46]

If there is any indication that the jurisdiction in which the project is being constructed would treat the owner's or contractor's interest in stored materials as a security interest, the safe course of action is to file a UCC financing statement to protect the security interest from being voided under the strong-arm provision of the Code.

17.24 STATUS OF CONTRACT FUNDS

At any given moment on a project, construction funds will be flowing through the system for payment to the contractor, subcontractors, laborers and suppliers. If one of the parties in the payment process files for bankruptcy, any funds in the system could be claimed by the debtor in possession or trustee as property of the estate. It is possible, though unlikely, that payment will be made downstream in the ordinary course of business. On the other hand, the debtor in possession or trustee may hold or seize funds intended to be paid to those downstream in the payment process. Unless those entities downstream gain control of the construction funds in the payment system at the time of bankruptcy, the funds may be absorbed into the debtor's estate and used in a Chapter 11 reorganization or a Chapter 7 liquidation.

---

[44] *Matter of American Boiler Works,* 220 F.2d 319 (3rd Cir. 1955) (ships and shipbuilding materials became property of the Government under a contract clause passing title, and therefore, stored materials were not part of the debtor's estate).

[45] 11 U.S.C. § 544.

[46] *In re A-1 Hydro Mechanics Corp.,* fn. 42, *supra,* at 451.

From the point of view of the nonbankrupt participants in the construction project, the best result is for payments to be made downstream in the ordinary course of business. The filing of a bankruptcy petition, however, can set off an intense competition among the debtor in possession or trustee, those downstream seeking payment for labor and materials already provided, those upstream asserting backcharges, and banks, guarantors, and sureties who have put money into the project to make up for the debtor's financial shortcomings.

To a great degree and in an ideal world, all of the claimants are entitled to be made whole. The reality is that only claimants with valid claims under the Code and applicable state law will be successful. Numerous Code provisions and state laws apply in the process of sorting out the competing rights and interests in contract funds.

17.25   Unearned Contract Funds

Problems arise only for funds earned for work performed. The debtor in possession or trustee cannot claim portions of the contract price for work that has not been performed any more than a contractor, subcontractor or supplier not in bankruptcy is entitled to payment for work not performed or for materials not supplied.

17.26   Earned but Unpaid Contract Funds

A number of theories have been advanced to claim funds flowing through the payment pipeline at the time one of the parties on the project files a petition in bankruptcy. Most of these theories involve the concept that it is more equitable for the parties downstream, who have spent time and money on the project, to be paid the funds than it is for the debtor to keep the funds for use of the debtor's estate in a reorganization or a liquidation.

17.27   Constructive Trust

One of the most important theories of capturing contract funds is the constructive or "construction" trust doctrine. The constructive trust doctrine holds that the construction funds are held in trust for the benefit of contractors, subcontractors, materialmen and laborers. If contract funds are treated as being held in trust, a debtor does not have any property interest in the funds.[47] The existence of a constructive trust depends upon state law.

The trust may be created by a builder's trust fund statute,[48] or it may be created by the terms of the owner/general contractor contract creating a retainage fund for the payment of subcontractors and suppliers.[49] At least

---

[47] *Georgia Pacific Corp. v. Sigma Serv. Corp.*, 712 F.2d 962 (5th Cir. 1983).

[48] *Selby v. Ford Motor Co.*, 592 F.2d 642 (6th Cir., 1979); *In re D & B Electric Inc.*, 4 B.R. 263 (Bankr. W.D. Ky. 1980).

[49] *In re La Follette Sheet Metal, Inc.*, 35 B.R. 34 (Bankr. E.D. Tenn. 1983).

one court has held that owner/general contractor contract terms obligating the general contractor to pay for labor and materials in performing the work creates a fund for payment of subcontractors and suppliers.[50]

17.28 Equitable Lien

Rather than treating the contract funds as being held in trust, certain courts give claimants an equitable lien on the funds.[51] Third-party beneficiary entitlement to funds is another theory that may be applied. The debtor's contract may contain terms that expressly make downstream claimants third-party beneficiaries of the payment terms of the contract. In that event, the claimants could claim funds as beneficiaries of rights created under the contract.[52]

17.29 Joint Check Agreements

Joint check agreements are entered into routinely by some owners and general contractors, but completely avoided by others. If joint check agreements are used, the wording of the agreement will have an impact on whether joint check funds can be seized by a debtor who is a joint payee on the check. A joint check agreement that expressly states that joint check funds are the property of an ultimate recipient of the funds and not the property of the other joint payee (the debtor) will make it very difficult for the debtor or trustee to claim that the funds are property of a debtor's estate rather than the property of the claimant.[53]

17.30 Setoff

Cases involving constructive trust or other equitable theories focus on the rights of claimants downstream in the payment process. Equally valid and often superior rights to funds of parties upstream of a debtor also exist. These rights include setoffs and backcharges for claims against the debtor and also the right to insist that contract funds be paid to downstream claimants rather than be seized by a debtor in midstream as property of the debtor's estate.

The Code provides parties upstream of the debtor a valuable right to set off certain claims against the debtor's right to payment of contract funds.[54] The right of setoff is available for mutual prepetition debts.[55] Setoff is available

---

[50] *In re Arnold,* 908 F.2d 52 (6th Cir. 1990).

[51] *Matter of GEBCO Investment Corp.,* 641 F. 2d 143 (3rd Cir. 1981).

[52] *Id.* at 147.

[53] *See Mid-Atlantic Supply Inc. of Va. v. Three Rivers Aluminum Co.,* 790 F.2d 1121 (4th Cir. 1986); *T & B Scottdale Contractors, Inc. v. United States,* 866 F.2d 1372 (11th Cir. 1989) (joint check agreement specified that funds in construction account were to pay sub-subs and suppliers); *but see Georgia Pacific Corp.,* fn. 47, *supra* (joint check funds held to be part of the Debtor's estate).

[54] 11 U.S.C. § 553.

[55] *In re Fulghum Constr. Corp.,* 23 B.R. 147 (Bankr. M.D. Tenn. 1982).

even though the mutual debts arise out of different transactions or contracts.[56] The right of setoff is allowed by the Code but not created by the Code; setoff is available only if allowed under applicable state law.

Setoff is most important for a party upstream of the debtor in the payment process when the upstream party wants to pay contract funds to claimants downstream of the debtor, thus bypassing the debtor in possession or the trustee. A general contractor may pay off claimants with claims against a debtor-subcontractor and set them off against the debtor's claim for contract payments arising out of the subcontract.[57] A project owner may set off amounts paid to a debtor–general contractor's subcontractors and suppliers against balances due to the debtor–general contractor.[58] Setoff is limited, however, to cases where the party paying off the claims has an independent obligation, such as under a payment bond or mechanics' lien statute, to make the payments. Setoff is allowed even though the claims of subcontractors and suppliers are not liquidated at the time of the petition of bankruptcy. It is sufficient that the claimants have claims that may be liquidated at some later point in settling up with the owner or general contractor.[59]

Setoff is prohibited by the automatic stay.[60] The party seeking to pay claims and set them off against amounts owed to the debtor must obtain relief from the automatic stay before asserting a right of setoff.[61] Prior to making any payments to claimants, the safe course is first to develop a list of all outstanding claims and then to petition the court to allow the payment of those claims with the amount of the payments being set off against the debtor's claims against contract funds.

17.31   Recoupment

Another valuable right that can be asserted by parties upstream from the debtor in the payment process is known as "recoupment." Recoupment is available for claims arising out of the same transaction or contract. Recoupment is not subject to any of the Code requirements governing setoff. Recoupment allows an owner, a general contractor or a subcontractor to reduce claims

---

[56] *In re Mohawk Industries, Inc.,* 82 B.R. 174 (Bankr. D. Mass. 1987).

[57] *In re Flanagan Bros. Inc.,* 47 B.R. 299 (Bankr. D. N.J. 1985). In *Flanagan,* a general contractor paid off claimants of an electrical subcontractor for work performed prior to the petition of bankruptcy. Because the general contractor had provided a payment bond and was obligated to pay off the subcontractor's debts, the general contractor was allowed to pay the debts and then set off the amounts of the payments against the debtor-subcontractor's claim for payments due from the general contractor. The rationale for allowing setoff is that the debtor would have its liability extinguished by the general contractor's direct payments to suppliers under the payment bond and would achieve a windfall if allowed to collect those amounts from the general contractor for the benefit of the debtor's estate.

[58] *In re Fulghum Construction Corp.,* fn. 55, *supra,* at 152. In *Fulghum,* the project owner had an independent obligation to pay off claimants under the state mechanic's lien law.

[59] *Id.* at 151–152.

[60] 11 U.S.C. § 362.

[61] *In re A-1 Hydro Mechanics Corp.,* fn. 42, *supra,* at 453.

for contract funds by the debtor by deducting backcharges or other claims against the debtor arising out of the same contract.[62] Recoupment is available for prepetition and postpetition obligations. Mutuality of debt is not required.[63] An owner or general contractor can assert recoupment as a matter of right to reimburse itself for backcharges for supplementing the debtor's forces. The right of recoupment also applies to completion costs in the event the debtor stops work and the owner or general contractor is forced to complete the work.[64]

17.32   Surety Claims to Funds

A bond surety often will be obligated to step in and pay off claimants on a payment bond provided by a contractor or subcontractor that petitions for bankruptcy. The surety then is held to have stepped into the shoes of those claimants, which entitles the surety to assert all of the constructive trust and equitable lien theories for recovery of contract funds, which the claimants themselves would have had.[65] Because the surety's rights "relate back" to the date of the surety bond, the surety's rights often are held to be superior to those of other claimants, such as construction lenders, seeking to use construction funds to pay off other obligations of the debtor.[66]

17.33   OTHER SOURCES OF FUNDS

Because of the difficulties and costs inherent in battling over construction project funds, parties on a construction project generally will seek to recover from any other available source of funds. An added advantage to recovering from alternate sources of funds is that the assertion of claims against parties other than the debtor usually does not require relief from the automatic stay. Alternate sources of funds and theories of recovery against those sources are reviewed in the following sections.

17.34   Payment Bond Claims

A claim may be asserted against a payment bond surety even though the principal on the bond is in bankruptcy.[67] Because the automatic stay does not

---

[62] *In re Clowards, Inc.*, 42 B.R. 627 (Bankr. D. Idaho. 1984).

[63] *In re Mohawk Industries, Inc.*, fn. 56, *supra*, at 174.

[64] *In re Clowards, Inc.*, fn. 62, *supra*, at 627.

[65] *In re Massart Company*, 105 B.R. 610 (Bankr. W.D. Wash. 1989).

[66] *Framingham Trust Co. v. Gould-Nat'l Batteries, Inc.*, 427 F.2d 856 (1st Cir. 1970).

[67] *In re Kora & Williams Corp.*, 97 B.R. 258 (Bankr. D. Md. 1988) (stay did not extend to Little Miller Act surety).

extend to actions against parties other than the debtor, relief from the automatic stay is not needed to pursue a payment bond claim.[68]

Sureties, however, sometimes seek an injunction against a payment bond claim under the court's equitable powers. A court may issue an injunction preventing a payment bond claim against a surety where the debtor's officers and employees are necessary and essential to assist the surety in defense of the claim.[69] The rationale is that the involvement of the officers and employees in the surety lawsuit would unnecessarily distract them from participation in reorganization or liquidation of the debtor's estate. The injunction prevents such an adverse impact on the debtor's estate. Once the plan of reorganization is approved or liquidation is completed, however, the injunction should be lifted to allow the suit to proceed against the surety.

17.35   Mechanics' Liens

On private projects, contractors, subcontractors, laborers and materialmen ordinarily have the right to file a mechanic's lien under applicable state law to collect unpaid sums due on a construction project. The impact of bankruptcy on mechanics' lien rights depends upon which party files the petition in bankruptcy and the nature of the mechanics' lien right under underlying state law.

In the case of an owner bankruptcy, the automatic stay may prohibit filing a mechanic's lien against the owner's property, depending upon the nature of the lien under the applicable state law. In many states, filing a notice of a mechanic's lien is retroactive to the date when the services and materials were first supplied. In these states, filing a notice of mechanic's lien does not violate the automatic stay. The reason is that the filing is said to "relate back" to the date prior to the filing of the petition.[70] If state law does not provide that filing the notice relates back to the date services were first provided, the filing of a lien violates the automatic stay.[71] In states where the filing does not relate back, a motion for relief from the stay should be filed immediately to seek permission to file the lien prior to the expiration of the period allowed under state law for filing the notice of lien.

If a mechanic's lien already was filed prior to the owner's bankruptcy, the automatic stay prohibits filing an action against the owner to foreclose the lien.[72] The Code allows filing of a notice to temporarily satisfy a state law requirement of filing suit to perfect the lien.[73] The Code also tolls the running of the period for filing suit to perfect the lien until thirty days after relief from

---

[68] *U.S. for use and benefit of Central Bldg. Supply, Inc. v. William F. Wilke, Inc.,* 685 F. Supp. 936 (D. Md. 1988).

[69] *Id.* at 938–39.

[70] *Matter of Peek Constr. Co.,* 80 B.R. 226 (Bankr. N.D. Ala. 1986) (mechanic's lien relates back under Alabama law).

[71] *Matter of Gotta,* 47 B.R. 198 (Bankr. W.D. Wis. 1985).

[72] *In re Bain,* 64 B.R. 581, 583 (Bankr. W.D. Va. 1986).

[73] 11 U.S.C. § 546(b).

the stay is granted or the underlying bankruptcy case is discharged.[74] Some states allow perfection of a mechanic's lien by filing a proof of claim in the bankruptcy court. In these states, no other action is necessary to perfect the lien after the proof of claim is filed.

In the case of a general contractor bankruptcy, claimants downstream may file a lien against the owner's property without violating the automatic stay because the automatic stay extends only to the debtor and the debtor's property. Whether the claimants can file suit to foreclose on the lien depends upon underlying state law. In states where the general contractor is treated as a necessary party to the foreclosure action, filing suit to foreclose a mechanic's lien violates the automatic stay. The claimant must obtain relief from the automatic stay in order to foreclose on the lien.[75] In these cases the claimant should act immediately to obtain relief from the automatic stay.

17.36 Guarantors

The parties on a construction project sometimes obtain guarantees of performance from the other parties with whom they contract. This may take the form of a personal guarantee by a corporate shareholder or a guarantee by a parent company of a subsidiary. A debtor's guarantor is not treated as being the same entity as the debtor and therefore is not protected by the automatic stay.[76] As with bond sureties, some courts will issue an injunction precluding an action against a guarantor where the guarantor is a principal of the debtor and its full attention is needed for a reorganization or liquidation of the estate.[77]

POINTS TO REMEMBER

The Bankruptcy Codes

· There are two types of bankruptcy, Chapter 11 reorganization and Chapter 7 liquidation. A Chapter 11 debtor is discharged from its debt and can continue to run its business with a court-approved plan of reorganization. A Chapter 7 debtor has its business liquidated by a court-appointed trustee.

The Automatic Stay

· The automatic stay prevents any creditor from taking a step which is hostile towards the debtor, including filing a lawsuit, terminating a contract, filing a lien, etc.

---

[74] 11 U.S.C. § 108.

[75] *In re Nash Phillips/Copus, Inc.,* 78 B.R. 798 (Bankr. W.D. Tex. 1987).

[76] *Browning Seed, Inc. v. Bayles,* 812 F.2d 999 (5th Cir. 1987)

[77] *In re Otero Mills, Inc.,* 25 B.R. 1018 (Bankr. D. N.M. 1982) (debtor's shareholder); *In re Johns-Manville Corp.,* 26 B.R. 420 (Bankr. S.D. N.Y. 1983) (debtor's key employees); *In re Comark,* 53 B.R. 945 (Bankr. C.D. Cal. 1985) (general partners of the debtor).

- The stay does not require a court order and persons violating it are subject to sanctions.
- Relief from the automatic stay can be obtained "for cause" such as when the creditor has no equity in the property, fails to maintain insurance on the property, fails to maintain or secure the property, or when proceedings are necessary to determine the debt owed by the debtor.

Preferential Transfers

- Under certain conditions, a debtor can have a "pre-bankruptcy" transfer of property to the creditor voided.
- A contemporaneous exchange of property for new value is not a voidable preference.
- Where the debtor receives valuable property in exchange for its transfer made in the ordinary course of business, the transfer cannot be voided.

Discharge

- After bankruptcy, the debtor is discharged of all its remaining debts and a permanent injunction is placed against all creditors. Debts arising from fraud or false statement tend to be nondischargeable, leaving the debtor liable to them after bankruptcy.

STATUS OF THE DEBTOR'S CONTRACTS

Executory Contracts

- All construction contracts remain in effect after bankruptcy until substantial completion.
- The debtor has the right to affirm or reject any executory contracts.
- To affirm a contract in default, the default must be cured and adequate assurances of future performance must be given by the debtor.
- Debts and expenses incurred by the debtor for an affirmed contract are treated as administrative expenses of the estate.
- Debtors can assign executory contracts.

Minimizing the Impact on Executory Contracts

- The following methods can minimize the impact of contracting with a debtor: (1) terminate the contract before bankruptcy, (2) exercise the right to protect yourself as provided for under the contract, (3) seek relief from the automatic stay, (4) seek a time limit on affirming or rejecting the executory contract.

Status of Material and Equipment

- Materials and equipment slated for installation into the project may be used by the debtor for the reorganization or liquidation of its estate.

- A party can recover unpaid-for goods that have not been incorporated into the project and are in possession of the debtor.
- Precautions must be taken to prevent a debtor from claiming property in its possession that another party has already paid for.

Voiding Unperfected Security Interests

- This strong-arm provision of the Bankruptcy Code allows a trustee to void an unperfected security loan in construction materials.

Status of Contract Bonds

- The following represent methods a party can use to rcover contract funds from a debtor:
- The debtor cannot seize contract funds that are held in constructive trust for the benefit of the nonbankrupt parties;
- Pursuant to specific contract provisions, parties may have an equitable lien on contract funds held by the debtor;
- The use of joint check procedures can prevent the ultimate seizure by the debtor of contract funds slated for a lower tier subcontractor or supplier;
- Owners and general contractors can set off monies paid to lower tier subcontractors and suppliers against contract funds owed to the debtor subcontractor where the parties have an independent obligation to pay the claims of the lower tier parties. The party can recoup contract funds it owes to the debtor in an amount representing back charges or other claims it has against the debtor;
- The surety of the debtor has the same rights against the debtor that the bond claimant has.

Other Sources of Funds

- Parties can seek relief from a debtor's surety unless the surety secures an injunction preventing the claim.
- Depending upon state law, the filing of a mechanic's lien against a bankrupt owner may violate the automatic stay.
- The automatic stay prevents filing an action against a bankrupt owner to foreclose a valid lien.
- State law determines whether an action to foreclose a lien for monies owed by a bankrupt contractor violates the automatic stay.
- An action on the personal guarantee of the debtor does not violate the automatic stay.

18

ALTERNATIVE CONTRACTING METHODS:MULTIPRIME CONTRACTING, CONSTRUCTION MANAGEMENT AND DESIGN-BUILD

Construction projects have traditionally been designed, bid, built and paid for within a framework of strictly defined roles, relationships and procedures. The traditional structure for construction contracting has proved its overall effectiveness, but perceived weaknesses or opportunities for improvement have lead to consideration and use of new, alternative methods. The development of new methods has provided many advantages, but has also raised new questions about the altered roles, relationships and procedures involved in these options.

Under some of these alternative approaches to construction, the classic relationship between the owner, the general contractor and subcontractors can be dramatically changed or eliminated altogether. A subcontractor in the traditional model may become a *trade contractor* under a construction management approach to project administration or a *parallel prime contractor* under a multiprime contracting approach. Although the subcontractor's actual work in the field may be precisely the same as under the traditional approach, the subcontractor's relationship with the owner, the design professional and other subcontractors is changed. Fast-track construction introduces additional uncertainties and ambiguities about the rights and responsibilities of various parties in the altered contractual structures. Design-build contracting involves perhaps the most fundamental departure from the traditional approach to construction by vesting one party with the responsibility to both design and build the project. The apparent simplicity of this approach should not lull anyone into the false sense that such an undertaking is simple and without risk.

The manner in which these alternative contracting methods diverge from clearly defined practices and roles requires careful attention to make certain that the advantages sought through their employment are not lost through unanticipated problems and disputes. Despite significant use of these alternative methods in the last decade, questions remain about how they affect otherwise established theories of liability among project participants. Consequently, it is difficult, and perhaps dangerous, to make generalizations about the impact of the alternative methods on the role of the traditional subcontractor. Each situation depends on the parties specific roles on a given project; Those roles ultimately can be defined only by reference to the specific framework and contract terms involved.

18.1 TRADITIONAL APPROACH TO CONSTRUCTION: ADVANTAGES AND DISADVANTAGES

Construction industry professionals are familiar with the traditional construction contract structure and the roles of the parties under that structure: owner, design professional, independent general contractor and subcontractors. In the traditional structure, design and construction proceed sequentially, with construction commencing only after the design is complete.

The process is initiated by the owner's recognition of a need or an opportunity for construction. The owner then contracts with a design professional to transform the owner's general concept ultimately into a complete set of plans and specifications for the entire project—from site preparation to finishes. The prepared plans and specifications are then used to solicit bids or proposals from general contractors, who rely on the scope of work defined by the plans and specifications as the basis for their pricing, and to solicit subcontractor quotes. Ultimately, the construction contract is awarded to one general contractor, usually the one with the lowest price. The general contractor then procures subcontractors for the portion of the work it will not perform with its own forces. After the owner makes the site available and issues a notice to proceed, construction starts. The general contractor's work is financed by regular monthly progress payments from the owner. The designer generally maintains a review and inspection role throughout construction, but the owner continues to maintain control over both the design professional and the general contractor.

The traditional approach and sequence to construction is reflected in and reinforced by industry customs and practices, by statutes, and by standard contract documents. Although not welcome, the problems that arise are fairly predictable and can be resolved through established procedures and remedies. It is well established, for example, that the owner will generally be liable to the general contractor for additional costs associated with defects in the project plans and specifications. The subcontractors are responsible to the general contractor for their work, but also look to the general contractor or through it to the owner for resolution of problems. The familiarity and predictability arising from the long use of this traditional approach to construction has generated standard procedures for obtaining insurance and bonding, dealing with unexpected conditions, making changes, and generally resolving unforeseen contingencies. A well-defined model of rights, duties and remedies is in place.

The traditional mode affords many advantages. It provides the owner with a complete design and a stated maximum price before construction begins. Also, the owner maintains exclusive control over the design professional and the contractor throughout construction. The traditional approach to construction has generally proven reliable and satisfactory.

Nevertheless, there are certain disadvantages to the traditional approach. The sequence of completing the design before construction arguably is not the most effective use of time and money. Waiting for a complete design before getting price commitments from contractors or starting any construction may expose the owner to inflation and delayed occupancy. That long lead time also denies the owner the ability to react quickly to changing market conditions and immediate needs. Use of completed plans and specifications to generate competition solely on a price basis may also be counterproductive. The practice tends to encourage contractors to employ the lowest acceptable standards, and it frequently generates disputes as to what is acceptable under the plans and specifications and what is an extra requiring additional payment. The manner in which the traditional approach to construction relies so heavily on the owner's management of the design professional and the general contractor often presumes far greater expertise than the owner possesses.

Certainly, none of these or other perceived shortcomings are fatal flaws. The general success and effectiveness of the traditional approach to construction is evident. Nonetheless, new approaches do suggest ways around these shortcomings. As new approaches are tested and applied, the roles and relationships of subcontractors and others can change dramatically.

18.2   MULTIPRIME CONTRACTING AND FAST-TRACKING

Multiprime contracting, sometimes referred to as *parallel prime contracting,* differs from the traditional method of construction by displacing the general contractor. The owner no longer contracts directly with one general contractor who, in turn, subcontracts out portions of the work to various subcontractors. In multiprime contracting, the owner contracts directly with a number of *specialty* or *trade* contractors, formerly subcontractors. Each trade contractor is responsible for the performance of a discrete portion of the work.

Cost savings is frequently cited as a justification for a multiprime contracting approach. One source of savings is the elimination of the general contractor's markup and profit. Further savings may be available by employing multiple prime contractors in conjunction with other alternative approaches to construction, such as fast-track or phased construction. The hope is that the compressed time frames associated with these techniques will save borrowing costs and blunt the impact of inflation on the construction budget.

Multiprime contracting is often employed with fast-track construction. The goal of *fast-track construction* is to phase the design and construction so that construction can begin on preliminary items of work, such as site work, foundations, and even the structure, as design of the mechanical and electrical systems, interior partitions and finishes continues. The goal of this phasing is to constrict the time required to complete a project from commencement of design to final completion by overlapping the end of the design process with the beginning of construction.

In many instances, however, the use of multiprime contracting is unrelated to reducing the time of construction. Instead, the sequence of design and construction may be the same as under the traditional approach, with no bidding or construction on any of the work commencing until the entire design is complete. Much multiprime contracting is employed on public projects under state statutes intended to reduce opportunities for bid shopping, and not to reduce the time required for design and construction. Regardless of the lack of any time savings, this approach to multiprime contracting is promoted by subcontractors, who emphasize the cost benefits of increased competition on multiple contracts and the elimination of the general contractor's markup and profit. However, the cost effectiveness of this approach is subject to serious debate. A 1995 report commissioned by the New York City School Construction Authority concluded that mandatory multiprime laws *increase* construction costs by five percent to ten percent and require one to two years more to go from the start of design to project completion. Another report, jointly sponsored by the Electrical Contracting Foundation and the Mechanical Contracting Foundation, concluded just the opposite—that multiprime contracting *reduces* costs by five percent.

Regardless of the conflicting studies in statistics, multiprime contracting, even without fast-track, does offer at least theoretical benefits. Whether those benefits are realized on a particular project depends on how the actual construction work is executed and administered. Here is where experience counsels caution and where the success or failure of a multiprime approach is determined on a case by case basis.

The most significant hazard is the coordination problem that multiprime contracting seems to create. Without a general contractor who has clear responsibility for coordination for the entire project, some other party must fill that void and provide those essential management, administrative and scheduling functions. As the party bringing the trade contractors together on the project, the owner, by implication, assumes the coordination duties and the liability that flows with them, just as the general contractor does with its subcontractors. Scheduling and coordinating trade contractors on a major project is a formidable task, which most owners are ill equipped to handle. The owner who does not possess the requisite expertise and resources must recognize the need to pay someone else to perform the required services. The owner's employment of a construction manager (see Section 18.3) can largely offset the owner's lack of ability to manage a construction project. Hiring a construction manager, however, does not guarantee that the coordination function is fully addressed or that the owner can avoid liability if coordination is a failure.

Unfortunately, some owners refuse to acknowledge the need for one party with the expertise and authority to provide that essential coordination in a multiprime approach. Instead, these owners simply seek to shift the responsibility and liability for coordination to the unwary trade contractors, who often do not recognize the scope of such an undertaking. Owners have succeeded in refusing coordination responsibilities by designating one of the prime contractors as being responsible for management and control of the project[1] or simply by expressly requiring the trade contractors to coordinate with each other.[2] The owner is not always successful, and can be exposed to significant liability if it fails to make an effort to coordinate.[3]

The amount of litigation over this issue of responsibility for coordination in a multiprime contracting approach to construction demonstrates that there is great uncertainty about where ultimate responsibility will rest. The litigation also suggests that uncertainty on a project about who possesses the responsibility for coordination will likely breed problems with coordination. Experience also shows that even if a particular party is designated as being responsible for coordination, that party must possess a "big stick" for enforcements, usually in the form of some authority or substantial influence on key management, scheduling and payment issues.

18.3 CONSTRUCTION MANAGEMENT

Construction management departs from the traditional model of construction contracting by replacing the general contractor with a construction manager who typically offers diverse expertise in design, construction and management. The construction manager (CM) emerged as a new concept in the late 1960s, though it did not gain industrywide approval or broad use and support until the late 1970s. In the last twenty-five years, however, there has been a tremendous growth in the use of construction management.

Ironically, although *construction management* is used very much as a term of art, it means different things to different people. The term actually describes a broad range of services and contractual frameworks that may be applied to a particular project. Consequently, great caution must be exercised when

---

[1] *Broadway Maintenance Corp. v. Rutgers*, 90 N.J. 253, 447 A.2d 906 (1982).

[2] *Hanberry Corp. v. State Bldg. Comm'n*, 390 So.2d 277 (Miss. 1980).

[3] *Id.; Broadway Maintenance Corp.*, fn. 1, *supra*.

discussing construction management, either in abstract terms or in its use and impact on a particular project, to make certain everyone is clear about the specific parameters of the concept being discussed.

The CM's role will be as diverse and extensive as the expertise the individual or entity brings to the project, and as determined by the owner's needs on the project. The CM may be a general contractor hired to supervise and coordinate work of specialty contractors during construction. The CM may also be a multifaceted team—supervising design; having important input into site selection, financing and accounting; providing necessary expertise in the areas of cost control and quality control; and serving as supervisor and coordinator of construction activities. The CM may act exclusively as the owner's agent, having responsibility without risk, or may have to assume some of the risks borne by the general contractor in the traditional model, such as guaranteeing a maximum price for the project. Within these two extremes, there are any number of variations or combinations of services provided or roles filled by the CM. Because general principles regarding construction management are lacking and because someone operating under a title and position designated CM performs many and varied roles, it is always necessary to examine the specific contractual obligations undertaken by the CM and the owner through the contract at issue.

Generally, the role of the CM appears to depend on whether the CM most closely resembles the architect or the general contractor in traditional construction. The key distinction is whether the risk of completion of the project on time and within budget has been shifted from the owner to the CM.

18.4 Agency Construction Management

The definition employed when a CM is described from an architect's perspective usually involves construction management in its purest form—the CM is acting solely as the owner's agent. In this pure form, generally referred to as *agency CM,* the construction manager takes no entrepreneurial risk for costs, timeliness or quality of construction, and all subcontractors contract directly with the owner.

The agency CM acts as the owner's agent in supervising and coordinating all aspects of the construction project from beginning of design to the end of construction. Because the management expertise is being provided by the agency CM, the role of the general contractor is typically eliminated. However, because the agency CM assumes no financial risks of construction, the owner will directly enter into contracts with the trade contractors. The agency CM may execute those contracts, but does so only as an agent of the owner.

As discussed above in the context of multiprime contracting, the owner's direct contractual relationship with the specialty contractors changes the owner's relationship to the construction process by creating increased owner responsibility for coordinating and solving problems among the contractors. Although the agency CM assumes some of this responsibility, the owner may ultimately be liable to the specialty contractors if lack of coordination generates claims. The owner may pursue rights against the agency CM for such extra costs based on the agency CM's failure to coordinate, but the owner's ability to succeed in such a claim is impeded by the fact that the agency CM generally does not guarantee a maximum price for the construction; thus the owner bears the risk of such cost overruns.

18.5 Construction Manager/General Contractor

At the other extreme from the agency CM is the construction manager that offers its services during the design phase and then also acts as the general contractor during the construction phase—the construction manager/general contractor (CM/GC). This variation makes the CM/GC's duties and rights resemble those of a typical general contractor.

The CM/GC will frequently become involved early in the design of the project. Although the design professional remains solely responsible for the design in this form of construction management, the CM/GC will offer its practical construction expertise to suggest more effective approaches to the design and methods to save costs. Frequently, the CM/GC immediately begins estimating and scheduling functions, both to expedite the design process and to provide the owner and design professional with feedback about the construction cost and time implications of the evolving design.

Once construction is ready to commence, the CM/GC, very much like a general contractor, will enter into fixed-priced subcontracts on its own behalf and not on behalf of the owner. These subcontract prices, together with the CM/GC's costs of performance and markups, will be the basis of the CM/GC's guaranteed maximum price (GMP). It is these two features—that the CM/GC binds itself to subcontracts and to a GMP—that serve as the principal distinctions from the agency CM approach.

Although the CM/GC may be the party entering into the subcontracts, it is common for the owner to be afforded considerable involvement in the selection of subcontractors. In addition, cost reporting requirements often found in the CM/GC's contract with the owner typically require the subcontractors to provide more job cost information than a firm fixed-price contract usually requires. Finally, consistent with the CM/GC's more extensive dealings with the design professional and owner, subcontractors may perceive that the CM/GC is much more closely aligned with the owner than is the case with a general contractor.

Once construction begins, the coordination duties owed to the subcontractors by the CM/GC are virtually identical to those owed by a general contractor. Indeed, as part of its contractually defined services, the CM/GC may assume even greater coordination and scheduling responsibility than would a typical general contractor, although these additional services would primarily be for the benefit of the owner.

18.6 DESIGN-BUILD CONTRACTING

The basic and traditional approach to construction can be described as the design professional designs, the contractor builds, and the owner pays. Design-build contracting dramatically alters this approach by placing the design and the construction in the hands of one party. The owner who has the flexibility to pursue design-build can potentially obtain many benefits from this approach. However, due to the extent of the departure from the traditional approach, caution is required for those engaged in design-build contracting to make certain all parties understand their responsibilities on the project.

One of the most significant changes represented by the realignment of the parties in design-build contracting involves liability for defective design. Understandably, by accepting responsibility for design, the contractor in the design-build role generally assumes the risks of any defects or deficiency in the design.[4] This responsibility requires the design-build contractor not only to absorb its own costs arising from defective design, but also to accept liability to the owner and possibly other third parties for design defects.

This single source of liability for design and construction has obvious appeal to owners. Whether the problem is defective design or faulty construction, the contractor is liable. It is the design-build contractor that must determine the cause of the problem and resolve it. This stands in stark contract to the traditional approach described above in which the owner can be stuck in the middle between the design professional and the general contractor.

The protection afforded the owner in a design-build approach is illustrated in *Brunson Assocs., Inc.*[5] The project involved a design-build contract with the Corps of Engineers for two fabric structures to be used as training buildings. Several months after final acceptance, both structures collapsed, with both failures taking place at the same location. The Corps concluded that the failures were due to defective design and that the contractor was responsible for the resulting damages.

At the Board, the contractor argued that the Corps should share in the liability on the theory of "comparative fault." The contractor alleged the shared liability arose from the Corps' participation in the design review and approval process, including the listing of recommended fabrics and insisting on the use of particular cables. The contractor also argued that any defects in the design were apparent to the Corps through inspections.

The Board rejected the contractor's theory that the Corps' review of the design was negligent. The Corps personnel were not actively involved in the design efforts and had no experience with these types of structures. Moreover, the defect which the Board found to be the cause of the collapse had not been a subject of any design review comments by the Corps or discussed in the two design meeting in which the Corps was involved. Finally, the Board

---

[4] *See, e.g., Mobile Housing Environments v. Barton and Barton,* 432 F. Supp. 1343 (D.Colo. 1977).
[5] ASBCA 41201, 94-2 BCA ¶ 26,936.

relied on a contract clause which stated that the government's review, approval, and acceptance of the contractor's design did not relieve the contractor from liability.

In addition to design liability, the design-build contractor is generally deemed to assume the economic risk that the construction will cost more than anticipated at the time of contracting, provided the owner's performance criteria, on which the design-build contract is based, is not impracticable.[6] A design-build contractor can even bear the risk of differing site conditions if a differing site conditions clause is not expressly included in the contract.[7]

A design-build contract does not guarantee an owner complete immunity from design liability. The level of the owner's own technical expertise and active participation in the design process can earn the owner a share of liability for defective design.[8] Moreover, the information the owner provides the contractor at the outset of the design-build process may create liability for the owner if that information is in error.

This point is illustrated in *M.A. Mortenson Co.*,[9] which involved the design-build contract for a medical clinic at an Air Force base. The solicitation for the contract included a conceptual design, which represented approximately thirty-five percent of complete working drawings. The contract required the contractor to complete the construction documents to one hundred percent and construct the facility according to that design. The scope of work included the requirement that the contractor "verify and validate the accuracy of the preliminary design information and submit complete design documents." The conceptual design included alternative structural systems that could be employed on the project.

The solicitation reported that the minimum requirements of the project were stated in the project drawings and that those drawings "may be used to form the basis for the pricing proposal." The solicitation further noted that the four alternative structural systems presented had been "investigated and presented as viable alternatives for pricing."

In preparing its price proposal, the contractor used the conceptual drawings to "take-off" the quantities of structural concrete and reinforcing steel needed for the project. The contract was awarded based on that pricing approach. The final design, however, required more concrete and steel than represented in the conceptual design or the contractor's original take-off and price proposal. Based upon this increased quantity, the contractor presented a claim under the "Changes" clause, which was applicable to the construction phase of the project.

The owner opposed the claim contending that it was not reasonable for the contractor to rely on the information provided with the solicitation in this

---

[6] *Ruscon Const. Co.* ASBCA 39,586, 90-2 BCA ¶ 22,768; *Maddox Industrial Contractors, Inc.,* ASBCA 36091, 88-3 BCA ¶ 21,037.

[7] *Drillers, Inc.,* EBCA 358-5-86, 90-3 BCA ¶ 23,056.

[8] *See, e.g., Clovis Heimsath & Assocs.,* NASABCA 180-1, 83-1 BCA ¶ 16,133.

[9] ASBCA 39978, 93-3 BCA ¶ 26,189

design-build context without having a structural engineer review the adequacy of the alternate structural systems. The owner further argued that, in any event, the contractor should have included a contingency in its pricing to cover increased quantities.

The Board granted the contractor relief. The Board found that the reasonableness of the contractor's approach to the proposal had to be viewed "from the perspective of a construction contractor." Indeed, the Board disregarded the design-build context stating: "In deciding this question, we are 'to put ourselves into the shoes' of a 'reasonable and prudent' construction contractor." It was therefore unreasonable to expect the contractor to undertake a preproposal engineering analysis of the alternative structural designs. The Board noted: "The contract required . . . [the contractor] to verify and validate the design as part of the design work, not the proposal effort." Finally, the Board pointed out the inclusion of the standard "changes" clause in the contract governing the construction phase. To adopt the owner's view that the contractor assumed the risk of increased quantity for concrete and structural steel would effectively remove the changes clause and the relief it provided from the project.

The result in *M.A. Mortenson Co.* demonstrates that in design-build construction, as in other construction disputes, the specific facts of the case and specific contract terms will ultimately dictate the outcome. As design-build is such a deviation from the allocation of design risks in the traditional approach, special attention needs to be provided to the contract terms to make certain that the expectations and understanding of the parties are mutual and clearly stated.

18.7 DESIGN-BUILD ASPECTS OF TRADITIONAL CONSTRUCTION

Even within the traditional "design-bid-build" approach, contractors must be aware of the extent to which they can assume design-build responsibility through performance specifications, the shop drawing process, and clauses which impose design review responsibilities on the contractor.

18.8 Performance Specifications

Specifications fall in two general categories: performance specifications and design specifications. Design specifications precisely describe the work the contractor is to accomplish including dimensions, tolerances, and materials. The design specifications are the recipe the contractor is required to follow in constructing the work. Performance specifications do not tell the contractor how to accomplish the result, but only dictate what the result must be. This distinction is of critical importance because design liability under performance specifications is generally allocated as it would be if the entire project was design-build. The contractor is responsible for all the costs associated with achieving the end result described in the performance specifications.

Often, a specification is not exclusively a performance specification. Instead, the desired end result is described, but at least some design information is offered. When problems result from the contractor's inability to meet the performance criteria when using the design data provided, liability for the design defect is unclear. The *M. A. Mortenson Co.* case discussed earlier indicates how even limited information can get the owner in trouble, even in a pure design-build context. Liability may ultimately be allocated on the basis of which party had superior knowledge. A contractor, on its own or through some specialty subcontractor or supplier, may be deemed to have sufficient knowledge to recognize the conflict between the design outlined and the performance required so that the defect constituted a patent defect. In which case, the contractor is, at a minimum, required to call the defect to the attention of the owner. In *Brunson Assocs, Inc.,* discussed earlier, the owner's lack of superior knowledge was a factor in holding the design-build contractor liable for the design defect.

In *Regan Construction Co. & Nager Electric Co.,*[10] the project specifications included performance criteria for air handling units. At trial, the contractor proved that the only air handling unit on the market that met the performance criteria was the one provided by the contractor. Unfortunately, that unit did not fit into the space allotted for the air handling unit in the overall design. Thus, although the contractor was able to establish that the performance specification was defective within the context of the overall design, the contractor was nonetheless found liable for the extra cost associated with accommodating the unit because the contractor should have discovered the conflict earlier and called it to the attention of the owner.

Contractors need to be aware of the risk of performance specifications may take somewhat unconventional forms. *Florida Board of Regents v. Mycon Corp.*[11] involved what appeared to be a "brand name or equal" specification for architectural concrete. Under the specifications, the contractor was to "provide a skin plate with a smooth, non-corded 'true-radius' forming surface, equal to that manufactured by Symons." The contractor used the referenced Symons system not only for the "skin plate" but also throughout the project, thinking that a Symons forming system would provide a suitable result. The owner concluded, however, that the concrete work failed to achieve the required tolerances. The contractor argued that its use of the specified Symons system was subject to the owner's implied warranty of the adequacy of the specifications so that the contractor could not be liable if the finished product did not meet specifications. The Florida Court of Appeals disagreed.

The court initially noted that if only one brand of product was specified so that the contractor had no discretion but to use that one product, then the

[10] PSBCA 633, 80-2 BCA ¶ 14,802
[11] 651 So.2d 149 (Fla. 1st D.C.A. 1995).

owner's implied warranty of the specifications would apply and the contractor would be entitled to relief. Moreover, the court recognized that if there was true "or equal" language in the contract, the contractor would be able to meet the contract by proposing a system equal to the brand specified. In this case, however, the court pointed out that the "or equal" references in the specifications related solely to the "skin plate" portion of the work, not to the entire steel concrete forming system that would need to be used on the project. While the court appeared to agree that there was an implied warranty of the plans by use of the Symons system in connection with the "skin plate," the contractor nevertheless had to meet the specific tolerances for other concrete surfaces and there was no representation in the contract that the Symons forming system would be adequate.

18.9 Shop Drawings

Shop drawings are an essential element of construction, bridging the gap between the design set forth in the plans and specifications and the details and specifics necessary to fabricate material and install the work in the field. There is the ever-present risk that in translating the design to shop drawings the contractor may intentionally or unintentionally alter the design. If that occurs and the change results in a design defect that impacts construction, the contractor assumes the liability for that defective design even if the design professional generally approved the shop drawing incorporating the change.

Most construction contracts contain a shop drawing clause which states that the design professional's approval does not relieve the contractor from responsibility for complying with the plans and specifications.[12] Unless there is some basis to argue an ambiguity in the plans of specifications, this clause will likely shift responsibility to the contractor for any changes to the design in the shop drawing process, at least as between the owner, contractor, and designer.[13] The design liability for such changes can, however, be shifted back to the owner and designer if they are clearly identified and called to the attention of the owner or the designer who reviews and approves the shop drawing.[14] The standard clauses state that changes in or deviations from the plans and specifications must be specifically identified in writing as changes and deviations and must be specifically approved.

The numerous factual issues of what constitutes a change or deviation, whether it was sufficiently highlighted as such to the designer, and whether there was specific acceptance and approval, are each fertile grounds for disagreement and litigation. Structural steel shop drawings, including the detailing of fabrication, erection, and welding details, as compared to information contained in the structural drawings and specifications, generates a tremendous

---

[12] See AIA Documents A201 (1987 ed.), ¶¶ 3.12.7 and 3.12.8, EJCDC No. 1910-8, ¶¶ 6.27 and 6.25.1.1.

[13] *See, e.g., Fauss Const. Inc. v. City of Hooper,* 197 Neb. 398, 249 N.W.2d 478 (1977).

[14] *See, e.g., Montgomery Ross Fisher & H. A. Lewis,* GSBCA, 85-2 BCA ¶ 18,108.

number of disputes because the stakes are so high and the technical issues so complex. Steel fabricators and erectors frequently feel an unreasonable amount of design responsibility is being shifted to them as they perceive structural drawings omits so much critical detail that is necessary to fabricate and install the structural steel frame.

The extent of the problems and pressures described by steel fabricators are not imagined. The seriousness of the problem is highlighted by the infamous Kansas City Hyatt disaster. In litigation arising from the disaster, the Missouri Court of Appeals held that the design of a structural steel connection could not be delegated to the steel fabricator. To have done so was grounds for revoking the license of the professional engineer who was deemed to be grossly negligent for making only a cursory review of the involved shop drawings.[15]

Another area of frequent dispute in the shop drawing process involves dimensional errors in the plans and specifications. The standard shop drawing clauses require the contractor to verify field dimensions when preparing shop drawings. A failure to verify existing field conditions can therefore transfer liability for dimensional errors on the plans from the owner to the contractor even if the owner's designer included the erroneous dimensions in the original design and approved the shop drawing which repeated the erroneous dimension.[16]

18.10   Secondary Design Review

Compliance with performance specifications and providing details in the shop drawing process are affirmative acts that hopefully alert the contractor to potential design liability. There are other standard contract clauses, however, that seek to shift farther design responsibility to the contractor. These clauses are not based upon the contractor's actions, but on the contractor's failure to take affirmative action to identify and correct defects in the design. Such boilerplate language is generally unnoticed and often not even an issue. Unfortunately, if there is a major design bust and more than enough damages and blame to go around, the contractor is likely to hear arguments about how it assumed some of that liability through these stealthy risk-shifting clauses.

The Interpretations Clause: Plans and specifications often lack all the details and specifics necessary to translate the design into construction, hence the need for shop drawings and material and equipment submittals. The requirement for the contractor to detail the design for construction purposes may also require the contractor to "fill in the gaps" of the design. Recognizing that all details cannot be addressed, many construction contracts contain a catch-all clause that requires the contractor to not only supply and construct the work specifi-

---

[15] *Duncan v. Missouri Board for Architects, Professional Engineers & Land Surveyors,* 744 S.W. 2d 524 (Mo. App. 1988).
[16] *KAM Electric Ent.,* VABCA, 89-1 BCA ¶ 21,558.

cally set forth in the plans and specifications, but also to furnish all necessary labor and materials that may be "reasonably inferred" from the plans and specifications in order to achieve a complete and functional project.[17] Disputes over the coverage of this clause frequently involve responsibility for piping and control wiring and whether the contractor is responsible to provide them at no additional cost. The stakes can be considerably higher than simply the cost of the omitted detail if the omission of the procurement or installation creates a major delay to the project or requires completed work to be torn out.

What the contractor is required to provide is tied to the circumstances of the project and what a reasonable contractor would do. If a reasonable contractor would have included the work in its bid or at least inquired about it, then the contractor will generally be responsible for the cost of providing the work, regardless of the fact that the work was not detailed on the plans and specifications.

Identification of Patent Defects: Even the most carefully designed and engineered project is not going to be perfect. The plans and specifications are too voluminous to not contain some errors. In recognition of this reality, many construction contracts attempt to impose upon the contractor the responsibility to review the design and to call to the attention of the owner or design professional any errors or omissions it finds.[18] Failure to disclose such errors renders the contractor potentially liable for them. Under AIA Document A201, the contractor's liability extends only to those errors which the contractor knowingly fails to report. The EJCDC Document, on the other hand, imposes liability on the contractor for errors that the contractor knew or *should have* known.

These clauses basically shift the liability for defective design for patent or obvious design defects to the contractor, while maintaining the owner's liability for hidden defects. What is patent or obvious will depend on the specific circumstances of the project and the relative expertise of the contractor.

Compliance with Permits, Codes and Regulations: It is the responsibility of the design professional to design the project in accordance with applicable building codes and regulations. In most construction contracts, the contractor also assumes a separate and additional duty to obtain necessary permits, and comply with applicable building codes and regulations.[19] These clauses are primarily intended to hold the contractor liable for the means and methods of construction. However, they can also be used to hold the contractor liable for design defects arising from conflicts with building codes. As a practical matter, however, the contractor will be unlikely to assume that liability unless the design defect was patent and the contractor failed to notify the owner.

[17] See, AIA Document A201 ¶1.2.3 and EJCDC No. 1910-8 ¶ 3.2.
[18] See e.g., EJCDC, No. 1910-8 ¶ 2.5; AIA Document A201, ¶3.2.1.
[19] See e.g., AIA Document A201, ¶ 3.7; EJCDC No. 1910-8 ¶¶ 6.13-6.14.

POINTS TO REMEMBER

- The traditional approach to construction of design-bid-build has many strengths, but also weaknesses that prompted pursuit of other approaches to the construction process.
- The manner in which alternative contracting methods divert from clearly defined and accepted practices and roles requires careful attention to avoid unanticipated problems and disputes.
- Multiprime contracting, particularly when employed with fast-track construction, can offer opportunities to reduce the time and cost of construction.
- All parties to a multiprime project must recognize that with the elimination of the general contractor, another party with the appropriate power should be designated to assume the coordination responsibilities generally fulfilled by the general contractor. Without some express disclaimer, the owner assumes the duty to coordinate in the multiprime setting.
- Construction management generally entails involving in the design and construction process an entity with diverse expertise in design, construction and management. The precise role of a construction manager on any project, however, can only be determined by reference to specific contract language.
- The role of the construction manager can range from a traditional general contractor, who provides some estimating and constructibility input during the design phase but is still required to guarantee time and price of performance, to a traditional design firm, which simply provides a higher level of construction adminstration and scheduling services for a fixed fee, without any guarantee of time or cost of performance.
- Design-build contracting represents the most radical departure from the traditional approach to construction by vesting all design and construction responsibilities and resulting liabilities in one party. The dramatic alteration of the traditional roles of the parties in design-build requires special attention to make certain the contract sets out the mutually understood and specific rights and responsibilities of each party.
- Even in the traditional build to design approach, contractors can assume discrete design liability as the result of performance specifications, the shop drawing process, and where secondary design review responsibility is imposed by standard contract clauses.

19

FEDERAL GOVERNMENT CONSTRUCTION CONTRACT DISPUTES

19.1 THE SCOPE AND IMPORTANCE OF FEDERAL CONSTRUCTION CONTRACTING

The Federal Government is the largest consumer of construction services in the world today. The procurement, administration and resolution of disputes on federal construction projects are governed by voluminous statutes and regulations, which are rigorously enforced. An extensive array of administrative boards of contract appeals and special courts have operated for decades for the sole purpose of resolving disputes on federal contracts. These various tribunals have generated a tremendous number of decisions and provide one of the largest areas of law in the area of construction disputes. Many of the citations in this book arise from federal construction contracts and many of the fundamental principles of construction law have their genesis in federal government construction contracts. It is impractical to speak of construction law without federal procurement law and the discussion of that law is interlaced in each chapter of this book. Considering the volume of federal construction contracts, it is also appropriate to provide this general outline of the legal framework applicable to federal construction contracts.

Disputes arising out of or related to the performance of a government construction contract are governed by the Contract Disputes Act of 1978 (hereinafter CDA or Act).[1] The CDA and its implementing regulations set forth a comprehensive approach to the resolution of claims by contractors and the government. The Act applies to contracts executed on or after March 1, 1979.

---

[1] U.S.C. §§ 601–613 (1987) (unless otherwise indicated, all references are to the 1987 version of the United States Code).

The citations in this chapter are to the appropriate provisions of the CDA, to other relevant statutes and the applicable regulations, particularly the Federal Acquisition Regulations (FAR), as well as to the cases. The CDA and the other cited statutes are found in West Publishing Company's United States Code Annotated. FAR citations are from Title 48 of the Code of Federal Regulations (CFR).

Government contract case law is found in a variety of sources. Since 1921 selected bid protest decisions issued by the General Accounting Office (GAO) have been published in the Decisions of the Comptroller General of the United States. Beginning in 1974, Federal Publications, Inc. (Fed. Pub.) issued the *Comptroller General's Procurement Decisions* (CPD) service containing the full text of all of the GAO's procurement decisions.[2] Court decisions regarding bid protests have been issued by the federal district courts, the various federal circuit courts of appeals, the United States Claims Court (now the United States Court of Federal Claims)[3] and the United States Court of Appeals for the Federal Circuit. The case law involving claims and disputes arising out of or related to the performance of a contract basically consist of the decisions of the various boards, United States Court of Claims, United States Claims Court, United States Court of Federal Claims, and the United States Court of Appeals for the Federal Circuit.[4]

The Court of Claims, which was abolished in 1982, had jurisdiction to entertain suits involving government contract claims, including claims under the CDA. When Congress abolished the Court of Claims, it created the Claims Court, now the Court of Federal Claims,[5] and granted to it all of the original jurisdiction of the Court of Claims.[6] At the same time, Congress also created a new United States Court of Appeals for the Federal Circuit.[7] The Federal Circuit reviews decisions of boards of contract appeals and the Court of Federal Claims.[8] The Court of Federal Claims and the Federal Circuit view decisions of the old Court of Claims as binding precedent.[9]

---

[2] Until 1974, the vast majority of the GAO's decisions on bid protests were not published and were not readily available.

[3] Pub. L. 102-572, 106 Stat. 4516, 28 U.S.C. § 1491 (1992).

[4] These forums dispose of the vast majority of all contract related issues. However, Congress has also granted the Executive Branch extraordinary powers to be used in the course of procurements related to the national defense. One of these laws, Public Law 85-804, 72 Stat. 972, 50 U.S.C. §§1431–1435, permits certain procuring activities to grant relief to contractors who may have no legal right to such relief, e.g., an amendment without consideration. This avenue for relief is not a substitute for relief under the CDA and will only be considered after it is determined that the CDA does not provide an adequate remedy. The procedures related to extraordinary contractual actions are found in 48 C.F.R. Part 50.

[5] 28 U.S.C. § 171.

[6] 28 U.S.C. § 1491. The United States Court of Federal Claims has the same basic jurisdiction, but broadened to include nonmonetary claims. See Section 19.22, below.

[7] 28 U.S.C. § 41.

[8] 41 U.S.C. § 607(g)(1); 28 U.S.C. § 1295(a)(10), (a)(3).

[9] *South Corp. v. United States,* 690 F.2d 1368, 1369 (Fed. Cir. 1982) (en banc); United States Court of Federal Claims Gen. Order No. 33, 27 Fed. Cl. xyv (1992).

19.2 SCOPE OF THE CONTRACT DISPUTES ACT

Prior to the enactment of the CDA, the government contract disputes process was a mixture of statutes, regulations, and interpretive case law. Government contracts contained a disputes clause[10] and every federal agency utilized a board of contract appeals. Reflecting a series of United States Supreme Court decisions,[11] the boards became the principle forum for the resolution of contractor claims, while the United States Court of Claims assumed the more limited role of an appellate court under the Wunderlich Act.[12] Except for the relatively unusual circumstance that could be characterized as a claim for breach of contract, nearly all claims arising under a contract had to be brought to the boards. However, the boards' jurisdiction was limited to those claims, and any suit alleging breach of contract had to be filed in the United States Court of Claims.

Each board had its own rules and procedures, which had varying degrees of formality. In some agencies, board members served only on a part-time basis. In those cases, the members had other duties within the agency. In addition, due to the decision of the United States Supreme Court in *S&E Contractors, Inc. v. United States,*[13] the government had no right of appeal from an adverse decision of a board. The *S&E* decision also had the effect of precluding a review of board decisions by the GAO, which review had the potential effect of negating a decision that was adverse to the agency's interests.

Attempting to improve the overall disputes process, the CDA created a comprehensive statutory basis for the disposition of contract disputes. The Act applies to any express or implied contract that is entered into by an "executive agency" of the federal government for the "procurement of [the] construction, alteration, repair, or maintenance of real property."[14] The Act applies to "the executive agency contracts for the procurement of property, other than real property, for the procurement of services and for the disposal of personal property, as well as for supplies."[15]

---

[10] *See* Shedd, "Disputes and Appeals: The Armed Services Board of Contract Appeals," 29 *Law & Contemp. Probs.* 39 (1964).

[11] *United States v. Holpuch,* 328 U.S. 234 (1946); *United States v. Moorman,* 338 U.S. 457 (1950); *United States v. Wunderlich,* 342 U.S. 98 (1951).

[12] The reaction to the *Moorman* and *Wunderlich* decisions resulted in the passage of the Wunderlich Act, which limited the finality of board decisions: 44 U.S.C. §§ 321–22; *United States v. Bianchi,* 373 U.S. 709 (1963); *United States v. Grace & Sons, Inc.,* 384 U.S. 424 (1966). *Grace* and *Bianchi* establish that a court reviewing a board decision was confined to the record at the board and could not conduct an independent evidentiary hearing into issues not addressed by the board. Thus the boards became the primary fact-finding bodies with significant emphasis placed on the development of a record that would support the finding with substantial evidence.

[13] 406 U.S. 1 (1972).

[14] 41 U.S.C. § 602(a).

[15] It is well established that the Act applies to leases for real property: *Robert J. DiDomenico,* GSBCA No. 5539, 80-1 BCA ¶ 14,412; *Goodfellow Bros. Inc.,* AGBCA No. 80-189-3, 81-1 BCA ¶ 14,917; *George Ungar,* PSBCA No. 935, 82-1 BCA ¶ 15,549. However, jurisdiction over a dispute outside of the terms of the lease, such as a decision to expand the area subject to the lease, has been rejected by a board. *See John Barrar and Marilyn Hunkler,* ENG BCA No. 5918, 92-3 BCA ¶ 25,074.

The term "executive agency" is defined in 41 U.S.C. § 601(2). It encompasses those entities that are commonly thought of as government agencies such as Department of Defense (DOD), the General Services Administration (GSA), the Department of Energy (DOE), and the Department of Veterans Affairs (VA). It also encompasses the U.S. Postal Service, the Postal Rate Commission, and various independent bodies in government corporations.[16] The comprehensive statutory basis for the disposition of disputes created by the CDA made significant changes in the process. It made the boards and board members more professional by requiring that all board memberships be full-time positions. In other words, it was no longer possible for a board member to function as an attorney for the agency on a part-time basis. Secondly, it gave the contractor a choice of forums with respect to the appeal of a final decision by the contracting officer. The contractor could elect either to appeal to a board or to file a suit on the final decision in the United States Court of Federal Claims (formerly Claims Court). This concept became known as contractor's right of direct access. Furthermore, the Act's provisions applied "notwithstanding any contract provision, regulation, or rules of law to the contrary" (41 U.S.C. § 609(b)). Accordingly, it is not possible to agree by contract to limit the right of appeal to a particular forum.[17] In addition, the Act effectively reversed the *S&E* decision by giving the government the right to appeal an adverse board decision to the United States Court of Appeals for the Federal Circuit.

The CDA seeks to address the processing of claims from their initiation to final disposition and payment. It describes the manner in which claims are asserted and seeks to provide time frames for decisions on such claims by the contracting officer. The Act also provides for a contractor's right to appeal the contracting officer's final decision or the lack of a final decision, as well as the time frames for appeals to each of the alternate forums (boards or Court of Federal Claims) and any appellate review of those decisions. Since the primary focus of the Act is the disposition of a claim, this chapter begins with a discussion of an assertion of a claim and follows the processing of that claim through a decision and any appeal. It will also review provisions of the CDA dealing with fraudulent or inflated claims,[18] small claims,[19] interest on amounts found due the contractor,[20] and payment of claims.[21]

Under the contract provisions utilized prior to the CDA, the typical disputes clause extended only to disputes "arising under" the contract. Typically, this meant that breach of contract claims were not subject to the disputes clause and were outside the jurisdiction of the boards.[22] The Act extends to all

---

[16] The Act also contains provisions covering the Tennessee Valley Authority. *See* 41 U.S.C. § 602(b).

[17] *OSHCO-PAE-SOMC v. United States,* 16 Cl. Ct. 614 (1989).

[18] 41 U.S.C. § 604.

[19] 41 U.S.C. § 608.

[20] 41 U.S.C. § 611.

[21] 41 U.S.C. § 612.

[22] *United States v. Utah Constr. & Mining Co.,* 384 U.S. 394 (1966).

disputes arising under or related to a contract. This broader formulation of the scope of the disputes process clearly includes claims for breach of contract. However, by its terms, and as its name implies, the Act is only applicable to contract disputes, and tort claims are not subject to the Act.[23] While the Act is specifically applicable to any "express or implied contract," the Federal Circuit has held that the CDA did not give the boards jurisdiction to hear claims based upon an implied contract by the government to treat bids fairly and honestly,[24] which is the basis for bid protest and bid preparation cost actions. The Federal Circuit held that the implied contract to treat bids fairly and honestly is not a contract for the procurement of "goods or services"; thus it does not fall within the definition contained in § 3(a) of the Act.

While § 605(a) of the Act provides that all claims related to a contract shall be submitted to the contracting officer for a decision, the Act also states that the authority of that subsection did not extend to "a claim or dispute for penalty of forfeitures prescribed by statute or regulation which another federal agency is specifically authorized to administer, settle, or determine." Therefore, disputes arising under the Walsh-Healey Act,[25] the Davis-Bacon Act[26] and the Service Contract Act of 1965[27] are not subject to the CDA. These Acts involve labor laws that are administered by the Secretary of Labor, and disputes related to the enforcement of these statutes are generally beyond the jurisdiction of the boards or the Court of Federal Claims.[28]

19.3 THE FREEDOM OF INFORMATION ACT—A CLAIM PREPARATION AND PROSECUTION AID

Often agency files contain documents that can provide support for a contractor's request for a contract adjustment or for the contractor's understanding of its contract obligations or the agency's responsibilities. Typically, these materials are available during discovery. However, this is after a claim has been submitted, a final decision has been issued, and an appeal or suit has been initiated. The Freedom of Information Act (FOIA)[29] often provides a means for a contractor to obtain access to the records maintained by the government prior to the submission of a claim. Contractors and their counsel should consider using FOIA requests as a means of obtaining additional information pertaining to the contract. Agencies subject to the FOIA include: (1) any department or agency of the Executive Branch; (2) government corpo-

---

[23] 41 U.S.C. § 602(a); *Malnak Assoc. v. United States,* 223 Ct. Cl. 783 (1980); *Siska Constr. Co.,* VABCA No. 3524, 92-2 BCA ¶ 24,825.

[24] *Coastal Corp. v. United States,* 713 F.2d 728 (Fed. Cir. 1983).

[25] 41 U.S.C. § 35 *et seq.*

[26] 40 U.S.C. § 276(a).

[27] 41 U.S.C. § 351 *et seq.*

[28] *Emerald Maintenance, Inc. v. United States,* 925 F.2d 1425 (Fed. Cir. 1991); *Tele-Sentry Security, Inc.,* GSBCA No. 10945, 91-2 BCA ¶ 23,880.

[29] 5 U.S.C. § 552.

rations; (3) government controlled corporations; or (4) any independent regulatory branch.[30] The FOIA does not apply to the federal courts or to the Congress.

Basically, information is made available to the public in three ways: (1) by publication in the Federal Register;[31] (2) by sale to the public or availability for examination in public reading rooms;[32] or (3) upon request for documents that are reasonably described.[33] This third category of records is generally the best source of information pertaining to contract performance issues. To obtain these documents in the third category, it is necessary to submit a written FOIA request. Each agency's procedures governing the submission should be carefully reviewed and followed when making a FOIA request.[34] The regulations usually identify the FOIA officer to whom a request should be sent and that person's address. In addition, these procedures set forth time limits for agency responses and appeal procedures if the request is denied. Following these procedures will save time in processing the request. In addition, it will avoid having a court decline jurisdiction over a suit to compel disclosure due to a failure to follow these rules.[35]

Generally, a request for agency documents should clearly state that it is an FOIA request and acknowledge that the government may be entitled to be paid certain fees and costs for responding to the request.[36] In addition, it is necessary to provide a "reasonable description" of the desired records.[37] A "reasonable description" is one that enables a professional employee of the agency who is familiar with the subject area of the request to locate the record with a reasonable amount of effort.[38] However, broad categorical requests that make it impossible for the agency to reasonably determine what is sought are not permissible.[39] If the agency denies the initial request, the person seeking disclosure may file an action in an United States district court to compel disclosure, after exhausting the applicable administrative procedures (including any appeal process) set forth in the agency's FOIA regulations.[40]

FOIA requests can be a means of expeditious, informal discovery to assist in the preparation of a claim. Even after an appeal or suit is pending, contractors and their counsel should consider the potential for appropriate contemporaneous FOIA requests and formal discovery requests. For example, many

---

[30] 5 U.S.C. § 552 (e).
[31] 5 U.S.C. § 552(a)(1); 1 CFR Part 51.
[32] 5 U.S.C. § 552(a)(2).
[33] 5 U.S.C. § 552(a)(3)(A).
[34] 5 U.S.C. § 552(a)(3)(B).
[35] *Television Wisc., Inc. v. NLRB,* 410 F. Supp. 999 (W.D. Wis. 1976).
[36] If the requesting party is not sure of the cost (scope) associated with the FOIA request, it is possible to advise the agency to contact the party making the request prior to conducting a search that is expected to cost more than a stated amount.
[37] H.R. Rep. No. 93-876, 93rd Congress, 2nd Sess. (1974).
[38] 5 U.S.C. § 552(a)(3)(A).
[39] S. Rep. No. 93-854, 93rd Congress, 2nd Sess. (1974).
[40] 5 U.S.C. § 552(a)6(c); *Oglesby v. United States,* 920 F.2d 57 (D.C. Cir. 1990).

projects involve federal agencies other than the contracting agency. An appropriate FOIA request to the noncontracting agency may provide quicker access to records than the use of subpoenas on nonparty federal agencies. Similarly, in a case involving issues related to the performance by, or positions asserted by an architect-engineer firm, a FOIA request to view the records on other projects designed or administered by the same firm may reveal contradictory views and positions.

19.4 CONTRACTOR CLAIMS

The Act provides that "[a]ll claims by a contractor against the government relating to a contract shall be in writing and shall be submitted to the contracting officer for a decision."[41] The Act further provides that claims by a contractor in excess of $100,000 must be certified.[42] The existence of a claim in dispute and the submission of that claim to the contracting officer for a decision are prerequisites to the contractor's ability to invoke the disputes resolution procedures of the CDA. Until a claim is submitted, the contracting officer has no obligation to issue a final decision and the contractor has no right of access to either a board of contract appeals or to the Court of Federal Claims. If a contractor initiates either a board or court proceeding prior to the submission of a proper claim, the proceeding will either be dismissed or stayed, depending upon the deficiency in the contractor's claim submission. Even though a dismissal would be without prejudice to the right of the contractor to reinitiate the process,[43] the contractor must begin the process by resubmitting the claim to the contracting officer for a decision.[44] This costs time and money. Moreover, under certain circumstances, interest does not begin to accrue on the submission until a CDA claim is submitted. Failure to understand and to follow the requirements of the CDA can be very costly.

19.5 WHO MAY SUBMIT A CLAIM?

Generally, under the CDA, only a prime contractor may assert claims against the government. The Act refers to "contractor claims"[45] and states that the term "contractor means a party to a government contract other than the government. . . ."[46] Similarly, § 33.201 of the FAR defines the claim as a

---

[41] 41 U.S.C. § 605(a).

[42] 41 U.S.C. § 605(c). Prior to 1994, the threshold for certification was $50,000.

[43] *Thoen v. United States,* 765 F.2d 1110, 1116 (Fed. Cir. 1985).

[44] *Skelly & Loy, Inc. v. United States,* 231 Ct. Cl. 370, 177, 685 F.2d, 414, 419 (1982); *Technassociates, Inc. v. United States,* 14 Cl. Ct. 200, 212 (1988); *T.J.D. Servs., Inc. v. United States,* 6 Cl. Ct. 257, 260 (1984).

[45] 41 U.S.C. § 605(a).

[46] 41 U.S.C. § 601(4).

demand or assertion "by one of the contracting parties."[47] This requirement for privity of contract is strictly enforced in government contracts. Generally, subcontractors are not considered to be one of the contracting parties and are not in privity of contract with the government. Accordingly, subcontractors may not assert claims directly against the government under the Act.[48] Only in rare situations does privity of contract exist between a subcontractor and the government, such as when the government utilizes an agent to enter into a contract "by and for" the government, or there is an assignment of a subcontractor's contract to the government pursuant to a clause such as the Termination for Convenience clause.[49] Similarly, a noncompleting performance bond surety is not a contractor for the purposes of the CDA.[50] However, a surety who expressly or implicitly assumes contract performance is in privity with the government and may assert claims under the Act. Finally, unless the government is a party to the assignment transaction, the assignee of a contractor's rights under a government contract does not attain the status of a contractor, and is not in the position to assert a claim under the CDA.[51]

Given the nature of most construction projects, subcontractor performance is often a key issue, and subcontractor claims are common. While subcontractors do not have the right to directly assert a claim against the government, subcontractor claims are routinely considered in the context of the disputes process. With the prime contractor's consent and cooperation, a subcontractor claim can be submitted to the contracting officer for decision and appealed through the disputes process. In that situation, the prime contractor acts as a "sponsor" for the subcontractor's claim.[52]

19.6 WHAT CONSTITUTES A CLAIM?

The Act states that all claims "shall be in writing and shall be submitted to the contracting officer for a decision."[53] However, the CDA does not define a claim. Moreover, while it would seem that the definition of a "claim" would be uniform in government contracts, there is a marked lack of uniformity. There are differing definitions of a claim for the purpose of the disputes

---

[47] 48 C.F.R. § 33.201 (all references are to the 1995 edition of the Code of Federal Regulations).
[48] *Erickson Air Crane Co. of Wash., Inc. v. United States,* 731 F.2d 810, 813 (Fed. Cir. 1984); *United States v. Johnson Controls, Inc.,* 713 F.2d 1541 (Fed. Cir. 1983); *G. Schneider,* ASBCA No. 333021, 87-2 BCA ¶ 19,865.
[49] *Kern-Limerick v. Scurlock,* 347 U.S. 110 (1954); *Deltec Corp. v. United States,* 326 F.2d 1004 (Ct. Cl. 1964).
[50] *See Universal Sur. Co. v. United States,* 10 Cl. Ct. 794, 799–800 (1986).
[51] *See Fireman's Fund/Underwater Constr., Inc.* ASBCA No. 33018, 87-3 BCA ¶ 20,007.
[52] *Erickson Air Crane,* fn. 48, *supra,* at 810, 813–14. However, if a prime contractor refuses to authorize prosecution of a claim in its name, the claim will be dismissed. *Divide Constructors, Inc.,* IBCA No. 1134-12-76, 77-1 BCA ¶ 14,430.
[53] 41 U.S.C. § 605(a). *See Reflectone, Inc. v. United States,* 60 F.3d 1572 (Fed. Cir. 1995) for a discussion of the elements constituting a CDA "claim."

clause,[54] the disallowance of certain costs associated with the prosecution of a "claim" against the government,[55] and for the purpose of contractor liability under the False Claims Act.[56]

FAR § 33.214 provides that absent specific circumstances, each government contract must contain the disputes clause set forth at FAR § 52.233-1.[57] That Disputes clause provides, in pertinent part, the following definition of a claim:

> (c) "Claim," as used in this clause, means a written demand or written assertion by one of the contracting parties seeking, as a matter of right, the payment of money in a sum certain, the adjustment or interpretation of contract terms, or other relief arising under or relating to this contract. . . . [A] written demand or written assertion by the Contractor seeking the payment of money in excess of $100,000 is not a claim under the Act until certified as required by subparagraph (d)(2) below. . . .
>
> (d)(1) A claim by the Contractor shall be made in writing and submitted to the Contracting Officer for a written decision.

Thus in order for a contractor's claim to be properly filed under the CDA, there must be submitted to the contracting officer in writing: (1) a demand or assertion; (2) which seeks, as matter of right, the payment of money in a sum certain, the adjustment or other interpretation of contract terms, or other relief arising under or related to the contract; (3) with respect to which a contracting officer's written decision is requested; (4) and which is certified if the amount involved exceeds $100,000.

19.7 Written Submission to the Contracting Officer

As indicated in the Disputes clause quoted above, the claim for the purposes of the CDA must be in writing and must be submitted to the contracting officer for a written decision. Accordingly, oral demands or assertions for compensation are not claims for the purposes of the CDA. Similarly, a written demand or submission that is submitted to a person who is not the contracting officer is not a claim for the purposes of the Act. The CDA defines a contracting officer as "[A]ny person who, by appointment in accordance with applicable regulations, has the authority to enter into and administer contracts and make determinations and findings with respect thereto." This definition also includes the authorized representative of the contracting officer, acting within the limits of that person's authority.[58]

---

[54] FAR §52.233-1, 48 C.F.R. § 52.233-1.

[55] *See Bill Strong Enterprises, Inc. v. Shannon*, 49 F.3d 1541 (Fed. Cir. 1995); *Reflectone, Inc. v. United States*, fn. 53, *supra*; *Betancourt & Gonzales S.E.*, DOT BCA Nos. 2785 *et al.*, 96-1 BCA ¶ 28,033.

[56] 18 U.S.C. § 287; *United States v. Neifert-White Co.*, 390 U.S. 228 (1968).

[57] 48 C.F.R. § 33.214.

[58] 41 U.S.C. § 601(3).

Under certain circumstances, the submission of a written claim to a subordinate of the contracting officer has been held to be ineffective for the purposes of the Act.[59] A contractor should be able to avoid the problem of misdirected claims by ascertaining at the outset of performance the specific individuals, in addition to the contracting officer, who are authorized to receive claims. Moreover, if there is any doubt regarding whether the submission to the contracting officer's subordinate will be deemed appropriate under the Act, the contracting officer should be copied on the submission. This removes any doubt regarding the date when the contracting officer received the submission for the purposes of the Act.

19.8 Elements of a Claim

In submitting a claim, a contractor is not required to use any particular wording or format.[60] However, the contractor is required to give the contracting officer sufficient information that the contracting officer has adequate notice of the basis for, and the amount of the claim.[61] Therefore, there are basically two elements of any claim: entitlement and quantum. The entitlement portion establishes the factual and contractual basis supporting the contractor's right to recover from the government. For example, in a claim involving the alleged misinterpretation of a specification by the government, the entitlement portion would describe how the government misinterpreted the specification, as contrasted to the contractor's reasonable understanding of the contract's requirements. In addition, that section would also describe the extra work and delay, if any, caused by the misinterpretation. The second part of the claim is quantum. In that, the contractor describes the amount of money or time to which it is entitled and attempts to relate cause (act by the government) to effect (expenditure of money). The relation of cause and effect can be quite difficult as it often encompasses issues of scheduling, cost accounting, and the support for estimates. As with any contract, project documentation is often critical to establishing cause and effect. See Chapter 10 for a discussion of project documentation.

There is no clear test to determine the degree of detail necessary to constitute a claim. In general, the boards and courts have adopted a standard similar to notice pleadings. That is, the contractor must provide the contracting officer with adequate notice of the basis and the amount of the claim *and* a request for the contracting officer to render a final decision.[62] In other words, the contractor should assert specific rights and request specific relief. Ultimately, whether a contractor's submission constitutes a claim depends upon the totality

---

[59] *Lakeview Constr. Co. v. United States,* 21 Cl. Ct. 269 (1990).
[60] *Contract Cleaning Maintenance, Inc. v. United States,* 811 F.2d 586, 592 (Fed. Cir. 1986).
[61] *Gauntt Constr. Co.,* ASBCA No. 33323, 87-3 BCA ¶ 20,221; *Mitcho, Inc.,* ASBCA No. 41847, 91-2 BCA ¶ 23,860; *Holk Dev., Inc.,* ASBCA No. 40579 et al., 90-3 BCA ¶ 23,086.
[62] *Metric Constr. Co. v. United States,* 1 Cl. Ct. 383, 392 (1983); *I.B.A. Co.,* ASBCA No. 37182, 89-1 BCA ¶ 21,576.

of the circumstances and communications between the parties.[63] For example, the following submissions have been found to be claims:

(1) A letter in which a contractor specified various items that a government audit had disallowed, but to which the contractor claimed entitlement. (The letter was viewed together with a prior letter from the contractor giving a detailed breakdown of the additional amounts to which the contractor believed it was entitled, and referring to the contractor's previous request for "funding of [a] back-wage demand.")[64]

(2) A letter sent by a company having a contract for transportation services at an Air Force base stating that the company viewed certain newly demanded bus service as beyond the contract's requirements, and specifically seeking "compensation of $11,000.04 per year, to be billed at $916.67 per month."[65]

(3) A letter from the contractor's attorney to the contracting officer that "expressed interest" in a final decision with respect to the contractor's request for contract reformation and that stated that the contractor was seeking a decision so that it could pursue its appeal routes under the CDA, if necessary.[66]

(4) Letters that, when taken together, showed the contractor protesting the payment of additional sums under a contract to purchase crude oil from the government and demanding that certain identified wire transfer payments comprising those sums be returned to the contractor.[67]

However, the claim must be made "by the contractor"; accordingly, a letter from the contractor's lawyer to the contracting officer has been held to be insufficient to establish a claim.[68] The burden is on the claimant to identify, specify and perfect its claims. For example, in *Mingus Constructors, Inc. v. United States*,[69] the contractor had complained of malicious harassment by the government's project representative during the construction of a road and had stated an intention to claim the added costs resulting from the alleged harassment. These complaints were made only in letter form. At the conclusion of the project, the contractor executed a standard final release form and added a notation to the release that it did not apply to "claims" stated in the earlier correspondence. The Federal Circuit affirmed the summary judgment granted

[63] *Transamerica Ins. Corp., Inc. v. United States*, 973, F.2d 1573 (Fed. Cir. 1992); *Winding Specialists Co., Inc.*, ASBCA No. 37765, 89-2 BCA ¶ 21,737; *Atlas Elevator Co., Inc. v. General Servs. Admin.*, GSBCA No. 11655, 93-1 BCA ¶ 25,216; *Penn Environmental Control, Inc.*; VABCA No. 3599, 93-3 BCA ¶ 26,021.
[64] *Contract Cleaning Maintenance*, fn. 60, *supra*.
[65] *Tecom, Inc. v. United States*, 732 F.2d 935, 937 (Fed. Cir. 1984).
[66] *Paragon Energy Corp. v. United States*, 645 F.2d 966, 976 (Ct. Cl. 1981).
[67] *Alliance Oil & Refining Co. v. United States*, 13 Cl. Ct. 496, 499–500 (1987).
[68] *Construction Equip. Lease v. United States*, 26 Cl. Ct. 341 (1992).
[69] 812 F.2d 1387 (Fed. Cir. 1987).

to the government, finding that the contractor had never properly identified, specified, or perfected its claims. As the claims were never properly made, the release barred the contractor from making a valid claim after it was executed.

Some decisions of the Claims Court and the Federal Circuit have emphasized the need for an explicit request for a final decision as part of the submission of a claim. However, in *Transamerica Ins. Corp., Inc. v. United States,*[70] the Federal Circuit specifically rejected a rule that a "claim" must include a specific request for a final decision. In particular, a formal demand for final decision has been held to be unnecessary if the claim gave a clear indication that a decision was desired.[71]

The existence of a dispute is an essential element of a claim.[72] Even though there is case law that there is no absolute requirement for a specific request for a final decision, there is a risk that the failure to make a specific request for a final decision will be viewed as evidence that there was no dispute between the parties sufficient to constitute a "claim" under the Act. For this reason, correspondence from a contractor that contains information detailing costs and, rather than demanding or requesting that the contracting officer issue a final decision, that merely expresses a willingness to reach an agreement, may not constitute a claim.[73] Similarly, the passage of time may not convert a proposal into a CDA claim. In *Santa Fe Eng'rs, Inc. v. Garrett,*[74] the contractor's certified proposal had been pending for more than two years, during which time parties met on several occasions to discuss the proposal and the contractor submitted additional information for the government's consideration. During that period of time, the contractor never asked for a contracting officer's final decision. The Federal Circuit affirmed the board decision,[75] which had concluded that the failure to ask for a contracting officer's final decision was an indication that the parties had not reached *an impasse* and that the matter was not sufficiently in dispute to constitute a CDA claim.

Often the decision whether a particular submission is a claim depends upon the totality of the circumstances. For example, in one case, a certified request for an equitable adjustment accompanied by a letter requesting a final decision did constitute a valid claim even though the letter also suggested the possibility,

---

[70] 973 F.2d at 1572 (Fed. Cir. 1992).

[71] *Cable Antenna Sys.,* ASBCA No. 36184, 90-3 BCA ¶ 23,203.

[72] *Esprit Corp. v. United States,* 6 Cl. Ct. 546, 549 (1984) ("The plaintiff's requests for contract modifications were never in dispute; they are therefore not claims"), *aff'd mem.,* 776 F.2d 1062 (Fed. Cir. 1985); *Dawco Constr., Inc. v. United States,* 930 F.2d 872 (F.2d. Cir. 1991); *CYR Constr. Co. v. United States,* 27 Fed. Cl. 153, 161–62 (1992).

[73] *Hoffman Constr. Co. v. United States,* 7 Cl. Ct. 518, 525 (1985). *See also Technassociates,* fn. 44, *supra,* at 209–10 (letters the contractor sent in order to get the contracting officer to negotiate with it "on the future direction of the contract" did not constitute claims).

[74] 991 F.2d 579, 1583–84 (Fed. Cir. 1993). However, in *D. H. Blattner & Sons, Inc.,* IBCA Nos. 2589, 2643, 89-3 BCA ¶ 22,230, the board held that a properly certified letter using the term "proposal" was not a claim. The Federal Circuit reversed this decision in an unpublished decision. *See Blattner & Sons, Inc. v. United States,* 909 F.2d 1495 (Fed. Cir. 1990).

[75] *Santa Fe Eng'rs, Inc.,* ASBCA No. 36292, 92-2 BCA ¶ 24,795.

or hope, of a negotiated resolution to the dispute.[76] In contrast, a letter sent to the contracting officer during negotiations on a proposal requesting that the matter be referred to an auditor did not qualify as a claim, because a contracting officer had not been asked to issue a decision.[77] Finally, the contractor may not submit a claim in an unspecified amount or in an amount that is open-ended.[78] A proper claim and request for a final decision exists only when the amount sought is either set forth in a "sum-certain"[79] or is determinable by a simple mathematical calculation or from the information provided by the contractor.[80]

19.9 CERTIFICATION REQUIREMENT

The CDA requires that a claim in excess of $100,000 be certified.[81] The purpose of the certification requirement is to discourage the submission of unwarranted or inflated contractor claims, to decrease litigation, and to encourage settlements.[82] Prior to October 29, 1992, compliance with the certification requirement was a prerequisite to invoking the disputes resolution procedures of the CDA. Until a claim in excess of $100,000 had been properly certified, interest did not begin to accrue,[83] the contracting officer could not issue a valid final decision,[84] and the contractor had no right of access to either a board or to the United States Court of Federal Claims (previously United States Claims Court).[85] Because the contracting officer did not have the authority to issue a final decision on a claim that had not been properly certified, a decision

[76] *Isles Eng'g & Constr., Inc. v. United States,* 26 Cl. Ct. 240, 243 (1992).

[77] *G.S.&L. Mechanical & Constr., Inc.,* DOT BCA No. 1856, 87-2 BCA ¶ 19,882; *see also Huntington Builders,* ASBCA No. 33945, 87-2 BCA ¶ 19,898, at 100,654–655 (letters to contracting officer that, when taken together, alleged defective specifications and requested a thirty-day time extension to contract and the release of monies withheld for liquidated damages did not constitute a claim because no specific monetary relief was requested for costs incurred as a result of the contractor's having to comply with the allegedly defective specifications).

[78] *Metric Constr. Co. v. United States,* 14 Cl. Ct. 177, 179–80 (1988) (contractor's submissions made it clear that contractor was seeking to recover extended home office overhead and third-party indemnification fees, but the submissions did not constitute a claim because the amount was not specified.

[79] Disputes clause ¶ (c), FAR § 52.233-1, 48 C.F.R. § 52.233-1. A claim for a "sum certain" that reserved the right to include additional line items to "modify the presentation" was, in fact, deemed to be a predicate for negotiations, rather than a CDA claim. *McElroy Machine & Mfg. Co., Inc.,* ASBCA No. 39416, 92-3 BCA ¶ 25,107.

[80] *Metric Constr. Co.* fn. 62, *supra,* at 392.

[81] 41 U.S.C. § 605(c)(1), (c)(2).

[82] *Paul E. Lehman, Inc. v. United States,* 230 Ct. Cl. 11, 14, 673 F.2d 352, 354 (1982).

[83] *Fidelity Constr. Co. v. United States,* 700 F.2d, 1379, 1382–85 (Fed. Cir. 1983).

[84] 41 U.S.C. § 605(c)(2); *Paul E. Lehman, Inc. v. United States,* 230 Ct. Cl. at 16, 673 F.2d at 355; *Paragon Energy Corp. v. United States,* 227 Ct. Cl. at 183–84, 645 F.2d at 971; *Conoc Constr. Corp. v. United States,* 3 Cl. Ct. 146, 147–48 (1983).

[85] *W. M. Schlosser Co. v. United States,* 705 F.2d 1336, 1338–39 (Fed. Cir. 1983); *Romala Corp. v. United States,* 12 Cl. Ct. 411, 412–13 (1987).

issued on an uncertified claim or an improperly certified claim was a nullity, and any appeal or suit was subject to dismissal.[86] The existence of a properly certified claim was a jurisdictional requirement that could not be waived or cured retroactively.[87]

Section 907(a) of the Federal Courts Administration Act of 1992, Pub. L. No. 102-572, which was signed into law on October 29, 1992 (1992 Amendment), significantly changed the Act regarding the certification of claims. The 1992 Amendment broadened the class of individuals who may certify claims to include anyone who is duly authorized to bind the contractor with respect to the claim. However, the 1992 Amendment required that the certification state that the individual signing the submission is authorized to do so. In addition, the Amendment provided that a defective certification would not operate to deprive a board or court of jurisdiction over the claim; however, the defective certification must be corrected before a decision can be rendered on the claim by the board or court. If the contracting officer receives a claim with a defective certification, the contracting officer is not required to issue a final decision on the claim if the contractor is advised in writing of the basis for the conclusion that the certification is inadequate within sixty days of the date of the contracting officer's receipt of the claim. Interest accrues on those claims subject to the 1992 Amendment from the later of October 29, 1992 or the date of receipt of the claim. Although the 1992 Amendment has general application, it expressly provides that it does not apply to claims pending at the boards of contract appeals or the United States Court of Federal Claims as of October 29, 1992. Accordingly, the preexisting case law continues to apply to those pending appeals or suits.

In connection with the certification requirement of government contract claims, it is important to understand the monetary threshold at which a claim must be certified, how it must be certified, who can certify it, and the relationship of that certification to other government contract certifications.

19.10 Monetary Threshold for Certification

The Act requires a certification when the contractor asserts a claim exceeding $100,000, therefore, it is not possible to bypass a certification requirement by breaking a claim into a series of separate claims each of which is $100,000 or less.[88] The test is whether these exists a "single, unitary claim based upon a common and related set of operative facts" that the contractor, unintentionally or otherwise, divided into separate and distinct claims.[89] However, if the claims

---

[86] *Paul E. Lehman, Inc. v. United States,* 230 Ct. Cl. 11, 673 F.2d 352.

[87] *W. H. Moseley Co. v. United States,* 677 F.2d 850 (Ct. Cl. 1982); *Echo West Constr.,* VABCA No. 3186, 90-3 BCA ¶ 23,106; *Chogging Ltd. v. United States,* 24 Cl. Ct. 407, 409 (1991); *Kaco Contracting Co.,* ASBCA No. 43066, 92-1 BCA ¶ 24,603.

[88] *Fidelity & Deposit Co. of Md. v. United States,* 2 Cl. Ct. 137, 143–43 (1983).

[89] *Warchol Constr. Co. v. United States,* 2 Cl. Ct. 384, 389 (1983). *See also LDG Timber Enters., Inc. v. United States,* 8 Cl. Ct. 445, 452 (1985).

are distinct and independent, with one claim having no relationship to the operative facts of the other claim, each independent claim of $100,000 or less need not be certified.[90] Even if the contractor submits a single letter to the contracting officer that reflects claims totaling more than $100,000, the certification is not required unless the claims arose from a common or related set of operative facts and are therefore truly a unitary claim.[91] In other words, does the claim or claims submitted by the contractor arise from the same or different events or causes of action?[92]

The following examples illustrate the application of this test. In one case, the contractor alleged that one differing site condition gave rise to three separate claims—one for additional paving costs, one for additional insurance, supervision and maintenance costs, and one for loss of interest on funds spent to perform additional work. The court concluded that, in fact, there was just one claim.[93] Similarly, when a contract was terminated for the convenience of the government, the court concluded that a contractor's demand for "pre-termination and post-termination items" constituted one claim because both items were directly related to the government's termination of the contract and the resolution of both items depended upon what, if any, liability the government incurred as a result of its action.[94] In another case, where the contract involved security guard services at five different locations in Boston, the court held that the contractor could not fragment its total dollar claim into separate claims based upon each of the different locations. The rationale was that the amounts claimed from the various locations were based upon the same operative facts (a total number of hours of services performed for which a total number of dollars allegedly was due).[95] In contrast, the Armed Services Board of Contract Appeal determined that where eighteen different claims arose from different causative events and were brought under different legal theories, such as differing site conditions and defective specifications, it was proper to separate the claims.[96]

19.11 Modification of Claim Amount

Sometimes a claim that initially does not exceed the certification threshold (and therefore is not certified) increases in amount after a contracting officer's decision is issued. In these circumstances, the question arises whether the contractor can still proceed on the basis of the increased claim before the court or board of contract appeals, or whether it is necessary for the contractor

[90] *Walsky Constr. Co. v. United States,* 3 Cl. Ct. 615, 619 (1983); *Little River Lumber Co. v. United States,* 21 Cl. Ct. 527 (1990); *C.B.C. Enter., Inc.,* ASBCA No. 43496, 92-2 BCA ¶ 24,803.
[91] *Placeway Constr. Corp. v. United States,* 910 F.2d 835 (Fed. Cir. 1990); *Spirit Leveling Contractors v. United States,* 19 Cl. Ct. 84 (1989).
[92] *Zinger Constr. Co.,* ASBCA No. 28788, 86-2 BCA ¶ 18,920.
[93] *Warchol Constr. Co.* fn. 89, *supra.*
[94] *Palmer & Sicard, Inc. v. United States,* 4 Cl. Ct. 420, 422–23 (1984).
[95] *Black Star Sec., Inc. v. United States,* 5 Cl. Ct. 110 (1984).
[96] *Zinger Constr. Co.,* fn. 92, *supra.*

to certify the claim in the increased amount and resubmit it to the contracting officer for a decision.

The question was addressed in *Tecom, Inc. v. United States.*[97] There, the contractor's claim was in an amount below the threshold for certification when it was submitted to the contracting officer. However, by the time the company filed its complaint before the Armed Services Board of Contract Appeals, the amount of the claim exceeded the threshold for certification. This increase was the result of two events that occurred after the contracting officer's decision: a reevaluation of the claim by the contractor and the government's exercise of an option to extend the contract for an additional year. Under these circumstances, the court held that it was not necessary for the contractor to certify and resubmit its claim.

Tecom stands for the proposition that a monetary claim properly considered by a contracting officer "need not be certified or recertified if that very same claim (but in an increased amount reasonably based on further information) comes before a board or a court."[98] The Federal Circuit stated that it would be disruptive of normal litigation procedures "if any increase in the amount of a claim based on matters developed in litigation before the court [or board] had to be submitted to the contracting officer before the court [or board] could continue to final resolution on the claim."[99] In a footnote, however, the *Tecom* court pointed out that its decision should not be taken as an invitation to seek to evade the certification requirement.[100] Thus a contractor who deliberately understates the amount of its original claim (with the intention of raising the amount on appeal on the basis of information that was readily

---

[97] Fn. 65, *supra,* at 935.

[98] *Id.* at 938.

[99] *Id.* at 937–38 (quoting *J. F. Shea Co. v. United States,* 4 Cl. Ct. 46, 54 (parentheticals in *Tecom*)). *Kunz Constr. Co. v. United States,* 12 Cl. Ct. 74, 79 (1987) (The court stated a contractor can enlarge dollar amount of its claim in court over what was presented to the contracting officer under two conditions: (1) if the increase is based on the same set of operative facts previously submitted to the contracting officer and (2) if the court finds that the contractor neither knew, nor reasonably should have known, at the time when the claim was presented to the contracting officer of the factors justifying the increase). *See also E. C. Schleyer Pump Co.,* ASBCA No. 33900, 87-3 BCA ¶ 19,986 (costs that were merely an additional area of damages from the same facts that were alleged in the claim could be brought before board even though not presented to the contracting officer); *Glenn v. United States,* 858 F.2d 1577, 1580 (Fed. Cir. 1988) (The contractor submitted a claim to the contracting officer in the amount of $31,500. Because the claim was less than $50,000, the contractor did not certify it. The contracting officer issued a final decision denying the claim, which the contractor appealed to the Armed Services Board of Contract Appeals. Thereafter, the contracting officer issued a second final decision. In that decision, the contracting officer stated that he was withholding $66,570.32 from the contractor (consisting of the $31,500 which the contractor previously had sought to recover and an additional $35,070.32). Relying on its prior decision in *Tecom,* the Federal Circuit held that it was not necessary for the contractor to certify its $66,570.32 claim before bringing suit in the Claims Court. "Because Glenn was not required to certify his $31,500 claim before the C.O., he need not have certified the $66,570.32 resulting from the denial of his initial claim . . . and [the] additional setoffs".)

[100] *Tecom,* fn. 65, supra at 938, n.2. *See D.E.W., Inc.,* ASBCA No. 35173, 89-3 BCA ¶ 22,008.

available at the time the claim first was submitted) may well find its subsequent suit in the Court of Federal Claims or its board appeal dismissed.[101]

19.12 CDA Certification Language

The CDA sets forth the language to be used in the certification. The contractor must certify "that the claim is made in good faith, that the supporting data are accurate and complete to the best of [the contractor's] knowledge and belief, and that the amount requested accurately reflects the contract adjustment for which the contractor believes the Government is liable."[102] The procurement regulations,[103] as well as the Disputes clause utilized in contracts covered by the CDA,[104] contain identical language. The 1992 Amendment to the Act added a fourth element to the certification. This element requires that the person signing the certification state that "the certifier is duly authorized to certify the claim on behalf of the contractor."[105]

Under the pre-1992 statutory language, the boards, the United States Claims Court and the Court of Appeals for the Federal Circuit developed strict rules applicable to the certification requirements. These rules, in conjunction with the holding that the submission of a proper certification for any claim in excess of $50,000 (now $100,000) was a jurisdictional requirement,[106] created extensive problems for claimants and their counsel. While the 1992 Amendment reversed the rule that the submission of a valid certification was a jurisdictional requirement that could not be waived, it is possible that questions regarding the form of the certification will remain. To the extent that the cases interpreting the pre-Amendment Act provide guidance regarding the proper wording of a certification, it is probable that these decisions will still be relied upon by the boards and the courts.

Prior to the 1992 Amendment, there was a split in authority regarding the contractor's obligation to strictly track the statutory certification language in order to submit a valid certification. One line of cases took a very formalistic view and held that any deviation from the statutory language would be subject to strict scrutiny. In those cases, a contractor's attempt to deviate from the statutory language by substituting alternate language was usually held to invalidate the certification.[107] A second line of cases held that *substantial*

---

[101] *Id.* Even the reduction of a claim below the $50,000 threshold at the board will not eliminate the need for a certification if the claim, as submitted to the contracting officer, exceeded $50,000. *Building Sys. Contractors,* VABCA Nos. 2749 et al., 89-2 BCA ¶ 21,678.

[102] 41 U.S.C. § 605(c)(1).

[103] FAR § 33.207(a); 48 C.F.R. § 33.207(a).

[104] FAR § 52.233-1; 48 C.F.R. § 52.233-1.

[105] 41 U.S.C. § 605(c)(7).

[106] *Skelly & Loy,* fn. 44, *supra; Paul E. Lehman v. United States,* fn. 82, *supra; Environmental Specialists, Inc. v. United States,* 23 Cl. Ct. 751 (1991); *Guilanani Contracting Co., Inc.,* ASBCA No. 41435, 91-2 BCA ¶ 23,774; *Kaco Contracting,* fn. 87, *supra.*

[107] *Centex Constr. Co., Inc.,* ASBCA No. 35338, 89-1 BCA ¶ 21,259; *Liberty Envtl Specialties, Inc.,* VABCA No. 2948, 89-3 BCA ¶ 21,982.

compliance was sufficient and that the inadvertent omission of a few words in the certification and the omission of the claimed amount, which was stated elsewhere in the claim, were not fatal defects.[108] In general, any certification must simultaneously state all elements of the statutory requirements, and an effort to satisfy the certification requirement by reference to multiple letters or by piecemeal submissions has not been deemed to be sufficient to satisfy the statutory requirement.[109]

In endorsing the substantial compliance approach, the GSBCA accepted a certification that omitted any reference to "knowledge or belief." The board held that this unqualified certification "more fully exposed [the contractor] to potential liability" for false statements than "if it had mimicked the words of the statute."[110] In contrast, the ASBCA has held that a failure to state that the contractor "believes" the government is liable invalidates the certification.[111] In addition, the following submissions were found not to meet the requirements of the Act:

(1) A certification that varied from the language of the statute and the Disputes clause by referring to "all data used" instead of the "supporting data" for the claim (thereby restricting the certification to "unidentified data [which the contractor] chose to use while the statute requires certification of all data that support the claim").[112]

(2) A certification that omitted the assertion that the supporting data was accurate and complete.[113]

(3) A letter in which a contractor demanded money damages that "probably exceeded $150,000" and in which the contractor's president stated that the claim was being made in good faith and wrote, "the supporting data is accurate and complete to the best of my knowledge and belief, and . . . the amount(s), unknown at this time, accurately reflect the contract adjustment for which the government is liable."[114]

(4) A certification in which the contractor stated that it would not assume any legal obligations that it would not have without the certification, that the data submitted was "as accurate and complete as practicable," and that the contractor was not demanding a "particular amount."[115]

---

[108] *United States v. General Elec. Corp.*, 727 F.2d 1567, 1569 (Fed. Cir. 1984); *Young Enter., Inc. v. United States*, 26 Cl. Ct. 858, 862 (1992); *P. J. Dick, Inc. v. General Serv. Admin.*, GSBCA No. 11847, et al., 93-1 BCA ¶ 25,263.

[109] *W. H. Moseley Co. v. United States*, fn. 87, *supra*, at 852; *Parriono Enters. v. United States*, 230 Ct. Cl. 1052 (1982); *Black Star Sec.* fn. 95, *supra* at 110,117.

[110] *P. J. Dick, Inc.*, fn. 108, *supra*, at 126,605.

[111] *C. F. Elecs.*, ASBCA No. 4077, 91-2 BCA ¶ 23,746.

[112] *Gauntt Constr.*, fn. 61, *supra*, at 102,412.

[113] *Raymond Kaiser Eng'rs, Inc./Kaiser Steel Corp., A Joint Venture*, ASBCA No. 34133, 87-3 BCA ¶ 20,140, at 101,940-41.

[114] *T.J.D. Servs.*, fn. 44, *supra*, at 257, 259.

[115] *Cochran Constr. Co.*, ASBCA No. 34378, 87-3 BCA ¶ 19,993 at 101,280-81, *aff'd on reconsideration*, 87-3 BCA ¶ 20,114.

By contrast in another case, a contractor whose certification did not contain the amount of the claim involved and did not have the words "the amount requested accurately reflects the contract adjustment for which the contractor believes the government is liable" still was found to be in substantial compliance with the certification requirement. The statement in which the certification was contained did have the remainder of the elements required by the Act, and, when the statement was read in its entirety and together with documents that accompanied it, all of the information and statements required by the statute were found to be present.[116] Notwithstanding the degree of flexibility that *may* be allowed, the prudent course is to track the language of the Act when certifying a claim.

19.13 Supporting Data

A contractor who certifies its claim by tracking the language of the statute may still find itself confronted with the argument that the data supporting its claim is inadequate for purposes of the certification requirement. For the most part, though, neither the courts nor the boards have taken an overly stringent attitude with respect to the extent of the supporting data.

In *Metric Constr. Co. v. United States,*[117] the government argued that the contractor's certification was defective because the contractor had failed to attach copies of the pertinent change order modifications to its claim. In rejecting the government's argument, the court observed that the certification requirement "was not intended, nor should it be so construed, to require a full evidentiary presentation before the contracting officer."[118] The court noted that the contracting officer had not denied the contractor's claim for lack of supporting data and that the data that had been presented had assisted the contracting officer "in making a meaningful determination on the dispute before him."[119]

The DOE Board of Contract Appeals took a similar position and cited *Metric* with approval in *Newhall Refining Co.*[120] There, in response to the government's argument that the contractors involved had not submitted accurate and complete supporting data when they certified their claims, the board noted that, on their face, the certifications met the requirements of the Act, that the claims were "articulated in a clear and concise fashion," that the contractors had notified the contracting officer of the basis for their claims prior to submitting them, and that the contracting officer already was in possession of information relating to the claims.[121] The board also noted the fact that the claims before it involved a legal issue of contract interpretation,

---

[116] *General Elec. Corp.*, fn. 108, *supra,* at 1569.
[117] 1 Cl. Ct. 383 (1983).
[118] *Id.* at 391.
[119] *Id.*
[120] EBCA Nos. 363-7-86, et al., 87-1 BCA ¶ 19,340.
[121] 87-1 BCA ¶ 19,340 at 97,583.

and it found "highly persuasive" the fact that the contracting officer had not requested additional information from the contractors.[122] Under these circumstances, the board determined that the data submitted with the claims was "adequate."[123]

These cases suggest that when the language of the contractor's certification meets the requirements of the Act and the contracting officer is provided with the needed information to render a final decision and has issued a final decision, the contractor probably does not have to worry about having its case derailed by the contention at the board or court that it failed to submit adequate supporting data.

19.14 Who May Certify the Claim?

The CDA is silent on the question of who must sign the certification on behalf of the contractor and the degree of personal knowledge that the person certifying the claim must have regarding the underlying facts set forth in the claim. The regulations and the Disputes clause, however, address the question of who must certify the claim. Prior to the 1992 Amendment to the Act, they provided as follows:

(c)(1) If the contractor is an individual, the certification shall be executed by that individual.

(2) If the contractor is not an individual, the certification shall be executed by

(i) A senior company official in charge at the contractor's plant or location involved; or

(ii) An officer or general partner of the contractor having overall responsibility for the conduct of the contractor's affairs.[124]

Since nearly all contractors are corporations, the cases have focused on certifications under (c)(2) above. Under one element of the pre-1992 regulation and clause, the claim could be certified by a corporate official with overall responsibility for the contractor's affairs. The Federal Circuit held that a corporate officer—a senior vice president and treasurer—whose responsibility was limited to financial affairs and who could not pursue a claim without his superiors' approval was not qualified to certify the claim because he did not have sufficient "overall responsibility" and was not truly "in charge."[125] This ruling led to extensive litigation regarding the authority of the person certifying the claim. While the boards and the courts did *not* adopt a rule that only

---

[122] *Id.*
[123] *Id.*
[124] 48 C.F.R. § 33.207(c)(2).
[125] *United States v. Grumman Aerospace,* 927 F.2d 575 (Fed. Cir. 1991). However, it is possible to have "overall responsibility" and still report to another individual. *See Johnson Controls World Service v. United States,* 987 F.2d 738 (Fed. Cir. 1993).

the CEO could certify claims, the boards carefully examined the facts and circumstances to determine the extent of the certifier's actual authority in order to determine whether the individual certifying the claim met the "overall responsibility" standard.[126]

The alternate standard required that the certifier be a senior company official in charge at the plant or a location involved. Again, the boards and the Federal Circuit adopted rather strict standards to determine whether the person satisfied the test of being both a senior company official and "in charge" at the plant or location involved. Thus in some cases a project manager with overall responsibility for a single significant contract was not considered to be a senior company official.[127] In other cases, a vice president for operations who was a senior company official was not considered to be "in charge" at the plant or location involved because that person made relatively infrequent visits to the actual project site and maintained contact with the project primarily by means of telephone calls with the on-site project manager.[128] In any event, it does not appear to be permissible for the contractor's attorney to certify the claim.[129]

Except for claims pending at the boards or Court of Federal Claims on the date of the enactment of the 1992 Amendment to the CDA,[130] questions of a person's authority to certify a claim should be minimal, so long as the certifier follows the language of the Amendment that requires the express representation that the person signing the certification is authorized to do so. In that context, it is not necessary for the person certifying the claim to have personal knowledge of the facts and data supporting the claim. Rather, it is sufficient for the person certifying the claim to rely upon data and facts developed by others within the contractor's organization.[131]

19.15 Other Certification Requirements

The complexity of the CDA certification is only compounded by the fact that there are at least two other claim related certifications that a contractor may be required to submit under other statutes. The DOD Appropriations Authorization Act of 1979[132] required that any claim, request for equitable

---

[126] *Newport News Shipbuilding & Dry Dock Co.*, ASBCA No. 33244, 91-2 BCA ¶ 23,865; *Ingalls Shipbuilding, Inc.*, ASBCA No. 38323, 91-2 BCA ¶ 23,904; *Fireman's Fund Ins. Co.*, ASBCA No. 38284, 91-1 BCA ¶ 23,439. *But see PCL Civil Constructors, Inc.*, ASBCA No. 41881, 91-2 BCA ¶ 23,906.

[127] *J. A. Jones Constr. Co.*, ASBCA No. 38827, 92-1 BCA ¶ 24,377; *Harbert Int'l, Inc.*, ASBCA Nos. 41144, 41571, 91-3 BCA ¶ 24,121; *Al Johnson Constr. v. United States*, 19 Cl. Ct. 732 (1990); *but see Western States Constr. Co.*, ASBCA No. 37611, 91-2 BCA ¶ 24,418.

[128] *Pizzagalli Constr. Co.*, ASBCA No. 43309, 92-2 BCA ¶ 24,834; *Clearwater Constructors, Inc.*, ASBCA No. 42665, 92-1 BCA ¶ 24,450; *See Reliance Ins. Co. v. United States*, 23 Cl. Ct. 108 (1991), *aff'd*, 932 F.2d 981 (Fed. Cir. 1991).

[129] *Romala Corp.*, fn. 85, *supra*, at 412–13; *T.J.D. Servs.*, fn. 44, *supra*, at 261–62.

[130] 41 U.S.C. § 605(c)(7).

[131] *Fischbach & Moore Int'l Corp. v. Christopher*, 987 F.2d 759, 762 (Fed. Cir. 1993).

[132] 10 U.S.C. § 2410.

adjustment to the contract terms, or request for relief under Public Law 85-804 that exceeds $100,000 must be certified. In addition to following the language of the CDA certification, the DFARS Regulation[133] that implements this certification requirement has been expanded to require that if a claim for an equitable adjustment is made under a completed or substantially completed contract, the certification must state that the claim only includes the cost for performing the change, that the claim is not for already reimbursed costs, and that all claimed indirect costs are allowable. In addition, the certification on a completed contract must state that the person who signs the claim is aware that the submission of a false claim can result in significant criminal and civil penalties and fines.

A third certification is required by the Truth in Negotiations Act.[134] There are significant differences between the Truth in Negotiations certificate and the two certificates previously discussed. Under the Truth in Negotiations Act, the certificate is not provided until the parties reach agreement on a price—at the time of the handshake. The basic threshold for a Truth in Negotiations certificate is $500,000 for contracts as well as subcontracts and modifications under such contracts.[135] The Truth in Negotiations Act provides a specific remedy when the data does not meet the requirements of accuracy, currency and completeness. Under the Act and the related regulations, the government is entitled to a price reduction if the data is found to be defective, that is inaccurate, not current, or not complete.[136]

These certification requirements overlap to some extent. However, there are sufficient differences that confusion can develop. Table 1 on the facing page contains a chart which compares the current requirements set forth in each of these statutes and their implementing regulations.

19.16   SUBCONTRACTOR CLAIM CERTIFICATION

Submission and CDA certification of subcontractor claims can present problems for prime contractors. To varying degrees, the prime may not fully agree with the positions asserted by the subcontractor. In addition, it is likely that the prime contractor must, to some extent, rely on data and information developed outside of its organization. Notwithstanding these practical problems, both the boards and the courts have held that the certification of a subcontractor's claim must be signed by the prime contractor.[137]

---

[133] 48 C.F.R. § 252.233–7000.

[134] 10 U.S.C. § 2306a. This statute applies only to the Department of Defense and the National Aeronautical and Space Administration (NASA). By regulation, the requirements of this statute have been extended to the civilian agencies. 48 C.F.R. § 15.804; 48 C.F.R. § 52.215-22; 48 C.F.R. § 52.215-2; 48 C.F.R. § 52.215-24 and 48 C.F.R. § 52.215-25.

[135] 10 U.S.C. § 2306a. The threshold amount is subject to adjustment every five years beginning on October 1, 1995.

[136] *Id.*

[137] *Harrington Assoc., Inc.,* GSBCA No. 6795, 82-2 BCA ¶ 16,103; *Johnson Controls,* fn. 48, *supra.*

Table 1   Claim/proposal certification comparison

	Contract Disputes Act (CDA)	Defense Authorization Act (DOD Contracts)	Truth in Negotiations Act
Language:	1) Claim made in good faith.	1) Claim made in good faith.	Data in support of proposal is accurate, current, and complete.
	2) Supporting data accurate and complete to best of contractor's knowledge and belief.	2) Supporting data accurate and complete to the best of contractor's knowledge and belief.	
	3) Amount requested accurately reflects adjustment for which contractor believes government liable.	3) Amount requested accurately reflects adjustment for which contractor believes government liable.	
	4) Certifier is duly authorized to certify the claim on behalf of the contractor.	4) Certifier is duly authorized to certify the claim on behalf of the contractor.	
$ Threshold:	Claim > $100,000.	Claim or request for adjustment > $100,000.	Price or adjustment: Over $500,000 (subject to adjustment for inflation to nearest $50,000 every five years).
Certified by:	"Any person duly authorized to bind the contractor with respect to the claim."	"Any person duly authorized to bind the contractor with respect to the claim."	"The contractor"—anyone authorized to sign contractual documents.
Date Required:	When submitted as a "claim" under CDA.	Upon submission of a claim, request for equitable adjustment, or request for extraordinary relief.	At time of agreement ("handshake") on price.

The prime contractor is not entitled to qualify its certificate by stating that it is "based on" a certificate provided by the subcontractor.[138] Absolute agreement with the subcontractor's claim is not essential, as the prime contractor may certify a claim with which it does not fully agree, if it concludes the subcontractor's claim is made in good faith and is not frivolous.[139] However, in *Arnold M. Diamond, Inc.*,[140] the prime contractor, which had previously attacked the subcontractor's claim, certified it only on the order of a federal bankruptcy court. Even though the wording of the certification was proper, the ASBCA held that compliance with the order of a bankruptcy court was not sufficient to demonstrate a contractor's good faith in certifying the subcontractor's claim because the prime contractor's actions and assertions in the bankruptcy court demonstrated that it did not believe that there was sufficient ground to support the claim. The Federal Circuit reversed the board and held that a certification made at the direction of the court satisfied the good faith certification requirement and supplanted requirement that the prime contractor endorse the basic validity of the subcontractor's claim.[141]

Efforts to soften this rule by application of substantial compliance principles was rejected by the Claims Court in *Century Constr. Co. v. United States*.[142] In *Century*, the prime contractor submitted the necessary certification for the subcontractor's claim but, as to the third element of the certification, certified that the amount reflected the adjustment for which the "subcontractor," rather than the "contractor," believed the government is liable. The Claims Court held that this was insufficient because it failed to provide the "requisite assurance" of the contractor's belief in the legitimacy of the sub's claim, that is that there was good ground for the amount sought.

19.17 GOVERNMENT CLAIMS

The CDA also covers government claims. The Act provides that "[a]ll claims by the Government against a contractor relating to a contract shall be the subject of a decision by the contracting officer."[143] The one exception to this

---

[138]*Cox Constr. Co.*, ASBCA No. 31072, 85-3 BCA ¶ 18,507.

[139] *United States v. Turner Constr. Co.*, 827 F.2d 1554 (Fed. Cir. 1987).

[140] ASBCA No. 40885, 93-2 BCA ¶ 25,680.

[141] *Arnold M. Diamond v. Dalton*, 25 F.3d 1006 (Fed. Cir. 1994).

[142] 22 Cl. Ct. 63 (1990).

[143] 41 U.S.C. § 605(a). The cases indicated that the boards may decline jurisdiction over a government counterclaim where the counterclaim was never presented to the contractor nor was the contractor given an opportunity to comment on it. These decisions seem to reflect an application of the rule that it is necessary for the matter to be "in dispute" in order to have a CDA claim. *See, Instruments & Controls Serv. Co.*, ASBCA No. 38332, 89-3 BCA ¶ 22,237, *Osborn Eng'g Co.*, DOT CAB No. 2165, 90-2 BCA ¶ 22,749. *But see Security Servs., Inc.*, GSBCA No. 11052, 92-1 BCA ¶ 24,704. In *Security Servs.*, the GSBCA concluded that the contracting officer had the discretion to either first negotiate the claim *or* issue a final decision. Similarly, a contracting officer's refusal to negotiate a government claim before issuing a final decision did not negate the finality of that decision. *Siebe North, Inc. & Norton Co.*, ASBCA No. 34366, 89-1 BCA ¶ 21,487.

rule is the situation where the government asserts a fraud claim against a contractor. Such a claim need not be the subject of a contracting officer's final decision.[144] Moreover, such claims are generally beyond the jurisdiction of the boards or the Court of Federal Claims.[145]

All government demands are not government claims. For example, the ASBCA has refused to consider an appeal in which the government demanded that a contractor repair defective work. Although the government directed the contractor to perform the work and the contractor disputed that it was required to do so without additional compensation, the board held that there was no government claim that could be appealed until the government either defaulted the contractor or the contractor did the work and submitted a claim.[146]

The question of when a claim is a government claim or a contractor's claim requiring certification to obtain a final decision has not been answered consistently by the boards and the courts. The ASBCA, GSBCA, AGBCA, and NASA BCA have held that the government's withholding of payment due a contractor is a government claim that does not require contractor certification.[147] Similarly, a demand for repayment of money allegedly paid to the contractor by mistake is a government claim and no contractor certification is required.[148]

Certain boards have held that where a contracting officer assesses liquidated damages in a final decision, a government claim exists and no certification is required.[149] One board has indicated that the burden of proof determines whose claim it is.[150] The Claims Court, however, has required a contractor to certify a claim for the return of liquidated damages that the government withheld from payments due the contractor, apparently because undisputed delays occurred that the contractor claimed were caused by the government.[151] Thus, although a government claim for liquidated damages need not be certified, a contractor's claim to recover amounts withheld as liquidated damages must be certified.[152]

Even if the contractor is not required to submit or certify a claim because it is considered to be the government's claim, submission of a claim by the contractor is probably needed in order to create the basis to recover CDA

---

[144] *Martin J. Simko Constr., Inc. v. United States,* 852 F.2d 540 (Fed. Cir. 1988).

[145] *Warren Beaves d/b/a/ Commercial Marine Servs.,* DOT CAB No. 1324, 83-1 BCA ¶ 16,232; *Comada Corp.,* ASBCA No. 26599, 83-2 BCA ¶ 16,681. *But see, Martin J. Simko* fn. 144, *supra.*

[146] *H. B. Zachry Co.,* ASBCA No. 39209, 90-1 BCA ¶ 22,342.

[147] *Mutual Maintenance Co., Inc.,* GSBCA No. 7496, 85-2 BCA ¶ 18,098; *Perkins & Will,* ASBCA No. 28335, 84-1 BCA ¶ 16,953; *General Dynamics Corp.,* ASBCA No. 31359, 86-3 BCA ¶ 19,008; *TEM Assocs., Inc.,* NASA BCA No. 33-0990, 91-2 BCA ¶ 23,730; *Alaska Lumber & Pulp Co., Inc.* AGBCA No. 83-301-1, et al., 91-2 BCA ¶ 23,890.

[148] *PX Eng'g Co., Inc.,* ASBCA No. 40714, 90-3 BCA ¶ 23,253.

[149] *Evergreen Intern. Aviation, Inc.,* PSBCA No. 2468, 89-2 BCA ¶ 21,712.

[150] *Equitable Life Ins. Soc'y of the United States,* GSBCA No. GS-7699R, 87-2 BCA ¶ 19,733.

[151] *Warchol Constr.,* fn. 89, *supra,* at 392–93.

[152] *Sun Eagle Corp. v. United States,* 23 Cl. Ct. 465 (1991).

interest on the funds held by the government. Many government claims, for example, the assessment of liquidated damages or deductive changes, may result in the government withholding funds that are otherwise due under the contract. Even if the government's position is eventually determined to have no merit, the contractor is not entitled to receive CDA interest on those funds *unless* it submits a CDA claim.[153]

19.18   NOTICE REQUIREMENTS

Lack of timely notice of a potential claim is often a costly omission for contractors. Factual and objective notice is good business. It provides an opportunity for the agency to address a problem before it becomes a costly dispute. To assist with the identification of notice requirements, a Notice Checklist should be prepared for each project. The checklist should be based on a thorough review of the contract. The checklist should identify the clause, the time requirements for notice, the subject matter of the notice, whether the notice must be in writing, and the stated consequences for failing to give timely notice.

Regardless of your general familiarity with government construction contracts and their clauses, each contract should be reviewed as "standard" contracts often contain special notice requirements. A notice checklist can be easily summarized on a single sheet of paper that is three hole punched and retained in the project manual. A few hours of review time at the project's start may save you thousands of dollars later. While a notice checklist can take various formats, the sample checklist on the facing page reflects a summary of three of the standard government contract clauses with critical notice requirements.

19.19   STATUTE OF LIMITATIONS ON CLAIMS BY THE CONTRACTOR OR THE GOVERNMENT

Initially, the CDA contained no statute of limitations. Consequently, the primary issue related to the timeliness of claims related to the obligation to provide timely notice. In 1994, the CDA was amended to establish a statute of limitations on claims by either the contractor or the government.

As amended, the CDA provides that "each claim" relating to a contract shall be submitted within six years after the accrual of the claim."[154] However, in amending the CDA, Congress did not define the term "accrual." Initially, the Federal Acquisition Regulatory Council ("FAR Council") proposed a definition of "accrual" that would have required a contractor to submit its

---

[153] *General Motors Corp.,* ASBCA No. 35634, 92-3 BCA ¶ 25,149.
[154] 41 U.S.C. § 605(a).

Notice Checklist - Government Construction Contract				
Clause Reference	Subject Matter of Notice	Time Requirements for Notice	Writing Required	Stated Consequences of a Lack of Notice
Changes FAR 52.243-4	Proposal for adjustment.	30 DAYS from receipt of a written change order from the Government or written notification of a constructive change by the contractor.	Yes	Claim may not be allowed. Notice requirement may be waived until final payment
Constructive Changes FAR 52.243-4	Date, circumstances and source of the order and that the contractor regards the Government's order as a contract change.	No starting point stated, but notice within 20 DAYS of incurring any additional costs due to the constructive change fully protects the contractor's rights.	Yes	Costs incurred more than 20 DAYS prior to giving notice cannot be recovered, except in the case of defective specifications.
Differing Site Conditions FAR 52.236-2	Existence of unknown or materially different conditions affecting the contractor's cost.	From the time such conditions are identified, notice must be furnished "promptly" and before such conditions are disturbed.	Yes	Claim not allowed. Lack of notice may be waived until final payment.

claims within six years after the contractor "knew or should have known the facts and circumstances giving rise to the issue in controversy."[155] The proposed definition of "accrual" failed to mention whether it applied to government claims of any type. Public comments criticizing the proposed regulation focused on the failure to state a single test for "accrual" that applied to claims by either the government or the contractor, the use of the "giving rise to the issue" standard, and the failure of the proposed regulation to address the application of the new statute of limitations to existing contracts.[156]

The FAR Council's final regulations substantively addressed many of these concerns.[157] The final regulation states that the six-year period does *not* apply to contracts awarded prior to October 1, 1995. In adopting a final regulatory definition of "accrual," the FAR Council expressly made the term "accrual" applicable to claims by either the contractor or the government, except for government claims based on a contractor claim involving fraud. The final regulation defined "accrual of a claim" as follows:

> [T]he date when all events, which fix the alleged liability of either the Government or the contractor and permit assertion of the claim, were known or should have been known. For liability to be fixed, some injury must have occurred. However, monetary damages need not have been incurred.[158]

This definition of "accrual" may still stimulate questions regarding what constitutes "injury" when monetary damages have not been incurred. In any event, contractors must remember that there can be a distinction between the submission of an equitable adjustment proposal and a CDA claim. Submission of the former may not satisfy the six year submission requirement if it is determined that the equitable adjustment proposal was not a "CDA claim."[159]

19.20   LACHES AS A DEFENSE

Even if a contractor is not subject to a statute of limitations defense for the untimely submission of a claim, the government may be able to establish that the late submission of the claim sufficiently prejudiced the government and that the claim should be barred by the doctrine of laches. In *Rudolf Bieraeugel*,[160] the contractor submitted its final invoice for payment in 1983. It was apparently not paid by the agency. In 1986, the contractor raised the issue of nonpayment, at which time the contracting officer asserted that the invoice had been paid. Six years later the contractor retained an agent to assist in the

---

[155] 60 Fed. Reg. 2630 (January 10, 1995).
[156] 63 Fed. Cont. Rep. 375 (1995).
[157] 60 Fed. Reg. 48.224 (1995).
[158] FAR 33.201.
[159] *See Reflectone, Inc. v. Dalton*, 60 F.3d 1572 (Fed. Cir. 1995).
[160] ASBCA No. 47145, 95-1 BCA ¶ 27,536.

resolution of the issue and a formal claim was not presented until 1993. The board rejected the claim relying on the doctrine of laches. The board concluded that the government's ability to defend against the claim was prejudiced by the destruction of records in 1989, 1990, or 1991 in accordance with established policy, the death of the key employee of the contractor, and the disappearance of the contracting officer's representative.

19.21 CONTRACTING OFFICER'S DECISION

Once a claim meeting all the requirements of the CDA has been submitted, the next step in the dispute resolution process is the issuance of a contracting officer's decision. The issuance of a valid contracting officer's decision, or the failure to issue such a decision within the time allowed by the Act, is a prerequisite to bringing suit on the claim in the Court of Federal Claims or filing an appeal with an agency board of contract appeals.[161]

19.22 Time Allowed for Issuing the Decision

The CDA provides that in the case of claims of $100,000 or less, the contracting officer will issue a decision within sixty days of receipt of a written request from the contractor that a decision be issued within that period.[162] For claims over $100,000, the Act provides that, within sixty days of receipt of a certified claim, the contracting officer will issue a decision or notify the contractor of the time within which a decision will be issued.[163] With regard to claims submitted after, or pending before the contracting officer as of October 29, 1992, the contracting officer has no obligation to render a decision on a claim accompanied by a defective certification so long as the contracting officer notifies the contractor in writing of the basis for the conclusion that the certification is defective within sixty days of the date of receipt of the claim.

The Act states that contracting officer's decisions are to be issued "within a reasonable time" in accordance with agency regulations, taking into account such factors as the size and complexity of the claim and the adequacy of the information in support of the claim.[164] Thus although the CDA does not require a full evidentiary submission in order to recognize a claim,[165] it is in a contractor's interest to make its claim submission clear, persuasive and understandable.

The CDA also provides that, in the event of undue delay on the part of the contracting officer in issuing a decision, a contractor may request the appropriate agency board of contract appeals to direct that a final decision

---

[161] *Milmark Servs., Inc. v. United States,* 231 Ct. Cl. 954, 956 (1982).
[162] 41 U.S.C. § 605(c)(1).
[163] 41 U.S.C. § 605(c)(2).
[164] 41 U.S.C. § 605(c)(3).
[165] *Metric Constr.,* fn. 62, *supra,* at 391.

be issued in a specified period of time, as determined by the board.[166] In making such a request to a board, the contractor should be sure that it has provided the contracting officer with all the information reasonably necessary for a proper review of the claim and the issuance of a decision.

Any failure by a contracting officer to issue a decision on a claim within the period required by the Act or directed by a board of contract appeals is deemed to be a decision by the contracting officer denying the claim ("deemed denied" decision), and such failure authorizes the commencement of suit in the Court of Federal Claims or an appeal to the appropriate board.[167] The fact that contracting officer fails to issue a decision, however, does not mean that the government is barred from contesting the claim in subsequent proceedings. Failure to issue a decision is deemed a denial, not a default.[168]

A contractor should be aware, however, that even when a claim is properly submitted and the contracting officer fails to issue a decision, the Court of Federal Claims or a board of contract appeals still has the option of staying proceedings for the purpose of obtaining a decision on the claim.[169] It is reasonable to expect, however, that the Court of Federal Claims or a board will not be inclined to exercise this option in the situation where the contracting officer involved has been directed by a board to issue a decision but has failed to do so, or in a situation where the contracting officer gave no reason for the failure to issue a decision.

19.23   Contents of the Decision

The CDA requires that each contracting officer's decision "state the reasons for the decision reached and . . . inform the contractor of his rights as provided in [the Act]. Specific findings of fact are not required, but, if made, shall not be binding in any subsequent proceeding."[170]

FAR § 33.211[171] also sets forth the procedure that the contracting officer is to follow if a claim by or against a contractor cannot be settled by mutual agreement. In preparing the final decision, the contracting officer is directed to include the following:

(1) Description of the claim or dispute
(2) Reference to pertinent contract terms
(3) Statement of the factual areas of agreement and disagreement
(4) Statement of the final decision, with supporting rationale

---

[166] 41 U.S.C. § 605(c)(4).
[167] 41 U.S.C. § 605(c)(5).
[168] *Maki v. United States,* 13 Cl. Ct. 779, 782 (1987).
[169] 41 U.S.C. § 605(c)(5).
[170] 41 U.S.C. § 605(a).
[171] 48 C.F.R. § 38.211.

(5) In the case of a final decision that the contractor is indebted to the government, a demand for payment in accordance with FAR § 32.610(b)

As a practical matter, the extent of the findings of fact and the rationale provided in the final decision can vary greatly, depending upon the nature of the dispute and the specific contracting officer. While the degree of detail and explanation may vary, every final decision is required by regulation[172] to contain a paragraph that reads substantially as follows:

> This is the final decision of the Contracting Officer. You may appeal this decision to the Board of Contract Appeals. If you decide to appeal, you must, within 90 days from the date you receive this decision, mail or otherwise furnish written notice to the Board of Contract Appeals and provide a copy to the Contracting Officer from whose decision the appeal is taken. The notice shall indicate that an appeal is intended, reference this decision, and identify the contract by number. Instead of appealing to the Board of Contract Appeals, you may bring an action directly in the United States Court of Federal Claims (except as provided in the Contract Disputes Act of 1978, 41 U.S.C. 603, regarding Maritime Contracts) within 12 months of the date you receive this decision. If you appeal to the Board of Contract Appeals, you may, solely at your election, proceed under the Board's small claims procedure for claims of $50,000 or less or its accelerated procedure for claims of $100,000 or less.

A contracting officer's final decision that fails to contain this paragraph may be defective.[173] A final decision that fails to correctly notify a contractor of its appeal rights may not trigger the running of the period for filing an appeal with the appropriate board of contract appeals or filing suit in the Court of Federal Claims if the contractor was prejudiced by the omission of that information from the final decision.[174] Since the receipt of the final decision generally triggers the time periods for an appeal or filing of a suit, the FAR directs the contracting officer to furnish the contractor a copy of the decision by certified mail, return receipt requested, or any other method that provides evidence of receipt.[175]

Notwithstanding the statutory requirement that the contracting officer act on claims within specific time frames, a contractor and its counsel must consider whether to petition the board to set a deadline for a final decision or to commence formal proceedings by filing an appeal or a suit on a deemed

---

[172] *Id.* If the required language regarding appeal rights is incorrect or absent, the decision is defective and not final. *Wolverine Supply Co.*, ASBCA No. 39250, 90-2 BCA ¶ 22,706. However, the contractor may appeal a defective decision. *Technical Support Servs., Inc.*, ASBCA No. 37976, 89-1 BCA ¶ 21,518.

[173] *Pathman Constr. v. United States*, 817 F.2d 1573, 1578 (Fed. Cir. 1987).

[174] *Decker & Co. v. West* 76 F.3d 1573 (Fed. Cir. 1996).

[175] 48 C.F.R. § 33.211.

denied basis if the contracting officer fails to act on the claim.[176] One practical consideration is that a board or the court may stay the proceedings to await the issuance of a final decision,[177] particularly if there is an indication that the agency is attempting to comply with the Act's requirements.

In order to provide the necessary foundation to: (1) appeal or file an action from the lack of a final decision; or (2) petition a board to set a deadline for the issuance of a final decision, certain basic documentation should be available to clearly establish the key events and their dates. This would include a letter notifying the agency that the matter is in dispute and that a final decision is requested. If the value of the claim is in excess of $100,000 the request for a final decision must be certified. If the proposal in excess of $100,000 has been previously certified and nothing has occurred that would require a new certification,[178] a basic request for a final decision is sufficient.

Once it is apparent that no final decision will be received, it is necessary to decide whether to: (1) petition the board to set a date by which the contracting officer is required to issue a final decision[179] or (2) file an appeal (institute a suit). The latter involves making an election regarding the forum that will eventually decide the matter. Regardless of whether a petition or appeal (suit) is filed, it is important to set forth the history of the efforts to obtain a final decision. While this approach is more detailed than notice pleadings, a detailed event-by-event statement of the facts with supporting documents enables the board or court to quickly evaluate the reasons why an action was instituted prior to the receipt of a final decision.

19.24 APPEAL DEADLINES

The CDA provides that a contracting officer's final decision on a claim (whether a contractor or a Government claim) is "final and conclusive and not subject to review by any forum, tribunal, or Governmental agency unless an appeal or suit is timely commenced as provided in the [Act]."[180] Once a contractor receives a contracting officer's final decision, it has two possible alternatives. The contractor can take no action on the appeal, in which event it becomes binding on both parties, or it can appeal the decision.

Under the CDA, a contractor has two avenues of appeal from a contracting officer's final decision. Within ninety days of the date of receipt of the decision,

---

[176] *Boeing Co. v. United States,* 26 Cl. Ct. 257 (1992); *Mitcho,* fn. 61, *supra.*

[177] *Titan Group, Inc.,* ASBCA No. 28584, 83-2 BCA ¶ 16,803; *Continental Maritime,* ASBCA No. 37820, 89-2 BCA ¶ 21,694.

[178] *Santa Fe v. Garrett,* fn. 74 *supra.*

[179] 41 U.S.C. § 605(c)(4).

[180] 41 U.S.C. § 605(b). The government may not appeal a final decision of its own contracting officer. *Douglas Indust., Inc.,* GSBCA No. 9630, 90-2 BCA ¶ 22,676. However, a final decision favoring a contractor can be rescinded and a new final decision denying the claim may be issued so long as it is done within the CDA appeal period. *Daniels & Shanklin Constr. Co.,* ASBCA No. 37102, 89-3 BCA ¶ 22,060.

the contractor may appeal the decision to the appropriate board of contract appeals.[181] Alternatively, within twelve months of the date of receipt of the decision, the contractor may initiate an action in the Court of Federal Claims.[182]

With respect to either an appeal to a board of contract appeals or an action in the Court of Federal Claims, it is important to consider three basic points. First, there can be no appeal or suit unless there has been a valid contracting officer's final decision or the failure to issue such a decision within the period required under the Act. Second, once a valid final decision has been issued, it is essential that a board appeal, or Court of Federal Claims suit, whichever the contractor wishes to pursue, be timely commenced. Third, the contractor should realize that, once it has elected either a board or the Court of Federal Claims as the forum in which to challenge the contracting officer's decision, it may not switch to the other forum.

As noted above, the contracting officer is directed to obtain evidence of the date on which the contractor received a final decision.[183] This regulatory directive reflects the requirement for strict compliance with the time limits set forth in the CDA for appealing to boards and the Court of Federal Claims. Neither a board nor the court can consider an appeal that is not timely presented to it,[184] as the periods for challenging a contracting officer's decision set forth in the CDA are jurisdictional and cannot be waived.[185]

The boards' rules typically provide that filing of the appeal occurs when it is mailed or otherwise furnished to the board.[186] "Mailing" has been interpreted as meaning the United States Postal Service. Thus an appeal that was submitted to a commercial carrier before the expiration of the ninety-day appeal period but received after that period expired was untimely.[187] Some-

---

[181] 41 U.S.C. § 606.

[182] 41 U.S.C. § 609(a)(1), (a)(2). *See Opalack v. United States*, 5 Cl. Ct. 349, 361 (1984).

[183] *See* fn. 174, *supra.* When the government alleges that an appeal is untimely, it bears the burden of proving the date of the contractor's receipt of the final decision. *Alco Machine Co.*, ASBCA No. 38183, 89-3 BCA ¶ 21,955; *Atlantic Petroleum Corp.*, ASBCA No. 36207, 89-1 BCA ¶ 21,199.

[184] *Cosmic Constr. Co. v. United States*, 697 F.2d 1389 (Fed. Cir. 1982); *Gregory Lumber Co. v. United States*, 229 Ct. Cl. 762 (1982); *Contract Servs. Co.*, ASBCA No. 34438, 87-2 BCA ¶ 19,850.

[185] *Id.*

[186] *See* ASBCA Rule 1(a), CCH Cont. App. Dec. ¶ 133. Some boards, but not all, will accept facsimile notices of appeal. *See J. C. Equip. Corp.*, IBCA No. 2885-89, 91-3 BCA ¶ 24,322.

[187] *Associated Eng'g. Co.*, VABCA No. 2673, 88-2 BCA ¶ 20,709; *North Coast Remanufacturing, Inc.*, ASBCA No. 38599, 89-3 BCA ¶ 22,232; *C. R. Lewis Co.*, ASBCA No. 37200, 90-2 BCA ¶ 23,152. The AGBCA has held that the notice of appeal must be mailed to the board, not the contracting officer, within the appeal period in order to be timely. *Doris Bookout*, AGBCA No. 89-147-1, 89-1 BCA ¶ 21,750. Other boards may not be as strict. For example, the Engineer Board has held that a notice of appeal inadvertently sent to the wrong board will not be deemed untimely because misdirected appeals are routinely transferred to the proper board. *Inventory Accounting Serv.*, ENG BCA No. 5797, 93-1 BCA ¶ 25,230. Confusion regarding the proper board in which to file an appeal is not uncommon. For example, the U.S. Army Corps of Engineers is responsible for construction projects utilizing military construction appropriations and civil works appropriations. The ASBCA has jurisdiction over the former, while the ENG BCA has jurisdiction over the latter. To determine which type of project is being performed requires an understanding of the abbreviations used in the specific contract's numeric designation.

times, contracting officers send out a copy of the final decision by facsimile followed by a copy sent via certified mail. Unless the facsimile copy clearly indicates that it is an "advance" copy, the ninety-day period has been calculated from the date of receipt of the facsimile.[188]

Often counsel participate directly in the transmission of a claim and may correspond with the agency regarding the claim. If the contracting officer sends the final decision to the contractor's attorney, that attorney may be treated by the boards or the court as the contractor's representative for the purpose of receiving the final decision. Accordingly, the time period for filing an appeal or suit would begin to run upon the attorney's receipt of the final decision.[189] Even if the real party in interest is a subcontractor and the prime contractor is only sponsoring the subcontractor's claim, the period for an appeal or suit begins to run when the prime contractor receives the final decision.[190]

A contracting officer cannot waive the filing deadlines.[191] However, reconsideration of final decision by a contracting officer can have the effect of starting a new appeal period, which would allow the board to assume jurisdiction over a timely appeal of the second final decision[192] or, under certain circumstances, even the lack of a second final decision.[193] However, relying upon postfinal decision communications to extend the appeal period can be very risky, as such communications do not revive appeal rights unless they clearly constitute a reconsideration of the final decision.[194] If both parties are interested in further negotiations after a final decision is issued, a safer course is to file an appeal or suit and then mutually seek a brief stay to explore a negotiated resolution unless there is a clear written record that the decision is being "reconsidered" by the contracting officer.

Although strict compliance is required with the limitation periods set forth in the CDA, those periods may not begin to run if a contracting officer issues a decision that fails to advise the contractor of its appeal rights under the Act and the contractor is prejudice by the lack of this information.[195] However, no limitations period is triggered in the situation where the contractor's right to proceed to either a board or the Court of Federal Claims arises because the contracting officer has failed to issue a decision on a proper claim within the period of time required by the Act and the claim therefore is deemed denied.[196]

---

[188] *Tyger Constr. Co.*, ASBCA No. 36100 et al., 88-3 BCA ¶ 21,149.

[189] *Structural Finishing, Inc. v. United States,* 14 Cl. Ct. 447 (1988).

[190] *Colton Constr. Co., Inc.*, ASBCA No. 30313, 85-3 BCA ¶ 18,262.

[191] *Watson Rice & Co.*, AGBCA No. 82-126-3, 82-2 BCA ¶ 16,009 at 79,359.

[192] *Summit Contractors v. United States*, 15 Cl. Ct. 806 (1988); *Nash Janitorial Serv., Inc.*, GSBCA No. 7338-R, 89-2 BCA ¶ 21,615.

[193] *Westland Builders*, VABCA No. 1664, 83-1 BCA ¶ 16,235.

[194] However, ongoing negotiations without clear evidence of an agreement to reconsider the decision will not prevent the appeal period from running. *Compare Birken Mfg. Co.*, ASBCA No. 36587, 89-2 BCA ¶ 21,581; *Colfax, Inc.*, AGBCA No. 89-159-1, 89-3 BCA ¶ 22,130 *with Royal Int'l Builders Co., Inc.*, ASBCA No. 42637, 92-1 BCA ¶ 24,684.

[195] *Decker & Co.*, fn. 173, *supra.*

[196] *Id.* at 1573.

Finally, in the case of a termination for default, the circumstances may be such that the time the contractor has to challenge the termination does not begin to run when the contracting officer issues the final decision terminating the contract, but at a later date. This exception to the general basic requirement for strict compliance with the appeal deadlines reflects the continuing application of the doctrine set forth in *Fulford Mfg. Co.*[197] The proposition embodied by the *Fulford* doctrine is that when a contractor makes a timely appeal to an assessment of excess reprocurement costs, the propriety of the default termination can be challenged even though the default termination was not appealed.[198] The *Fulford* doctrine was not expressly altered by the CDA and the boards, as well as the Claims Court (Court of Federal Claims), have continued to follow it.[199] Thus the limitations periods set forth in the CDA do not "bar a contractor from contesting the propriety of a default termination in an action appealing a contracting officer's decision assessing excess reprocurement costs" if such an action is filed within ninety days (a board appeal) or twelve months (Court of Federal Claims) of the decision assessing excess costs.[200] Failure to seek review of a default termination within the ninety-day or twelve-month period, however, bars a contractor from challenging the default termination if excess costs are not assessed.[201]

19.25 CHOOSING A FORUM—BOARD OR UNITED STATES COURT OF FEDERAL CLAIMS

When it becomes apparent that the agency will or is likely to issue an adverse final decision, it is essential that the contractor and its counsel give careful consideration to the election of the forum (board or Court of Federal Claims). The CDA gives the contractor the basic right to seek a *de novo* review of a final decision in either forum.[202] Under a *de novo* review, there is *no* presumption given to any of the contracting officer's findings and conclusions even those that favor the contractor's position.[203] When considering whether to elect to go to the board or to the court, there are a number of factors to consider such as:

---

[197] ASBCA Nos. 2143, 2144 (May 20, 1955), Cont. Cas. Fed. (CCH) ¶ 61,815 (May 20, 1955) (digest only); a timely appeal of the default action will also preserve the right to contest the excess cost assessment even though the second final decision is not appealed in a timely manner. *El-Tronics, Inc.,* ASBCA No. 5457, 61-1 BCA ¶ 2961; *T.E. Deloss Equip. Rentals,* ASBCA No. 35374, 88-1 BCA ¶ 20,497. However, failure to timely appeal a default termination final decision will preclude a challenge to the default in a subsequent appeal from a government claim for recovery of unliquidated progress payments or property damages. *Dailing Roofing, Inc.,* ASBCA No. 34739, 89-1 BCA ¶ 21,311. *See also Guidance Sys.,* ASBCA No. 34690, 88-3 BCA ¶ 20,914.

[198] *D. Moody & Co. v. United States,* 5 Cl. Ct. 70, 72 (1984).

[199] *Id.* at 760; *Tom Warr,* IBCA No. 2360, 88-1 BCA ¶ 20,231.

[200] *Id.*

[201] *Id.*

[202] 41 U.S.C. § 606, 609(a)(1), (a)(2).

[203] *Wilner v. United States,* 24 F.3d 1397 (Fed. Cir. 1994).

(1) *Time and Money:* Ordinarily, board proceedings are believed to be less time consuming and costly than court proceedings. Often this perception reflects the fact that the boards' formal rules of procedure are not as extensive as the court's rules. However, some board judges issue extensive prehearing orders that mirror, to a large degree, orders issued by a federal district court or the Court of Federal Claims.

(2) *Judicial Background Experience:* In accordance with the CDA, board judges must have at least five years of experience in government contract law. Typically, they have much more than that minimum level of experience in government contracting.[204] There is no parallel specialized experience requirement for Court of Federal Claims judges. Board judges hear only government contract cases. Judges on the Court of Federal Claims hear a wide range of matters besides contract cases.

(3) *Case Issues:* If the case involves a particular issue or contract provision, it is important to learn how that board or the court views that issue. For example, a board or the court may have recently issued a decision reflecting its views on the proof of delay and the use of a CPM to demonstrate delay. If the case warrants the investment, this type of research should be conducted as part of the forum selection process.[205]

(4) *Agency Involvement:* If a case is appealed to a board, the agency will provide the government trial counsel. Accordingly, the counsel representing the government may be the same person who advised the contracting officer when the claim was being denied. When a case is filed in the Court of Federal Claims, the Civil Division of the Justice Department represents the government and controls the litigation. Under certain circumstances, the Justice Department can, in theory, settle a case over the procuring agency's objections.

(5) *Hearing/Trial Location:* All of the boards and the Court of Federal Claims are located in Washington, D.C. In practice, the boards and the court can and often do hold hearings outside of Washington. Location usually depends upon the convenience of all of the parties.

(6) *Counsel's Involvement:* Board practice permits an officer of the corporation to represent it. At the Court of Federal Claims, a corporation must be represented by an attorney admitted to practice before that court.[206]

(7) *Monetary/Non-monetary Claims:* Prior to the 1992 Amendment to the CDA, only the boards had jurisdiction over disputes that did not involve a

---

[204] 41 U.S.C. § 607(b)(1).

[205] A comparison of the recent decisions of the ASBCA and the Claims Court concerning the interpretation of essentially the same specification illustrates the value of this type of research. *Compare Western States Constr. Co. v. United States,* 26 Cl. Ct. 818 (1992) *with Tomahawk Const. Co.,* ASBCA No. 41717, 93-3 BCA ¶ 26,219.

[206] *Alchemy, Inc. v. United States,* 3 Cl. Ct. 727 (1983).

monetary claim. For example, in *Overall Roofing & Constr. Inc. v. United States,*[207] the Federal Circuit held that the Claims Court did not have jurisdiction to consider the contractor's suit challenging the validity of a default termination absent a related monetary claim. The 1992 Amendment to the CDA effectively reversed *Overall Roofing* and extended the Court of Federal Claims' jurisdiction to nonmonetary claims such as "termination of contracts, rights intangible or intangible property, compliance with cost accounting standards, and other nonmonetary disputes."[208] Accordingly, this historical jurisdictional division is no longer an issue in selecting a forum.

Once a contractor has elected either a board or the Court of Federal Claims as the forum in which to challenge a contracting officer's final decision, it may not switch to the other forum. In this regard, a contractor who is poised to proceed to either a board or the court should be aware of the "Election Doctrine." The term "Election Doctrine" refers to the body of law related to the contractor's right to initially select the forum in which to challenge a contracting officer's decision. However, the Act does not allow the contractor to pursue its claim in both forums.[209] Thus once a contractor makes a binding election to appeal a contracting officer's decision to the appropriate board of contract appeals, the contractor cannot change course and pursue its claim in the court.[210] The converse is also true.

A binding election takes place when a contractor files an appeal or initiates a suit in a *"forum with jurisdiction over the proceeding."*[211] This means that when a contractor initiates proceedings on its claim before a board of contract appeals in a timely manner, it has made a binding election to proceed before the board and it is barred from initiating suit in the court; any suit it files in the court will be dismissed.[212] However, the filing of an appeal with the appropriate board of contract appeals is not a binding election if it is determined by the board that the contractor's appeal was untimely, and hence the subsequent filing of a claim in the Court of Federal Claims is not barred.[213] The rationale is that a contractor's choice of forums in which to contest the contracting officer's decision is a binding election only if that choice is truly available, which it is not if resort to a board of contract appeals is untimely.[214] In those circumstances, the untimely appeal to the board was an absolute nullity and the Election Doctrine is not applicable.[215]

---

[207] 929 F.2d 687 (Fed. Cir. 1991); *See also, Page Constr. v. United States,* 26 Cl. Ct. 198 (1992).
[208] 28 U.S.C. § 149(a)(2).
[209] *Tuttle/White Constructors, Inc. v. United States,* 28 Cl. Ct. 354, 361, 656 F.2d 644, 649 (1981).
[210] *Id.* However, a notice of appeal to a board that was retrieved before docketing did not constitute a binding election. *Blake Constr. Co., Inc. v. United States,* 13 Cl. Ct. 250 (1987).
[211] *Id.*
[212] *National Neighbors, Inc. v. United States,* 839 F.2d at 1541–42.
[213] *Id.*
[214] *Id.*
[215] *Id.*

19.26 TRANSFER AND CONSOLIDATION OF CASES

The CDA provides that, if two or more suits arising from one contract are filed in the Court of Federal Claims and one or more boards, the court is authorized to order the consolidation of the suits before it or to transfer suits to or among the boards involved "for the convenience of parties or witnesses or in the interest of justice."[216] In deciding whether a case should be consolidated or transferred, the court will take into account a number of factors; whether the disputes in the different forums arise out of the same contract; whether the cases present overlapping or the same issues; whether the plaintiff initially elected to initiate proceedings at the board; whether substantial effort in the case already has been expended in one forum but not the other; which proceeding involves the most money; and which proceeding presents the more difficult and complex claims.[217]

19.27 ADR AND FEDERAL GOVERNMENT CONTRACT DISPUTES

There has long been a need for alternatives to the traditional manner in which government contract disputes are resolved. The Administrative Conference of the United States (Conference), whose purpose is to promote efficiency and fairness in federal agency procedures, is a major proponent of alternative dispute resolution (ADR) in government contracts. The Conference has strongly supported ADR and has several publications that discuss the contract disputes dilemma and various ADR efforts.[218]

FAR § 33.214[219] states that the objective of using ADR procedures is to increase the opportunity for relatively inexpensive and expeditious resolution of issues in controversy. Essential elements of ADR include: (1) existence of an issue in controversy; (2) a voluntary election by both parties to participate in the ADR process; (3) an agreement on alternative procedures and terms to be used in lieu of formal litigation; (4) participation in the process by officials of both parties who have the authority to resolve the issue in controversy; and (5) certification by the contractor in accordance with FAR § 33.207.

ADR procedures may be used at any time that the contracting officer has authority to settle the issue in controversy and may be applied to a portion of a claim. When ADR procedures are used subsequent to issuance of a contracting officer's final decision, their use does not alter any of the time

---

[216] 41 U.S.C. § 609(d). *See, Glendale Joint Venture v. United States,* 13 Cl. Ct. 325, 327 (1987); *Multi-Roof Sys. Co. v. United States,* 5 Cl. Ct. 245, 248 (1984); *E.D.S. Fed. Corp. v. United States,* 2 Cl. Ct. 739 (1983).

[217] *Glendale,* fn. 208, *supra; Multi-Roof Sys.,* fn. 208, *supra; E.D.S. Fed.* fn. 208, *supra,* at 735, 739.

[218] 1987 Sourcebook: Federal Agency Use of Alternative Means of Dispute Resolution (Office of the Chairman 1987) and its report on Appealing Government Contract Decisions: *Reducing the Cost and Delay of Procurement Litigation.*

[219] 48 C.F.R. § 33.214.

limitations or procedural requirements for filing an appeal of the contracting officer's final decision and does not constitute a reconsideration of the final decision.

The CDA states that the boards shall provide, to the fullest extent practicable, informal, expeditious, and inexpensive resolution of disputes, and this is the authority for their use of ADR.[220] The boards of contract appeals have implemented ADR procedures and issued a Notice Regarding Alternative Methods of Dispute Resolution that strongly endorses the use of ADR and suggests several techniques. Many of the procedures outlined by that Notice come from the recommendations made by the Administrative Conference of the United States. Boards routinely provide a notice of the availability of ADR procedures when the docketing notice is sent out to the parties together with a copy of the board's rules of procedure.

Use of ADR is a decision made jointly by the parties, and a board will not accept a unilateral request. However, the board may take the initiative in suggesting ADR as an option in dispute resolution. There are a number of ADR methods, and both the parties and the board may agree to the use of any of these methods, such as Settlement Judge, Minitrial, Summary Trial with Binding Decision and Other Agreed Methods.

The United States Court of Federal Claims has formally approved the voluntary use of ADR. As described in the Deskbook for Practitioners published by the Court's Bar Association,[221] the court is sensitive to rising litigation costs and the delay often inherent in the traditional judicial resolution of complex legal claims. Accordingly, General Order 13 established two alternative methods of dispute resolution: the settlement judge and the minitrial.

These techniques are voluntary and both parties must agree to their use. The court expects the techniques to be invoked in complex cases where the amount in controversy exceeds $100,000.00, the parties anticipate a lengthy period of discovery, and a trial is expected to consume more than one week.

When both parties agree to utilize one of these ADR methods, they notify the presiding judge as early as possible in the proceedings or concurrently with the submission of a joint preliminary status report.

If the presiding judge agrees, the case will be referred to the clerk, who will assign the case to another court judge who will preside over the procedure and who will exercise final authority, within the general guidelines adopted by the court, to determine the form and function of each method. If the ADR method utilized by the parties fails to produce a satisfactory settlement, the case will be returned to the docket of the presiding judge. All representations made in the course of utilizing a method of ADR are confidential, and except as permitted by Federal Rule of Evidence 408, may not be utilized for any reason in subsequent litigation.

---

[220] 41 U.S.C. § 605(d).
[221] The United States Claims Court, *A Deskbook for Practitioners,* United States Claims Court Bar Association, 1992.

POINTS TO REMEMBER

- While the Contract Disputes Act (CDA) addresses the procedures for the processing of claims on a government contract, it is essential that you understand your obligations and rights under the standard clauses such as the Changes, Differing Site Conditions, and Suspension of Work clauses.
- Compliance with the contract's notice provisions, as well as consideration of the six year statute of limitations, is essential to preserving your right to recovery on a claim.
- Every request for an equitable adjustment is not necessarily a claim. A "claim" is a nonroutine written submission or demand that seeks, as a matter of right, the payment of money in a sum certain.
- Every claim in excess of $100,000 must be certified by an authorized representative of the prime contractor in order to be considered a "claim" and entitle you to recovery CDA interest.
- Prime contractors must provide unqualified certifications of their subcontractors' claims. In that context, consider obtaining an appropriate indemnity agreement.
- A defective claim certification may delay action by the contracting officer, a board of contract appeals, or the Court of Federal Claims.
- The CDA specifies time frame for action by the contracting officer on all claims and provides a means for a contractor to compel consideration of the claim if the contracting officer is unreasonably slow in acting.
- Once a final decision is received, you have ninety days to file an appeal at the board of contract appeals or one year to file a suit in the Court of Federal Claims. If these periods are allowed to pass, the final decision is, in almost all cases, final and binding.
- Carefully consider whether you wish to have your appeal heard at a board of contract appeals or in the Court of Federal Claims. Once an election is made, it is, in almost all cases, binding on the parties.
- Whether you appeal the final decision to a board of contract appeals or file a suit in the Court of Federal Claims, the claim receives "de novo" consideration. That means that no presumption of correctness is attached to the decision—even those portions favorable to the contractor.

INDEX